ABBREVIATED RAIL TIMES

FOR GREAT BRITAIN

for Principal Stations on Main Lines and Rural Routes

Summer Edition

21 May to 9 December 2017

Cut here or use a photocopier to make a bookmark to save memorising details.

KEY·

...ING

...lays

...ys

...ys

...days

... Wednesdays, Thursdays

⑤⑥ Fridays, Saturdays

⑦ Sundays

①–④ Mondays to Thursdays

SERVICES

[12] Through service (first and standard class seats)

[2] Through service (standard class seats only)

🛏 Sleeping car

🍴 Restaurant car

🍸 Snacks and drinks available

2 Standard class only

🚌 Bus or coach service

⛴ Shipping service

OTHER SYMBOLS

[R] Reservation compulsory

✈ Airport

| Train does not stop

▬ Separates two trains in the same column between which no connection is possible

→ Continued in later column

← Continued from earlier column

v.v. Vice Versa

D1579776

Cover picture: This panorama from 24th July 2012 features the Caldon Canal and the waiting shelter cantilevered over it at Consall, on the reopened Churnet Valley Railway. Arriving at 13.48 is no. 33102, piloting no. 33021. This is reproduced from the latest Middleton Press album, Uttoxeter to Macclesfield. *(David Gibson)*

Compiled by:

European Rail Timetable Ltd

Director and Editor-in-Chief: John Potter, 28 Monson Way, Oundle, Northamptonshire, PE8 4QG

Tel: 01832 270198 (Monday to Friday 0900-1700) *www.europeanrailtimetable.eu*

Published by:

MP Middleton Press

Easebourne Lane
Midhurst, West Sussex, GU29 9AZ
Tel: 01730 813169
sales@middletonpress.co.uk www.middletonpress.co.uk

ISBN 978 1 910356-07-4

Data and monochrome diagrams
Copyright © 2017 European Rail Timetable Ltd

Printed and bound by CPI Group (UK) Ltd, Croydon, CR0 4YY

Every care has been taken to render the t... being made by the administrations concerned and neither the publishers nor the comp... accuracies.

80003440947

Heritage Railways

Keith & Dufftown
Alford
Strathspey
Royal Deeside
Caledonian Rly (Brechin)
Kerrs
Almond
Prestongrange
PSPS Bo'ness & Kinneil
Summerlee EDINBURGH
Glasgow Museum
Heatherslaw
Leadhills
Scottish
North Tyneside/Stephenson Bowes
Tanfield
South Tynedale Beamish Monkwearmouth
Weardale Locomotion Saltburn
Giant's Causeway Head of Steam (Darlington) North Bay
County Donegal RPSI Haig Eden North Yorkshire Moors
Fintown Ulster Wensleydale
BELFAST Ravenglass & Eskdale Lightwater
Snaefell Mountain Lakeside & Haverthwaite National Railway Museum
Downpatrick Great Laxey Keighley & Worth Valley
Groudle Glen Embsay & Bolton Abbey Abbey Derwent
Manx Electric Light
Cavan & Leitrim I.O.M. Steam Railway VCT
Blackpool Middleton Leeds Museum Appleby Frodingham (Scunthorpe)
West Lancashire Ribble Elsecar Lincolnshire Wolds
Windmill Farm National Coal North Ings
DUBLIN Museum (Manchester) Lakeside East Lancashire Kirklees Cleethorpes Coast North Norfolk
Rheilffordd Eryri Penrhyn Rhyl Astley Green Ashmanhaugh
West Clare Great Orme Wirral Brookside Peak Rail Wells & Walsingham Bure Valley
Moseley Hills Barrow Hill Whitewell
Welsh Highland Snowdon Mountain Llanberis Lake Crich Midland/Golden Valley Mid Norfolk
Irish Steam Conwy Churnet Valley Nottingham EATM
Ffestiniog Llangollen Crewe Rudyard Ecclesbourne
Fairbourne Bala Lake Rudyard Foxfield Great Central Bressingham
Irish Traction Group Corris Oswestry Amerton Silk Mill Abbey
Welshpool Chasewater Battlefield Line Snibston Rutland Railworld Mid-Suffolk
Waterford Talyllyn & Llanfair Cambrian Ironbridge Nene Valley
Vale of Rheidol Telford Tyseley Northampton & Lamport
Kidderminster Irchester
Severn Valley Coventry Northants Ironstone
Evesham Great Whipsnade
Gloucestershire Leighton Audley End
Warwickshire Buzzard
Telfi Brecon Winchcombe Buckinghamshire Colne Valley
Gwili Mountain Didcot EARM
Perrygrove National Chinnor Waltham Abbey Mangapps Farm
Llanelli Dean Forest Waterways Ruislip Epping
Pontypool Cholsey
Gawr Swindon Steam LONDON
CARDIFF Bristol & Cricklade Great Cockcrow
West Somerset Avon Valley Sittingbourne & Kemsley
Lynton Midsomer Norton Spa Valley Bredgar East Kent
Longleat Kent &
S&DJRT East Somerset Mid-Hants Old Kiln Bluebell East Sussex
Yeovil Gartell Hollycombe Lavender Rother Romney, Hythe
Amberley Valley & Dymchurch
Devon Railway Shillingstone Moors Hayling Volks
Launceston Centre Seaton South Downs
Dartmoor Beer Swanage Exbury Royal Victoria
Bicton Burlesdon
Bodmin & Bickington Eastleigh
Lappa Wenford South Paignton & Dartmouth Isle of Wight
Devon Alderney
Plym Pallot (Jersey)
Valley
Helston

LONDON
Kew Bridge, LT Depot
Science Museum,
Southall, LT Museum

CONTENTS

FOREWORD

The dismissive attitude of so many authorities to the printed timetable continues, but the demand remains substantial and our slim edition was well received by most. Requests for the *Comprehensive Rail Times* justified its production in two volumes. Additionally, the *National Rail Passenger Network Diagram* is still available (see page 5 for more details).

We apologise to customers of W.H.Smith for any inconvenience following our withdrawal of supply to them of the *Abbreviated Rail Times*, due to display issues of theirs.

The content of individual timetables was decided by the producers of the European Rail Timetable many years ago and thus the *Abbreviated Rail Times* has to be confined to ERT's international design. We are producing the Comprehensive version again for those needing full details.

Delays in the production of both publications are due to Network Rail producing their National Rail Timetable files later than ever before. Complaints about the train service offered should be directed to the operating company concerned. The *European Rail Timetable* is produced six times per annum and thus British updates are available therein, if required.

We always recommend confirmation of train times by visiting *www.nationalrail.co.uk* **or telephoning 03457 484950.**

Vic Bradshaw-Mitchell

NEWSLINES

Virgin Trains East Coast (Table 180) has increased the frequency of its services to and from Leeds to half hourly on Saturdays.

East Midlands Trains has increased the number of trains serving Corby on Sunday afternoons with three new direct services to and from London (Table 170). As a consequence of this, journey times of three services in each direction between London and Sheffield have been reduced by up to 15 minutes by omitting the stops now served by the Corby trains.

The Bedford to Bletchley service has been re-cast (Table 143b).

Services in Tables 132, 133 and 136 are severely affected by ongoing work in the Severn Tunnel during weekends from September 16 to October 22 (some services in Tables 120a and 140 are also affected with no trains running through to Cardiff on Saturdays). A special version of Table 136 is included on page 30 with details of the amended service between Bristol Temple Meads, Bristol Parkway and Newport on Saturdays and Sundays during this period.

The Exeter to Okehampton service is once again running on summer Sundays, this year until September 10 (Table 118).

We have inserted a new Table 131a, showing journeys between Slough and Windsor. Slough has also been added to Table 131.

Table 173 shows new timings for the recently restored Settle to Carlisle through service.

INDEX OF PLACES by table number

🚃 Connection by train from the nearest station shown in this timetable.
⚓ Connection by boat from the nearest station shown in this timetable.

🚌 Connection by bus from the nearest station shown in this timetable.
180/186 Consult both indicated tables to find the best connecting services.

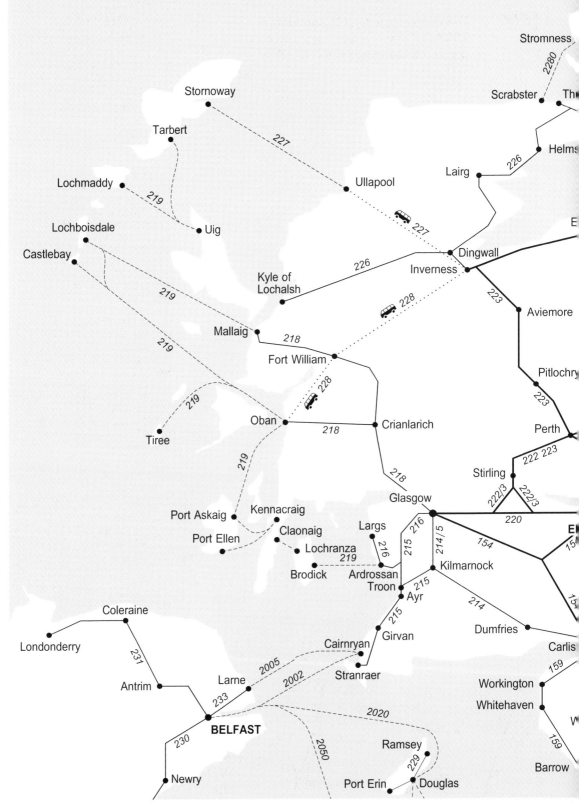

The Eurostar route (10) and table nos 100 to 229 are herein. Nos 230 onwards are in the *European Rail Timetable*.

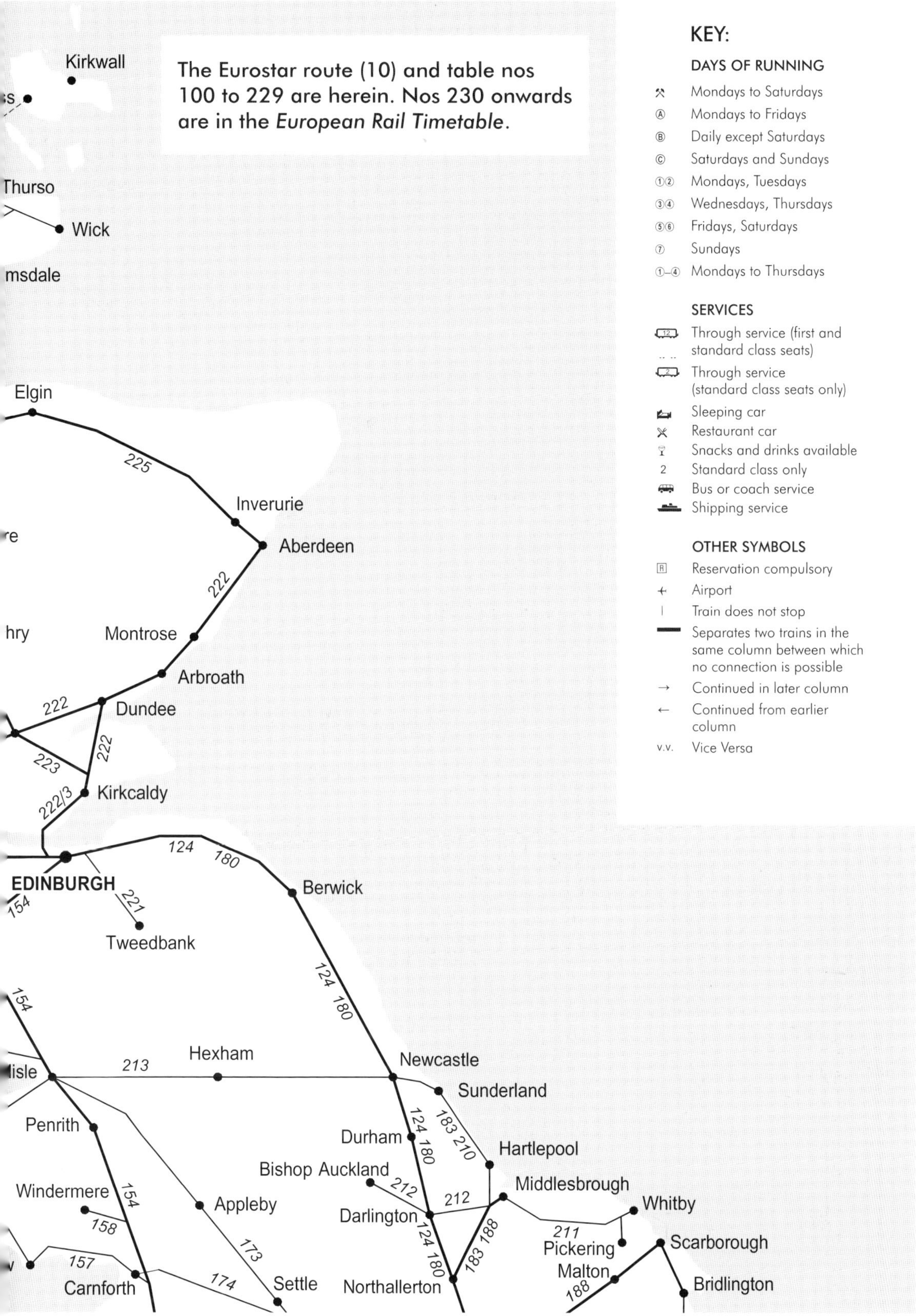

KEY:

DAYS OF RUNNING

- ⚒ Mondays to Saturdays
- Ⓐ Mondays to Fridays
- Ⓑ Daily except Saturdays
- Ⓒ Saturdays and Sundays
- ①② Mondays, Tuesdays
- ③④ Wednesdays, Thursdays
- ⑤⑥ Fridays, Saturdays
- ⑦ Sundays
- ①–④ Mondays to Thursdays

SERVICES

- [12] Through service (first and standard class seats)
- [2] Through service (standard class seats only)
- 🛏 Sleeping car
- 🍴 Restaurant car
- 🍸 Snacks and drinks available
- 2 Standard class only
- 🚌 Bus or coach service
- ⛴ Shipping service

OTHER SYMBOLS

- [R] Reservation compulsory
- ✈ Airport
- | Train does not stop
- ▬ Separates two trains in the same column between which no connection is possible
- → Continued in later column
- ← Continued from earlier column
- v.v. Vice Versa

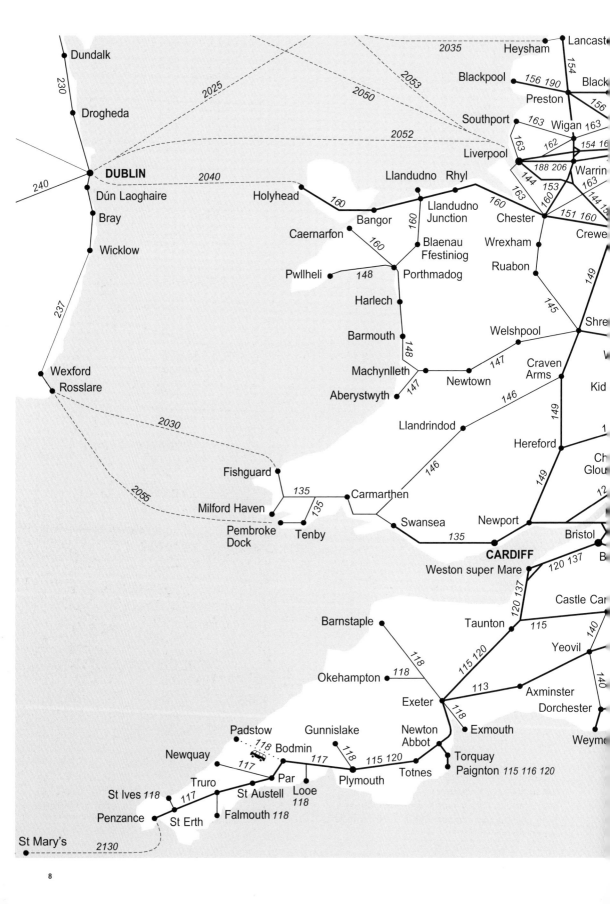

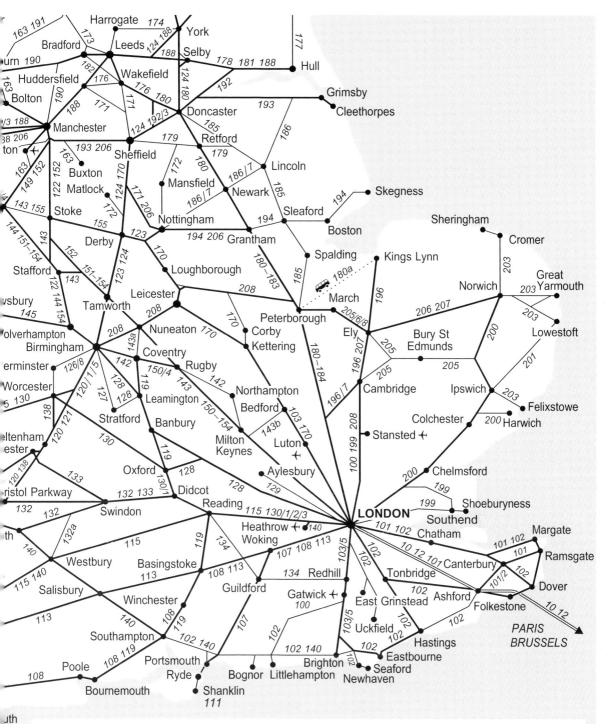

Crossing London

London termini are linked by buses and underground trains, but some journeys involve a change. Those travelling between the Midlands and most of Sussex are likely to be advised to travel by Underground, via Victoria. However, those using King's Cross can cross the road to St. Pancras, where there is a regular service to East Croydon. Mid-Surrey and many Sussex stations are served from there. See table no. 103.

LONDON - LILLE - PARIS and BRUSSELS *by Eurostar*

**Minimum check-in time is 30 minutes, but passengers are advised to allow longer due to immigration procedures.
Not available for London - Ebbsfleet - Ashford or v.v. Special fares payable that include three classes of service: business premier, standard premier and standard. All times shown are local times (France and Belgium are one hour ahead of Great Britain).
All Eurostar services are [R], non-smoking and convey 🍴 in Business Premier and Standard Premier, 🍸 in Standard.**

Service May 28 - November 4. Subject to alteration November 5 - December 9.

Due to engineering work until July 22 (also July 29), on the high speed line between Calais and Paris, services will arrive Paris 6 - 21 minutes later.

km	*km*	*train number*	**9080**	**9108**	**9002**	**9110**	**9110**	**9004**	**9008**	**9008**	**9114**	**9010**	**9010**	**9116**	**9116**	**9014**	**9018**	**9126**	**9126**	**9020**	**9022**	**9060**	**9024**
		notes	①–⑤	①⑤	⑥	②③④	⑥	①–⑤	⑥	①–⑤		⑦					Ⓑ	①–⑥	⑦	⑥			
		notes	**O**	**P**		**L**		**j**		**j**	**J**	**y**	**R**	**V**	**X**			**j**	**y**		**S**	**Z**	
0	*0*	**London** St Pancras d.	0540	0613	0618	0650	0657	0701	0752	0755	0804	0819	0831	0854	0858	0924	1024	1058	1104	1101	1131	1201	1224
35	*35*	Ebbsfleet International d.	0558	0630	│	0707	│	│	0812	0812	│	0838	│	0912	0915	0941	1042	1115	│	│	│	│	1242
90	*90*	Ashford International d.	0624	0653	0655	0728	0728	│	│	│	│	│	│	│	│	│	│	│	│	│	│	│	│
166	*166*	Calais Fréthun a.	│	│	│	0859	│	│	│	│	│	│	│	│	1059	│	│	│	│	│	│	│	│
267	*267*	Lille Europe a.	│	│	│	0930	0926	│	│	│	1026	│	│	1123	1130	│	│	1326	1326	│	│	│	│
	373	**Brussels** Midi / Zuid a.	│	0922	│	1007	1005	│	│	│	1105	│	│	1202	1208	│	│	1405	1405	│	│	│	│
492		**Paris** Nord a.	0917	...	0947	...	...	1017	1117	1117	...	1147	1147	...	...	1248	1347	...	...	1417	1447	1529	1547

train number	**9132**	**9028**	**9030**	**9032**	**9140**	**9036**	**9038**	**9144**	**9040**	**9148**	**9044**	**9152**	**9046**	**9152**	**9048**	**9050**	**9156**	**9158**	**9054**	**9162**	**9056**		
notes					Ⓑ		⑤⑦	⑥				⑦	①–⑤				⑥⑦	①–⑤		⑦	⑦		
notes		**Q**	**AA**				**B**			**E**		**y**	**j**	**G**	**C**	**U**	**y**	**j**	❦	**p**	**y**		
London St Pancras d.	1258	1331	1401	1422	1504	1531	1601	1604	1631	1704	1731	1755	1801	1804	1831	1901	1904	1934	2001	2003	2031	...	...
Ebbsfleet International d.	1315	│	│	│	│	│	│	│	│	│	│	│	│	│	│	│	│	│	│	│	│	...	...
Ashford International d.	│	│	│	1455	│	│	│	│	│	│	│	1828	│	│	│	│	│	│	│	│	│	...	...
Calais Fréthun a.	1459	│	│	│	│	│	│	│	│	│	│	│	│	│	│	│	2059	2129	│	│	│	...	...
Lille Europe a.	1530	│	│	│	1726	│	│	1826	│	1926	│	2026	│	2026	│	│	2130	2200	│	2226	│	...	...
Brussels Midi / Zuid a.	1608	│	│	│	1805	│	│	1905	│	2005	│	2105	│	2105	│	│	2208	2238	│	2305	│	...	...
Paris Nord a.	...	1647	1717	1747	...	1847	1917	...	1947	...	2047	...	2117	...	2147	2217	...	...	2317	...	2347	...	...

train number	**9109**	**9005**	**9007**	**9113**	**9009**	**9011**	**9117**	**9013**	**9015**	**9019**	**9125**	**9023**	**9129**	**9027**	**9029**	**9133**	**9029**	**9031**	**9031**	**9035**	**9037**	**9141**	**9141**
notes	①	①	①–⑥	①–⑥	①–⑤	⑥⑦							⑦			①–⑥	⑦	⑦	①–⑥	⑥⑦		⑦	①–⑥
notes	**j**	**BB**	**h**	**f**	**j**	**y**		**CC**		**T**	**K**		**g**	**F**	**M**	**j**	**y**	**D**	**j**	**g**	**Y**	**y**	**j**
Paris Nord d.	...	0643	0713	...	0743	0813	...	0843	0913	1013	...	1113	...	1213	1231	...	1243	1313	1313	1413	1443	...	...
Brussels Midi / Zuid d.	0656	│	│	0756	│	│	0852	│	│	│	1056	│	1156	│	│	1252	│	│	│	│	│	1452	1456
Lille Europe d.	0735	│	│	0835	│	│	0930	│	│	│	1135	│	1235	│	│	1330	│	│	│	│	│	1530	1535
Calais Fréthun d.	│	│	│	│	│	│	1001	│	│	│	│	│	│	│	│	1401	│	│	│	│	│	1601	│
Ashford International a.	│	│	│	│	│	│	│	│	│	│	│	1208	│	│	│	│	│	│	│	│	│	│	│
Ebbsfleet International a.	│	│	│	│	│	│	│	│	1018	│	│	│	│	│	│	1345	1348	│	1418	│	│	1545	1545
London St Pancras a.	0759	0802	0832	0857	0900	0930	0957	1000	1039	1130	1157	1239	1258	1330	1400	1405	1409	1430	1439	1530	1602	1605	1605

train number	**9039**	**9043**	**9045**	**9149**	**9149**	**9047**	**9153**	**9153**	**9051**	**9157**	**9053**	**9055**	**9161**	**9059**	**9061**	**9063**							
notes			⑦	⑦	①–⑥		①–⑤	⑦	Ⓑ						⑦	Ⓑ							
notes	**x**		**y**	**y**	**j**		**j**	**y**		**H**	**A**				**w**								
Paris Nord d.	1513	1613	1643	...	...	1713	...	...	1813	...	1843	1913	...	2013	2043	2113	...	...	...	...	...	...	...
Brussels Midi / Zuid d.	│	│	│	1656	1656	│	1756	1756	│	1856	│	│	1952	│	│	│	...	...	...	...	...	...	...
Lille Europe d.	│	│	│	1734	1735	│	1835	1835	│	1935	│	│	2030	│	│	│	...	...	...	...	...	...	...
Calais Fréthun d.	│	│	│	│	│	│	│	│	│	│	│	│	2101	│	│	│	...	...	...	...	...	...	...
Ashford International a.	│	│	1737	│	1734	│	│	1835	│	│	│	2007	│	│	│	│	...	...	...	...	...	...	...
Ebbsfleet International a.	1618	1718	│	1745	│	│	1845	│	1918	│	│	│	2045	2118	│	2218	...	...	...	...	...	...	...
London St Pancras a.	1639	1739	1812	1805	1806	1832	1903	1910	1939	1957	2004	2039	2103	2139	2200	2239	...	...	...	...	...	...	...

A – ②③④⑤⑦ May 28 - July 22. ⑤⑦ July 23 - Sept. 2. ④⑤⑦ Sept. 3 - Nov. 4.

B – ①④⑤⑦ May 28 - July 22. ⑤⑦ July 23 - Nov. 4.

C – Daily May 28 - July 22. ⑤⑥⑦ July 23 - Sept. 2 (also Aug. 28). ⑤⑦ Sept. 3 - Nov. 4.

D – ⑦ May 28 - July 22, Sept. 3 - Nov. 4.

E – Daily May 28 - Sept. 2. Ⓑ Sept. 3 - Nov. 4.

F – ①④⑤⑦ May 28 - July 22. ⑦ July 23 - Sept. 2 (also Aug. 28). ⑤⑦ Sept. 3 - Nov. 4.

G – ①–⑤ May 28 - Sept. 2 (not Aug. 28). ④⑤ Sept. 3 - Nov. 4.

H – Ⓑ May 28 - July 22. ①④⑤⑦ July 23 - Nov. 4.

J – ①–⑤ May 28 - July 22 (not May 29, June 5). ①④⑤ July 23 - Sept. 2 (not Aug. 28). ①⑤ Sept. 3 - Nov. 4.

K – ①–⑥ May 28 - Sept. 2. ⑤ Sept. 3 - Nov. 4.

L – ②③④ May 28 - Nov. 4 (not Aug. 15, Nov. 1).

M – ⑤ May 26 - July 22.

O – ①–⑤ (not May 29, June 5, July 23 - Sept. 2, Nov. 1).

P – ①⑤ May 28 - Nov. 4 (not May 29, June 5, Aug. 14, 28).

Q – Daily May 26 - July 22. ①④⑤⑥⑦ July 23 - Sept. 2. ①⑤⑦ Sept. 3 - Nov. 4.

R – ①–⑥ May 28 - July 22. ①⑤⑥ July 23 - Sept. 2. ①④⑤⑥ Sept. 3 - Nov. 4.

S – ①④⑤⑦ May 28 - July 22. ⑤⑥⑦ Sept. 3 - Nov. 4.

T – Daily May 28 - July 22. ①④⑤⑥ July 23 - Sept. 2 (not Aug. 28). ①–⑥ Sept. 3 - Nov. 4.

U – ⑦ May 28 - July 22. Ⓑ July 23 - Nov. 4 (not July 24 - 28).

V – ②③④ May 28 - Nov. 4.

X – ①⑤⑥⑦ May 28 - Nov. 4.

Y – ①④⑤ May 28 - July 22. ⑤ July 23 - Nov. 4.

Z – ⑤ May 26 - July 22.

AA – ⑤⑦ May 28 - July 22 (also July 28).

BB – ① (not May 29, June 5, July 23 - Sept. 2).

CC – ①–⑤ May 28 - July 22 (not May 29, June 5). ① July 23 - Sept. 2 (not Aug. 28). ①⑤ Sept. 3 - Nov. 4.

f – Not Aug. 15, 28.

g – Also May 29, June 5.

h – Not May 29, June 5, Aug. 28, Nov. 1.

j – Not May 29, June 5, Aug. 28.

p – Not Aug. 27.

w – Also Aug. 28; not May 27, June 5, Aug. 27.

x – Not May 28, Aug. 27.

y – Also May 29, June 5, Aug. 28.

❦ – May 28 - July 28 (not July 23) depart London 1925 on ①–⑤.

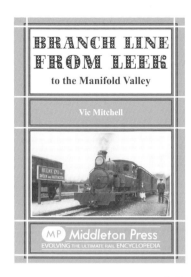
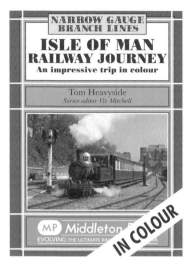
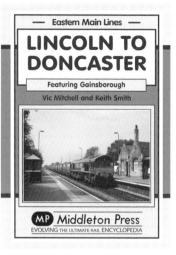
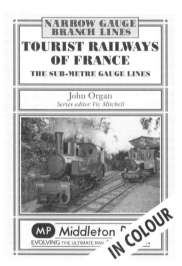
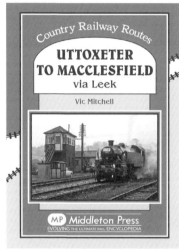
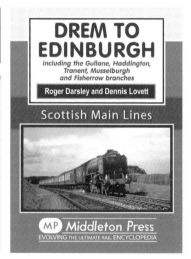
Leisurely armchair journeys back in time.
Each station is visited in geographical order.
Photographs give a visual history of each location.
Over 400 albums bound in attractive glossy hardback covers.

Please request our brochure or visit our website. The latter
includes an Index to Stations contained in all Middleton Press albums.
This now extends to over 140 pages and is updated regularly.

MP Middleton Press

Easebourne Lane, Midhurst, West Sussex, GU29 9AZ
Tel: 01730 813169 ● sales@middletonpress.co.uk ● www.middletonpress.co.uk

GREAT BRITAIN

Operators: Passenger services are provided by a number of private passenger train companies operating the **National Rail** (www.nationalrail.co.uk) network on lines owned by the British national railway infrastructure company **Network Rail**. The following Network Rail codes are used in the table headings to indicate the operators of trains in each table:

AW	Arriva Trains Wales	GR	Virgin Trains East Coast	ME	Merseyrail	SW	South West Trains
CC	c2c	GW	Great Western Railway	NT	Arriva Rail North	TL	Thameslink Railway
CH	Chiltern Railways	HT	Hull Trains	NY	North Yorkshire Moors Railway	TP	TransPennine Express
CS	Caledonian Sleeper	IL	Island Line	SE	Southeastern	VT	Virgin Trains West Coast
EM	East Midlands Trains	LE	Greater Anglia	SN	Southern	XC	Arriva Cross Country
GC	Grand Central Railway	LM	London Midland	SR	Abellio ScotRail		

Timings: Except where indicated otherwise, timings are valid **May 21 - December 9, 2017.**
As service patterns at weekends (especially on ⑦) usually differ greatly from those applying on Mondays to Fridays, the timings in most tables are grouped by days of operation: Ⓐ = Mondays to Fridays; ⚒ = Mondays to Saturdays; ⑥ = Saturdays; ⑦ = Sundays. Track engineering work, affecting journey times, frequently takes place at weekends, so it is advisable to confirm your journey details locally if planning to travel in the period between the late evening of ⑥ and the late afternoon of ⑦. Confirm timings, too, if you intend travelling on public holidays (see page **2**) as there may be alterations to services at these times. Suburban and commuter services are the most likely to be affected; the majority of long-distance and cross-country trains marked Ⓐ and ⚒ run as normal on these dates. No trains (except limited Gatwick and Heathrow Express services) run on **December 25**, with only a limited service on certain routes on **December 26**. In Scotland only trains between Edinburgh / Glasgow and England run on **January 1**.

Services: Unless indicated otherwise (by '2' in the train column or '2nd class' in the table heading), trains convey both **first** (1st) and **standard** (2nd) classes of seated accommodation. Light refreshments (snacks, hot and cold drinks) are available from a **buffet car** or a **mobile trolley service** on board those trains marked 🍷 and 🍴: the latter also convey a **restaurant car** or serve meals to passengers at their seats (this service is in some cases available to first-class ticket holders only). Note that catering facilities may not be available for the whole of a train's journey. **Sleeping-cars** (🛏) have one berth per compartment in first class and two in standard class.

Reservations: Seats on most long-distance trains and berths in sleeping-cars can be reserved in advance when purchasing travel tickets at rail stations or directly from train operating companies (quote the departure time of the train and your destination). Seat reservation is normally free of charge.

100 LONDON AIRPORT LINKS

Gatwick ✈

GATWICK EXPRESS: Daily non-stop rail service from / to **London Victoria**. Journey time: 30 minutes (35 minutes on ⑦).

From **London** Victoria: 0002, 0030, 0500 and every 15 minutes until 2045, 2100⑥, 2115Ⓑ, 2130⑥, 2145Ⓑ, 2200, 2215, 2230, 2300, 2330, 2345.
From **Gatwick Airport**: 0020, 0035, 0050, 0135, 0545, 0600 and every 15 minutes until 2045, then 2-3 trains per hour until 2330⑥, 2335Ⓐ, 2350⑦.

Other rail services via Gatwick Airport: London Victoria - Eastbourne Table **102**; Bedford - Brighton Table **103**; London Victoria - Brighton Table **105**; Reading - Gatwick Airport Table **134**.

Heathrow ✈

HEATHROW EXPRESS: Daily non-stop rail service **London** Paddington - **Heathrow** Terminal 5 and v.v. Journey times: **Heathrow** Central ♣, 15 minutes, **Heathrow** Terminal 5, 21 minutes.
From **London** Paddington: 0510⚒/0625⑦ and every 15 minutes until 2155, then every 30 minutes (15 minutes on ⑤⑦) until 2325.
From **Heathrow** Terminal 5 (5 mins. later from Heathrow Central): 0507⚒/0618⑦ and every 15 minutes until 2212, then every 30 minutes (15 mins. on ⑤⑦) until 2342⚒ / 2348⑦.

HEATHROW CONNECT: Daily rail service **London** Paddington - **Heathrow** Central ♣ and v.v. Journey time 32 minutes.
From **London** Paddington: on ⚒ at 0442, 0513, 0533 and every 30 minutes until 2103 (additional later trains on ⑤⑥); on ⑦ at 0612, 0712, 0812, 0907 and hourly until 2312.
From **Heathrow** Central ♣: on ⚒ at 0529, 0557 and every 30 minutes until 2127 (additional later trains on ⑤⑥); on ⑦ at 0713 and hourly until 2313.

♣ – Heathrow Central serves Terminals 1, 2 and 3. A free rail transfer service operates every 15 minutes Heathrow Central - Heathrow **Terminals 4 and 5 and v.v.**

PICCADILLY LINE: London Underground service between **Kings Cross St Pancras** and all Heathrow terminals via Central London. Journey time: 50 - 58 minutes.
Frequent trains (every 4 - 10 minutes) 0530⚒/0730⑦ - 2300⚒/2330⑦.

RAILAIR LINK 🚌 **Reading** railway station - **Heathrow Airport** (Service **X25**).
From **Reading**: Services call at Heathrow Terminal 5 (±40 minutes), Heathrow Terminal 1 (±50 minutes) and Heathrow Terminal 3 (±56 minutes):
On Ⓐ at 0400, 0500, 0530, 0555, 0608, 0620, 0640, 0700, 0720, 0740, 0800, 0820, 0840, 0905 and every 20 minutes until 1805, 1835, 1905, 1935, 2005, 2035, 2105, 2205, 2305.
On Ⓒ at 0400, 0500, 0545, 0615, 0645 and every 30 minutes until 1915, 1945, 2025, 2055, 2205, 2305.
From **Heathrow Airport** Bus Station: Services call at Heathrow Terminal 5 (±10 minutes) and Reading Railway Station (±50 minutes).
On Ⓐ at 0005, 0500, 0600, 0630, 0657, 0720 and every 20 minutes until 1000, 1015, and every 20 minutes until 1755, 1815, 1835, 1855, 1915, 1940, 2010, 2040, 2110, 2140, 2215, 2305.
On Ⓒ at 0005, 0500, 0600, 0700, 0730 and every 30 minutes until 1900, 1920, 1950, 2020, 2050, 2130, 2200, 2305.

RAILAIR LINK 🚌 **Woking** rail station - **Heathrow Airport** (Service **701**).
From **Woking**: Services call at Heathrow Terminal 5 (±25 - 45 minutes) and Heathrow Central Bus Station (±40 - 60 minutes).
0300, 0400, 0500, 0600, 0640, 0740, 0845, 0945, 1050, 1135 and hourly until 1735, 1845, 1945, 2045, 2130, 2220.
From **Heathrow** Central Bus Station: Services call at Heathrow Terminal 5 (±15 minutes) and Woking (±45 - 65 minutes).
0545, 0645, 0745, 0845, 0950, 1040, 1140, 1230 and hourly until 1630, 1735, 1835, 1940, 2040, 2130, 2215, 2315.

Luton ✈

Thameslink Railway services Brighton - Gatwick Airport - London St Pancras - Luton Airport Parkway ◧ - Luton ◧ - Bedford: Table **103**.
East Midlands Trains services London St Pancras - Luton Airport Parkway ◧ - Luton ◧ - Leicester - Nottingham / Derby / Sheffield: Table **170**.
◧ – A frequent shuttle 🚌 service operates between each of the railway stations and the airport terminal.

🚌 service **Milton Keynes** - **Luton Airport** and v.v. (Stagecoach route **99**. Journey 55 minutes) for connections from / to **Birmingham**, **Liverpool** and **Manchester** (Table **150**).
From **Milton Keynes** railway station: on Ⓐ at 0645, 0745, 0900 and hourly until 1600, 1710, 1740, 1810, 1910, 2010, 2110, 2210; on ⑥ at 0635, 0755, 0900 and hourly until 1600, 1710, 1810, 1910, 2010, 2110; on ⑦ at 0900 and hourly until 2100.
From **Luton Airport**: on Ⓐ at 0545, 0655, 0755, 0915 and hourly until 1715, 1820, 1920, 2020, 2120; on ⑥ at 0535, 0700, 0800, 0915 and hourly until1715, 1820, 1920, 2020; on ⑦ at 0815 and hourly until 2015.

Stansted ✈

STANSTED EXPRESS: Daily rail service from / to **London** Liverpool St. Journey time ± 45 minutes.
From **London** Liverpool Street: on ⚒ at 0440, 0510 and every 15 minutes until 2255, 2325; on ⑦ at 0410, 0440, 0510, 0540, 0610 and every 15 minutes until 2255, 2325.
From **Stansted Airport**: on ⚒ at 0030, 0600 and every 15 minutes until 2345, 2359; on ⑦ at 0030, 0530, 0600, 0630, 0700 and every 15 minutes until 2345, 2359.

Most trains call at **Tottenham Hale** for London Underground (Victoria Line) connections to / from Kings Cross, St Pancras, Euston, and Victoria stations.
For *Cross Country* services to / from Cambridge, Peterborough, Leicester and Birmingham see Table **208**.

City ✈

DOCKLANDS LIGHT RAILWAY from / to **Bank** (interchange with London Underground: Central, Circle, District, Northern, and Waterloo & City Lines).
Trains run every 7 - 10 minutes 0530 - 0030 on ⚒, 0700 - 2330 on ⑦. Journey time: ± 22 minutes.

Inter - Airport 🚌 links

Operator: National Express ✆ 08717 81 81 81. www.nationalexpress.com

Gatwick North Terminal - **Heathrow** Central. Journey 1½ hours
0015, 0035, 0240, 0340, 0535, 0540, 0600, 0615, 0635, 0700, 0720Ⓐ, 0735Ⓒ, 0800Ⓐ, 0815Ⓒ, 0820Ⓐ, 0835, 0905, 0935, 0940, 1015, 1025, 1035, 1100, 1120, 1135, 1140, 1215, 1235, 1245, 1300, 1315, 1335, 1340, 1415, 1435, 1455, 1515, 1530, 1535, 1540, 1545, 1615, 1635, 1645, 1705Ⓐ, 1715Ⓒ, 1720, 1735, 1740, 1815, 1835, 1900, 1920, 1935, 1950, 1955, 2015, 2030, 2035, 2130, 2205, 2225, 2230, 2240, 2305, 2315, 2340, 2355.

Heathrow Central - **Gatwick** North Terminal.
0055, 0155, 0245, 0300, 0320, 0335, 0400, 0430, 0440, 0510, 0535, 0540, 0605, 0630, 0640, 0700, 0715, 0730Ⓐ, 0740, 0805, 0825, 0840, 0925, 0945Ⓒ, 0955, 1000Ⓐ, 1005, 1025, 1040, 1055, 1110, 1125, 1155, 1205, 1215, 1225, 1240, 1255, 1325, 1340, 1355, 1405, 1415, 1425, 1440, 1455, 1525, 1555, 1605, 1610, 1630, 1640, 1655, 1710, 1735, 1755Ⓒ, 1805, 1825, 1910Ⓒ, 1920Ⓒ, 1925Ⓐ, 1935Ⓐ, 1945Ⓒ, 1955Ⓒ, 2005, 2040, 2055, 2110, 2200, 2255, 2355.

Gatwick North Terminal - **Stansted**. Journey 3 hours
0340, 0535, 0720Ⓐ, 0735Ⓒ, 0935, 1135, 1335, 1535, 1735, 1935, 2205.

Stansted - **Gatwick** North Terminal.
0140, 0405, 0605, 0815, 1015, 1215, 1415, 1615Ⓒ, 1625Ⓐ, 1815Ⓒ, 1825Ⓐ, 2115.

Heathrow Central - **Luton**. Journey 1–1½ hours
0005, 0550Ⓐ, 0605Ⓒ, 0730, 0750Ⓐ, 0805Ⓒ, 1005, 1205, 1405, 1605, 1805, 2005, 2205.

From **Luton** to **Heathrow** Central.
0355, 0555, 0740Ⓐ, 0755Ⓒ, 0955, 1155, 1355, 1555, 1755, 1955, 2155.

Heathrow Central - **Stansted**. Journey 1½ hours
0505, 0705, 0905, 1105, 1305, 1505, 1705, 1905, 2105, 2335.

Stansted - **Heathrow** Central.
0140, 0405, 0605, 0815, 1015, 1215, 1415, 1615Ⓒ, 1625Ⓐ, 1815Ⓒ, 1825Ⓐ, 2115.

Stansted - **Luton**. Journey 1½ hours
0100, 0615Ⓐ, 0645Ⓒ, 0920, 1200, 1400, 1630, 1900, 2200.

Luton - **Stansted**.
0300, 0630, 0910, 1130, 1355, 1620, 1855Ⓒ, 1905Ⓐ, 2055.

Special fares are payable for high-speed services. For slower services see Table **102**.

Via Faversham

km			Ⓐ	ⒶF	Ⓐ	ⒶF		ⒶF	Ⓐ	Ⓐ	Ⓐ	Ⓐ	Ⓐ	Ⓐ	Ⓐ		Ⓐ	Ⓐ	ⒶA	Ⓐ	Ⓐ	Ⓐ		⑥F	⑥	⑥F	⑥
0	**London** St Pancras d.	Ⓐ	0655	0722	0755	0825		1525	1555	1625	1658	1725	1755	1825	1855		2125	2155	2225	2255	2325	2355	⑥	0725	0755	0825	0852
9	Stratford Int'l d.		0702	0729	0805	0832	and at	1532	1602	1632	1705	1732	1802	1832	1902	and at	2132	2202	2232	2302	2332	0002		0732	0802	0832	0859
35	Ebbsfleet Int'l d.		0713	0740	0816	0843	the same	1543	1613	1643	1716	1743	1813	1844	1913	the same	2143	2213	2243	2313	2343	0013		0743	0813	0843	0913
52	Rochester d.		0731	0758	0834	0901	minutes	1601	1631	1701	1734	1758	1830	1902	1931	minutes	2201	2231	2301	2331	0001	0031		0801	0831	0901	0931
54	Chatham d.		0735	0801	0837	0904	past each	1604	1634	1704	1738	1802	1834	1906	1934	past each	2204	2234	2304	2334	0004	0034		0804	0834	0904	0934
70	Sittingbourne d.		0752	0818	0854	0921	hour until	1621	1651	1721	1755	1820	1852	1924	1953	hour until	2221	2251	2321	2351	0021	0051		0821	0851	0921	0951
83	Faversham a.		0801	0826	0903	0929	♣	1629	1700	1730	1803	1828	1900	1932	2006	♣	2229	2300	2329	0002	0030	0100		0829	0900	0929	1000
100	Herne Bay a.		...	0842	...	0944		1646	...	...	...	1843	1915	1948	...		2246	...	2346	...	...	...		0844	...	0944	...
118	**Margate** a.		...	0859	...	0959		1702	...	...	..	1857	1931	2004	...		2302	...	0002	...	...	...		0859	...	0959	...

	⑥F	⑥	⑥F		⑥F	⑥	⑥	⑥	⑥	⑥	⑥	⑥		⑦F	⑦F	⑦F	⑦F	⑦F	⑦		⑦K	⑦	⑦	⑦	⑦	⑦	⑦
London St Pancras d.	0927	0955	1022		2025	2055	2125	2155	2225	2255	2325	2355	⑦	0825	0927	1027	1125	1225	1252		2025	2055	2125	2155	2225	2255	2325
Stratford Int'l d.	0934	1002	1032	and at	2032	2102	2132	2202	2232	2302	2332	0002		0832	0934	1034	1132	1232	1259	and at	2032	2102	2132	2202	2232	2302	2332
Ebbsfleet Int'l d.	0945	1013	1043	the same	2043	2113	2143	2213	2243	2313	2343	0013		0843	0945	1045	1143	1243	1313	the same	2043	2113	2143	2213	2243	2313	2343
Rochester d.	1002	1031	1101	minutes	2101	2131	2201	2231	2301	2331	0001	0031		0901	1002	1102	1201	1301	1331	minutes	2101	2131	2201	2231	2301	2334	0001
Chatham d.	1005	1034	1104	past each	2104	2134	2204	2234	2304	2334	0004	0034		0904	1005	1105	1204	1304	1334	past each	2104	2134	2204	2234	2304	2337	0004
Sittingbourne d.	1022	1051	1121	hour until	2121	2151	2221	2251	2321	2351	0021	0051		0921	1022	1122	1221	1321	1351	hour until	2121	2151	2221	2251	2321	2355	0021
Faversham a.	1030	1100	1129	♣	2129	2200	2229	2300	2329	0001	0030	0100		0929	1030	1130	1229	1329	1404	♣	2129	2204	2229	2304	2329	0004	0030
Herne Bay a.	1044	...	1144		2144	...	2244	...	2344	*0040*	...	...		0944	1044	1144	1244	1344	...		2144	...	2244	...	2344	...	...
Margate a.	1059	...	1159		2159	...	2259	...	2359	*0057*	...	...		0959	1059	1159	1259	1359	...		2159	...	2259	...	2359	...	...

		Ⓐ	Ⓐ	Ⓐ	Ⓐ	Ⓐ	Ⓐ	Ⓐ	Ⓐ	Ⓐ	Ⓐ	ⒶG	Ⓐ	ⒶG		ⒶG	Ⓐ	Ⓐ	ⒶG	Ⓐ	Ⓐ	Ⓐ	Ⓐ	ⒶG		⑥	⑥	⑥
Margate d.	Ⓐ	...	*0443*	*0517*	0605	0634	0703	...	...	0826	...	0926	...	1030		1730	...	1826	1838	1930	...	2030	...	2130	⑥	...	...	0630
Herne Bay d.		...	*0459*	*0533*	0619	0648	0717	...	...	0843	...	0943	...	1044	and at	1744	...	1843	1854	1944	...	2044	...	2144		...	...	0644
Faversham d.		0458	0528	0558	0634	0702	0731	0759	0828	0859	0926	0959	1026	1059	the same	1759	1829	1859	1928t	1959	2028	2059	2126	2159		0528	0628	0659
Sittingbourne d.		0507	0537	0607	0642	0710	0739	0807	0837	0907	0937	1007	1037	1107	minutes	1807	1837	1907	1937	2007	2037	2107	2137	2207		0537	0637	0707
Chatham d.		0524	0554	0624	0659	0727	0758	0824	0854	0924	0954	1024	1054	1124	past each	1824	1854	1924	1954	2024	2054	2124	2154	2224		0554	0654	0724
Rochester d.		0528	0558	0628	0703	0730	0802	0828	0858	0928	0958	1028	1058	1128	hour until	1828	1858	1928	1958	2028	2058	2128	2158	2228		0558	0658	0728
Ebbsfleet Int'l a.		0546	0616	0646	0717	0747	0817	0847	0916	0946	1016	1046	1116	1146	♣	1849	1916	1946	2016	2046	2116	2146	2216	2246		0616	0716	0746
Stratford Int'l a.		0558	0628	0658	0729	0800	0830	0859	0928	0959	1028	1058	1129	1159		1902	1928	1959	2028	2102	2128	2159	2228	2258		0628	0728	0758
London St Pancras a.		0606	0636	0707	0737	0807	0838	0907	0936	1006	1036	1106	1140	1206		1910	1936	2006	2036	2109	2136	2207	2236	2306		0636	0736	0806

	⑥	⑥H	⑥	⑥G		⑥	⑥G	⑥	⑥G	⑥	⑥G	⑥	⑥G		⑦	⑦		⑦	⑦H	⑦G	⑦	⑦G		⑦	⑦G	⑦	⑦G
Margate d.	...	0730	...	0830		...	1830	...	1930	...	2030	...	2130	⑦	...	...	...	0830	0930	1030	...	1130		...	2030	...	2130
Herne Bay d.	...	0744	...	0844	and at	...	1844	...	1944	...	2044	...	2144		...	...	...	0844	0944	1044	...	1144	and at	...	2044	...	2144
Faversham d.	0728	0759	0828	0859	the same	1826	1859	1926	1959	2026	2059	2126	2159		0659	0759	...	0859	0959	1059	1129	1159	the same	2029	2059	2129	2159
Sittingbourne d.	0737	0807	0837	0907	minutes	1837	1907	1937	2007	2037	2107	2137	2207		0707	0807	...	0907	1007	1107	1137	1207	minutes	2037	2107	2137	2207
Chatham d.	0754	0824	0854	0924	past each	1854	1924	1954	2024	2054	2124	2154	2224		0724	0824	...	0924	1024	1124	1154	1224	past each	2054	2124	2154	2224
Rochester d.	0758	0828	0858	0928	hour until	1858	1928	1958	2028	2058	2128	2158	2228		0728	0828	...	0928	1028	1128	1158	1228	hour until	2058	2128	2158	2228
Ebbsfleet Int'l a.	0816	0846	0916	0946	♣	1916	1946	2016	2046	2116	2146	2216	2246		0746	0846	...	0946	1046	1146	1216	1246	♣	2116	2146	2216	2246
Stratford Int'l a.	0829	0858	0929	0958		1928	1958	2028	2102	2128	2158	2228	2258		0758	0858	...	0958	1058	1159	1228	1258		2128	2159	2228	2258
London St Pancras a.	0836	0906	0936	1006		1936	2006	2036	2109	2136	2206	2236	2306		0806	0906	...	1006	1106	1207	1236	1306		2136	2207	2236	2306

Via Ashford and Dover

km			②–⑤	Ⓐ	Ⓐ	ⒶD	Ⓐ	Ⓐ	ⒶD	Ⓐ	ⒶD		Ⓐ	ⒶD	Ⓐ	Ⓐ	Ⓐ	Ⓐ	Ⓐ	Ⓐ	Ⓐ	Ⓐ	Ⓐ	Ⓐ	Ⓐ	ⒶD
0	**London** St Pancras d.	Ⓐ	0012	0640	0704	0725	0737	0812	0837	0909	0937		1612	1637	1650	1707	1720	1737	1750	1807	1820	1837	1850	1907	1920	1937
9	Stratford International d.		0019	0647	0711	0732	0744	0819	0844	0916	0944	and at	1619	1644	1657	1714	1727	1744	1757	1814	1827	1845	1857	1914	1927	1944
35	Ebbsfleet International d.		0030	0659	0722	|	0755	0830	0855	0927	0955	the same	1630	1655	|	1726	|	1756	|	1826	|	1856	|	1926	|	1955
90	Ashford International d.		0050	0722	0742	0801	0817	0852	0915	0952	1015	minutes	1652	1718	1726	1747	1756	1817	1826	1847	1856	1917	1926	1947	1956	2015
112	**Folkestone** Central d.		...	|	|	0819	0837	|	0930	|	1030	past each	|	1733	|	1803	|	1835	|	1903	|	1934	|	2003	|	2030
124	**Dover** Priory a.		...	|	|	0830	0847	|	0941	|	1041	hour until	|	1744	|	1815	|	1845	|	1915	|	1945	|	2015	|	2041
112	Canterbury West d.		...	0740	0758	|	|	0909	|	1009	|	♠	1709	|	1742	...	1812	|	1842	...	1912	...	1942	...	2012	|
140	Ramsgate a.		...	0803	0818	0910	0924	0927	1018	1027	1118		1729	1823	1801	...	1831	1925	1901	...	1931	...	2001	...	2031	2118
149	**Margate** a.		...	...	0831	0926	...	0939	1030	1039	1130		1741	1837	1815	...	1845	...	1915	...	1945	...	2015	...	2045	2130

	Ⓐ	Ⓐ	Ⓐ	Ⓐ	ⒶB	Ⓐ	②–⑤	①	Ⓐ		⑥	⑥D	⑥D	⑥		⑥D	⑥	⑥	⑥	⑥	⑥	⑥	⑥	⑥		⑦
London St Pancras d.	2012	2037	2112	2137	2212	2237	2312	2312	2337	⑥	0012	...	0637	0708		1937	2012	2037	2112	2137	2212	2237	2312	2337	⑦	0012
Stratford International d.	2019	2044	2119	2144	2219	2244	2319	2319	2344		0019	...	0644	0715	and at	1944	2019	2044	2119	2144	2219	2244	2319	2344		0019
Ebbsfleet International d.	2030	2055	2130	2155	2230	2255	2330	2330	2355		0030	...	0655	0726	the same	1955	2030	2055	2130	2155	2230	2255	2330	2355		0030
Ashford International d.	2052	2115	2152	2215	2252	2315	2352	2352	0015		0050	0615	0715	0752	minutes	2015	2052	2115	2152	2215	2252	2315	2352	0015		0050
Folkestone Central d.	|	2130	|	2230	|	2330	|	|	0030		...	0630	0730	|	past each	2030	|	2130	|	2230	|	2330	|	0030		...
Dover Priory a.	|	2141	|	2241	|	2341	|	|	0041		...	0641	0741	|	hour until	2041	|	2141	|	2241	|	2341	|	0041		...
Canterbury West d.	2109	|	2209	|	2309	|	0009	*0034*p	|		...	|	|	0809	♠	|	2109	|	2209	|	2309	|	0009	|		...
Ramsgate a.	2131	2219	2227	2321	2330	0019	0030	0043	0121		...	0718	0818	0827		2119	2127	2219	2227	2321	2327	0021	0027	0121		...
Margate a.	2142	...	2239	...	2339	...	0039r	0058	...		...	0730	0830	0839		2130	2139	...	2239	...	2339	...	0039	...		...

	⑦D	⑦D	⑦		⑦D	⑦	⑦	⑦	⑦	⑦	⑦	⑦	⑦
London St Pancras d.	...	0837	0909		1937	2012	2037	2112	2137	2212	2237	2312	2337
Stratford International d.	...	0844	0916	and at	1944	2019	2044	2119	2144	2219	2244	2319	2344
Ebbsfleet International d.	...	0855	0927	the same	1955	2030	2055	2130	2155	2230	2255	2330	2355
Ashford International d.	0815	0915	0952	minutes	2015	2052	2115	2152	2215	2252	2315	2352	0015
Folkestone Central d.	0830	0930	|	past each	2030	|	2130	|	2230	|	2330	|	...
Dover Priory a.	0841	0941	|	hour until	2041	|	2141	|	2241	|	2341	|	...
Canterbury West d.	|	|	1009	♠	|	2109	|	2209	|	2309	|	0009	...
Ramsgate a.	0918	1018	1029		2118	2129	2218	2229	2318	2329	0018	0029	...
Margate a.	0930	1030	1041		2130	2141	...	2241	...	2341	...	0041	...

		Ⓐ	Ⓐ	Ⓐ	Ⓐ	Ⓐ	Ⓐ	Ⓐ	Ⓐ
Margate d.	Ⓐ	...	...	...	0546	...	0615	...	0646
Ramsgate d.		...	0455	...	0558	...	0628	0614	0658
Canterbury West d.		...	0518	...	0618	...	0648	|	0718
Dover Priory d.		...	|	0545	|	0618	|	0648	|
Folkestone Cent. d.		...	|	0556	|	0629	|	0659	|
Ashford Int'l d.		0513	0543	0613	0636	0646	0706	0716	0736
Ebbsfleet Int'l a.		0532	0602	0632	0655	0705	|	0735	|
Stratford Int'l a.		0544	0614	0644	0707	0717	0734	0747	0804
London St Pancras a.		0551	0621	0651	0714	0725	0742	0754	0813

	Ⓐ	Ⓐ	Ⓐ	Ⓐ	Ⓐ	Ⓐ	Ⓐ	ⒶE	Ⓐ		ⒶE	Ⓐ	Ⓐ	Ⓐ	Ⓐ	Ⓐ	Ⓐ	Ⓐ	Ⓐ	Ⓐ	Ⓐ	Ⓐ		⑥	⑥	⑥
Margate d.	...	0716	0656	0749	...	0851	...	0859	0953		1702	1753	...	1853	...	1953	...	2053	2100	2153	...	2253	⑥	...	...	0553
Ramsgate d.	...	0728	0712	0801	...	0903	0932	0912	1005	and at	1713	1805	...	1905	...	2005	...	2105	2112	2205	2212	2305		0505	...	0605
Canterbury West d.	...	0748	|	0825	...	0923	0952	|	1025	the same	|	1825	...	1925	...	2025	...	2125	|	2225	|	2325		0525	...	0625
Dover Priory d.	0716	|	0748	|	0849	|	|	0949	|	minutes	1749	|	1849	|	1949	|	2049	|	2149	|	2249	|		|	0549	|
Folkestone Central d.	0727	|	0759	|	0900	|	|	1000	|	past each	1800	|	1900	|	2000	|	2100	|	2200	|	2300	|		|	0600	|
Ashford International d.	0744	0806	0816	0843	0916	0943	1010	1016	1043	hour until	1816	1843	1916	1943	2016	2043	2116	2143	2216	2243	2316	2341		0543	0616	0643
Ebbsfleet International a.	|	|	0835	0902	0935	1002	|	1035	1102	♠	1835	1902	1935	2002	2035	2102	2135	2202	2235	2302	2335	...		0602	0635	0702
Stratford International a.	0812	0834	0847	0914	0947	1014	1038	1047	1114		1847	1914	1947	2014	2047	2114	2147	2214	2247	2314	2347	...		0614	0647	0714
London St Pancras a.	0820	0842	0854	0921	0954	1021	1046	1055	1121		1854	1921	1954	2021	2054	2121	2154	2221	2254	2321	2354	...		0621	0654	0721

	⑥	⑥	⑥	⑥	⑥	⑥	⑥E		⑥	⑥E	⑥		⑦	⑦	⑦		⑦	⑦	⑦	⑦	⑦E		⑦E	⑦	⑦E
Margate d.	...	0653	0657	0753	...	0853	0859		2153	2159	2253	⑦	...	...	0753	...	...	0853	...	0953	0959		2059	2153	2159
Ramsgate d.	0612	0705	0712	0805	0812	0905	0912	and at	2205	2212	2305		...	0712	0805	...	0812	0905	0912	1005	1012	and at	2112	2205	2212
Canterbury West d.	|	0725	|	0825	|	0925	|	the same	2225	|	2325		...	|	0825	...	|	0925	|	1025	|	the same	|	2225	|
Dover Priory d.	0649	|	0749	|	0849	|	0949	minutes	|	2249	|		...	0749	|	...	0849	|	0949	|	1049	minutes	2149	|	2249
Folkestone Central d.	0700	|	0800	|	0900	|	1000	past each	|	2300	|		...	0800	|	...	0900	|	1000	|	1100	past each	2200	|	2300
Ashford International d.	0716	0743	0816	0843	0916	0943	1016	hour until	2243	2316	2341		0743	0816	0843	...	0916	0943	1016	1043	1116	hour until	2216	2243	2315
Ebbsfleet International a.	0735	0802	0835	0902	0935	1002	1035	♠	2302	2335	...		0802	0835	0902	...	0935	1002	1035	1102	1135	♠	2235	2302	...
Stratford International a.	0747	0814	0847	0914	0947	1014	1047		2314	2347	...		0814	0847	0914	...	0947	1014	1047	1114	1147		2247	2314	...
London St Pancras a.	0754	0821	0855	0921	0954	1021	1055		2321	2354	...		0821	0854	0921	...	0954	1021	1054	1121	1154		2254	2321	...

A – ② departure from London St Pancras is operated by 🚌 after Faversham (Faversham d. 2336, Herne Bay d. 0012, Margate a. 0043).
B – ② departure from London St Pancras is operated by 🚌 after Ramsgate (Ramsgate d. 2335, Margate a. 2354).
D – To London St Pancras (see upper table).
E – From London St Pancras (see upper table).
F – To London St Pancras (see lower table).
G – From London St Pancras (see lower table).
H – From Ashford International (see lower table).
K – To Ashford International (see lower table).
p – Connection by 🚌 from Ashford; continues to Ramsgate (arr. 0112) and Margate (arr. 0131).
r – Not ②.
t – Arrives 1910.
♠ – Timings may vary by up to ± 4 minutes.
♣ – Timings may vary by up to ± 3 minutes.

Typical off-peak journey time in hours and minutes
READ DOWN ↓ READ UP ↑

Journey times may be extended during peak hours on Ⓐ (0600 - 0900 and 1600 - 1900) and also at weekends.
The longest journey time by any train is noted in the table heading.

LONDON VICTORIA - RAMSGATE

Longest journey: 2 hours 10 minutes SE

km	Read down ↓	Station	Read up ↑
0	0h00	d.**London** Victoria.....a.	1h57
18	0h17	d.Bromley South.......d.	1h40
53	0h47	d.Rochester..............d.	1h12
55	0h50	d.Chatham................d.	1h10
72	1h09	d.Sittingbourne..........d.	0h50
84	1h21	d.Faversham.............d.	0h42
101	1h36	d.Herne Bay.............d.	0h26
119	1h49	d.Margate.................d.	0h10
128	1h59	a.**Ramsgate**.............d.	0h00

From London Victoria: on Ⓐ at 0007②–⑥ **f**, 0522, 0552, 0622 **g**, 0652 **g**, 0736, 0837 and hourly until 1537, 1607, 1637 **g**, 1636 **c**, 1657, 1727, 1730 **c m**, 1752 **c m**, 1757 **m**, 1812 **c**, 1827, 1844 **c**, 1857, 1937, 2037, 2137, 2207 **f g**, 2237 **f**, 2307 **f**; on ⑥ at 0007, 0707 **g**, 0737 and hourly until 2237, 2307; on ⑦ at 0007, 0745 and hourly until 2045, 2104 **h**, 2145, 2204 **h**, 2245, 2304 **h**, 2345 **h**.

From Ramsgate: on Ⓐ at 0432, 0506, 0539, 0608, 0629 **m c**, 0632, 0651 **m c**, 0703, 0708 **m c**, 0719 **b**, 0754 and hourly until 1354, 1450, 1545, 1648, 1705, 1748, 1848, 1954, 2050, 2154, 2310 **h**; on ⑥ at 0430, 0554 and hourly until 2154, 2310 **h**; on ⑦ at 0705, and hourly until 2105, 2120 **g**, 2235.

b – To London Blackfriars, not Victoria.
c – From / to London Cannon Street, not Victoria.
f – On Tuesday nights / Wednesday mornings does not call at Herne Bay or Margate.
h – To Faversham.
g – Change at Faversham.
m – To / from Margate.

LONDON VICTORIA - DOVER

Longest journey: 2 hours 10 minutes SE

km	Read down ↓	Station	Read up ↑
0	0h00	d.**London** Victoria.....a.	2h02
18	0h17	d.Bromley South.......d.	1h43
53	0h47	d.Rochester..............d.	1h17
55	0h50	d.Chatham................d.	1h15
72	1h09	d.Sittingbourne..........d.	0h58
84	1h21	d.Faversham.............d.	0h47
99	1h37	d.Canterbury East.....d.	0h27
124	1h58	a.**Dover** Priory..........d.	0h00

From London Victoria: on Ⓐ at 0522 **g**, 0552 **g**, 0622, 0652, 0734, 0807, 0834 and at the same minutes past each hour until 1407, 1437 **g**, 1507, 1537 **g**, 1607, 1636 **c g**, 1637, 1657 **g**, 1708 **c**, 1727, 1730 **c g**, 1757, 1827, 1857, 1927 **b**, 1937 **g**, 2007, 2034 **e**, 2107, 2134 **e**, 2207; on ⑥ at 0522, 0634, 0707, 0734 and at the same minutes past each hour until 1934, 2007, 2034 **e**, 2107, 2134 **e**, 2207; on ⑦ at 0745, 0804 **e**, 0845, 0904 **e** and at the same minutes past each hour until 2004 **e**, 2045, 2104 **h**, 2145.

From Dover Priory: on Ⓐ at 0430, 0500 **g**, 0545 **b**, 0605 **g**, 0628 **g**, 0702, 0735, 0820, 0852, 0920, 0952 and at the same minutes past each hour until 1520, 1551, 1620, 1651 **g**, 1720, 1751, 1820, 1851, 1920, 2005, 2105, 2205, 2305 **h**; on ⑥ at 0520, 0620, 0652 and at the same minutes past each hour until 1920, 2005, 2105, 2205, 2305 **h**; on ⑦ at 0705, 0805, 0903 **e**, 0905 and at the same minutes past each hour until 2005, 2103 **e**, 2105, 2203 **e**, 2235 **g**.

b – From / to London Blackfriars, not Victoria. **c** – From London Cannon Street, not Victoria. **e** – To / from Canterbury East. **g** – Change at Faversham. **h** – To Faversham.

LONDON CHARING CROSS - CANTERBURY WEST

Longest journey: 1 hour 55 minutes SE

km	Read down ↓	Station	Read up ↑
0	0h00	d.**London** C Cross ...a.	1h46
1	0h03	d.**London** Waterloo ‡ a.	1h42
3	0h08	d.**London** Bridge ......a.	1h36
36	0h32	d.Sevenoaks.............d.	1h13
48	0h40	d.Tonbridge..............d.	1h04
90	1h20	a.Ashford Int'l...........d.	0h27
113	1h38	a.**Canterbury** West....d.	0h00

From London Charing Cross: on Ⓐ at 0530 **d**, 0636 **c g**, 0709, 0738, 0817 **g**, 0923 **g**, 0940 **d**, 1010, 1040 **d** and at the same minutes past each hour until 1609, 1638, 1709, 1738, 1800 **d**, 1808 **c g**, 1840, 1910, 1940 **d**, 2010, 2110, 2210 **e**, 2310 **e**, 2340 **e h**; on ⑥ at 0602, 0710, 0740 **d**, 0810 and at the same minutes past each hour until 1910, 2010, 2110, 2210, 2310, 2340 **d**; on ⑦ at 0810, 0840 **d** and at the same minutes past each hour until 1710 then hourly until 2210.

From Canterbury West: on Ⓐ at 0518 **d**, 0600, 0634 **c g**, 0703, 0718 **d**, 0736, 0806 **d**, 0836 **d**, 0906 **d**, 0937, 1006 **d**, 1042 and at the same minutes past each hour until 1506 **d g**, 1542 **g**, 1606 **d**, 1641, 1706 **d**, 1740, 1806 **d**, 1836, 1939, 2039, 2139; on ⑥ at 0539, 0637, 0737, 0806 **d**, 0840, 0906 **d**, 0938, 1006 **d**, 1042 at the same minutes past each hour until 1942, 2006 **d**, 2039, 2139, 2239 **k**; on ⑦ at 0740, 0840, 0906 **d**, 0943 and at the same minutes past each hour until 1843, 1906 **d**, 1940, 2040, 2140.

c – To / from London Cannon Street.
d – Change trains at Ashford.
e – On ① change trains at Ashford for 🚌 connection to Canterbury.
g – Does not call at London Bridge.
h – On ②–⑤ change trains at Ashford.
k – To Tonbridge.
‡ – London Waterloo East.

LONDON CHARING CROSS - DOVER

Longest journey: 2 hours 06 minutes SE

km	Read down ↓	Station	Read up ↑
0	0h00	d.**London** C Cross ...a.	1h58
1	0h03	d.**London** Waterloo ‡ a.	1h53
3	0h08	d.**London** Bridge ......a.	1h42
36	0h32	d.Sevenoaks.............d.	1h18
48	0h40	d.Tonbridge..............d.	1h06
90	1h20	d.Ashford Int'l...........d.	0h29
113	1h40	d.Folkstone Central...d.	0h12
124	1h52	a.**Dover** Priory..........d.	0h00

From London Charing Cross: on Ⓐ at 0530, 0636 **c d**, 0709, 0738, 0836 **b**, 0940 and hourly until 1240, 1310 **d**, 1340, 1410, 1440, 1510, 1540, 1609, 1638, 1650 **f**, 1724 **b c**, 1738 **d**, 1745 **c f**, 1800, 1832 **b c**, 1910, 1940, 2040, 2140, 2240, 2340; on ⑥ at 0740 and hourly until 2340; on ⑦ at 0840 and hourly until 2240.

From Dover Priory: on Ⓐ at 0429 **b c**, 0529, 0559 **b c**, 0628, 0711 **b c f**, 0725, 0758, 0825, 0858, 0925, 0958 and hourly until 1458 **b**, 1558 **b**, 1625, 1658, 1725, 1758, 1825, 1858, 1958, 2058, 2158 **e**; on ⑥ at 0458 and hourly until 2058, 2158 **e**; on ⑦ at 0759 and hourly until 2059.

b – Does not call at London Bridge.
c – From / to London Cannon Street.
d – Change trains at Ashford.
e – Terminates at Tonbridge.
f – To / from Folkestone Central.
‡ – London Waterloo East.

LONDON VICTORIA - ASHFORD INTERNATIONAL

Longest journey: 1 hours 40 minutes SE

km	Read down ↓	Station	Read up ↑
0	0h00	d.**London** Victoria.....a.	1h29
18	0h17	d.Bromley South.......d.	1h14
28	0h28	d.Swanley.................d.	1h03
56	0h52	d.West Malling..........d.	0h42
64	1h03	d.Maidstone East......d.	0h30
68	1h09	d.Bearsted................d.	0h25
95	1h31	a.**Ashford** Int'l..........d.	0h00

From London Victoria: on Ⓐ at 0022 ②–⑤, 0555, 0637, 0707, 0752, 0822, 0852 and every 30 minutes until 1622, 1652, 1712, 1742, 1747 **b**, 1818, 1842, 1904 **b**, 1922, 1952, 2022, 2052, 2122, 2152, 2222, 2252, 2322; on ⑥ at 0022, 0622, 0722, 0752 and every 30 minutes until 2322; on ⑦ at 0022, 0736 and hourly until 2336.

From Ashford International: on Ⓐ at 0514, 0532 **b**, 0547, 0601, 0617, 0624 **b**, 0640, 0656, 0711, 0748, 0830, 0910, 0930, 1010, 1038 and at the same minutes past each hour until 1538, 1602, 1638, 1702, 1738, 1802, 1838, 1900, 1938, 2002, 2038, 2102, 2132, 2232; on ⑥ at 0532, 0610, 0638 and at the same minutes past each hour until 2038, 2110, 2132, 2232; on ⑦ at 0646 and hourly until 2146.

b – From / to Blackfriars, not Victoria.

LONDON CHARING CROSS - HASTINGS

Longest journey: 1 hour 53 minutes SE

km	Read down ↓	Station	Read up ↑
0	0h00	d.**London** C Cross ...a.	1h43
1	0h03	d.**London** Waterloo ‡ a.	1h39
3	0h08	d.**London** Bridge ......a.	1h35
36	0h34	d.Sevenoaks.............d.	1h09
48	0h43	d.Tonbridge..............d.	1h00
55	0h55	d.Tunbridge Wells.....d.	0h49
89	1h33	d.Battle.....................d.	0h16
100	1h45	a.**Hastings**...............d.	0h00

From London Charing Cross: on Ⓐ at 0628, 0715, 0745 **c d**, 0819 **d**, 0842 **c d**, 0914 **c d**, 0945 and every 30 minutes until 1545, 1612, 1622 **c d** *, 1642, 1702 **c d**, 1714 *, 1737 **c d** *, 1756 *, 1828 **c d** *, 1845, 1905 **c d**, 1915, 1945, 2015, 2045, 2145, 2245, 2345; on ⑥ at 0715, 0745, 0815, 0845 and every 30 minutes until 2015, 2045, 2145, 2245, 2345; on ⑦ at 0825, 0855, and every 30 minutes until 1925, 1955, 2025, 2125, 2225, 2325.

From Hastings: on Ⓐ at 0517, 0537 **c d**, 0548 **c d**, 0604 *, 0620 *, 0628 *, 0643 **c d** *, 0703 *, 0725 **c d** *, 0744, 0804 **c d** *, 0814, 0847, 0929, 0947, 1031, 1050 and at the same minutes past each hour until 1450 **d**, 1531 **d**, 1545 **c d**, 1619 **d**, 1645, 1719, 1750, 1819, 1846, 1950, 2050, 2150; on ⑥ at 0548, 0620, 0650, 0720, 0750, 0820, 0850, 0931, 0950 and at the same minutes past each hour until 1650, 1720, 1750, 1820, 1850, 1950, 2050, 2150; on ⑦ at 0650, 0720, 0750, 0831, 0850 and at the same minutes past each hour until 1831, 1850, 1950, 2050, 2150.

c – From / to London Cannon Street.
d – Does not call at London Bridge.
* – Does not call at Sevenoaks and Tonbridge. Frequent trains call at these stations.
‡ – London Waterloo East.

LONDON VICTORIA - EASTBOURNE

Longest journey: 1 hour 44 minutes SN

km	Read down ↓	Station	Read up ↑
0	0h00	d.**London** Victoria.....a.	1h26
17	0h16	d.East Croydon.........d.	1h09
43	0h33	d.Gatwick Airport ......d.	0h53
61	0h50	d.Haywards Heath ....d.	0h34
81	1h06	d.Lewes....................d.	0h19
106	1h27	a.**Eastbourne**...........d.	0h00

From London Victoria: on Ⓐ at 0005 ②–⑤, 0532, 0647, 0747, 0817, 0847, 0917 and every 30 minutes until 1647, 1723 **b**, 1727, 1757, 1823 **b**, 1846, 1917, 1947, 2017, 2047, 2117, 2147, 2247; on ⑥ at 0005, 0747 and every 30 minutes until 2147, 2247; on ⑦ at 0005, 0847 and hourly until 2247.

From Eastbourne: on Ⓐ at 0508, 0543 **b**, 0621 **b**, 0654 **g**, 0712 **g b**, 0731 **g**, 0757, 0818, 0853, 0931, 0955, 1035, 1055 and at the same minutes past each hour until 1435, 1453, 1535, 1553, 1635, 1653, 1733, 1755, 1831, 1859, 1931, 1955, 2031, 2131, 2216; on ⑥ at 0503, 0628, 0655, 0735, 0755 and at the same minutes past each hour until 1935, 1955, 2035, 2135, 2218; on ⑦ at 0658, 0755, 0859 and hourly until 2059.

b – From / to London Bridge, not Victoria.
g – Does not call at Gatwick Airport.

ASHFORD - HASTINGS - EASTBOURNE - BRIGHTON

Longest journey: 2 hours 07 minutes SN

km	Read down ↓	Station	Read up ↑
0	0h00	d.**Ashford** Int'l ‡.......a.	1h46
25	0h23	d.Rye ‡......................d.	1h24
42	0h42	d.**Hastings**...............d.	1h04
50	0h52	d.Bexhill....................d.	0h52
67	1h07	a.**Eastbourne**...........d.	0h37
67	1h15	d.**Eastbourne**...........a.	0h32
93	1h35	d.Lewes....................d.	0h12
106	1h48	a.**Brighton**...............d.	0h00

From Ashford International: on Ⓐ at 0614, 0715, 0833, 0853 **h**, 0933 and hourly until 1933, 1959 **h**, 2033, 2133, 2234 **h**; on ⑥ at 0615, 0733 and hourly until 2133, 2234 **h**; on ⑦ at 0811, 0916 and hourly until 2116, 2234 **h**.

From Brighton: on Ⓐ at 0450 **k**, 0512 **e**, 0546 **h**, 0554 **k**, 0615, 0732 and hourly until 1532, 1632, 1709 **h**, 1730, 1832, 1932, 2030; on ⑥ at 0510 **e**, 0520 **h**, 0553 **k**, 0632 and hourly until 2032; on ⑦ at 0722 **h**, 0748 **k**, 0812 and hourly until 2012.

e – Change at Eastbourne. **h** – Ashford - Hastings and v.v. **k** – Eastbourne - Hastings.
‡ – Additional services operate on Ⓐ: Ashford - Rye at 0635, 0741, 1800, 1902; Rye - Ashford at 0706, 0814, 1831, 1933.
☛ Additional local services are available Brighton / Lewes - Eastbourne - Hastings v.v.

For explanation of standard symbols see page 1

Typical off-peak journey time in hours and minutes
READ DOWN ↓ READ UP ↑

Journey times may be extended during peak hours on Ⓐ (0600 - 0900 and 1600 - 1900) and also at weekends.
The longest journey time by any train is noted in the table heading.

LONDON BRIDGE - UCKFIELD

Longest journey: 1 hour 19 minutes SN

km					
0	0h00	↓	d.**London** Bridge......a.	↑	1h15
16	0h16		d.East Croydon.........d.		0h59
32	0h29	↓	d.Oxted.....................d.	↑	0h44
57	0h55		d.Eridge △ ....d.		0h17
70	1h01	↓	d.Crowborough ....d.	↑	0h12
74	1h15		a.**Uckfield** ....d.		0h00

From London Bridge: on Ⓐ at 0526 **e**, 0602, 0638, 0703, 0755, 0902, 1008 and hourly until 1508, 1538, 1608, 1638, 1708, 1806, 1817 **x**, 1908, 2004, 2104, 2204, 2304; on ⑥ at 0608 and hourly until 2208, 2304.

From Uckfield: on Ⓐ at 0516, 0540, 0630, 0705, 0731, 0801, 0833, 0934 and hourly until 1534, 1633, 1732, 1832, 1900, 1933, 2004, 2034, 2134, 2234; on ⑥ at 0634 and hourly until 2234.

On ⑦ services run Oxted - Uckfield and v.v. only. Connections available from/to London Victoria (see East Grinstead Table). From Oxted at 0937 ⑦ and hourly until 2237 ⑦. From Uckfield at 1034 ⑦ and hourly until 2134 ⑦, 2234 ⑦ **e**.

e – East Croydon - Uckfield and v.v. **x** – Change at Oxted. △ – **Spa Valley Railway** (🚂 Eridge - Tunbridge Wells West: *8 km*). ☎ 01892 537715. www.spavalleyrailway.co.uk

LONDON VICTORIA - EAST GRINSTEAD

Longest journey: 60 minutes SN

km					
0	0h00	↓	d.**London** Victoria.....a.	↑	0h56
17	0h17		d.East Croydon.........d.		0h37
33	0h37		d.Oxted.....................d.		0h16
42	0h43	↓	d.Lingfield.................d.	↑	0h12
48	0h54		a.**East Grinstead** ▽.d.		0h00

From London Victoria: on Ⓐ at 0526, 0547, 0624, 0654, 0710, 0718 **b**, 0732, 0750 **b**, 0824 **b**, 0853 and every 30 minutes until 1653, 1713 **b**, 1723, 1745 **b**, 1753, 1817 **b**, 1823, 1847 **b**, 1853 and every 30 minutes until 2323; on ⑥ at 0523, 0623, 0653 and every 30 minutes until 2253, 2324; on ⑦ at 0747, 0853, 0923, 0953 and every 30 minutes until 1953, 2053, 2153, 2236.

From East Grinstead: on Ⓐ at 0545 **b**, 0555, 0613 **b**, 0632, 0640 **b**, 0702, 0716 **b**, 0733, 0749 **b**, 0807, 0817 **b**, 0837 and every 30 minutes until 1807, 1817 **b**, 1837, 1847 **c**, 1907, 1947 **c**, 1937, 1947 **c**, 2007, 2037, 2107, 2137, 2207, 2237, 2254; on ⑥ at 0637 and every 30 minutes until 2237, 2257; on ⑦ at 0820, 0912, and every 30 minutes until 2012, 2112, 2212, 2309.

b – From/to London Bridge (not Victoria).
c – East Grinstead - East Croydon.
▽ – **Bluebell Railway** (🚂 East Grinstead - Sheffield Park: *18 km*). ☎ 01825 720800. www.bluebell-railway.com

LONDON VICTORIA - LITTLEHAMPTON

Longest journey: 1 hour 47 minutes SN

km					
0	0h00	↓	d.**London** Victoria.....a.	↑	1h42
17	0h16		d.East Croydon.........a.		1h25
43	0h33	↓	d.Gatwick Airport ......a.	↑	1h09
61	0h50		d.Haywards Heath ....a.		0h54
82	1h06	↓	d.Hove......................a.	↑	0h35
96	1h21		d.Worthing ....d.		0h21
114	1h41	↓	a.**Littlehampton**.......d.	↑	0h00

From London Victoria: on Ⓐ at 0747, 0817, 0847 and every 30 minutes until 1617, 1657 **bg**, 1718, 1741 **bg**, 1746, 1810 **bg**, 1817 **g**, 1846, 1917, 1947, 2017, 2047, 2147; on ⑥ at 0747, 0817, 0847 and every 30 minutes until 2017, 2047, 2147; on ⑦ at 0817 and hourly until 2117.

From Littlehampton: on Ⓐ at 0552 **b**, 0629 **bg**, 0640 **g**, 0700 **g**, 0729, 0814, 0851, 0914, 0947, 1014, 1051 and at the same minutes past each hour until 1514, 1549, 1614, 1651, 1714, 1751, 1814, 1914, 2014, 2114 ⑤; on ⑥ at 0545, 0614, 0651 and at the same minutes past each hour until 1814, 1914, 2014, 2114; on ⑦ at 0715 and hourly until 2015.

b – From/to London Bridge (not Victoria). **g** – Does not call at Gatwick Airport.

LONDON VICTORIA - BOGNOR REGIS

Longest journey: 1 hour 57 minutes SN

km					
0	0h00	↓	d.**London** Victoria.....a.	↑	1h50
17	0h16		d.East Croydon.........d.		1h30
43	0h37	↓	d.Gatwick Airport ......d.	↑	1h08
61	1h03		d.Horsham................d.		0h50
94	1h30	↓	d.Arundel..................d.	↑	0h16
110	1h40		d.Barnham.................d.		0h07
116	1h46	↓	a.**Bognor Regis**.......d.	↑	0h00

From London Victoria: on Ⓐ at 0602, 0803, 0832, 0902, 0932, 1006 and every 30 minutes until 1636, 1702 **g**, 1734 **g**, 1803 **g**, 1834 **g**, 1902, 1932, 2002, 2102, 2117 **k**, 2217 **k**; on ⑥ at 0736, 0806, 0836 and every 30 minutes until 1836, 1902, 1932, 2002, 2032, 2117 **k**, 2217 **k**; on ⑦ at 0702 and hourly until 2202.

From Bognor Regis: on Ⓐ at 0605, 0640 **g**, 0717 **g**, 0755, 0826, 0856, 0930, 0956 and at the same minutes past each hour until 1456, 1527, 1556, 1630, 1656, 1730, 1756, 1833 **k**, 1936 **k**, 2033 **k**; on ⑥ at 0630, 0656 and at the same minutes past each hour until 1756, 1833 **k**, 1930, 1940 **k**, 2040 **k**; on ⑦ at 0652, 0759 and hourly until 2159.

g – Does not call at Gatwick Airport. **k** – Does not call at Arundel and Horsham.

SEAFORD - BRIGHTON

Longest journey: 42 minutes SN

km					
0	0h00	↓	d.**Seaford**.................a.	↑	0h36
4	0h05		d.Newhaven Harbour..d.		0h30
5	0h07	↓	d.Newhaven Town ....d.	↑	0h28
15	0h19		d.Lewes.....................d.		0h18
22	0h26	↓	d.Falmer....................d.	↑	0h09
28	0h35		a.**Brighton** ....d.		0h00

From Seaford: on Ⓐ at 0509, 0544, 0627, 0717, 0733, 0759, 0855, 0925, 0954 and at the same minutes past each hour until 1654, 1720, 1757, 1824, 1841, 1859, 1917, 1937, 1957, 2028, 2057, 2128, 2157, 2220, 2257, 2325; on ⑥ at 0505, 0628, 0657, 0725, 0757 and at the same minutes past each hour until 1957, 2028, 2057, 2128, 2157, 2220, 2257, 2325; on ⑦ at 0757, 0828, 0857, 0928, 0957 and every 30 minutes until 2127, 2154, 2227, 2253.

From Brighton: on Ⓐ at 0545, 0639, 0652, 0717, 0740, 0810, 0845, 0910 and every 30 minutes until 1710, 1745, 1802, 1822, 1838, 1908, 1940, 2010, 2040, 2104, 2140, 2204, 2234, 2336; on ⑥ at 0552, 0610, 0640 and every 30 minutes until 2040, 2104, 2140, 2204, 2236, 2336; on ⑦ at 0715, 0749, 0817, 0849, 0917, 0947 and every 30 minutes until 2147, 2209, 2239.

BRIGHTON - PORTSMOUTH HARBOUR

Longest journey: 1 hour 49 minutes SN

km	⚒	⑦				⚒	⑦
0	0h00	0h00	↓	d.**Brighton**..............d.	↑	1h19	1h36
2	0h04	0h10		d.Hove......................d.		1h15	1h31
16	0h22	0h31	↓	d.Worthing ....d.	↑	0h57	1h10
35	0h39	0h54		d.Barnham ....d.		0h39	0h48
45	0h47	1h02	↓	d.Chichester ....d.	↑	0h31	0h39
59	1h02	1h23		d.Havant ....d.		0h17	0h19
71	1h14	1h37	↓	a.**Portsmouth** S ▽.d.	↑	0h04	0h04
72	1h18	1h41		a.**Portsmouth** Hbr ..d.		0h00	0h00

From Brighton: on Ⓐ at 0553, 0635, 0715, 0737 **t**, 0803, 0904, 1003 and hourly until 1503, 1603 **p**, 1705, 1800 **t**, 1900 **pt**, 2003 **t**, 2103 **t**, 2133 **t**, 2203 **t**; on ⑥ at 0601, 0703 and hourly until 1903 **t**, 1956 **t**, 2103 **t**, 2133 **t**, 2203 **t**; on ⑦ at 0715 **r**, 0719, 0820 **r**, 0830 and hourly until 2030, 2125, 2146 **r**.

From Portsmouth Harbour: on Ⓐ at 0528 **t**, 0604, 0701, 0720, 0829 and hourly until 1629, 1640, 1729, 1827, 1932 **p**, 2032 **p**, 2115 **pt**, 2215 **t**, 2240 **t**; on ⑥ at 0629, 0648, 0729 and hourly until 1929, 2028, 2111 **t**, 2215 **t**, 2244 **t**; on ⑦ at 0714 and hourly until 1914, 2011, 2114, 2144.

p – To/from Portsmouth & Southsea only. **t** – Runs in ⑦ (slower) timings.
r – Runs in ⚒ (faster) timings. ▽ – Portsmouth and Southsea.

BRIGHTON - SOUTHAMPTON CENTRAL

Longest journey: 2 hours 1 minute SN

km	⚒	⑦				⚒	⑦
0	0h00	0h00	↓	d.**Brighton**..............d.	↑	1h45	1h50
2	0h04	0h04		d.Hove......................d.		1h41	1h46
16	0h18	0h25	↓	d.Worthing ....d.	↑	1h23	1h25
35	0h39	0h48		d.Barnham ....d.		1h00	1h03
45	0h46	0h56	↓	d.Chichester.............d.	↑	0h52	0h54
59	1h04	1h08		d.Havant ....d.		0h38	0h42
75	1h19	1h25	↓	d.Fareham ....d.	↑	0h23	0h24
98	1h52	1h56		a.**Southampton** C ..d.		0h00	0h00

From Brighton: on Ⓐ at 0512 **t**, 0530 **t**, 0627, 0705, 0730, 0833, 0859, 0933 and hourly until 1633, 1702, 1733, 1828, 1930 **t**, 2030 **t**; on ⑥ at 0515, 0527 **t**, 0634, 0733, 0833, 0900, 0933 and hourly until 1633, 1700, 1733, 1833, 1929 **t**, 2030 **t**; on ⑦ at 0800, 0900, 1000, 1100, 1110 **r**, 1200, 1300, 1400, 1500, 1546 **r**, 1600, 1700, 1746 **r**, 1800, 1900, 2000, 2100.

From Southampton Central: on Ⓐ at 0610, 0733, 0832 and hourly until 1332, 1426, 1434, 1532 and hourly until 2032 **t**, 2113 **t**; on ⑥ at 0632 and hourly until 1332, 1426, 1434, 1532 and hourly until 1732, 1832 **t**, 1932 **t**, 2032 **t**, 2113 **t**; on ⑦ at 0730, 0827, 0831 **r**, 0930, 1030, 1130, 1230, 1304 **r**, 1330, 1430, 1506 **r**, 1530, 1630, 1730, 1830, 1927 **r**, 1930, 2029, 2130.

r – Runs in ⚒ (faster) timings. **t** – Runs in ⑦ (slower) timings.

LONDON WATERLOO - READING

Longest journey: 1 hour 35 minutes SW

km					
0	0h00	↓	d.**London** Waterloo ..a.	↑	1h22
16	0h16		d.Richmond ....d.		1h03
18	0h20	↓	d.Twickenham...........d.	↑	0h58
30	0h33		d.Staines ....d.		0h36
46	0h53	↓	d.Ascot.....................d.	↑	0h28
70	1h20		a.**Reading** ....d.		0h00

From London Waterloo: on Ⓐ at 0505, 0550, 0620, 0650, 0720, 0750, 0807, 0820, 0837, 0850 and every 30 minutes until 1550, 1605, 1620, 1635, 1650, 1720, 1735, 1750, 1805, 1820, 1835, 1850, 1905, 1920, 1935, 1950 and every 30 minutes until 2350; on ⑥ at 0505, 0550 and every 30 minutes until 2350; on ⑦ at 0709, 0809 and every 30 minutes until 2339.

From Reading: on Ⓐ at 0620, 0654, 0709, 0720, 0739, 0839, 0909, 0922, 0939, 0953, 1009 and every 30 minutes until 1639, 1709, 1723, 1739, 1753, 1809, 1839, 1849, 1909 and every 30 minutes until 2239, 2312; on ⑥ at 0539 and every 30 minutes until 2239, 2312; on ⑦ at 0751, 0821, 0851 and every 30 minutes until 2151, 2221, 2254.

LONDON WATERLOO - WINDSOR

Longest journey: 1 hour 09 minutes SW

km					
0	0h00	↓	d.**London** Waterloo ..a.	↑	0h56
16	0h20		d.Richmond ....d.		0h34
18	0h24	↓	d.Twickenham...........d.	↑	0h30
30	0h39		d.Staines ....d.		0h15
41	0h53	↓	a.**Windsor** ▷ ....d.	↑	0h00

From London Waterloo: on Ⓐ at 0558 and every 30 minutes until 2328; on ⑥ at 0558 and every 30 minutes until 2328; on ⑦ at 0644, 0744, 0825, 0844 and at the same minutes past each hour until 1944, 2025, 2044, 2144, 2244.

From Windsor and Eton Riverside: on Ⓐ at 0551, 0621 and every 30 minutes until 2221, 2253; on ⑥ at 0551, 0621 and every 30 minutes until 2221, 2253; on ⑦ at 0659, 0759, 0859, 0932, 0959 and at the same minutes past each hour until 2059, 2159, 2301.

▷ – Windsor and Eton Riverside.

103 BEDFORD - LUTON ✈ - LONDON - GATWICK ✈ - BRIGHTON

Additional trains are available London Bridge - Brighton and v.v.

Other services: Bedford - Luton Airport - London St Pancras see Table **170**; London Victoria - Gatwick Airport - Brighton see Table **105**; London Victoria - Gatwick Airport *Gatwick Express* see Table **100**.

km			Ⓐ	Ⓐ	Ⓐ	Ⓐ	Ⓐ	Ⓐ	Ⓐ	Ⓐ	Ⓐ	Ⓐ	Ⓐ	Ⓐ	Ⓐ	Ⓐ	Ⓐ	Ⓐ	Ⓐ	Ⓐ	Ⓐ	Ⓐ	Ⓐ	Ⓐ		Ⓐ	Ⓐ	Ⓐ
0	**Bedford** d.	Ⓐ	0040	0140	0220	0240	0320	0340	0416	0446	0518	0544	0600	0618	0654	0658	0730	0734	0748	0804	0824	0840	0854	0910	and at	1440	1454	1510
31	Luton d.		0104	0204	0244	0304	0344	0404	0440	0510	0542	0604	0624	0638	0714	0722	0750	0758	0812	0828	0848	0904	0918	0934	the same	1504	1518	1534
33	Luton Airport ✈ d.		0107	0207	0247	0307	0347	0407	0443	0513	0544	|	0627	0641	|	0725	|	0800	0815	0831	0851	0907	0921	0937	minutes	1507	1521	1537
48	St Albans City d.		0119	0219	0259	0319	0359	0419	0455	0525	0556	0616	0638	0652	0726	0738	0802	0812	0828	0843	0903	0918	0933	0948	past	1518	1533	1548
80	**London** St Pancras d.		0154	0254	0324	0354	0424	0454	0524	0552	0620	0634	0656	0714	0744	0756	0820	0832	0848	0904	0924	0940	0954	1010	each	1540	1554	1610
85	**London** Blackfriars d.		0205	0305	0335	0405	0435	0505	0535	0603	0633	0646	0708	0728	0756	0808	0832	0844	0900	0918	0938	0952	1008	1022	hour	1552	1608	1622
101	East Croydon d.		0236	0336	0406	0436	0506	0532	0602	0632	0702	0716	0736	0758	0826	0838	0858	0912	0931	0949	1004	1019	1034	1049	until	1619	1634	1651
127	Gatwick Airport ✈ d.		0255	0355	0425	0457	0527	0548	0618	0648	0717	0732	0754	0814	0842	0854	0914	0928	0958	1005	1034	1035	1102	1105		1635	1702	1707
145	Haywards Heath d.		...	...	...	0512	0542	0602	0634	0704	0731	0748	0808	0830	0858	...	0928	0945	...	1019	...	1049	...	1119	♣	1649	...	1721
166	**Brighton** a.		...	...	...	0534	0602	0622	0654	0726	0750	0808	0823	0850	0918	...	0948	1005	...	1039	...	1109	...	1139		1709	...	1743

	Ⓐ	Ⓐ	Ⓐ	Ⓐ	Ⓐ	Ⓐ	Ⓐ	Ⓐ	Ⓐ	Ⓐ	Ⓐ	Ⓐ	Ⓐ	Ⓐ	Ⓐ	Ⓐ	Ⓐ	Ⓐ	Ⓐ	Ⓐ	Ⓐ	Ⓐ	Ⓐ	Ⓐ		⑥	⑥	⑥	⑥
Bedford d.	1524	1550	1608	1626	1640	1708	1720	1734	1800	1810	1824	1840	1854	1908	1940	2010	2040	2110	2140	2152	2222	2240	2310	2340	⑥	0040	0140	0220	0240
Luton d.	1548	1610	1632	1650	1704	1732	1744	1758	1819	1834	1848	1904	1918	1932	2004	2034	2104	2134	2204	2216	2246	2306	2334	0004		0104	0204	0244	0304
Luton Airport ✈ d.	1551	1613	1635	1652	1707	1735	1747	1801	1822	1837	1851	1907	1921	1935	2007	2037	2107	2137	2207	2219	2249	2309	2337	0007		0107	0207	0247	0307
St Albans City d.	1603	1624	1647	1704	1718	1748	1758	1812	1834	1848	1903	1918	1933	1946	2018	2048	2118	2148	2218	2230	2300	2321	2349	0019		0119	0219	0259	0319
London St Pancras d.	1624	1646	1708	1728	1740	1808	1818	1834	1854	1910	1924	1940	1954	2010	2040	2110	2140	2210	2240	2254	2324	2354	0024	0054		0154	0254	0324	0354
London Blackfriars d.	1638	1658	1720	1740	1752	1820	1830	1846	1908	1922	1938	1952	2008	2022	2052	2122	2152	2222	2252	2308	2336	0005	0035	0105		0205	0305	0335	0405
East Croydon d.	1704	1726	1748	1809	1825	1850	1901	1918	1939	1951	2010	2021	2039	2051	2121	2151	2221	2251	2321	2339	0006	0032	0106	0136		0236	0336	0406	0436
Gatwick Airport ✈ d.	1729	1742	1814	1824	1852	1906	1927	1935	2000	2007	2026	2037	2054	2107	2137	2207	2237	2307	2340	2357	0026	0054	0127	0155		0256	0356	0426	0456
Haywards Heath d.	...	1758	1832	1840	...	1920	...	1949	...	2021	...	2051	2110	2121	2153	2221	2253	2321	2355	0011	0043	...	...	...		...	...	...	...
Brighton a.	...	1819	1852	1903	...	1942	...	2010	...	2041	...	2111	2124	2141	2213	2241	2313	2341	0015	0031	0103	...	...	...		...	...	...	...

	⑥	⑥	⑥	⑥	⑥	⑥	⑥	⑥	⑥	⑥		⑥	⑥	⑥	⑥	⑥	⑥	⑥	⑥		⑥	⑥	⑥	⑥	⑥	⑥	⑥	⑥
Bedford d.	0320	0340	0412	0450	0520	0540	0554	0610	0624	0640	and at	1754	1810	1824	1840	1854	1910	1940	2010	...	2040	2110	2140	2152	2222	2240	2310	2340
Luton d.	0344	0404	0436	0514	0544	0604	0618	0634	0648	0704	the same	1818	1834	1848	1904	1918	1934	2004	2034	...	2104	2134	2204	2216	2246	2306	2334	0004
Luton Airport ✈ d.	0347	0407	0439	0517	0547	0607	0621	0637	0651	0707	minutes	1821	1837	1851	1907	1921	1937	2007	2037	...	2107	2137	2207	2219	2249	2309	2337	0007
St Albans City d.	0359	0419	0451	0528	0558	0618	0633	0648	0703	0718	past	1833	1848	1903	1918	1933	1948	2018	2048	...	2118	2148	2218	2230	2300	2321	2349	0019
London St Pancras d.	0424	0454	0524	0554	0624	0640	0654	0710	0724	0740	each	1854	1910	1924	1940	1954	2010	2040	2110	...	2140	2210	2240	2254	2324	2354	0024	0054
London Blackfriars d.	0435	0505	0535	0608	0638	0652	0708	0722	0738	0752	hour	1908	1922	1938	1952	2008	2022	2052	2122	...	2152	2222	2252	2308	2336	0005	0035	0105
East Croydon d.	0506	0532	0602	0634	0704	0719	0734	0749	0804	0819	until	1934	1951	2004	2021	2034	2051	2121	2151	...	2221	2251	2321	2339	0004	0032	0106	0136
Gatwick Airport ✈ d.	0526	0548	0618	0650	0720	0735	0802	0805	0834	0835		2002	2007	2034	2037	2102	2107	2137	2207	...	2237	2307	2337	2357	0024	0054	0126	0156
Haywards Heath d.	0544	0603	0633	0703	0733	0751	...	0819	...	0849	♣	...	2021	...	2051	2116	2121	2153	2221	...	2253	2321	2353	0011	0041	0109	...	...
Brighton a.	0606	0624	0654	0724	0754	0811	...	0839	...	0909		...	2041	...	2111	2132	2141	2213	2241	...	2313	2341	0013	0031	0101	0129	...	...

		⑦	⑦	⑦	⑦	⑦	⑦	⑦	⑦	⑦		⑦	⑦	⑦	⑦	⑦	⑦	⑦	⑦	⑦	⑦	⑦	⑦	⑦	⑦	⑦	⑦	⑦
Bedford d.	⑦	...	0558	0628	0658	0728	0750	0806	0820	0836	and at	1636	1650	1706	1720	1736	1806	1836	1906	1936	2006	2028	2058	2128	2158	2228	2300	2340
Luton d.		...	0622	0652	0722	0752	0814	0830	0844	0900	the same	1700	1714	1730	1744	1800	1830	1900	1930	2000	2030	2052	2122	2152	2222	2252	2324	0004
Luton Airport ✈ d.		...	0625	0655	0725	0755	0817	0833	0847	0903	minutes	1703	1717	1733	1747	1803	1833	1903	1933	2003	2033	2055	2125	2155	2225	2255	2327	0007
St Albans City d.		...	0637	0707	0737	0807	0829	0845	0859	0915	past	1715	1729	1745	1759	1815	1845	1915	1945	2015	2045	2107	2137	2207	2237	2307	2339	0019
London St Pancras d.		...	0710	0740	0810	0840	0854	0910	0924	0940	each	1740	1754	1810	1824	1840	1910	1940	2010	2040	2110	2140	2210	2240	2310	2340	0014	0054
London Blackfriars d.		0652	0722	0752	0822	0852	0906	0922	0936	0952	hour	1752	1806	1822	1836	1852	1922	1952	2022	2052	2122	2152	2222	2252	2322	2352	0025	0105
East Croydon d.		0723	0753	0821	0856	0926	0939	0956	1009	1026	until	1826	1839	1856	1909	1926	1956	2026	2056	2126	2156	2226	2256	2326	2357	0029	0059	0136
Gatwick Airport ✈ d.		0744	0818	0842	0912	0942	0956	1012	1026	1042		1842	1856	1912	1926	1942	2012	2042	2112	2142	2212	2242	2312	2342	0020	0049	0119	0156
Haywards Heath d.		0758	0834	0856	0926	0956	...	1028	...	1056	♣	1856	...	1928	...	1956	2028	2056	2128	2156	2228	2256	2328	2356	0036	...	...	...
Brighton a.		0818	0854	0916	0948	1016	...	1048	...	1116		1916	...	1948	...	2016	2048	2116	2148	2216	2248	2316	2348	0016	0056	...	...	...

		②–⑤	Ⓐ	Ⓐ	Ⓐ	Ⓐ	Ⓐ	Ⓐ	Ⓐ	Ⓐ	Ⓐ	Ⓐ	Ⓐ	Ⓐ	Ⓐ	Ⓐ	Ⓐ	Ⓐ	Ⓐ	Ⓐ	Ⓐ	Ⓐ	Ⓐ	Ⓐ	Ⓐ	Ⓐ	Ⓐ	
Brighton d.	Ⓐ	0010	...	...	...	...	...	...	...	0510	0530	0544	0606	0619	0657	0722	0748	0800	0818	0833	0905	0935	1005	1035	...	1105	...	and at
Haywards Heath d.		0025	...	...	...	...	...	...	...	0531	0551	0603	0629	0642	0720	0746	0809	0822	0839	0856	0926	0956	1026	1056	...	1126	...	the same
Gatwick Airport ✈ d.		0039	0121	0221	0321	0351	0421	0455	0525	0548	0608	0617	0643	0700	0738	0801	0823	0839	0853	0910	0940	1010	1040	1110	1108	1140	1138	minutes
East Croydon d.		0100	0140	0240	0340	0410	0440	0517	0547	0603	0623	0639	0658	0723	0754	0824	0839	0854	0910	0925	0955	1025	1055	1125	1138	1155	1208	past
London Blackfriars d.		0129	0209	0309	0409	0439	0509	0546	0612	0630	0652	0708	0726	0754	0822	0850	0910	0922	0938	0954	1024	1054	1124	1154	1208	1224	1238	each
London St Pancras d.		0140	0220	0320	0420	0450	0520	0556	0622	0640	0702	0718	0736	0804	0832	0900	0920	0932	0948	1004	1034	1104	1134	1204	1218	1234	1248	hour
St Albans City d.		0214	0254	0354	0454	0514	0554	0618	0644	0703	0723	0743	0757	0825	0852	0920	0940	0952	1009	1025	1055	1125	1155	1225	1239	1255	1309	until
Luton Airport ✈ d.		0226	0306	0406	0506	0526	0606	0630	0656	0714	0734	0754	0808	0837	0903	0929	0952	1003	1021	1037	1107	1137	1206	1237	1251	1307	1321	
Luton d.		0229	0309	0409	0509	0529	0609	0633	0659	0717	0737	0757	0811	0840	0906	0932	0955	1006	1024	1040	1110	1140	1210	1240	1254	1310	1324	♣
Bedford a.		0255	0337	0435	0535	0557	0637	0701	0725	0743	0803	0823	0837	0905	0926	0957	1020	1025	1053	1105	1135	1205	1235	1305	1319	1335	1349	

	Ⓐ	Ⓐ	Ⓐ	Ⓐ	Ⓐ	Ⓐ	Ⓐ	Ⓐ	Ⓐ	Ⓐ	Ⓐ	Ⓐ	Ⓐ	Ⓐ	Ⓐ	Ⓐ	Ⓐ	Ⓐ	Ⓐ	Ⓐ	Ⓐ	Ⓐ	Ⓐ	Ⓐ	Ⓐ	Ⓐ	Ⓐ	Ⓐ	Ⓐ
Brighton d.	...	1505	...	1535	...	1602	...	1635	...	1701	...	1735	...	1805	1835	...	1905	...	1933	...	2003	...	2033	2105	2133	2205	2233	2305	2337
Haywards Heath d.	...	1526	...	1556	...	1623	...	1656	...	1722	...	1756	...	1826	1856	...	1926	...	1954	...	2026	...	2054	2126	2154	2226	2254	2326	2358
Gatwick Airport ✈ d.	1508	1540	1538	1610	1608	1640	1638	1710	1710	1740	1745	1810	1815	1840	1910	1917	1940	1947	2010	2018	2040	2047	2110	2140	2210	2240	2310	2340	0015
East Croydon d.	1538	1555	1608	1625	1638	1656	1703	1725	1739	1755	1804	1825	1834	1855	1925	1934	1955	2008	2025	2038	2055	2108	2125	2155	2225	2255	2325	2356	0038
London Blackfriars d.	1608	1622	1638	1652	1708	1722	1736	1752	1810	1822	1836	1852	1906	1924	1954	2008	2024	2038	2054	2108	2124	2138	2154	2222	2252	2322	2352	0024	0104
London St Pancras d.	1618	1632	1648	1702	1718	1732	1746	1802	1820	1832	1846	1902	1916	1934	2004	2018	2034	2048	2104	2118	2134	2148	2204	2232	2302	2332	0002	0034	0114
St Albans City d.	1639	1650	1709	1720	1736	1750	1806	1820	1842	1850	1906	1920	1936	1955	2025	2039	2055	2109	2125	2139	2155	2209	2225	2257	2327	2357	0027	0108	0148
Luton Airport ✈ d.	1651	|	1721	|	1748	|	1818	|	1854	|	1919	|	1948	2007	2037	2051	2107	2121	2137	2151	2207	2221	2237	2309	2339	0009	0039	0120	0200
Luton d.	1654	1702	1724	1732	1751	1802	1821	1832	1857	1902	1922	1932	1951	2010	2040	2054	2110	2124	2140	2154	2210	2224	2240	2312	2342	0012	0042	0123	0203
Bedford a.	1719	1723	1749	1753	1813	1823	1846	1853	1926	1923	1948	1953	2013	2035	2105	2119	2135	2150	2205	2219	2235	2249	2305	2340	0008	0038	0108	0149	0229

		⑥	⑥	⑥	⑥	⑥	⑥	⑥	⑥	⑥	⑥	⑥	⑥	⑥	⑥	⑥	⑥	⑥	⑥	⑥		⑥	⑥	⑥	⑥	⑥	⑥	⑥
Brighton d.	⑥	0010	...	...	...	...	...	...	0533	0605	0602	0635	0632	0705	0737	0734	0805	...	0835	...	and at	2005	...	2033	...	2105	2133	2205
Haywards Heath d.		0025	...	...	...	...	...	...	0554	0626	0620	0656	0647	0726	0756	0751	0826	...	0856	...	the same	2026	...	2054	...	2126	2154	2226
Gatwick Airport ✈ d.		0039	0121	0221	0321	0421	0455	0525	0610	0640	0638	0710	0708	0740	0810	0808	0840	0838	0910	0908	minutes	2040	2038	2110	2108	2140	2210	2240
East Croydon d.		0100	0140	0240	0340	0440	0517	0547	0625	0655	0708	0725	0738	0755	0825	0838	0855	0908	0925	0938	past	2055	2108	2125	2138	2155	2225	2255
London Blackfriars d.		0129	0209	0309	0409	0509	0542	0614	0654	0724	0738	0754	0808	0824	0854	0908	0924	0938	0954	1008	each	2124	2138	2154	2208	2224	2252	2322
London St Pancras d.		0140	0220	0320	0420	0520	0552	0624	0704	0734	0748	0804	0818	0834	0904	0918	0934	0948	1004	1018	hour	2134	2148	2204	2218	2234	2302	2332
St Albans City d.		0214	0254	0354	0454	0554	0625	0645	0725	0755	0809	0825	0839	0855	0925	0939	0955	1009	1025	1039	until	2155	2209	2225	2239	2259	2327	2357
Luton Airport ✈ d.		0226	0306	0406	0506	0606	0637	0657	0737	0807	0821	0837	0851	0907	0937	0951	1007	1021	1037	1051		2207	2221	2237	2251	2311	2339	0009
Luton d.		0229	0309	0409	0509	0609	0640	0700	0740	0810	0824	0840	0854	0910	0940	0954	1010	1024	1040	1054	♣	2210	2224	2240	2254	2314	2342	0012
Bedford a.		0255	0335	0436	0537	0635	0708	0725	0805	0835	0849	0905	0919	0935	1005	1019	1035	1049	1105	1119		2235	2249	2305	2319	2340	0008	0038

	⑥	⑥	⑥		⑦	⑦	⑦	⑦	⑦	⑦	⑦	⑦	⑦	⑦		⑦	⑦	⑦	⑦	⑦	⑦	⑦	⑦	⑦	⑦	⑦	⑦	⑦
Brighton d.	2233	2305	2337	⑦	0010	0606	0636	0703	0736	0804	...	0844	...	0914	and at	...	1844	...	1914	1944	2014	2044	2114	2144	2214	2244	2312	2342
Haywards Heath d.	2254	2326	2358		0026	0624	0654	0724	0754	0824	...	0903	...	0933	the same	...	1903	...	1933	2003	2033	2103	2133	2203	2233	2303	2331	0002
Gatwick Airport ✈ d.	2310	2340	0015		0039	0638	0708	0738	0808	0838	0859	0917	0929	0947	minutes	1859	1917	1929	1947	2017	2047	2117	2147	2217	2247	2317	2345	0015
East Croydon d.	2325	2356	0038		0100	0657	0727	0757	0827	0856	0917	0933	0947	1003	past	1917	1933	1947	2003	2033	2103	2133	2203	2233	2303	2333	0002	0038
London Blackfriars d.	2352	0024	0104		0129	0724	0754	0824	0854	0924	0954	1008	1022	1038	each	1952	2008	2022	2038	2108	2138	2208	2238	2308	2338	0008	0032	0104
London St Pancras d.	0002	0034	0114		0140	0734	0804	0834	0904	0934	1004	1018	1032	1048	hour	2002	2018	2032	2048	2118	2148	2218	2248	2318	2348	0018	0044	0114
St Albans City d.	0027	0108	0148		0214	0808	0838	0908	0938	1008	1038	1043	1057	1113	until	2027	2043	2057	2113	2143	2213	2243	2322	2352	0022	0052	0118	0148
Luton Airport ✈ d.	0039	0120	0200		0226	0820	0850	0920	0950	1020	1050	1055	1109	1125		2039	2055	2109	2125	2155	2225	2255	2334	0004	0034	0104	0130	0200
Luton d.	0042	0123	0203		0229	0823	0853	0923	0953	1023	1053	1058	1112	1128	♣	2042	2058	2112	2128	2158	2228	2258	2337	0007	0037	0107	0133	0203
Bedford a.	0108	0149	0229		0255	0849	0919	0949	1019	1049	1119	1125	1138	1154		2108	2124	2138	2154	2226	2254	2324	0003	0033	0103	0133	0159	0229

♣ – Timings may vary by up to 5 minutes.

LONDON - GATWICK ✈ - BRIGHTON

km			②–⑤	Ⓐ	Ⓐ	Ⓐ	Ⓐ	Ⓐ	Ⓐ	Ⓐ	Ⓐ	Ⓐ	Ⓐ	Ⓐ	Ⓐ	Ⓐ	Ⓐ	Ⓐ	Ⓐ	Ⓐ	Ⓐ		Ⓐ	Ⓐ	Ⓐ	Ⓐ	Ⓐ
0	**London** Victoria d.	Ⓐ	0005	0100	0400	0452	0606	0615	0617	0630	0715	0736	0800	0807	0821	0830	0838	0900	0920	0930	0950	and at the same	1550	1600	1620	1630	1647
17	East Croydon d.		0027	0124	0427	0519	0623	|	0635	|	|	0752	|	0823	0841	|	0854	|	0936	|	1006	minutes past	1606	|	1636	|	1703
43	Gatwick Airport ✈ d.		0045	0150	0452	0548	|	0646	0706	0704	0750	0808	0833	|	0857	0902	0910	0932	0952	1002	|	each hour until	|	1632	1652	1702	1719
82	**Brighton** a.		0118	0225	0523	0626	0705	0716	0741	0735	0820	0838	0857	0912	0938	0927	0942	0954	1017	1024	1046	❖	1646	1654	1720	1732	1756

	Ⓐ	Ⓐ	Ⓐ	Ⓐ	Ⓐ	Ⓐ	Ⓐ	Ⓐ	Ⓐ	Ⓐ	Ⓐ	Ⓐ	Ⓐ	Ⓐ	Ⓐ	Ⓐ	Ⓐ	Ⓐ	Ⓐ	Ⓐ	Ⓐ	Ⓐ	Ⓐ	Ⓐ	Ⓐ		⑥	⑥	⑥
London Victoria d.	1706	1730	1742	1800	1815	1830	1844	1900	1920	1930	1950	2000	2020	2030	2050	2100	2120	2130	2150	2200	2220	2230	2250	2307	2332	⑥	0005	0100	0400
East Croydon d.	1723	|	|	|	|	1847	|	|	1936	|	2007	|	2036	|	2106	|	2136	|	2206	|	2238	|	2306	2323	2350		0027	0124	0424
Gatwick Airport ✈ d.	|	1807	1815	1837	1847	|	1917	1932	1952	2002	2023	2032	2051	2102	2122	2132	2152	2202	2222	2232	2254	2302	2322	|	0015		0045	0151	0449
Brighton a.	1812	1839	1848	1912	1921	1939	1953	2002	2019	2027	2049	2057	2119	2127	2148	2158	2216	2230	2246	2257	2319	2327	2346	0003	0053		0118	0226	0517

	⑥	⑥	⑥	⑥	⑥	⑥	⑥	⑥	⑥	⑥	⑥	⑥		⑥	⑥	⑥	⑥	⑥	⑥	⑥	⑥	⑥	⑥	⑥	⑥	⑥	⑥
London Victoria d.	0502	0532	0600	0630	0700	0720	0730	0750	0800	0820	0830	0850	and at the same	2000	2020	2030	2050	2100	2120	2130	2150	2200	2220	2230	2250	2307	2332
East Croydon d.	0524	0548	|	|	|	0736	|	0806	|	0836	|	0906	minutes past	|	2036	|	2106	|	2136	|	2206	|	2236	|	2306	2324	2349
Gatwick Airport ✈ d.	0553	0622	0632	0702	0732	0751	0802	|	0832	0852	0902	|	each hour until	2032	2052	2102	2122	2132	2152	2202	2222	2232	2252	2302	2322	|	0013
Brighton a.	0630	0706	0702	0727	0757	0816	0824	0846	0854	0916	0924	0946	❖	2054	2118	2124	2146	2157	2221	2227	2247	2259	2318	2327	2346	0003	0050

		⑦	⑦	⑦	⑦	⑦	⑦	⑦	⑦	⑦	⑦	⑦	⑦	⑦	⑦		⑦	⑦	⑦	⑦	⑦	⑦	⑦	⑦	⑦	⑦	
London Victoria d.	⑦	0005	0100	0400	0502	0547	0632	0726	0832	0907	0927	0932	1006	1027	1032	and at the same	1906	1927	1932	2006	2027	2032	2106	2127	2227	2332	...
East Croydon d.		0028	0126	0426	0525	0610	0655	0748	0853	0923	0942	0949	1023	1042	1049	minutes past	1923	1942	1949	2023	2042	2049	2123	2142	2242	2353	...
Gatwick Airport ✈ d.		0046	0154	0453	0550	0633	0723	0813	0913	0939	1006	|	1039	1106	|	each hour until	1939	2006	|	2039	2106	|	2139	2207	2306	0015	...
Brighton a.		0117	0225	0522	0620	0709	0759	0851	0951	1003	1043	1024	1103	1143	1124	❖	2003	2043	2024	2103	2143	2124	2203	2243	2345	0052	...

		Ⓐ	Ⓐ	Ⓐ	Ⓐ	Ⓐ	Ⓐ	Ⓐ	Ⓐ	Ⓐ	Ⓐ	Ⓐ	Ⓐ	Ⓐ	Ⓐ	Ⓐ	Ⓐ		Ⓐ	Ⓐ	Ⓐ	Ⓐ	Ⓐ		Ⓐ	Ⓐ	Ⓐ
Brighton d.	Ⓐ	0350	0523	0614	0630	0640	0646	0712	0729	0744	0815	0830	0846	0918	0928	0948	0958	and at the same	1418	1428	1448	1458	1518	...	1526	1548	1618
Gatwick Airport ✈ d.		0505	0555	0652	0704	0719	|	0749	0802	0820	0849	0906	0914	0945	0953	1015	|	minutes past	1445	1453	1515	|	1545	...	1553	1615	1645
East Croydon d.		0532	0611	0716	|	|	0739	|	|	|	|	|	0929	|	1008	|	1038	each hour until	|	1508	|	1538	|	...	1608	|	|
London Victoria a.		0552	0629	0735	0741	0754	0758	0823	0839	0855	0923	0939	0949	1016	1026	1045	1056	❖	1515	1524	1546	1554	1615	...	1626	1647	1717

	Ⓐ	Ⓐ	Ⓐ	Ⓐ	Ⓐ	Ⓐ	Ⓐ	Ⓐ	Ⓐ	Ⓐ	Ⓐ	Ⓐ	Ⓐ	Ⓐ	Ⓐ	Ⓐ	Ⓐ	Ⓐ	Ⓐ	Ⓐ	Ⓐ	Ⓐ	Ⓐ	Ⓐ			⑥	⑥	⑥
Brighton d.	1648	1720	1728	1750	1758	1818	1828	1848	1859	1915	1928	1948	1958	2020	2028	2048	2058	2120	2128	2149	2158	2226	2255	2310	...	⑥	0350	0523	0550
Gatwick Airport ✈ d.	1716	1748	1753	1817	1823	1850	1853	1921	1940	1945	1953	2015	2023	2045	2053	2115	2123	2145	2153	2215	2223	2250	2320	2353	...		0503	0553	0626
East Croydon d.	|	|	1808	|	1838	|	1909	|	2003	|	2009	|	2039	|	2108	|	2138	|	2208	|	2238	|	|	0020	...		0529	0608	0641
London Victoria a.	1747	1822	1824	1852	1856	1926	1928	1951	2020	2015	2026	2044	2056	2117	2125	2144	2156	2214	2224	2243	2256	2321	2354	0042	...		0556	0624	0657

	⑥	⑥	⑥	⑥	⑥	⑥	⑥	⑥	⑥		⑥	⑥	⑥	⑥	⑥	⑥	⑥	⑥	⑥	⑥	⑥	⑥	⑥	⑥	⑥	⑥	⑥
Brighton d.	0556	0618	0628	0648	0658	0718	0728	0748	0758	and at the same	1818	1828	1848	1858	1918	1928	1948	1958	2018	2028	2048	2058	2118	2128	2148	2158	2218
Gatwick Airport ✈ d.	0633	0645	0653	0715	|	0745	0753	0815	|	minutes past	1845	1853	1915	1923	1945	1953	2015	2024	2045	2053	2115	2124	2145	2153	2215	2225	2245
East Croydon d.	0653	|	0708	|	0738	|	0808	|	0838	each hour until	|	1908	|	1938	|	2008	|	2039	|	2109	|	2139	|	2208	|	2240	|
London Victoria a.	0710	0715	0724	0746	0754	0815	0824	0845	0854	❖	1915	1924	1945	1954	2015	2024	2045	2055	2115	2125	2145	2155	2215	2224	2245	2256	2315

	⑥	⑥		⑦	⑦	⑦	⑦		⑦	⑦	⑦	⑦	⑦	⑦	⑦	⑦		⑦	⑦	⑦	⑦	⑦	⑦		⑦	⑦	⑦
Brighton d.	2255	2308	⑦	0350	0613	0706	0747	...	0825	0838	0910	0859	0935	1010	0959	1035	and at the same	1910	1859	1935	2010	1959	2035	...	2104	2204	2305
Gatwick Airport ✈ d.	2321	2354		0502	0648	0743	0830	...	|	0901	|	0941	0957	|	1041	1057	minutes past	|	1941	1957	|	2041	2057	...	2141	2241	2346
East Croydon d.	|	0020		0527	0706	0804	0858	...	0908	0916	0946	1001	1014	1046	1101	1114	each hour until	1946	2001	2014	2046	2101	2114	...	2201	2301	0018
London Victoria a.	2355	0041		0555	0727	0825	0914	...	0924	0932	1003	1018	1030	1103	1118	1130	❖	2003	2018	2031	2105	2118	2130	...	2218	2319	0040

❖ – Timings may vary by ± 3 minutes.

☛ For other services London - Gatwick Airport - Brighton and v.v. see Tables **100** and **103**.

🍷 on most trains

LONDON - GUILDFORD - PORTSMOUTH

km			①	Ⓐ	Ⓐ	Ⓐ	Ⓐ	Ⓐ	Ⓐ	Ⓐ	Ⓐ	Ⓐ	Ⓐ		Ⓐ	Ⓐ	Ⓐ	Ⓐ	Ⓐ	Ⓐ	Ⓐ	Ⓐ	Ⓐ	Ⓐ	Ⓐ
0	**London** Waterloo 113 d.	Ⓐ	0050	...	0500	0520	0615	0645	0730	0800	0830	0900	0930	and at	1600	1630	1700	1730	1800	1815	1830	1900	1930	2000	2030
39	Woking 113 d.		0118	...	0553	0611	0643	0713	0755	0825	0855	0925	0955	the same	1625	1655	1725	1756	|	|	1858	1925	1955	2025	2055
49	Guildford d.		0126**s**	0509	0604	0630**a**	0655	0725	0804	0840	0907	0934	1004	minutes	1634	1704	1737	1808	1834	1851	1908	1937	2004	2034	2104
69	Haslemere d.		|	0524	0628	0655	0720	0753	0825	0856	0925	0949	1021	past each	1651	1724	1754	1826	1852	1906	1926	1953	2023	2055	2122
88	Petersfield d.		|	0545	0645	0711	0736	0811	0836	0907	0936	1000	1032	hour until	1702	1735	1805	1837	1903	1923	1937	2004	2034	2106	2133
107	Havant a.		0200**s**	0600	0659	0727	0751	0826	0849	0919	0949	1014	1049		1714	1749	1819	1850	1915	1940	1951	2016	2048	2118	2145
118	**Portsmouth** & Southsea a.		0214**s**	0616	0716	0746	0807	0843	0902	0932	1003	1028	1102	♥	1728	1802	1832	1903	1929	1959	2004	2029	2101	2132	2158
120	**Portsmouth** Harbour a.		0219	0620	0720	0751	0812	0848	0907	0937	1008	1033	1107		1738	1809	1839	1910	1936	...	2010	2034	2106	2137	2202

	Ⓐ	Ⓐ	Ⓐ	Ⓐ**k**	Ⓐ	Ⓐ**k**	Ⓐ		⑥	⑥	⑥	⑥	⑥	⑥		⑥	⑥	⑥	⑥	⑥		⑥	⑥	⑥	⑥
London Waterloo 113 d.	2100	2130	2200	2230	2245	2315	2345	⑥	...	0520	0645	0730	0800	0830		1900	1930	2000	2030	2100	...	2130	2200	2230	2245
Woking 113 d.	2125	2155	2225	2256	2313	2343	0013		...	0613	0713	0755	0825	0855	and at	1925	1955	2025	2055	2125	...	2155	2225	2255	2313
Guildford d.	2134	2204	2234	2305	2325	2352	0025		0515	0625	0725	0804	0834	0904	the same	1934	2004	2034	2104	2134	...	2204	2234	2304	2325
Haslemere d.	2155	2225	2255	2325	2350	0012	0050		0530	0645	0745	0821	0849	0921	minutes	1949	2021	2049	2121	2155	...	2225	2255	2325	2350
Petersfield d.	2206	2236	2306	2336	0006	0023	0106		0546	0701	0801	0832	0900	0932	past each	2000	2032	2100	2132	2206	...	2236	2306	2336	0006
Havant a.	2218	2248	2318	2348	0020	0036	0121		0601	0719	0816	0849	0915	0949	hour until	2015	2049	2115	2144	2218	...	2248	2318	2348	0020
Portsmouth & Southsea a.	2232	2303	2331	0002	0038	0050	0138		0618	0735	0832	0902	0928	1002		2028	2102	2128	2158	2232	...	2302	2331	0002	0037
Portsmouth Harbour a.	2237	2308	2336	0007	...	0055	...		0622	0740	0837	0907	0933	1007		2033	2107	2133	2203	2236	...	2308	2336	0007	...

	⑥	⑥		⑦	⑦	⑦	⑦		⑦	⑦	⑦		⑦	⑦	⑦	⑦		⑦	⑦	⑦	⑦	⑦	⑦	⑦	⑦
London Waterloo 113 d.	2315	2345	⑦	...	0800	0830	0900	...	0930	1000	1030	and at	1800	1830	1900	1930	...	2000	2030	2100	2130	2200	2230	2300	2330
Woking 113 d.	2343	0013		[illegible]	0833	0904	0935	...	1004	1032	1102	the same	1832	1902	1932	2002	...	2032	2102	2132	2202	2232	2302	2332	0003
Guildford d.	2352	0025		0741	0845	0914	0945	...	1014	1042	1112	minutes	1842	1912	1942	2012	...	2042	2112	2142	2212	2242	2312	2342	0012
Haslemere d.	0012	0050		0807	0912	0929	1012	...	1029	1107	1127	past each	1907	1927	2007	2027	...	2107	2127	2207	2227	2307	2327	0007	0027
Petersfield d.	0023	0106		0823	0928	0940	1028	...	1040	1123	1138	hour until	1923	1938	2023	2038	...	2123	2138	2223	2238	2323	2338	0023	0038
Havant a.	0036	0121		0838	0943	0952	1043	...	1052	1138	1150		1938	1950	2038	2050	...	2138	2150	2238	2250	2338	2350	0038	0050
Portsmouth & Southsea a.	0049	0137		0853	0958	1006	1058	...	1105	1153	1204	♥	1953	2004	2053	2104	...	2153	2204	2253	2304	2353	0004	0053	0104
Portsmouth Harbour a.	0054	...		0857	1003	1011	1103	...	1111	1158	1211		1958	2011	2058	2109	...	2158	2208	2258	2309	2358	0009	0058	0109

		Ⓐ	Ⓐ**r**	Ⓐ**k**	Ⓐ**k**	Ⓐ	Ⓐ	Ⓐ	Ⓐ	Ⓐ	Ⓐ	Ⓐ	Ⓐ	Ⓐ	Ⓐ	Ⓐ		Ⓐ	Ⓐ	Ⓐ	Ⓐ	Ⓐ	Ⓐ	Ⓐ	Ⓐ
Portsmouth Harbour d.	Ⓐ	0425	0514	0519	0550	0615	...	0642	...	0713	0745	0815	0845	0915	0945	1015	and at	1445	1515	...	1545	1615	...	1645	1715
Portsmouth & Southsea d.		0430	0519	0524	0555	0620	...	0647	...	0718	0750	0820	0850	0920	0950	1020	the same	1450	1520	...	1550	1620	...	1650	1720
Havant d.		0446	0535	0540	0611	0634	0650	0700	0711	0732	0804	0834	0904	0934	1004	1034	minutes	1504	1534	1554	1604	1634	1656	1704	1734
Petersfield d.		0503	0552	0557	0629	0648	0707	0714	0725	0746	0818	0848	0918	0948	1018	1048	past each	1518	1548	1610	1618	1648	1710	1718	1748
Haslemere d.		0521**f**	0614	0616	0647	0702	0726	0735	0740	0800	0832	0902	0932	1002	1032	1102	hour until	1532	1602	1624	1637	1702	1732	1737	1802
Guildford d.		0550	0631	0631	0707	0717	0745	0754	0803	0815	0854	0917	0947	1017	1047	1117		1547	1617	1647	1700	1717	1747	1800	1817
Woking 113 a.		0600	0640	0640	0715	0725	0755	|	0811	0826	|	0927	0959	1025	1057	1125	♥	1557	1625	1657	1711	1725	1758	1811	|
London Waterloo 113 a.		0629	0712	0712	0745	0754	0824	0832	0841	0856	0931	0955	1027	1054	1124	1151		1624	1651	1727	1743	1754	1827	1843	1859

	Ⓐ	Ⓐ	Ⓐ	Ⓐ	Ⓐ	Ⓐ	Ⓐ	Ⓐ	Ⓐ	Ⓐ		⑥**g**	⑥**h**	⑥**g**	⑥**h**	⑥	⑥	⑥	⑥		⑥	⑥	⑥	⑥	⑥
Portsmouth Harbour d.	1745	1815	1845	1915	1945	2015	2045	2119	2219	2319	⑥	0438	0443	0514	0519	0619	0645	0715	0745	and at	1615	1645	...	1719	1745
Portsmouth & Southsea d.	1750	1820	1850	1920	1950	2020	2050	2124	2224	2324		0443	0448	0519	0524	0624	0650	0720	0750	the same	1620	1650	1710	1724	1750
Havant d.	1804	1834	1904	1934	2004	2034	2104	2140	2240	2340		0459	0504	0535	0540	0640	0704	0734	0804	minutes	1634	1704	1726	1740	1804
Petersfield d.	1818	1848	1918	1948	2018	2048	2118	2157	2257	2357		0515	0520	0552	0557	0657	0718	0748	0818	past each	1648	1718	1743	1757	1818
Haslemere d.	1832	1902	1932	2002	2032	2102	2132	2215	2315	0015		0534	0539	0613	0615	0715	0732	0802	0832	hour until	1702	1732	1802	1815	1832
Guildford d.	1855	1921	1947	2017	2047	2117	2147	2239	2339	0037		0602	0602	0634	0634	0734	0747	0817	0847		1717	1747	1817	1834	1847
Woking 113 a.	1903	1929	1957	2025	2058	2125	2157	2249	2349	...		0611	0611	0644	0644	0744	0757	0826	0857	♣	1725	1757	1825	1844	1857
London Waterloo 113 a.	1929	1959	2024	2050	2129	2150	2227	2319	0033	...		0640	0640	0713	0713	0813	0823	0851	0923		1751	1823	1851	1913	1923

	⑥	⑥	⑥	⑥	⑥	⑥	⑥	⑥	⑥		⑦**b**	⑦**n**	⑦	⑦	⑦	⑦	⑦	⑦	⑦	⑦		⑦	⑦	⑦	⑦
Portsmouth Harbour d.	1815	1845	1915	1945	2015	2045	2119	2219	2319	⑦	0643	0648	0729	0748	0829	0848	0932	0948	1032	1048		2132	2148	2232	2248
Portsmouth & Southsea d.	1820	1850	1920	1950	2020	2050	2124	2224	2324		0648	0653	0734	0753	0834	0853	0937	0953	1037	1053	and at	2137	2153	2237	2253
Havant d.	1834	1904	1934	2004	2034	2104	2140	2240	2340		0702	0707	0747	0807	0847	0907	0950	1007	1050	1107	the same	2150	2207	2250	2307
Petersfield d.	1848	1918	1948	2018	2048	2118	2157	2257	2357		0719	0724	0801	0824	0901	0924	1004	1024	1104	1124	minutes	2204	2224	2304	2324
Haslemere d.	1902	1932	2002	2032	2102	2132	2215	2315	0015		0737	0742	0814	0842	0914	0942	1017	1042	1117	1142	past each	2217	2242	2317	2342
Guildford d.	1917	1947	2017	2047	2117	2149	2239	2339	0037		0805	0805	0835	0905	0935	1005	1035	1106	1135	1205	hour until	2235	2305	2335	0005
Woking 113 a.	1925	1957	2025	2059	2125	2157	2249	2349	...		0813	0813	0842	0915	0942	1015	1042	1113	1142	1213		2242	2313	2342	0013
London Waterloo 113 a.	1951	2023	2050	2127	2151	2227	2318	0032	...		0850	0850	0916	0948	1014	1046	1114	1149	1214	1244		2314	2344	0014	...

a – Arrives 0621.
b – From Oct. 8.
f – Departs 5 minutes later May 22 - Oct. 6.
g – From Oct. 14.
h – May 27 - Oct. 7.
k – May 22 - Aug. 25.
n – May 21 - Oct. 1.
r – From Oct. 9.
♣ – London Waterloo arrivals may vary by ± 6 minutes.
♥ – Timings may vary by ± 3 minutes.

① – Mondays ② – Tuesdays ③ – Wednesdays ④ – Thursdays ⑤ – Fridays ⑥ – Saturdays ⑦ – Sundays Ⓐ – Monday to Fridays, not holidays

7

LONDON - SOUTHAMPTON - BOURNEMOUTH - WEYMOUTH

🍷 on most trains. SW

km			②–⑤t	Ⓐ	Ⓐ	Ⓐ	Ⓐ	Ⓐ	Ⓐ	Ⓐ	Ⓐ	Ⓐ	Ⓐ		Ⓐ	Ⓐ	Ⓐ	Ⓐ	Ⓐ	Ⓐ	Ⓐ	Ⓐ	Ⓐ	Ⓐ	Ⓐt
0	**London** Waterloo 113 d.	Ⓐ	0005	...	...	...	0530	0630	0703	0735	0805	0835	0905		1635	1705	1735	1805	1835	1905	1935	2005	2035	2105	2135
39	Woking 113 d.		0037	...	...	...	0601	0657	0730	0800	|	0900	|	and	1700u	|	|	|	|	|	2000	|	2100	2132	2200
77	Basingstoke 119 d.		0056	...	...	0540	0621	0718	0750	0820	0849	|	0949	at	|	|	|	|	|	1949	|	2049	|	2152	|
107	Winchester 119 d.		0113	...	...	0559	0638	0734	0806	0837	0905	0933	1005	the	1733	1800	1830	1900	1930	2005	2033	2105	2133	2208	2233
120	**Southampton** Airport 119 d.		0126	...	...	0613	0653	0749	0815	0852	0914	0942	1014	same	1742	1809	1839	1909	1939	2014	2042	2115	2142	2222	2242
128	**Southampton** Central 119 d.		0137	...	...	0625	0701	0759	0827	0901	0924	0951	1024	minutes	1753r	1821	1851	1919	1951r	2024	2051	2125	2151	2231	2251
149	Brockenhurst 119 d.		0153s	...	0615	0644	0718	0820	0846	0918	0938	1005	1038	past	1808	|	|	1936	|	2038	2108	2144	2205	2250	2305
174	**Bournemouth** 119 d.		0215	0611	0644	0711	0746	0848	0913	0945	1004r	1024r	1104r	each	1824	1850	1921	2007r	2021	2104r	2127r	2212	2224r	2317	2329r
183	Poole d.		...	0624	0657	0724	0758	0900	0926	0958	1014	1037	1114	hour	1837	1903	1934	2019	2034	2115	2139	2223	2237	2329	2342
193	Wareham d.		...	0638	0711	0738	0812	0912	0940	1010	1028	1050	1128	until	1849	1917	1946	2033	2046	2127	2151	...	2249	...	2354
219	Dorchester South d.		...	0658	0731	0758	0833	0933	1000	1026	1054	1106	1149	♠	1908	1937	2003	2054	2102	2147	2212	...	2309	...	0014
230	**Weymouth** a.		...	0709	0742	0809	0844	0944	1011	1035	1106	1115	1202		1919	1950	2015	2107	2115	2200	2223	...	2320	...	0025

	Ⓐ	Ⓐ	Ⓐ		⑥	⑥	⑥	⑥	⑥z	⑥	⑥	⑥	⑥	⑥	⑥		⑥	⑥	⑥	⑥	⑥	⑥	⑥	⑥	⑥
London Waterloo 113 d.	2205	2235	2305	⑥	0005	...	...	...	0530	...	0630	...	0735	0805	0835		1835	1905	1935	2005	2035	2105	2135	2205	2235
Woking 113 d.	2232	2300	2332		0037	...	...	...	0601	...	0657	...	0800	|	0900	and	1900	|	2000	|	2100	2132	2200	2232	2300
Basingstoke 119 d.	2252	|	2353		0056	...	...	...	0621	...	0718	...	0821	0849	|	at	|	1949	|	2049	|	2152	|	2252	|
Winchester 119 d.	2308	2333	0012		0113	...	...	...	0641	...	0734	...	0838	0905	0933	the	1933	2005	2033	2105	2133	2208	2233	2308	2333
Southampton Airport 119 d.	2322	2342	0028		0126	...	...	...	0656	...	0748	...	0851	0914	0942	same	1942	2014	2042	2114	2142	2222	2242	2322	2342
Southampton Central 119 d.	2330	2351	0038		0137	...	...	0621	0705	0721	0800r	0819	0900	0924	0951	minutes	1951	2024	2051	2124	2151	2230	2251	2330	2351
Brockenhurst 119 d.	2349	0005	0054s		0153s	...	0615	0640	0722	0740	0817	0840	0917	0938	1005	past	2005	2038	2105	2143	2205	2249	2305	2349	0005
Bournemouth 119 d.	0016	0022	0118		0215	0611	0644	0711r	0749	0811r	0844	0911r	0944	1004r	1024r	each	2024r	2104r	2124r	2210	2224r	2317	2326	0016	0022
Poole d.	0028	0035	0130		...	0624	0657	0724	0802	0824	0857	0924	0957	1014	1037	hour	2037	2114	2137	2223	2237	2329	2339	0030	0035
Wareham d.	...	...	...		...	0638	0711	0738	0814	0838	0909	0938	1009	1028	1049	until	2049	2128	2149	...	2249	...	2350	...	...
Dorchester South d.	...	...	...		...	0658	0731	0758	0834	0858	0929	0958	1027	1049	1105	♠	2105	2149	2209	...	2309	...	0011	...	...
Weymouth a.	...	...	...		...	0709	0742	0809	0845	0909	0940	1009	1035	1100	1113		2113	2200	2220	...	2320	...	0022	...	...

	⑥		⑦	⑦	⑦	⑦	⑦	⑦	⑦	⑦	⑦		⑦	⑦	⑦	⑦	⑦		⑦	⑦	⑦	⑦	⑦	⑦
London Waterloo 113 d.	2305	⑦	0005	...	...	...	0754	0835	0854	0935	0954		1435	1454	1535	1605	1635		2005	2035	2105	2135	2205	2305
Woking 113 d.	2332		0037	...	...	...	0828	0909	0928	1009	1028	and	1507	1528	1607	1637	1707	and	2037	2107	2137	2207	2237	2337
Basingstoke 119 d.	2352		0056	...	0748	...	0848	0929	0948	1029	1048	at	1528	1548	1628	1657	1728	at	2057	2128	2157	2228	2257	2357
Winchester 119 d.	0011		0113	...	0808	...	0908	0946	1008	1046	1108	the	1544	1608	1644	1714	1744	the	2114	2144	2214	2244	2314	0014
Southampton Airport 119 d.	0025		0126	...	0827	...	0927	0955	1027	1055	1127	same	1553	1627	1653	1727	1753	same	2127	2153	2227	2253	2327	0028
Southampton Central 119 d.	0035		0137	...	0835	0903	0935	1003	1035	1103	1135	minutes	1603	1635	1703	1736	1803	minutes	2136	2203	2236	2303	2336	0042
Brockenhurst 119 d.	0051s		0153s	...	0857	0917	0957	1018	1057	1118	1157	past	1617	1657	1717	1757	1817	past	2157	2217	2257	2317	2355	0058s
Bournemouth 119 d.	0115		0215	0839	0927	0939r	1024	1039r	1124	1139r	1224	each	1639r	1724	1739r	1825	1839r	each	2225	2239r	2325	2339r	0022	0122
Poole d.	0127		...	0851	0936	0951	1033	1051	1133	1151	1233	hour	1651	1733	1751	1834	1851	hour	2234	2251	2334	2351	0034	0134
Wareham d.	...		...	0903	...	1003	...	1103	...	1203	...	until	1703	...	1803	...	1903	until	...	2303	...	0003	...	...
Dorchester South d.	...		...	0924	...	1024	...	1124	...	1224	...		1724	...	1824	...	1924		...	2325	...	0025	...	...
Weymouth a.	...		...	0935	...	1035	...	1135	...	1235	...		1735	...	1835	...	1935		...	2336	...	0036	...	...

		Ⓐ	Ⓐ	Ⓐ	Ⓐ	Ⓐ	Ⓐ	Ⓐ	Ⓐ	Ⓐ	Ⓐ	Ⓐ	Ⓐ	Ⓐ		Ⓐ	Ⓐ	Ⓐ	Ⓐ	Ⓐ	Ⓐ	Ⓐ	Ⓐ	Ⓐ	Ⓐ
Weymouth d.	Ⓐ	...	...	...	0550f	...	0620f	...	0650f	...	0725	0755	0820	0903		1703	1720	1803	1820	1903	1920	2010	2110	2210	2310
Dorchester South d.		...	...	...	0602f	...	0632f	...	0702f	...	0737	0807	0833	0913	and	1713	1733	1813	1833	1913	1937	2022	2122	2222	2322
Wareham d.		...	...	...	0622f	...	0652f	...	0722f	...	0757	0827	0853	0928	at	1728	1753	1828	1853	1928	1957	2042	2142	2242	2342
Poole d.		0457	0542	*0608*	0639	...	0709	...	0739	0755	0811	0841	0907	0940	the	1740	1807	1840	1907	1940	2009	2054	2154	2254	2354
Bournemouth 119 d.		0512	0554	*0625*	0656	0634	0726	0704	0759r	0810	0825	0859r	0918	0955	same	1759r	1822r	1859r	1922r	1959r	2022r	2112r	2212r	2312r	0003
Brockenhurst 119 d.		0538	0614	|	|	0703	|	0733	0815	0841	0852	0915	0941	1011	minutes	1815	1845	1915	1945	2015	2045	2140	2240	2340	...
Southampton Central 119 d.		0555	0630	0700	0725	0730j	0755	0800j	0830	0900	*0916*	0930	1000	1030	past	1830	1900	1930	2000	2030	2100	2200	2300	2359	...
Southampton Airport 119 d.		0603	0638	0708	...	0738	...	0808	0838	0908	*0923*	0938	1008	1038	each	1838	1908	1938	2008	2038	2108	2208	2308	0010	...
Winchester 119 d.		0618	0648	0718	...	0748	...	0818	0848	0918	*0932*	0948	1018	1048	hour	1848	1918	1948	2018	2048	2118	2218	2324	...	...
Basingstoke 119 a.		0634	|	|	...	|	...	0834	|	0935	*0946*	|	1034	|	until	|	1934	|	2034	|	2134	2234	2343	...	...
Woking 113 a.		0653	|	|	...	|	...	0853	0922	0954	...	1020	|	1119	♠	1925	|	2019	|	2119	|	2254	0018	...	...
London Waterloo 113 a.		0724	0747	0816	...	0850	...	0925	0953	1023	...	1049	1120	1149		1952	2020	2049	2125	2149	2222	2323	0104	...	...

		⑥	⑥	⑥	⑥	⑥	⑥	⑥	⑥	⑥	⑥	⑥	⑥		⑥	⑥	⑥	⑥	⑥	⑥	⑥	⑥	⑥	⑥	⑥
Weymouth d.	⑥	...	...	...	0537f	0615f	0650f	0720	0758f	0820	0903	0920	1003		1703	1720	1803	1820	1903	1920	2010	...	2110	2210	2310
Dorchester South d.		...	...	...	0547f	0628f	0702f	0733	0808f	0833	0913	0933	1013	and	1713	1733	1813	1833	1913	1933	2022	...	2122	2222	2322
Wareham d.		...	...	...	0605f	0648f	0722f	0753	0823f	0853	0928	0953	1028	at	1728	1753	1828	1853	1928	1953	2042	...	2142	2242	2342
Poole d.		...	...	0528	0622	0707	0741	0807	0835f	0907	0940	1007	1040	the	1740	1807	1840	1907	1940	2007	2054	...	2154	2254	2354
Bournemouth 119 d.		...	...	0542	0642r	0722r	0759r	0822r	0859r	0922r	0959r	1022r	1059r	same	1759r	1822r	1859r	1922r	1959r	2022r	2112r	...	2212r	2312r	0003
Brockenhurst 119 d.		...	...	0610	0710	0745	0815	0845	0915	0945	1015	1045	1115	minutes	1815	1845	1915	1945	2015	2045	2140	...	2240	2340	...
Southampton Central 119 d.		0512	0600	0630	0730	0800	0830	0900	0930	1000	1030	1100	1130	past	1830	1900	1930	2000	2030	2100	2200	2230	2300	2359	...
Southampton Airport 119 d.		0520	0608	0638	0738	0808	0838	0908	0938	1008	1038	1108	1138	each	1838	1908	1938	2008	2038	2108	2208	2238	2308	0010	...
Winchester 119 d.		0534	0623	0652	0748	0818	0848	0918	0948	1018	1048	1118	1148	hour	1848	1918	1948	2018	2048	2118	2218	2255	2324	...	...
Basingstoke 119 a.		0550	0639	0708	|	0834	|	0934	|	1034	|	1134	|	until	|	1934	|	2034	|	2134	2234	2311	2343	...	...
Woking 113 a.		0628	0658	0727	0821	|	0919	|	1019	|	1119	|	1219	♠	1919	|	2019	|	2120	|	2253	2332	0018	...	...
London Waterloo 113 a.		0708	0731	0753	0849	0920	0949	1020	1049	1120	1149	1221	1251		1949	2020	2049	2124	2149	2222	2322	0003	0104	...	...

		⑦	⑦	⑦	⑦	⑦	⑦	⑦	⑦		⑦	⑦	⑦	⑦	⑦		⑦	⑦	⑦	⑦	⑦	⑦	⑦	⑦
Weymouth d.	⑦	...	...	...	0743f	...	0843f	...	0948		...	1248	...	1348	...		1748	...	1848	...	1958	2058	2158	2258
Dorchester South d.		...	...	...	0755f	...	0855f	...	1000	and	...	1300	...	1400	...	and	1800	...	1900	...	2010	2110	2210	2310
Wareham d.		...	...	...	0815f	...	0915f	...	1020	at	...	1320	...	1420	...	at	1820	...	1920	...	2030	2130	2230	2330
Poole d.		...	0650	0750	0830	0855	0930	0955	1032	the	1255	1332	1355	1432	1455	the	1832	1855	1932	1955	2050j	2150j	2250j	2350j
Bournemouth 119 d.		...	0706r	0806r	0850r	0906	0950r	1006	1050r	same	1306	1350r	1406	1450r	1506	same	1850r	1906	1950r	2006	2106	2206	2306	0003
Brockenhurst 119 d.		...	0734	0834	0909	0934	1009	1034	1109	minutes	1334	1409	1434	1509	1534	minutes	1909	1934	2009	2034	2134	2234	2334	...
Southampton Central 119 d.		0655	0755	0855	0925	0955	1025	1055	1125	past	1355	1425	1455	1525	1555	past	1925	1955	2025	2055	2155	2255	2353	...
Southampton Airport 119 d.		0703	0803	0903	0933	1003	1033	1103	1133	each	1403	1433	1503	1533	1603	each	1933	2003	2033	2103	2203	2303	...	...
Winchester 119 d.		0723	0823	0923	0942	1023	1042	1123	1142	hour	1423	1442	1523	1542	1617	hour	1942	2017	2042	2117	2218	2323	...	...
Basingstoke 119 a.		0742	0842	0942	0958	1042	1058	1142	1158	until	1442	1458	1542	1558	1633	until	1958	2033	2058	2133	2235	2342	...	...
Woking 113 a.		0802	0902	1002	1019	1102	1118	1202	1218		1502	1518	1602	1618	1653		2018	2053	2118	2153	2254	0002	...	...
London Waterloo 113 a.		0846	0941	1039	1050	1139	1150	1237	1249		1537	1549	1637	1649	1724		2049	2124	2149	2224	2325	0033	...	...

Brockenhurst - Lymington Pier (for ⛴ to Isle of Wight).
Journey 11 minutes. Trains call at Lymington Town 6 minutes later:
Ⓐ: 0559 and every 30 minutes until 0929, 1012 and every 30 minutes until 1812, 1848 and every 30 minutes until 2218.
⑥: 0612, 0642 and every 30 minutes until 2112, 2148, 2218.
⑦: 0859, 0929 and every 30 minutes until 2059, 2129, 2159.

Lymington Pier - Brockenhurst.
Journey 11 minutes. Trains call at Lymington Town 2 minutes later:
Ⓐ: 0614 and every 30 minutes until 0944, 1027 and every 30 minutes until 1827, 1903 and every 30 minutes until 2203, 2236.
⑥: 0627, 0657 and every 30 minutes until 2127, 2203, 2236.
⑦: 0914, 0944 and every 30 minutes until 2114, 2144, 2214.

f – Departs 5 minutes later May 21 - Oct. 7.
j – Arrives 8–9 minutes earlier.
r – Arrives 4–5 minutes earlier.
s – Calls to set down only.
t – May 22 - Aug. 25.
u – Calls to pick up only.
z – May 27 - Oct. 7.
♠ – Timings may vary by ± 4 minutes.
☛ For ⛴ services Weymouth / Poole – Jersey / Guernsey / St Malo and v.v., see Table **2100**.

111 PORTSMOUTH - RYDE - SHANKLIN

2nd class IL

Through fares including ferry travel are available. Allow 10 minutes for connections between trains and ferries. Operator: Wightlink ✆ 0871 376 4342. www.wightlink.co.uk

Portsmouth Harbour - Ryde Pierhead: ⛴
0515Ⓐ, 0615⚒, 0715 and hourly until 1815, 1920, 2020, 2120, 2245.

Ryde Pierhead - Portsmouth Harbour Journey time: ± 20 minutes
0547Ⓐ, 0647⚒, 0747 and hourly until 2147, 2310.

Service until December 17, 2017. Additional services operate on Ⓐ and on public holidays.

Ryde Pierhead - Shanklin: *14 km*
⚒: 0549, 0607, 0649, 0707, 0749, 0807, 0849, 0907, 0949, 1007, 1049*, 1107, 1149*, 1207*, 1249*, 1307*, 1349, 1407, 1449*, 1507*, 1549*, 1607*, 1649, 1707, 1749, 1807, 1849, 1907, 1949, 2007, 2049, 2149.
⑦: 0649, 0749, 0849, 0907 **a**, 0949, 1007 **a**, 1049*, 1107 **a**, 1149*, 1207***a**, 1249*, 1307*, 1349, 1407, 1449*, 1507*, 1549*, 1607*, 1649, 1707, 1749, 1807, 1849, 1907 **a**, 1949, 2049, 2149.

Shanklin - Ryde Pierhead Journey time: ± 24 minutes
⚒: 0618, 0638, 0718, 0738, 0818, 0838, 0918, 0938, 1018, 1038*, 1118, 1138*, 1218*, 1238*, 1318*, 1338, 1418, 1438*, 1518*, 1538*, 1618*, 1638, 1718, 1738, 1818, 1838, 1918, 1938, 2018, 2118, 2238.
⑦: 0718, 0818, 0838 **a**, 0918, 0938 **a**, 1018, 1038***a**, 1118, 1138***a**, 1218*, 1238***a**, 1318*, 1338, 1418, 1438*, 1518*, 1538*, 1618*, 1638, 1718, 1738, 1818, 1838 **a**, 1918, 1938 **a**, 2018, 2118, 2238.

a – Until Sept. 24.
* – Also calls at Smallbrook Junction (connection with **Isle of Wight Steam Railway**, see note △) 9 minutes from Ryde / 15 minutes from Shanklin, when Steam Railway is operating.
△ – **Isle of Wight Steam Railway** (🚂 Smallbrook Junction - Wootton: *9 km*). ✆ 01983 882204. www.iwsteamrailway.co.uk

km	Ⓐ	Ⓐ	Ⓐ	Ⓐ	Ⓐ	Ⓐ	Ⓐ	Ⓐ	Ⓐ B	Ⓐ	Ⓐ	Ⓐ B	Ⓐ	Ⓐ	Ⓐ	Ⓐ	Ⓐ	Ⓐ	Ⓐ	Ⓐ W	Ⓐ	Ⓐ	Ⓐ	Ⓐ W	Ⓐ B
0	**London** W'loo.... **108** d.	...	...	...	...	*0630*	0710	0820	0920	1020	1120	1220	1250	1320	1350	1420	1520	1550	1620	1650	1720	1750	1820	1850	1920
39	Woking .... **108** d.	...	...	...	...	*0657*	0736	0846	0946	1046	1146	1246	1316	1346	1416	1446	1546	1616	1646	1716**u**	1746**u**	|	1846	1918	1946
77	Basingstoke .... **108** d.	...	...	...	...	0722	0757	0907	1007	1107	1207	1307	1338	1407	1438	1507	1607	1638	1707	1738	1807	1838	1907	1939	2007
107	Andover .... d.	...	...	...	...	0744	0819	0924	1024	1124	1224	1324	1400	1424	1500	1524	1624	1700	1729	1800	1829	1900	1929	2001	2029
134	**Salisbury** .... a.	...	...	...	...	0803	0839	0943	1042	1142	1242	1343	1419	1442	1520	1542	1642	1720	1748	1820	1850	1920	1948	2021	2049
134	**Salisbury** .... d.	...	...	0608	0740	0808	0847	0947	1047	1147	1247	1347	1424	1447	1523	1547	1647	1723	1753	1823	1854	1923	1953	2025	2053
169	Gillingham .... d.	...	0551	0642	0811	0837	0917	1017	1117	1217	1317	1417	|	1517	1552**f**	1617	1717	1753**f**	1819	1851	1919	1954**f**	2022	2052	2119
190	Sherborne .... d.	...	0606	0657	0826	...	0932	1032	1132	1232	1332	1432	◧	1532	1607	1632	1732	1808	1834	1906	1934	2009	2037	2107	2134
197	**Yeovil** Junction .... a.	...	0611	0703	0832	...	0938	1038	1138	1238	1338	1438	|	1538	1613	1638	1738	1813	1840	1912	1939	2015	2043	2113	2140
197	**Yeovil** Junction .... d.	...	0615	0707	0839	...	0939	1039	1139	1239	1339	1439	|	1539	1620	1639	1739	...	1843	1917	1941	2020	2044	2117	2141
200	**Yeovil** Pen Mill **140** a.	...	|	|	|	...	|	|	|	|	|	|	1539	|	1627	|	|	...	|	1925	|	2025	|	2123	|
211	Crewkerne .... d.	...	0624	0716	0849	...	0949	1049	1149	1249	1349	1449	...	1549	▬	1649	1749	...	1853	...	1950	...	2054	...	2151
233	Axminster................. d.	0552	0656**c**	0737	0903	...	1003	1103	1203	1303	1403	1503	...	1603	Ⓐ	1703	1803	...	1907	...	2004	...	2108	...	2205
249	Honiton .... d.	0607	0712	0753**f**	0916	...	1016	1116	1216	1316	1416	1516	...	1616	1707	1716	1818	...	1919	...	2017	...	2120	...	2219
277	**Exeter** St Davids ..△ a.	0635	0742	0821	0944	...	1042	1143	1243	1343	1443	1544	...	1643	1736	1742	1843	...	1946	...	2043	...	2147	...	2247

	Ⓐ	Ⓐ	Ⓐ	①–④	⑤	⑥	⑥	⑥	⑥	⑥	⑥	⑥ B	⑥		⑥		⑥ B	⑥	⑥	⑥	⑥	⑥	⑥	⑥ B	⑥
London Waterloo **108** d.	2020	2120	2220	2340	2340	...	...	...	...	0710	0820	0920	1020	...	1120	...	1220	1320	1420	1520	1620	1720	1820	1920	2020
Woking .... **108** d.	2046	2149	2249	0008	0008	...	...	...	...	0736	0846	0946	1046	...	1146	...	1246	1346	1446	1546	1646	1746	1846	1946	2046
Basingstoke .... **108** d.	2107	2214	2311	0028	0028	...	...	...	...	0759	0907	1007	1107	...	1207	...	1307	1407	1507	1607	1707	1807	1907	2007	2107
Andover .... d.	2129	2236	2333	0050	0050	...	...	...	...	0821	0924	1024	1124	...	1224	...	1324	1424	1524	1624	1724	1824	1924	2024	2129
Salisbury .... a.	2148	2255	2353	0110	0110**s**	...	...	...	...	0842	0942	1042	1142	...	1242	...	1342	1442	1542	1642	1742	1843	1943	2042	2148
Salisbury .... d.	2206	2303	...	...	|	...	...	0615	0745	0847	0947	1047	1147	...	1247	...	1347	1447	1547	1647	1747	1847	1947	2047	2153
Gillingham .... d.	2235	2327**s**	...	...	0136**s**	...	...	0642	0811	0917	1017	1117	1217	...	1317	...	1417	1517	1617	1717	1817	1919	2017	2117	2220
Sherborne.................. d.	2250	2342**s**	...	...	0151**s**	...	...	0657	0826	0932	1032	1132	1232	...	1332	...	1432	1532	1632	1732	1832	1934	2032	2132	2235
Yeovil Junction.......... a.	2255	2348	...	...	0157	...	...	0703	0832	0938	1038	1138	1238	...	1338	...	1438	1538	1638	1738	1838	1939	2038	2138	2241
Yeovil Junction.......... d.	2257	...	...	...	...	...	0615	0707	0839	0939	1039	1139	1239	...	1339	...	1439	1539	1639	1739	1839	1941	2039	2139	2242
Yeovil Pen Mill.**140** a.	|	...	...	...	...	...	|	|	|	|	|	|	|	...	|	...	|	|	|	|	|	|	|	|	|
Crewkerne .... d.	2306	...	...	...	...	...	0624	0716	0849	0949	1049	1149	1249	...	1349	...	1449	1549	1649	1749	1849	1950	2049	2149	2252
Axminster .... d.	2320	...	...	...	...	0552	0656**c**	0738	0903	1003	1103	1203	1303	...	1403	...	1503	1603	1703	1803	1903	2005	2103	2203	2305
Honiton...................... d.	2332	...	...	...	...	0607	0712	0754**f**	0916	1016	1116	1216	1316	...	1416	...	1516	1616	1716	1817	1916	2017	2117	2217	...
Exeter St Davids ... △ a.	0001	...	...	...	...	0635	0742	0822	0944	1042	1142	1242	1342	...	1442	...	1542	1642	1742	1842	1942	2044	2142	2245	...

	⑥	⑥	⑥	⑦	⑦	⑦	⑦	⑦	⑦	⑦ B	⑦	⑦	⑦	⑦	⑦	⑦	⑦ B	⑦	⑦	⑦	⑦	⑦	⑦ e	⑦	⑦
London Waterloo **108** d.	2120	2220	2340	...	...	0815	0915	1015	1115	1215	1315	1415	1515	1615	1715	1745	1815	1845	1915	1945	2015	2045	2115	2215	2335
Woking .... **108** d.	2149	2249	0008	...	...	0847	0947	1046	1146	1246	1346	1446	1546	1646	1746	|	1846	|	1946	|	2046	|	2146	2246	0008
Basingstoke .... **108** d.	2214	2311	0028	...	0805	0908	1008	1107	1207	1307	1407	1507	1607	1707	1807	|	1907	|	2007	|	2107	|	2207	2307	0040
Andover.................... d.	2236	2333	0050	...	0827	0930	1025	1129	1224	1329	1424	1529	1624	1729	1824	1849	1929	1949	2024	2049	2129	|	2226	2329	0102
Salisbury .... a.	2255	2353	0110	...	0846	0946	1045	1145	1245	1345	1445	1545	1645	1745	1845	1905	1945	2005	2045	2105	2145	2205	2245	2348	0122
Salisbury .... d.	2303	...	...	0706	0851	0951	1051	1151	1251	1351	1451	1551	1651	1751	1851	...	1951	...	2051	...	2151	...	2251	...	...
Gillingham .... d.	2327**s**	...	...	0731	0921	1021	1121	1221	1321	1421	1521	1621	1721	1821	1921	...	2021	...	2121	...	2221	...	2322	...	...
Sherborne.................. d.	2342**s**	...	...	0746	0936	1036	1136	1236	1336	1436	1536	1636	1736	1836	1936	...	2036	...	2136	...	2236	...	2337	...	...
Yeovil Junction.......... a.	2349	...	...	0751	0941	1041	1141	1241	1341	1441	1541	1641	1741	1841	1941	...	2041	...	2141	...	2242	...	2343	...	...
Yeovil Junction.......... d.	...	...	...	0753	0943	1043	1143	1243	1343	1443	1543	1643	1743	1843	1943	...	2043	...	2143	...	...	...	2344	...	...
Yeovil Pen Mill.**140** a.	...	...	...	|	|	|	|	|	|	|	|	|	|	|	|	...	|	...	|	...	...	...	|	...	...
Crewkerne .... d.	...	...	...	0802	0952	1052	1152	1252	1352	1452	1552	1652	1752	1852	1952	...	2052	...	2152	...	...	...	2354	...	...
Axminster .... d.	...	...	...	0816	1006	1106	1206	1306	1406	1506	1606	1706	1806	1906	2006	...	2106	...	2206	...	...	...	0008	...	...
Honiton...................... d.	...	...	...	0831	1018	1118	1218	1318	1418	1518	1618	1718	1818	1918	2018	...	2118	...	2220	...	...	...	0020	...	...
Exeter St Davids ... △ a.	...	...	...	0859	1045	1145	1245	1345	1445	1545	1645	1745	1845	1945	2045	...	2146	...	2248	...	...	...	0046	...	...

	Ⓐ	Ⓐ	Ⓐ	Ⓐ	Ⓐ	Ⓐ	Ⓐ	Ⓐ	Ⓐ	Ⓐ B	Ⓐ	Ⓐ	Ⓐ	Ⓐ B	Ⓐ	Ⓐ	Ⓐ	Ⓐ B	Ⓐ	Ⓐ	Ⓐ	Ⓐ	Ⓐ	Ⓐ	Ⓐ
Exeter St Davids ... ▽ d.	...	...	...	...	0510	...	0641	0725	...	0823	0925	1025	1125	1225	1325	1425	...	1525	...	...	1624	1725	1746	1825	...
Honiton...................... d.	...	...	...	...	0541	0619	0712	0752	...	0855	0955	1055	1155	1255	1355	1455	...	1555	...	...	1656**f**	1755	1819	1859	...
Axminster .... d.	...	...	...	...	0552	0630	0723	0803	...	0906	1006	1106	1206	1306	1406	1506	...	1606	...	...	1707	1806	1829	1910	...
Crewkerne .... d.	...	...	...	...	0605	0643	0736	0816	...	0919	1019	1119	1219	1319	1419	1519	...	1619	...	...	1720	1819	...	1923	...
Yeovil Pen Mill.**140** d.	...	...	...	0541	|	|	|	|	...	|	|	|	|	|	|	|	1544	|	1631	1653	|	|	...	|	1927
Yeovil Junction.......... a.	...	...	...	0546	0614	0652	0745	0825	...	0927	1027	1127	1227	1327	1427	1527	1549	1627	1636	|	1728	1827	...	1931	|
Yeovil Junction.......... d.	...	...	0511**r**	0550	0620	0653	0750	0829	...	0929	1029	1129	1229	1329	1429	1529	1553	1629	...	1646**b**	1730	1829	...	1933	1917**b**
Sherborne.................. d.	...	...	0517**r**	0556	0626	0700	0756	0835	...	0935	1035	1135	1235	1335	1435	1535	1559	1635	...	◧	1736	1835	...	1939	◧
Gillingham .... d.	...	...	0533**r**	0612	0642	0715	0812	0851	0918	0951	1051	1151	1251	1351	1451	1551	1617	1651	...	|	1752	1851	...	1955	|
Salisbury .... a.	...	...	0558**r**	0639	0707	0740	0837	0916	0942	1016	1116	1216	1316	1416	1516	1616	1643	1716	...	1817	1822	1923	...	2022	2042
Salisbury .... d.	0512**r**	0540**r**	0603**r**	0645	0715	0745	0847	0921	0947	1021	1121	1221	1321	1421	1521	1621	1647	1721	...	1827	1827	1926	...	2026	...
Andover.................... d.	0532**r**	0600**r**	0623**r**	0705	0735	0805	0906	0938	1006	1038	1138	1238	1338	1438	1538	1638	1706	1738	...	1844	1844	1945	...	2045	...
Basingstoke .... **108** a.	0558	0626	0649	0728	0758	0828	0928	0955	1028	1055	1155	1255	1355	1455	1555	1655	1729	1755	...	1901	1901	2008	...	2108	...
Woking .... **108** a.	0618	0646	|	|	0818	0848	0949	1015	1049	1115	1215	1315	1415	1515	1615	1715	1749	1815	...	1921	1921	2029	...	2129	...
London Waterloo **108** a.	0649	0714	0739	0812	0846	0917	1019	1049	1119	1149	1249	1349	1449	1549	1649	1749	1821**h**	1849	...	1950	1950	2100	...	2204	...

	Ⓐ	Ⓐ	Ⓐ	Ⓐ	Ⓐ	⑥	⑥	⑥	⑥	⑥	⑥	⑥	⑥	⑥ B	⑥	⑥	⑥	⑥ B	⑥	⑥	⑥ B	⑥	⑥	⑥	⑥
Exeter St Davids ... ▽ d.	1925	...	2025	2125	2257	...	...	...	...	0510	...	0641	0725	0824	0925	1025	1125	1225	1325	1425	1525	1625	1725	1825	1925
Honiton...................... d.	1955	...	2057	2159	2332**f**	...	...	...	...	0541	0619	0713	0755	0855	0955	1055	1155	1255	1355	1455	1555	1655	1757	1855	1955
Axminster .... d.	2006	...	2108	2210	2343	...	...	...	...	0552	0630	0724	0806	0906	1006	1106	1206	1306	1406	1506	1606	1706	1808	1906	2006
Crewkerne .... d.	2019	...	2121	2223	2356	...	...	...	...	0605	0643	0737	0819	0919	1019	1119	1219	1319	1419	1519	1619	1719	1821	1919	2019
Yeovil Pen Mill.**140** d.	|	2030	|	|	|	...	...	...	...	|	|	|	|	|	|	|	|	|	|	|	|	|	|	|	|
Yeovil Junction.......... a.	2028	2035	2129	2231	0004	...	...	...	...	0614	0652	0745	0827	0927	1027	1127	1227	1327	1427	1527	1627	1727	1829	1927	2027
Yeovil Junction.......... d.	2029	...	2131	2233	0006	...	...	...	...	0620	0653	0750	0829	0929	1029	1129	1229	1329	1429	1529	1629	1729	1831	1929	2029
Sherborne.................. d.	2036	...	2137	2239	|	...	...	...	...	0626	0700	0756	0835	0935	1035	1135	1235	1335	1435	1535	1635	1735	1837	1935	2035
Gillingham .... d.	2051	...	2153	2255	|	...	...	...	...	0642	0715	0812	0851	0951	1051	1151	1251	1351	1451	1551	1651	1751	1853	1951	2051
Salisbury .... a.	2122	...	2218	2329	0043	...	...	...	...	0707	0740	0837	0916	1016	1116	1216	1316	1416	1516	1616	1716	1816	1918	2016	2116
Salisbury .... d.	2126	...	2226	...	...	0512**r**	0544**r**	0618**r**	0647	0721	0747	0847	0921	1021	1121	1221	1321	1421	1521	1621	1721	1821	1926	2026	2126
Andover.................... d.	2145	...	2245	...	...	0532**r**	0603**r**	0635**r**	0706	0738	0806	0906	0938	1038	1138	1238	1338	1438	1538	1638	1738	1838	1945	2045	2145
Basingstoke .... **108** a.	2207	...	2307	...	...	0558	0628	0655	0728	0755	0828	0928	0955	1055	1155	1255	1355	1455	1555	1655	1755	1855	2008	2108	2207
Woking .... **108** a.	2228	...	*2331*	...	...	0618	0649	0715	0749	0817	0849	0949	1015	1115	1215	1315	1415	1515	1615	1715	1815	1915	2029	2129	2228
London Waterloo **108** a.	2258	...	*0008*	...	...	0649	0719	0749	0819	0849	0919	1019	1049	1149	1249	1349	1449	1549	1649	1749	1849	1949	2104	2204	2257

	⑥	⑥	⑥	⑦	⑦	⑦	⑦	⑦	⑦	⑦	⑦	⑦	⑦	⑦	⑦	⑦ B	⑦	⑦	⑦ F	⑦	⑦	⑦	⑦	⑦	⑦
Exeter St Davids ... ▽ d.	2025	2125	2257	...	...	...	...	...	0925	1025	1125	1225	1325	1425	...	1525	...	1625	...	1725	1825	1925	2025	2125	2315
Honiton...................... d.	2056	2157	2332**f**	...	...	...	...	0858	0957	1057	1157	1257	1357	1457	...	1557	...	1657	...	1757	1857	1957	2057	2159	2340**s**
Axminster .... d.	2107	2208	2343	...	...	...	...	0909	1009	1109	1209	1309	1409	1509	...	1609	...	1709	...	1809	1909	2009	2109	2210	2351**s**
Crewkerne .... d.	2120	2221	2356	...	...	...	...	0922	1022	1122	1222	1322	1422	1522	...	1622	...	1722	...	1822	1922	2022	2122	2223	0012**s**
Yeovil Pen Mill.**140** d.	|	|	|	...	...	...	...	|	|	|	|	|	|	|	...	|	...	|	...	|	|	|	|	|	|
Yeovil Junction.......... a.	2129	2229	0004	...	...	...	...	0930	1030	1130	1230	1330	1430	1530	...	1630	...	1730	...	1830	1930	2030	2131	2232	0021**s**
Yeovil Junction.......... d.	2130	2231	0006	...	...	0732	...	0932	1032	1132	1232	1332	1432	1532	...	1632	...	1732	...	1832	1932	2032	2132	2233	|
Sherborne.................. d.	2137	2237	|	...	...	0738	...	0938	1038	1138	1238	1338	1438	1538	...	1638	...	1738	...	1838	1938	2038	2138	2240	|
Gillingham .... d.	2152	2253	|	...	...	0754	0854	0954	1054	1154	1254	1354	1454	1554	1621	1654	1721	1754	...	1854	1954	2054	2154	2256	|
Salisbury .... a.	2223	2329	0041	...	...	0820	0920	1020	1120	1220	1320	1420	1520	1620	1647	1720	1747	1820	...	1920	2020	2120	2220	2321	0057
Salisbury .... d.	2227	...	...	0642**r**	0724**r**	0827	0927	1027	1129	1227	1327	1427	1527	1627	1652	1727	1752	1827	1852	1927	2027	2127	2227	...	...
Andover.................... d.	2247	...	...	0659**r**	0743**r**	0846	0946	1044	1146	1244	1346	1444	1546	1644	1709	1746	1809	1844	1909	1946	2044	2146	2246	...	...
Basingstoke .... **108** a.	2309	...	...	0719	0808	0908	1002	1106	1204	1306	1402	1506	1602	1706	1726	1802	1826	1906	1926	2002	2106	2203	2308	...	...
Woking .... **108** a.	*2332*	...	...	0739	0828	0928	1028	1128	1228	1328	1428	1528	1628	1728	1748	1828	1848	1928	1948	2028	2128	2228	*0002*	...	...
London Waterloo **108** a.	*0003*	...	...	0820	0912	1011	1104	1204	1304	1359	1459	1559	1659	1759	1819	1859	1919	1959	2019	2059	2159	2259	*0033*	...	...

☛ Full service **London** Waterloo - **Salisbury** and v.v.:

From **London** Waterloo on ⚒ at 0710, 0750, 0820, 0850 and every 30 minutes until 1920, 1950, 2020, 2120, 2220, 2340; on ⑦ at 0815 and hourly until 2215, 2335 (also 1745, 1845, 1945, 2045. Please see timings above for calling points between London and Salisbury).

From **Salisbury** on Ⓐ at 0512**r**, 0540**r**, 0603**r**, 0645, 0715, 0745, 0815, 0847, 0921, 0947 and at the same minutes past each hour until 1747, 1827, 1847, 1926, 2026, 2126; on ⑥ at 0512**r**, 0544**r**, 0618**r**, 0647, 0721, 0747, 0821, 0847, 0947, 1021, 1047 and at the same minutes past each hour until 1847, 1926, 2026, 2126; on ⑦ at 0642**r**, 0724**r**, 0827, 0927, 1027, 1129, 1227 and hourly until 2127 (also 1652, 1752, 1852).

B – Conveys [12] London Waterloo - Bristol and v.v. (Table **140**).
F – From Frome (Table **140**).
W – To Westbury (Table **140**).
b – Calls at Yeovil Junction before Yeovil Pen Mill.
c – Arrives 0643.
e – Does not call at Exeter Central.
f – Arrives 5–7 minutes earlier.
h – Arrives 1816 from Aug. 28.
r – Runs 3 minutes later May 21 - Oct. 7.
s – Calls to set down only.
u – Calls to pick up only.
◧ – Via Westbury (Table **140**).
△ – Trains to Exeter St Davids also call at **Exeter Central** 5–6 minutes earlier.
▽ – Trains from Exeter St Davids also call at **Exeter Central** 4–5 minutes later.

115 — LONDON - EXETER - PAIGNTON and PLYMOUTH (GW)

km		②2	②2	②	②	②2	②	②2	②2	①	④	④	④	④	⑤	⑤	④
		B★	★	2	⚒	⚒★	2	D★	⚒	Dn	Dr	⚒	⚒★	⚒	✕	2	✕	D2	2★	⚒	2	⚒e	⚒
0	London Paddington 132 d.	...	...	...	0706	0730	...	...	0906	...	★	1006	1000	1106	1134	1205	...	1305	...	...	1407	...	1434	1506	1606
58	Reading 132 d.	...	...	...	0733	0759	...	...	0935	...		1032	1028	1133	1201	1233u	...	1333	...	...	1434	...	1501u	1533	1632
85	Newbury d.	...	...	...	0749		...	...		...					1223		...		...	...		...			
154	Westbury 139 d.	...	...	...	0826		...	...		...				1221	1300		...		...	...		...	1520	1610	1623
186	Castle Cary 139 d.	...	...	...			...	1031		...				1240			...		...	...		...	1550	1628	1641
	Bristol T M 132 120a 120 d.	...	0524	0642		0913	...	0855		0955	0955	1147				1319		1357		...		...			
230	Taunton 120a 120 d.	...	0619	0738	0902	0945	...	1000	1052	1100	1100	1229	1302	1340		1400	1447	1458		...	1549	1621	1650	1705	1750
253	Tiverton Parkway 120 d.	...	0634	0754	0915		...	1105	1116	1116		1315				1415	1500	1514		...	1602	1637	1703	1718	1803
279	Exeter St Davids 120 a.	...	0651	0812	0930	1009	...	1031	1120	1132	1132	1205	1254	1332	1404	1406	1432	1515	1532	...	1617	1658	1718	1733	1818
279	Exeter St Davids 116 120 d.	0628	0655	0814	0933	1010	1018	1032	1125	1135	1135	1208	1257	1332		1410		1519		...	1550	1620	...	1737	1822
311	Newton Abbot 116 120 d.	0655	0728	0835	0955	1038	1041	1101	1145	1157	1214	1229	1323	1352		1429		1542		...	1621	1641	...	1758	1843
321	Torquay 116 120 d.					1050		1113		1209	1227		1337							...			...		
324	Paignton 116 120 d.					1057		1120		1242	1301		1345							...			...		
325	Totnes 120 d.	0709	0742	0849	1007		1053		1158					1405				1554		...	1633	1653	...	1811	1856
363	Plymouth 120 d.	0740	0811	0919	1033		1124		1227			1305		1435		1505		1623		...	1705	1721	...	1839	1926
	Newquay 117 a.	1009d					1419e													...			...		
	Penzance 117 a.	1016e	1126	1237		1325						1511				1712		1833j		...	1933		...	2042	2131

	①	⑤	④	④	④	①④	⑤	①④	④	④	④	④	A	⑥2	⑥2	⑥⚒	⑥★	⑥	⑥	⑥	⑥⚒
	⚒	⚒	★	⚒★	⚒	⚒	⚒	✕	✕	⚒	2	2	A	★	n★	r★	⚒	n2	r2	⚒	⚒
London Paddington 132 d.	1636	1636	1703	1733	1803	1805	1835	1835	1903	1903	1945	2035	...	2145	2345½	⑥	...	...	...	0706	...	0730	0806	0835
Reading 132 d.	1704	1704	1730	1801	1831	1838	1903	1933u	2012	2102			2212	0046u		...	...	0735u	...	...	0759	0835	0903u
Newbury d.	1719	1719	1748	1819	1849	1904	1919	1919	1950	1950	2028	2119	...				...	...	...			0859	0920
Westbury 139 d.	1803	1803		1900		1955	2006	2006		2106	2156		...				...	...	...			0943	0958
Castle Cary 139 d.	1822	1822		1919			2024	2024		2126	2215		...				...	...	...			1002	1017
Bristol T M 132 120a 120 d.													2156	2306	2336		0524	0636	0644		0918		
Taunton 120a 120 d.	1843	1843	1851	1941	1951		2045	2045	2053	2053	2148	2236	2303	0013s	0036s	0235	0618	0725	0730	0851		0952	1025	1039
Tiverton Parkway 120 d.	1856	1856	1904	1954			2058	2058	2106	2106	2202	2249	2319	0030s	0049s		0633	0741	0743			1038	1052
Exeter St Davids 120 a.	1912	1912	1920	2008	2015		2114	2114	2121	2121	2217	2304	2337	0052	0106	0307	0652	0759	0758	0916		1015	1053	1106
Exeter St Davids 116 120 d.	...	1916	1922	2021	2017		2117	2125	2125	2219	2308			0411			0653	0800	0800	0920	0928	0946	1017	1110
Newton Abbot 116 120 d.	...	1936	1942	2059	2037		2137	2145	2145	2040	2328			0433			0727	0831	0832	0948	1000	1008	1040	1144
Torquay 116 120 d.	...		2113																				1157
Paignton 116 120 d.	...		2123																				1207
Totnes 120 d.	...	1956		2050			2158	2158	2253	2342							0740	0845	0846	1001	1001	1021	1053	
Plymouth 120 d.	...	2015	2024	2118			2215	2226	2226	2325	0011			0514			0813	0916	0916	1028	1032	1051	1120	
Newquay 117 a.	...																			1239			
Penzance 117 a.	...	2228		2313				0046	0045					0753			1018n	1126	1127	1240	1236		1324t

	⑥	⑥	⑥	⑥	⑥	⑥	⑥	⑥	⑥	⑥	⑥	⑥	⑥	⑥	⑥	⑥	⑥	⑥	⑥	⑥	⑥	⑥	⑥	⑥
	n⚒	r⚒	⚒	2★	n★	n⚒	r⚒	r⚒	⚒	p⚒	r★	p⚒	r⚒	q⚒	⚒	⚒	n★	r★	⚒	⚒	⚒	⚒★	E2
London Paddington 132 d.	0906	0906	1006		1035	1106	1106	1135	1206	1218	1235	1306	1306	1306	1406	1506		1606	1706	1630	1806	1906	2006	2030
Reading 132 d.	0933	0933u	1035u		1105u	1133u	1133	1205u	1235u	1249	1305u	1333	1333u	1333	1435	1534u		1635u	1733	1659	1835u	1933	2035	2059
Newbury d.									1313	1321										1949	2050	
Westbury 139 d.			1154			1222	1250		1359	1400		1424		1624		1823		2027	2129	
Castle Cary 139 d.			1212			1240			1417	1418		1442		1642		1841		2045	2147	
Bristol T M 132 120a 120 d.			1144										1644	1644		1818			2159	2217
Taunton 120a 120 d.	1049	1049		1216	1235		1303	1330		1439	1440	1449	1449	1505	1550	1705	1717	1717	1749	1904	1907	1950	2108	2209	2305	2318
Tiverton Parkway 120 d.	1102	1102		1228	1248		1316				1502	1502	1518	1603	1718	1730	1730	1802	1917	1922		2121	2222	2331
Exeter St Davids 120 a.	1116	1116	1208	1243	1302	1306	1331	1353	1409		1504	1516	1516	1532	1617	1731	1743	1743	1817	1932	1938	2012	2135	2235	2339	2347
Exeter St Davids 116 120 d.	1119	1122	1212	1252	1308	1314	1333	1356	1413		1507	1518	1521	1536	1619	1738	1753	1753	1817	1939	2015	2139	
Newton Abbot 116 120 d.	1140	1146	1236	1321	1349	1336	1354		1434		1540	1539	1544	1555	1640	1759	1822	1823	1840	1955	2000	2036	2200	2306	
Torquay 116 120 d.			1401								1553							2014		
Paignton 116 120 d.			1412								1603							2024		
Totnes 120 d.	1153	1159		1334		1350	1407				1553	1557	1609	1653	1812	1835	1836	1853	2008		2050	2213	2319	
Plymouth 120 d.	1224	1226	1315	1405		1417	1434	1451	1510		1620	1624	1649	1724	1839	1905	1904	1924	2035		2118	2243	2346	
Newquay 117 a.							1647															
Penzance 117 a.	...	1429	1518	1621		1618		1711		1824	1825	1854	1924	2041n	2108	2111	2128r	2242n		2322		

	⑦	⑦	⑦	⑦	⑦	⑦	⑦	⑦	⑦	⑦	⑦	⑦	⑦	⑦	⑦	⑦	⑦	⑦	⑦	⑦	⑦	⑦	⑦	A
	2★	2★	⚒★	r⚒	n⚒	2			2★					2		⚒★	n⚒	r⚒				A
London Paddington 132 d.	...	0800	0851	0857		0957	1057	1127w	1157	1257	1300	...	1357	1457	1557	1657	...	1757	1857	1903	1903	1957	2057	2350½
Reading 132 d.	...	0837	0932	0932		1032	1132	1208	1232	1331	1338	...	1432	1532	1632	1732	...	1832	1932	1938	1938	2032	2132	0038u
Newbury d.	...		0948	0948			1248				...	1448		1648		...	1848			2048	
Westbury 139 d.	...		1022	1022			1305		1418		...	1724		1927		...				2127	
Castle Cary 139 d.	...				1134		1324			...	1536		1743		...	2029			2144	
Bristol T M 132 120a 120 d.	0726	0828	1000							1455		1830x			2055	2100	
Taunton 120a 120 d.	0820	0932	1034	1058	1058	1156	1247	1345	1354	1455	1529	...	1557	1651	1805	1850	1933	2001	2149	2152	2206	2246s
Tiverton Parkway 120 d.	0835	0947	1048	1112	1112			1359	1407			1704	1818	1903	1949	2016	2105	2203	2206	2219	2300s
Exeter St Davids 120 a.	0853	1004	1102	1126	1126	1221	1314	1413	1422	1518	1553	...	1718	1834	1918	2007	2029	2120	2219	2222	2235	2319	0305
Exeter St Davids 116 120 d.	0905	1006	1105	1126	1126	1215	1223	1315	1415	1424	1521	1555	1605	1625	1721	1836	1920	...	2030	2121	...	2236	0435
Newton Abbot 116 120 d.	0928	1032	1133	1147	1147	1236	1244	1337	1442	1447	1542	1616	1637	1644	1740	1858	1939	...	2053	2148	...	2257	0456
Torquay 116 120 d.									1453										2014		
Paignton 116 120 d.									1502										2024		
Totnes 120 d.	0941	1044	1145	1201	1201	1248	1257		1459	1554		1651	1700	1754		1953		...	2106	2202	...	2310	
Plymouth 120 d.	1012	1113	1212	1230	1230	1318	1325	1413		1528	1622	1653	1721	1730	1821	1934	2020	...	2133	2231	...	2340	0535
Newquay 117 a.						1512v															
Penzance 117 a.	1224	1315	1418	1433	1447	1525v		1612		1729	1824	...	1937	1937	2028	2142	2222	...	2335				0859

A – THE NIGHT RIVIERA – Conveys 🛏 1, 2. cl and �car🚗 . See also note ‡.
B – Continues to Par until June 30 and from Sept. 1 (Table 117).
D – To / from Cardiff (Table 120a).
E – Starts from Cardiff until Sept. 9 and from Oct. 28 (Table 120a).

a – Via Trowbridge (Table 140).
b – Also calls at Dawlish 0621.
c – Also calls at Teignmouth 0555.
d – To June 30 and from Sept. 4.
e – July 3 - Sept. 1.

j – May 21 - Aug. 31.
k – 6 minutes later from Sept. 16.
n – From Sept. 11.
p – From Oct. 28.
q – Sept. 16 - Oct. 21.

r – May 21 - Sept. 10.
s – Stops to set down only.
u – Stops to pick up only.

NOTES CONTINUE ON NEXT PAGE →

---

116 — EXETER - PAIGNTON (2nd class, GW)

km		Ⓐ	Ⓐ	Ⓐ	Ⓐ	Ⓐ	Ⓐ	Ⓐ	Ⓐ		Ⓐ	Ⓐ	Ⓐ	Ⓐ	Ⓐ	Ⓐ	Ⓐ	Ⓐ	Ⓐ	Ⓐ	Ⓐ	Ⓐ	Ⓐ
0	Exeter St Davids 115 120 d.	0534	0611	0718	0750	0842	0900	1001	1032	...	1058	1158	1249	1303	1358	1503	1558	1628	1655	1728	1751	1836	1933
20	Dawlish 115 120 d.	0555	0631	0738	0810	0907	0924	1034	1048	...	1118	1228		1324	1428	1523	1619	1648	1715	1755	1812	1902	1959
24	Teignmouth 115 120 d.	0600	0636	0743	0815	0902	0929	1039	1053	...	1123	1233		1329	1433	1528	1624	1653	1720	1800	1817	1907	2004
32	Newton Abbot 115 120 d.	0609	0645	0752	0824	0911	0937	1049	1101	...	1132	1241	1313	1338	1442	1537	1632	1702	1729	1810	1826	1916	2013
42	Torquay 115 120 d.	0620	0656	0803	0836	0922	0948	1101	1113	...	1143	1253	1324	1349	1453	1548	1644	1713	1740	1821	1837	1927	2024
45	Paignton 🚂 115 120 a.	0628	0706	0812	0844	0929	1110	1120	...	1152	1301	1333	1358	1500	1557	1654	1750	1830	1846	1934	2032

		Ⓐ	Ⓐ	Ⓐ		⑥	⑥	⑥	⑥	⑥	⑥	⑥	⑥	⑥	⑥	⑥e	⑥d	⑥	⑥	⑥	⑥	⑥	⑥
	Exeter St Davids 115 120 d.	2021	2129	2249	⑥	0518	0530	0611	0750	0837	0856	0956	1025	1035	1059	1157	1157	1228	...	1359	1430	1458	1558	1655	1727
	Dawlish 115 120 d.	2044	2149	2309		0539	0557	0631	0810	0851	0925	1016		1051	1119	1217	1219	1318	...	1429	1446	1518	1617	1715	1753
	Teignmouth 115 120 d.	2051	2154	2314		0544	0602	0636	0815	0856	0930	1021		1056	1124	1222	1224	1323	...	1434	1451	1523	1622	1720	1758
	Newton Abbot 115 120 d.	2059	2203	2334b		0552	0611	0645	0824	0906	0939	1031	1048	1104	1136	1238b	1234	1332	...	1443	1500	1532	1631	1729	1808
	Torquay 115 120 d.	2113	2214	2344		0603	0622	0656	0835	0916	0950	1042	1059	1114	1147	1248	1244	1343	...	1454	1511	1543	1642	1740	1819
	Paignton 🚂 115 120 a.	2123	2223	2353		0611	0630	0704	0844	0925	0958	1052	1107	1123	1157	1256	1252	1351	...	1504	1519	1553	1652	1750	1826

		⑥	⑥	⑥	⑥	⑥		⑦	⑦	⑦	⑦	⑦	⑦	⑦	⑦	⑦	⑦	⑦	⑦	⑦	⑦	⑦	⑦	⑦
	Exeter St Davids 115 120 d.	1827	1856	1913	2019	2150	⑦	0849	0954	1053	1158	1302	1326	1359	1415	1505	1531	1600	1657	1713	1757	1857	1957	2102	2202
	Dawlish 115 120 d.	1846	1909	1933	2039	2210		0909	1014	1113	1218	1317	1339	1417	1435	1517	1543	1615	1710	1725	1817	1917	2017	2115	2222
	Teignmouth 115 120 d.	1851	1914	1938	2044	2215		0914	1019	1118	1223	1322	1344	1424	1435	1522	1548	1620	1715	1730	1822	1922	2022	2120	2227
	Newton Abbot 115 120 d.	1901	1922	1947	2053	2223		0924	1037b	1127	1232	1330	1352	1435	1446	1530	1556	1629	1723	1738	1831	1931	2031	2128	2236
	Torquay 115 120 d.	1912	1932	1958	2104	2234		0935	1048	1138	1243	1341	1404	1446	1453	1607	1640	1735	1749	1842	1942	2042	2140	2247
	Paignton 🚂 115 120 a.	1921	1940	2006	2111	2242		0942	1054	1145	1251	1348	1412	1455	1502	1615	1647	1742	1756	1849	1949	2049	2147	2255

b – Arrives 7 – 10 minutes earlier.   d – May 27 - Sept. 9.   e – From Sept. 16.   🚂 – Dartmouth Steam Railway (Paignton - Kingswear). See page 99 for contact details.

GW PLYMOUTH and PAIGNTON - EXETER - LONDON 115

km		Ⓐ	Ⓐ 🍷a	Ⓐ 🍷	Ⓐ 🍷	Ⓐ 2	Ⓐ 🍷	Ⓐ 🍷b	Ⓐ 🍷c	Ⓐ 🍴	Ⓐ 🍷	Ⓐ 🍷☆	Ⓐ2 D☆	Ⓐ 🍷	Ⓐ 🍷	Ⓐ 🍷	Ⓐ 🍷☆	Ⓐ 🍴	Ⓐ2 D☆	Ⓐ 🍴	Ⓐ e2	Ⓐ 🍷☆	Ⓐ 🍷	Ⓐ 🍷	Ⓐ 🍷	Ⓐ 🍷
	Penzance 117 d.		...	...	...	...	...	...	...	0505	0541	...	0600	0645	0741	0844	...	1000	...	1047e	1141	...	...	1303	...	...
	Newquay 117 d.		...	...	...	...	...	...	...	|	|	...	|	|	|	|	...	|	...	|	|	...	...	|	...	1506e
0	**Plymouth** 120 d.		...	...	...	...	0553	0530	0509	0655	0748	...	0809	0853	0948	1044	...	1201	...	1256	1343	...	...	1503	1602	1657
38	Totnes 120 d.		...	...	...	...	|	0558	|	|	0816	...	0839	0923	1019	|	...	1229	...	1324	1412	...	...	|	1629	1728
	Paignton 116 120 d.		...	...	...	...	|	|	|	|	|	0740	|	|	|	|	1132	|	1248	|	|	1413	...	|	|	|
	Torquay 116 120 d.		...	...	...	...	|	|	|	|	|	0746	|	|	|	|	1138	|	1254	|	|	1419	...	|	|	|
52	Newton Abbot 116 120 d.		...	...	...	...	0631	0611	0547	0732	0829	0806	0852	0936	1032	|	1150	1242	1308	1337	1426	1432	...	1541	1642	1741
84	**Exeter** St Davids 116 120 a.		...	...	...	...	0650	0632	0610	0751	0849	0838	0918	0955	1054	1137	1215	1301	1332	1357	...	1457	...	1600	1702	1800
84	**Exeter** St Davids 120 d.		...	...	0546	0600	0652	0635	0613	0753	0852	0841	0933	0958	1056	1139	1217	1304	1336	1359	...	1501	1453	1603	1708	1803
110	Tiverton Parkway 120 d.		...	...	0602	0617	|	0651	0628	|	0907	|	0950	1013	1111	|	1232	1319	1353	|	...	1516	1508	1618	1723	1818
133	Taunton 120a 120 d.		...	...	0617	0633	0718	0706	0655	0818	0921	0905	1006	1028	1125	|	1246	1334	1410	1424	...	1531	1523	1633	1737	1833
205	**Bristol** T M. 132 120a 120 a.		0518	...	|	0741	|	|	0757	|	|	0957	1108	|	1158	|	|	|	1513	|	...	|	|	|	|	|
	Castle Cary d.		|	...	0639	...	|	0727	|	|	0942	|	...	|	|	|	1306	|	...	1446	...	1553	|	|	|	1854
	Westbury d.		0603	0616	0701	...	|	0751	|	|	1002	|	...	1105	|	|	1327	|	...	1504	...	|	1608	|	|	1914
	Newbury a.		0648	0706	0745	...	|	0829	|	|	|	|	...	|	|	|	1403	|	...	|	...	|	1649	|	|	1951
337	**Reading** 132 a.		0716	0737	0806	...	0832	0847	0914	0931	1050	1108	...	1150	1308	1316	1420	1450	...	1549	...	1650	1716	1749	1851	2008
395	**London** Paddington 132 a.		0748	0811	0838	...	0900	0921	0942	1000	1124	1140	...	1221	1339	1344	1454	1521	...	1622	...	1724	1745	1821	1921	2039

	⑤ e🍷	Ⓐ 🍴	Ⓐ 2☆	①–④	⑤	①–④ 🍷	⑤ 🍷	Ⓐ 🍷	Ⓐ 🍷	Ⓐ 2☆	Ⓐ 2☆	Ⓐ A		⑥	⑥ 2	⑥ 🍷	⑥ 🍷	⑥ 🍷	⑥ r2	⑥ 🍷	⑥ 2☆	⑥ 🍷	⑥🍷 r☆	⑥🍷 p☆	⑥🍷 q☆	⑥ r🍷
Penzance 117 d.	...	1559	...	1644	1644	...	...	1742	...	...	*1913*	2145‡	...		...	...	...	...	0527	*0537*n	...	0650	...	...	...	0718
Newquay 117 d.	...	|	...	|	|	...	...	|	...	...	|	|	...		...	...	...	...	|	|	...	|	...	...	...	|
Plymouth 120 d.	...	1803	...	1844	1844	...	...	1944	...	...	2125	2354	...		...	0540	0655	...	0735	0747	0806	0852	...	...	...	0930
Totnes 120 d.	...	1831	...	1913	1913	...	...	2012	...	...	2154	0022	...		...	0607	|	...	0803	0814	0835	0919	...	...	...	0959
Paignton 116 120 d.	...	|	1852	|	|	...	...	|	*2014*	*2035*	|	|	...		...	|	|	...	|	|	|	|	0918	0918	0918	|
Torquay 116 120 d.	...	|	1857	|	|	...	...	|	*2020*	*2040*	|	|	...		...	|	|	...	|	|	|	|	0925	0925	0925	|
Newton Abbot 116 120 d.	...	1844	1909	1926	1926	...	...	2025	*2031*	*2053*	2206	0036	...		...	0620	0732	...	0815	0827	0848	0932	0939	0939	0939	1012
Exeter St Davids 116 120 a.	...	1903	1939	1948	1948	...	...	2044	*2050*	*2128*	2240	0058	...		...	0640	0752	...	0842	0847	0914	0952	1013	1013	1013	1032
Exeter St Davids 120 d.	1817	1906	1939	...	1948	1955	...	2046	*2052*	2149	...	0106	...		0600	0641	0754	0729	...	0849	...	0954	1015	1015	1015	1035
Tiverton Parkway 120 d.	|	1921	|	...	2005	2010	...	2101	*2105*	2206	...	|	...		0617	0656	0809	0744	...	0904	...	1009	1030	1030	1030	|
Taunton 120a 120 d.	1842	1936	2010	...	2021	2025	2027	2115	2129	2223	...	0142	...		0634	0711	0824	0759	...	0919	...	1024	1045	1045	1045	1100
Bristol T M.. 132 120a 120 a.	|	|	2054	...	...	|	|	2145	2232	2313	...	|	...		0743	|	|	0857	...	|	...	|	1122	1127	1131	|
Castle Cary d.	|	|	...	...	...	2046	2046	|	|	...	...	|	...		...	0733	|	|	...	0940	...	|	|	|	|	1121
Westbury d.	|	|	...	...	...	2105	2105	|	|	...	...	|	...		...	0756	|	|	...	1001	...	1102	|	|	|	1143
Newbury a.	|	|	...	...	...	2142	2142	|	|	...	...	|	...		...	0833	|	|	...	|	...	|	|	|	|	|
Reading 132 a.	2018	2050	...	...	...	2159	2159	2308	0023	...	...	0401s	...		...	0851	0942	1011	...	1050	...	1147	1245	1245	1246	1237
London Paddington 132 a.	2052	2122	...	...	...	2239	2230	2342	0107	...	...	0523z	...		...	0922	1010	1041	...	1121	...	1221	1314	1314	1315	1309

	⑥ n🍷	⑥ 🍷	⑥ n🍷	⑥ 🍷	⑥ n🍷	⑥ r🍷	⑥ p🍷	⑥ r🍷	⑥ p🍷	⑥ q🍷	⑥ p🍷	⑥🍷 r☆	⑥ n🍷	⑥ r🍷	⑥ 🍷	⑥🍷 r☆	⑥ n🍷	⑥ 🍷	⑥2 n☆	⑥ r2	⑥ r🍷	⑥ 🍷	⑥ 2☆	⑦	⑦ 2	⑦ 🍷
Penzance 117 d.	0759	0838k	...	0954k	1058	1100	...	1158	...	...	...	...	...	1307	1359	...	...	1552	1641	1655	...	1740	1906		...	...
Newquay 117 d.	|	|	...	|	|	|	...	|	...	...	...	...	...	|	|	...	...	|	|	|	1726	|	|		...	...
Plymouth 120 d.	1001	1043	...	1159	1254	1304	...	1359	1400	1400	...	...	1504	1510	1600	...	1656	1754	1851	1904	1918	1942	2115		...	...
Totnes 120 d.	1031	|	...	1229	1322	|	...	|	|	|	...	...	1531	|	1628	...	1727	1821	1922	1934	|	2009	2144		...	...
Paignton 116 120 d.	|	|	...	|	|	|	...	|	|	|	*1355*	1448	|	|	|	1700	|	|	|	|	|	|	|		...	...
Torquay 116 120 d.	|	|	...	|	|	|	...	|	|	|	*1401*	1455	|	|	|	1707	|	|	|	|	|	|	|		...	...
Newton Abbot 116 120 d.	1044	|	...	1242	1335	|	...	1435	1435	1435	*1412*	1507	1544	1546	1641	1719	1740	1834	1935	1946	1955	2022	2156		...	...
Exeter St Davids 116 120 a.	1104	1136	...	1302	1355	1401	...	1456	1456	1456	*1435*	1533	1604	1606	1701	1751	1800	1854	2001	...	2015	2042	2223		...	...
Exeter St Davids 120 d.	1106	1138	1154	1304	1357	1404	...	1459	1459	1459	*1437*	1536	1606	1608	1703	1802	1802	1856	...	...	2017	2045	...		0801	0837
Tiverton Parkway 120 d.	1121	|	1209	1319	|	|	...	1514	1514	1514	*1450*	|	1621	1623	1718	1817	1817	1911	...	...	|	2100	...		0818	0852
Taunton 120a 120 d.	1136	|	1224	1334	1423	1429	1519	1529	1529	1529	1519	1601	1636	1637	1733	1832	1832	1926	...	...	2042	2114	...		0835	0906
Bristol T M.. 132 120a 120 a.	|	|	|	|	|	|	|	|	|	|	|	|	|	|	|	|	|	|	...	...	|	2147	...		0938	|
Castle Cary d.	|	|	1246	|	1444	|	|	1550	1550	1550	|	1623	|	|	|	1853	1853	1947	...	...	|	|	...		...	0928
Westbury d.	|	|	1305	|	1502	|	1607	|	|	1616	1607	1642	|	|	|	1913	1913	2006	...	...	|	|	...		...	0950
Newbury a.	|	|	1351	|	|	|	1653	|	|	1654	1653	|	|	|	|	1946	1946	|	...	...	|	|	...		...	1027
Reading 132 a.	1251	1315	1419	1449	1549	1546	1721	1648	1648	1711	1721	1734	1751	1753	1848	2004	2004	2056	...	...	2157	2304	...		...	1045
London Paddington 132 a.	1321	1344	1450	1521	1621	1621	1751	1721	1721	1741	1751	1807	1821	1821	1921	2037	2037	2130	...	...	2232	2344	...		...	1123

	⑦ r2	⑦ n2	⑦ 🍷☆	⑦ 🍷	⑦ r🍷	⑦ n🍷	⑦ 🍷	⑦ 🍷	⑦ 🍷	⑦ 2☆	⑦ 🍷	⑦ 🍷	⑦ 🍷	⑦ 🍷☆	⑦ 2	⑦ 🍷	⑦ 2☆	⑦ 🍷	⑦ r🍷	⑦ n🍷	⑦ r🍷	⑦ n🍷	⑦ 🍷	⑦ 🍷	⑦ 2☆	⑦ A
Penzance 117 d.	...	...	...	...	0830	0830	0947	1100	1140r	1205	1256	...	...	...	1339	...	1437	1500	1550	...	...	1613	1731	...	1900	2115‡
Newquay 117 d.	...	...	...	...	|	|	|	|	|	|	|	...	...	...	|	...	|	|	|	...	1621	|	|	...	|	|
Plymouth 120 d.	...	...	0840	1010	1038	1035	1145	1300	1345	1407	1455	1510	1542	...	1551	1610	1638	1700	1745	1749	1810	1815	1930	2000	2115	2320
Totnes 120 d.	...	...	0907	1040	1105	1103	1214	1328	1413	1436	1525	|	1609	...	1620	1637	1707	1728	1816	1816	1840	1842	1957	|	2144	2348
Paignton 116 120 d.	...	...	|	|	|	|	|	|	|	|	|	|	|	1545	|	|	|	|	|	|	|	|	|	|	|	|
Torquay 116 120 d.	...	...	|	|	|	|	|	|	|	|	|	|	|	1550	|	|	|	|	|	|	|	|	|	|	|	|
Newton Abbot 116 120 d.	...	...	0921	1054	1119	1119	1227	1341	1426	1449	1538	1547	1623	1605	1633	1655	1720	1740	1829	1829	1853	1854	2010	2036	2157	0001
Exeter St Davids 116 120 a.	...	...	0947	1114	1139	1139	1248	1401	1448	1515	1558	1607	1643	1631	1654	1715	1746	1801	1850	1850	1913	1915	2030	2057	2222	0023
Exeter St Davids 120 d.	0936	0936	0949	1118	1141	1141	1248	1403	1449	...	1601	1609	1644	1633	...	1717	1747	1802	1852	1852	1915	1917	2031	2059	...	0059
Tiverton Parkway 120 d.	0953	0953	|	1133	1156	1156	|	1417	|	...	1616	1624	1700	|	...	1732	|	1819	|	|	1930	1932	2047	2114	...	|
Taunton 120a 120 d.	1009	1018	1013	1148	1210	1210	1314	1432	1513	...	1631	1639	1713	1658	...	1746	1818	1834	1916	1916	1944	1946	2100	2127	...	|
Bristol T M.. 132 120a 120 a.	1108	1119	|	1221	|	|	|	|	|	...	|	1720	|	1757	...	1822	1919	|	|	|	|	|	|	2159	...	|
Castle Cary d.	...	...	|	|	1231	1231	|	|	1535	...	|	|	1735	|	...	|	...	|	|	|	2006	2008	2124	|	...	|
Westbury d.	...	...	1049	|	1251	1251	1359	|	1553	...	|	|	1755	|	...	|	...	|	1955	1955	2027	2028	2144	|	...	|
Newbury a.	...	...	1123	|	1328	1328	|	|	1632	...	|	|	1832	|	...	|	...	|	2028	2028	|	|	2219	|	...	|
Reading 132 a.	...	...	1144	1344	1348	1349	1446	1549	1650	...	1749	1845	1850	1914	...	1944	...	1949	2049	2049	2114	2116	2240	2327	...	0403s
London Paddington 132 a.	...	...	1223	1423	1426	1429	1529	1629	1729	...	1829	1924	1930	1958	...	2024	...	2030	2126	2129	2155	2201	2328	0007	...	0503

← **NOTES** (continued from previous page)

w – 1133 from Sept. 17.
x – 1823 July 9 - Sept. 3.
z – Arrives 0512 on ⑥.

★ – Also calls at Dawlish (10 – 15 minutes after Exeter) and Teignmouth (15 – 18 minutes after Exeter).
☆ – Also calls at Teignmouth (7 – 10 minutes after Newton Abbot) and Dawlish (12 – 15 minutes after Newton Abbot).
‡ – Passengers may occupy cabins at London Paddington from 2230 and at Penzance from 2045⑦ / 2115Ⓐ.

GW 2nd class PAIGNTON - EXETER 116

	Ⓐ	Ⓐ	Ⓐ	Ⓐ	Ⓐ	Ⓐ	Ⓐ	Ⓐ	Ⓐ	Ⓐ	Ⓐ	Ⓐ	Ⓐ	Ⓐ	Ⓐ	Ⓐ	Ⓐ	Ⓐ	Ⓐ	Ⓐ	Ⓐ	Ⓐ	Ⓐ	Ⓐ	Ⓐ
Paignton 🚂 115 120 d.		0603	0634	0711	0740	0820	0912	0934	1021	1033	1115	1213	1308	1421	1513	1612	1630	1657	1726	1752	1834	1937	2035	2135	2245
Torquay 115 120 d.		0608	0639	0716	0746	0825	0917	0939	1026	1038	1120	1218	1313	1426	1518	1617	1635	1702	1731	1757	1839	1942	2040	2141	2250
Newton Abbot 115 120 d.		0621	0652	0737b	0806b	0838	0939b	0950	1039	1051	1133	1231	1326	1439	1531	1631	1648	1715	1744	1810	1852	1954	2053	2200	2303
Teignmouth 115 120 d.		0628	0659	0745	0813	0845	0945	|	1046	1058	1140	1238	1333	1446	1538	1638	1656	1722	1751	1817	1859	2002	2100	*2213*	2310
Dawlish 115 120 d.		0633	0704	0750	0819	0850	0950	|	1051	1103	1145	1243	1338	1451	1543	1643	1701	1727	1756	1822	1904	2007	2105	*2218*	2315
Exeter St Davids 115 120 a.		0703	0733	0814	0838	0912	1014	*1020*	1113	1128	1208	1313	1408	1513	1612	1711	1718	1751	1819	1845	1932	2029	2128	*2240*	2337

	Ⓐ	⑥	⑥	⑥	⑥	⑥	⑥	⑥	⑥d	⑥e	⑥e	⑥d	⑥	⑥	⑥	⑥d	⑥e	⑥	⑥d	⑥e	⑥	⑥	⑥e	⑥d	⑥
Paignton 🚂 115 120 d.	2355		0613	0634	0711	0806	0904	0930	1015	1015	1058	1058	1120	1213	1243	1300	1313	1412	1508	1513	1543	1613	1711	1718	1751
Torquay 115 120 d.	2359		0618	0639	0716	0811	0909	0935	1020	1020	1103	1103	1125	1218	1248	1305	1318	1417	1513	1518	1548	1618	1716	1723	1756
Newton Abbot 115 120 d.	0013		0631	0652	0727	0834c	0935c	0949	1033	1033	1122b	1122b	1138	1232	1307	1318	1338b	1439b	1526	1533	1606b	1631	1729	1736	1809
Teignmouth 115 120 d.	0020		0638	0659	|	0841	0942	0956	1040	1040	1130	1130	1145	1239	1314	1325	1346	1447	1534	1541	1613	1638	1736	1744	1817
Dawlish 115 120 d.	0025		0643	0704	|	0846	0947	1002	1045	1045	1135	1135	1150	1244	1319	1330	1351	1452	1539	1546	1618	1643	1741	1749	1822
Exeter St Davids 115 120 a.	0048		0706	0733	*0752*	0909	1009	1018	1007	1114	1148	1157	1213	1313	1336	1353	1413	1513	1602	1613	1632	1714	1810	1813	1845

	⑥	⑥	⑥	⑥	⑥e	⑥	⑥	⑦	⑦	⑦	⑦	⑦	⑦	⑦		⑦	⑦	⑦	⑦	⑦	⑦	⑦	⑦	⑦	⑦
Paignton 🚂 115 120 d.	1856	1921	1951	2020	2047	2120	2330		0949	1058	1149	1257	1352	1419	...	1457	1555	1619	1654	1749	1855	1955	2055	2152	2300
Torquay 115 120 d.	1901	1926	1956	2025	2053	2125	2335		0954	1103	1154	1302	1357	1424	...	1501	1600	1624	1659	1754	1900	2000	2100	2157	2305
Newton Abbot 115 120 d.	1914	1940	2008	2038	2105	2138	2347		1007	1122b	1207	1315	1409	1437	...	1516	1613	1637	1712	1807	1913	2014	2113	2209	2318
Teignmouth 115 120 d.	1921	1947	2015	2045	|	2145	2354		1014	1128	1214	1322	1416	1444	...	1523	1620	1644	1719	1814	1920	2021	2120	2216	2325
Dawlish 115 120 d.	1926	1952	2020	2050	|	2150	2359		1019	1133	1219	1327	1421	1449	...	1528	1625	1649	1724	1819	1925	2026	2125	2221	2330
Exeter St Davids 115 120 a.	1948	2025	2037	2112	2125	2212	0022		1040	1147	1242	1340	1442	1512	...	1541	1638	1711	1741	1840	1948	2049	2138	2242	2352

b – Arrives 7 – 10 minutes earlier.
c – Arrives 12 – 15 minutes earlier.
d – May 27 - Sept. 9.
e – From Sept. 16.
🚂 – Dartmouth Steam Railway (Paignton - Kingswear). ☎ 01803 555 872. www.dartmouthrailriver.co.uk

117 PLYMOUTH - NEWQUAY and PENZANCE — GW, XC

km	Ⓐ	②–⑤ A	①	②–⑤	① A	Ⓐ 🍷	Ⓐ 2B	Ⓐ 2b	Ⓐ 2a	Ⓐ 2a	Ⓐ b	Ⓐ 2a	Ⓐ 2b	Ⓐ 🍷	Ⓐ 2	Ⓐ 2K	Ⓐ b	Ⓐ2 Gb	Ⓐ 2a	Ⓐ 🍷	Ⓐ 2a	Ⓐ 2	Ⓐ 🍷	Ⓐ 2	Ⓐ 2a	Ⓐ 🍷b	Ⓐ 2	Ⓐ 🍷
	London Pad. **115** d.	2345p	...	...	2350p	...	...	...	...	...	...	...	...	0706	...	*0730*e	0906	...	*0906*	1006	...	...	1205	...	...	1305	...	1407
	Bristol § **115 120** d.	|	...	...	|	...	...	0524	0524	...	...	0642	0642	|	...	*0913*e	*0944*	...	*0944*	*1045*	...	*1144*	*1245*	...	*1345*	*1345*	*1445*	*1513*e
0	**Plymouth** d.	0543	0600	0628	0628	0702	0753	0814	0814	...	0820	0921	0924	1039	...	1125	1228	...	1239	1311	...	1349	1512	...	1557	1628	1701	1723
7	Saltash d.	|	|	|	|	0715	0802	|	0824	...	0832	0931	0934	|	...	1134	1238	...	1248	|	...	1358	|	...	1612	|	1714	1734
29	Liskeard d.	0608	0623	0651	0709	0736	0820	0839	0843	...	0853	0950	0953	1103	...	1153	1258	...	1307	1335	...	1417	1537	...	1633	1653	1738	1754
43	Bodmin Parkway 🚂 d.	0622	0635	0703	0723	0749	0833	0851	0855	...	|	1002	1005	1116	...	1205	1312	...	1319	1348	...	1429	1549	...	1645	1706	...	1807
49	Lostwithiel d.	0628	0641	0708	0729	0755	0840	0856	0900	...	|	1007	1010	|	...	1211	1318	...	1324	|	...	1434	|	...	1650	1712	...	1813
56	Par ♡ d.	0637	0648	0715	0738	0803	0854	0917	0908	0917	0914	1015	1018	1128	1140	1218	1328	1338	1332	1400	1407	1442	1601	1610	1658	1728	...	1822
89	**Newquay** ♡ a.	|	|	|	|	|	...	1009	|	1009	|	|	|	|	1231	|	1419	|	|	|	1459	|	|	1702	|	|	...	|
63	St Austell d.	0646	0655	0721	0746	0811	...	...	0916	...	0923	1022	1025	1136	...	1225	...	1345	1339	1407	...	1449	1608	...	1706	1728	...	1829
86	Truro d.	0706	0711	0738	0806	0829	...	...	0934	...	0940	1040	1043	1154	...	1242	...	1403	1357	1425	...	1507	1626	...	1723	1746	...	1847
101	Redruth d.	0718	0723	0749	0820	0841	...	...	0947	...	0953	1053	1056	1206	...	1256	...	1416	1410	1437	...	1520	1638	...	1736	1759	...	1859
107	Camborne d.	0726	0730	0755	0827	0848	...	...	0953	...	1000	1059	1102	1214	...	1302	...	1422	1416	1445	...	1526	1646	...	1742	1807	...	1907
119	St Erth d.	0742	0743	0807	0845	0902	...	...	1008	...	1014	1110	1113	1225	...	1314	...	1433	1428	1459	...	1538	1700	...	1754	1822	...	1921
128	**Penzance** a.	0753	0752	0816	0859	0912	...	...	1016	...	1027	1123	1126	1237	...	1325	...	1444	1439	1511	...	1549	1712	...	1806	1833	...	1933

	Ⓐ 2	Ⓐ 2	Ⓐ 2	Ⓐ 🍷	Ⓐ C	Ⓐ 🍷	Ⓐ 2	Ⓐ D	Ⓐ 🍷	Ⓐ C	Ⓐ 🍷	⑤ 🍷	①–④ 2	⑥	⑥ 2c	⑥ A	⑥ 2c	⑥ c	⑥ d	⑥ 2c	⑥ 2c	⑥ 🍷d	⑥ 2c	⑥ 🍷d	⑥ 2c	⑥2 Kc	⑥ 🍷d	⑥2 Kd	⑥ 🍷
London Pad. **115** d.	...	...	...	1506	...	1606	...	...	1703	...	1803	1903	*1903*		...	2345p	...	...	...	...	...	...	...	...	...	...	0706	...	0730
Bristol § **115 120** d.	...	*1544*	...	|	1645	|	...	1744	|	1844	|	*1945*	*1945*		...	|	...	...	...	0524	...	*0524*	0636	0644	...	*0812*e	*0812*e	*0845*	0918
Plymouth d.	...	1755	1817	1842	1901	1931	...	1949	2026	2050	2120	2229	2242		...	0543	...	0628	0725	0818	...	0818	0919	0923	0951	1033	1032	1053	1123
Saltash d.	...	1804	1831	|	|	1940	...	|	2037	|	|	2239	2251		...	|	...	|	|	0828	...	0828	0928	0933	1001	1044	1043	1105	|
Liskeard d.	...	1820	1854	1907	1924	1957	...	2012	2056	2113	2145	2259	2310		...	0608	...	0651	1749	0847	...	0848	0949	0950	1022	1103	1104	1124	1148
Bodmin Parkway 🚂 d.	...	1832	...	1919	1936	2010	...	2024	2109	2125	2159	2313	2326		...	0622	...	0703	0802	0859	...	0901	1002	1003	1034	1115	1117	1136	1201
Lostwithiel d.	...	1837	...	|	|	|	...	|	|	2131	|	2319	2331		...	0628	...	0708	0808	0904	...	0907	|	1009	1039	1120	1123	|	|
Par ♡ d.	1829	1845	...	1931	1946	2022	2028	2034	2121	2137	2211	2328	2339		0609	0637	0652	0714	0818	0912	0918	0916	1014	1016	1046	1128	1132	1148	1212
Newquay ♡ a.	1921	|	...	|	|	|	2120	|	|	|	|	|	|		|	|	0744	|	0908	|	1010	|	|	|	|	|	|	1239	|
St Austell d.	...	1853	...	1939	1952	2029	...	2041	2128	2144	2218	2335	2346		0616	0646	...	0721	...	0920	...	0923	1022	1024	1054	1137	1139	...	1220
Truro d.	...	1910	...	2000	2018	2047	...	2102	2146	2203	2237	2356	0005		0635	0706	...	0737	...	0937	...	0942	1040	1042	1110	1155	1158	...	1239
Redruth d.	...	1923	...	2010	2029	2059	...	2118	2158	2214	2248	0011	0018		0648	0718	...	0748	...	0950	...	0955	1055	1054	1124	1208	1210	...	1251
Camborne d.	...	1929	...	2018	2035	2107	...	2125	|	2220	|	0019	0024		0654	0726	...	0755	...	0956	...	1002	1102	1101	1130	1214	1217	...	1258
St Erth d.	...	1942	...	2028	2046	2120	...	2135	2214	2232	|	0033	0035		0704	0742	...	0807	...	1008	...	1018	1117	1116	1142	1225	1230	...	1310
Penzance a.	...	1954	...	2042	2054	2131	...	2143	2228	2241	2313	0045	0046		0716	0753	...	0815	...	1018	...	1028	1126	1127	1155	1236	1240	...	1324

	⑥ 2c	⑥ 🍷d	⑥ Md	⑥ 2c	⑥ 🍷	⑥ 2c	⑥ Hd	⑥ 🍷d	⑥ 2c	⑥ 🍷d	⑥ 🍷	⑥ 2c	⑥ 2	⑥ 🍷h	⑥ 🍷g	⑥🍷 Jd	⑥ 🍷	⑥ 2c	⑥ Cd	⑥ 2c	⑥ 2d	⑥ 🍷c	⑥ C	⑥ 2d	⑥ 2K	⑥ 2c	⑥ 🍷d	⑥ D	⑥ 🍷c
London Pad. **115** d.	...	0906	...	*0906*	1006	...	...	1106	...	1135	1206	...	...	1306	1306	...	1406	...	...	...	...	1506	...	...	...	...	1606	*1606*	1706
Bristol § **115 120** d.	...	|	1020	*1044*	|	...	1144	|	*1144*	*1244*	*1244*	...	*1345*c	|	|	1444	*1512*e	...	1544	*1544*	...	|	1644	...	...	...	|	1744	|
Plymouth d.	...	1228	1239	1245	1316	...	1348	1420	1415	1458	1513	...	1603	1626	1649	1650	1726	...	1742	1752	1752	1843	1855	...	1907	...	1930	1948	2040
Saltash d.	...	1239	|	1254	|	...	|	|	1424	|	|	...	1612	|	|	|	|	...	|	1806	1805	|	|	...	1917	...	|	|	2051
Liskeard d.	...	1255	1305	1313	1341	...	1411	1445	1445	|	1538	...	1633	1651	1714	1713	1751	...	1805	1826	1828	1908	1921	...	1936	...	1955	2011	2111
Bodmin Parkway 🚂 d.	...	1308	1320	1325	1354	...	1424	1458	1458	|	1551	...	1645	1704	1729	1729	1804	...	1817	1838	1841	1921	1933	...	1948	...	2008	2023	2124
Lostwithiel d.	...	|	|	1330	|	...	|	|	1504	1537	|	...	1650	|	|	|	|	...	|	1844	1847	|	|	...	1953c	...	|	2028	|
Par ♡ d.	1215	|	1333	1337	1406	1410	1434	|	1512	1548	1603	1615	1657	|	|	1741	1816	1821	1828	1852	1855	1932	1944	1948	2001	2015	2020	2035	2136
Newquay ♡ a.	1307	|	1431	|	|	1457	|	|	|	1647	|	1707	|	|	|	1839	|	1913	|	|	|	|	|	2040	|	2107	|	|	|
St Austell d.	...	1324	...	1345	1414	...	1442	1513	1521	...	1610	...	1704	1721	1746	...	1824	...	1834	1859	1902	1941	1952	...	2008	...	2027	2041	2144
Truro d.	...	1342	...	1402	1432	...	1500	1532	1539	...	1629	...	1723	1739	1804	...	1842	...	1852	1917	1921	2000	2015	...	2026	...	2046	2102	2203
Redruth d.	...	1355	...	1415	1445	...	1512	1544	1553	...	1641	...	1736c	1752	1817	...	1855	...	1908	1930	1933	2012	2027	...	2043	...	2058	2113	2215
Camborne d.	...	1402	...	1421	1452	...	1519	1552	1600	...	1649	...	1742c	1759	1824	...	1902	...	1915	1936	1941	2020	2035	...	2049	...	2106	2119	|
St Erth d.	...	1419	...	1433	1507	...	1529	1608	1612	...	1700	...	1754c	1814	1844	...	1914	...	1927	1948	1955	2030	2046	...	2058	...	2118	2131	2232
Penzance a.	...	1429	...	1442	1518	...	1538	1618	1621	...	1711	...	1803c	1825	1854	...	1924	...	1936	1957	2005	2041	2056	...	2111	...	2128	2140	2242

	⑥ 2d	⑥ Cc	⑥ 🍷	⑦	⑦ 2q	⑦ 2f	⑦ 2r	⑦ 2	⑦ 2q	⑦ 2	⑦ 🍷	⑦ 2r	⑦ 🍷q	⑦ F	⑦ 🍷q	⑦2 Kr	⑦ 🍷		⑦ 2	⑦ 🍷	⑦ 2	⑦ 🍷	⑦ 2K	⑦ 🍷	⑦ E	⑦ 2	⑦ 🍷	⑦ C	⑦ 🍷
London Pad. **115** d.	*1706*	...	1806		...	...	...	...	...	...	0800	...	0851	*0857*r	0957	*0957*	1057	...	...	1157	...	1257	*1300*	1457	...	*1557*	1657	...	1757
Bristol § **115 120** d.	|	1844	|		...	...	...	0726	...	0828	1000	...	|	1057	|	|	*1154*	...	...	*1254*	...	*1344*	*1455*	*1614*e	1644	|	*1744*	1844	|
Plymouth d.	2040	2058	2121		0901	0909	...	1020	...	1113	1215	...	1235	1255	1328	1331	1415	...	1450	1530	...	1625	1735	1825	1853	1943	2024	2050	2135
Saltash d.	2054	|	|		|	0917	...	1030	...	1124	|	...	|	|	|	1339	|	...	1459	|	...	|	1745	|	|	1952	|	|	|
Liskeard d.	2113	2125	2146		0925	0939	...	1051	...	1143	1239	...	1301	1318	1353	1358	1439	...	1518	1555	...	1650	1806	1853	1916	2011	2049	2113	2200
Bodmin Parkway 🚂 d.	2125	2137	2200		0938	0951	...	1103	...	1155	1252	...	1314	1330	1405	1410	1453	...	1530	1609	...	1703	1818	1906	1928	2023	2102	2125	2213
Lostwithiel d.	2130	|	|		|	1957	...	1108	...	1200	|	...	|	|	1411	|	|	...	1536	|	...	|	1823	|	|	2028	|	|	|
Par ♡ d.	2138	2147	2212		0955	1005	1018	1116	1149	1208	1304	1315	1325	1340	1422	1421	|	...	1544	1621	1634	1714	1831	1917	1938	2036	2113	2135	2226
Newquay ♡ a.	|	|	|		1100	|	1110	|	1247	|	|	1407	|	|	1512	|	|	...	|	|	1734t	|	|	|	|	|	|	|	|
St Austell d.	2145	2201	2219		...	1012	...	1125	...	1215	1311	...	1333	1351	...	1429	1509	...	1551	1629	...	1722	1838	1925	1945	2043	2120	2143	2234
Truro d.	2203	2218	2238		...	1031	...	1144	...	1233	1331	...	1351	1409	...	1445	1526	...	1610	1647	...	1740	1856	1941	2001	2100	2137	2200	2249
Redruth d.	2217	2229	2250		...	1044	...	1157	...	1246	1343	...	1404	1420	...	1459	1537	...	1623	1659	...	1753	1909	1954	2012	2114	2151	2211	2304
Camborne d.	2223	2235	2258		...	1050	...	1203	...	1252	1351	...	1411	1427	...	1505	1545	...	1629	1707	...	1801	1915	2004	2021	2120	2157	2220	2311
St Erth d.	2234	2245	2312		...	1102	...	1214	...	1305	1403	...	1423	1437	...	1516	1559	...	1639	1719	...	1813	1925	2016	2031	2132	2210	2230	2323
Penzance a.	2244	2254	2322		...	1117	...	1224	...	1315	1418	...	1433	1447	...	1525	1612	...	1650	1729	...	1824	1937	2028	2039	2142	2222	2242	2335

A – THE NIGHT RIVIERA – Conveys 🛏 1, 2. cl and [2]. See also note ‡ on page 99.
B – Starts from Exeter St. Davids until June 30 and from Sept. 4 (Table **115**).
C – From Glasgow Central (Table **120**).
D – From Aberdeen (Tables **222** / **120**).
E – From Edinburgh (Table **120**).
F – From Birmingham New Street (Table **120**).
G – From Newquay.

H – From York (Table **120**).
J – From Dundee (Tables **222** / **120**).
K – From Exeter St Davids (Table **115**).
M – From Manchester Piccadilly (Table **120**).

a – Until June 30 and from Sept. 4.
b – July 3 - Sept. 1.
c – From Sept. 16.
d – May 27 - Sept. 9.

e – Change at Exeter St Davids.
f – Timings may vary by up to 4 minutes.
g – Sept. 16 - Oct. 21.
h – May 27 - Sept. 9 and from Oct. 28.
p – Previous night.
q – May 21 - Sept. 10.
r – From Sept. 17.

s – Stops to set down only.
t – Arrives 1726 from Sept. 17.
u – Stops to pick up only.

§ – Bristol Temple Meads
♡ – Par - Newquay: *'The Atlantic Coast Line'*.
🚂 – Bodmin & Wenford Railway (Bodmin Parkway - Bodmin General - Boscarne Junction *10 km*). ✆ 01208 73555. www.bodminrailway.co.uk

118 BRANCH LINES and BUS CONNECTIONS IN DEVON and CORNWALL — 2nd class GW

EXETER - EXMOUTH *'The Avocet Line'* *18 km*

From Exeter St Davids: on ⚒ at 0544, 0606Ⓐ, 0629, 0708, 0736, 0815, 0845, 0915, 0948 and at the same minutes past each hour until 1616, 1646, 1715, 1745⑥, 1753Ⓐ, 1816⑥, 1821Ⓐ, 1847⑥, 1850Ⓐ, 1931, 2031⑥, 2034Ⓐ, 2131Ⓐ, 2141⑥, 2231Ⓐ, 2241⑥, 2309⑥, 2328Ⓐ; on ⑦ at 0830, 0940, 1013, 1044, 1122**a**, 1151, 1226**a**, 1247, 1322**a**, 1348, 1446, 1518, 1546, 1622**a**, 1642, 1716, 1746, 1846, 1951, 2052, 2148, 2248, 2325.

From Exmouth: on ⚒ at 0001①, 0004②–⑥, 0614, 0643Ⓐ, 0712, 0751, 0821, 0852, 0921, 0953 and at the same minutes past each hour until 1653, 1723, 1753⑥, 1801Ⓐ, 1825⑥, 1832Ⓐ, 1854⑥, 1859Ⓐ, 1939, 2007⑥, 2015Ⓐ, 2111Ⓐ, 2116⑥, 2207Ⓐ, 2219⑥, 2307Ⓐ, 2317⑥, 2345⑥; on ⑦ at 0910, 1019, 1054**b**, 1124, 1200**b**, 1228, 1255, 1324, 1358, 1427, 1523, 1555**b**, 1623, 1655, 1723, 1755, 1823, 1923, 2028, 2128, 2227, 2329.

Journey: 37–40 minutes. Trains call at Exeter Central 3–4 minutes from Exeter St Davids.

a – Starts from Exeter Central. **b** – Terminates at Exeter Central.

EXETER - BARNSTAPLE *'The Tarka Line'* *63 km*

From Exeter St Davids: on ⚒ at 0550Ⓐ, 0554⑥, 0648Ⓐ, 0655⑥, 0831, 0927, 1027, 1127, 1227, 1327, 1427, 1527, 1657⑥, 1702Ⓐ, 1757, 1859, 2100, 2253⑤; on ⑦ at 0843, 0954, 1203, 1408, 1604, 1807, 2001.

From Barnstaple: on ⚒ at 0700Ⓐ, 0705⑥, 0843, 0943, 1043, 1143, 1243, 1343, 1443, 1543, 1708⑥, 1713Ⓐ, 1813, 1916, 2024, 2216Ⓐ, 2230⑥; on ⑦ at 1000, 1129, 1323, 1529, 1721, 1926, 2130.

Journey: 65 minutes. Trains call at ***Crediton*** *(11 minutes from Exeter / 54 minutes from Barnstaple) and* ***Eggesford*** *(40 minutes from Exeter / 25 minutes from Barnstaple).*

PLYMOUTH - GUNNISLAKE *'The Tamar Valley Line'* *24 km*

From Plymouth: on Ⓐ at 0506, 0641, 0840, 1054, 1254, 1454, 1637, 1823, 2131; on ⑥ at 0627**a**, 0640**b**, 0854, 1054**b**, 1059**a**, 1254, 1448**a**, 1454**b**, 1639, 1823, 2131; on ⑦ at 0920, 1106, 1306, 1511, 1741, 2001**a**.

From Gunnislake: on Ⓐ at 0551, 0731, 0929, 1145, 1345, 1545, 1729, 1913, 2221; on ⑥ at 0717**a**, 0731**b**, 0945, 1145**b**, 1154**a**, 1345, 1545, 1729, 1913**b**, 1920**a**, 2221; on ⑦ at 1018, 1207, 1358, 1604, 1835, 2050**a**.

Journey: 45–60 minutes. **a** – Until Sept. 10. **b** – From Sept. 16.

LISKEARD - LOOE *'The Looe Valley Line'* *14 km*

From Liskeard: on Ⓐ at 0605, 0714, 0833, 0959, 1111, 1216, 1321, 1425, 1541, 1641, 1806, 1920; on ⑥ at 0550**a**, 0601**b**, 0713, 0835, 0958, 1108, 1212, 1324, 1428, 1543, 1656, 1801, 1928, 2040**a**; on ⑦ May 21 - Oct. 22 at 1012, 1126, 1247, 1400, 1503**d**, 1523**e**, 1610**d**, 1635**e**, 1745, 2015.

From Looe: on Ⓐ at 0637, 0746, 0909, 1030, 1143, 1248, 1353, 1459, 1613, 1715, 1840, 1952; on ⑥ at 0622**a**, 0633**b**, 0747, 0909, 1032, 1137, 1244, 1356, 1456, 1615, 1728, 1833, 2000, 2121**a**; on ⑦ May 21 - Oct. 22 at 1044, 1158, 1319, 1432, 1535**d**, 1555**e**, 1642**d**, 1712**e**, 1819, 2050.

Journey: 28–33 minutes. **a** – May 27 - Sept. 9. **b** – From Sept. 16. **d** – May 21 - Sept. 10. **e** – Sept. 17 - Oct. 22.

EXETER - OKEHAMPTON *Service runs only summer ⑦.* 40 km

From Exeter St. Davids: On ⑦ until Sept. 10 at 0907, 1107, 1433, 1635.
From Okehampton: On ⑦ until Sept. 10 at 0955, 1212, 1523, 1759.

Journey: 40–42 minutes. Trains call at ***Crediton*** *(approx. 10 minutes from Exeter).*

For explanation of standard symbols see page 1

PENZANCE and NEWQUAY - PLYMOUTH

		Ⓐ 🍷	Ⓐ 2	Ⓐ 🍷	Ⓐ 2L	Ⓐ D	Ⓐ 🍷	Ⓐ 🍷	Ⓐ D	Ⓐ 🍷	Ⓐ E	Ⓐ 2	Ⓐ 🍷	Ⓐ 2a	Ⓐ 🍷b	Ⓐ 2M	Ⓐ 2b	Ⓐ 2a	Ⓐ 🍷	Ⓐ 2	Ⓐ 2a	Ⓐ 2a	Ⓐ 2b	Ⓐ 🍷b	Ⓐ 2b	Ⓐ 🍷	Ⓐ 2	①–④ 2B
Penzance d.	Ⓐ	0505	0520	0541	0600	0628	0645	0741	0828	0844	0935	...	1000	1046	1047	1141	...	...	1303	1345	...	1449	1452	...	...	1559	...	1644
St Erth d.		|	|	|	0609	0636	0655	0751	0836	0854	0943	...	1010	1055	1057	1150	...	...	1313	1354	...	1458	1501	...	...	1610	...	1653
Camborne d.		|	0539	0559	0622	0646	0707	0806	0846	0907	0956	...	1023	1108	1112	1203	...	...	1325	1407	...	1511	1514	...	...	1621	...	1706
Redruth d.		0526	|	0606	0628	0652	0714	0813	0852	0914	1003	...	1030	1114	1119	1209	...	...	1332	1413	...	1517	1520	...	...	1629	...	1712
Truro d.		0538	0554	0619	0640	0704	0727	0826	0904	0927	1015	...	1043	1126	1132	1220	...	...	1345	1424	...	1528	1531	...	...	1642	...	1725
St Austell d.		0556	...	0636	0657	0720	0745	0844	0920	0944	1031	...	1100	1143	1150	1237	...	...	1402	1441	...	1545	1548	...	...	1659	...	1742
Newquay ♡ d.		|	...	|	|	|	|	|	|	|	|	1013	|	|	|	|	1240	1303	|	|	1501	|	|	1506	...	|	...	|
Par ♡ d.		|	...	0643	0703	0727	0752	0851	0927	0951	1038	1102	1108	1150	1157	1244	1335	1352	1410	1448	1547	1552	1554	1600	...	1707	...	1748
Lostwithiel d.		|	...	0651	0710	|	0800	|	|	|	1045	...	|	1156	|	1250	...	...	|	1455	...	1558	...	1609	...	1714	...	1755
Bodmin Parkway 🚂 d.		0614	...	0657	0716	0737	0806	0903	0937	1003	1051	...	1119	1202	1208	1256	...	...	1421	1501	...	1604	...	1616	...	1721	...	1801
Liskeard d.		0627	...	0711	0729	0753	0820	0916	0950	1016	1104	...	1133	1217	1221	1309	...	...	1434	1514	...	1617	...	1629	1643	1734	1749	1814
Saltash d.		|	...	0730	0747	|	0839	0934	|	|	|	...	|	1234	1241	1328	...	...	|	1532	...	1637	...	|	1703	|	1806	1832
Plymouth a.		0651	...	0741	0804	0820	0849	0946	1018	1040	1127	...	1157	1244	1252	1338	...	...	1459	1543	...	1651	...	1654	1718	1758	1818	1842
Bristol § **115 120** a.		*0926*	...	|	1108	1025	*1124*	1158	1224	*1324*	1355	...	*1426*	*1523*	*1523*	*1623*	...	...	*1724*	*1823*	...	*1925*	...	|	*1925*	*2025*	*2025*	|
London Pad **115** a.		1002	...	1124	...	...	1221	1339	...	1344	...	...	1521	*1622*	1622	...	...	...	1821	*1921*	...	*2039*	...	2039	...	2122	...	*2239*e

	⑤ 2C	Ⓐ 2	Ⓐ 🍷	Ⓐ 2	Ⓐ 2b	Ⓐ 2a	①–④ 2	⑤ 🍷	Ⓐ 2	Ⓐ A	Ⓐ		⑥ 2k	⑥2 Bd	⑥ 2c	⑥ D	⑥ 🍷	⑥ 🍷d	⑥ 2c	⑥ 2c	⑥ 🍷c	⑥ D	⑥ 🍷d	⑥ 🍷c	⑥ Hd	⑥ Ec	⑥ 2c	⑥ 🍷
Penzance d.	1644	...	1742	...	1913	1916	2018	2018	...	2145	2210	⑥	0510	0527	0537	0630	0650	0718	...	0735	0759	0828	0838	0844	...	0943	...	0954j
St Erth d.	1653	...	1752	...	1923	1925	2027	2027	...	2155	2218		|	0535	0545	0638	0700	1729	...	0748	0809	0836	0849	0854	...	0951	...	1005j
Camborne d.	1706	...	1807	...	1939	1938	2042	2042	...	2209	2231		0528	0549	0559	0651	0712	1745	...	0803	0824	0846	0905	0906	...	1001	...	1021
Redruth d.	1712	...	1815	...	1946	1944	2050	2050	...	2217	2238		0534	0555	0605	0657	0719	1752	...	0810	0831	0852	0912	0913	...	1007	...	1028
Truro d.	1725	...	1827	...	1959	1956	2103	2103	...	2230	2249		0546	0606	0616	0709	0732	0806	...	0821	0844	0904	0925	0926	...	1019	...	1041
St Austell d.	1742	...	1844	...	2016	2013	2120	2120	...	2248	2305		...	0623	0633	0725	0749	0823	...	0837	0902	0920	0943	0944	...	1035	...	1059
Newquay ♡ d.	|	1722	|	1924	|	|	|	|	2126	|	|		...	|	|	|	|	|	0748	|	|	|	|	|	0935	|	1012	|
Par ♡ d.	1748	1813	1852	2013	2024	2019	2127	2127	2216	2257	2312		...	0629	0639	0732	0756	0830	0839	0844	0909	0927	0950	0951	1031	1041	1101	1107
Lostwithiel d.	1755	...	|	...	2031	2026	2134	2134	...	|	2319		...	0636	0646	0739	0804	0838	...	0851	|	|	|	|	|	1048	...	|
Bodmin Parkway 🚂 d.	1801	...	1904	...	2038	2032	2140	2140	...	2309	2325		...	0642	0652	0746	0810	0844	...	0857	0920	0937	1001	1002	1043	1055	...	1118
Liskeard d.	1814	...	1917	...	2051	2045	2153	2153	...	2325	2337		...	0656	0707	0758	0823	0857	...	0910	0933	0950	1014	1015	1055	1107	...	1131
Saltash d.	1832	...	|	...	|	2104	2211	2211	...	|	|		...	0715	0726	|	|	0917	...	0929	|	|	|	|	|	|	...	|
Plymouth a.	1842	...	1941	...	2116	2119	2224	2224	...	2348	0001		...	0731	0742	0821	0848	0926	...	0940	0958	1017	1038	1039	1118	1130	...	1156
Bristol § **115 120** a.	|	...	2145	...	...	...	...	...	...	|	...		...	|	|	1025	*1130*	|	...	...	|	1225	|	|	1325	1355	...	*1425*
London Pad **115** a.	*2230*n	...	2342	...	...	...	...	...	...	0527t	...		...	*1121*	*1121*	...	1221	1309	...	...	1321	...	1344	1344	...	...	...	1521

	⑥ 2d	⑥ 2c	⑥ 🍷c	⑥ 🍷d	⑥ 🍷d	⑥ 2c	⑥ 2c	⑥ 🍷d	⑥ 2c	⑥ 🍷d	⑥ 2d	⑥ 🍷	⑥ 2c	⑥ 2c	⑥ 🍷d	⑥🍷 Ed	⑥ 🍷	⑥🍷 Gd	⑥2 Bc	⑥ 2c	⑥ 🍷d	⑥ 🍷	⑥ d	⑥ 2c	⑥ 2B	⑥ 2d	⑥ 2c	⑥
Penzance d.	...	1037	1058	1100	...	1146	...	1158	1300	1307	...	1359	...	1452	1500	...	1552	1625	1641	...	...	1740	...	...	1906	...	...	2129
St Erth d.	1028	1045	1108	1111	...	1155	...	1209	1309	1317	...	1409	...	1501	1510	...	1602	1634	1651	...	...	1750	...	...	1915	...	...	2138
Camborne d.	1043	1059	1120	1127	...	1209	...	1225	1322	1333	...	1421	...	1515	1526	...	1614	1645	1706	...	...	1805	...	...	1928	...	...	2149
Redruth d.	1050	1105	1127	1134	...	1215	...	1232	1328	1340	...	1428	...	1521	1533	...	1621	1652	1713	...	...	1812	...	...	1934	...	...	2156
Truro d.	1103	1116	1140	1147	...	1227	...	1244	1339	1353	...	1441	...	1532	1546	...	1634	1705	1726	...	...	1825	...	...	1945	...	...	2209
St Austell d.	1120	1133	1157	1204	...	1244	...	1302	1356	1410	...	1458	...	1549	1604	...	1652	1722	1744	...	...	1842	...	...	2002	...	...	2226
Newquay ♡ d.	|	|	|	|	1130	|	1309	|	|	|	1323	|	1459	|	|	1530	|	|	|	1721	1726	|	1900	1917	|	2045	2118	|
Par ♡ d.	1128	1139	|	|	1226	1253	1358	|	1403	1418	1428	1505	1548	1555	1611	1627	1659	1729	1751	1810	1822	1849	1954	2003	2009	2140	2209	2233
Lostwithiel d.	1136	1146	|	|	|	1300	...	|	1409	|	1434	|	...	1602	1619	|	1706	|	1758	...	|	|	|	...	2015	2149	2218	|
Bodmin Parkway 🚂 d.	1142	1152	1213	1220	|	1306	...	1318	1415	1429	1441	1517	...	1608	1625	1638	1713	1741	1805	...	1835	1901	2006	...	2021	2155	2224	2244
Liskeard d.	1157	1207	1226	1233	|	1319	...	1331	1428	1442	1454	1533	...	1621	1638	1651	1726	1754	1819	...	1848	1914	2020	...	2035	2208	2237	2258
Saltash d.	1220	1226	|	|	|	1339	...	|	1447	|	1514	|	...	1640	1659	|	|	|	1838	...	|	|	|	...	2054	2226	2255	|
Plymouth a.	1231	1237	1251	1259	1311	1350	...	1355	1458	1507	1525	1557	...	1650	1710	1714	1750	1818	1849	...	1914	1938	2047	...	2110	2242	2312	2322
Bristol § **115 120** a.	...	...	*1525*	|	*1525*	*1625*	...	*1625*	*1725*	*1725*	...	*1825*c	...	*1924*	*1924*	1923	*2022*c	2024	...	...	|	2147	...	...	...	...	...	...
London Pad **115** a.	...	...	1621	1621	1631	...	...	1721	*1821*	1821	...	1921	...	*2037*	...	...	2130	...	...	...	2232	2344	...	...	...	...	...	...

		⑦ 🍷	⑦ F	⑦ 2q	⑦ 🍷	⑦ 2r	⑦ 🍷	⑦🍷 Fq	⑦ 🍷q	⑦ 2B	⑦ E	⑦ 🍷		⑦2 B	⑦ 2	⑦ 2r	⑦ 🍷	⑦ G	⑦ 🍷q	⑦ 🍷q	⑦ 🍷r	⑦ 2	⑦ 🍷	⑦ 2q	⑦ 2B	⑦ 2q	⑦ 2	⑦ A
Penzance d.	⑦	0830	0930	...	0947	...	1100	...	1140	1205	1230	1256	...	1339	1437	...	1500	1530	1550	...	1613	...	1731	1750	1900	...	2005	2115
St Erth d.		0839	0938	...	0956	...	1110	...	1149	1214	1238	1306	...	1349	1447	...	1510	1538	1559	...	1625	...	1740	1800	1909	...	2014	2125
Camborne d.		0856	0948	...	1008	...	1124	...	1201	1226	1251	1320	...	1402	1500	...	1523	1549	1612	...	1636	...	1753	1813	1921	...	2027	2139
Redruth d.		0902	0954	...	1014	...	1130	...	1207	1232	1258	1326	...	1408	1506	...	1530	1555	1618	...	1645	...	1800	1819	1927	...	2033	2146
Truro d.		0916	1006	...	1027	...	1143	...	1221	1244	1309	1339	...	1419	1517	...	1542	1607	1633	...	1658	...	1812	1831	1939	...	2045	2201
St Austell d.		0932	1022	...	1044	...	1200	...	1237	1300	1326	1357	...	1436	1534	...	1600	1623	1649	...	1715	...	1831	1848	1956	...	2102	2219
Newquay ♡ d.		|	|	0952	|	1112	|	1132	|	|	|	|	...	|	|	1510	|	|	|	1621	|	1738	|	|	|	2015	|	|
Par ♡ d.		0940	1029	1039	1052	1201	1207	1224	1245	1306	1332	1403	...	1443	1540	1559	1607	1630	1656	1715	1721	1827	1838	1855	2003	2102	2109	|
Lostwithiel d.		|	|	...	|	...	|	|	|	1313	1339	|	...	1449	1547	...	|	|	|	|	|	...	|	1901	2009	...	2115	|
Bodmin Parkway 🚂 d.		0952	1039	...	1105	...	1219	1237	1258	1319	1346	1416	...	1455	1553	...	1618	1640	1709	1727	1733	...	1849	1908	2015	...	2122	2235
Liskeard d.		1005	1052	...	1118	...	1233	1251	1311	1333	1358	1429	...	1508	1609	...	1631	1652	1722	1741	1747	...	1902	1922	2028	...	2136	2250
Saltash d.		1021	|	...	|	...	|	|	|	1354	|	|	...	1526	1626	...	|	|	|	1758	1803	...	|	1940	2047	...	2154	|
Plymouth a.		1029	1115	...	1143	...	1257	1314	1336	1403	1423	1454	...	1534	1636	...	1657	1715	1745	1810	1812	...	1926	1951	2100	...	2204	2314
Bristol § **115 120** a.		|	1323	...	*1354*	...	*1526*	1526	|	*1625*	1647	*1720*	...	*1822*	1919	...	|	1922	|	|	*2025*	...	*2159*	*2159*	...	...	...	|
London Pad **115** a.		1429	...	...	1529	...	1629	...	1729	...	...	1829	...	*2024*	...	...	2030	*2129*	2126	2155	2201	...	2328	*0007*	...	...	...	0503

A – THE NIGHT RIVIERA – Conveys 🛏 1, 2. cl and 2-class seated carriage. See also note ‡ on page 99.
B – To Exeter St Davids (Table **115**).
C – To Taunton (Table **115**).
D – To Glasgow Central (Table **120**).
E – To Manchester Piccadilly (Table **120**).
F – To Edinburgh (Table **120**).
G – To Leeds (Table **120**).
H – To Dundee (Tables **120** / **222**).
J – To Penzance.
K – To Newton Abbot (Table **115**).
L – To Cardiff Central (Table **120a**).
M – Continues to Newton Abbot July 3 - Sept. 1 (Table **117**).
a – Until June 30 and from Sept. 4.
b – July 3 - Sept. 1.
c – From Sept. 16.
d – May 27 - Sept. 9.
e – Change at Exeter St Davids.
g – Sept.16 - Oct. 21.
j – 5 minutes later from Sept. 16.
k – Runs 10 minutes later from Sept. 16.
q – May 21 - Sept. 10.
r – From Sept. 17.
n – Change at Taunton.
t – Arrives 0512 on ⑥ mornings.
§ – Bristol Temple Meads.
♡ – Par - Newquay: *'The Atlantic Coast Line'*.
🚂 – Bodmin & Wenford Railway (Bodmin Parkway - Bodmin General - Boscarne Junction *10 km*). ✆ 01208 73555. www.bodminrailway.co.uk

BRANCH LINES and BUS CONNECTIONS IN DEVON and CORNWALL — 118

GW 2nd class

Rail tickets are generally not valid on 🚌 services shown in this table.

BODMIN PARKWAY - PADSTOW — *Plymouth City Bus 🚌 service 11A*

Service valid until June 3.

From Bodmin Parkway station: on ⚒ at 0612, 0707, 0807, 0907, 1007, 1107, 1207, 1307, 1407, 1507, 1607, 1707⑥, 1722Ⓐ, 1802⑥, 1807Ⓐ; on ⑦ at 0804, 0957, 1157, 1357, 1557, 1754.

From Padstow Bus Terminus: on ⚒ at 0625, 0725, 0825, 0925, 1025, 1125, 1225, 1325, 1425, 1525⑥, 1535Ⓐ, 1630, 1730, 1830⑥, 1835Ⓐ, 1925; on ⑦ at 0905, 1105, 1305, 1505, 1705, 1905.

Journey: 68 minutes. Buses also make calls in Bodmin town centre and at Bodmin General station, and call at ***Wadebridge*** *(35 minutes after Bodmin / 25 minutes after Padstow).*

TRURO - FALMOUTH DOCKS — *'The Maritime Line'* — *20 km*

From Truro: on ⚒ at 0605, 0631, 0714, 0747, 0820, 0851 and at the same minutes past each hour until 1620, 1651, 1727, 1759, 1831, 1902, 2004, 2105, 2244Ⓐ, 2212⑥;
on ⑦ at 0901, 1037, 1134**a**, 1209**b**, 1238**a**, 1308**b**, 1344**a**, 1412**b**, 1440**a**, 1535**b**, 1547**a**, 1705, 1815, 1946, 2103, 2204.

From Falmouth Docks: on ⚒ at 0632, 0715, 0747, 0820, 0850 and at the same minutes past each hour until 1620, 1650, 1727, 1759, 1831, 1902, 1929, 2031, 2132, 2239⑥, 2311Ⓐ;
on ⑦ at 0935, 1104, 1202**a**, 1236**b**, 1305**a**, 1335**b**, 1411**a**, 1439**b**, 1509**a**, 1602**b**, 1617**a**, 1735, 1842, 2013, 2130, 2233.

Trains call at ***Falmouth Town*** *22 minutes after Truro and 3 minutes after Falmouth Docks.*

Journey: 25 minutes.

a – May 21 - Sept. 17.
b – From Sept. 10.
c – From Oct. 29.
d – From Sept. 16.
e – May 27 - Sept. 9 and from Oct. 28.
f – May 21 - Sept. 10.
g – From Sept. 17.
h – Sept. 16 - Oct. 21.
k – May 21 - Oct. 22.
n – Sept. 17 - Oct. 22.

ST AUSTELL - EDEN PROJECT — *First Kernow 🚌 service 101*

From St Austell bus station: on Ⓐ at 0847, 0930, 1040, 1147, 1242, 1412, 1454, 1550, 1735;
on ⑥ at 0846, 0930, 1040, 1143, 1235, 1417, 1504, 1553, 1642, 1735;
on ⑦ at 0846, 0937, 1030, 1130, 1225, 1330, 1441, 1539, 1627, 1735.

From Eden Project: on Ⓐ at 0908, 1110, 1210, 1330, 1432, 1515, 1615, 1715, 1800;
on ⑥ at 0908, 1105, 1205, 1330, 1436, 1525, 1620, 1705, 1800;
on ⑦ at 0908, 0958, 1055, 1150, 1250, 1355, 1505, 1559, 1649, 1800.

Journey: 20 minutes.

ST ERTH - ST IVES — *'The St Ives Bay Line'* — *7 km*

From St Erth: on Ⓐ at 0706, 0759, 0905, 0938 and every 30 minutes until 1648, 1717, 1748 and every 30 minutes until 2048, 2123, 2158; on ⑥ at 0650, 0800, 0903, 0935, 1013, 1048, 1119, 1148 and every 30 minutes until 1648, 1717, 1759, 1859**e**, 1904**h**, 1953, 2033, 2106, 2147; on ⑦ at 0853**f**, 0927**f**, 1000**f**, 1030**k**, 1113**k**, 1142**k**, 1156**c**, 1218**k**, 1230**c**, 1248**n**, 1318, 1348, 1418, 1448, 1518**g**, 1548, 1618, 1648, 1723, 1755, 1830, 1930.

From St Ives: on Ⓐ at 0725, 0815, 0922, 0953, 1033 and every 30 minutes until 1703, 1731, 1803, 1833, 1905, 1932, 2003, 2033, 2103, 2137, 2231; on ⑥ at 0712, 0814, 0920, 0950, 1027, 1103, 1203, 1233, 1303, 1333**d**, 1403 and every 30 minutes until 1703, 1732, 1817, 1926, 2010, 2049, 2124, 2205; on ⑦ at 0910**f**, 0941**f**, 1015**f**, 1050**k**, 1127**k**, 1157**k**, 1213**c**, 1233**n**, 1248**c**, 1303**k**, 1333, 1403, 1432, 1503**g**, 1533, 1603, 1633, 1703, 1739, 1810**d**, 1812**f**, 1850, 1950.

Journey: 15 minutes.

① – Mondays ② – Tuesdays ③ – Wednesdays ④ – Thursdays ⑤ – Fridays ⑥ – Saturdays ⑦ – Sundays Ⓐ – Monday to Fridays, not holidays 3

```
km
                                         ⚒   ⚒   ⑥   Ⓐ   ⑥   Ⓐ   ⚒   ⑥   Ⓐ   ⚒   Ⓐ   ⑥   ⚒   Ⓐ   ⑥   Ⓐ   ⑥   ⚒   ⚒   ⚒           ⚒   ⚒
                                                                      A                                                  E
     Manchester Piccadilly 122 ..d. ⚒  ...  ... 0511 0511 ...  ...  ...  ... 0727  ...  ... 0827  ...  ... 0927 0927  ... 1027  ...  ...      1127
     Newcastle 124 ...............d.     ...  ...  |    |   ...  ...  ...  ...  |  0625 0623  |  0725 0735  |       |  0835   |   ...  0935      1035
     York 124 ......................d.   ...  ...  |    |   ...  ...  ...  ...  |  0727 0727  |  0826 0835  |       |  0935   |   ...  1035
     Leeds 124..................d.       ...  ...  |    |   ...  ...  0616 0616  |
     Sheffield 124................d.     ...  ...  |    |  0545d 0601 ... 0718 0718  |  0821 0820  |  0924 0924   |       |  1024   |   ...  1124
     Derby 124....................d.     ...  ...  |    |  0648 0648 0706 0751 0750 ...  0853 0853  |  0953 0953   |       |  1053   |   ...  1153
  0  Birmingham New St. 142 150 d.  0604 0633 0704 0704 0733 0733 0804 0833 0833 0904 0933 0933 1004 1033 1033 1104 1104 1133 1204  ... 1233 1304
 13  Birmingham Intl + . 142 150 d.  0614  ... 0714 0714  ... 0814  ... 0914  ... 1014  ... 1114 1114  ... 1214  ... 1314
 30  Coventry ............ 142 150 d.  0625  ... 0725 0725  ... 0825  ... 0925  ... 1025  ... 1125 1125  ... 1225  ... 1325
 45  Leamington Spa....... 128 d.    0637 0700 0738 0738 0800 0759 0838 0900 0900 0938 1000 1000 1038 1100 1100 1138 1138 1200 1238  ... 1300 1338
 77  Banbury................. 128 d.   0654 0719 0755 0755 0819 0816 0855 0919 0920 0955 1019 1019 1055 1119 1119 1155 1155 1219 1255  ... 1319 1355
114  Oxford ......................a.   0714 0741 0814 0814 0839 0839 0914 0940 0941 1015 1040 1041 1114 1141 1141 1214 1214 1241 1314  ... 1341 1414
114  Oxford ...................131 d.  0716 0743 0816 0816 0843 0843 0916 0943 0943 1016 1043 1043 1116 1143 1143 1216 1216 1243 1316  ... 1343 1415
158  Reading ................131 a.   0741 0809 0841 0840 0909 0908 0941 1008 1010 1041 1109 1111 1140 1209 1206 1241 1241 1309 1340  ... 1409 1441
158  Reading ....................d.  0746a 0820 0846 0846  ... 0946b 1020 1020 1046a  ...  ... 1146 1220 1220 1250 1246  ... 1346  ... 1418 1446b
183  Basingstoke .......... 108 a.    0808 0841 0908 0908  ... 1008 1039 1039 1108  ...  ... 1208 1239 1240 1308 1308  ... 1408  ... 1440 1508
213  Winchester ........... 108 a.    0824 0856 0924 0925  ... 1024 1054 1054 1124  ...  ... 1224 1254 1255 1323 1324  ... 1424  ... 1455 1524
226  Southampton Airport +.108 a.    0833 0908 0932 0933  ... 1032 1108 1107 1133  ...  ... 1232 1308 1308 1332 1332  ... 1434  ... 1509 1532
234  Southampton Central .. 108 a.   0844 0917 0940 0943  ... 1043 1117 1117 1143  ...  ... 1241 1317 1317 1341 1341  ... 1441  ... 1517 1541
255  Brockenhurst ......... 108 a.    0859  ... 0957 0958  ... 1058  ... 1158  ...  ... 1257  ... 1356 1357  ... 1457  ... 1557
280  Bournemouth ......... 108 a.     0914  ... 1011 1013  ... 1113  ... 1213  ...  ... 1312  ... 1411 1412  ... 1512  ... 1612
```

```
                                         ⚒   ⚒        ⚒   ⚒   Ⓐ   ⑥        ⚒   ⚒        ⚒   ⚒   ⚒   ⚒        ⑥   Ⓐ   ⚒   ⑥   Ⓐ        Ⓐ   ⑥   Ⓐ
                                                                     G
     Manchester Piccadilly 122 ...d.  ... 1227  ... 1327  ...  ... 1427  ... 1527  ...  ... 1627  ... 1727  ...  ... 1827  ...  ...  ... 1927 1927  ...
     Newcastle 124 ...............d. 1035  ...  ... 1135  ... 1234 1235  ... 1335  ...  ... 1435  ... 1505  ... 1635 1635  ... 1732 1732  ...
     York 124 ......................d. 1135  ...  ... 1235  ... 1335 1335  ... 1435  ...  ... 1535  ... 1605  ... 1735 1735  ... 1835 1835  ...
     Leeds 124..................d.    ...  ...  ...  ...  ...  |    |   ...  ...  ...  ...  |   ... 1640  ...  |    |   ...  |    |   ...
     Sheffield 124................d. 1224  ...  ... 1324  ... 1424 1424  ... 1524  ...  ... 1624  ... 1724  ... 1824 1824  ... 1924 1924  ...
     Derby 124....................d. 1253  ...  ... 1353  ... 1453 1453  ... 1553  ...  ... 1653  ... 1753  ... 1853 1853  ... 1954 1954  ...
     Birmingham New St. 142 150 d. 1333 1404  ... 1433 1504 1533 1533 1604 1633 1704  ... 1733 1804 1833 1904 1933 1933 2004 2033 2033  ... 2104 2104 2204
     Birmingham Intl + . 142 150 d.  ... 1414  ...  ... 1514  ...  ... 1614  ... 1714  ...  ... 1814  ... 1914  ...  ... 2014  ...  ... 2114 2114 2214
     Coventry ............ 142 150 d.  ... 1425  ...  ... 1525  ...  ... 1625  ... 1725  ...  ... 1825  ... 1925  ...  ... 2025  ...  ... 2125 2125 2225
     Leamington Spa....... 128 d. 1400 1438  ... 1500 1538 1601 1602 1638 1700 1738  ... 1801 1838 1900 1938 2003 2004 2038 2100 2100  ... 2138 2138 2238
     Banbury................. 128 d. 1419 1455  ... 1519 1555 1619 1620 1655 1719 1755  ... 1819 1855 1919 1955 2020 2022 2055 2120 2119  ... 2155 2155 2255
     Oxford ......................a. 1440 1514  ... 1541 1614 1640 1640 1714 1740 1814  ... 1841 1914 1941 2014 2040 2040 2114 2141 2140  ... 2214 2214 2314
     Oxford ...................131 d. 1443 1516  ... 1543 1616 1643 1643 1716 1743 1816  ... 1843 1915 1943 2016 2043 2042 2116 2143 2143  ... 2216 2218 2316
     Reading ................131 a. 1508 1541  ... 1611 1641 1708 1710 1740 1810 1842  ... 1910 1941 2009 2041 2108 2107 2142 2214 2216  ... 2242 2245 2347
     Reading ....................d.  ... 1546a  ... 1620 1646  ...  ... 1750  ... 1850  ...  ... 1946c  ... 2046c  ...  ... 2150 2222 2222  ... 2248 2250  ...
     Basingstoke .......... 108 a.  ... 1608  ... 1640 1708  ...  ... 1808  ... 1908  ...  ... 2009  ... 2109  ...  ... 2209 2239 2239  ... 2305 2307  ...
     Winchester ........... 108 a.  ... 1624  ... 1658 1724  ...  ... 1824  ... 1924  ...  ... 2024  ... 2124  ...  ... 2226 2256 2256  ... 2324 2324  ...
     Southampton Airport +.108 a.  ... 1632  ... 1708 1732  ...  ... 1833  ... 1932  ...  ... 2033  ... 2133  ...  ... 2234 2312 2312  ... 2336 2332  ...
     Southampton Central .. 108 a.  ... 1641  ... 1717 1741  ...  ... 1843  ... 1941  ...  ... 2041  ... 2140  ...  ... 2242 2320 2320  ... 2343 2341  ...
     Brockenhurst ......... 108 a.  ... 1657  ...  ... 1757  ...  ... 1857  ... 1957  ...  ... 2058  ... 2156  ...  ... 2258  ...  ...
     Bournemouth ......... 108 a.  ... 1712  ...  ... 1815  ...  ... 1912  ... 2012  ...  ... 2115  ... 2215  ...  ... 2319  ...  ...
```

```
                                      ⑦    ⑦   ⑦   ⑦   ⑦   ⑦   ⑦   ⑦   ⑦   ⑦   ⑦   ⑦   ⑦   ⑦   ⑦   ⑦   ⑦   ⑦   ⑦   ⑦   ⑦   ⑦   ⑦
                                                                                                               E                   G
     Manchester Piccadilly 122 ...d. ⑦ ...  ... 0827 0927 1027  ... 1127  ... 1226  ... 1327  ... 1427  ... 1527  ... 1627  ... 1727  ... 1827  ... 1927
     Newcastle 124 ...............d.   ...  ...  |    |    |   ...  |   ...  |   ...  |   ...  |  1335  ... 1435  ... 1524  ... 1635  ... 1735  |
     York 124 ......................d.   ...  ...  |    |    |   ...  |   ...  |   ...  |   ...  | 1435  ... 1535  ... 1625  ... 1735  ... 1835  |
     Leeds 124..................d.     ...  ...  |    |    |   ...  |   ...  |   ...  |   ...  |   |    ...  |    ...  |    ...  |    ...  |    |
     Sheffield 124................d.    ...  ...  |    |    |   ...  |   ...  |   ...  | 1422  ... 1524  ... 1624  ... 1724  ... 1824  ... 1924  |
     Derby 124....................d.    ...  ...  |    |    |   ...  |   ...  |   ... 1355 1453  ... 1553  ... 1654  ... 1754  ... 1854  ... 1956  |
     Birmingham New St. 142 150 d.  ... 0904 1004 1104 1204 1233 1304 1333 1404 1433 1504 1533 1604 1633 1704 1733 1804 1833 1904 1933 2004 2033 2104
     Birmingham Intl + . 142 150 d.  ... 0914 1014 1114 1214 1245 1314  ... 1414 1445 1514  ... 1614 1645 1714  ... 1814 1845 1914 1945 2014  ... 2114
     Coventry ............ 142 150 d.  ... 0925 1025 1125 1225 1255 1325  ... 1425 1455 1525  ... 1625 1655 1725  ... 1825 1855 1925 1955 2025  ... 2124
     Leamington Spa....... 128 d.  ... 0938 1038 1138 1238 1308 1338 1359 1438 1508 1538 1559 1638 1708 1738 1759 1838 1908 1938 2008 2038 2100 2136
     Banbury................. 128 d.  ... 0955 1055 1155 1255 1325 1355 1416 1455 1526 1555 1616 1655 1725 1755 1817 1855 1925 1955 2025 2119 2153
     Oxford ......................a.  ... 1014 1114 1214 1314 1343 1414 1435 1514 1544 1614 1635 1714 1743 1814 1835 1914 1944 2014 2043 2114 2138 2211
     Oxford ...................131 d.  ... 1016 1116 1216 1316 1345 1416 1436 1516 1546 1616 1636 1716 1746 1816 1838 1916 1946 2016 2044 2116 2140 2212
     Reading ................131 a.  ... 1042 1140 1240 1341 1409 1440 1504 1540 1611 1640 1701 1739 1809 1840 1906 1939 2008 2040 2113 2140 2206 2238
     Reading ....................d. 0952 1052 1152 1252 1352  ... 1452  ... 1552  ... 1652  ... 1752  ... 1852  ... 1952  ... 2052  ... 2152  ...
     Basingstoke .......... 108 a. 1011 1109 1208 1308 1408  ... 1508  ... 1608  ... 1708  ... 1808  ... 1909  ... 2009  ... 2108  ... 2209  ...
     Winchester ........... 108 a. 1026 1124 1224 1324 1424  ... 1524  ... 1624  ... 1724  ... 1824  ... 1924  ... 2024  ... 2124  ... 2223  ...
     Southampton Airport +.108 a. 1035 1133 1233 1333 1433  ... 1533  ... 1633  ... 1733  ... 1833  ... 1933  ... 2033  ... 2133  ... 2233  ...
     Southampton Central .. 108 a. 1042 1142 1242 1342 1442  ... 1542  ... 1642  ... 1740  ... 1842  ... 1940  ... 2041  ... 2142  ... 2242  ...
     Brockenhurst ......... 108 a. 1106 1206 1306 1406 1506  ... 1603  ... 1706  ... 1806  ... 1903  ... 2006  ... 2106  ... 2206  ...
     Bournemouth ......... 108 a. 1126 1226 1326 1426 1526  ... 1626  ... 1726  ... 1826  ... 1926  ... 2026  ... 2126  ... 2226  ...
```

A – From Nottingham (Table **121**).
E – From Edinburgh Waverley (Table **124**).
G – To Guildford (Table **134**).

a – Departs 6 minutes later on Ⓐ.
b – Departs 6 minutes later on ⑥.
c – Departs 4 minutes later on Ⓐ.
d – May 27 - Sept. 9.

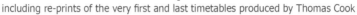

BOURNEMOUTH - SOUTHAMPTON - READING - BIRMINGHAM

⚒

	⑥	Ⓐ	Ⓐ G	⑥ G	Ⓐ	⑥	Ⓐ	⑥	Ⓐ	⑥	Ⓐ	⑥	Ⓐ	⑥	⑥	Ⓐ	⚒	⚒	⚒	⚒	⚒	Ⓐ	⑥	⚒	Ⓐ
Bournemouth 108 d.	...	...	...	...	...	...	...	0625	0630	0637	...	...	0730	0747	...	...	0845	...	0945	...	1045	...	...	1145	...
Brockenhurst 108 d.	...	...	...	...	...	...	...	0639	0645	0655	...	...	0750	0802	...	...	0900	...	1000	...	1100	...	...	1200	...
Southampton Central 108 d.	0509	0515	...	...	0615	0620	...	0653	0715	0720	...	0747	0815	0820	...	...	0916	0946	1017	...	1117a	1146	1147	1217a	...
Southampton Airport ✈ 108 d.	0516	0522	...	...	0622	0627	...	0701	0722	0727	...	0754	0822	0827	...	...	0923	0954	1024	...	1124a	1153	1154	1224a	...
Winchester 108 d.	0525	0531	...	...	0631	0636	...	0709	0731	0736	0812	0803	0831	0836	...	...	0932	1003	1033	...	1133a	1202	1203	1233a	...
Basingstoke 108 d.	0541	0547	...	...	0647	0652	...	0725	0747	0752	0828	0819	0847	0852	...	...	0949a	1019	1049a	...	1149a	1218	1219	1249a	...
Reading a.	0600	0605	...	...	0704	0708	...	0742	0804	0808	0844	0835	0904	0908	...	...	1007	1037	1107	...	1208b	1237	1235	1308b	...
Reading 131 d.	0615	0615	0645	0645	0715	0715	0746	0747	0815	0815	0850	0845	0915	0912	0945	0945	1015	1045	1115	1145	1215	1245	1245	1315	1345
Oxford 131 a.	0637	0637	0706	0710	0736	0738	0810	0810	0838	0838	0913	0910	0937	0934	1010	1013	1038	1110	1138	1210	1238	1311	1310	1338	1411
Oxford d.	0639	0638	0708	0712	0739	0740	0812	0812	0839	0840	0915	0912	0939	0936	1012	1015	1039	1112	1139	1212	1239	1313	1312	1339	1413
Banbury 128 d.	0657	0657	0725	0729	0757	0757	0830	0829	0857	0857	0933	0929	0957	0953	1029	1032	1057	1129	1157	1229d	1257	1331	1329	1357	1431
Leamington Spa 128 d.	0714	0714	0743	0747	0814	0814	0847	0847	0914	0914	0950	0947	1014	1011	1047	1050	1114	1147	1214	1247d	1314	1348	1347	1414	1450
Coventry 142 150 d.	0727	0727	|	|	0827	0827	|	|	0927	0927	|	|	1027	1027	|	|	1127	|	1227	|	1327	|	|	1427	|
Birmingham Intl ✈ 142 150 d.	0738	0738	|	|	0838	0838	|	|	0938	0938	|	|	1038	1038	|	|	1138	|	1238	|	1338	|	|	1438	|
Birmingham New St. 142 150 a.	0748	0748	0812	0818	0848	0848	0918	0918	0948	0948	1018	1018	1048	1048	1118	1118	1148	1218	1248	1318	1348	1418	1418	1448	1518
Derby 124 a.	|	|	0905	0905	|	|	1005	1006	|	|	1105	1105	|	|	1205	1205	|	1305	|	1405	|	1505	1505	|	1605
Sheffield 124 a.	|	|	0944	0944	|	|	1044	1044	|	|	1144	1144	|	|	1244	1244	|	1344	|	1444	|	1544	1544	|	1644
Leeds 124 a.	|	|	|	|	|	|	|	|	|	|	|	|	|	|	|	|	|	|	|	|	|	|	|	|	|
York 124 a.	|	|	1039	1039	|	|	1139	1139	|	|	1240	1239	|	|	1339	1340	|	1439	|	1539	|	1639	1639	|	1740
Newcastle 124 a.	|	|	1145	1146	|	|	1245	1246	|	|	1345	1345	|	|	1446	1445	|	1545	|	1646	|	1745	1745	|	1847
Manchester Piccadilly 122 a.	0926	0939	...	...	1026	1026	...	...	1126	1126	...	...	1226	1226	...	...	1326	...	1426	...	1526	...	...	1626	...

	⑥	⚒	Ⓐ E	⑥	⚒	⚒	⚒	Ⓐ	⑥	⚒	Ⓐ	⑥	⚒	⑥	Ⓐ	Ⓐ	⑥ e	⑥ g	⑥	Ⓐ	Ⓐ	⑥	Ⓐ	⑥	Ⓐ	⑥
Bournemouth 108 d.	...	1245	...	...	1345	...	1445	...	...	1545	...	...	1645	...	...	1745	1747	1747	...	...	1845	1847	...	...	1945	1947
Brockenhurst 108 d.	...	1300	...	...	1400	...	1500	...	...	1600	...	...	1700	...	...	1800	1802	1802	...	...	1900	1902	...	...	2000	2002
Southampton Central 108 d.	...	1315a	1346	1347	1417a	...	1515a	1546	1547	1617a	...	...	1716a	1747	1746	1815	1820	1820	...	...	1916	1920	...	...	2017	2019
Southampton Airport ✈ 108 d.	...	1322a	1354	1354	1424a	...	1522a	1553	1554	1624a	...	...	1723a	1754	1753	1822	1827	1827	...	...	1923	1927	...	...	2024	2026
Winchester 108 d.	...	1331a	1403	1403	1433a	...	1531a	1602	1603	1633a	...	...	1732a	1803	1802	1831	1836	1836	...	...	1932	1936	...	...	2033	2036
Basingstoke 108 d.	...	1348a	1419	1419	1449a	...	1547a	1618	1618	1649a	...	...	1748a	1818	1818	1847	1852	1852	...	...	1949	1952	...	...	2049	2052
Reading a.	...	1403c	1436	1435	1507	...	1607b	1634	1634	1708	...	...	1807b	1835	1835	1904	1908	1908	...	...	2005	2008	...	...	2106	2108
Reading 131 d.	1345	1415	1445	1445	1515	1545	1615	1645	1645	1715	1745	1745	1815	1845	1845	1915	1915	1915	1945	1945	2015	2015	2045	2045	2111	2115
Oxford 131 a.	1410	1438	1509	1510	1538	1611	1638	1708	1710	1738	1808	1810	1838	1910	1911	1938	1938	1938	2010	2009	2036	2038	2112	2110	2134	2138
Oxford d.	1412	1439	1513	1512	1539	1612	1639	1713	1712	1739	1810	1812	1839	1912	1913	1939	1940	1940	2012	2013	2039	2040	2114	2112	2136	2139
Banbury 128 d.	1429	1457	1532	1529	1557	1629	1657	1732	1729	1757	1827	1829	1857	1929	1930	1957	1957	1957	2030	2032	2057	2057	2133	2129	2154	2157
Leamington Spa 128 d.	1447	1514	1550	1547	1614	1647	1714	1750	1747	1814	1845	1847	1914	1947	1948	2014	2015	2015	2048	2050	2114	2115	2152	2147	2211	2214
Coventry 142 150 d.	|	1527	|	|	1627	|	1727	|	|	1827	|	|	1927	|	|	2027	2027	2027	|	|	2127	2127	|	2159	2225	2226
Birmingham Intl ✈ 142 150 d.	|	1538	|	|	1638	|	1738	|	|	1838	|	|	1938	|	|	2038	2038	2038	|	|	2138	2138	|	2211	2235	2237
Birmingham New St. 142 150 a.	1518	1548	1618	1618	1648	1718	1748	1818	1818	1848	1918	1918	1948	2018	2018	2048	2048	2048	2116	2123	2148	2148	2218	2221	2245	2247
Derby 124 a.	1606	|	1705	1705	|	1805	|	1905	1905	|	2005	2005	|	2124	2109	|	2142	|	...	...	|	|	...	...	...	...
Sheffield 124 a.	1644	|	1742	1745	|	1844	|	1940	1947	|	2040	2049	|	2159	2150	|	2223	|	...	...	|	|	...	...	...	...
Leeds 124 a.	|	|	1834	1829	|	|	|	|	|	|	|	|	|	|	|	|	2325	|	...	...	|	|	...	...	...	...
York 124 a.	1739	|	1901	1901	|	1939	|	2038	2040	|	2141	2144	|	2246	2252	|	...	|	...	...	|	|	...	...	...	...
Newcastle 124 a.	1841	|	2001	2001	|	2042	|	2144	2145	|	2247	2247	|	...	...	|	...	|	...	...	|	|	...	...	...	...
Manchester Piccadilly 122 a.	...	1726	...	...	1826	...	1925	...	...	2026	...	...	2126	...	...	2227	...	2233	...	...	2326	2329	...	...	...	...

	⑥	Ⓐ	⑦	⑦	⑦	⑦	⑦ G	⑦	⑦	⑦	⑦	⑦	⑦ E	⑦	⑦	⑦	⑦	⑦	⑦	⑦	⑦	⑦	⑦	⑦	⑦
Bournemouth 108 d.	...	...	...	...	0940	1040	...	1140	...	1240	...	1340	...	1440	...	1540	...	1640	...	1740	...	1840	...	1940	...
Brockenhurst 108 d.	...	...	...	...	0957	1057	...	1157	...	1257	...	1357	...	1457	...	1557	...	1657	...	1757	...	1857	...	1957	...
Southampton Central 108 d.	...	...	...	0915	1015	1115	...	1215	...	1315	...	1415	...	1515	...	1615	...	1715	...	1815	...	1915	...	2015	...
Southampton Airport ✈ 108 d.	...	...	...	0922	1022	1122	...	1222	...	1322	...	1422	...	1522	...	1622	...	1722	...	1822	...	1922	...	2022	...
Winchester 108 d.	...	...	...	0931	1031	1131	...	1231	...	1331	...	1431	...	1531	...	1631	...	1731	...	1831	...	1931	...	2031	...
Basingstoke 108 d.	...	...	...	0947	1047	1147	...	1247	...	1347	...	1447	...	1547	...	1647	...	1747	...	1847	...	1947	...	2047	...
Reading a.	...	...	...	1004	1103	1203	...	1304	...	1404	...	1505	...	1604	...	1703	...	1803	...	1903	...	2003	...	2103	...
Reading 131 d.	2145	2145	0912	1011	1111	1211	1254	1311	1341	1411	1441	1511	1541	1611	1641	1711	1741	1811	1841	1911	1941	2011	2041	2111	2141
Oxford 131 a.	2210	2223	0935	1035	1135	1235	1315	1335	1404	1435	1504	1535	1604	1635	1704	1735	1804	1835	1903	1935	2003	2035	2104	2135	2202
Oxford d.	2212	2230	0937	1037	1137	1237	1317	1337	1406	1437	1506	1537	1606	1637	1706	1737	1806	1837	1906	1937	2006	2037	2106	2137	2206
Banbury 128 d.	2229	2248	0955	1055	1155	1255	1335	1355	1424	1455	1524	1555	1624	1655	1724	1755	1824	1855	1924	1955	2024	2055	2124	2154	2224
Leamington Spa 128 d.	2247	2305	1012	1112	1212	1312	1352	1412	1442	1512	1540	1612	1640	1712	1740	1812	1842	1912	1941	2012	2041	2112	2141	2212	2242
Coventry 142 150 d.	|	2317	1029	1129	1228	1327	|	1427	1454	1527	1554	1627	1654	1727	1754	1827	1855	1927	1954	2027	2054	2127	2153	2224	2254
Birmingham Intl ✈ 142 150 d.	|	2327	1040	1141	1240	1338	|	1438	1504	1538	1604	1638	1704	1738	1804	1838	1905	1938	2004	2038	2104	2138	2203	2234	2304
Birmingham New St. 142 150 a.	2317	2356	1050	1151	1250	1348	1419	1448	1514	1548	1614	1648	1714	1748	1814	1848	1915	1948	2014	2048	2115	2148	2214	2243	2314
Derby 124 a.	...	...	|	|	|	|	1501	|	1601	|	1702	|	1802	|	1903	|	2001	|	...	|	...	|	...	...	...
Sheffield 124 a.	...	...	|	|	|	|	1547	|	1648	|	1749	|	1845	|	1940	|	2041	|	...	|	...	|	...	...	...
Leeds 124 a.	...	...	|	|	|	|	|	|	|	|	1851	|	|	|	|	|	|	|	...	|	...	|	...	...	...
York 124 a.	...	...	|	|	|	|	1638	|	1740	|	1921	|	1939	|	2039	|	2143	|	...	|	...	|	...	...	...
Newcastle 124 a.	...	...	|	|	|	|	1744	|	1841	|	2019	|	2041	|	2144	|	2312	|	...	|	...	|	...	...	...
Manchester Piccadilly 122 a.	...	...	1240	1329	1429	1524	...	1629	...	1730	...	1829	...	1928	...	2028	...	2129	...	2226	...	2324	...	...	...

E – To Edinburgh Waverley (Table **124**).
G – From Guildford (Table **134**).
a – Departs 3–5 minutes later on ⑥.
b – Arrives 3 minutes earlier on Ⓐ.
c – Arrives 5 minutes earlier on Ⓐ.
d – Departs 3 minutes later on Ⓐ.
e – May 27 - Sept. 9.
g – From Sept. 16.

GW 2nd class

BRISTOL - TAUNTON

120a

km		Ⓐ B	Ⓐ B	Ⓐ A	Ⓐ	Ⓐ B	Ⓐ B	Ⓐ	Ⓐ	Ⓐ	Ⓐ B	Ⓐ	Ⓐ	Ⓐ	Ⓐ	Ⓐ	Ⓐ	Ⓐ	Ⓐ B	Ⓐ B	Ⓐ C	⑥ B	⑥	⑥	⑥ 🍷
	Cardiff Central 136 d.	...	...	...	...	0759	0900	0959	1059	1159	1300	1359	1500	1600	1700	1800	1900	2000	...	...	...	...	...	**Ba**	**Bd**
0	**Bristol** T Meads 120 132 d.	0524	0642	0718	0826	0855	0955	1053	1152	1253	1357	1453	1553	1653	1755	1856	1955	2055	2156	2306	2336	0524	0618	0636	0644
31	Weston-super-Mare 132 d.	0547	0706f	0749	0901	0929f	1024	1122	1221	1323	1425	1528f	1627	1728	1830	1930	2029	2133f	2231	2342	0006s	0545	0646	0656	0707f
43	Highbridge and Burnham d.	0557	0717	0800	0911	0940	1035	1133	1232	1334	1436	1538	1638	1739	1841	1940	2039	2144	2242	2354	0017s	0555	0657	|	|
53	Bridgwater d.	0605	0725	0808	0919	0948	1043	1141	1240	1342	1444	1546	1646	1747	1849	1948	2047	2152	2250	0002	0025s	0603	0705	|	|
72	**Taunton** 120 132 a.	0617	0737	0823	0932	1000	1059	1155	1255	1358	1457	1600	1701	1801	1902	2003	2102	2206	2302	0013	0036	0616	0719	0724	0728

	⑥	⑥	⑥	⑥	⑥	⑥	⑥	⑥	⑥	⑥	⑥	⑥	⑥	⑥	⑥ B	⑥	⑦ B	⑦ B	⑦	⑦ A	⑦	⑦	⑦	⑦ B	⑦	⑦
Cardiff Central 136 d.	**Ae**	0800r	0900r	1000r	1100r	1200r	1300r	1400r	1500r	1600r	1700r	1800r	1900r	...	2100r	...	...	...	...	...	...	...	...	...	...	...
Bristol T Meads 120 132 d.	0718	0857	0953	1054	1153	1254	1356	1453	1553	1654	1753	1853	1953	2054	2159	2217	0726	0828	1022	1110	1305	1555	1655	1823g	1905	2025
Weston-super-Mare 132 d.	0751	0932	1022	1122	1222	1322	1424	1524	1622	1723	1822	1924	2023	2128	2233	2247s	0749	0858	1053	1137	1333	1629	1726	1900t	1940	2059f
Highbridge and Burnham d.	0802	0944	1033	1133	1233	1333	1435	1536	1633	1734	1833	1935	2034	2139	2244	2258s	|	0909	1103	1147	1344	1639	1739	1911	1950	2109
Bridgwater d.	0810	0952	1041	1141	1241	1341	1443	1544	1641	1742	1841	1943	2042	2147	2252	2305s	0805	0917	1111	1155	1352	1647	1744	1919	1958	2117
Taunton 120 132 a.	0824	1006	1057	1156	1257	1358	1500	1600	1656	1759	1855	1958	2059	2159	2305	2317	0818	0930	1124	1209	1404	1702	1759	1933	2012	2132

	Ⓐ	Ⓐ	Ⓐ B	Ⓐ D	Ⓐ	Ⓐ	Ⓐ	Ⓐ B	Ⓐ	Ⓐ	Ⓐ	Ⓐ B	Ⓐ	Ⓐ	Ⓐ	Ⓐ	Ⓐ	Ⓐ A	Ⓐ	Ⓐ	⑥	⑥ B	⑥	⑥	⑥ C
Taunton 120 132 d.	0512	0602	0633	0655	0712	0836	0938	1006	1104	1207	1307	1410	1457	1607	1706	1808	1917	2030	2129	2245	0539	0634	0654	0735	0759
Bridgwater d.	0524	0614	0646	0706	0723	0848	0950	1018	1116	1219	1319	1422	1509	1619	1717	1819	1929	2042	2140	2257	0551	0646	0705	0747	0810
Highbridge and Burnham d.	0532	0621	0654	0714	0731	0856	0957	1026	1124	1227	1327	1431	1516	1627	1725	1827	1936	2050	2148	2305	0559	0654	0712	0755	0817
Weston-super-Mare 132 d.	0543f	0636f	0709f	0725	0749f	0911	1010	1038	1146c	1239	1339	1443	1543b	1639	1738	1839	1951f	2102	2201	2317	0611	0708	0724	0805	0830
Bristol T Meads 120 132 a.	0620	0709	0741	0757	0825	0943	1042	1108	1212	1309	1412	1513	1612	1711	1812	1913	2020	2136	2232	2351	0644	0743	0758	0840	0857
Cardiff Central 136 a.	...	0824	...	...	...	...	...	1221	1323	1417	1525	1618	1727	1817	1921	2020	...	...	...	...	...	...	...	...	...

	⑥	⑥ a	⑥ d	⑥	⑥	⑥	⑥	⑥	⑥	⑥	⑥	⑥	⑥	⑥	⑦ B	⑦ B h	⑦ B k	⑦	⑦	⑦	⑦ E	⑦	⑦ B	⑦	⑦	⑦
Taunton 120 132 d.	0910	1012	1017	1104	1207	1307	1407	1507	1607	1707	1807	1907	2017	2135	0835	1009	1018	1136	1334	1519	1658	1719	1818	1856	2025	2136
Bridgwater d.	0922	1024	1029	1116	1219	1319	1419	1519	1619	1719	1819	1919	2029	2147	0847	1021	1030	1148	1346	1531	1709	1730	1830	1906	2037	2148
Highbridge and Burnham d.	0930	1032	1037	1124	1227	1327	1427	1527	1627	1727	1827	1927	2037	2155	0855	1028	1037	1155	1353	1538	1717	1737	1837n	1913	2045	2155
Weston-super-Mare 132 d.	0944	1043	1048	1139f	1239	1339	1439	1539	1639	1739	1841	1939	2050	2206	0906	1040	1051f	1211f	1406	1550	1729	1750	1848	1925	2058	2207
Bristol T Meads 120 132 a.	1012	1112	1116	1211	1309	1411	1510	1609	1712	1811	1910	2009	2124	2240	0938	1108	1119	1243	1436	1620	1757	1819	1919	1950	2131	2238
Cardiff Central 136 a.	1120r	1217r	1217	1318r	1419r	1518r	1618r	1717r	1815r	1918r	2015r	...	2231r	...	...	...	...	...	...	...	...	...	...	...	...	...

A – To/from Gloucester (Table **140**).
B – To/from Penzance, Paignton, Plymouth or Exeter St Davids (see Table **115**).
C – (12) 🍷 London Paddington - Exeter St Davids and v.v. (Table **115**).
D – (12) 🍷 Plymouth - London Paddington (Table **115**).
E – (12) 🍷 Paignton - London Paddington (Table **115**).
a From Sept. 16.
b – Arrives 1527.
c – Arrives 1134.
d – May 27 - Sept. 9.
e – Runs 4 minutes later May 27 - Sept. 9.
f – Arrives 4–6 minutes earlier.
g – Departs 1830 May 27 - Sept. 9 and from Oct. 28.
h – May 21 - Sept. 10.
k – From Sept. 17.
n – Not July 9 - Sept. 3.
r – May 27 - Sept. 9 and from Oct. 28.
s – Calls to set down only.
t – Arrives 1850 July 9 - Sept. 3.

km	Ⓐ	Ⓐ	Ⓐ	Ⓐ	Ⓐ	Ⓐ	Ⓐ	Ⓐ	Ⓐ	Ⓐ	Ⓐ	Ⓐ	Ⓐ	Ⓐ	Ⓐ	Ⓐ	Ⓐ	Ⓐ	Ⓐ	Ⓐ	Ⓐ	Ⓐ	Ⓐ	Ⓐ	Ⓐ
								★d							A					★	B			
	Glasgow Central **124** d.	...	...	...	...	...	...	...	...	...	...	...	...	0601	...	...	...	0750	...	0900	...	...	...	1100	...
	Edinburgh Waverley **124** d.	...	...	...	...	...	...	...	...	...	...	0606	...	0707	...	0810	...	0908	...	1010	...	1106	...	1208	...
	Newcastle **124** d.	...	...	...	...	...	...	...	...	0645	...	0740	...	0841	...	0942	...	1042	...	1144	...	1241	...	1343	...
	York **124** d.	...	...	...	...	...	...	0640	...	0743	...	0845	...	0944	...	1045	...	1145	...	1245	...	1345	...	1445	...
	Leeds **124** d.	...	...	...	...	0600	...	0705	...	0811	...	0911	...	1011	...	1111	...	1211	...	1311	...	1411	...	1511	...
	Sheffield **124** d.	...	...	...	...	0652	...	0753	...	0854	...	0954	...	1054	...	1154	...	1255	...	1355	...	1455	...	1555	...
	Derby **124** d.	...	...	0610	...	0727	...	0828	...	0928	...	1030	...	1130	...	1230	...	1328	...	1428	...	1528	...	1628	...
	Manchester P'dilly **122** d.	...	...	|	0600	|	0707	|	0807	|	0907	|	1007	|	1107	|	1207	|	1307	|	1407	|	1507	|	1607
0	**Birmingham** New St **121** d.	...	0642	0712	0742	0812	0842	0917	0942	1017	1042	1117	1142	1217	1242	1317	1342	1417	1442	1517	1542	1612	1642	1712	1742
73	Cheltenham Spa **121** a.	...	0721	0751	0824	0850	0924	0958	1024	1059	1124	1157	1224	1259	1324	1357	1424	1458	1524	1558	1624	1649	1724	1751	1824
135	**Bristol** Parkway a.	...	0754	0826	0854	0925	0954	1030	1054	1131	1154	1229	1254	1331	1354	1429	1454	1529	1554	1630	1654	1724	1754	1828	1854
145	**Bristol** Temple Meads a.	...	0805	0839	0910	0939	1008	1042	1110	1141	1205	1242	1309	1342	1408	1442	1510	1541	1611	1643	1710	1739	1807	1841	1906
145	**Bristol** Temple M **120a 115** d.	0634	0810	0844	...	0944	...	1045	1115	1144	...	1245	...	1345	...	1445	1513	1544	...	1645	1713	1744	...	1844	...
217	Taunton **120a 115** a.	0707	0842	0914	...	1015	...	1116	1158	1214	...	1316	...	1416	...	1516	1544	1614	...	1716	1744	1815	...	1915	...
240	Tiverton Parkway **115** a.	0719	0854	0926	...	1028	...	1129	1210	1226	...	1328	...	1428	...	1528	1556	1626	...	1728	1756	1827	...	1927	...
266	**Exeter** St Davids **115** a.	0732	0907	0940	...	1042	...	1143	1224	1240	...	1343	...	1443	...	1543	1612	1640	...	1742	1811	1841	...	1942	...
298	Newton Abbot **115** a.	0754	0927	0959	...	1104	...	1204	1248	1259	...	1403	...	1503	...	1603	...	1704	...	1811	1835	1905	...	2002	...
308	Torquay **115** a.	|	0939	|	...	|	...	|	1300	|	...	|	...	|	...	|	...	|	...	|	1847	|	...	|	...
311	**Paignton** **115** a.	|	0947	|	...	|	...	|	1308	|	...	|	...	|	...	|	...	|	...	|	1855	|	...	|	...
312	Totnes **115** a.	0807	...	1014	...	1117	...	1218	...	1311	...	1416	...	1516	...	1619	...	1716	...	1823	...	1917	...	2014	...
350	**Plymouth** **115** a.	0833	...	1042	...	1144	...	1247	...	1338	...	1443	...	1543	...	1648	...	1742	...	1849	...	1943	...	2040	...
	Newquay **117** a.	...	...	...	...	...	...	...	...	...	...	...	...	...	...	...	...	...	...	|	...	|	...	|	...
	Penzance **117** a.	...	...	...	...	...	...	...	...	...	...	...	...	...	...	...	...	...	...	2054	...	2143	...	2241	...

	Ⓐ	Ⓐ	Ⓐ	Ⓐ	Ⓐ	Ⓐ	Ⓐ	Ⓐ	⑥	⑥	⑥	⑥	⑥	⑥	⑥	⑥	⑥	⑥	⑥	⑥	⑥	⑥	⑥	⑥	⑥
	b	D					c						e	★g	e	g		★d	e	g		g	e		e
Glasgow Central **124** d.	...	...	1300	...	...	...	1500	...	...	...	...	...	...	...	...	...	...	...	...	...	...	...	...	...	0601
Edinburgh Waverley **124** d.	1307	...	1408	...	1508	...	1606	1707	...	...	...	...	...	...	...	...	...	...	...	...	...	0608	0606	...	0707
Newcastle **124** d.	1442	...	1541	...	1641	...	1741	1843	...	...	...	...	...	...	...	...	...	...	0645	...	...	0741	0741	...	0843
York **124** d.	1545	...	1645	...	1745	...	1845	1945	...	...	...	...	...	...	...	...	0620g	...	0745	0745	...	0845	0845	...	0945
Leeds **124** d.	1611	...	1711	...	1811	...	1911	2011	...	...	...	...	0600	0600	...	...	0711	...	0811	0811	...	0911	0911	...	1011
Sheffield **124** d.	1655	...	1758	...	1858	...	1958	2058	...	...	...	...	0650	0650	...	...	0756	...	0854	0854	...	0955	0954	...	1055
Derby **124** d.	1729	...	1829	...	1930	...	2029	2129	...	...	0610	...	0726	0726	...	...	0828	...	0930	0930	...	1028	1029	...	1130
Manchester P'dilly **122** d.	|	1705	|	1805	|	1907	|	|	...	...	|	0600	|	|	0707	0707	|	0807	|	|	0907	|	|	1007	|
Birmingham New St **121** d.	1812	1842	1912	1942	2012	2042	2112	2212	...	0642	0712	0742	0812	0812	0842	0842	0912	0942	1012	1012	1042	1112	1112	1142	1212
Cheltenham Spa **121** a.	1850	1924	1950	2024	2052	2125	2151	2251	...	0724	0750	0824	0851	0851	0924	0924	0951	1024	1051	1051	1124	1153	1153	1224	1251
Bristol Parkway a.	1932	1954	2030	2054	2125	2201	2233	2322	...	0753	0824	0853	0924	0924	0953	0953	1029	1054	1125	1125	1153	1229	1229	1253	1324
Bristol Temple Meads a.	1942	2009	2041	2105	2136	2214	2243	2340	...	0805	0838	0906	0939	0939	1004	1004	1042	1109	1138	1138	1204	1242	1242	1307	1338
Bristol Temple M **120a 115** d.	1945	...	2044	2113	2144	...	...	...	0608	0812	0845	...	0944	0944	...	1020	1044	1112	1144	1144	...	1244	1244	...	1345
Taunton **120a 115** a.	2016	...	2115	2143	2215	...	...	...	0715	0842	0915	...	1017	1017	...	1100	1115	1159	1215	1216	...	1315	1316	...	1415
Tiverton Parkway **115** a.	2029	...	2127	2155	2227	...	...	...	0727	0854	0927	...	1030	1030	...	1112	1127	1211	1227	1229	...	1327	1329	...	1427
Exeter St Davids **115** a.	2043	...	2144	2209	2241	...	...	...	0740	0907	0940	...	1044	1044	...	1126	1141	1225	1241	1243	...	1341	1343	...	1441
Newton Abbot **115** a.	2103	...	2205	2228	2301	...	...	...	0759	0928	1000	...	1109	1111	...	1151	1201	1250	1300	1304	...	1400	1403	...	1502
Torquay **115** a.	|	...	|	|	|	...	...	...	|	0939	|	...	|	1125	...	|	|	1302	|	|	...	|	|	...	|
Paignton **115** a.	|	...	|	|	|	...	...	...	|	0947	|	...	|	1135	...	|	|	1310	|	|	...	|	|	...	|
Totnes **115** a.	2116	...	2217	2241	2313	...	...	...	0812	...	1012	...	1122	...	...	1204	1213	...	1312	1317	...	1412	1417	...	1514
Plymouth **115** a.	2146	...	2243	2313	2339	...	...	...	0838	...	1039	...	1151	...	...	1234	1240	...	1339	1345	...	1439	1445	...	1541
Newquay **117** a.	...	...	...	...	...	...	...	...	...	...	...	...	...	...	...	1431	...	...	...	|	...	...	...	...	...
Penzance **117** a.	...	...	...	...	...	...	...	...	...	...	...	...	...	...	...	...	...	...	...	1538	...	...	...	...	...

	⑥	⑥	⑥	⑥	⑥	⑥	⑥	⑥	⑥	⑥	⑥	⑥	⑥	⑥	⑥	⑥	⑥	⑥	⑥	⑥	⑥	⑥	⑥	⑦	⑦
	★g		Ag	Ae	★g	e				g	★e	B					E		g	e			c		
Glasgow Central **124** d.	0601	...	...	...	...	...	0750	...	0900	...	...	...	...	1100	...	...	...	1300	...	...	...	...	1500	...	...
Edinburgh Waverley **124** d.	0707	...	0805	0805	...	...	0908	...	1005	...	...	1108	...	1204	...	1309	...	1405	...	...	1508	...	1605	...	...
Newcastle **124** d.	0843	...	0942	0942	...	...	1044	...	1142	...	...	1244	...	1344	...	1444	...	1544	...	...	1644	...	1744	...	...
York **124** d.	0945	...	1045	1045	...	...	1145	...	1245	...	...	1345	...	1445	...	1545	...	1645	...	...	1745	...	1845	...	...
Leeds **124** d.	1011	...	1111	1111	...	...	1211	...	1311	...	...	1411	...	1511	...	1611	...	1711	...	...	1811	...	1911	...	...
Sheffield **124** d.	1055	...	1155	1155	...	...	1255	...	1355	...	...	1455	...	1555	...	1655	...	1755	...	...	1858	...	1955	...	...
Derby **124** d.	1130	...	1230	1230	...	...	1328	...	1430	...	...	1528	...	1628	...	1728	...	1829	...	...	1929	...	2028	...	...
Manchester P'dilly **122** d.	|	1107	|	|	1207	1207	|	1307	|	1407	1407	|	1507	|	1607	|	1706	|	1805	1805	|	1907	|	...	...
Birmingham New St **121** d.	1212	1242	1312	1312	1342	1342	1412	1442	1512	1542	1542	1612	1642	1712	1742	1812	1842	1912	1942	1942	2012	2042	2112	...	...
Cheltenham Spa **121** a.	1251	1325	1350	1350	1424	1424	1451	1524	1550	1624	1624	1650	1724	1750	1824	1850	1924	1950	2024	2024	2051	2124	2150	...	...
Bristol Parkway a.	1324	1354	1426	1426	1454	1454	1524	1554	1629	1653	1653	1725	1753	1829	1853	1925	1954	2029	2053	2053	2122	2158	2231	...	...
Bristol Temple Meads a.	1338	1405	1440	1440	1509	1509	1538	1607	1642	1707	1707	1738	1807	1842	1904	1938	2005	2042	2104	2104	2135	2212	2241	...	...
Bristol Temple M **120a 115** d.	1345	...	1444	1444	1512	1512	1544	...	1644	...	1710	1744	...	1844	...	1944	...	2044	...	2111	2144	...	...	0844	0948
Taunton **120a 115** a.	1416	...	1515	1516	1542	1542	1614	...	1716	...	1740	1815	...	1915	...	2015	...	2115	...	2141	2215	...	...	0915	1019
Tiverton Parkway **115** a.	1429	...	1527	1528	1554	1554	1626	...	1729	...	1752	1827	...	1927	...	2027	...	2127	...	2153	2229	...	...	0927	1031
Exeter St Davids **115** a.	1443	...	1540	1543	1607	1609	1640	...	1743	...	1805	1841	...	1944	...	2040	...	2143	...	2207	2244	...	...	0939	'1044
Newton Abbot **115** a.	1511	...	1604	1603	1647	...	1700	...	1810	...	1830	1904	...	2005	...	2100	...	2204	...	2226	2311	...	...	0959	1103
Torquay **115** a.	1523	...	|	|	1659	...	|	...	|	...	1841	|	...	|	...	|	...	|	...	|	|	...	...	|	|
Paignton **115** a.	1533	...	|	|	1710	...	|	...	|	...	1849	|	...	|	...	|	...	|	...	|	|	...	...	|	|
Totnes **115** a.	...	...	1616	1616	...	...	1712	...	1823	...	...	1916	...	2017	...	2112	...	2220	...	2238	2327	...	...	1012	1116
Plymouth **115** a.	...	...	1643	1643	...	...	1739	...	1851	...	...	1942	...	2043	...	2138	...	2250	...	2305	2356	...	...	1037	1142
Newquay **117** a.	...	...	1839	...	...	...	|	...	|	...	...	|	...	|	...	...	...	...	...	...	...	...	...	...	...
Penzance **117** a.	...	...	...	...	...	...	1936g	...	2056	...	...	2140	...	2254e	...	...	...	...	...	...	...	...	...	...	...

	⑦	⑦	⑦	⑦	⑦	⑦	⑦	⑦	⑦	⑦	⑦		⑦	⑦	⑦	⑦	⑦k	⑦n		⑦	⑦	⑦	⑦	⑦	⑦	⑦
								★									★a	★a		B				c		
Glasgow Central **124** d.	...	...	...	...	...	...	...	...	...	...	...	...	...	1055	...	1200	...	...	...	...	...	1348	...	1455	...	...
Edinburgh Waverley **124** d.	...	...	...	...	...	...	0908	...	1008	...	1105	...	...	1208	...	1308	...	...	...	1408	...	1508	...	1608	...	1708
Newcastle **124** d.	...	...	...	...	0935	...	1039	...	1140	...	1240	...	...	1340	...	1440	...	...	...	1540	...	1640	...	1740	...	1840
York **124** d.	...	...	...	0933	1033	...	1141	...	1241	...	1341	...	...	1441	...	1541	...	...	...	1641	...	1741	...	1841	...	1941
Leeds **124** d.	...	0810	0900	1000	1100	...	1211	...	1311	...	1411	...	...	1511	...	1611	...	...	...	1711	...	1811	...	1911	...	2011
Sheffield **124** d.	...	0854	0957	1057	1157	...	1257	...	1357	...	1455	...	...	1555	...	1654	...	...	...	1754	...	1855	...	1955	...	2054
Derby **124** d.	...	0928	1033	1129	1229	...	1332	...	1429	...	1526	...	...	1627	...	1727	...	...	...	1826	...	1927	...	2027	...	2126
Manchester P'dilly **122** d.	...	|	|	|	|	...	|	1307	|	1407	|	...	1507	|	1607	|	1707	1707	...	|	1807	|	1907	|	2007	|
Birmingham New St **121** d.	0930	1030	1130	1212	1312	1342	1412	1442	1512	1542	1612	...	1642	1712	1742	1812	1842	1842	...	1912	1942	2012	2042	2112	2142	2212
Cheltenham Spa **121** a.	1008	1109	1208	1251	1351	1423	1450	1524	1550	1624	1650	...	1724	1751	1824	1851	1924	1924	...	1951	2024	2051	2124	2151	2223	2252
Bristol Parkway a.	1037	1139	1238	1320	1420	1453	1523	1559	1620	1654	1720	...	1803	1820	1854	1921	2003	2003	...	2020	2056	2120	2159	2233	2252	2322
Bristol Temple Meads a.	1048	1151	1249	1331	1431	1508	1534	1611	1631	1708	1733	...	1814	1835	1908	1932	2014	2014	...	2031	2106	2130	2210	2244	2302	2333
Bristol Temple M **120a 115** d.	1057	1154	1254	1344	1444	...	1544	1614	1644	...	1744	...	...	1844	...	1944	2019	2019	...	2044	...	2144	...	...	...	...
Taunton **120a 115** a.	1129	1225	1325	1414	1514	...	1614	1644	1714	...	1817	...	...	1916	...	2017	2058	2058	...	2114	...	2214	...	...	...	...
Tiverton Parkway **115** a.	1141	1235	1336	1426	1526	...	1626	1656	1726	...	1829	...	...	1928	...	2029	2111	2111	...	2126	...	2227	...	...	...	...
Exeter St Davids **115** a.	1154	1252	1352	1439	1539	...	1640	1709	1739	...	1845	...	...	1945	...	2043	2127	2127	...	2139	...	2245	...	...	...	...
Newton Abbot **115** a.	1214	1312	1412	1459	1600	...	1701	1736	1800	...	1905	...	...	2007	...	2101	2153	2153	...	2159	...	2304	...	...	...	...
Torquay **115** a.	|	|	|	|	|	...	|	1748	|	...	|	...	...	|	...	|	2204	|	...	|	...	|	...	...	...	...
Paignton **115** a.	|	|	|	|	|	...	|	1756	|	...	|	...	...	|	...	|	2213	|	...	|	...	|	...	...	...	...
Totnes **115** a.	1226	1325	1425	1511	1612	...	1714	...	1812	...	1917	...	...	2019	...	2113	...	|	...	2217	...	2317	...	...	...	...
Plymouth **115** a.	1252	1352	1452	1537	1638	...	1742	...	1838	...	1943	...	...	2045	...	2141	...	2237	...	2245	...	2346	...	...	...	...
Newquay **117** a.	|	...	...	...	...	...	...	...	|	...	...	...	...	|	...	...	...	...	...	...	...	...	...	...	...	...
Penzance **117** a.	1447	...	...	...	...	...	...	...	2039	...	...	...	...	2242	...	...	...	...	...	...	...	...	...	...	...	...

A – From Dundee (Table **222**).
B – From Aberdeen (Table **222**).
D – To Cardiff Central (Table **121**).
E – To Cardiff Central May 27 - Sept. 9 and from Oct. 28 (Table **121**).

a – Also calls at Weston-super-Mare (a. 2036).
b – Also calls at Gloucester (a. 1901).
c – Also calls at Gloucester (a. 2202 on Ⓐ and ⑦, 2200 on ⑥).

d – Also calls at Weston-super-Mare (a. 1132 on Ⓐ, 1129 on ⑥).
e – From Sept. 16.
g – May 27 - Sept. 9.
h – 0645 May 27 - Sept 9.
k – May 21 - Sept. 10.
n – From Sept. 17.
★ – Also calls at Dawlish (10–15 minutes after Exeter) and Teignmouth (15–18 minutes after Exeter).

Ⓐ	Ⓐ E	Ⓐ	Ⓐ	Ⓐ D	Ⓐ	Ⓐ ☆e	Ⓐ	Ⓐ	Ⓐ	Ⓐ	Ⓐ B	Ⓐ ☆	Ⓐ	Ⓐ	Ⓐ A	Ⓐ	Ⓐ	Ⓐ	Ⓐ	Ⓐ ☆a	Ⓐ	Ⓐ	Ⓐ
Penzance **117** d.	...	...	...	...	...	...	...	...	0628	...	...	...	0828	...	...	0935	...	...	...	...	...	...	...
Newquay **117** d.	...	...	...	...	...	...	...	...	|	...	...	...	|	...	...	|	...	...	...	...	...	...	...
Plymouth **115** d.	...	...	0520	...	0625	...	0725	...	0825	...	0925	...	1025	...	1125	1150	1225	...	1325	...	1425	...	1525
Totnes **115** d.	...	...	0545	...	0650	...	0750	...	0850	...	0950	...	1050	...	1150	1215	1251	...	1351	...	1450	...	1551
Paignton **115** d.	...	...	|	...	|	0702	|	...	|	...	|	1007	|	...	|	|	|	...	|	1404	|	...	|
Torquay **115** d.	...	...	|	...	|	0708	|	...	|	...	|	1013	|	...	|	|	|	...	|	1410	|	...	|
Newton Abbot **115** d.	...	...	0602	...	0703	0719	0803	...	0903	...	1003	1024	1103	...	1203	1228	1304	...	1404	1421	1503	...	1604
Exeter St Davids **115** d.	...	...	0624	...	0724	0745	0824	...	0924	...	1024	1050	1124	...	1224	1250	1324	...	1424	1448	1524	...	1624
Tiverton Parkway **115** d.	...	...	0637	...	0737	0758	0837	...	0938	...	1037	1103	1137	...	1238	1306	1338	...	1438	1502	1537	...	1638
Taunton **120a 115** d.	...	...	0651	...	0751	0812	0851	...	0951	...	1051	1117	1151	...	1251	1322	1351	...	1451	1515	1551	...	1651
Bristol Temple M .. **120a 115** a.	0620	...	0726	...	0827	0854	0926	...	1025	...	1124	1152	1224	...	1324	1355	1426	...	1523	1556	1623	...	1724
Bristol Temple Meads d.	0627	0700	0730	0800	0830	0900	0930	1000	1030	1100	1130	1200	1230	1300	1330	1400	1430	1500	1530	1600	1630	1700	1730
Bristol Parkway d.	0638	0709	0739	0809	0839	0909	0939	1009	1039	1109	1139	1209	1239	1309	1339	1409	1440	1509	1540	1609	1639	1709	1740
Cheltenham Spa **121** d.	0710	0740	0811	0840	0912	0942	1010	1041	1111	1142	1211	1240	1311	1342	1410	1441	1511	1542	1611	1641	1711	1742	1811
Birmingham New Street **121** a.	0756	0826	0856	0926	0958	1023	1056	1126	1158	1226	1256	1326	1356	1423	1456	1523	1556	1623	1656	1723	1756	1823	1856
Manchester P'dilly **122** a.	|	0959	|	1059	|	1159	|	1259	|	1359	|	1459	|	1559	|	1659	|	1800	|	1859	|	1959	|
Derby **124** a.	0841	...	0939	...	1038	...	1138	...	1241	...	1339	...	1440	...	1540	...	1641	...	1739	...	1839	...	1940
Sheffield **124** a.	0917	...	1017	...	1118	...	1217	...	1317	...	1418	...	1517	...	1618	...	1718	...	1818	...	1918	...	2018
Leeds **124** a.	1001	...	1101	...	1201	...	1301	...	1401	...	1501	...	1601	...	1704	...	1802	...	1903	...	2005	...	2106
York **124** a.	1030	...	1130	...	1230	...	1330	...	1430	...	1530	...	1630	...	1730	...	1831	...	1930	...	2030	...	...
Newcastle **124** a.	1129	...	1230	...	1329	...	1431	...	1529	...	1629	...	1730	...	1833	...	1932	...	2033	...	2128	...	...
Edinburgh Waverley **124** a.	1306	...	1410	...	1507	...	1606	...	1706	...	1807	...	1906	...	2009	...	2108	...	2215	...	2303	...	...
Glasgow Central **124** a.	1412	...	...	...	1612	...	...	...	1811	...	...	...	2015	...	...	...	2224	...	...	...	...	...	...

Ⓐ / ⑥	Ⓐ	Ⓐ	Ⓐ	Ⓐ	Ⓐ b	Ⓐ	Ⓐ	⑥ c	⑥	⑥	⑥ C	⑥		⑥ ☆	⑥	⑥	⑥	⑥ gk	⑥ h	⑥☆ Bg	⑥ Bh	⑥ ☆	⑥
Penzance **117** d.	...	...	...	...	...	...	...	...	...	...	...	...	...	...	...	...	0630	...	...	...	...	...	0828
Newquay **117** d.	...	...	...	...	...	...	...	...	...	...	...	...	...	...	...	...	|	...	...	...	...	...	|
Plymouth **115** d.	...	1625	...	1725	...	1825	...	...	...	0525	...	0625	...	...	0725	...	0825	0839	...	0918	0925	...	1025
Totnes **115** d.	...	1651	...	1751	...	1850	...	...	...	0550	...	0650	...	...	0750	...	0850	0904	...	0943	0950	...	1050
Paignton **115** d.	...	|	...	|	...	|	2014	...	...	|	...	|	...	0702	|	...	|	|	...	|	|	1006	|
Torquay **115** d.	...	|	...	|	...	|	2020	...	...	|	...	|	...	0708	|	...	|	|	...	|	|	1012	|
Newton Abbot **115** d.	...	1704	...	1804	...	1903	2031	...	...	0603	...	0703	...	0719	0803	...	0903	0917	...	0956	1003	1023	1103
Exeter St Davids **115** d.	1654	1725	...	1825	...	1924	2052	...	...	0623	...	0723	...	0745	0823	...	0923	0945	...	1025	1024	1049	1123
Tiverton Parkway **115** d.	1708	1739	...	1839	...	1937	2105	...	...	0637	...	0737	...	0758	0837	...	0937	0958	...	1038	1037	1102	1137
Taunton **120a 115** d.	1722	1751	...	1851	...	1951	2119	...	...	0650	...	0750	...	0811	0850	...	0950	1011	...	1051	1051	1117	1150
Bristol Temple M .. **120a 115** a.	1754	1823	...	1925	...	2025	2152	...	...	0722	...	0824	...	0849	0925	...	1025	1051	...	1126	1123	1154	1225
Bristol Temple Meads d.	1800	1830	1900	1930	2000	2030	2200	0615	0700	0730	0800	0830	...	0900	0930	1000	1030	1100	1100	1130	1130	1200	1230
Bristol Parkway d.	1809	1840	1909	1940	2009	2040	2210	0624	0709	0739	0809	0839	...	0909	0939	1009	1039	1109	1109	1139	1139	1209	1239
Cheltenham Spa **121** d.	1841	1911	1940	2011	2056	2117	2242	0711	0741	0811	0841	0911	...	0941	1011	1041	1111	1141	1141	1211	1211	1241	1311
Birmingham New Street **121** a.	1923	1956	2022	2051	2137	2202	2343	0756	0825	0856	0926	0956	...	1025	1056	1126	1156	1226	1226	1256	1256	1326	1356
Manchester P'dilly **122** a.	2058	|	2200	|	...	...	...	|	0959	|	1059	|	...	1159	|	1259	|	1359	1359	|	|	1459	|
Derby **124** a.	...	2040	...	2143	...	...	...	0841	...	0939	...	1038	...	...	1138	...	1238	...	...	1338	1338	...	1438
Sheffield **124** a.	...	2118	...	2224	...	...	...	0917	...	1017	...	1117	...	...	1217	...	1317	...	...	1418	1418	...	1517
Leeds **124** a.	...	2204	...	2315	...	...	...	1001	...	1101	...	1200	...	...	1302	...	1401	...	...	1501	1501	...	1601
York **124** a.	...	...	...	...	...	...	...	1030	...	1130	...	1230	...	...	1330	...	1430	...	...	1530	1530	...	1630
Newcastle **124** a.	...	...	...	...	...	...	...	1129	...	1229	...	1329	...	...	1428	...	1529	...	...	1629	1629	...	1729
Edinburgh Waverley **124** a.	...	...	...	...	...	...	...	1302	...	1406	...	1504	...	...	1604	...	1707	...	...	1803	1803	...	1906
Glasgow Central **124** a.	...	...	...	...	...	...	...	1412	...	...	...	1612	...	...	...	...	1811	...	...	...	...	...	2012

⑥	⑥	⑥ A	⑥ h	⑥ g	⑥ ☆g	⑥ h		⑥	⑥	⑥ ☆a	⑥	⑥	⑥	⑥ h	⑥ g	⑥ ☆g	⑥ h	⑥	⑥ g	⑥ h	⑥ g	⑥ h	⑥ h	⑥ g
Penzance **117** d.	...	...	0943	...	...	...	...	...	...	...	...	...	...	...	...	...	...	...	...	...	...	...	...	1625
Newquay **117** d.	...	0935g	|	...	...	...	...	...	...	...	...	...	...	...	...	...	...	...	1530	...	...	...	...	|
Plymouth **115** d.	...	1125	1148	...	...	1225	...	...	1325	...	1425	...	1525	...	...	...	1625	...	1725	1725	...	...	1825	1825
Totnes **115** d.	...	1150	1213	...	...	1251	...	...	1350	...	1450	...	1551	...	...	...	1650	...	1750	1751	...	...	1850	1851
Paignton **115** d.	...	|	|	...	1235	|	...	...	|	1355	|	...	|	...	...	1637	|	...	|	|	1811	...	|	|
Torquay **115** d.	...	|	|	...	1242	|	...	...	|	1401	|	...	|	...	...	1644	|	...	|	|	1818	...	|	|
Newton Abbot **115** d.	...	1203	1225	...	1254	1304	...	...	1403	1412	1503	...	1604	...	...	1656	1703	...	1803	1804	1830	...	1903	1904
Exeter St Davids **115** d.	...	1223	1248	...	1323	1323	...	...	1425	1437	1523	...	1624	1653	...	1723	1723	...	1823	1824	1850	...	1923	1924
Tiverton Parkway **115** d.	...	1237	1302	...	1337	1337	...	...	1438	1450	1537	...	1638	1707	...	1737	1737	...	1837	1838	1904	...	1937	1938
Taunton **120a 115** d.	...	1250	1315	...	1350	1350	...	...	1451	1503	1550	...	1651	1721	...	1750	1750	...	1850	1851	1917	...	1950	1951
Bristol Temple M .. **120a 115** a.	...	1325	1355	...	1425	1425	...	...	1525	1549	1625	...	1725	1755	...	1825	1825	...	1923	1924	1953	...	2022	2024
Bristol Temple Meads d.	1300	1330	1400	1400	1430	1430	...	1500	1530	1600	1630	1700	1730	1800	1800	1830	1830	1900	1930	1930	2000	2000	2030	2030
Bristol Parkway d.	1309	1339	1409	1409	1440	1440	...	1509	1539	1609	1639	1709	1740	1809	1809	1839	1839	1909	1940	1940	2009	2009	2039	2040
Cheltenham Spa **121** d.	1341	1411	1441	1441	1511	1511	...	1541	1611	1641	1711	1741	1813	1841	1841	1911	1911	1941	2013	2013	2041	2041	2111	2111
Birmingham New Street **121** a.	1426	1456	1526	1526	1556	1556	...	1626	1656	1726	1756	1826	1856	1926	1926	1958	1958	2026	2050	2052	2138	2138	2152	2151
Manchester P'dilly **122** a.	1559	|	1659	1659	|	|	...	1759	|	1859	|	1959	|	2059	2059	|	|	2202	2233	|	...	...	...	|
Derby **124** a.	...	1540	...	...	1640	1640	...	...	1738	...	1840		1930	...	...	2040	2040	...	...	2143	...	...	...	2229
Sheffield **124** a.	...	1618	...	...	1717	1717	...	...	1817	...	1917	...	2021	...	...	2119	2119	...	...	2223	...	...	...	2309
Leeds **124** a.	...	1701	...	...	1802	1802	...	...	1901	...	2004	...	2105	...	...	2202	2202	...	...	2325	...	...	...	2351
York **124** a.	...	1729	...	...	1830	1830	...	...	1930	...	2030	...	2155	...	...	...	...	...	...	...	...	...	...	...
Newcastle **124** a.	...	1831	...	...	1932	1932	...	...	2028	...	2128	...	...	...	...	...	...	...	...	...	...	...	...	...
Edinburgh Waverley **124** a.	...	2006	...	...	2108	2108	...	...	2208	...	2257	...	...	...	...	...	...	...	...	...	...	...	...	...
Glasgow Central **124** a.	...	...	...	...	2220	2220	...	...	...	...	...	...	...	...	...	...	...	...	...	...	...	...	...	...

⑦	⑦ c	⑦	⑦ B	⑦	⑦ ☆a	⑦	⑦	⑦ p	⑦ n	⑦	⑦	⑦	⑦	⑦ d		⑦	⑦	⑦	⑦	⑦	⑦	⑦	⑦
Penzance **117** d.	...	...	...	...	...	0930	...	...	...	...	...	...	...	1230	...	...	...	...	...	1530	...	...	...
Newquay **117** d.	...	...	...	...	...	|	...	...	...	...	1132n	...	...	|	...	...	...	...	...	|	...	...	...
Plymouth **115** d.	...	...	0925	1025	...	1125	1200	1225	1225	1252	1325	...	1425	1435	...	1524	...	1625	...	1725	...	1825	...
Totnes **115** d.	...	...	0950	1050	...	1150	|	1250	1251	|	1351	...	1451	1501	...	1550	...	1650	...	1750	...	1852	...
Paignton **115** d.	...	...	|	|	1050	|	|	|	|	|	|	...	|	|	...	|	...	|	...	|	1820	|	...
Torquay **115** d.	...	...	|	|	1056	|	|	|	|	|	|	...	|	|	...	|	...	|	...	|	1826	|	...
Newton Abbot **115** d.	...	...	1003	1103	1108	1203	1236	1303	1304	1327	1404	...	1504	1513	...	1603	...	1703	...	1803	1837	1905	...
Exeter St Davids **115** d.	...	...	1023	1123	1133	1223	1256	1323	1324	1347	1424	...	1524	1532	...	1624	...	1726	...	1823	1858	1925	...
Tiverton Parkway **115** d.	...	...	1037	1137	1147	1237	1310	1337	1338	|	1438	...	1537	1546	...	1637	...	1739	...	1837	1911	1938	...
Taunton **120a 115** d.	...	...	1050	1152	1200	1250	1323	1350	1350	|	1451	...	1551	1559	...	1651	...	1753	...	1850	1924	1952	...
Bristol Temple M .. **120a 115** a.	...	...	1124	1227	1244	1323	1354	1421	1422	1440	1526	...	1625	1647	...	1726	...	1827	...	1922	1957	2025	...
Bristol Temple Meads d.	0915	1030	1130	1230	1300	1330	1400	1430	1430	1500	1530	1600	1630	1700	...	1730	1800	1830	1900	1930	2000	2030	2210
Bristol Parkway d.	0924	1039	1139	1239	1309	1339	1409	1439	1440	1509	1540	1609	1640	1709	...	1740	1809	1839	1909	1939	2009	2040	2220
Cheltenham Spa **121** d.	1012	1110	1210	1310	1341	1410	1441	1510	1511	1540	1611	1640	1712	1741	...	1811	1840	1910	1941	2010	2040	2111	2249
Birmingham New Street **121** a.	1049	1148	1249	1348	1427	1448	1527	1548	1550	1627	1649	1726	1749	1827	...	1848	1926	1948	2027	2049	2118	2148	2340
Manchester P'dilly **122** a.	|	|	|	|	1559	|	1659	|	|	1759	|	1859	|	1959	...	|	2100	|	2200	|	...	|	...
Derby **124** a.	1137	1238	1337	1439	...	1537	...	1638	1640	...	1740	...	1839	...	...	1940	...	2039	...	2141	...	2240	...
Sheffield **124** a.	1218	1318	1417	1517	...	1618	...	1717	1719	...	1819	...	1920	...	...	2018	...	2116	...	2218	...	2318	...
Leeds **124** a.	1301	1401	1501	1602	...	1701	...	1801	1803	...	1904	...	2005	...	...	2107	...	2204	...	2301	...	0008	...
York **124** a.	1327	1427	1527	1627	...	1727	...	1827	1829	...	1929	...	2030	...	...	2132	...	...	...	...	...	...	...
Newcastle **124** a.	1426	1526	1625	1725	...	1825	...	1925	1930	...	2031	...	2131	...	...	...	...	...	...	...	...	...	...
Edinburgh Waverley **124** a.	1602	1656	1757	1856	...	1957	...	2056	2105	...	2212	...	2304	...	...	...	...	...	...	...	...	...	...
Glasgow Central **124** a.	...	1812	...	2019	...	...	...	2213	2213	...	...	...	...	...	...	...	...	...	...	...	...	...	...

A – To Dundee (Table **222**).
B – To Aberdeen (Table **222**).
C – From Cardiff Central May 27 - Sept. 9 and from Oct. 28 (Table **121**).
D – From Cardiff Central (Table **121**).
E – From Bath Spa (d. 0609).

a – Also calls at Weston-super-Mare (d. 1538 on Ⓐ, 1529 on ⑥, 1221 on ⑦).
b – Also calls at Gloucester (d. 2046).
c – Also calls at Gloucester (d. 0700 on ⑥, 1000 on ⑦).
d – Also calls at Weston-super-Mare (d. 1628).
e – Also calls at Weston-super-Mare (d. 0833).
g – May 27 - Sept. 9.

h – From Sept. 16.
k – Also calls at Weston-super-Mare (d. 1033).
n – May 21 - Sept. 10.
p – From Sept. 17.

☆ – Also calls at Teignmouth (7 – 10 minutes after Newton Abbot) and Dawlish (12 –15 minutes after Newton Abbot).

① – Mondays ② – Tuesdays ③ – Wednesdays ④ – Thursdays ⑤ – Fridays ⑥ – Saturdays ⑦ – Sundays Ⓐ – Monday to Fridays, not holidays 7

km		Ⓐ	Ⓐ	Ⓐ	Ⓐ	Ⓐ	Ⓐ	Ⓐ	Ⓐ		Ⓐ	Ⓐ	Ⓐ	Ⓐ	Ⓐ	Ⓐ	Ⓐ	Ⓐ	Ⓐ 2	Ⓐ	Ⓐ	Ⓐ
			2			2	🍷	2			🍷	2	🍷	2	🍷	🍷	2	🍷	**B**	🍷	🍷	2
	Nottingham **123** d.	Ⓐ	...	...	...	...	0600	...	0704	...	0812	...	0910	...	1010	1110	...	1210	...	1310	1410	...
	Derby **123** d.		...	...	...	...	0636	...	0736	...	0837	...	0936	...	1037	1137	...	1237	...	1337	1436	...
0	**Birmingham** New Street **120** d.		...	0500	0537	...	0730	...	0830	...	0930	...	1030	...	1130	1230	...	1330	...	1430	1530	...
73	Cheltenham **120** d.		0537	0602	0643	0746	0811	0846	0910	...	1010	1045	1110	1146	1210	1310	1345	1410	...	1510	1610	1645
83	Gloucester d.		0550	0614	0701**d**	0758	0825**c**	0858	0925**c**	...	1025**c**	1058	1125**c**	1159	1225**c**	1325**c**	1358	1425	1448	1525**c**	1625**c**	1658
115	Lydney 🚂 d.		0609	0633	0720	0817	|	0917	|	...	1044	1117	|	1218	|	1344	1417	|	1507	|	1644	1717
127	Chepstow d.		0619	0642	0729	0827	0851	0927	0951	...	|	1127	1151	1228	1251	|	1427	1451	1517	1551	1653	1727
138	Caldicot d.		0626	0651	0738	0835	|	0935	|	...	|	1135	|	1236	|	|	1435	|	1525	|	|	1735
155	Newport **132 136 149** a.		0641	0705	0752	0850	0912	0951	1011	...	1111	1150	1210	1251	1309	1410	1450	1510	1540	1612	1711	1750
174	**Cardiff** Central **132 136 149** a.		0700	0721	0808	0907	0929	1011	1028	...	1128	1212	1226	1308	1330	1426	1515	1530	1558	1630	1730	1810

	Ⓐ	Ⓐ	Ⓐ	Ⓐ	Ⓐ	Ⓐ	Ⓐ	Ⓐ	Ⓐ	⑤	①–④	⑤		⑥	⑥	⑥	⑥	⑥		⑥	⑥	⑥
	🍷	2		2		**A**	2			2	2	2		2			2	🍷		2		🍷
Nottingham **123** d.	1510	...	1610	...	1710	...	...	1810	1910	...	...	...	⑥	...	...	...	...	0558	...	...	0658	0809
Derby **123** d.	1537	...	1637	...	1737	...	...	1837	1937	*2129*	*2129*	...		...	...	...	...	0636	...	...	0736	0837
Birmingham New Street **120** d.	1630	...	1730	...	1830	1842	...	1930	2030	*2212*	*2212*	2300		...	0500	0542	...	0730	...	...	0830	0930
Cheltenham **120** d.	1714	1745	1817	1845	1913	1925	1945	2011	2110	2300	2300	0008		...	0603	0642	0745	0810	...	0845	0910	1010
Gloucester d.	1725	1758	1831	1900	1925	|	1958	2025**c**	2121	2313	2313	0019		0550	0614	0657**c**	0758	0822	...	0858	0922	1022
Lydney 🚂 d.	1744	1817	|	1920	|	|	2017	|	2140	2333	2333	...		0609	0633	0716	0817	|	...	0917	|	1041
Chepstow d.	|	1827	|	1929	|	|	2027	|	2149	2342	2342	...		0619	0642	0726	0827	0848	...	0927	0948	|
Caldicot d.	|	1835	|	1937	|	|	2035	|	2158	2351	2351	...		0627	0651	0734	0835	|	...	0935	|	|
Newport **132 136 149** a.	1811	1849	1914	1953	2011	2047	2050	2110	2212	0006	0006	...		0642	0705	0748	0850	0906	...	0950	1005	1106
Cardiff Central **132 136 149** a.	1828	1909	1933	2012	2028	2103	2110	2128	2235**a**	0025	0034	...		0703	0721	0804	0910	0925	...	1009	1021	1124

	⑥	⑥	⑥	⑥	⑥		⑥	⑥	⑥	⑥		⑥	⑥	⑥	⑥	⑥	⑥	⑥	⑥	⑥	⑥	⑥
	2	🍷	2	🍷	🍷		2	🍷	**B**	🍷		🍷	2	🍷	2		2		**E**	2		
Nottingham **123** d.	...	0910	...	1010	1110	...	...	1210	...	1310	...	1410	...	1510	...	1610	...	1710	...	...	1810	1910
Derby **123** d.	...	0936	...	1037	1137	...	...	1237	...	1337	...	1437	...	1537	...	1637	...	1737	...	...	1837	1937
Birmingham New Street **120** d.	...	1030	...	1130	1230	...	...	1330	...	1430	...	1530	...	1630	...	1730	...	1830	1842	...	1930	2030
Cheltenham **120** d.	1045	1110	1146	1210	1310	...	1345	1410	...	1510	...	1610	1645	1710	1745	1816	1845	1910	1925	1945	2010	2110
Gloucester d.	1058	1122	1158	1222	1322	...	1358	1422	1440	1522	...	1622	1658	1722	1758	1827	1858	1922	|	1958	2022	2121
Lydney 🚂 d.	1117	|	1217	|	1341	...	1417	|	1459	|	...	1641	1717	1741	1817	|	1917	|	|	2017	|	2140
Chepstow d.	1127	1148	1227	1248	|	...	1427	1449	1509	1548	...	1651	1727	|	1827	|	1927	|	|	2027	|	2150
Caldicot d.	1135	|	1235	|	|	...	1435	|	1517	|	...	|	1735	|	1835	|	1934	|	|	2035	|	2158
Newport **132 136 149** a.	1150	1205	1250	1305	1406	...	1450	1509	1535	1606	...	1708	1750	1806	1850	1910	1950	2003	2044	2050	2109	2217
Cardiff Central **132 136 149** a.	1206	1223	1307	1321	1422	...	1509	1526	1553	1625	...	1724	1810	1824	1912	1930	2011	2020	2100	2108	2126	2242

	⑥	⑥		⑦	⑦	⑦	⑦	⑦	⑦	⑦	⑦		⑦	⑦	⑦	⑦	⑦	⑦	⑦	⑦	⑦	⑦
	🍷	2		2	🍷	🍷	2	🍷	🍷	2	🍷		🍷	2		🍷	2	🍷	🍷	2	🍷	2
Nottingham **123** d.	...	...	⑦	...	...	0954	...	1111	1210	...	1310	...	1410	...	1510	1610	...	1710	1810	...	...	...
Derby **123** d.	2028	...		...	...	1018	...	1136	1236	...	1338	...	1434	...	1534	1634	...	1735	1835	...	2027	...
Birmingham New Street **120** d.	2112	...		...	1012	1112	...	1230	1330	...	1430	...	1530	...	1630	1730	...	1830	1930	...	2112	...
Cheltenham **120** d.	2151	...		...	1052	1152	1219	1310	1410	1419	1510	...	1610	1619	1711	1810	1835	1912	2010	2019	2152	...
Gloucester d.	2200	2309		1048	1105	1205	1232	1323	1424**c**	1434	1523	...	1623	1637**c**	1723	1823	1848	1928	2022	2033	2202	2233
Lydney 🚂 d.	...	2328		1107	|	|	1251	|	|	1453	|	...	|	1656	|	|	1907	|	|	2052	...	2252
Chepstow d.	...	2338		1117	|	|	1301	|	|	1503	|	...	|	1707	|	|	1917	|	|	2102	...	2302
Caldicot d.	...	2346		1125	|	|	1309	|	|	1511	|	...	|	1713	|	|	1925	|	|	2110	...	2310
Newport **132 136 149** a.	...	0011		1139	1147	1244	1324	1406	1501	1526	1606	...	1704	1729	1806	1906	1947	2006	2106	2125	...	2330
Cardiff Central **132 136 149** a.	...	0035		1206	1209	1307	1350	1427	1528	1551	1629	...	1726	1752	1829	1927	2014	2030	2127	2148	...	2351

		Ⓐ	Ⓐ	Ⓐ	Ⓐ	Ⓐ	Ⓐ		Ⓐ	Ⓐ	Ⓐ	Ⓐ	Ⓐ		Ⓐ	Ⓐ	Ⓐ	Ⓐ	Ⓐ	Ⓐ	Ⓐ	Ⓐ
		C	2		2	**A**				2	🍷	2			🍷	2	🍷	2	🍷	🍷	2	🍷
Cardiff Central **132 136 149** d.	Ⓐ	...	0612	0640	0705	0700	0745	...	0845	0912	0945	1009	1045	...	1145	1212	1245	1312	1345	1445	1512	1545
Newport **132 136 149** d.		...	0628	0655	0723	0715	0802	...	0900	0928	1000	1027	1100	...	1200	1228	1301	1327	1400	1500	1528	1600
Caldicot d.		...	0641	0708	0738	|	|	...	|	0939	|	1040	|	...	|	1242	|	1341	|	|	1541	|
Chepstow d.		...	0650	0716	0749	|	|	...	0918	0948	1018	1049	|	...	1218	1251	1318	1350	|	1518	1550	1618
Lydney 🚂 d.		...	0659	0725	0758	|	0825	...	|	0957	|	1058	1125	...	|	1300	|	1359	1425	|	1559	|
Gloucester d.		0710	0722	0746	0821	|	0849**c**	...	0950**c**	1020	1050**c**	1121	1150**c**	...	1248**c**	1322	1350**c**	1421	1450**c**	1550**c**	1622	1650**c**
Cheltenham **120** d.		0721	0734	0757	0834	0840	0900	...	1001	1031	1101	1132	1201	...	1258	1333	1401	...	1501	1601	1631	1701
Birmingham New Street **120** a.		0816	*0826*	0845	...	0926	0945	...	1045	...	1145	...	1245	...	1345	...	1445	...	1545	1645	...	1745
Derby **123** a.		...	...	0934	...	...	1034	...	1134	...	1234	...	1334	...	1434	...	1534	...	1634	1734	...	1834
Nottingham **123** a.		...	...	1003	...	...	1103	...	1203	...	1303	...	1403	...	1503	...	1603	...	1703	1803	...	1903

	Ⓐ	Ⓐ		Ⓐ	Ⓐ	Ⓐ	Ⓐ	Ⓐ	Ⓐ	Ⓐ	Ⓐ	Ⓐ		⑥	⑥	⑥	⑥	⑥	⑥	⑥	⑥	⑥
	2	🍷		2	🍷	2	🍷			2		2			**C**	2		2	**E**			2
Cardiff Central **132 136 149** d.	1610	1645	...	1712	1745	1808	1845	1950	2105	2112	2150	2320	⑥	...	...	0610	0640	0707	0700	0745	0845	0910
Newport **132 136 149** d.	1627	1700	...	1728	1800	1824	1900	2005	2121	2127	2205	2338		...	...	0626	0655	0723	0715	0800	0900	0925
Caldicot d.	1640	|	...	1741	|	1837	|	2018	|	2141	|	0001		...	...	0639	0708	0736	|	|	|	0937
Chepstow d.	1649	|	...	1750	1818	1846	1917	2026	|	2150	|	0010		...	...	0648	0716	0745	|	|	0918	0947
Lydney 🚂 d.	1658	1725	...	1759	|	1855	|	2035	|	2159	|	0019		...	...	0657	0725	0754	|	0825	|	0955
Gloucester d.	1723**c**	1750**c**	...	1821	1846	1921**c**	1945	2059**c**	2204	2223	2247	0039		0700	0707	0721	0746	0822	|	0850**c**	0950**c**	1021
Cheltenham **120** d.	1732	1801	...	1830	1857	1931	1957	2111	2215	2234	2258	...		0711	0718	0734	0757	0835	0841	0901	1001	1032
Birmingham New Street **120** a.	...	1845	...	...	1945	...	2040	2151	2305	...	2359	...		0756	0808	...	0845	...	0926	0945	1045	...
Derby **123** a.	...	1934	...	...	2034	...	2132	...	...	...	...	...		0841	...	...	0934	...	...	1034	1134	...
Nottingham **123** a.	...	2004	...	...	2103	...	2208	...	...	...	...	...		...	...	...	1003	...	...	1103	1203	...

	⑥	⑥	⑥		⑥	⑥	⑥	⑥	⑥	⑥	⑥	⑥	⑥	⑥	⑥	⑥	⑥	⑥	⑥	⑥	⑥	⑥
	🍷	2			🍷	2	🍷	2 🍷	🍷	🍷	2	🍷	2	🍷	2	🍷	2	🍷			2	2
Cardiff Central **132 136 149** d.	0945	1010	1045	...	1145	1209	1245	1312	1345	1445	1508	1545	1608	1645	1709	1745	1808	1845	2000	2050	2111	2318
Newport **132 136 149** d.	1000	1027	1100	...	1200	1227	1300	1327	1400	1500	1527	1600	1624	1700	1725	1800	1827	1900	2015	2105	2127	2337
Caldicot d.	|	1040	|	...	|	1240	|	1341	|	|	1538	|	1637	|	1738	|	1840	|	2028	|	2140	2359
Chepstow d.	1018	1049	|	...	1218	1249	1318	1350	|	1518	1547	1618	1646	|	1747	1818	1849	1918	2036	|	2149	0008
Lydney 🚂 d.	|	1058	1125	...	|	1258	|	1359	1425	|	1556	|	1655	1725	1756	|	1858	|	2045	|	2158	0017
Gloucester d.	1050**c**	1122	1150**c**	...	1248**c**	1322	1350**c**	1420	1450**c**	1550**c**	1621	1650**c**	1723**c**	1750**c**	1824**c**	1846	1921	1946	2107	2149	2219	0040
Cheltenham **120** d.	1101	1132	1201	...	1259	1332	1401	...	1501	1601	1632	1701	1733	1801	1833	1857	1931	1957	2118	2200	...	...
Birmingham New Street **120** a.	1145	...	1245	...	1345	...	1445	...	1545	1645	...	1745	...	1845	...	1945	...	2042	2207	2242	...	...
Derby **123** a.	1235	...	1334	...	1434	...	1535	...	1634	1734	...	1835	...	1932	...	2034	...	2133	2253	...	...	...
Nottingham **123** a.	1303	...	1403	...	1503	...	1603	...	1703	1803	...	1903	...	2004	...	2103	...	2208	2327	...	...	...

		⑦	⑦	⑦	⑦	⑦	⑦		⑦	⑦	⑦	⑦	⑦		⑦	⑦	⑦		⑦	⑦	⑦	⑦
		2	🍷	🍷	2	🍷	🍷		2	🍷	🍷	2	🍷		🍷	2	🍷		**D**	2		2
Cardiff Central **132 136 149** d.	⑦	1030	1045	1145	1225	1245	1345	...	1425	1445	1545	1625	1645	...	1745	1824	1845	...	1945	2024	2045	2226
Newport **132 136 149** d.		1048	1106	1205	1247	1305	1405	...	1445	1505	1605	1645	1703	...	1804	1846	1903	...	2003	2046	2105	2246
Caldicot d.		1101	|	|	1300	|	|	...	1458	|	|	1658	|	...	|	1859	|	...	|	2059	|	2259
Chepstow d.		1110	|	|	1309	|	|	...	1507	|	|	1707	|	...	|	1908	|	...	|	2108	|	2308
Lydney 🚂 d.		1119	|	|	1318	|	|	...	1516	|	|	1716	|	...	|	1917	|	...	|	2117	|	2317
Gloucester d.		1142	1150	1248	1340	1348	1448	...	1540	1548	1648	1740	1748	...	1848	1942**c**	1950	...	2049	2142	2148	2342
Cheltenham **120** d.		1155	1201	1258	1352	1358	1458	...	1550	1558	1658	1750	1758	...	1858	1955	2000	...	2100	...	2159	...
Birmingham New Street **120** a.		...	1243	1341	...	1441	1541	...	...	1641	1741	...	1841	...	1941	...	2043	...	2144	...	2242	...
Derby **123** a.		...	1333	1434	...	1533	1634	...	...	1733	1833	...	1933	...	2034	...	2133	...	*2240*	...	...	...
Nottingham **123** a.		...	1400	1500	...	1600	1700	...	...	1800	1900	...	2000	...	2100	...	2200	...	...	...	...	...

A – (12) Manchester Piccadilly - Bristol Temple Meads - Cardiff Central and v.v. (Tables **120 / 122**).
B – (2) 🍷 Gloucester - Fishguard Harbour (Table **135**).
C – (12) Gloucester - Stansted Airport (Table **208**).
D – (12) Cardiff - Leicester (Table **208**).
E – May 27 - Sept 9 and from Oct. 28. (12) Manchester Piccadilly - Bristol Temple Meads - Cardiff Central and v.v. (Tables **120 / 122**).

a – Arrives 2230 on ⑤.
c – Arrives 4 – 6 minutes earlier.
d – Arrives 8 minutes earlier.

🚂 – DEAN FOREST RAILWAY (Lydney Junction - Parkend. *7 km*). ✆ 01594 845840. www.deanforestrailway.co.uk. Lydney Junction station is 10 minutes walk from the National Rail station.

XC — Most services convey 🍷 — BIRMINGHAM - MANCHESTER — 122

km		Ⓐ	Ⓐ	Ⓐ	Ⓐ	Ⓐ	Ⓐ	Ⓐ	Ⓐ	Ⓐ	Ⓐ	Ⓐ	Ⓐ	Ⓐ	Ⓐ	Ⓐ	Ⓐ	Ⓐ	Ⓐ	Ⓐ	Ⓐ	Ⓐ	Ⓐ
									A												H		
	Bournemouth **119** d.	...	...	...	...	...	...	...	...	0630	...	0730	...	0845	...	0945	...	1045	...	1145	...	1245	...
	Southampton Central **119** d.	...	...	...	...	0515	...	0615	...	0715	...	0815	...	0916	...	1017	...	1117	...	1217	...	1315	...
	Reading **119** d.	...	...	...	...	0615	...	0715	...	0815	...	0915	...	1015	...	1115	...	1215	...	1315	...	1415	...
	Paignton **120** d.	...	...	...	...	|	...	|	...	|	0702	|	...	|	...	|	1007	|	...	|	...	|	...
	Exeter St Davids **120** d.	...	..	...	...	|	...	|	...	|	0745	|	...	|	...	|	1050	|	...	|	1250	|	...
	Bristol T Meads **120** d.	...	...	...	...	|	0700	|	0800	|	0900	|	1000	|	1100	|	1200	|	1300	|	1400	|	1500
0	**Birmingham** New Street **150** d.	0557	0622	0657	0731	0757	0831	0857	0931	0957	1031	1057	1131	1157	1231	1257	1331	1357	1431	1457	1531	1557	1631
20	Wolverhampton **150** d.	0616	0641	0715	0750	0815	0849	0915	0949	1015	1049	1115	1149	1215	1249	1315	1349	1415	1449	1515	1549	1615	1649
46	Stafford d.	0632	0655	0731	0802	0833	0902	0928	1002	1028	1102	1128	1202	1228	1302	1328	1402	1428	1502	1528	1603	1628	1702
72	Stoke on Trent **152** d.	0651	0714	|	0820	0854	0920	0944	1020	1044	1120	1144	1220	1244	1320	1344	1420	1444	1520	1544	1620	1644	1720
104	Macclesfield **152** d.	0712	0731	|	0837	0911	|	1002	|	1102	|	1202	|	1302	|	1402	|	1502	|	1602	|	1702	|
123	Stockport **152** d.	0726	0750	0824	0850	0927	0950	1014	1050	1114	1150	1214	1250	1314	1350	1414	1450	1514	1550	1614	1650	1714	1751
132	**Manchester** Piccadilly **152** a.	0734	0800	0834	0859	0939	0959	1026	1059	1126	1159	1226	1259	1326	1359	1426	1459	1526	1559	1626	1659	1726	1800

	Ⓐ	Ⓐ	Ⓐ	Ⓐ	Ⓐ	Ⓐ	Ⓐ	Ⓐ	Ⓐ	Ⓐ	Ⓐ	⑥	⑥	⑥	⑥	⑥	⑥	⑥	⑥	⑥	⑥	⑥	⑥
																			B				
Bournemouth **119** d.	1345	...	1445	...	1545	...	1645	...	1745	1845	...	...	...	...	...	...	...	...	...	0637	...	0747	...
Southampton Central **119** d.	1417	...	1515	...	1617	...	1716	...	1815	1916	...	...	...	...	...	0509	...	0620	...	0720	...	0820	...
Reading **119** d.	1515	...	1615	...	1715	...	1815	...	1915	2015	...	...	...	...	...	0615	...	0715	...	0815	...	0912	...
Paignton **120** d.	|	1404	|	...	|	...	|	...	|	|	...	...	...	...	...	|	...	|	...	|	0702	|	...
Exeter St Davids **120** d.	|	1448	|	...	|	1654	|	...	|	|	...	...	...	...	...	|	...	|	...	|	0745	|	...
Bristol T Meads **120** d.	|	1600	|	1700	|	1800	|	1900	|	|	...	...	...	...	...	|	0700	|	0800	|	0900	|	1000
Birmingham New Street **150** d.	1657	1731	1757	1831	1857	1931	1957	2031	2057	2157	2230	0557	0631	0657	0731	0757	0831	0857	0931	0957	1031	1057	1131
Wolverhampton **150** d.	1715	1749	1815	1849	1915	1949	2015	2049	2115	2215	2248	0615	0649	0715	0749	0815	0849	0915	0949	1015	1049	1115	1149
Stafford d.	1728	1802	1828	1902	1928	2002	2028	2102	2129	2228	2301	0628	0702	0731	0802	0828	0902	0928	1002	1028	1102	1128	1202
Stoke on Trent **152** d.	1744	1820	1844	1920	1944	2020	2044	2119	2146	2244	2320	0645	0720	|	0820	0844	0920	0944	1020	1044	1120	1144	1220
Macclesfield **152** d.	1802	|	1902	|	2002	|	2102	|	2203	2302	|	0706	0737	|	0837	0902	|	1002	|	1102	|	1202	|
Stockport **152** d.	1815	1850	1914	1951	2014	2049	2114	2150	2216	2316	|	0719	0750	0816	0850	0914	0950	1014	1050	1114	1150	1214	1250
Manchester Piccadilly **152** a.	1825	1859	1924	1959	2026	2058	2126	2200	2227	2326	0011	0728	0759	0829	0859	0926	0959	1026	1059	1126	1159	1226	1259

	⑥	⑥	⑥	⑥	⑥	⑥	⑥	⑥	⑥	⑥	⑥	⑥	⑥	⑥	⑥	⑥	⑥	⑥	⑥	⑥	⑥	⑥	⑥	⑥
		b	F a						H b	a											b	C a		
Bournemouth **119** d.	0847	...	...	0947	...	1047	...	1147	...	...	1247	...	1347	...	1447	...	1547	...	1647	...	1747	...	1847	...
Southampton Central **119** d.	0918	...	...	1017	...	1120	...	1220	...	...	1318	...	1420	...	1518	...	1620	...	1720	...	1820	...	1920	...
Reading **119** d.	1015	...	...	1115	...	1215	...	1315	...	...	1415	...	1515	...	1615	...	1715	...	1815	...	1915	...	2015	...
Paignton **120** d.	|	...	...	|	1006	|	...	|	...	...	|	...	|	1355	|	...	|	...	|	...	|	...	|	...
Exeter St Davids **120** d.	|	...	0945	|	1049	|	...	|	1248	...	|	...	|	1437	|	...	|	1653b	|	...	|	1823	|	...
Bristol T Meads **120** d.	|	1100	1100	|	1200	|	1300	|	1400	1400	|	1500	|	1600	|	1700	|	1800	|	1900	|	1930	|	...
Birmingham New Street **150** d.	1157	1231	1231	1257	1331	1357	1431	1457	1531	1531	1557	1631	1657	1731	1757	1831	1857	1931	1957	2031	2057	2057	2157	2231
Wolverhampton **150** d.	1215	1249	1249	1315	1349	1415	1449	1515	1549	1549	1615	1649	1715	1749	1815	1849	1915	1949	2015	2049	2117	2117	2215	2249
Stafford d.	1228	1302	1302	1328	1402	1428	1502	1528	1602	1602	1628	1702	1728	1802	1828	1902	1928	2002	2028	2102	2130	2130	2228	2302
Stoke on Trent **152** d.	1244	1320	1320	1344	1420	1444	1520	1544	1620	1620	1644	1720	1744	1820	1844	1920	1944	2020	2044	2120	2147	2147	2244	2320
Macclesfield **152** d.	1302	|	|	1402	|	1502	|	1602	|	|	1702	|	1802	|	1902	|	2002	2037	2102	2138	2205	2205	2302	2339
Stockport **152** d.	1314	1350	1350	1414	1450	1514	1550	1614	1650	1650	1714	1750	1814	1850	1914	1950	2014	2050	2114	2153	2221	2221	2314	2354
Manchester Piccadilly **152** a.	1326	1359	1359	1426	1459	1526	1559	1626	1659	1659	1726	1759	1826	1859	1925	1959	2026	2059	2126	2202	2233	2233	2329	0010

	⑦	⑦	⑦	⑦	⑦	⑦	⑦	⑦	⑦	⑦		⑦	⑦	⑦	⑦	⑦	⑦	⑦	⑦	⑦	⑦	⑦	⑦
										F			F				H						
Bournemouth **119** d.	...	...	...	...	0940	...	1040	...	1140	...	...	1240	...	1340	...	1440	...	1540	...	1640	...	1740	1840
Southampton Central **119** d.	...	...	...	0915	1015	...	1115	...	1215	...	...	1315	...	1415	...	1515	...	1615	...	1715	...	1815	1915
Reading **119** d.	...	...	0912	1011	1111	...	1211	...	1311	...	...	1411	...	1511	...	1611	...	1711	...	1811	...	1911	2011
Paignton **120** d.	...	...	|	|	|	...	|	1050	|	...	...	|	...	|	...	|	...	|	...	|	...	|	|
Exeter St Davids **120** d.	...	...	|	|	|	...	|	1133	|	1256	...	|	1347	|	...	|	1532	|	...	|	...	|	|
Bristol T Meads **120** d.	...	...	|	|	|	...	|	1300	|	1400	...	|	1500	|	1600	|	1700	|	1800	|	1900	|	|
Birmingham New Street **150** d.	0901	1001	1101	1157	1257	1331	1357	1431	1457	1531	...	1557	1631	1657	1731	1757	1831	1857	1931	1957	2031	2057	2157
Wolverhampton **150** d.	0919	1019	1119	1216	1316	1349	1415	1449	1515	1549	...	1615	1649	1715	1749	1815	1849	1915	1949	2015	2053	2117	2215
Stafford d.	0933	1033	1132	1229	1329	1402	1428	1502	1528	1602	...	1628	1702	1729	1802	1828	1902	1928	2002	2028	2106	2130	2228
Stoke on Trent **152** d.	|	1052	1152	1246	1345	1420	1445	1521	1545	1619	...	1645	1721	1746	1821	1847	1921	1947	2021	2045	2122	2146	2245
Macclesfield **152** d.	|	1109	1210	1305	1405	|	1502	|	1605	|	...	1705	|	1805	|	1905	|	2005	|	2103	|	2204	2302
Stockport **152** d.	1026	1123	1230	1317	1417	1451	1515	1550	1617	1650	...	1717	1750	1817	1850	1918	1950	2017	2050	2115	2151	2216	2315
Manchester Piccadilly **152** a.	1037	1133	1240	1329	1429	1500	1524	1559	1629	1659	...	1730	1759	1829	1859	1928	1959	2028	2100	2129	2200	2226	2324

	Ⓐ	Ⓐ	Ⓐ	Ⓐ	Ⓐ	Ⓐ	Ⓐ	Ⓐ	Ⓐ	Ⓐ	Ⓐ	Ⓐ	Ⓐ	Ⓐ	Ⓐ	Ⓐ	Ⓐ	Ⓐ	Ⓐ	Ⓐ	Ⓐ	Ⓐ	Ⓐ
Manchester Piccadilly **152** d.	0511	0600	0627	0707	0727	0807	0827	0907	0927	1007	1027	1107	1127	1207	1227	1307	1327	1407	1427	1507	1527	1607	1627
Stockport **152** d.	|	0608	0635	0716	0736	0816	0836	0916	0935	1016	1036	1116	1136	1216	1236	1316	1336	1416	1436	1516	1536	1616	1636
Macclesfield **152** d.	|	|	0648	|	0749	|	0849	|	0949	|	1049	|	1149	|	1249	|	1349	|	1449	|	1549	|	1649
Stoke on Trent **152** d.	0607	|	0706	0744	0807	0844	0907	0944	1007	1045	1107	1144	1207	1244	1307	1344	1407	1444	1507	1544	1607	1644	1707
Stafford d.	0625	0700	0724	0801	0825	0902	0925	1000	1025	1102	1125	1201	1225	1301	1325	1401	1425	1501	1525	1603	1625	1702	1725
Wolverhampton **150** d.	0641	0716	0745	0816	0841	0916	0942	1017	1041	1116	1141	1216	1241	1317	1341	1417	1441	1517	1541	1617	1641	1717	1741
Birmingham New Street **150** a.	0657	0733	0807	0833	0858	0933	0958	1033	1058	1133	1158	1233	1258	1333	1358	1433	1458	1533	1558	1633	1658	1733	1758
Bristol T Meads **120** a.	|	0910	...	1008	|	1110	|	1205	|	1309	|	1408	|	1510	|	1611	|	1710	|	1807	|	1906	|
Exeter St Davids **120** a.	|	...	...	...	|	1224	|	...	|	...	|	...	|	1612	|	...	|	1811	|	...	|	...	|
Paignton **120** a.	|	...	...	...	|	1308	|	...	|	...	|	...	|	...	|	...	|	1855	|	...	|	...	|
Reading **119** a.	0840	...	...	...	1041	...	1140	...	1241	...	1340	...	1440	...	1541	...	1640	...	1740	...	1842	...	1940
Southampton Central **119** a.	0943	...	...	...	1143	...	1241	...	1341	...	1441	...	1541	...	1641	...	1741	...	1843	...	1940	...	2041
Bournemouth **119** a.	1013	...	...	...	1213	...	1311	...	1411	...	1511	...	1611	...	1711	...	1815	...	1912	...	2011	...	2115

	Ⓐ	Ⓐ	Ⓐ	Ⓐ	Ⓐ	Ⓐ	Ⓐ	Ⓐ	Ⓐ	Ⓐ		⑥	⑥	⑥	⑥	⑥	⑥	⑥	⑥	⑥	⑥	⑥	⑥
	A		F											b	C a								
Manchester Piccadilly **152** d.	1705	1727	1805	1827	1907	1927	2007	2027	2127	2207	...	0511	0600	0707	0707	0727	0807	0827	0907	0927	1007	1027	1107
Stockport **152** d.	1714	1735	1813	1836	1916	1936	2017	2036	2136	2216	...	|	0608	0716	0716	0736	0816	0836	0916	0937	1016	1036	1116
Macclesfield **152** d.	1728	|	1826	|	|	1949	|	2049	2149	2229	...	|	0621	|	|	0749	|	0849	|	0950	|	1049	|
Stoke on Trent **152** d.	1745	|	1844	1907	1944	2007	2045	2107	2208	2247	...	0608	0640	0744	0744	0807	0844	0907	0944	1008	1044	1107	1144
Stafford d.	1802	1825	1901	1925	2001	2025	2102	2125	2226	2304	...	0626	0700	0801	0801	0825	0901	0925	1001	1025	1101	1125	1201
Wolverhampton **150** d.	1816	1841	1917	1941	2017	2044	2116	2141	2242	2318	...	0641	0716	0817	0817	0841	0917	0941	1017	1041	1117	1141	1217
Birmingham New Street **150** a.	1833	1858	1933	1958	2033	2100	2132	2200	2259	2336	...	0657	0733	0833	0833	0858	0933	0958	1033	1058	1133	1159	1233
Bristol T Meads **120** a.	2009	|	2105	|	2214	|	...	...	...	...	...	|	0906	1004	1004	|	1109	|	1204	|	1307	|	1405
Exeter St Davids **120** a.	...	|	2209	|	...	|	...	...	...	...	...	|	...	...	1126	|	1225	|	...	|	...	|	...
Paignton **120** a.	...	|	...	|	...	|	...	...	...	...	...	|	...	...	...	|	1310	|	...	|	...	|	...
Reading **119** a.	...	2041	...	2142	...	2242	...	...	...	...	...	0841	...	...	...	1041	...	1138	...	1241	...	1340	...
Southampton Central **119** a.	...	2140	...	2242	...	2343	...	...	...	...	...	0940	...	...	...	1141	...	1241	...	1341	...	1441	...
Bournemouth **119** a.	...	2215	...	2319	...	...	...	...	...	...	...	1011	...	...	...	1212	...	1312	...	1412	...	1512	...

A – To / from Cardiff (Table **121**).
B – May 27 - Sept. 9 and from Oct. 28 conveys 12 from Cardiff Central (Table **121**).
C – To / from Newquay (Tables **117** and **120**).
F – To / from Plymouth (Table **120**).
H – From Penzance (Tables **117** and **120**).

a – May 27 - Sept. 9.
b – From Sept. 16.

122 MANCHESTER - BIRMINGHAM

Most services convey 🍸 XC

	⑥	⑥ a	⑥ b	⑥	⑥	⑥	⑥ b	⑥ a	⑥	⑥	⑥	⑥	⑥	⑥ B	⑥	⑥ a	⑥ Gb	⑥	⑥	⑥	⑥	⑥	⑥	⑥
Manchester Piccadilly .... **152** d.	1127	1207	1207	1227	1307	1327	1407	1407	1427	1507	1527	1607	1627	1706	1727	1805	1805	1827	1907	1927	2007	2027	2107	2127
Stockport .... **152** d.	1136	1216	1216	1236	1316	1336	1416	1416	1436	1516	1536	1616	1636	1715	1736	1813	1813	1836	1916	1936	2016	2035	|	2135
Macclesfield .... **152** d.	1149	|	|	1249	|	1349	|	|	1449	|	1549	|	1649	1727	|	1826	1826	|	|	1949	|	2049	|	2149
Stoke on Trent .... **152** d.	1207	1244	1244	1307	1344	1407	1444	1444	1507	1544	1607	1644	1707	1745	1807	1844	1844	1907	1944	2007	2045	2107	2144	2207
Stafford .... d.	1225	1301	1301	1325	1401	1425	1501	1501	1525	1601	1625	1701	1725	1801	1825	1901	1901	1925	2001	2025	2102	2125	2202	2230
Wolverhampton .... **150** d.	1241	1317	1317	1341	1417	1441	1517	1517	1541	1617	1641	1717	1741	1817	1841	1917	1917	1941	2017	2041	2115	2142	2217	2245
Birmingham New Street **150** a.	1258	1333	1333	1358	1433	1458	1533	1533	1558	1633	1658	1733	1758	1833	1858	1933	1933	1959	2033	2058	2131	2159	2233	2301
Bristol T Meads **120** .... a.	|	1509	1509	|	1607	|	1707	1707	|	1807	|	1904	|	2005	|	2104	2104	|	2212	|	...	...	...	...
Exeter St Davids **120** .... a.	|	1607	1609	|	...	|	1805	...	|	...	|	...	|	...	|	...	2207	|	...	|	...	...	...	...
Paignton **120** .... a.	|	1710	...	|	...	|	1849	...	|	...	|	...	|	...	|	...	...	|	...	|	...	...	...	...
Reading **119** .... a.	1441	...	...	1540	...	1641	...	...	1739	...	1841	...	1941	...	2041	...	...	2142	...	2245	...	...	...	...
Southampton Central **119** ... a.	1541	...	...	1641	...	1741	...	...	1841	...	1941	...	2041	...	2140	...	...	2242	...	2341	...	...	...	...
Bournemouth **119** .... a.	1612	...	...	1712	...	1812	...	...	1912	...	2012	...	2112	...	2215	...	...	2319	...	...	...	...	...	...

⑦	⑦	⑦	⑦	⑦	⑦	⑦	⑦	⑦	⑦	⑦	⑦	⑦	⑦	⑦ a	⑦ Gb	⑦	⑦	⑦	⑦	⑦	⑦	⑦	⑦
Manchester Piccadilly .... **152** d.	0827	0927	1027	1127	1226	1307	1327	1407	1427	1507	1527	1607	1627	1707	1707	1727	1807	1827	1907	1927	2007	2107	2207
Stockport .... **152** d.	0836	0936	1036	1136	1235	1316	1336	1416	1436	1516	1536	1616	1636	1716	1716	1736	1816	1836	1916	1936	2016	2116	2216
Macclesfield .... **152** d.	|	0949	1049	1149	1249	|	1349	|	1449	|	1549	|	1649	|	|	1749	|	1849	|	1949	2029	2129	2229
Stoke on Trent .... **152** d.	|	1007	1107	1207	1307	1344	1407	1444	1507	1544	1607	1644	1707	1744	1744	1807	1844	1907	1944	2007	2047	2147	2247
Stafford .... d.	0926	1025	1127	1225	1325	1401	1425	1501	1525	1601	1625	1701	1725	1801	1801	1825	1901	1925	2001	2025	2104	2204	2304
Wolverhampton .... **150** d.	0941	1041	1142	1241	1341	1415	1441	1515	1541	1615	1641	1715	1741	1815	1815	1841	1915	1941	2015	2041	2117	2222	2319
Birmingham New Street **150** a.	0957	1057	1158	1257	1357	1431	1457	1531	1557	1631	1657	1731	1757	1831	1831	1857	1931	1957	2031	2057	2133	2240	2336
Bristol T Meads **120** .... a.	|	|	|	|	|	1611	|	1708	|	1814	|	1908	|	2014	2014	|	2106	|	2210	|	2302	...	...
Exeter St Davids **120** .... a.	|	|	|	|	|	1709	|	...	|	...	|	...	|	2127	2127	|	...	|	...	|	...	...	...
Paignton **120** .... a.	|	|	|	|	|	1756	|	...	|	...	|	...	|	2213	...	|	...	|	...	|	...	...	...
Reading **119** .... a.	1140	1240	1341	1440	1540	...	1640	...	1739	...	1840	...	1939	...	...	2040	...	2140	...	2238	...	...	...
Southampton Central **119** ... a.	1242	1342	1442	1542	1642	...	1740	...	1842	...	1940	...	2041	...	...	2142	...	2242	...	...	...	...	...
Bournemouth **119** .... a.	1326	1426	1526	1626	1726	...	1826	...	1926	...	2026	...	2126	...	...	2226	...	...	...	...	...	...	...

B – May 27 - Sept. 9 and from Oct. 28 conveys 🚃 to Cardiff Central (Table **121**).
G – To Plymouth (Table **120**).
a – May 27 - Sept. 9.
b – From Sept. 16.

123 BIRMINGHAM - NOTTINGHAM

XC

km		Ⓐ	Ⓐ	Ⓐ	Ⓐ	Ⓐ	Ⓐ	Ⓐ	Ⓐ		Ⓐ	Ⓐ	Ⓐ	Ⓐ	Ⓐ		⑥	⑥	⑥	⑥	⑥
	Cardiff Central **121** .... d.	...	...	...	...	...	0640	...	0745	and at	...	1745	1845	*1950*	...	...	...	...	...	...	...
0	**Birmingham** New Street **124** d.	0619	0649	0719	0749	0819	0849	0919	0949	the same	1919	1949	2049	2203	2309	...	0619	0649	0719	0749	0819
28	Tamworth .... **124** d.	0639	0707	0739	0807	0836	0909	0936	1007	minutes	1936	2009	2109	2227	2328	...	0639	0707	0739	0807	0836
48	Burton-on-Trent .... **124** d.	0651	0720	0750	0819	0848	0921	0948	1019	past each	1948	2021	2121	2239	2340	...	0651	0719	0750	0819	0848
67	**Derby** .... **124** a.	0704	0735	0805	0836	0900	0934	1000	1034	hour until	2000	2034	2132	2251	2353	...	0703	0734	0805	0835	0900
67	**Derby** .... d.	0708	0743	0810	0840	0908	0940	1008	1040		2008	2040	2138	2259	2357	...	0709	0740	0809	0840	0908
93	**Nottingham** .... a.	0738	0809	0834	0906	0928	1003	1028	1103		2028	2103	2208	2327	0016	...	0738	0806	0834	0906	0928

	⑥	⑥	⑥	⑥		⑥	⑥	⑥	⑥	⑥	⑥	⑦	⑦	⑦	⑦	⑦	⑦	⑦	⑦	⑦	⑦	⑦
Cardiff Central **121** .... d.	0640	...	0745	...	and at	1645	...	1745	1845	2000	...	...	1045	1145	1245	1345	1445	1545	1645	1745	1845	*1945*
Birmingham New Street **124** d.	0849	0919	0949	1019	the same	1849	1919	1949	2049	2210	2249	1149	1249	1349	1449	1549	1649	1749	1849	1949	2049	2203
Tamworth .... **124** d.	0909	0936	1007	1036	minutes	1909	1936	2009	2109	2227	2308	1207	1307	1407	1509	1607	1707	1807	1909	2007	2106	2219
Burton-on-Trent .... **124** d.	0921	0948	1019	1048	past each	1921	1948	2021	2121	2239	2320	1219	1319	1419	1521	1619	1719	1819	1921	2019	2119	|
Derby .... **124** a.	0934	1000	1034	1100	hour until	1932	2000	2034	2133	2253	2333	1234	1333	1434	1533	1634	1733	1833	1933	2034	2133	2240
Derby .... d.	0940	1008	1040	1108	▽	1940	2008	2040	2140	2259	...	1240	1340	1440	1540	1640	1740	1840	1940	2040	2140	...
Nottingham .... a.	1003	1028	1103	1128		2004	2028	2103	2208	2327	...	1300	1400	1500	1600	1700	1800	1900	2000	2100	2200	...

	Ⓐ	Ⓐ A	Ⓐ	Ⓐ	Ⓐ	Ⓐ	Ⓐ		Ⓐ	Ⓐ	Ⓐ	Ⓐ	Ⓐ	Ⓐ	⑥	⑥ A	⑥	⑥	⑥	⑥	⑥
Nottingham .... d.	0600	0637	0704	0737	0812	0841	0910	and at	1841	1910	1940	2040	2139	...	0558	0637	0658	0737	0809	0841	0910
Derby .... a.	0632	0659	0731	0802	0833	0907	0931	the same	1906	1931	2006	2104	2208	...	0630	0659	0729	0802	0829	0909	0931
Derby .... **124** d.	0636	0706	0736	0806	0837	0910	0936	minutes	1910	1937	2010	2110	2212	2245	0636	0706	0736	0806	0837	0912	0936
Burton-on-Trent .... **124** d.	0648	0717	0750	0818	0849	0922	0950	past each	1921	1949	2021	2124	2223	2256	0648	0717	0750	0818	0849	0924	0949
Tamworth .... **124** d.	0701	0730	0803	0830	0902	0934	1002	hour until	1933	2003	2033	2134	2235	2307	0701	0730	0802	0830	0902	0935	1002
Birmingham New Street **124** a.	0725	0753	0825	0855	0924	0955	1024	▲	1955	2025	2055	2157	2301	2325	0724	0752	0824	0855	0924	0956	1024
Cardiff Central **121** .... a.	0929	...	1028	...	1128	...	1230		...	2235a	...	...	...	...	0925	...	1021	...	1124	...	1223

		⑥	⑥	⑥	⑥	⑥	⑥	⑦	⑦	⑦		⑦	⑦	⑦		⑦	⑦	⑦	⑦	⑦	⑦	⑦
Nottingham .... d.	and at	1841	1910	1941	2037	2139	...	0954	1111	1210	...	1310	1410	1510	...	1610	1710	1810	1910	2010	2110	...
Derby .... a.	the same	1906	1932	2007	2102	2208	...	1012	1131	1230	...	1330	1429	1530	...	1630	1729	1830	1930	2030	2130	...
Derby .... **124** d.	minutes	1910	1937	2011	2110	2212	2226	1018	1136	1236	...	1338	1434	1534	...	1634	1735	1835	1935	2035	2137	2226
Burton-on-Trent .... **124** d.	past each	1921	1949	2022	2124	2222	2237	1029	1147	1247	...	1349	1447	1547	...	1647	1747	1847	1947	2047	2148	2237
Tamworth .... **124** d.	hour until	1933	2002	2034	2135	2235	2247	1042	1200	1300	...	1400	1500	1600	...	1700	1800	1900	1959	2059	2200	2247
Birmingham New Street **124** a.		1955	2024	2055	2156	2302	2306	1102	1221	1320	...	1422	1520	1621	...	1719	1819	1921	2021	2118	2223	2305
Cardiff Central **121** .... a.	△	...	2242	...	...	...	...	1307	1427	1528	...	1629	1726	1829	...	1927	2030	2127	...	...	...	...

A – To Bournemouth (Table **119**).
a – On ⑤ arrives 2230.
▲ – Cardiff arrivals may vary ± 4 minutes.
△ – Cardiff arrivals may vary ± 6 minutes.
▽ – Nottingham arrivals may be up to 3 minutes later after 1700.

136 CARDIFF - BRISTOL (special service during Severn Tunnel closure)

GW 2nd class

⑥⑦ Service Sept. 16 - Oct. 22. See page 119 for other dates.

	⑥	⑥	⑥	⑥	⑥🚌	⑥	⑥	⑥	⑥🚌	⑥	⑥	⑥🚌	⑥	⑥	⑥	⑥	⑥	⑥	⑥🚌	⑥	⑥	⑥	⑥	⑥	⑥🚌	⑥
Newport ⁘ .... d.	...	0543*	0620*	0711*	0750	0811*	0850*	0911*	0942	1042*	1102*	1142	1202*	1240*	1302*	1340*	1440*	1502*	1542	1602*	1640*	1702*	1742*	1802*	1840	1912*
Bristol Parkway ... a.	...	0653*	0730*	0751*	0830	0851*	0930*	0951*	1032	1132*	1152*	1232	1252*	1330*	1352*	1430*	1530*	1552*	1232	1652*	1730*	1752*	1832*	1852*	1930	1952*
Bristol Parkway ... d.	0542	0704	0801	0820	...	0901	0930	1001	...	1135	1201	...	1301	1330	1401	1501	1535	1601	...	1701	1730	1801	1901	1901	...	2001
Bristol Temple M .... a.	0553	0719	0819	0834	...	0919	0943	1019	...	1152	1219	...	1319	1346	1419	1519	1549	1619	...	1718	1746	1819	1919	1919	...	2019

	⑥🚌	⑥	⑥🚌	⑥🚌	⑥🚌	⑥🚌	⑦🚌	⑦	⑦	⑦🚌	⑦	⑦	⑦	⑦	⑦	⑦	⑦	⑦	⑦	⑦	⑦	⑦🚌	⑦🚌	⑦	⑦🚌	⑦🚌
Newport ⁘ ▲ .... d.	1957	2010*	2050	2140	2230	2320	0830	0900*	0950*	1030	1055*	1203*	1305*	1345*	1450*	1530*	1620*	1650*	1750*	1905*	2005*	2034	2114	2200*	2255	2343
Bristol Parkway ▲ a.	2037	2050*	2130	2220	2315	|	0930	0940*	1030*	1110	1135*	1243*	1345*	1425*	1530*	1640*	1700*	1730*	1830*	1945*	2045*	2114	2154	2240*	2350s	|
Bristol Parkway ... d.	...	2101	...	...	...	|	0930	0955	1101	...	1151	1252	1355	1448	1549	1648	1715	1750	1830	1952	2101	...	...	2247	|	|
Bristol Temple M .... a.	...	2117	...	...	...	0010	0950	1009	1112	...	1203	1304	1406	1500	1601	1702	1728	1803	1842	2006	2112	...	...	2257	0012	0038

	⑥	⑥🚌	⑥🚌	⑥	⑥🚌	⑥🚌	⑥	⑥🚌	⑥	⑥🚌	⑥	⑥	⑥🚌	⑥	⑥🚌	⑥	⑥🚌	⑥	⑥🚌	⑥	⑥	⑥🚌	⑥	⑥🚌	⑥	⑥
Bristol Temple M .... d.	0137	...	...	0741	...	...	0854	...	0953	...	1054	1104	...	1152	...	1254	...	1352	...	1545	1504	...	1553	...	1655	1705
Bristol Parkway ... a.	|	...	...	0752	...	...	0905	...	1005	...	1105	1116	...	1205	...	1305	...	1405	...	1505	1516	...	1605	...	1705	1717
Bristol Parkway △ d.	|	0706	0744	0815*	0815	0845	0926*	0944	1015*	1045	...	1126*	1144	1215*	1243	1328*	1342	1415*	1440	...	1526*	1542	1613*	1644	...	1726*
Newport ⁘ △ .... a.	0220	0746	0824	0855*	0855	0925	1016*	1034	1105*	1135	...	1216*	1234	1305*	1331	1418*	1432	1505*	1528	...	1616*	1630	1703*	1734	...	1816*

	⑥🚌	⑥	⑥🚌	⑥	⑥	⑥🚌	⑥	⑥	⑥🚌	⑥	⑥🚌	⑥	⑥	⑦🚌	⑦	⑦	⑦	⑦	⑦	⑦	⑦	⑦	⑦	⑦	⑦	⑦
Bristol Temple M .... d.	...	1753	...	1838	1841	...	1954	2003	...	2054	...	2157	2255	0800	1040	1147	1341	1448	1548	1648	1748	1848	1948	2048	2148	2248
Bristol Parkway ... a.	...	1805	...	1852	1905	...	2005	2016	...	2106	...	2209	2307	0825	1052	1200	1401	1500	1600	1700	1800	1900	2000	2059	2202	2300
Bristol Parkway △ d.	1742	1815*	1843	...	1918*	1944	...	2026*	2044	2115*	2151	2219	2315	0830	1100*	1209*	1415*	1510*	1615*	1715*	1815*	1915*	2015*	2110*	2212*	2310*
Newport ⁘ △ .... a.	1832	1905*	1933	...	1958*	2024	...	2106*	2124	2155*	2231	2324	0020	0925	1140*	1249*	1455*	1620*	1655*	1755*	1855*	1955*	2055*	2150*	2307*	0005*

s – Stops to set down only.
* – Connection by 🚌.
⁘ – For connections from Cardiff Central to Newport and v.v. see Tables **121**, **132** and **149**.
▲ – Additional buses run Newport - Bristol Parkway on ⑦ at 1420, 1520, 1720 and 1935 (Journey time 40 minutes).
△ – Additional buses run Bristol Parkway - Newport on ⑦ at 0940, 1000, 1145, 1239, 1310, 1515, 1645, 1745, 1845, 1945, 2045 (Journey time 40 minutes).

km	Ⓐ	Ⓐ	Ⓐ	Ⓐ	Ⓐ	Ⓐ	Ⓐ	Ⓐ	Ⓐ	Ⓐ	Ⓐ	Ⓐ	Ⓐ	Ⓐ	Ⓐ	Ⓐ	Ⓐ	Ⓐ	Ⓐ	Ⓐ	Ⓐ	Ⓐ	Ⓐ	Ⓐ
							H	G				A			B		C		B		D		
	Plymouth **120** d.	...	...	...	...	...	...	...	...	0520	...	0625	...	0725	...	0825	...	0925	...	1025	...	1125	...	1225
	Bristol T Meads **120** d.	...	...	...	...	...	...	0627	...	0730	...	0830	...	0930	...	1030	...	1130	...	1230	...	1330	...	1430
	Southampton Central **119** d.	...	...	...	...	...	...	|	...	|	...	|	...	|	...	|	0946	|	...	|	1146	|	...	|
	Reading **119** d.	...	...	...	...	...	...	|	0645	|	0746	|	0850	|	0945	|	1045	|	1145	|	1245	|	1345	|
0	**Birmingham** New Street **123** d.	...	...	0600	0630	0703	0730	0803	0830	0903	0930	1003	1030	1103	1130	1203	1230	1303	1330	1403	1430	1503	1530	1603
28	Tamworth **123** d.	...	...	|	|	0719	|	0819	|	|	|	1019	|	|	|	1219	|	|	|	1419	|	|	|	1620
48	Burton on Trent **123** d.	...	...	|	|	0731	|	0829	|	0927	|	|	|	1126	|	|	|	1328	|	|	|	1526	|	|
67	**Derby** **123 170** d.	...	0556	0635	0713	0744	0813	0844	0916**a**	0944	1016**a**	1044**b**	1116**a**	1144**b**	1216**a**	1244	1316**a**	1344**b**	1416**a**	1444	1516**a**	1544	1616**a**	1643
105	Chesterfield **170** d.	...	0617	0654	0732	0803	0832	0903	|	1003	|	1103	|	1203	|	1303	|	1403	|	1503	|	1603	|	1704
125	**Sheffield** **170** d.	...	0633	0709	0754**d**	0822**b**	0847	0921	0947	1021	1047	1121	1147	1221	1247	1321	1347	1421	1447	1521	1547	1621	1647	1721
154	Doncaster **180** d.	...	0703**b**	|	0825	|	0919	|	1019	|	1119	|	1219	|	1319	|	1419	|	1519	|	1619	|	1720	|
171	Wakefield Westgate **180** d.	...	|	0737	|	0848	|	0947	|	1047	|	1147	|	1247	|	1347	|	1447	|	1547	|	1650	|	1749
187	**Leeds** **190 180** d.	...	|	0757**d**	|	0908**d**	|	1008**d**	|	1108**d**	|	1208**d**	|	1308**d**	|	1408**d**	|	1508**d**	|	1608**d**	|	1708	|	1808**b**
199	**York** **190 180** a.	...	0723	0822	0847	0930	0940	1030	1039	1130	1139	1230	1240	1330	1340	1430	1439	1530	1539	1630	1639	1730	1740	1831
	York **180** d.	...	0732	0829	0850	0932	0950	1032	1048	1132	1150	1232	1248	1332	1350	1432	1448	1532	1548	1632	1648	1732	1748	1833
270	Darlington **180** d.	...	0800	0858	0917	0958	1016	1100	1115	1159	1216	1300	1315	1400	1416	1500	1515	1600	1615	1700	1715	1800	1815	1901
305	Durham **180** d.	...	0818	0915	0934	1016	1033	1117	1132	1216	1233	1317	1332	1416	1433	1517	1532	1617	1632	1718	1732	1817	1833	1919
328	**Newcastle** **180** a.	...	0838	0927	0947	1029	1046	1129	1145	1230	1245	1329	1345	1431	1445	1529	1545	1629	1645	1730	1745	1833	1847	1932
	Newcastle **180** d.	0735	...	0935	...	1035	...	1140	...	1239	...	1338	...	1435	...	1537	...	1637	...	1737	...	1840	...	1935
384	Alnmouth **180** a.	|	...	0958	...	|	...	|	...	|	...	1401	...	|	...	1600	...	1700	...	1800	...	|	...	2000
436	Berwick upon Tweed **180** a.	0818	...	1019	...	|	...	1221	...	|	...	1422	...	|	...	1621	...	|	...	1821	...	1921	...	2023
528	**Edinburgh** Waverley **180 220** a.	0900	...	1106	...	1204	...	1306	..	1410	...	1507	...	1606	...	1706	...	1807	...	1906	...	2009	...	2108
599	Motherwell **220** a.	1002	...	1152	...	...	...	1353	...	...	...	1552	...	...	...	1752	...	...	...	1953	...	...	...	2207
620	**Glasgow** Central **220** a.	1025	...	1212	...	...	...	1412	...	...	...	1612	...	...	...	1811	...	...	...	2015	...	...	...	2224

	Ⓐ	Ⓐ	Ⓐ	Ⓐ	Ⓐ	Ⓐ	Ⓐ	Ⓐ	Ⓐ	Ⓐ	⑥	⑥	⑥	⑥	⑥	⑥	⑥	⑥	⑥	⑥	⑥	⑥	⑥	⑥
																		G		E				
Plymouth **120** d.	...	1325	...	1425	...	1525	...	1625	...	725	...	...	...	...	...	...	...	...	0525	...	0625	...	0725	...
Bristol T Meads **120** d.	...	1530	...	1630	...	1730	...	1830	...	1930	...	...	...	...	...	...	0615	...	0730	...	0830	...	0930	...
Southampton Central **119** d.	1346	|	...	|	1546	|	...	|	1746	|	...	...	...	...	...	...	|	...	|	0653	|	0747	|	...
Reading **119** d.	1445	|	1545	|	1645	|	1745	|	1845	|	...	...	...	...	...	...	|	0645	|	0747	|	0845	|	0945
Birmingham New Street **123** d.	1630	1703	1730	1803	1830	1903	1930	2003	2030	2103	...	...	0557	0630	0703	0730	0803	0830	0903	0930	1003	1030	1103	1130
Tamworth **123** d.	|	|	|	1819	|	|	|	2019	|	2119	...	...	0613	0646	0719	0746	0819	|	|	|	1019	|	|	|
Burton on Trent **123** d.	|	1726	|	|	|	1929	|	|	|	2130	...	...	0624	0656	0731	0756	0829	|	0928	|	|	|	1128	|
Derby **123 170** d.	1711**b**	1742	1816**a**	1844**b**	1909	1943	2009	2043	2119**a**	2144	...	0556	0638	0713	0744	0813**b**	0844	0916**a**	0944**b**	1016**a**	1044**b**	1116**a**	1144**b**	1216**a**
Chesterfield **170** d.	|	1803	|	1903	1928	2004	|	2104	2138	2207	...	0631	0657	0732	0803	0832	0903	|	1003	|	1103	|	1203	|
Sheffield **170** d.	1747**b**	1821	1847	1926**d**	1956**g**	2021	2053**a**	2121	2154	2230**b**	...	0649**b**	0712	0754**d**	0822**b**	0847	0921	0947	1021	1047	1121	1147	1221	1247
Doncaster **180** d.	|	|	1918	|	2018	|	2121	|	2231	|	...	0719	|	0825	|	0919	|	1019	|	1119	|	1219	|	1319
Wakefield Westgate **180** d.	1819	1848	|	1951	|	2048	|	2149	|	2301	...	|	0740	|	0848	|	0947	|	1047	|	1147	|	1247	|
Leeds **190 180** d.	1838	1908**b**	|	2008	|	2106	|	2204	|	2315	...	|	0757	|	0908**d**	|	1008**d**	|	1108**d**	|	1208**d**	|	1308**b**	|
York **190 180** a.	1901	1930	1939	2030	2038	...	2141	...	2252	...	...	0743	0819	0847	0930	0940	1030	1039	1130	1139	1230	1239	1330	1339
York **180** d.	1904	1933	1945	2032	2048	...	2147	...	...	...	...	0748	0829	0850	0932	0948	1032	1048	1132	1150	1232	1248	1332	1350
Darlington **180** d.	1932	2002	2012	2059	2115	...	2213	...	...	...	...	0815	0858	0917	0959	1018	1100	1115	1158	1216	1300	1315	1359	1417
Durham **180** d.	1949	2020	2029	2116	2132	...	2230	...	...	...	...	0832	0915	0934	1016	1035	1117	1132	1215	1233	1317	1332	1416	1434
Newcastle **180** a.	2001	2033	2042	2128	2144	...	2247	...	...	...	...	0845	0927	0947	1029	1047	1129	1146	1229	1246	1329	1345	1428	1446
Newcastle **180** d.	2003	2036	...	2135	...	...	...	...	...	..	0738	...	0935	...	1035	...	1136	...	1236	...	1335	...	1433	...
Alnmouth **180** a.	2026	|	...	2158	...	...	...	...	..	...	|	...	0958	...	|	...	|	...	|	...	1358	...	|	...
Berwick upon Tweed **180** a.	|	2124	...	|	...	...	...	...	....	...	0821	...	1019	...	|	...	1219	...	|	...	1419	...	|	...
Edinburgh Waverley **180 220** a.	2128	2215	...	2303	...	...	...	...	...	...	0907	...	1103	...	1205	...	1302	...	1406	...	1504	...	1604	...
Motherwell **220** a.	...	...	...	...	...	...	...	...	...	...	0954	...	1152	...	...	...	1353	...	...	...	1552	...	...	...
Glasgow Central **220** a.	...	...	...	...	...	...	...	...	...	...	1015	...	1212	...	...	...	1412	...	...	...	1612	...	...	...

	⑥	⑥	⑥	⑥	⑥	⑥	⑥	⑥	⑥	⑥	⑥	⑥	⑥	⑥	⑥	⑥	⑥	⑥	⑥	⑥	⑥	⑥	⑥	⑦
	B		C		B		DF		Jc	e								Jc	e		Ec	e	Bc	
Plymouth **120** d.	0825	...	0918**f**	...	1025	...	1125	...	...	1225	...	1325	...	1425	...	1525	...	...	1625	...	...	1725	1825	...
Bristol T Meads **120** d.	1030	...	1130	...	1230	...	1330	...	1430	1430	...	1530	...	1630	...	1730	...	1830	1830	...	...	1930	2030	...
Southampton Central **119** d.	|	0947	|	...	|	1147	|	...	|	|	1347	|	...	|	1547	|	...	|	|	1747	1820	|	|	...
Reading **119** d.	|	1045	|	1145	|	1245	|	1345	|	|	1445	|	1545	|	1645	|	1745	|	|	1845	1915	|	|	...
Birmingham New Street **123** d.	1203	1230	1303	1330	1403	1430	1503	1530	1603	1603	1630	1703	1730	1803	1830	1903	1930	2003	2003	2030	2103	2103	2156	...
Tamworth **123** d.	1219	|	|	|	1419	|	|	|	1619	1619	|	|	|	1819	|	|	|	2019	2019	|	2119	2119	|	...
Burton on Trent **123** d.	|	|	1327	|	|	|	1527	|	|	|	1654	1726	|	|	|	1927	|	|	|	|	2130	2130	|	...
Derby **123 170** d.	1244**b**	1316**a**	1344**b**	1416**a**	1444**b**	1516**a**	1544	1616**a**	1643	1643	1716**a**	1744**b**	1816**a**	1844	1916**a**	1943	2016**a**	2044	2044	2127	2146	2146	2233	...
Chesterfield **170** d.	1303	|	1403	|	1503	|	1603	|	1704	1704	|	1803	|	1903	1935	2004	2035	2105	2105	2147	2208	2208	2255	...
Sheffield **170** d.	1321	1347	1421	1447	1521	1547	1621	1647	1721	1721	1747	1821	1847	1921	1956**d**	2023	2053	2121	2121	2203	2230**d**	2230**d**	2312	...
Doncaster **180** d.	|	1419	|	1519	|	1619	|	1719	|	|	|	|	1919	|	2019	|	2124	|	|	2226	2253	2253	|	...
Wakefield Westgate **180** d.	1347	|	1447	|	1547	|	1647	|	1748	1748	1815	1848	|	1951	|	2051	|	2148	2148	|	2311	2311	|	...
Leeds **190 180** d.	1408**d**	|	1508**d**	|	1608**d**	|	1708**d**	|	1808**b**	1808**b**	1838**d**	1908**d**	|	2008	|	2119**g**	|	2202	2202	|	2325	2325	2351	...
York **190 180** a.	1430	1439	1530	1539	1630	1639	1729	1739	1830	1830	1901	1930	1939	2030	2040	2155	2144	...	...	2246	...	...	...	...
York **180** d.	1432	1448	1532	1546	1632	1648	1731	1746	1832	1832	1904	1932	1945	2032	2048	...	2148	...	...	...	...	...	...	...
Darlington **180** d.	1500	1515	1600	1616	1700	1715	1757	1812	1901	1901	1932	1959	2012	2059	2115	...	2215	...	...	...	...	...	...	...
Durham **180** d.	1517	1532	1617	1633	1717	1732	1814	1829	1919	1919	1949	2016	2029	2116	2132	...	2232	...	...	...	...	...	...	...
Newcastle **180** a.	1529	1545	1629	1646	1729	1745	1829	1841	1932	1932	2001	2028	2042	2128	2145	...	2247	...	...	...	...	...	...	...
Newcastle **180** d.	1535	...	1634	...	1735	...	1837	...	1935	1935	...	2035	...	2132	...	...	...	...	...	...	...	...	...	0945
Alnmouth **180** a.	1558	...	1657	...	1759	...	|	...	2000	2000	...	|	...	2155	...	...	...	...	...	...	...	...	...	1011
Berwick upon Tweed **180** a.	1619	...	|	...	1819	...	1918	...	2023	2023	...	2118	...	|	...	...	...	...	...	...	...	...	...	|
Edinburgh Waverley **180 220** a.	1707	...	1803	...	1906	...	2006	...	2108	2108	...	2208	...	2257	...	...	...	...	...	...	...	...	...	1111
Motherwell **220** a.	1752	...	...	...	1953	...	...	...	2159	2159	...	...	...	...	...	...	...	...	...	...	...	...	...	...
Glasgow Central **220** a.	1811	...	...	...	2012	...	...	...	2220	2220	...	...	...	...	...	...	...	...	...	...	...	...	...	...

	⑦	⑦	⑦	⑦	⑦	⑦	⑦	⑦	⑦	⑦	⑦	⑦	⑦	⑦	⑦	⑦	⑦	⑦	⑦	⑦	⑦	⑦	⑦	⑦	⑦
								C			G	B		k	h									B	
Plymouth **120** d.	...	...	...	...	...	...	...	0925	...	1025	...	1125	...	1225	1225	...	1325	...	1425	...	1524	...	1625	1725	1825
Bristol T Meads **120** d.	...	...	...	...	0915	1030	...	1130	...	1230	...	1330	...	1430	1430	...	1530	...	1630	...	1730	...	1830	1930	2030
Southampton Central **119** d.	...	...	...	...	|	|	...	|	...	|	...	|	...	|	|	...	|	...	|	...	|	...	|	|	|
Reading **119** d.	...	...	...	...	|	|	...	|	...	|	1254	|	1341	|	|	1441	|	1541	|	1641	|	1741	|	|	|
Birmingham New Street **123** d.	...	...	0903	1003	1103	1203	1230	1303	1330	1403	1430	1503	1530	1603	1603	1630	1703	1730	1803	1830	1903	1930	2003	2103	2203
Tamworth **123** d.	...	...	0919	1018	|	1219	|	|	|	1419	|	|	|	1619	1619	|	|	|	1819	|	|	|	2019	2119	2219
Burton on Trent **123** d.	...	...	0928	1029	1125	|	|	1326	|	|	|	1525	|	|	|	|	1728	|	|	|	1926	|	|	2129	|
Derby **123 170** d.	...	...	0944	1044	1144**d**	1244**b**	1311**a**	1344**d**	1411**a**	1444**b**	1511**a**	1544**d**	1611**a**	1644**b**	1643	1712**a**	1743	1812**a**	1843	1906	1942	2009**d**	2044**b**	2144	2242
Chesterfield **170** d.	...	...	1003	1103	1203	1303	1330	1403	1430	1503	|	1603	|	1703	1704	|	1804	|	1905	|	2003	|	2103	2203	2303
Sheffield **170** d.	...	0921	1021**b**	1121	1221	1321	1351**d**	1421	1451**b**	1521	1551	1621	1651	1721	1721	1752	1821	1852**d**	1921	1952**a**	2021	2052**a**	2121**b**	2221	2319
Doncaster **180** d.	...	|	|	|	|	|	1417	|	1522**d**	|	1618	|	1719**b**	|	|	1817	|	1919	|	2018	|	2123	|	|	|
Wakefield Westgate **180** d.	...	0946	1046	1146	1246	1346	|	1446	|	1546	|	1646	|	1745	1747	1835	1849	|	1950	|	2053	|	2148	2244	|
Leeds **190 180** d.	0920	1008**b**	1105**b**	1205	1305	1405	|	1505	|	1605	|	1705	|	1805	1807**b**	1859**d**	1908	|	2008	|	2108	|	2204	2301	0008
York **190 180** a.	0942	1029	1127	1227	1327	1427	1437	1527	1543	1627	1638	1727	1740	1827	1829	1921	1929	1939	2030	2039	2132	2143	...	...	...
York **180** d.	0944	1032	1129	1229	1329	1429	1448	1529	1545	1629	1647	1729	1745	1829	1831	1923	1932	1945	2032	2048	...	2149	...	...	...
Darlington **180** d.	1011	1059	1156	1256	1357	1457	1515	1556	1612	1656	1714	1756	1811	1856	1859	1950	2000	2012	2100	2115	...	2226	...	...	...
Durham **180** d.	1028	1116	1213	1313	1414	1514	1532	1613	1629	1713	1731	1813	1828	1913	1917	2007	2018	2029	2118	2132	...	2243	...	...	...
Newcastle **180** a.	1040	1128	1225	1325	1426	1526	1544	1625	1642	1725	1744	1825	1841	1925	1930	2019	2031	2041	2131	2144	...	2312	...	...	...
Newcastle **180** d.	1042	1134	1230	1328	1432	1528	...	1628	...	1728	...	1828	...	1928	1933	...	2034	2056	2134	...	...	...	...	...	...
Alnmouth **180** a.	|	|	|	1351	|	1552	...	1651	...	1751	...	|	...	1951	1958	...	|	|	2159	...	...	...	...	...	...
Berwick upon Tweed **180** a.	1123	1217	|	1412	|	1612	...	|	...	1812	...	1909	...	2012	2020	...	2121	|	|	...	...	...	...	...	...
Edinburgh Waverley **180 220** a.	1207	1259	1400	1456	1602	1656	...	1757	...	1856	...	1957	...	2056	2105	...	2212	2221	2304	...	...	...	...	...	...
Motherwell **220** a.	1258	1353	...	1554	...	1755	...	...	...	1959	...	...	...	2156	2156	...	...	...	...	...	...	...	...	...	...
Glasgow Central **220** a.	1318	1412	...	1611	...	1812	...	...	...	2019	...	...	...	2213	2213	...	...	...	...	...	...	...	...	...	...

A – From Winchester (Table **119**).
B – From Penzance (Tables **117**/**120**).
C – To Aberdeen (Table **222**).
D – To Dundee (Table **222**).
E – From Bournemouth (Table **119**).
F – From Newquay May 27 - Sept. 9 (Tables **117**/**120**).
G – From Guildford (Table **134**).
H – From Bath Spa (Table **120**).
J – From Paignton (Table **120**).
a – Arrives 10–12 minutes earlier.
b – Arrives 5–6 minutes earlier.
c – May 27 - Sept. 9.
d – Arrives 7–9 minutes earlier.
e – From Sept. 16.
f – Departs 0925 from Sept. 16.
g – Arrives 15–16 minutes earlier.
h – May 21 - Sept. 10.
k – From Sept. 17.

① – Mondays ② – Tuesdays ③ – Wednesdays ④ – Thursdays ⑤ – Fridays ⑥ – Saturdays ⑦ – Sundays Ⓐ – Monday to Fridays, not holidays

		Ⓐ	Ⓐ	Ⓐ	Ⓐ	Ⓐ	Ⓐ	Ⓐ	Ⓐ	Ⓐ	Ⓐ	Ⓐ	Ⓐ	Ⓐ	Ⓐ	Ⓐ	Ⓐ	Ⓐ	Ⓐ	Ⓐ	Ⓐ	Ⓐ	Ⓐ	Ⓐ	Ⓐ
														D				**B**		**CB**	**G**	**B**			
Glasgow Central 220 d.	Ⓐ	...	...	...	...	...	...	...	...	...	...	0601	...	...	...	0750	...	0900	...	...	...	1100	...	...	...
Motherwell 220 d.		...	...	...	...	...	...	...	...	...	...	0617	...	...	...	0805	...	0915	...	...	...	1116	...	...	...
Edinburgh Waverley 180 220 d.		...	...	...	...	...	...	...	...	0606	0700	0707	...	0810	...	0908	...	1010	...	1106	...	1208	...	1307	...
Berwick upon Tweed 180 d.		...	...	...	...	...	...	...	...	0647	0741	|	...	0851	...	0951	...	1049	...	1149	...	1248	...	|	...
Alnmouth 180 d.		...	...	...	...	...	...	...	...	0708	0801	|	...	|	...	|	...	|	...	1209	...	|	...	1411	...
Newcastle 180 a.		...	...	...	...	...	...	...	...	0738	0832	0836	...	0939	...	1038	...	1137	...	1238	...	1334	...	1439	...
Newcastle 180 d.		...	...	...	...	...	0625	0645	0725	0740	0835	0841	0935	0942	1035	1042	1135	1144	1234	1241	1335	1343	1436	1442	1505
Durham 180 d.		...	...	...	...	...	0638	0658	0738	0755	0848	0855	0949	0956	1048	1055	1149	1157	1248	1254	1349	1356	1449	1456	1518
Darlington 180 d.		...	...	...	...	...	0655	0715	0755	0812	0905	0912	1007	1013	1105	1113	1206	1214	1305	1313	1407	1413	1506	1513	1534
York 180 a.		...	...	...	...	...	0722	0741	0823	0840	0932	0940	1033	1041	1132	1141	1232	1240	1331	1340	1433	1440	1533	1541	1601
York 190 180 d.		...	...	...	...	0640	0727	0743	0826	0845	0935	0944	1035	1045	1135	1145	1235	1245	1335	1345	1435	1445	1535	1545	1605
Leeds 190 180 d.		...	...	0600	0616	0705	|	0811	|	0911	|	1011	|	1111	|	1211	|	1311	|	1411	|	1511	|	1611	1640**c**
Wakefield Westgate 180 d.		...	...	0612	0628	0719	|	0823	|	0923	|	1023	|	1124	|	1223	|	1323	|	1423	|	1523	|	1623	1652
Doncaster 180 d.		...	...	|	0646	|	0756**b**	|	0851	|	0959	|	1059	|	1159	|	1259	|	1359	|	1459	|	1559	|	|
Sheffield 170 d.		...	0601	0652**e**	0718**d**	0753	0821	0854	0924**d**	0954	1024	1054	1124	1154	1224	1255	1324	1355	1424	1455	1524	1555	1624	1655	1724
Chesterfield 170 d.		...	0626	0706	0730	0806	0833	0907	|	1008	|	1108	|	1208	|	1307	|	1407	|	1507	|	1607	|	1708	|
Derby 123 170 d.		0610	0648**b**	0727	0750	0828	0853	0928	0953	1030	1053	1130	1153	1230	1253	1328	1353	1428	1453	1528	1553	1628	1653	1729	1753
Burton on Trent 123 d.		0620	0658	0738	0800	0838	|	0938	|	|	|	|	|	|	|	1338	|	|	|	1538	|	|	|	1740	|
Tamworth 123 d.		0631	0709	0750	0811	0850	|	|	|	1050	|	|	|	1249	|	|	|	1447	|	|	|	1647	|	|	|
Birmingham New Street 123 a.		0652	0727	0808	0827	0910	0927	1008	1027	1109	1127	1207	1227	1308	1327	1408	1427	1508	1527	1602	1628	1708	1728	1806	1827
Reading **119** a.		|	0908	|	1010	|	1109	|	1209	|	1307	|	1409	|	1508	|	1611	|	1708	|	1808	|	1910	|	2009
Southampton Central **119** a.		|	...	|	1117	|	...	|	1317	|	...	|	1517	|	...	|	1716	|	...	|	...	|	...	|	...
Bristol T Meads **120** a.		0839	...	0939	...	1042	...	1141	...	1242	...	1341	...	1442	...	1541	...	1643	...	1739	...	1841	...	1942	...
Plymouth **120** a.		1042	...	1144	...	1247	...	1338	...	1443	...	1540	...	1648	...	1742	...	1849	...	1943	...	2040	...	2146	...

	Ⓐ	Ⓐ	Ⓐ	Ⓐ	Ⓐ	Ⓐ	Ⓐ	Ⓐ	Ⓐ	Ⓐ		⑥	⑥	⑥	⑥	⑥	⑥	⑥	⑥	⑥	⑥	⑥	⑥	⑥	⑥
													a	**g**	**g**	**Ha**		**g**	**a**		**g**	**Ba**			
Glasgow Central 220 d.	1300	...	...	...	1500	...	...	...	1700	1900	⑥	...	...	...	...	...	...	...	...	...	...	...	...	...	...
Motherwell 220 d.	1316	...	...	...	1516	...	...	...	1716	1916		...	...	...	...	...	...	...	...	...	...	...	...	...	...
Edinburgh Waverley 180 220 d.	1408	...	1508	...	1606	...	1707	...	1805	2002		...	...	...	...	...	...	...	...	...	...	...	...	0606	0700
Berwick upon Tweed 180 d.	1450	...	|	...	|	...	1751	...	1852	2045		...	...	...	...	...	...	...	...	...	...	...	...	0647	0740
Alnmouth 180 d.	|	...	|	...	1702	...	|	...	1910	2105		...	...	...	...	...	...	...	...	...	...	...	...	0707	0800
Newcastle 180 a.	1534	...	1634	...	1734	...	1837	...	1939	2134		...	...	...	...	...	...	...	...	...	...	...	...	0738	0831
Newcastle 180 d.	1541	1635	1641	1732	1741	1835	1843	1935	1942	...		...	...	...	...	...	...	...	...	0623	0645	...	0735	0741	0835
Durham 180 d.	1554	1648	1653	1748	1754	1848	1856	1950	1955	...		...	...	...	...	...	...	...	...	0638	0658	...	0748	0754	0848
Darlington 180 d.	1613	1706	1712	1805	1813	1907	1913	2007	2013	...		...	...	...	...	...	...	...	...	0655	0715	...	0805	0812	0905
York 180 a.	1640	1731	1740	1832	1839	1933	1940	2032	2040			...	...	...	...	...	...	...	...	0721	0741	...	0831	0840	0932
York 190 180 d.	1645	1735	1745	1835	1845	1936	1945	2035	2045	...		...	...	...	...	...	...	0620	0645	0727	0745	0745	0835	0845	0935
Leeds 190 180 d.	1711	|	1811	|	1911	|	2011	|	2111	...		...	...	...	0600	0600	0616	0711**e**	0711	|	0811	0811	|	0911	|
Wakefield Westgate 180 d.	1723	|	1823	|	1923	|	2024	|	2123	...		...	...	...	0612	0612	0629	0723	0723	|	0824	0824	|	0923	|
Doncaster 180 d.	|	1759	|	1859	|	2000	|	2102	|	...		...	...	...	|	|	0647	|	|	0756**d**	|	|	0859	|	0959
Sheffield 170 d.	1758**d**	1824	1858**d**	1924	1958**d**	2024	2058**b**	2129	2201**d**	...		...	0545	...	0650**c**	0650**c**	0718**d**	0756**b**	0756**b**	0820	0854	0854	0924	0954	1024
Chesterfield 170 d.	1810	|	1911	|	2010	|	2110	2141	2225	...		...	0557	...	0704	0704	0730	0808	0808	0832	0907	0907	|	1007	|
Derby 123 170 d.	1829	1853	1930	1954	2029	2054	2129	2202	2245	...		0610	0648**h**	0648	0726	0726	0751	0828	0828	0853	0930**b**	0930**b**	0953	1028	1053
Burton on Trent 123 d.	|	|	1941	|	|	|	2140	|	2256	...		0620	0658	0658	0737	0737	0800	0838	0838	|	0941	0941	|	|	|
Tamworth 123 d.	1848	|	|	|	2047	|	2150	|	2307	...		0631	0709	0709	0748	0748	0812	0849	0849	|	|	|	|	1048	|
Birmingham New Street 123 a.	1908	1927	2007	2027	2107	2129	2209	2251	2325	...		0650	0728	0728	0808	0808	0827	0908	0908	0927	1006	1006	1027	1108	1127
Reading **119** a.	|	2107	|	2216	|	...	|	...	...	...		|	0909	0909	|	|	1008	|	|	1111	|	|	1206	|	1309
Southampton Central **119** a.	|	...	|	2320	|	...	|	...	...	...		|	...	...	|	|	1117	|	|	...	|	|	1317	|	...
Bristol T Meads **120** a.	2041	...	2136	...	2243	...	2340	...	...	...		0838	...	...	0939	0939	...	1042	1042	...	1138	1138	...	1242	...
Plymouth **120** a.	2243	...	2339	...	...	...	...	...	...	...		1039	...	...	1151	...	...	1240	1241	...	1339	1345	...	1444**f**	...

	⑥	⑥	⑥	⑥	⑥	⑥	⑥	⑥	⑥	⑥	⑥	⑥	⑥	⑥	⑥	⑥	⑥	⑥	⑥	⑥	⑥	⑥	⑥	⑥	⑥
	g	**Ha**		**DF**		**Ba**	**g**		**B**		**CB**	**G**	**Bg**	**a**											
Glasgow Central 220 d.	0601	0601	...	...	...	0750	0750	...	0900	...	...	...	1100	1100	...	...	...	1300	...	...	...	1500	...	...	...
Motherwell 220 d.	0617	0617	...	...	...	0805	0805	...	0915	...	...	...	1116	1116	...	...	...	1316	...	...	...	1516	...	...	...
Edinburgh Waverley 180 220 d.	0707	0707	...	0805	...	0908	0908	...	1005	...	1108	...	1204	1204	...	1309	...	1405	...	1508	...	1605	...	1708	...
Berwick upon Tweed 180 d.	|	|	...	0847	...	0951	0951	...	1045	...	1151	...	1246	1246	...	|	...	1447	...	|	...	|	...	1752	...
Alnmouth 180 d.	|	|	...	0909	...	|	|	...	|	...	1211	...	|	|	...	1409	...	|	...	|	...	1703	...	|	...
Newcastle 180 a.	0836	0836	...	0939	...	1038	1038	...	1138	...	1240	...	1334	1334	...	1348	...	1532	...	1634	...	1734	...	1838	...
Newcastle 180 d.	0843	0842	0935	0942	1035	1044	1044	1135	1142	1235	1244	1335	1344	1344	1435	1444	1505	1544	1635	1644	1732	1744	1835	1844	1935
Durham 180 d.	0856	0856	0949	0956	1048	1056	1056	1149	1155	1248	1256	1349	1356	1356	1448	1456	1518	1556	1648	1656	1749	1756	1849	1857	1950
Darlington 180 d.	0913	0913	1006	1013	1105	1113	1113	1206	1212	1305	1313	1406	1413	1413	1505	1513	1535	1613	1705	1713	1806	1813	1906	1914	2007
York 180 a.	0941	0941	1032	1041	1131	1140	1140	1232	1240	1331	1341	1432	1440	1440	1531	1540	1601	1640	1731	1740	1831	1841	1932	1941	2033
York 190 180 d.	0945	0945	1035	1045	1135	1145	1145	1235	1245	1335	1345	1435	1445	1445	1535	1545	1606	1645	1735	1745	1835	1845	1936	1945	2035
Leeds 190 180 d.	1011	1011	|	1111	|	1211	1211	|	1311	|	1411	|	1511	1511	|	1611	1640**c**	1711	|	1811	|	1911	|	2011	|
Wakefield Westgate 180 d.	1024	1024	|	1123	|	1223	1223	|	1323	|	1423	|	1523	1523	|	1623	1652	1723	|	1823	|	1924	|	2023	|
Doncaster 180 d.	|	|	1059	|	1159	|	|	1259	|	1359	|	1459	|	|	1559	|	|	|	1759	|	1859	|	2000	|	2059
Sheffield 170 d.	1055	1054	1124	1155	1224	1255	1255	1324	1355	1424	1455	1524	1555	1555	1624	1655	1724	1755	1824	1858**d**	1924	1955	2024	2055	2125
Chesterfield 170 d.	1107	1107	|	1209	|	1307	1307	|	1408	|	1507	|	1607	1607	|	1707	|	1807	|	1910	|	2007	|	2107	2137
Derby 123 170 d.	1130**b**	1130**b**	1153	1230	1253	1328	1328	1353	1430	1453	1528	1553	1628	1628	1653	1728	1753	1829**b**	1853	1929	1954	2028	2053	2128	2156
Burton on Trent 123 d.	1141	1141	|	|	|	1338	1338	|	|	|	1538	|	|	|	|	1738	|	|	|	1939	|	|	|	2138	|
Tamworth 123 d.	|	|	|	1249	|	|	|	|	1449	|	|	|	1648	1648	|	|	|	1847	|	|	|	2046	|	2149	|
Birmingham New Street 123 a.	1208	1208	1227	1308	1327	1402	1402	1426	1508	1527	1602	1627	1707	1707	1727	1807	1827	1907	1927	2006	2027	2104	2125	2206	2244
Reading **119** a.	|	|	1408	|	1508	|	|	1609	|	1710	|	1810	|	|	1910	|	2009	|	2108	|	2214	|	...	...	...
Southampton Central **119** a.	|	|	1517	|	...	|	|	1717	|	...	|	...	|	|	...	|	...	|	...	|	2320	|	...	...	...
Bristol T Meads **120** a.	1338	1338	...	1440	...	1538	1538	...	1642	...	1738	...	1842	1842	...	1938	...	2042	...	2135	...	2241	...	...	...
Plymouth **120** a.	1541	...	...	1643	...	1739	1739	...	1851	...	1942	...	2043	2043	...	2138	...	2250	...	2356	...	...	...	...	...

	⑥		⑦	⑦	⑦	⑦	⑦	⑦	⑦	⑦	⑦	⑦	⑦	⑦	⑦	⑦	⑦	⑦	⑦	⑦	⑦	⑦	⑦	⑦	⑦
								B				**B**				**C**			**G**						
Glasgow Central 220 d.	1700	⑦	...	...	...	...	...	...	...	...	...	1055	...	1200	...	...	...	1348	...	1455	...	...	...	1655	1900
Motherwell 220 d.	1716		...	...	...	...	...	...	...	...	...	1113	...	1217	...	...	...	1404	...	1512	...	...	...	1712	1914
Edinburgh Waverley 180 220 d.	1808		...	...	...	...	0908	1008	...	1105	...	1208	...	1308	1355	1408	...	1508	...	1608	...	1708	...	1808	2018
Berwick upon Tweed 180 d.	1851		...	...	...	...	0949	|	...	1148	...	1248	...	|	1434	1447	...	|	...	|	...	1751	...	1851	2039
Alnmouth 180 d.	1911		...	...	...	...	|	1105	...	1208	...	|	...	1408	|	|	...	|	...	1705	...	|	...	|	2103
Newcastle 180 a.	1940		...	...	...	...	1036	1136	...	1237	...	1335	...	1437	1520	1535	...	1634	...	1736	...	1837	...	1937	2149
Newcastle 180 d.	1945		...	...	...	0935	1039	1140	...	1240	1335	1340	1435	1440	1524	1540	1635	1640	1735	1740	1825	1840	1926	1940	...
Durham 180 d.	1957		...	...	...	0948	1053	1153	...	1253	1348	1353	1449	1454	1537	1553	1648	1653	1748	1754	1837	1853	1939	1953	...
Darlington 180 d.	2014		...	...	...	1005	1110	1210	...	1310	1406	1410	1506	1511	1554	1610	1705	1710	1806	1811	1854	1910	1956	2010	...
York 180 a.	2041		...	...	...	1031	1138	1237	...	1337	1432	1437	1532	1537	1622	1636	1731	1737	1832	1838	1920	1937	2022	2037	...
York 190 180 d.	2045		...	...	0933	1033	1141	1241	...	1341	1435	1441	1535	1541	1625	1641	1735	1741	1835	1841	1924	1941	2024	2041	...
Leeds 190 180 d.	2111		0810	0900	1000	1100	1211**b**	1311**d**	...	1411**d**	|	1511**d**	|	1611**d**	|	1711**b**	|	1811**b**	|	1911**d**	|	2011**b**	|	2111**d**	...
Wakefield Westgate 180 d.	2123		0823	0911	1012	1112	1224	1324	...	1423	|	1523	|	1623	|	1723	|	1823	|	1923	|	2023	|	2123	...
Doncaster 180 d.	|		|	0932	1030	1130	|	|	...	|	1459	|	1559	|	1651	|	1759	|	1859	|	1954**b**	|	2051	|	...
Sheffield 170 d.	2155		0854	0957	1057	1157	1257	1357	1422	1455	1524	1555	1624	1654	1724	1754	1824	1855	1924	1955	2021	2054	2120	2154	...
Chesterfield 170 d.	2207		0907	1009	1109	1209	1309	1409	1432	1507	|	1607	|	1707	|	1807	|	1907	|	2007	|	2106	2132	2206	...
Derby 123 170 d.	2226		0928	1033	1129	1229	1332	1429	1453	1526	1553	1627	1654	1727	1754	1826	1854	1927	1956	2027	2054**b**	2126	2153	2226	...
Burton on Trent 123 d.	2237		|	|	1140	|	1343	|	|	1537	|	|	|	1737	|	|	|	1938	|	|	|	2137	2203	2237	...
Tamworth 123 d.	2247		|	1053	|	1248	|	1448	|	|	|	1648	|	|	|	1845	|	|	|	2046	|	2147	2214	2247	...
Birmingham New Street 123 a.	2306		1018	1121	1205	1306	1409	1505	1526	1602	1626	1705	1726	1802	1826	1904	1928	2005	2027	2103	2126	2205	2231	2305	...
Reading **119** a.	...		|	|	|	|	|	|	1701	|	1809	|	1906	|	2008	|	2113	|	2206	|	...	|	...	...	...
Southampton Central **119** a.	...		|	|	|	|	|	|	...	|	...	|	...	|	...	|	...	|	...	|	...	|	...	...	...
Bristol T Meads **120** a.	...		1151	1249	1331	1431	1534	1631	...	1733	...	1835	...	1932	...	2031	...	2130	...	2244	...	2333	...	...	...
Plymouth **120** a.	...		1352	1452	1537	1638	1742	1838	...	1943	...	2045	...	2141	...	2245	...	2346	...	...	...	...	...	...	...

A – To Winchester (Table **119**).
B – To Penzance (Tables **117** / **120**).
C – From Aberdeen (Table **222**).
D – From Dundee (Table **222**).
E – To Bournemouth (Table **119**).
F – From Newquay May 27 - Sept. 9 (Tables **117** / **120**).
G – To Guildford (Table **134**).
H – To Paignton (Table **120**).
a – May 27 - Sept. 9.
b – Arrives 5 – 6 minutes earlier.
c – Arrives 9 – 10 minutes earlier.
d – Arrives 7 – 8 minutes earlier.
e – Arrives 12 minutes earlier
f – Arrives 1439 May 27 - Sept. 9.
g – From Sept. 16.
h – Arrives 0633.

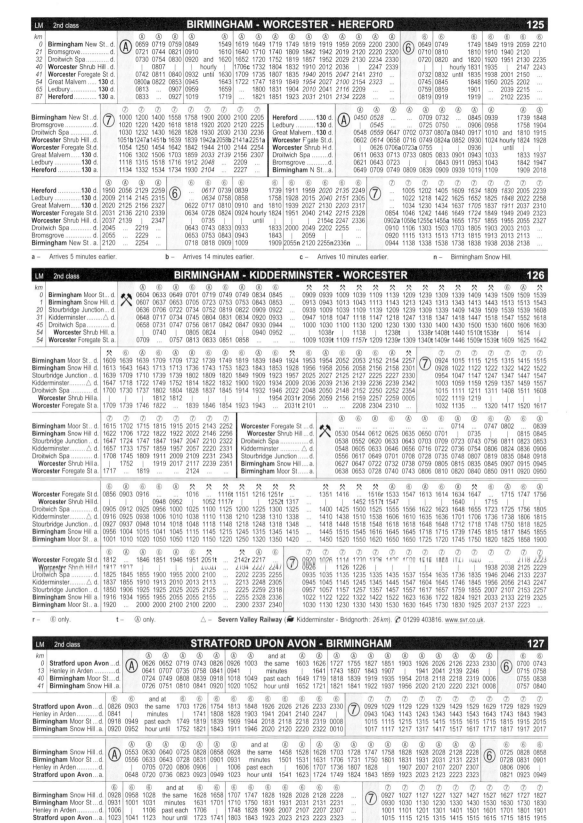

LM 2nd class BIRMINGHAM - WORCESTER - HEREFORD 125

km		Ⓐ	Ⓐ	Ⓐ	Ⓐ		Ⓐ	Ⓐ	Ⓐ	Ⓐ	Ⓐ	Ⓐ	Ⓐ	Ⓐ	Ⓐ	Ⓐ	Ⓐ	⑥	⑥		⑥	⑥	⑥	⑥	⑥
0	**Birmingham** New St.. d.	0659	0719	0759	0849		1549	1619	1649	1719	1749	1819	1919	1959	2059	2200	2300	0649	0749		1749	1849	1919	2059	2210
21	Bromsgrove................ d.	0721	0744	0821	0910		1610	1640	1710	1740	1809	1842	1942	2019	2120	2220	2320	0710	0810		1810	1910	1940	2120	|
32	Droitwich Spa............ d.	0730	0754	0830	0920	and	1620	1652	1720	1752	1819	1857	1952	2029	2130	2234	2330	0720	0820	and	1820	1920	1951	2130	2235
40	**Worcester** Shrub Hill . d.	|	0807	|	|	hourly	|	1706c	1732	1804	1832	1910	2012	2036	|	2247	2339	|	|	hourly	1831	1935	|	2147	2243
41	**Worcester** Foregate St d.	0742	0811	0840	0932	until	1630	1709	1735	1807	1835	1940	2015	2047	2141	2310	...	0732	0832	until	1835	1938	2001	2150	...
54	Great Malvern ..... **130** d.	0800a	0822	0853	0945		1643	1722	1747	1819	1849	1954	2027	2100	2154	2323	...	0745	0845		1848	1950	2025	2202	...
65	Ledbury.............. **130** d.	0813	...	0907	0959		1659	...	1800	1831	1904	2010	2041	2116	2209	...	...	0759	0859		1901	...	2039	2215	...
87	**Hereford**............ **130** a.	0833	...	0927	1019		1719	...	1821	1851	1923	2031	2101	2134	2228	...	...	0819	0919		1919	...	2102	2235	...

	⑦	⑦	⑦	⑦	⑦	⑦	⑦	⑦	⑦
Birmingham New St ..d.	1000	1200	1400	1558	1758	1900	2000	2100	2205
Bromsgrove ....d.	1020	1220	1420	1618	1818	1920	2020	2120	2225
Droitwich Spa ....d.	1030	1232	1430	1628	1828	1930	2030	2130	2236
Worcester Shrub Hill..d.	1051b	1247a	1451b	1639	1839	1942a	2058b	2141a	2251a
Worcester Foregate St.d.	1054	1250	1454	1642	1842	1944	2100	2144	2254
Great Malvern......**130** d.	1106	1302	1506	1703	1859	2033	2139	2156	2307
Ledbury ....**130** d.	1118	1315	1518	1716	1912	2048	...	2209	...
Hereford ....**130** a.	1134	1332	1534	1734	1930	2104	...	2227	...

	Ⓐ	Ⓐ	Ⓐ	Ⓐ	Ⓐ	Ⓐ	Ⓐ	Ⓐ	Ⓐ		Ⓐ	Ⓐ
Hereford ....**130** d.	0450	0528	...	...	0709	0732	...	0845	0939		1739	1848
Ledbury ....**130** d.	|	0545	...	...	0725	0750	...	0906	0958		1758	1904
Great Malvern..**130** d.	0548	0559	0647	0702	0737	0807a	0840	0917	1010	and	1810	1915
Worcester F'gate St.d.	0602	0614	0658	0716	0749	0824a	0852	0930	1024	hourly	1824	1928
Worcester Shrub H d.	|	0626	0706a	0723a	0755	|	|	0936	|	until	|	|
Droitwich Spa ....d.	0611	0633	0713	0733	0805	0833	0901	0943	1033		1833	1937
Bromsgrove ....d.	0621	0643	0723	|	|	0843	0911	0953	1043		1842	1947
Birmingham N St...a.	0649	0709	0749	0809	0839	0909	0939	1019	1109		1909	2018

	Ⓐ	Ⓐ	Ⓐ	Ⓐ	⑥	⑥	⑥	⑥		⑥	⑥	⑥	⑥	⑥	⑥	⑦	⑦	⑦	⑦	⑦	⑦	⑦	⑦	⑦	⑦
Hereford ....**130** d.	1950	2056	2129	2259	...	0617	0739	0839		1739	1911	1959	2020	2135	2249	...	1005	1202	1405	1609	1634	1809	1830	2005	2239
Ledbury ....**130** d.	2009	2114	2145	2315	...	0634	0758	0858		1758	1928	2015	2040	2151	2305	...	1022	1218	1422	1625	1652	1825	1848	2022	2258
Great Malvern......**130** d.	2020	2125	2156	2327	0622	0717	0810	0910	and	1810	1939	2027	2130	2203	2317	...	1034	1230	1434	1637	1705	1837	1911	2037	2310
Worcester Foregate St d.	2031	2136	2210	2339	0634	0728	0824	0924	hourly	1824	1951	2040	2142	2215	2328	0854	1046	1242	1446	1649	1724	1849	1949	2049	2323
Worcester Shrub Hill. d.	2037	2139	|	2347	|	0735	|	|	until	|	|	|	2154c	2247	2336	0902a	1058c	1255c	1455a	1655	1757	1855	1955	2055	2327
Droitwich Spa .... d.	2045	...	2219	...	0643	0743	0833	0933		1833	2000	2049	2202	2255	...	0910	1106	1303	1503	1703	1805	1903	2003	2103	...
Bromsgrove .... d.	2055	...	2229	...	0653	0753	0843	0943		1843	|	2059	|	|	...	0920	1115	1313	1513	1713	1815	1913	2013	2113	...
Birmingham New St . a.	2120	...	2254	...	0718	0818	0909	1009		1909	2055n	2120	2255n	2336n	...	0944	1138	1338	1538	1738	1838	1938	2038	2138	...

a – Arrives 5 minutes earlier. b – Arrives 14 minutes earlier. c – Arrives 10 minutes earlier. n – Birmingham Snow Hill.

LM 2nd class BIRMINGHAM - KIDDERMINSTER - WORCESTER 126

km		Ⓐ	⑥	Ⓐ	⑥	Ⓐ	⑥	Ⓐ	Ⓐ	⑥		⚒	⚒	⚒	⚒	⚒	⚒	⚒	⚒	⚒	⚒	⚒	⚒	⑥	Ⓐ	⚒
0	**Birmingham** Moor St... d.	0604	0633	0649	0701	0719	0749	0749	0834	0845	...	0909	0939	1009	1039	1109	1139	1209	1239	1309	1339	1409	1439	1509	1509	1539
1	**Birmingham** Snow Hill. d.	0607	0637	0653	0705	0723	0753	0753	0843	0853	...	0913	0943	1013	1043	1113	1143	1213	1243	1313	1343	1413	1443	1513	1513	1543
20	Stourbridge Junction... d.	0636	0706	0722	0734	0752	0819	0822	0909	0922	...	0939	1009	1039	1109	1139	1209	1239	1309	1339	1409	1439	1509	1539	1539	1608
31	Kidderminster.........△ d.	0648	0717	0734	0745	0804	0831	0834	0920	0933	...	0947	1018	1047	1118	1147	1218	1247	1318	1347	1418	1447	1518	1547	1552	1618
45	Droitwich Spa............ d.	0658	0731	0747	0756	0817	0842	0847	0930	0944	...	1000	1030	1100	1130	1200	1230	1300	1330	1400	1430	1500	1530	1600	1606	1630
54	**Worcester** Shrub Hill. a.	|	0740	|	0805	0824	|	|	0940	0952	...	|	1038r	|	1138	|	1238t	|	1338r	1408t	1440	1510t	1538r	|	1614	|
54	**Worcester** Foregate St. a.	0709	...	0757	0813	0833	0851	0858	...	...	...	1009	1039t	1109	1157r	1209	1239r	1309	1340t	1409r	1446	1509r	1539t	1609	1625	1642

	⚒	⑥	Ⓐ	⑥	Ⓐ	Ⓐ	⑥	Ⓐ	⑥	Ⓐ	⑥	⚒	⑥	Ⓐ	⑥	Ⓐ	⑥	Ⓐ	⚒	⑦	⑦	⑦	⑦	⑦	⑦	⑦
Birmingham Moor St.. d.	1609	1639	1639	1709	1709	1732	1739	1749	1819	1839	1849	1924	1953	1954	2052	2053	2152	2154	2257	0924	1015	1115	1215	1315	1415	1515
Birmingham Snow Hill d.	1613	1643	1643	1713	1713	1736	1743	1753	1823	1843	1853	1928	1956	1958	2056	2058	2156	2158	2301	0928	1022	1122	1222	1322	1422	1522
Stourbridge Junction .. d.	1639	1709	1710	1739	1739	1802	1809	1820	1849	1909	1923	1957	2025	2027	2125	2127	2225	2227	2330	0954	1047	1147	1247	1347	1447	1547
Kidderminster.........△ d.	1647	1718	1722	1749	1752	1814	1822	1832	1900	1920	1934	2009	2036	2039	2136	2139	2236	2239	2342	1003	1059	1159	1259	1357	1459	1557
Droitwich Spa .... d.	1700	1730	1737	1802	1804	1828	1837	1845	1914	1932	1946	2022	2048	2050	2148	2152	2250	2252	2354	1015	1111	1211	1311	1408	1511	1608
Worcester Shrub Hill a.	|	|	|	1812	1812	|	|	|	|	|	1954	2031r	2056	2059	2156	2159	2257	2259	0005	1022	1119	1219	|	|	|	|
Worcester Foregate St a.	1709	1739	1746	1822	...	1839	1846	1854	1923	1943	...	2031t	2101	...	...	2208	2304	2310	...	1032	1135	...	1320	1417	1520	1617

	⑦	⑦	⑦	⑦	⑦	⑦	⑦	⑦
Birmingham Moor St.. d.	1615	1702	1715	1815	1915	2015	2143	2252
Birmingham Snow Hill d.	1622	1706	1722	1822	1922	2022	2146	2256
Stourbridge Junction .. d.	1647	1724	1747	1847	1947	2047	2210	2322
Kidderminster.........△ d.	1657	1733	1757	1859	1957	2057	2220	2331
Droitwich Spa .... d.	1708	1745	1809	1911	2009	2109	2231	2343
Worcester Shrub Hill a.	|	1752	|	1919	2017	2117	2239	2351
Worcester Foregate St a.	1717	...	1819	...	...	2124	...	...

	Ⓐ	⑥	Ⓐ	⑥	Ⓐ	Ⓐ	⑥	Ⓐ	Ⓐ	⑥	Ⓐ	⑥	Ⓐ
Worcester Foregate St ... d.	...	...	...	...	...	...	...	0714	...	0747	0802	...	0839
Worcester Shrub Hill ... d.	0530	0544	0612	0625	0635	0650	0701	|	0735	|	|	0815	0845
Droitwich Spa .... d.	0538	0552	0620	0633	0643	0703	0709	0723	0743	0756	0811	0823	0853
Kidderminster .... △ d.	0548	0605	0633	0646	0656	0716	0722	0736	0754	0806	0824	0836	0906
Stourbridge Junction ...... d.	0556	0617	0649	0701	0708	0728	0735	0748	0807	0819	0835	0848	0918
Birmingham Snow Hill .... a.	0627	0647	0722	0732	0738	0759	0805	0815	0835	0845	0907	0915	0945
Birmingham Moor St ...... a.	0638	0653	0728	0740	0743	0806	0810	0820	0840	0850	0911	0920	0950

	⑥	Ⓐ	⑥	⑥	Ⓐ	⚒	⚒	⚒	⚒	⚒	⚒	⚒		⚒	⚒	⚒	⚒	Ⓐ	⑥	Ⓐ	⑥	Ⓐ	⚒	⑥	Ⓐ	⑥	Ⓐ
Worcester Foregate St d.	0856	0903	0916	...	...	1016	...	1116t	1151	1216	1251r	...	...	1351	1416	...	1516r	1533	1547	1613	1614	1634	1647	...	1715	1747	1756
Worcester Shrub Hill d.	|	|	|	0948	0952	|	1052	1117r	|	|	1252t	1317	...	|	|	1452	1517t	1547	|	|	|	1640	|	1715	|	|	|
Droitwich Spa .... d.	0905	0912	0925	0956	1000	1025	1100	1125	1200	1225	1300	1325	...	1400	1425	1500	1525	1555	1556	1622	1623	1648	1655	1723	1725	1756	1805
Kidderminster.........△ d.	0916	0925	0938	1006	1010	1038	1110	1138	1210	1238	1310	1338	...	1410	1438	1510	1538	1606	1610	1635	1636	1701	1706	1736	1738	1806	1815
Stourbridge Junction .. d.	0927	0937	0948	1014	1018	1048	1118	1148	1218	1248	1318	1348	...	1418	1448	1518	1548	1618	1618	1648	1648	1712	1718	1748	1750	1818	1825
Birmingham Snow Hill a.	0956	1004	1015	1041	1045	1115	1145	1215	1245	1315	1345	1415	...	1445	1515	1545	1616	1645	1645	1718	1715	1739	1745	1815	1817	1845	1855
Birmingham Moor St.. a.	1001	1010	1020	1050	1050	1120	1150	1220	1250	1320	1350	1420	...	1450	1520	1550	1620	1650	1650	1725	1720	1745	1750	1820	1825	1858	1900

	⑥	Ⓐ	Ⓐ	⑥	Ⓐ	⑥	⚒		⚒	Ⓐ	⑥	⑦	⑦	⑦	⑦	⑦	⑦	⑦	⑦	⑦	⑦	⑦	⑦	⑦	⑦	⑦
Worcester Foregate St d.	1812	...	1846	1851	1946	1951	2051t	...	2142r	2217	...	0920	1026	1114	1220	1326	1426	[illegible]	[illegible]	1620	1721	1820	...	...	2118	2223
Worcester Shrub Hill d.	1817	1827	|	|	|	|	2052t	...	2154	2227	2247	0926	|	1126	1226	|	|	|	|	|	|	|	1938	2038	2125	2229
Droitwich Spa .... d.	1825	1845	1855	1900	1955	2000	2100	...	2202	2235	2255	0935	1035	1135	1235	1335	1435	1537	1554	1635	1736	1835	1946	2046	2133	2237
Kidderminster.........△ d.	1837	1855	1910	1913	2010	2013	2113	...	2213	2248	2305	0945	1045	1145	1245	1345	1445	1547	1604	1645	1746	1845	1956	2056	2143	2247
Stourbridge Junction .. d.	1850	1906	1925	1925	2025	2025	2125	...	2225	2259	2318	0957	1057	1157	1257	1357	1457	1557	1617	1657	1759	1855	2007	2107	2153	2257
Birmingham Snow Hill a.	1916	1934	1955	1955	2055	2055	2155	...	2255	2328	2336	1022	1122	1222	1322	1422	1522	1623	1636	1722	1824	1921	2033	2133	2219	2325
Birmingham Moor St.. a.	1920	...	2000	2000	2100	2100	2200	...	2300	2337	2340	1030	1130	1230	1330	1430	1530	1630	1645	1730	1830	1925	2037	2137	2223	...

r – ⑥ only. t – Ⓐ only. △ – **Severn Valley Railway** (🚂 Kidderminster - Bridgnorth: *26 km*). ✆ 01299 403816. www.svr.co.uk.

LM 2nd class STRATFORD UPON AVON - BIRMINGHAM 127

km		Ⓐ	Ⓐ	Ⓐ	Ⓐ	Ⓐ	Ⓐ	Ⓐ		Ⓐ	Ⓐ	Ⓐ	Ⓐ	Ⓐ	Ⓐ	Ⓐ	Ⓐ	Ⓐ	Ⓐ	Ⓐ	Ⓐ	⑥	⑥
0	**Stratford upon Avon** ...d.	0626	0652	0719	0743	0826	0926	1003	and at	1603	1626	1727	1755	1827	1851	1903	1926	2026	2126	2233	2330	0700	0743
13	Henley in Arden ....d.	0641	0707	0735	0758	0841	0941	|	the same	|	1641	1743	1807	1843	1907	|	1941	2041	2139	2246	|	0715	0758
40	**Birmingham** Moor St....d.	0724	0749	0808	0839	0918	1018	1049	minutes past each	1649	1719	1818	1839	1919	1935	1954	2018	2118	2218	2319	0006	0755	0838
41	**Birmingham** Snow Hill .a.	0726	0751	0810	0841	0920	1020	1052	hour until	1652	1721	1821	1841	1922	1937	1956	2020	2120	2220	2321	0008	0757	0840

	⑥	⑥		⑥	⑥	⑥	⑥	⑥	⑥	⑥	⑥	⑥	⑥	⑦	⑦	⑦	⑦	⑦	⑦	⑦	⑦	⑦	⑦	⑦
Stratford upon Avon...d.	0826	0903	and at the same	1703	1726	1754	1813	1848	1926	2026	2126	2233	2330	0929	1029	1129	1229	1329	1429	1529	1629	1729	1829	1929
Henley in Arden............d.	0841	|	minutes	|	1741	1808	1828	1903	1941	2041	2140	2247	|	0943	1043	1143	1243	1343	1443	1543	1643	1743	1843	1943
Birmingham Moor St ...d.	0918	0949	past each	1749	1819	1839	1909	1944	2018	2118	2218	2319	0008	1015	1115	1215	1315	1415	1515	1615	1715	1815	1915	2015
Birmingham Snow Hill .a.	0920	0952	hour until	1752	1821	1843	1911	1946	2020	2120	2220	2322	0010	1017	1117	1217	1317	1417	1517	1617	1717	1817	1917	2017

	Ⓐ	Ⓐ	Ⓐ	Ⓐ	Ⓐ	Ⓐ	Ⓐ		Ⓐ	Ⓐ	Ⓐ	Ⓐ	Ⓐ	Ⓐ	Ⓐ	Ⓐ	Ⓐ	Ⓐ	Ⓐ	Ⓐ	⑥	⑥	⑥
Birmingham Snow Hill .d.	0553	0630	0640	0725	0828	0858	0928	and at the same	1458	1528	1628	1703	1728	1747	1758	1828	1928	2028	2128	2228	0725	0828	0858
Birmingham Moor St ...d.	0556	0633	0643	0728	0831	0901	0931	minutes	1501	1531	1631	1706	1731	1750	1801	1831	1931	2031	2131	2231	0728	0831	0901
Henley in Arden............d.	|	0705	0720	0806	0906	|	1006	past each	|	1606	1707	1736	1807	1828	|	1907	2007	2107	2207	2307	0806	0906	|
Stratford upon Avon...a.	0648	0720	0736	0823	0923	0949	1023	hour until	1541	1623	1724	1749	1824	1843	1859	1923	2023	2123	2223	2323	0821	0923	0949

	⑥	⑥	⑥		⑥	⑥	⑥	⑥	⑥	⑥	⑥	⑥	⑥		⑦	⑦	⑦	⑦	⑦	⑦	⑦	⑦	⑦	⑦
Birmingham Snow Hill .d.	0928	0958	1028	and at the same	1628	1658	1707	1747	1828	1928	2028	2128	2228	...	0927	1027	1127	1227	1327	1427	1527	1627	1727	1827
Birmingham Moor St ...d.	0931	1001	1031	minutes	1631	1701	1710	1750	1831	1931	2031	2131	2231	...	0930	1030	1130	1230	1330	1430	1530	1630	1730	1830
Henley in Arden............d.	1006	|	1106	past each	1706	|	1748	1828	1906	2007	2107	2207	2307	...	1001	1101	1201	1301	1401	1501	1601	1701	1801	1901
Stratford upon Avon...a.	1023	1041	1123	hour until	1723	1741	1803	1843	1923	2023	2123	2223	2323	...	1015	1115	1215	1315	1415	1515	1615	1715	1815	1915

🚂 – THE SHAKESPEARE EXPRESS – (12). ✕ (1st class only) and 🍷 Birmingham Snow Hill - Stratford upon Avon and v.v. Runs ⑦ July 16 - Sept. 3, 2017. National Rail tickets NOT valid. From Birmingham Snow Hill 1000 and 1356 (Birmingham Moor Street 5 minutes later). From Stratford upon Avon at 1236 and 1613. Journey time: 59–68 minutes. To book contact Vintage Trains Ltd. ✆ 0121 708 4960. www.shakespeareexpress.com.

LONDON - BIRMINGHAM

km	Ⓐ	Ⓐ	Ⓐ	Ⓐ	Ⓐ	Ⓐ	Ⓐ	Ⓐ	Ⓐ	Ⓐ	Ⓐ	Ⓐ	Ⓐ	Ⓐ	Ⓐ	Ⓐ	Ⓐ	Ⓐ	Ⓐ	Ⓐ	Ⓐ	Ⓐ
0	**London** Marylebone ◇ d.	...	0605	0711	0748	0814	0837	0910	0940	1010	1040	1110	1140	1210	1240	1310	1340	1410	1440	1510	1540	1615
45	High Wycombe ◇ d.	...	|	|	0814	|	|	0936	|	1036	|	1135	|	1234	|	1334	|	1434	|	1536	|	|
88	Bicester North ◇ d.	0546	0647	0754	0836	|	0926	|	1030	|	1131	|	1227	|	1327	|	1427	|	1527	|	1627	|
111	Banbury 119 ◇ d.	0604	0703	0807	0850	0908	0940	1008	1043	1107	1145	1207	1240	1307	1340	1410	1440	1507	1540	1609	1640	1708
143	Leamington Spa 119 d.	0624	0721	0825	0907	0926	0958	1025	1101	1125	1204	1226	1258	1325	1358	1427	1458	1525	1558	1626	1658	1726
146	Warwick d.	0629	0726	0829	0912	0930	1003	|	1105	|	1209	|	1302	|	1402	|	1502	|	1602	|	1702	|
147	Warwick Parkway d.	0632	0729	0833	0915	0934	1017	1032	1109	1132	1213	1232	1306	1332	1406	1433	1506	1530	1606	1632	1706	1732
169	Solihull a.	0648	0750	0844	0930	0945	1023	1044	1124	1144	1230	1244	1321	1344	1421	1444	1521	1544	1621	1643	1721	1744
180	**Birmingham** Moor Street 126 a.	0658	0802	0853	0942	0954	1035	1053	1133	1156	1241	1256	1333	1356	1433	1456	1533	1556	1633	1653	1736	1754
181	**Birmingham** Snow Hill 126 a.	0703	0807	0858	...	0959	...	1058	1139	...	1248	...	1338	...	1438	...	1538	...	1638	1658	1741	1757
198	Stourbridge Junction 126 a.	...	...	...	...	...	...	...	...	...	...	...	...	...	...	...	...	...	...	...	...	1825
210	Kidderminster 126 a.	...	...	...	...	...	...	...	...	...	...	...	...	...	...	...	...	...	...	...	...	1841

	Ⓐ	Ⓐ	Ⓐ	Ⓐ	Ⓐ	Ⓐ	Ⓐ	Ⓐ	Ⓐ	Ⓐ	Ⓐ	Ⓐ	Ⓐ	Ⓐ	Ⓐ	⑥	⑥	⑥	⑥	⑥	⑥	⑥
London Marylebone ◇ d.	1621	1647	1715	1747	1815	1847	1915	1947	2010	2040	2110	2140	2210	2237	2307	...	0700	0810	0840	0910	0940	1010
High Wycombe ◇ d.	1648	|	|	|	|	|	|	|	2034	2105	2136	2204	2235	2302	|	0612	0724	0834	|	0934	|	1034
Bicester North ◇ d.	1711	1734	|	1835	|	1936	2003	2034	2058	2126	2201	2228	2259	2327	2350	0645	0751	0857	0926	|	1024	|
Banbury 119 ◇ d.	1724	1747	1809	1848	1910	1951	2016	2047	2112	2139	2214	2241	2313	2341	0003	0703	0804	0910	0940	1007	1037	1107
Leamington Spa 119 d.	1741	1804	1827	1905	1928	2009	2035	2104	2130	2157	2231	2259	2331	2359	0021	0721	0823	0928	0958	1025	1055	1125
Warwick d.	|	1808	|	1909	|	2013	|	2108	|	2201	|	2303	|	0003	0025	0725	|	0932	1002	|	1059	|
Warwick Parkway d.	1747	1812	1834	1913	1934	2017	2043	2112	2136	2205	2238	2307	2337	0007	0029	0729	0829	0935	1006	1031	1103	1132
Solihull a.	1802	1826	1849	1928	1950	2032	2058	2133	2148	2220	2250	2330	2348	0023	0040	0747	0846	0950	1021	1043	1120	1144
Birmingham Moor Street 126 a.	1811	1838	1859	1938	2000	2041	2110	2143	2158	2230	2300	2339	0001	0036	0052	0803	0859	1001	1033	1058	1133	1159
Birmingham Snow Hill 126 a.	1819	...	1902	1943	2004	2046	...	2148	2206	2235	2304	2344	...	...	...	...	0907	1009	1041	...	1141	...
Stourbridge Junction 126 a.	...	...	1926	...	2033	...	...	...	2236	...	2349	...	...	...	...	...	...	...	...	...	...	...
Kidderminster 126 a.	...	...	1938	...	2045	...	...	...	2247	...	...	...	...	...	...	...	...	...	...	...	...	...

	⑥	⑥	⑥	⑥	⑥	⑥	⑥	⑥	⑥	⑥	⑥	⑥	⑥	⑥	⑥	⑥	⑥	⑥	⑥	⑥	⑥	⑥	⑥
London Marylebone ◇ d.	1040	1110	1140	1210	1240	1310	1340	1410	1440	1510	1540	1610	1640	1710	1740	1810	1840	1910	1940	2010	2040	2110	2210
High Wycombe ◇ d.	|	1134	|	1234	|	1334	|	1434	|	1534	|	1634	|	1734	|	1834	|	1934	|	2034	|	2134	2234
Bicester North ◇ d.	1127	|	1224	|	1324	|	1424	|	1524	|	1624	|	1724	|	1824	|	1924	|	2024	|	2124	2157	2257
Banbury 119 ◇ d.	1143	1210	1237	1307	1337	1409	1437	1507	1537	1609	1637	1707	1737	1809	1837	1907	1937	2009	2037	2107	2137	2210	2310
Leamington Spa 119 d.	1201	1227	1255	1325	1355	1426	1455	1525	1555	1626	1655	1725	1755	1826	1855	1926	1955	2027	2055	2125	2155	2228	2328
Warwick d.	1205	|	1259	|	1359	|	1459	|	1559	|	1659	|	1759	|	1859	|	1959	|	2059	|	2159	2232	2332
Warwick Parkway d.	1209	1234	1303	1332	1403	1433	1503	1532	1603	1633	1703	1732	1803	1833	1903	1933	2003	2033	2103	2132	2203	2236	2337
Solihull a.	1224	1245	1320	1344	1420	1444	1520	1544	1620	1644	1720	1744	1820	1847	1918	1946	2018	2045	2118	2144	2218	2256	2354
Birmingham Moor Street 126 a.	1233	1259	1333	1359	1433	1459	1533	1559	1633	1659	1733	1759	1833	1858	1927	1958	2027	2100	2127	2200	2227	2306	0009
Birmingham Snow Hill 126 a.	1241	...	1341	...	1441	...	1541	...	1641	...	1741	...	1841	1907	1935	2007	2035	...	2135	...	2235	2314	...
Stourbridge Junction 126 a.	...	...	...	...	...	...	...	...	...	...	...	...	...	...	...	...	...	...	...	...	...	...	...
Kidderminster 126 a.	...	...	...	...	...	...	...	...	...	...	...	...	...	...	...	...	...	...	...	...	...	...	...

	⑦	⑦	⑦	⑦	⑦	⑦	⑦	⑦	⑦		⑦	⑦	⑦	⑦	⑦		⑦	⑦	⑦	⑦	⑦
London Marylebone ◇ d.	0815	0910	0940	1010	1040	1110	1140	1210	1240		1710	1740	1810	1840	1910	...	1940	2010	2040	2110	2208
High Wycombe ◇ d.	0845	0934	|	1034	|	1134	|	1234	|	and at	1734	|	1835	|	1934	...	|	2034	|	2134	2234
Bicester North ◇ d.	0910	|	1024	|	1124	|	1224	|	1326	the	|	1826	|	1926	|	...	2026	|	2126	|	2256
Banbury 119 ◇ d.	0929	1007	1037	1107	1137	1207	1237	1307	1339	same	1807	1839	1907	1939	2007	...	2039	2107	2139	2207	2309
Leamington Spa 119 d.	0947	1025	1055	1125	1155	1225	1255	1325	1357	minutes	1825	1857	1925	1957	2025	...	2057	2125	2157	2225	2327
Warwick d.	0951	|	1059	|	1159	|	1259	|	1401	past	|	1901	|	2001	|	...	2101	|	2201	2229	2331
Warwick Parkway d.	0955	1032	1103	1132	1203	1232	1303	1332	1405	each	1832	1905	1932	2005	2032	...	2105	2132	2205	2234	2334
Solihull a.	1016	1044	1118	1144	1218	1244	1320	1344	1420	hour	1844	1920	1943	2020	2044	...	2128	2144	2220	2257	2349
Birmingham Moor Street a.	1024	1053	1127	1156	1227	1256	1329	1356	1429	until	1856	1929	1956	2029	2056	...	2137	2156	2229	2306	2358
Birmingham Snow Hill a.	1029	1058	1132	...	1232	...	1334	...	1434		...	1934	...	2034	...	...	2142	...	2234	2311	0004

	Ⓐ	Ⓐ	Ⓐ	Ⓐ	Ⓐ	Ⓐ	Ⓐ	Ⓐ	Ⓐ	Ⓐ	Ⓐ	Ⓐ	Ⓐ	Ⓐ	Ⓐ	Ⓐ	Ⓐ	Ⓐ	Ⓐ	Ⓐ	Ⓐ	Ⓐ
Kidderminster 126 d.	...	...	...	...	...	0609	...	0705	0730	...	0809	...	...	...	...	...	...	...	...	...	...	...
Stourbridge Junction 126 d.	...	...	...	...	...	0618	0638	0714	0738	...	0823	...	...	...	...	...	...	...	...	...	...	...
Birmingham Snow Hill 126 d.	...	...	...	...	...	0650	0707	0750	0807	0822	0852	0912	...	1012	...	1112	...	1212	...	1312	...	1412
Birmingham Moor Street 126 d.	...	0515	0542	0610	0628	0655	0711	0754	0810	0825	0855	0915	0955	1015	1055	1115	1155	1215	1255	1315	1355	1415
Solihull d.	...	0524	0551	0619	0638	0704	0720	0803	0819	0837	0907	0924	1004	1024	1104	1124	1204	1224	1304	1324	1404	1424
Warwick Parkway d.	...	0536	0605	0634	0659	0718	0739	0815	0834	0902	0919	0939	1016	1039	1116	1139	1216	1239	1316	1339	1416	1439
Warwick d.	...	|	0608	|	0702	|	|	|	0837	0906	|	0942	|	1042	|	1142	|	1242	|	1342	|	1442
Leamington Spa 119 d.	...	0541	0613	0641	0706	0724	0746	0821	0842	0912	0925	0946	1022	1046	1123	1146	1222	1246	1322	1346	1422	1446
Banbury 119 ◇ d.	0517	0559	0631	0659	0724	|	0806	0840	0900	0930	0944	1004	1040	1104	1140	1204	1240	1304	1340	1404	1440	1504
Bicester North ◇ d.	0533	0611	0646	0711	0739	|	|	|	0913	0942	|	1016	|	1116	|	1216	|	1317	|	1416	|	1516
High Wycombe ◇ d.	0600	0635	|	|	|	|	|	|	|	1008	|	|	1110	|	1210	|	1310	|	1410	|	1510	|
London Marylebone ◇ a.	0630	0703	0735	0802	0833	0834	0907	0938	0959	1036	1040	1108	1140	1208	1241	1308	1341	1408	1441	1508	1538	1608

	Ⓐ	Ⓐ	Ⓐ	Ⓐ	Ⓐ	Ⓐ	Ⓐ	Ⓐ	Ⓐ	Ⓐ	Ⓐ	Ⓐ	⑥	⑥	⑥	⑥	⑥	⑥	⑥	⑥	⑥	⑥
Kidderminster 126 d.	...	...	...	...	...	...	...	...	...	...	...	...	...	...	...	...	0637	0712	...	0813	...	0910
Stourbridge Junction 126 d.	...	...	...	...	...	...	...	...	...	...	...	...	...	...	...	...	0645	0722	...	0824	...	0920
Birmingham Snow Hill 126 d.	...	1512	...	1612	1652	1707	1752	1812	1840	1917	2015	2115	...	...	0612	0646	0712	0751	...	0853	0912	0951
Birmingham Moor Street 126 d.	1455	1515	1555	1615	1655	1710	1755	1815	1843	1920	2018	2118	...	...	0615	0649	0715	0755	0815	0856	0915	0955
Solihull d.	1504	1524	1604	1624	1704	1719	1806	1824	1852	1929	2027	2127	...	...	0624	0702	0724	0805	0824	0905	0924	1004
Warwick Parkway d.	1516	1539	1616	1639	1716	1736	1822	1845	1907	1949	2042	2147	...	...	0644	0714	0739	0818	0839	0916	0939	1019
Warwick d.	|	1542	|	1642	1719	1739	|	1848	|	1952	2045	2150	...	...	0647	|	0742	|	0842	|	0942	|
Leamington Spa 119 d.	1522	1546	1622	1646	1723	1743	1828	1853	1912	1957	2050	2155	...	...	0652	0720	0746	0824	0846	0922	0946	1025
Banbury 119 ◇ d.	1540	1604	1640	1704	1741	1801	1846	1912	1930	2015	2113	2213	0604	0629	0710	0739	0804	0844	0904	0940	1004	1044
Bicester North ◇ d.	|	1616	|	1716	|	1814	1858	1928	1946	2027	2125	2225	0618	0646	0722	0751	0816	|	0916	|	1016	|
High Wycombe ◇ d.	1610	|	1710	|	1811	1838	|	|	2013	|	2145	2245	0647	0710	0746	0811	|	0914	|	1014	|	1118
London Marylebone ◇ a.	1641	1712	1742	1813	1839	1911	1944	2023	2043	2113	2212	2311	0724	0736	0813	0840	0910	0941	1010	1041	1110	1146

	⑥	⑥	⑥	⑥	⑥	⑥	⑥	⑥	⑥	⑥	⑥	⑥	⑥	⑥	⑥	⑥	⑥	⑥	⑥	⑥	⑥	⑥	⑥
Kidderminster 126 d.	...	...	...	...	...	...	...	...	...	...	...	...	...	...	...	...	...	...	...	...	...	...	...
Stourbridge Junction 126 d.	...	...	...	...	...	...	...	...	...	...	...	...	...	...	...	...	...	...	...	...	...	...	...
Birmingham Snow Hill 126 d.	1012	...	1112	...	1212	...	1312	...	1412	...	1512	...	1612	...	1712	...	1812	...	1912	...	2012	...	2115
Birmingham Moor Street 126 d.	1015	1055	1115	1155	1215	1255	1315	1355	1415	1455	1515	1555	1615	1655	1715	1755	1815	1855	1915	1955	2015	2045	2118
Solihull d.	1024	1104	1124	1204	1224	1304	1324	1404	1424	1504	1524	1604	1624	1704	1724	1804	1824	1904	1924	2004	2024	2055	2127
Warwick Parkway d.	1039	1116	1139	1220	1239	1316	1339	1416	1439	1516	1539	1616	1639	1716	1739	1816	1839	1916	1939	2016	2039	2113	2149
Warwick d.	1042	|	1142	|	1242	|	1342	|	1442	|	1542	|	1642	|	1742	|	1842	|	1942	|	2042	2117	2152
Leamington Spa 119 d.	1046	1121	1146	1226	1246	1322	1346	1422	1446	1522	1546	1622	1646	1722	1746	1822	1846	1922	1946	2022	2046	2122	2157
Banbury 119 ◇ d.	1104	1139	1204	1244	1304	1340	1407	1440	1504	1540	1604	1640	1704	1740	1804	1840	1904	1940	2004	2040	2104	2140	2215
Bicester North ◇ d.	1116	|	1216	|	1316	|	1420	|	1516	|	1616	|	1716	|	1816	|	1916	|	2016	|	2116	2152	2230
High Wycombe ◇ d.	|	1214	|	1314	|	1414	|	1514	|	1614	|	1714	|	1814	|	1914	|	2014	|	2114	|	2214	2301
London Marylebone ◇ a.	1211	1241	1310	1341	1411	1441	1510	1541	1610	1646	1710	1741	1810	1841	1910	1941	2010	2041	2110	2141	2210	2241	2333

	⑦	⑦	⑦	⑦	⑦	⑦	⑦	⑦	⑦	⑦	⑦		⑦	⑦	⑦	⑦	⑦	⑦	⑦	⑦	⑦
Birmingham Snow Hill d.	...	...	...	0912	...	1012	...	1112	...	1212	...		...	1712	...	1812	...	1912	...	2012	2115
Birmingham Moor Street d.	...	0825	0855	0915	0955	1015	1055	1115	1155	1215	1255	and at	1655	1715	1755	1815	1855	1915	1939	2015	2118
Solihull d.	...	0834	0904	0924	1004	1024	1104	1124	1204	1224	1304	the	1704	1724	1804	1824	1904	1924	1948	2024	2127
Warwick Parkway d.	...	0849	0916	0939	1016	1039	1116	1139	1216	1239	1316	same	1716	1739	1816	1839	1916	1939	|	2039	2144
Warwick d.	...	0852	|	0942	|	1042	|	1142	|	1242	|	minutes	|	1742	|	1842	|	1942	2011	2042	2147
Leamington Spa 119 d.	...	0858	0922	0946	1022	1046	1122	1146	1222	1246	1322	past	1722	1746	1822	1846	1922	1946	2017	2046	2152
Banbury 119 ◇ d.	0849	0916	0940	1004	1040	1104	1140	1204	1240	1304	1340	each	1740	1805	1840	1904	1941	2004	2036	2104	2215
Bicester North ◇ d.	0903	0929	|	1016	|	1118	|	1216	|	1316	|	hour	|	1819	|	1916	1953	2016	2052	2116	2230
High Wycombe ◇ d.	0932	|	1013	|	1114	|	1213	|	1313	|	1413	until	1812	|	1913	|	2016	|	2116	|	2301
London Marylebone ◇ a.	1006	1018	1041	1108	1142	1210	1240	1310	1340	1410	1440		1840	1910	1940	2010	2043	2108	2153	2212	2342

◇ – Frequent additional services are available between these stations.

LONDON - STRATFORD UPON AVON

km		Ⓐ	Ⓐ	Ⓐ	Ⓐ	Ⓐ		Ⓐ	Ⓐ	Ⓐ	Ⓐ	⑥	⑥	⑥	⑥	⑥	⑥	⑥	⑦	⑦	⑦		⑦	⑦
0	**London** Marylebone d.	...	0617	0814	1010	1210	...	1410	1621	1824	2043	0700	1010	1210	1410	1610	1810	2010	0943	1210	1410	...	1610	1810
45	High Wycombe d.	...	0701	|	1036	1234	...	1434	1648	1900	2114	0724	1034	1234	1434	1634	1834	2034	1018	1234	1434	...	1634	1835
88	Bicester North d.	0546	0733	|	|	|	...	|	1711	1941	2143	0751	|	|	|	|	|	|	1047	|	|	...	|	|
111	Banbury 119 d.	0604	0749	0908	1107	1307	...	1507	1724	2006	2201	0804	1107	1307	1507	1707	1907	2107	1111	1307	1507	...	1707	1907
143	Leamington Spa 119 a.	0623	0808	0925	1124	1324	...	1524	1741	2025	2219	0822	1124	1324	1524	1724	1924	2124	1130	1324	1524	...	1724	1924
143	Leamington Spa d.	0653	0808	0940	1132	1332	...	1532	1811	2026	2220	0830	1132	1332	1532	1732	1932	2132	1132	1332	1532	...	1732	1932
146	Warwick d.	0658	0813	0945	1137	1337	...	1537	1816	|	2224	0834	1138	1337	1537	1737	1937	2137	1138	1337	1537	...	1737	1937
165	**Stratford u. Avon** Pkwy. a.	0722	0837	1008	1157	1401	...	1601	1846	2050	2245	0901	1155	1400	1558	1805	2000	2200	1157	1356	1556	...	1756	1956
167	**Stratford upon Avon** a.	0728	0843	1014	1203	1407	...	1607	1851	2054	2253	0912	1205	1409	1608	1815	2010	2210	1204	1403	1603	...	1803	2003

	Ⓐ	Ⓐ	Ⓐ	Ⓐ	Ⓐ	Ⓐ	Ⓐ	Ⓐ	Ⓐ	Ⓐ	⑥	⑥	⑥	⑥	⑥	⑥	⑥	⑥	⑦	⑦	⑦	⑦	⑦	⑦
Stratford upon Avon d.	0606	0733	0900	1037	1240	1437	1736	1912h	2139	2315	0756	1040	1242	1442	1641	1841	2042	2215	0938	1246	1446	1646	1846	2038
Stratford u. Avon Pkwy. d.	0610	0737	0904	1041	1244	1441	1740	1916h	2143	|	0800	1044	1246	1446	1645	1845	2046	|	0941	1250	1450	1650	1850	2042
Warwick d.	0640	0803	0927	1104	1304	1505	1803	1952	2206	2334	0824	1108	1309	1509	1709	1909	2109	2235	1001	1311	1511	1711	1911	2103
Leamington Spa a.	0645	0807	0934	1111	1311	1515	1807	1956	2210	2338	0828	1115	1316	1516	1716	1916	2115	2240	1005	1317	1517	1717	1917	2107
Leamington Spa 119 d.	0706	0808	0946	1123	1322	1546	1808	1957	2210	2339	0829	1146	1346	1546	1746	1946	2157	2241	1006	1346	1546	1746	1946	2108
Banbury 119 d.	0724	0827	1004	1140	1340	1604	1827	2015	2230	2357	0848	1204	1407	1604	1804	2004	2215	2302	1024	1404	1604	1805	2004	2128
Bicester North d.	0739	0841	1016	|	|	1616	1843	2027	2246	...	0903	1216	1420	1616	1816	2016	2230	...	1036	1416	1618	1819	2016	2142
High Wycombe d.	|	0905	|	1210	1410	|	|	|	2317	...	0930	|	|	|	|	|	2301	...	1103	|	|	|	|	2213
London Marylebone a.	0833	0935	1108	1241	1441	1712	1941	2113	2358	...	1005	1310	1510	1710	1910	2110	2333	...	1139	1510	1710	1910	2108	2253

LONDON - OXFORD via High Wycombe

km		Ⓐ	Ⓐ	Ⓐ	Ⓐ	Ⓐ	Ⓐ	Ⓐ	Ⓐ	Ⓐ	Ⓐ	Ⓐ	Ⓐ	Ⓐ	Ⓐ	Ⓐ	Ⓐ	Ⓐ	Ⓐ	Ⓐ	Ⓐ	Ⓐ	Ⓐ	Ⓐ	Ⓐ
0	**London** Marylebone d.	0609	0648	0714	0740	0811	0841	0900	0935	1006	1035	1107	1135	1207	1235	1307	1335	1407	1435	1507	1535	1618	1650	1718	1750
45	High Wycombe d.	0642	0713	0738	0804	|	0906	|	1001	|	1100	|	1200	|	1259	|	1359	|	1502	|	1559	|	1715	|	1815
90	Bicester Village d.	0711	0745	0802	0832	0855	0930	0952	1024	1053	1124	1154	1223	1254	1321	1353	1421	1453	1525	1554	1621	1706	1740	1805	1840
103	**Oxford** Parkway a.	0721	0753	0811	0839	0902	0937	1001	1032	1101	1132	1201	1230	1303	1329	1401	1429	1501	1532	1601	1630	1713	1749	1812	1848
108	**Oxford** 131 a.	0729	0802	0822	0847	0911	0946	1011	1038	1110	1139	1210	1238	1312	1338	1410	1438	1510	1546	1610	1638	1722	1756	1821	1854

	Ⓐ	Ⓐ	Ⓐ	Ⓐ	Ⓐ	Ⓐ	Ⓐ	Ⓐ	Ⓐ	Ⓐ	Ⓐ	⑥	⑥	⑥	⑥	⑥	⑥	⑥	⑥	⑥	⑥		⑥
London Marylebone d.	1818	1850	1921	1950	2007	2037	2102	2132	2207	2240	2310	0557	0625	0705	0735	0805	0835	0905	0935	1005	1035	and at	1835
High Wycombe d.	|	1916	1945	2014	|	|	|	2159	|	2307	2339	0627	0652	0729	0759	|	0859	|	0959	|	1059	the same	1859
Bicester Village d.	1909	1941	2011	2039	2055	2124	2155	2226	2256	2333	0010	0656	0724	0757	0827	0854	0922	0954	1022	1054	1124	minutes past each hour until	1922
Oxford Parkway a.	1916	1949	2018	2046	2104	2131	2202	2236	2303	2341	0018	0704	0734	0804	0836	0901	0931	1001	1029	1101	1131	♥	1929
Oxford 131 a.	1925	1957	2026	2055	2113	2145	2210	2242	2312	2349	0027	0711	0745	0812	0844	0910	0939	1009	1038	1109	1139		1936

	⑥	⑥	⑥	⑥	⑥	⑥	⑥	⑥	⑥		⑦		⑦	⑦	⑦		⑦	⑦	⑦	⑦		⑦	⑦
London Marylebone d.	1905	1935	2005	2035	2105	2135	2205	2235	2310	...	0735	...	0835	0905	0935	and at the same	2005	2035	2105	2135	...	2215	2315
High Wycombe d.	|	1959	|	2059	|	2159	|	2306	2336	...	0805	...	0859	|	0959	minutes past	|	2059	|	2159	...	|	2347
Bicester Village d.	1954	2022	2054	2122	2154	2222	2254	2331	2359	...	0834	...	0922	0953	1022	each hour until	2053	2122	2153	2222	...	2305	0018
Oxford Parkway a.	2001	2029	2101	2131	2201	2229	2301	2338	0009	...	0843	...	0929	1000	1031	♥	2100	2129	2200	2231	...	2312	0026
Oxford 131 a.	2009	2036	2110	2138	2210	2239	2309	2346	0017	...	0850	...	0936	1008	1038		2108	2136	2208	2238	...	2320	0034

	Ⓐ	Ⓐ	Ⓐ	Ⓐ	Ⓐ	Ⓐ		Ⓐ	Ⓐ	Ⓐ	Ⓐ	Ⓐ	Ⓐ	Ⓐ	Ⓐ	Ⓐ	Ⓐ	Ⓐ		Ⓐ	Ⓐ	Ⓐ	Ⓐ
Oxford 131 d.	0536	0602	0625	0643	0717	0744	...	0801	0821	0840	0910	0936	1010	1041	1110	1142	1211	1240	and at	1611	1638	1723	1803
Oxford Parkway d.	0542	0607	0631	0648	0725	0750	...	0808	0827	0850	0916	0946	1017	1047	1115	1147	1217	1247	the same minutes past	1617	1645	1729	1809
Bicester Village d.	0552	0617	0640	0657	0735	0759	...	0820	0836	0859	0925	0957	1026	1056	1124	1156	1226	1256	each hour until	1626	1656	1738	1822
High Wycombe d.	0625	0646	|	0725	|	0827	...	0850	0901	0927	0950	|	1051	|	1151	|	1251	|	♥	1651	|	1806	|
London Marylebone a.	0700	0723	0730	0757	0820	0857	...	0927	0930	0956	1019	1041	1118	1146	1218	1246	1318	1346		1721	1744	1835	1912

	Ⓐ	①–④	⑤	Ⓐ	Ⓐ	Ⓐ	Ⓐ	Ⓐ	Ⓐ	Ⓐ	Ⓐ	Ⓐ	⑥	⑥	⑥	⑥	⑥	⑥	⑥	⑥		⑥	⑥
Oxford 131 d.	1822	1902	1902	1920	2000	2026	2055	2115	2137	2215	2242	2315	0612	0635	0710	0738	0811	0840	0909	0943	and at the same	1911	1943
Oxford Parkway d.	1829	1909	1909	1929	2007	2031	2101	2121	2146	2221	2247	2320	0618	0641	0715	0745	0817	0847	0915	0948	minutes past	1917	1948
Bicester Village d.	1838	1918	1918	1939	2019	2040	2110	2130	2155	2230	2258	2330	0628	0650	0726	0755	0826	0857	0926	0957	each hour until	1926	1957
High Wycombe d.	1906	|	|	2007	|	2110	2138	|	2221	2300	2326	0004	0656	|	0754	|	0851	|	0951	|	♥	1951	|
London Marylebone a.	1933	2008	2015	2037	2109	2138	2205	2218	2253	2335	0011	...	0727	0740	0828	0854	0918	0946	1018	1047		2018	2048

	⑥	⑥	⑥		⑥	⑥	⑦	⑦	⑦	⑦	⑦	⑦	⑦		⑦	⑦	⑦	⑦	⑦	⑦	⑦	⑦	⑦
Oxford 131 d.	2011	2042	2109	...	2142	2209	0743	0810	0838	0901	0942	1011	1042	and at	1811	1841	1909	1941	2011	2049	2109	2148	2211
Oxford Parkway d.	2017	2048	2115	...	2148	2214	0749	0816	0844	0907	0948	1017	1048	the same minutes past	1817	1847	1915	1947	2017	2054	2114	2154	2216
Bicester Village d.	2026	2057	2126	...	2157	2225	0758	0825	0853	0918	0957	1026	1057	each hour until	1826	1856	1926	1956	2026	2103	2125	2203	2224
High Wycombe d.	2051	|	2151	...	2222	2251	0823	0850	|	0944	|	1051	|	♥	1851	|	1951	|	2051	|	2150	|	2251
London Marylebone a.	2118	2147	2218	...	2249	2327	0851	0925	0942	1011	1045	1118	1145		1918	1945	2017	2048	2118	2156	2216	2256	2316

h – Change at **Hatton** (a. 1936 / d. 1944).

♥ – Timings may vary by up to 2 minutes.

km		Ⓐ	Ⓐ	Ⓐ	Ⓐ	Ⓐ	Ⓐ	Ⓐ	Ⓐ	Ⓐ	Ⓐ	Ⓐ	Ⓐ	Ⓐ	Ⓐ	Ⓐ	Ⓐ	Ⓐ	Ⓐ	Ⓐ	Ⓐ	Ⓐ	Ⓐ	Ⓐ
0	**London** Marylebone △ d.	0633	0652	0757	0857	0957	1057	1157	1257	1357	1457	1527	1612	1642	1730	1759	1832	1859	1932	1956	2057	2157	2257	2357
38	Amersham △ d.	0708	0727	0832	0932	1032	1132	1232	1332	1432	1532	1602	1647	1717	|	1829	|	1934	2008	2031	2132	2232	2332	0032
60	**Aylesbury** △ d.	0730	0753	0854	0954	1054	1154	1254	1354	1454	1554	1626	1709	1739	1824	1855	1925	2003	2031	2053	2154	2254	2354	0054
65	**Aylesbury** Vale Parkway a.	0739	0804	0903	1003	1103	1203	1303	1403	1503	1603	1634	1718	1748	1832	1904	1933	2011	2039	2102	2203	2303	0003	0103

	⑥	⑥	⑥	⑥	⑥		⑥	⑥	⑥	⑥	⑦	⑦	⑦	⑦	⑦		⑦	⑦	⑦		⑦
London Marylebone △ d.	...	0727	0757	0857	0957	and at the same	2057	2157	2227	2257	0757	0857	0957	1057	1157	and at the same	1957	2057	2127	...	2227
Amersham △ d.	0702	0802	0832	0932	1032	minutes	2132	2232	2302	2332	0832	0932	1032	1132	1232	minutes	2032	2132	2202	...	2302
Aylesbury △ d.	0726	0824	0854	0954	1054	past each	2154	2254	2324	2354	0854	0954	1054	1154	1254	past each	2054	2154	2224	...	2324
Aylesbury Vale Parkway a.	...	0833	0903	1003	1103	hour until	2203	2303	2333	0003	0903	1003	1103	1203	1303	hour until	2103	2203	2233	...	2333

	Ⓐ	Ⓐ	Ⓐ	Ⓐ	Ⓐ	Ⓐ	Ⓐ	Ⓐ	Ⓐ	Ⓐ	Ⓐ	Ⓐ	Ⓐ	Ⓐ	Ⓐ	Ⓐ	Ⓐ	Ⓐ	Ⓐ	Ⓐ		Ⓐ	Ⓐ	Ⓐ
Aylesbury Vale Parkway d.	0513	0541	0616	0650	0722	0748	0809	0836	0915	1010	1110	1210	1310	1410	1510	1610	1640	1734	1809	1839	...	1940	2045	2110
Aylesbury ▽ d.	0518	0546	0621	0655	0727	0859	0814	0841	0920	1015	1115	1215	1315	1415	1515	1615	1645	1750	1818	1844	...	1945	2050	2115
Amersham ▽ d.	0540	0608	0644	0718	0750	0822	0836	0902	0941	1036	1136	1236	1336	1436	1536	1636	1706	1811	1839	1905	...	2006	2111	2136
London Marylebone ▽ a.	0616	0649	0722	0753	0826	0900	0916	0944	1023	1120	1220	1320	1420	1520	1620	1720	1748	1853	1921	1948	...	2049	2153	2219

	⑥	⑥	⑥	⑥		⑥	⑥	⑥	⑥	⑥	⑦	⑦	⑦	⑦	⑦		⑦	⑦	⑦	⑦	⑦
Aylesbury Vale Parkway d.	0613	0713	0813	0913	and at the same	1913	2013	2113	2213	...	0713	0813	0913	1013	1113	and at the same	1813	1913	2013	2113	2243
Aylesbury ▽ d.	0618	0718	0818	0918	minutes	1918	2018	2118	2218	2318	0718	0818	0918	1018	1118	minutes	1818	1918	2018	2118	2248
Amersham ▽ d.	0639	0739	0839	0939	past each	1939	2039	2139	2239	2342	0739	0839	0939	1039	1139	past each	1839	1939	2039	2139	2309
London Marylebone ▽ a.	0718	0818	0920	1020	hour until	2020	2120	2220	2320	...	0820	0920	1020	1120	1220	hour until	1920	2020	2120	2220	2348

△ – Additional trains London Marylebone - Aylesbury on Ⓐ at 0727 and hourly until 1427, 1557, 1627, 1711, 1742, 1812, 1843, 1918, 2023, 2127, 2227, 2327; on ⑥ at 0827 and hourly until 2127, 2327, 2357; on ⑦ at 1527 and hourly until 2027, 2157, 2257, 2327.

▽ – Additional trains Aylesbury - London Marylebone on Ⓐ at 0604, 0635, 0709, 0738, 0859, 0945 and hourly until 1545, 1712, 1915, 2018, 2145, 2245; on ⑥ at 0648 and hourly until 2148; on ⑦ at 0848, 0948, 1448 and hourly until 2148.

130 LONDON - WORCESTER - HEREFORD

Most trains convey 🍸 GW

Other services: London Paddington - Oxford see Table **131**; Worcester - Hereford see Table **125**.

km		Ⓐ	Ⓐ	Ⓐ	Ⓐ	Ⓐ	Ⓐ	Ⓐ	Ⓐ	Ⓐ	Ⓐ	Ⓐ	Ⓐ	Ⓐ	Ⓐ	Ⓐ	Ⓐ	Ⓐ	Ⓐ	Ⓐ	Ⓐ	Ⓐ	⑤	⑥	⑥	⑥
0	**London** Padd. **131 132** d.	...	0512	0545	0652	*0750*	0821	0921	1022	1120	1221	1322	1421	1522	1549	1622	1722	1749	1822	1922	2022	2148	2318	0517	0621	0721
58	Reading **131 132** d.	...	0550	0619	0722	*0822*	0853	0953	1052	1152	1251	1352	1453	1552	1620	1652**u**	1750	1822	1851	1952	2053	2223	0005	0554	0654	0754
103	**Oxford** **131** d.	0514	0621	0650	0801	0857	0924	1019	1119	1221	1321	1418	1520	1621	1646	1725	1817	1850	1922	2021	2121	2254	0036	0624	0723	0823
148	Moreton in Marsh d.	0542	0648	0727	0839	0931	1003	1055	1156	1259	1358	1456	1555	1656	1725	1812	1855	1929	2001	2059	2157	2335	0115	0701	0757	0857
172	Evesham a.	0559	...	0744	0856	0946	1022	1109	1216	1317	1416	1511	1612	1715	...	1831	1915	1945	2020	2118	2217	2355	...	0720	0816	0916
172	Evesham d.	0559	...	0751	0857	0946	1027	1110	1224	1318	1428	1511	1621	1717	...	1838	1915	1946	2022	2122	2218	2355	...	0724	0821	0921
194	**Worcester** Shrub Hill a.	0619	...	0810	0915	1001	1046	1128	1243	1338	1449	1525	1640	1736	...	1857	1935	2005	2041	2147	2240	0017	...	0743	0840	0940
195	**Worcester** Foregate St a.	0625	...	0816	0919	1004	1051	1134	1248	1342	...	1540	1644	1744	...	1911	1939	...	2045	2151	2244	...	...	0748	0844	0944
208	Great Malvern **125** a.	...	...	...	0932	1017	1107	...	1302	1357	...	...	...	1758	...	1926	1953	...	2059	2207	2301	...	...	0802	0901	1000
219	Ledbury **125** a.	...	...	...	...	...	1120	...	1323	...	...	...	...	...	...	...	2008	...	2114	2235	...	...	...	...	...	...
241	**Hereford** **125** a.	...	...	...	...	...	1141	...	1347	...	...	...	...	...	...	...	2031	...	2136	2257	...	...	...	...	...	..

	⑥	⑥	⑥	⑥	⑥	⑥	⑥	⑥	⑥	⑥	⑥**e**	⑥**c**	⑥	⑦	⑦**g**	⑦**n**	⑦	⑦	⑦	⑦	⑦	⑦	⑦	⑦	⑦	⑦	⑦
London Padd. **131 132** d.	0821	0922	1021	1122	1321	1421	1522	1621	1721	1821	1950	1950	2148	0803	0842	0842	0935	1042	1242	1342	1442	1542	1642	1742	1842	1942	2142
Reading **131 132** d.	0854	0954	1055	1153	1354	1454	1555	1654	1755	1854	2022	2022	2221	0845	0920	0924	1016	1122	1322	1422	1520	1622	1726	1825	1925	2022	2223
Oxford **131** d.	0925	1025	1123	1225	1425	1523	1623	1723	1823	1923	2049	2052	2253	0918	0949	0952	1051	1154	1352	1452	1556	1656	1759	1856	1959	2054	2254
Moreton in Marsh d.	1002	1100	1200	1303	1503	1557	1658	1804	1900	2000	2126	2129	2334	0953	1022	1025	1126	1230	1430	1526	1628	1728	1834	1933	2034	2131	2331
Evesham a.	1021	1119	1219	1321	1521	1616	1716	1823	1919	2019	2143	2146	2352	1011	1038	1041	1143	1249	1449	1544	1649	1744	1852	1954	2051	2150	2350
Evesham d.	1025	1131	1227	1323	1522	1621	1721	1824	1920	2023	2144	2147	2353	1012	1042	1045	1148	1250	1450	1545	1649	1744	1852	1955	2052	2151	2351
Worcester Shrub Hill a.	1044	1151	1246	1342	1541	1640	1740	1844	1939	2043	2203	2206	0015	1035	1100	1059	1207	1310	1510	1604	1708	1803	1911	2014	2112	2210	0014
Worcester Foregate St. a.	1049	1157	1250	1346	1545	1644	1744	1856	1944	2049	2206	2209	...	1039	1114	1103	1210	1314	1515	1607	1711	1806	1915	2018	...	2214	...
Great Malvern **125** a.	1102	...	1305	1404	1600	1700	1801	1910	...	2102	2221	2224	...	1056	1119	1117	1225	1327	1527	...	1723	...	1927	2032	...	2228	...
Ledbury **125** a.	1122	...	1321	...	...	...	...	1924	...	2116	...	...	...	...	1129	1132	...	1342	1542	...	1736	...	...	2046	...	...	...
Hereford **125** a.	1141	...	1339	...	...	...	...	1945	...	2135	...	...	...	...	1148	1151	...	1407	1601	...	1754	...	...	2104	...	...	...

	Ⓐ	Ⓐ	Ⓐ	Ⓐ	Ⓐ	Ⓐ	Ⓐ	Ⓐ	Ⓐ	Ⓐ	Ⓐ	Ⓐ	Ⓐ	Ⓐ	Ⓐ	Ⓐ	Ⓐ	Ⓐ	Ⓐ	Ⓐ	Ⓐ	Ⓐ	⑥	⑥	⑥	⑥
Hereford **125** d.	...	0450	0528	...	...	0642	...	...	...	...	...	1209	...	...	...	1514	...	...	...	...	...	2151	...	0617	0710	...
Ledbury **125** d.	...	|	0545	...	...	0659	...	...	...	...	...	1224	...	...	...	1531	...	...	...	...	...	2209	...	0634	0730	...
Great Malvern **125** d.	...	0517	0559	...	...	0712	...	...	0958	1059	...	1236	1425	...	...	1545	...	...	1835	1944	...	2222	0554	0649	0744	0843
Worcester Foregate St. d.	...	0531	0614	...	0653	0728	0826	...	1010	1115	1206	1256	1439	...	1550	1601	...	1728	1848	1956	2059	2234	0609	0704	0759	0858
Worcester Shrub Hill d.	0511	0536	0619	...	0655	0732	0839	...	1013	1122	1208	1258	1443	1521	1554	1605	...	1731	1852	2004	2103	2243	0613	0708	0804	0902
Evesham a.	0525	0553	0635	...	0712	0749	0854	...	1029	1136	1224	1316	1501	1535	1607	1622	...	1746	1908	2019	2120	2300	0630	0725	0821	0919
Evesham d.	0527	0558	0637	...	0712	0750	0905	...	1030	1136	1232	1330	1502	1535	1608	1625	...	1747	1908	2019	2121	2301	0631	0726	0825	0929
Moreton in Marsh d.	0547	0614	0656	0710	0727	0811	0923	1022	1048	1152	1250	1349	1522	1552	1624	1645	1732	1805	1926	2047	2141	2326	0651	0745	0845	0948
Oxford **131** a.	0624	0652	0732	0751	0812	0849	0959	1056	1127	1227	1325	1423	1559	1628	1653	1728	1801	1900	2000	2124	2226	2358	0728	0826	0925	1028
Reading **131 132** a.	0653	0725	0756	0822	...	0916	1024	1125	1153	1255	1354	1454	1625	1654	1724	1754	1825	1931	2024	2155	2253	0042**b**	0754	0852	0952	1054
London Padd. **131 132** a.	0730	0758	0829	0851	...	0945	1057	1201	1227	1330	1428	1530	1659	1727	1759	1829	1859	2006	2057	2242**a**	2337	0122	0827	0927	1025	1128

	⑥	⑥	⑥	⑥	⑥	⑥	⑥	⑥	⑥	⑥	⑥	⑥	⑦**h**	⑦**k**	⑦	⑦	⑦**n**	⑦**g**	⑦	⑦	⑦	⑦	⑦	⑦**h**	⑦**k**	⑦	⑦
Hereford **125** d.	...	...	...	1213	...	1513	...	...	...	...	2020	...	...	...	...	...	...	...	1332	1432	...	1634	...	1830	1830	...	...
Ledbury **125** d.	...	...	...	1231	...	1531	...	...	...	...	2040	...	...	...	...	...	...	...	1351	1452	...	1652	...	1848	1848	...	...
Great Malvern **125** d.	0951	1058	...	1246	1433	1544	1634	1749	1835	...	2053	2241	0920	0922	...	1115	1315	1320	1407	1509	...	1705	...	1910	1911	2015	...
Worcester Foregate St. d.	1004	1111	1206	1301	1457	1559	1655	1802	1849	2002	2111	2253	0932	0934	1023	1128	1327	1333	1422	1524	1628	1724	1826	1928	1929	2028	...
Worcester Shrub Hill d.	1008	1115	1210	1306	1501	1604	1702	1806	1902	2006	2115	2256	0935	0940	1028	1131	1331	1338	1429	1528	1632	1728	1830	1932	1933	2031	2128
Evesham a.	1024	1131	1225	1323	1518	1620	1718	1823	1917	2023	2132	2314	0951	0956	1045	1147	1347	1354	1446	1546	1646	1747	1848	1948	1948	2049	2145
Evesham d.	1030	1132	1230	1326	1526	1621	1726	1827	1927	2024	2133	...	0952	0957	1054	1151	1355	1357	1455	1554	1655	1755	1854	1953	1955	2049	2149
Moreton in Marsh d.	1049	1150	1248	1345	1546	1641	1744	1845	1944	2043	2152	...	1011	1016	1113	1210	1414	1417	1511	1613	1713	1816	1913	2014	2017	2108	2208
Oxford **131** a.	1124	1226	1322	1426	1623	1723	1823	1924	2022	2127	2235	...	1049	1049	1150	1249	1449	1455	1549	1654	1754	1851	1953	2049	2054	2148	2243
Reading **131 132** a.	1155	1257	1355	1456	1656	1756	1857	1957	2055	2156	2310	...	1125	1127	1230**t**	1330	1528	1527	1629	1728	1823	1929**t**	2026	2125**f**	2124	2221	2314
London Padd. **131 132** a.	1231	1333	1428	1530	1729	1831	1931	2031	2127	2229	2352	...	1206	1206	1309**t**	1409	1606	1609	1711	1808	1907	2006	2108**r**	2207	2207	2301	2359

a – 2236 on ⑤.
b – 0037 on ②–⑤ mornings.
c – Sept. 16 - Oct. 28.
e – May 27 - Sept. 9 and from Oct. 28.
f – Arrives 2119 May 21 - Sept 10.
g – May 21 - Sept. 10.
h – May 21 - Oct. 22.
k – From Oct. 29.
n – From Sept. 17.
r – Arrives 6–7 minutes earlier from Sept. 17.
t – Arrives 7–9 minutes earlier Sept. 17 - Oct. 22.
u – Calls to pick up only.

131 LONDON - OXFORD via Reading

GW

km		②–⑤	Ⓐ	Ⓐ	Ⓐ	Ⓐ	Ⓐ	Ⓐ	Ⓐ	Ⓐ	Ⓐ	Ⓐ	Ⓐ	Ⓐ	Ⓐ	Ⓐ	Ⓐ	Ⓐ	Ⓐ	Ⓐ	Ⓐ	Ⓐ	Ⓐ	Ⓐ	Ⓐ
0	**London** P ◇ **130 132** d.	0022	0512	0545	0620	0652	0721	0750	0821	0851	0921	0950	1022	1050	1120	1150	1221	1250	1322	1350	1421	1450	1522	1549	1622
30	Slough **131a** d.	0041	0530	0559	0633	0706	0736	0806	0835	0906	0937	1007	1036	1106	1136	1206	1236	1306	1336	1406	1437	1506	1536	1605	1637**u**
58	Reading **130 132** d.	0101	0550	0619	0651	0722	0753	0822	0853	0922	0953	1023	1052	1122	1152	1222	1251	1322	1352	1422	1453	1522	1552	1620	1652**u**
85	Didcot Parkway **132** d.	0119	0607	|	0708	0744	|	|	|	0938	|	|	|	1138	|	|	|	1338	|	|	|	1538	|	|	|
102	**Oxford** **130 128** a.	0134	0619	0648	0723	0758	0819	0848	0918	0952	1017	1048	1117	1151	1219	1248	1316	1350	1416	1447	1517	1550	1616	1644	1723

	Ⓐ	Ⓐ	Ⓐ	Ⓐ	Ⓐ	Ⓐ	Ⓐ	Ⓐ	Ⓐ	⑤	①–④	⑤	⑤	①–④	⑤	①–④	Ⓐ	⑤	Ⓐ	⑥	⑥	⑥	⑥	⑥	⑥
London P ◇ **130 132** d.	1649	1722	1749	1822	1850	1922	1950	2022	2048	2118	2148	2148	2219	2218	2248	2248	2318	2342	2333	0022	0517	0550	0621	0650	0721
Slough **131a** d.	1705	|	|	|	1906	1936	2006	2038	2105	2135	2204	2204	|	|	2305	2308	2339	0001	0001	0040	0534	0606	0637	0706	0737
Reading **130 132** d.	1721	1750	1822	1851	1923	1952	2022	2053	2122	2151	2223	2225	2250	2300	2333	2336	0005	0027	0027	0104	0554	0622	0654	0722	0754
Didcot Parkway **132** d.	1738	|	|	|	|	|	|	|	|	|	|	|	|	|	|	|	|	0046	0056	0122	0608	0638	|	|	|
Oxford **130 128** a.	1753	1814	1848	1919	1952	2020	2052	2117	2151	2218	2249	2253	2325	2330	2357	0001	0034	0102	0118	0137	0621	0652	0719	0748	0818

	⑥	⑥		⑥	⑥	⑥	⑥		⑥	⑥	⑥	⑥	⑦	⑦	⑦	⑦		⑦	⑦	⑦	⑦	⑦	⑦
London P ◇ **130 132** d.	0750	0821	and at the same	1950	2018	2050	2118	...	2148	2218	2250	2333	0803	0842	0935	1042	and	1842	1942	2042	2142	2203	2242
Slough **131a** d.	0806	0838	minutes past	2006	2035	2106	2135	...	2205	2235	2308	2351	0820	0859	0953	1059	hourly	1901	1959	2101	2205	|	2303
Reading **130 132** d.	0822	0854	each hour until	2022	2051	2122	2154	...	2221	2255	2328	0017	0845	0920	1016	1122	until	1925	2022	2120	2222	2246	2321
Didcot Parkway **132** d.	|	|	♥	|	|	2139	2210	...	2238	2312	2347	0033	0901	0937	1032	1138	♥	1942	2038	2137	2239	2302**a**	2339**a**
Oxford **130 128** a.	0847	0917		2050	2116	2151	2223	...	2250	2326	0001	0054	0913	0949	1045	1150		1954	2052	2150	2253	2355*	0015*

	②–⑤	②–⑤	Ⓐ	Ⓐ	Ⓐ	Ⓐ	Ⓐ	Ⓐ	Ⓐ	Ⓐ	Ⓐ	Ⓐ	Ⓐ	Ⓐ	Ⓐ	Ⓐ	Ⓐ	Ⓐ	Ⓐ	Ⓐ	Ⓐ	Ⓐ	Ⓐ	Ⓐ	Ⓐ
Oxford **130 128** d.	0007	0027	0400**b**	0501	0542	0559	0630	0655	0734	0753	0808	0851	0901	0931	1001	1031	1101	1130	1201	1231	1301	1329	1401	1431	1501
Didcot Parkway **132** d.	0021	0046	0412	0516	0600	0613	|	0710	|	|	0821	|	0916	|	|	|	|	|	|	|	|	|	|	|	|
Reading **130 132** a.	0037	0113	0440	0541	0616	0626	0653	0725	0756	0822	0834	0916	0932	0954	1024	1053	1125	1153	1225	1255	1325	1354	1425	1454	1524
Slough **131a** a.	0056	0139	0507	0608	|	0647	|	|	|	|	|	|	0952	1010	1038	1109	1141	1208	1240	1310	1341	1409	1440	1510	1539
London P ◇ **130 132** a.	0122	0207	0547	0644	0651	0708	0730	0758	0829	0851	0907	0945	1012	1029	1057	1128	1201	1227	1316	1330	1400	1428	1501	1530	1600

	Ⓐ	Ⓐ	Ⓐ	Ⓐ	Ⓐ	Ⓐ	Ⓐ	Ⓐ	Ⓐ	Ⓐ	Ⓐ	Ⓐ	⑤	①–④	Ⓐ	Ⓐ	Ⓐ	⑥	⑥	⑥	⑥	⑥	⑥	⑥	⑥
Oxford **130 128** d.	1531	1601	1631	1701	1730	1801	1831	1905	1931	2001	2031	2101	2132	2132	2211	2230	2309	0007	0027	0359	0514	0549	0631	0659	0730
Didcot Parkway **132** d.	|	|	|	|	|	|	|	|	|	|	|	|	|	|	2226	|	2323	0021	0046	0410	0531	0601	|	|	|
Reading **130 132** a.	1554	1625	1654	1724	1754	1825	1855	1931	1953	2024	2054	2126	2155	2155	2243	2253	2341	0042	0113	0430	0557	0627	0657	0723	0754
Slough **131a** a.	1609	1640	1709	1737	1810	1841	1909	1946	2010	2039	2111	2142	2214	2213	2301	2315	0002	0101	0139	0502	0628	0658	0714	0738	0809
London P ◇ **130 132** a.	1629	1659	1727	1759	1829	1859	1929	2006	2028	2057	2130	2201	2236	2242	2325	2337	0027	0122	0207	0531	0707	0737	0737	0758	0827

	⑥	⑥		⑥	⑥	⑥	⑥	⑥	⑥	⑥	⑥	⑥	⑦	⑦	⑦		⑦	⑦	⑦	⑦	⑦	⑦	⑦
Oxford **130 128** d.	0801	0829	and at the same	1929	2001	2027	2101	2128	2201	2235	2301	2310	0715*	0850	0955	and	1755	1854	1955	2055	2150	2245	2300*
Didcot Parkway **132** d.	|	|	minutes past	|	|	|	|	2142	2213	2251	2315	2337	0759	0903	1010	hourly	1808	1908	2008	2108	2204	2258	2350
Reading **130 132** a.	0825	0852	each hour until	1957	2025	2055	2125	2156	2228	2310	2332	0002	0818	0919	1028	until	1823	1922	2026	2125	2221	2315	0016
Slough **131a** a.	0840	0909	♥	2012	2040	2109	2140	2210	2243	2331	2349	0030	0839	0936	1046		1847	|	2047	2138	2238	2334	0040
London P ◇ **130 132** a.	0859	0927		2031	2059	2127	2159	2229	2302	2352	0017	0105	0902	0958	1106		1907	2006	2108	2207	2301	2359	0113

a – Arrival time. **b** – ②–⑤ only. **u** – Calls to pick up only. * – Connection by 🚌. ◇ – London Paddington. ♥ – Timings may vary by up to 5 minutes.

131a SLOUGH - WINDSOR

Journey time 6 minutes 2nd class GW

From Slough:
Ⓐ: 0538, 0558, 0618, 0637, 0655, 0713, 0731, 0754, 0813, 0831, 0854, 0914, 0933, 0953, 1011, 1030, 1050 and every 20 minutes until 1550; then 1621, 1643, 1701, 1721, 1740, 1758, 1816, 1840, 1858, 1916, 1940, 2000 and every 20 minutes until 2320.
⑥: 0617 and every 30 minutes until 0947, 1012, 1030, 1050 and every 20 minutes until 1850, 1917, 1947 and every 30 minutes until 2247; then 2322 and 2356.
⑦: 0822, 0852, 0922, 0952, 1012 and every 20 minutes until 1852, 1922 and every 30 minutes until 2322.

From Windsor & Eton Central:
Ⓐ: 0548, 0608, 0628, 0646, 0704, 0722, 0740, 0804, 0822, 0840, 0904, 0924, 0942, 1002, 1020, 1040 and every 20 minutes until 1600; then 1630, 1652, 1710, 1730, 1749, 1807, 1828, 1849, 1907, 1927, 1950, 2010 and every 20 minutes until 2330.
⑥: 0627 and every 30 minutes until 0957, 1021, 1040, 1100 and every 20 minutes until 1900, 1927, 1957, 2026, 2056 and every 30 minutes until 2256; then 2331.
⑦: 0005, 0832, 0902, 0932, 1002, 1022 and every 20 minutes until 1902, 1932 and every 30 minutes until 2332.

LONDON - BRISTOL TEMPLE MEADS - TAUNTON

km			ⒶQ	Ⓐ	Ⓐ	ⒶA	Ⓐ	Ⓐ	Ⓐ	Ⓐ	ⒶA	Ⓐ	Ⓐ	Ⓐ	Ⓐ	Ⓐ	Ⓐ	Ⓐ	Ⓐ	Ⓐ	Ⓐ	Ⓐ	Ⓐ	Ⓐ	Ⓐ
0	**London** Paddington 130 131 d.	Ⓐ	0518	0630	0700	0730	0800	0830	0900	0930	1000	1030	1100	1130	1200	1230	1300	1330	1400	1430	1500	1530	1600	1630	1700
58	Reading 130 131 d.		0555	0657	0730	0759	0828	0859	0928	0959	1028	1059	1127	1159	1227	1259	1328	1359	1428	1459	1527	1558	1628	1659	1727
85	Didcot Parkway 131 d.		0610	0712	0744	|	0841	|	0942	|	1043	|	1143	|	1242	|	1342	1413	|	1514	|	1612	|	1713	1742
124	Swindon 132a d.		0628	0730	0801	0830	0900	0933	1000	1025	1102	1126	1200	1229	1300	1328	1400	1430	1456	1530	1556	1629	1657	1732	1800
151	Chippenham 132a d.		0642	0744	0817	0843	0915	0945	1014	1039	1115	1140	1214	1244	1314	1343	1414	1444	1510	1544	1609	1644	1711	1746	1815
172	Bath a.		0655	0757	0829	0856	0927	0959	1028	1054	1129	1156	1228	1259	1327	1356	1428	1459	1524	1600	1623	1658	1724	1800	1828
190	**Bristol** Temple Meads 115 120 120a a.		0710	0817	0845	0910	0943	1015	1043	1111	1144	1213	1243	1315	1345	1412	1443	1515	1540	1615	1638	1714	1739	1814	1844
221	Weston-super-Mare 120 120a a.		...	...	...	|	...	...	...	...	1206	...	...	...	...	...	...	...	...	1652	...	1752	...	1851	...
262	**Taunton** 115 120 120a a.		...	...	...	0944	...	...	...	...	1229	...	...	...	...	...	...	...	...	...	...	...	...	1929	...

	Ⓐ	Ⓐ	Ⓐ	Ⓐ	⑤	Ⓐ	Ⓐ	Ⓐ	ⒶB	⑤	①–④	ⒶC		⑥	⑥	⑥D	⑥	⑥	⑥	⑥	⑥	⑥	⑥	⑥	⑥
London Paddington 130 131 d.	1730	1800	1830	1900	1912	1930	2000	2045	2145	2215	2215	2330	⑥	0630	0700	0730	0800	0830	0900	0930	1000	1030	1100	1130	1200
Reading 130 131 d.	1757	1828	1858	1928	1938	1959	2029	2112	2213	2243	2255	0010		0700	0729	0759	0828	0858	0928	0958	1028	1059	1128	1158	1228
Didcot Parkway 131 d.	1811	1842	1913	1942	1954	2012	2042	2127	2233	2303	2314	0028		0714	|	0813	|	0913	|	1012	|	1114	|	1212	|
Swindon 132a d.	1830	1900	1930	2001	2011	2030	2100	2144	2251	2322	2333	0048		0733	0757	0832	0857	0931	0955	1030	1056	1132	1156	1230	1255
Chippenham 132a d.	1845	1914	1946	2016	|	2044	2116	2158	2305	2336	2346	0103		0747	0811	0846	0910	0946	1010	1044	1110	1146	1211	1244	1310
Bath a.	1859	1928	1959	2029	k	2059	2129	2212	2319	2349	2358	0115		0800	0824	0900	0924	1000	1025	1058	1123	1200	1225	1258	1325
Bristol Temple Meads 115 120 120a a.	1913	1943	2014	2044	2059	2114	2144	2228	2333	0004	0014	0130		0815	0840	0915	0939	1015	1039	1115	1139	1215	1240	1313	1342
Weston-super-Mare 120 120a a.	1949	...	2053	...	...	2149	...	...	0006s	...	...	...		...	...	|	...	...	1107r	...	...	1235r	...	...	...
Taunton 115 120 120a a.	2023	...	...	...	...	...	...	...	0036	...	...	...		...	...	0950	...	...	...	...	...	...	...	...	...

	⑥	⑥	⑥	⑥	⑥	⑥	⑥	⑥	⑥A	⑥	⑥	⑥	⑥	⑥	⑥	⑥	⑥B	⑥	⑥	⑥		⑦Dd	⑦Db	⑦a	⑦e
London Paddington 130 131 d.	1230	1300	1330	1400	1430	1500	1530	1600	1630	1700	1730	1800	1830	1900	1930	2000	2030	2130	2235	2330	⑦	0800	0800	0900	0900
Reading 130 131 d.	1259	1328	1359	1428	1459	1528	1600	1628	1659	1728	1759	1828	1859	1928	1959	2028	2059	2159	2303	0006		0838	0840	0938	0938
Didcot Parkway 131 d.	1314	|	1414	|	1513	|	1614	|	1713	|	1812	|	1913	|	2013	2042	2114	2214	2320	0023		0854	0858	0953	0958
Swindon 132a d.	1332	1357	1432	1456	1531	1556	1633	1656	1731	1756	1831	1856	1931	1956	2031	2101	2132	2232	2339	0042		0913	0917	1011	1015
Chippenham 132a d.	1346	1410	1446	1510	1546	1610	1647	1710	1746	1810	1845	1910	1946	2010	2046	2116	2146	2247	2354	0056		0929	0932	1026	1029
Bath a.	1400	1424	1500	1525	1600	1625	1700	1725	1800	1825	1858	1925	2000	2025	2059	2129	2200	2300	0008	0110		0944	0946	1040	1044
Bristol Temple Meads 115 120 120a a.	1415	1439	1515	1541	1615	1640	1715	1740	1815	1841	1914	1939	2015	2042	2114	2145	2214	2315	0022	0124		0958	1000	1055	1059
Weston-super-Mare 120 120a a.	1436r	...	...	...	1636r	...	1737r	...	1837	...	1950	...	2036	2126	...	...	2247s	...	...	...		|	|	1119	...
Taunton 115 120 120a a.	...	...	...	...	...	...	...	...	1907	...	...	...	2102	2159	...	...	2317	...	...	...		1034	1034	...	...

	⑦	⑦	⑦	⑦E	⑦	⑦	⑦	⑦	⑦a	⑦e	⑦	⑦	⑦	⑦e	⑦a	⑦b	⑦B	⑦a	⑦b	⑦	⑦	⑦	⑦e	⑦	⑦
London Paddington 130 131 d.	1000	1100	1200	1300	1400	1500	1527	1600	1622	1627	1700	1727j	1800	1827	1827	1900	1903	1927	1930	2003	2103	2203	2237	2303	2337
Reading 130 131 d.	1038	1138	1238	1338	1438	1538	1603	1638	1700	1703	1738	1804	1838	1903	1903	1936	1938	2003	2006	2038	2143	2246	2317	2346	0020
Didcot Parkway 131 d.	1053	1153	1253	1353	1453	1553	|	1653	|	|	1753	|	1853	|	|	|	1953	|	|	2053	2200	2304	2332s	0002s	0035s
Swindon 132a d.	1111	1211	1311	1410	1511	1611	1630	1711	1728	1728	1811	1834	1911	1929	1934	2002	2011	2032	2032	2110	2218	2322	2348s	0021s	0053s
Chippenham 132a d.	1126	1226	1326	1425	1525	1625	1645	1725	1741	1744	1825	1848	1925	1944	1948	|	2025	2046	2046	2126	2232	2337	|	0035s	0106s
Bath a.	1140	1240	1340	1439	1539	1639	1659	1739	1757	1758	1839	1901	1939	1959	2001	m	2040	2103	2103	2140	2246	2352	h	0051s	0123s
Bristol Temple Meads 115 120 120a a.	1155	1255	1355	1455	1555	1655	1717	1756	1813	1813	1855	1920	1955	2013	2017	2043	2055	2116	2117	2155	2302	0007	0030	0105	0139
Weston-super-Mare 120 120a a.	1231	...	1429	|	...	1724	...	...	...	...	...	1957	...	...	...	...	2128c	...	...	2230	...	...	...	...	...
Taunton 115 120 120a a.	...	...	...	1528	...	1759	...	...	...	...	...	...	...	...	...	...	2151c	...	...	...	...	...	...	...	...

LONDON - BRISTOL PARKWAY - CARDIFF - SWANSEA

km			Ⓐ	Ⓐ	Ⓐ	Ⓐ	Ⓐ	Ⓐ	Ⓐ	Ⓐ	Ⓐ	Ⓐ✕	Ⓐ	Ⓐ	Ⓐ	Ⓐ	Ⓐ	Ⓐ	Ⓐ	Ⓐ	Ⓐ	Ⓐ	Ⓐ	Ⓐ	ⒶG	Ⓐ	Ⓐ
0	**London** Paddington 130 131 d.	Ⓐ	0518	0645	0715	0745	0815	0845	0915	0945	1015	1045	1115	1145	1215	1245	1315	1345	1415	1445	1515	1545	1615	1645	1715	1745	1815
58	Reading 130 131 d.		0555	0711	0742	0811	0844	0911	0941	1011	1042	1111	1142	1211	1241	1310	1341	1411	1441	1511	1541	1611	1642	1711	1742	1811	1840
85	Didcot Parkway 131 d.		0610	|	0757	|	0857	|	0956	|	1056	|	1156	|	1256	|	1356	|	1455	|	1556	|	1657	|	1758	|	1856
124	Swindon d.		0628	0739	0815	0841	0916	0940	1014	1042	1113	1140	1213	1242	1313	1338	1415	1442	1516	1539	1614	1641	1715	1739	1815	1845	1916
180	**Bristol** Parkway d.		0716t	0808	0841	0908	0943	1008	1041	1108	1143	1208	1242	1309	1341	1408	1442	1508	1544	1608	1640	1708	1741	1808	1842	1910	1942
215	Newport 136 149 a.		0748	0832	0907	0929	1005	1031	1106	1131	1204	1231	1304	1331	1402	1430	1505	1531	1607	1630	1706	1732	1803	1830	1910	1933	2005
234	**Cardiff** Central 135 136 149 a.		0803	0850	0922	0949	1022	1046	1123	1145	1221	1246	1322	1346	1422	1445	1523	1546	1622	1645	1723	1748	1821	1848	1925	1948	2021
266	Bridgend 135 a.		0826	0914	...	1010	...	1109	...	1208	...	1309	...	1409	...	1508	...	1609	...	1708	...	1811	1849	1909	1949	2010	2044
286	Port Talbot 135 a.		0839	0927	...	1023	...	1122	...	1221	...	1322	...	1423	...	1521	...	1622	...	1721	...	1824	1902	1922	2002	2025	2057
295	Neath 135 a.		0847	0934	...	1031	...	1130	...	1229	...	1330	...	1432	...	1529	...	1629	...	1729	...	1830	1910	1930	2009	2033	2104
307	**Swansea** 135 a.		0900	0948	...	1045	...	1143	...	1242	...	1343	...	1446	...	1542	...	1643	...	1742	...	1845	1923	1945	2021	2046	2118

	Ⓐ	①–④	⑤	⑤	①–④	Ⓐ	⑤	①–④	⑤	①–④		⑥	⑥	⑥	⑥	⑥	⑥	⑥	⑥	⑥	⑥	⑥	⑥G	⑥	⑥g	⑥	⑥
London Paddington 130 131 d.	1845	1915	1915	2015	2015	2115	2245	2245	2330	2330	⑥	...	0745	0845	0945	1045	1145	1245	1345	1445	1545	1645	1745	1845	1915	1945	2045
Reading 130 131 d.	1911	1943	1943u	2040	2040	2142	2311	2323	0010	0010		...	0812	0912	1012	1112	1212	1312	1412	1512	1612	1712	1812	1912	1942	2012	2112
Didcot Parkway 131 d.	|	1957	|	2056	2056	2201	2332	2343	0028	0028		...	|	|	|	|	|	|	|	|	|	|	|	|	1956	|	|
Swindon d.	1941	2016	2017	2115	2115	2219	2350	0001	0048	0048		...	0840	0939	1040	1139	1240	1341	1440	1539	1639	1740	1839	1940	2014	2039	2139
Bristol Parkway d.	2008	2043	2043	2141	2141	2247	0016	0027	0137t	0137t	★	0711	0909	1009	1109	1209	1309	1409	1509	1609	1709	1809	1909	2009	2043	2109	2212f
Newport 136 149 a.	2031	2104	2104	2203	2203	2319	0038	0055	0203s	0210s		0731	0930	1031	1131	1230	1331	1431	1531	1630	1730	1831	1930	2030	2104	2130	2244
Cardiff Central 135 136 149 a.	2051	2119	2120	2223	2224	2341	0054	0116	0220	0231	§	0747	0946	1046	1146	1245	1346	1445	1545	1645	1746	1846	1946	2045	2118	2144	2305
Bridgend 135 a.	2115	2145	2145	2246	2249	0003	0119	0141	...	...		0809	1009	1109	1209	1309	1409	1509	1609	1709	1809	1909	2009	2109	2145	2209	2328
Port Talbot 135 a.	2128	2158	2158	2300	2303	0017	0133	0155	...	...		0822	1021	1121	1221	1321	1421	1521	1621	1721	1821	1921	2021	2121	2157	2222	2341
Neath 135 a.	2135	2206	2206	2308	2310	0025	0141	0203	...	...		0830	1029	1129	1229	1329	1429	1529	1629	1729	1829	1929	2029	2129	2205	2230	2349
Swansea 135 a.	2150	2220	2220	2322	2324	0039	0155	0217	...	...		0844	1043	1143	1243	1343	1443	1543	1643	1743	1846	1943	2043	2143	2220	2245	0003

	⑥		⑥	⑥	⑥	⑥	⑥	⑥		⑥	⑥	⑥	⑥	⑥G	⑥	⑥	⑥	⑥	⑥		⑦	⑦G	⑦p	⑦n	⑦G	⑦	⑦G
London Paddington 130 131 d.	2200	⑥	0712	0812	0912	1012	1112	1212	...	1312	1412	1512	1612	1712	1812	1912	2012	2112	2200	⑦	0837	0930	1037	1037	1137	1237	1337
Reading 130 131 d.	2230		0740	0840	0940	1040	1140	1240	...	1340	1440	1540	1640	1740	1840	1940	2040	2140	2230		0916	1007	1113	1117	1213	1313	1413
Didcot Parkway 131 d.	2248		|	|	|	|	|	|	...	|	|	|	|	|	|	|	|	|	2248		0933	|	1129	1131	1229	1327	1429
Swindon d.	2306		0811	0908	1008	1108	1208	1308	...	1408	1508	1608	1708	1808	1908	2008	2109	2209	2308		0951	1041	1148	1148	1248	1346	1448
Bristol Parkway d.	2333	☆	|	|	|	|	|	|	...	|	|	|	|	|	|	|	|	|	|	♥	1017	1106	1214	1214	1314	1412	1514
Newport 136 149 a.	0001		0931	1030	1130	1233	1331	1429	...	1538	1633	1729	1833	1930	2033	2134	2235	2334	0034		1037	1125	1233	1233	1333	1434	1533
Cardiff Central 135 136 149 a.	0023		0945	1044	1145	1247	1345	1444	...	1552	1647	1745	1847	1946	2047	2149	2256	2355	0055		1100	1148	1258	1301	1401	1501	1601
Bridgend 135 a.	...		1009	1109	1209	1310	1409	1509	...	1615	1709	1809	1910	2009	2110	2212	2319	0020	...		1122	1213	1322	1322	1420	1520	1620
Port Talbot 135 a.	...		1021	1121	1221	1322	1421	1521	...	1627	1721	1821	1922	2021	2122	2224	2332	0033	...		1135	1226	1334	1334	1434	1534	1634
Neath 135 a.	...		1029	1129	1229	1329	1429	1529	...	1635	1729	1830	1930	2029	2130	2232	2340	0041	...		1144	1235	1341	1341	1441	1541	1641
Swansea 135 a.	...		1043	1144	1249	1349	1449	1549	...	1649	1749	1849	1944	2043	2144	2247	2354	0056	...		1159	1248	1355	1357	1457	1559	1657

	⑦	⑦	⑦	⑦	⑦	⑦n	⑦p	⑦	⑦	⑦		⑦	⑦	⑦	⑦	⑦	⑦G	⑦		⑦	⑦	⑦	⑦	⑦	⑦	⑦	⑦
London Paddington 130 131 d.	1437	1537	1637	1737	1837	1900	1900	1937	2037	2137	⑦	0751	0930	1030	1137	1237	1337	1437	...	1537	1637	1737	1837	1900	1937	2037	2137
Reading 130 131 d.	1513	1613	1713	1813	1913	1939	1936	2013	2113	2215		0831	1007	1106	1213	1313	1414	1513	...	1613	1713	1814	1914	1936	2013	2113	2215
Didcot Parkway 131 d.	1529	1629	1729	1829	1929	|	|	2029	2129	2232		0845	1023	1120	1227	1329	1429	1528	...	1627	1727	1829	1928	|	|	2129	2232
Swindon d.	1548	1648	1748	1848	1948	2005	2004	2048	2147	2250		0907	1044	1140	1246	1348	1448	1548	...	1644	1747	1846	1948	2002	2041	2148	2250
Bristol Parkway d.	1614	1714	1814	1914	2014	2033	2032	2112	2214	2317	♣	|	|	|	|	|	|	|	...	|	|	|	|	2030	|	|	|
Newport 136 149 a.	1633	1732	1833	1933	2033	2049	2049	2133	2237	2337		1025	1201	1256	1408	1507	1609	1706	...	1811	1909	2011	2116	...	2201	2314	0017
Cardiff Central 135 136 149 a.	1701	1759	1901	2000	2100	2116	2117	2158	2300	0004	§	1046	1224	1319	1430	1531	1632	1729	...	1834	1933	2033	2137	...	2220	2337	0037
Bridgend 135 a.	1720	1820	1924	2020	2120	2138	2140	2220	2324	0027		1109	1248	1343	1451	1555	1655	1753	...	1859	1956	2056	2200	...	2243	0001	0100
Port Talbot 135 a.	1734	1834	1938	2034	2135	2151	2153	2233	2339	0039		1122	1301	1400	1506	1607	1711	1805	...	1909	2007	2110	2212	...	2257	0011	0112
Neath 135 a.	1741	1842	1946	2041	2141	2159	2202	2240	2347	0047		1130	1308	1409	1514	1616	1719	1813	...	1918	2017	2118	2220	...	2305	0019	0120
Swansea 135 a.	1755	1857	2000	2057	2155	2213	2215	2256	0004	0102		1144	1322	1421	1528	1629	1731	1827	...	1932	2033	2131	2234	...	2318	0036	0135

A – To Paignton (Table **115**).
B – To Exeter St Davids (Table **115**).
C – To Cardiff Central (See lower panel).
D – To Penzance (Tables **115**/**117**).
E – To Plymouth (Table **115**).
G – To Carmarthen (Table **135**).
Q – To Swansea (See lower panel).

a – May 21 - Sept 10.
b – Sept 17 - Oct 22.
c – Arrives 3 minutes earlier from Sept. 17.
d – May 21 - Sept 10 and from Oct. 29.
e – From Sept. 17.
f – Arrives 9 minutes earlier.
g – From Oct. 28.
h – Also calls Bristol Parkway (to set down only) a. 0018.
j – Departs 3 minutes later from Sept.17.
k – Also calls Bristol Parkway a. 2036/d. 2038.
m – Also calls Bristol Parkway a. 2030/d. 2030.
n – May 21 - Sept. 10.
p – From Oct. 29.
r – May 27 - Sept. 9.

s – Calls to set down only.
t – Bristol Temple Meads.
u – Calls to pick up only.

★ – ⑥ May 27 - Sept. 9 and from Oct. 28.
☆ – ⑥ Sept. 16 - Oct. 21.
♥ – ⑦ May 21 - Sept. 10 and from Oct. 29.
♣ – ⑦ Sept. 17 - Oct. 22.
§ – For special service Bristol Parkway - Newport during Severn Tunnel closure see page 108.

TAUNTON - BRISTOL TEMPLE MEADS - LONDON

		ⒶR	Ⓐ	Ⓐ	Ⓐ	Ⓐ	Ⓐ	ⒶE	ⒶT	Ⓐ	Ⓐ	Ⓐ	ⒶA	Ⓐ	Ⓐ	Ⓐ	ⒶD	Ⓐ	Ⓐ	Ⓐ	Ⓐ	Ⓐ	Ⓐ	Ⓐ	Ⓐ	Ⓐ	Ⓐ	Ⓐ	Ⓐ
Taunton 115 120 120a d.		...	...	...	...	...	...	0655	...	0713	...	...	0905	...	...	...	1125	...	...	...	...	...	...	...	...	...	...	...	...
Weston-s-Mare . 120 120a d.	Ⓐ	...	...	...	...	0620	0648	0725	...	0749	...	...	0929	...	...	...	|	...	...	...	...	...	...	...	...	...	...	1710	...
Bristol T M 115 120 120a d.		0447	0529	0600	0633	0700	0730	0800	0812	0830	0900	0930	1000	1030	1100	1130	1200	1230	1300	1330	1400	1430	1500	1530	1600	1630	1700	1730	1800
Bath d.		|	0541	0613	0646	0713	0743	0813	0830	0843	0913	0943	1013	1043	1113	1143	1212	1243	1313	1343	1413	1443	1513	1543	1613	1643	1713	1743	1813
Chippenham 132a d.		|	0554	0625	0658	0725	0755	0825	0845	0855	0925	0955	1025	1055	1125	1155	1225	1255	1325	1355	1425	1455	1525	1555	1625	1655	1725	1755	1825
Swindon 132a d.		0523	0610	0641	0715	0741	0811	0841	0904	0911	0941	1011	1041	1111	1141	1211	1241	1311	1341	1411	1441	1511	1541	1611	1641	1711	1741	1811	1841
Didcot Parkway 131 a.		0541	0627	0658	|	0801	0828	0858	...	0928	|	1031	|	1128	|	1229	|	1328	|	1428	|	1528	|	1628	|	1728	1759	1828	|
Reading 130 131 a.		0556	0641	0713	0743	0816	0843	0914	...	0944	1008	1046	1108	1143	1208	1243	1308	1345	1408	1443	1509	1543	1608	1643	1708	1743	1813	1844	1909
London Padd 130 131 a.		0626	0717	0746	0814	0845	0912	0942	...	1015	1038	1114	1140	1215	1238	1312	1339	1414	1438	1514	1542	1614	1640	1714	1737	1814	1844	1914	1939

	Ⓐ	Ⓐ	Ⓐ	⑤D	qD	Ⓐ		⑥	⑥Q	⑥	⑥	⑥	⑥	⑥	⑥B	⑥b	⑥c	⑥	⑥b	⑥c	⑥	⑥Ab	⑥Ac	⑥	⑥b	⑥c	⑥	⑥b	⑥c
Taunton 115 120 120a d.	...	...	...	2115	2115	2129		...	...	...	...	...	0654	...	0759	...	...	...	...	...	...	1045	1045	...	...	...	...	...	...
Weston-s-Mare . 120 120a d.	1809	...	...	|	|	2201	⑥	...	...	...	0624	...	0724	...	0830	...	...	...	...	...	...	1107f	1107	1131r	...	...	...	1301r	...
Bristol T M 115 120 120a d.	1830	1930	2030	2150	2150	2235		0530	0600	0630	0700	0730	0800	0830	0900	0930	0933	1000	1030	1033	1100	1130	1133	1200	1230	1230	1300	1330	1330
Bath d.	1843	1943	2043	2202	2202	2247		0543	0613	0643	0713	0743	0813	0843	0913	0943	0946	1013	1043	1046	1113	1143	1146	1213	1243	1243	1313	1343	1343
Chippenham 132a d.	1855	1955	2055	2215	2215	2300		0555	0625	0655	0725	0755	0825	0855	0925	0955	0958	1025	1055	1058	1125	1155	1158	1225	1255	1255	1325	1355	1355
Swindon 132a d.	1911	2011	2111	2232	2233	2316		0611	0641	0711	0742	0811	0842	0911	0941	1011	1015	1042	1111	1115	1141	1211	1215	1242	1311	1315	1341	1411	1415
Didcot Parkway 131 a.	1928	2028	2128	2250	2248	2333		0628	0659	0728	0759	0828	0859	0928	|	1028	1032	|	1128	1132	|	1228	1232	|	1328	1332	|	1428	1432
Reading 130 131 a.	1943	2043	2144	2308	2306	2354		0642	0714	0743	0813	0843	0914	0943	1011	1044	1047	1108	1143	1146	1209	1245	1246	1309	1343	1346	1411	1443	1446
London Padd 130 131 a.	2014	2114	2213	2341	2345	0034		0714	0744	0814	0844	0914	0944	1015	1039	1114	1115	1138	1214	1215	1239	1314	1315	1338	1414	1415	1440	1514	1515

	⑥	⑥b	⑥c	⑥	⑥b	⑥c	⑥	⑥b	⑥c	⑥	⑥b	⑥c	⑥	⑥b	⑥c	⑥b	⑥c	⑥	⑥D	⑥		⑦	⑦d	⑦e	⑦	⑦	⑦k	⑦n	⑦d
Taunton 115 120 120a d.	...	...	...	...	...	...	...	...	...	...	...	...	...	...	...	...	...	...	2114	2130		...	...	...	...	...	...	...	...
Weston-s-Mare .. 120 120a d.	...	...	...	...	1501r	...	...	...	...	...	1701r	...	...	1801r	...	...	...	2010	|	2153	⑦	...	...	...	0811	...	0956	0956	...
Bristol T M 115 120 120a d.	1400	1430	1433	1500	1530	1533	1600	1630	1633	1700	1730	1733	1800	1830	1832	1930	1933	2033	2147	2228		0745	0815	0820	0845	0948	1030	1030	1100
Bath d.	1413	1443	1446	1513	1543	1546	1613	1643	1646	1713	1743	1746	1813	1843	1845	1943	1946	2046	2202	2246		0758	0828	g	0858	1001	1043	1043	1113
Chippenham 132a d.	1425	1455	1458	1525	1555	1558	1625	1655	1658	1725	1755	1758	1825	1855	1857	1955	1958	2058	2215	2258		0810	0840	|	0910	1013	1055	1055	1125
Swindon 132a d.	1442	1511	1515	1541	1611	1615	1641	1711	1715	1742	1811	1815	1841	1911	1915	2011	2015	2114	2231	2314		0826	0856	0856	0926	1029	1111	1111	1141
Didcot Parkway 131 a.	|	1528	1532	|	1628	1632	|	1728	1732	|	1828	1832	|	1928	1932	2027	2031	2132	2248	2332		0844	|	|	0943	1045	1127	1127	|
Reading 130 131 a.	1508	1543	1546	1610	1644	1646	1708	1743	1746	1808	1845	1846	1908	1943	1946	2043	2046	2146	2304	2348		0900	0927	0927	1000	1102	1146	1144	1210
London Padd 130 131 a.	1538	1614	1615	1638	1714	1715	1738	1814	1815	1838	1914	1915	1940	2014	2015	2114	2115	2215	2344	0033		0940	1009h	1005	1044j	1143	1225j	1229	1251

	⑦e	⑦n	⑦	⑦d	⑦e	⑦n	⑦E	⑦d	⑦p	⑦		⑦d	⑦p	⑦d	⑦e	⑦	⑦	⑦	⑦d	⑦e	⑦E	⑦A	⑦E	⑦d	⑦p	⑦	⑦	⑦	⑦E
Taunton 115 120 120a d.	...	...	...	...	...	...	1148	...	...	...	...	...	...	...	...	...	...	...	...	...	1639	1658	1746	...	...	...	1856	...	2127
Weston-s-Mare .. 120 120a d.	...	...	...	1139	...	...	|	...	...	...	...	1320	1320	...	...	1451	...	...	...	...	1701	1729	|	...	...	...	1925	2026	|
Bristol T M 115 120 120a d.	1105	1105	1130	1200	1205	1205	1230	1300	1305	1330	...	1400	1405	1500	1505	1530	1600	1630	1700	1705	1730	1800	1830	1900	1905	1930	2000	2100	2210
Bath d.	1118	1118	1143	1213	1218	1218	1243	1313	1318	1343	...	1412	1418	1513	1518	1543	1613	1643	1713	1718	1743	1813	1843	1913	1918	1943	2013	2113	2223
Chippenham 132a d.	1130	1130	1155	1225	1230	1230	1255	1325	1330	1355	...	1425	1430	1525	1530	1555	1625	1655	1725	1730	1755	1825	1855	1925	1930	1955	2025	2125	2235
Swindon 132a d.	1146	1146	1211	1241	1246	1245	1311	1341	1346	1411	...	1442	1445	1541	1546	1611	1641	1711	1740	1745	1811	1841	1911	1941	1946	2011	2040	2141	2252
Didcot Parkway 131 a.	|	1203	1227	|	|	1303	1327	|	|	1427	...	1458	|	1557	1602	|	1658	|	1756	1801	|	1858	1928e	1958	2003	|	2058	2158	2310
Reading 130 131 a.	1214	1219	1245	1310	1316	1319	1344	1412	1414	1444	...	1515	1514	1615	1620	1644	1714	1743	1815	1819	1845	1914	1944	2014	2019	2044	2116	2216	2327
London Padd 130 131 a.	1252	1258	1323	1344	1353	1359	1423	1451	1459	1523	...	1554	1558	1653	1659	1723	1758j	1823	1853	1859	1924	1958j	2024	2053	2058	2123	2159	2258	0007

SWANSEA - CARDIFF - BRISTOL PARKWAY - LONDON

		ⒶS	Ⓐ	Ⓐ	Ⓐ	Ⓐ✕	Ⓐ	Ⓐ	Ⓐ	Ⓐ	ⒶG	Ⓐ	Ⓐ	Ⓐ	Ⓐ	Ⓐ	Ⓐ	Ⓐ	Ⓐ	Ⓐ	Ⓐ	Ⓐ	Ⓐ	Ⓐ	Ⓐ	Ⓐ	Ⓐ	Ⓐ
Swansea 135 d.		...	0352	0458	0527	0559	0629	0658	0728	0759	0829	...	0929	...	1029	...	1128	...	1229	...	1328	...	1428	...	1529	...	1629	...
Neath 135 d.	Ⓐ	...	0404	0510	0539	0611	0641	0710	0740	0811	0841	...	0941	...	1041	...	1140	...	1241	...	1340	...	1440	...	1541	...	1641	...
Port Talbot 135 d.		...	0412	0518	0547	0619	0649	0718	0748	0819	0849	...	0949	...	1049	...	1148	...	1249	...	1348	...	1448	...	1549	...	1649	...
Bridgend 135 d.		...	0425	0531	0600	0632	0702	0731	0801	0832	0902	...	1002	...	1102	...	1201	...	1302	...	1401	...	1501	...	1602	...	1702	...
Cardiff Cent .. 135 136 149 d.		...	0512	0555	0625	0656	0726	0755	0826	0856	0926	0955	1026	1055	1126	1155	1226	1256	1326	1355	1426	1455	1526	1556	1626	1656	1726	1756
Newport 136 149 d.		...	0532	0609	0639	0710	0740	0808	0840	0910	0939	1008	1040	1108	1140	1208	1240	1309	1340	1408	1440	1508	1540	1609	1640	1709	1740	1809
Bristol Parkway d.		0457	0602	0631	0701	0734	0802	0832	0902	0932	1003	1033	1103	1132	1203	1232	1302	1332	1403	1433	1503	1532	1603	1633	1703	1733	1803	1832
Swindon d.		0523	0628	0658	0729	0801	0829	0858	0930	0959	1030	1059	1130	1159	1230	1259	1330	1359	1430	1500	1530	1559	1630	1700	1730	1800	1830	1859
Didcot Parkway 131 a.		0541	0646	|	0746	|	|	|	|	1015	1046	1116	|	1216	1246	1315	|	1416	1446	1517	|	1616	1646	1717	|	1817	1847	|
Reading 130 131 a.		0556	0700	0728	0801	|	0855	0925	0958	1030	1101	1131	1157	1231	1301	1330	1356	1431	1501	1531	1557	1630	1701	1732	1759	1831	1901	1925
London Padd 130 131 a.		0624	0732	0801	0833	0854	0924	0957	1032	1059	1131	1202	1229	1300	1332	1408	1432	1507	1533	1610	1632	1707	1730	1809	1832	1906	1932	1954

	Ⓐ	Ⓐ	Ⓐ	①–④	⑤		⑥	⑥	⑥	⑥	⑥	⑥	⑥	⑥	⑥	⑥	⑥G	⑥	⑥	⑥	⑥	⑥	⑥	⑥	⑥	⑥		⑥
Swansea 135 d.	1729	1829	1929	2029	2029		0359	0459	0529	0559	0629	0659	0729	0759	0829	0929	1029	1129	1229	1329	1429	1529	1629	1729	1829	1929		0419
Neath 135 d.	1741	1841	1940	2041	2041	⑥	0411	0511	0541	0611	0641	0711	0741	0811	0841	0941	1041	1141	1241	1341	1441	1541	1641	1741	1841	1941	⑥	0431
Port Talbot 135 d.	1749	1849	1948	2049	2049		0419	0519	0549	0619	0649	0719	0749	0819	0849	0949	1049	1149	1249	1349	1449	1549	1649	1749	1849	1949		0439
Bridgend 135 d.	1802	1902	2001	2102	2102		0431	0532	0602	0632	0702	0732	0802	0832	0902	1003	1102	1202	1302	1402	1502	1602	1702	1802	1902	2002		0451
Cardiff Cent .. 135 136 149 d.	1826	1926	2025	2126	2126	★	0456	0556	0626	0656	0726	0756	0826	0856	0926	1026	1126	1226	1326	1426	1526	1626	1726	1826	1926	2026	☆	0515
Newport 136 149 d.	1840	1940	2039	2140	2140		0510	0610	0640	0710	0740	0810	0840	0910	0940	1040	1140	1240	1340	1440	1540	1640	1740	1840	1940	2040		0529
Bristol Parkway d.	1903	2003	2103	2202	2202		0601t	0634	0704	0733	0804	0833	0904	0933	1004	1104	1204	1304	1404	1504	1604	1704	1804	1903	2004	2103	§	|
Swindon d.	1930	2030	2133	2229	2230		0642	0701	0731	0800	0831	0900	0931	0959	1031	1131	1231	1331	1431	1531	1631	1731	1831	1929	2031	2130		0701
Didcot Parkway 131 a.	1947	2047	2152	|	|		0659	|	|	0816	|	0917	|	1016	|	|	|	|	|	|	|	|	|	|	|	2147		|
Reading 130 131 a.	2001	2101	2211	2300	2302		0714	0727	0757	0832	0857	0932	0957	1031	1058	1157	1259	1357	1457	1557	1657	1758	1857	1957	2057	2201		0727
London Padd 130 131 a.	2032	2132	2251a	2343	2338		0744	0800	0830	0902	0930	1002	1028	1102	1132	1230	1333	1430	1532	1633	1731	1832	1930	2030	2126	2238		0800

	⑥	⑥	⑥	⑥	⑥	⑥	⑥	⑥	⑥	⑥	⑥	⑥	⑥	⑥	⑥	⑥		⑦v	⑦n	⑦v	⑦n	⑦v	⑦n	⑦v	⑦n	⑦	⑦	⑦
Swansea 135 d.	0449	0559	0659	0759	0843	0943	1043	1138	1243	1343	1443	1543	1643	1743	1843	1929		...	...	0810	0810	0924	0928	1024	1028	1124	1224	1324
Neath 135 d.	0501	0611	0711	0811	0855	0955	1055	1150	1255	1355	1455	1555	1655	1755	1855	1941	⑦	...	...	0822	0822	0936	0940	1036	1040	1136	1236	1336
Port Talbot 135 d.	0509	0619	0719	0819	0903	1003	1103	1158	1303	1403	1503	1603	1703	1803	1903	1949		...	...	0829	0829	0943	0947	1043	1047	1143	1243	1343
Bridgend 135 d.	0522	0632	0732	0832	0916	1016	1116	1211	1316	1416	1516	1616	1716	1816	1916	2002		...	...	0843	0843	0956	1000	1056	1100	1156	1256	1356
Cardiff Cent .. 135 136 149 d.	0545	0656	0756	0856	0941	1041	1141	1241	1341	1441	1541	1641	1741	1841	1945	2026	♥	0800	0805	0905	0905	1020	1024	1120	1125	1220	1320	1419
Newport 136 149 d.	0559	0710	0810	0910	0955	1057	1155	1256	1355	1455	1555	1655	1755	1855	2000	2040		0820	0828	0926	0927	1039	1041	1139	1144	1239	1339	1439
Bristol Parkway d.	|	|	|	|	|	|	|	|	|	|	|	|	|	|	|	|		0845	0851	0947	0950	1102	1104	1201	1205	1301	1401	1501
Swindon d.	0731	0832	0932	1042	1122	1222	1322	1422	1522	1622	1722	1822	1922	2022	2123	2159		0913	0919	1017	1018	1128	1129	1228	1233	1328	1428	1528
Didcot Parkway 131 a.	|	|	|	|	|	|	|	|	|	|	|	|	|	|	|	2216		|	|	|	1035	1145	|	1245	|	1346	1446	1546
Reading 130 131 a.	0757	0858	0958	1108	1151	1251	1351	1451	1551	1651	1751	1851	1951	2050	2151	2231		0949	0952	1048	1050	1201	1158	1300	1300	1400	1501	1602
London Padd 130 131 a.	0830	0930	1029	1138	1224	1327	1421	1525	1624	1721	1824	1924	2021	2122	2222	2308		1027	1029	1127	1128	1239	1243	1339	1343	1443	1543j	1643j

	⑦v	⑦n	⑦	⑦Gn	⑦Gv	⑦n	⑦v	⑦Gn		⑦Gv	⑦	⑦Gv	⑦Gn		⑦	⑦	⑦	⑦	⑦	⑦	⑦	⑦	⑦G	⑦	⑦G	⑦	⑦	⑦G
Swansea 135 d.	1424	1424	1524	1551	1551	1651	1651	1751	...	1751	1851	1955	1955		...	0808	0919	1044	1144	1250	1350	1450	1551	1623	1715	1815	1915	1953
Neath 135 d.	1436	1436	1536	1603	1603	1703	1703	1803	...	1803	1903	2007	2007	⑦	...	0820	0931	1056	1156	1302	1402	1502	1603	1635	1728	1827	1927	2005
Port Talbot 135 d.	1443	1443	1543	1610	1610	1710	1710	1810	...	1810	1910	2014	2014		...	0827	0938	1103	1203	1309	1409	1509	1610	1642	1735	1834	1934	2012
Bridgend 135 d.	1456	1456	1556	1623	1623	1723	1723	1823	...	1823	1923	2028	2028		...	0840	0951	1117	1216	1322	1422	1522	1623	1655	1748	1847	1947	2026
Cardiff Cent .. 135 136 149 d.	1517	1520	1620	1649	1650	1750	1750	1850	...	1850	1949	2050	2055	♣	0805	0905	1015	1140	1240	1350	1450	1550	1650	1715	1810	1910	2010	2049
Newport 136 149 d.	1538	1540	1639	1708	1709	1808	1809	1908	...	1909	2009	2110	2114		0823	0924	1034	1159	1259	1409	1507	1609	1709	1738	1831	1930	2030	2109
Bristol Parkway d.	1601	1601	1701	1728	1731	1828	1831	1929	...	1932	2032	2132	2138	§	|	|	|	|	|	|	|	|	|	|	|	|	|	|
Swindon d.	1629	1628	1728	1757	1800	1855	1858	1957	...	1959	2057	2159	2205		0949	1045	1153	1328	1428	1528	1628	1728	1827	1856	1957	2050	2150	2228
Didcot Parkway 131 a.	|	1646	1746	1814	1817	1914	1917	2014	...	2018	|	|	|		1006	1102	1211	1345	1446	1545	1647	1746	1845	|	2011	2108	|	|
Reading 130 131 a.	1656	1701	1801	1830	1833	1930	1932	2030	...	2034	2127	2234	2240		1021	1117	1227	1359	1502	1602	1702	1800	1901	1927	2027	2123	2223	2259
London Padd 130 131 a.	1735	1743	1843j	1907	1911	2007	2011	2107	...	2112	2207	2321	2321		1100	1158	1307	1443	1544	1643	1743	1844	1943	2003	2106	2204	2304	2354

A – From Paignton (Table **115**).
B – From Exeter St Davids (Table **115**).
D – From Penzance (Tables **115**/**117**).
E – From Plymouth (Table **115**).
G – From Carmarthen (Table **135**).
Q – From Swansea (See lower panel).
R – Via Bristol Parkway (See lower panel).
S – From Bristol Temple Meads (See upper panel).
T – From Gloucester (Table **138**).

a – Arrives 2244 on ⑤.

b – May 27 - Sept. 9 and from Oct. 28.
c – Sept. 16 - Oct. 21.
d – May 21 - Sept 10 and from Oct. 29.
e – Sept. 17 - Oct. 22.
f – From Oct. 28.
g – Also calls Bristol Parkway a. 0829 / d. 0830.
h – Arrives 5 minutes earlier from Oct. 29.
j – Arrives 4 – 5 minutes earlier May 21 - Sept. 10.
k – May 21 - Oct. 22.
v – May 21 - Sept. 10.
n – From Oct. 29.

p – From Sept. 17.
q – ①–④ only.
r – May 27 - Sept. 9.
t – Bristol Temple Meads.

★ – ⑥ May 27 - Sept. 9 and from Oct. 28.
☆ – ⑥ Sept. 16 - Oct. 21.
♥ – ⑦ May 21 – Sept. 10 and from Oct. 29.
♣ – ⑦ Sept. 17 - Oct. 22.
§ – For special service to Bristol Parkway during Severn Tunnel closure see page 108.

For explanation of standard symbols see page 1

GW 2nd class — SWINDON - WESTBURY — 132a

km		Ⓐ A	Ⓐ	Ⓐ	Ⓐ	Ⓐ	Ⓐ	Ⓐ	Ⓐ AB	Ⓐ	⑥	⑥	⑥	⑥	⑥	⑥	⑥	⑥ B	⑦ a	⑦	⑦	⑦	⑦	⑦
	Gloucester 133 140 d.	0517	...	...	...	...	...	...	1754	...	...	...	...	...	...	...	...	2014	...	...	...	...	...	...
0	**Swindon** 133 132 d.	0612	0849	1047	1247	1319	1512	1736	1848	2006	0836	1036	1236	1436	1522	1736	1936	2106	0926	1128	1328	1528	1718	1953
27	Chippenham 132 d.	0629	0906	1104	1304	1336	1529	1753	1905	2023	0853	1053	1253	1453	1539	1753	1953	2125	0943	1145	1345	1545	1735	2010
37	Melksham d.	0638	0915	1113	1313	1347	1539	1803	1915	2032	0902	1102	1302	1502	1548	1802	2002	2134	0952	1154	1354	1554	1744	2019
46	Trowbridge 140 d.	0648	0933	1124	1323	1359	1549	1813	1924	2042	0912	1112	1312	1511	1558	1812	2012	2144	1001	1203	1403	1603	1754	2029
52	**Westbury** 140 a.	0655	0942	1133	1332	1407	1557	1821	1931	2049	0920	1120	1320	1520	1605	1818	2020	2152	1008	1210	1410	1610	1801	2038

	Ⓐ B	Ⓐ	Ⓐ	Ⓐ	Ⓐ	Ⓐ	Ⓐ	Ⓐ	Ⓐ B	⑥	⑥	⑥ b	⑥ c	⑥ d	⑥	⑥	⑥	⑥	⑦	⑦	⑦	⑦	⑦	⑦ B
Westbury 140 d.	0704	0733	0948	1147	1220	1414	1621	1832	1932	0732	0822	0930	0939	1132	1332	1506	1633	1832	1030	1230	1435	1620	1839	1941
Trowbridge 140 d.	0710	0739	0954	1153	1226	1420	1627	1838	1938	0738	0828	0936	0946	1138	1338	1512	1639	1838	1035	1235	1440	1625	1845	1946
Melksham d.	0720	0749	1004	1203	1236	1430	1637	1848	1947	0748	0837	0946	0955	1148	1348	1521	1649	1848	1046	1246	1450	1635	1854	1957
Chippenham 132 a.	0730	0800	1014	1212	1245	1441	1646	1900	2000	0800	0847	1000	1005	1200	1400	1531	1703	1902	1100	1300	1500	1645	1904	2007
Swindon 133 132 a.	0748	0819	1034	1236	1305	1504	1706	1923	2021	0820	0906	1022	1024	1220	1420	1550	1723	1923	1120	1320	1520	1705	1922	2025
Gloucester 133 140 a.	0852	...	...	...	...	...	...	...	2123	...	...	...	...	...	...	...	...	...	...	...	...	...	...	2123

A – To Southampton Central (Table **140**).
B – From/to Cheltenham Spa (Table **133**).
a – May 21 - Sept. 10.
b – May 27 - Sept. 9 and from Oct. 28.
c – Sept. 16 - Oct. 21.
d – Runs 3–5 minutes later Sept. 16 - Oct. 21.

GW Most London trains convey 🍷 — LONDON - CHELTENHAM — 133

km		Ⓐ	Ⓐ 2A	Ⓐ	Ⓐ 2	Ⓐ	Ⓐ 2	Ⓐ	Ⓐ 2	Ⓐ	Ⓐ 2	Ⓐ	Ⓐ 2	Ⓐ	Ⓐ	Ⓐ 2A	Ⓐ	Ⓐ 2	Ⓐ 2	⑥ 2	⑥	⑥ 2	⑥	⑥ 2	⑥	⑥ 2
0	**London** Paddington 132 d.	...	...	0736	...	0936	...	1136	...	1336	...	1536	...	1741	1847	...	1948	...	...	...	0815r	...	1015r	...	1215r	...
58	Reading 132 d.	...	...	0802	...	1003	...	1203	...	1404	...	1602	...	|	1919	...	2018	...	...	...	0842r	...	1042r	...	1242r	...
85	Didcot Parkway 132 d.	...	...	0818	...	1018	...	1218	...	1419	...	1617	...	1821	1934	...	2034	...	...	...	0855r	...	1056r	...	1256r	...
124	**Swindon** 132 d.	0640	0750	0841	0936	1039	1136	1239	1336	1439	1536	1638	1754	1841	1955	2025	2055	2154	2336	0716	0914	1014	1114	1214	1314	1414
164	Stroud d.	0709	0820	0910	1005	1107	1205	1307	1405	1507	1605	1708	1822	1911	2025	2053	2124	2223	0005	0745	0945	1043	1145	1243	1345	1443
183	Gloucester a.	0731	0848	0931	1028	1131	1227	1331	1428	1531	1628	1730	1849	1931	2046	2115	2147	2246	0025	0806	1006	1105	1207	1303	1406	1503
194	**Cheltenham** Spa 138 a.	0749	0905	0953	1046	1152	1245	1352	1447	1552	1647	1752	1905	1947	2102	2133	2202	2304	0045t	0824	1022	1122	1222	1324	1422	1525
	Worcester Shrub Hill 138 a.	...	...	...	...	...	...	...	...	...	...	...	...	...	...	...	2224	...	...	...	...	...	...	...	...	...

	⑥	⑥ 2	⑥	⑥ 2	⑥	⑥ 2	⑥	⑥ 2	⑦	⑦ 2g	⑦ 2p	⑦ g	⑦ p	⑦ k	⑦ p	⑦ 2	⑦	⑦ n	⑦ q	⑦ 2g	⑦ 2p	⑦ n	⑦ q	⑦ 2A	⑦ n	⑦ q	⑦ 2
London Paddington 132 d.	1415r	...	1615r	...	1815r	...	2015r	...	0827	...	...	1027	1037	1228	1228	...	1427	1627	1630	...	...	1822	1830	...	2022	2027	...
Reading 132 d.	1442r	...	1642r	...	1842r	...	2042r	...	0903	...	...	1103	1112	1303	1303	...	1503	1703	1703	...	...	1901	1903	...	2059	2103	...
Didcot Parkway 132 d.	1456r	...	1656r	...	1855r	...	2055r	...	|	...	...	|	|	|	|	...	|	|	|	...	...	|	|	...	|	|	...
Swindon 132 d.	1514	1614	1714	1814	1914	2000	2117	2241	0937	1044v	1109	1137	1147	1333	1333	1425f	1533k	1733	1737	1843	1900	1930	1937	2029	2129	2133	2257
Stroud d.	1545	1643	1745	1843	1944	2029	2145	2310	1005	1113v	1138	1205	1214	1400	1400	1455f	1600k	1801	1804	1911	1928	1957	2005	2058	2158	2202	2326
Gloucester a.	1605	1703	1806	1903	2006	2050	2206	2331	1027	1136v	1158	1227	1234	1427	1422	1519	1627	1827	1827	1934	1950	2024	2027	2118	2219	2223	2346
Cheltenham Spa 138 a.	1621	1725	1822	1925	2022	2102	2221	...	1043	1149	1214	1244	1249	1446	1446	1533	1646	1846	1846	...	...	2046	2045	2131	2236	2240	0007
Worcester Shrub Hill 138 a.	...	...	...	...	...	...	...	...	...	...	...	...	...	...	...	...	...	...	...	...	...	...	...	...	...	...	...

	Ⓐ 2B	Ⓐ	Ⓐ	Ⓐ C	Ⓐ	Ⓐ	Ⓐ 2	Ⓐ	Ⓐ 2	Ⓐ	Ⓐ 2	Ⓐ	Ⓐ 2	Ⓐ	Ⓐ 2B	Ⓐ	Ⓐ 2	Ⓐ 2	Ⓐ 2	⑥ 2	⑥ g	⑥ p	⑥	⑥ 2	⑥	⑥ 2
Worcester Shrub Hill 138 d.	...	0528	...	...	0708	...	...	...	...	...	...	...	...	...	...	...	...	...	...	...	...	...	0836	...	...	...
Cheltenham Spa 138 d.	...	0554	0630	...	0731	0831	0918	1036	1120	1236	1320	1436	1520	1620	1740	1834	2001	2100	2201	0530	0731	0720	0859	1001	1100	1201
Gloucester d.	0517	0611	0646	0705	0746	0849	0934	1052	1134	1253	1334	1453	1534	1644	1755	1851	2013	2121	2215	0543	0747	0736	0915	1014	1115	1214
Stroud d.	0535	0631	0705	|	0806	0908	0952	1113	1153	1313	1352	1513	1552	1704	1812	1911	2031	2138	2232	0601	0806	0755	0935	1032	1135	1232
Swindon 132 d.	0605	0701	0735	0904	0836	0945	1023	1145	1225	1345	1424	1545	1624	1735	1842	1941	2105	2209	2305	0632	0837	0824	1005	1104	1205	1304
Didcot Parkway 132 a.	...	0719	0755	...	0853	1002	...	1202	...	1402	...	1602	...	|	...	1958	...	...	...	...	0853	...	1022r	...	1222r	...
Reading 132 a.	...	0735	0811	...	0908	1016	...	1217	...	1417	...	1617	...	1803	...	2014	...	...	...	...	0908	...	1036r	...	1236r	...
London Paddington 132 a.	...	0809	0842	...	0939	1047	...	1247	...	1446	...	1655	...	1839	...	2043	...	...	...	...	0937	...	1109r	...	1307r	...

	⑥	⑥ 2	⑥	⑥ 2	⑥	⑥ 2	⑥	⑥ 2A	⑥ 2	⑦ 2	⑦	⑦ p	⑦ 2g	⑦ 2p	⑦ n	⑦ a		⑦ n	⑦ a	⑦ 2g	⑦ 2p	⑦ n	⑦ a	⑦ g	⑦ p	⑦ 2	⑦ 2
Worcester Shrub Hill 138 d.	...	...	...	...	...	...	...	...	...	...	...	...	...	...	...	...	...	...	...	...	...	...	...	...	...	...	...
Cheltenham Spa 138 d.	1300	1401	1500	1601	1700	1801	1900	2001	2120	0924	1118	...	1232	1303	1333	1346	...	1533	1546	1632	1645	1733	1746	1932	1932	...	2147
Gloucester d.	1316	1414	1515	1614	1715	1814	1917	2014	2135	0937	1134	1244	1245	1316	1349	1402	...	1546	1602	1645	1704	1749	1802	1946	1946	2017	2159
Stroud d.	1335	1432	1535	1632	1735	1832	1936	2032	2153	0955	1154	|	1303	1334	1409	1422	...	1606	1622	1702	1721	1809	1822	2006	2006	2035	2217
Swindon 132 d.	1406	1504	1605	1704	1805	1904	2006	2103	2225	1024	1222	1328	1332	1403	1437	1450	...	1636	1652	1733	1752	1839	1852	2035	2035	2104	2247
Didcot Parkway 132 a.	1423r	...	1622r	...	1822r	...	2023r	...	...	...	|	1345	...	...	|	1509	...	|	|	...	...	|	|	|	|	...	...
Reading 132 a.	1437r	...	1636r	...	1836r	...	2037r	...	...	...	1252	1359	...	...	1507	1523	...	1706	1722	...	...	1907	1919	2105	2104	...	...
London Paddington 132 a.	1506r	...	1707r	...	1906r	...	2107r	...	...	...	1330	1443	...	...	1545	1601	...	1751	1801	...	...	1945	2001	2153	2153	...	...

A – To/from Westbury (Table **132a**).
B – To Southampton Central (Tables **132a** and **140**).
C – Via Bristol and Bath (Tables **132** and **138**).
a – From Sept. 17.
f – Departs 4 minutes later May 21 - Sept. 10.
g – May 21 - Sept. 10 and from Oct. 29.
k – Departs 4 minutes later May 21 - Sept. 10 and from Oct. 27.
n – May 21 - Sept. 10.
p – Sept. 17 - Oct. 22.
q – From Sept. 17.
r – Not Sept. 16 - Oct. 21.
t – On ②–⑤ mornings arrives 0040.
v – 3 minutes later May 21 - Sept. 10.

GW — GATWICK AIRPORT ✈ - READING — 134

Service to October 8. For services from October 9 please contact National Rail Enquiries on 044 (0) 3457 48 49 50.

km		Ⓐ A	Ⓐ	Ⓐ	Ⓐ	Ⓐ	Ⓐ	Ⓐ 🍷		Ⓐ 🍷	Ⓐ 🍷	Ⓐ	Ⓐ	Ⓐ	Ⓐ	Ⓐ	Ⓐ	Ⓐ	⑥ A	⑥	⑥	⑥		⑥
0	**Gatwick** Airport ✈ d.	...	0531	0556	0658	0758	0910	1003	and	1503	1603	1703	1803	1913	2003	2103	2222	2318	...	0531	0603	0703	and	1903
10	Redhill △ d.	...	0543	0613	0710	0808	0923	1014	hourly	1514	1614	1713	1813	1927	2014	2114	2232	2334	...	0542	0613	0713	hourly	1914
43	Guildford △ d.	0602	0613	0643	0743	0838	0954	1044	until	1544	1644	1744	1847r	1956	2044	2144	2314	0002	0609	0612	0644	0744	until	1944
84	**Reading** △ a.	0632	0658	0729	0828	0917	1023	1119		1619	1719	1824	1927	2034	2119	2221	0001	0040	0643	0701	0719	0819		2019

	⑥	⑥		⑥	⑥	⑦	⑦		⑦	⑦	⑦	⑦	⑦ A	⑦	⑦	⑦		⑦	⑦	⑦	⑦	⑦	⑦		⑦	⑦	⑦
Gatwick Airport ✈ d.	2003	2103	...	2219	2318	0611	0711	...	0811	0909	1009	1109	...	1209	1309	1409	...	1509	1609	1709	1809	1909	2009	...	2109	2209	2309
Redhill △ d.	2014	2114	...	2233	2329	0620	0720	...	0820	0920	1020	1120	...	1220	1320	1420	...	1520	1620	1720	1820	1920	2020	...	2120	2220	2320
Guildford △ d.	2044	2144	...	2314	0002	0651	0752	...	0900	0952	1100	1152	1214	1300	1352	1500	...	1552	1700	1752	1900	1952	2100	...	2152	2300	2352
Reading △ a.	2119	2219	...	0001	0037	0726	0835	...	0938	1035	1135	1235	1248	1335	1435	1535	...	1635	1735	1835	1935	2035	2136	...	2236	2336	0037

	Ⓐ	Ⓐ	Ⓐ	Ⓐ	Ⓐ 🍷	Ⓐ 🍷		Ⓐ 🍷	Ⓐ	Ⓐ	Ⓐ	Ⓐ A	Ⓐ	Ⓐ		Ⓐ	Ⓐ	Ⓐ	Ⓐ	⑥	⑥		⑥	⑥ A
Reading ▽ d.	0434	0524	0634	0734	0832	0934	and	1434	1528	1634	1734	1821	1834	1934	...	2034	2134	2234	2334	0434	0534	and	1734	1823
Guildford ▽ d.	0510	0600	0710	0818	0913	1010	hourly	1510	1610	1710	1818	1859	1910	2010	...	2110	2218	2318	0021	0510	0610	hourly	1810	1901
Redhill ▽ a.	0539	0629	0738	0846	0942	1038	until	1538	1640	1738	1847	...	1942	2038	...	2145	2248	2358	0049	0539	0639	until	1838	...
Gatwick Airport ✈ a.	0555	0642	0750	0859	0957	1050		1551	1659	1754	1900	...	1956	2050	...	2204	2304	0011	0103	0558	0650		1850	...

	⑥	⑥	⑥	⑥	⑥	⑥	⑦	⑦	⑦	⑦	⑦		⑦	⑦	⑦	⑦	⑦	⑦	⑦	⑦	⑦		⑦	⑦	⑦ A	⑦	⑦
Reading ▽ d.	1834	1934	2034	2134	2234	2334	0603	0703	0820	0918	1020	...	1118	1220	1318	1420	1518	1620	1718	1820	1918	...	2020	2118	2214	2217	2315
Guildford ▽ d.	1910	2010	2110	2218	2318	0021	0639	0747	0856	1001	1056	...	1201	1256	1401	1456	1601	1656	1801	1856	2001	...	2056	2201	2242	2256	2359
Redhill ▽ a.	1938	2038	2146	2253	2358	0049	0708	0816	0935	1035	1135	...	1235	1335	1435	1535	1635	1735	1835	1935	2035	...	2135	2235	...	2335	0030
Gatwick Airport ✈ a.	1950	2050	2159	2305	0008	0100	0728	0828	0947	1047	1147	...	1247	1347	1447	1547	1647	1747	1847	1947	2047	...	2147	2247	...	2347	0041

A – To/from Newcastle (Table **124**).
r – Arrives 1841.
△ – Additional trains Redhill - Reading on Ⓐ at 0624, 0728, 0833, 0934 and hourly until 1434, 1529, 1632, 1743, 1843, 2034, 2135; on ⑥ at 0634 and hourly until 2034, 2136. Journey time 80–92 minutes.
▽ – Additional trains Reading - Redhill on Ⓐ at 0554, 0704 and hourly until 1804, 2004; on ⑥ at 0604 and hourly until 2004. Journey time 85–90 minutes.

135 CARDIFF - SWANSEA - SOUTH WEST WALES

2nd class AW

km	Ⓐ	Ⓐ	Ⓐ	Ⓐ	Ⓐ 🍷	Ⓐ	Ⓐ 🍷	Ⓐ 🍷	Ⓐ	Ⓐ	Ⓐ	Ⓐ 🍷	Ⓐ 🍷	Ⓐ 🍷	Ⓐ 🍷	Ⓐ 🍷	Ⓐ 🍷	Ⓐ 🍷	Ⓐ 🍷	Ⓐ	Ⓐ	Ⓐ 🍷	Ⓐ 🍷	Ⓐ	Ⓐ 🍷 C	Ⓐ 🍷	Ⓐ 🍷 B
	Manchester Picc. **149** d.	...	...	...	...	...	...	...	...	...	...	...	...	0630	0730	...	...	0830	0930	...	...	1030	1130	...	...	1230	...
0	**Cardiff** Central **149 132** d.	...	...	...	...	...	...	0535	0642	...	0714	0750	0904	1004	1042	1058	...	1138	1239	...	1313	1340	1443	...	1513	1539	1604
32	Bridgend **132** d.	...	...	...	...	...	...	0607	0705	...	0739	0809	0924	1023	1101	1119	...	1159	1258	...	1334	1404	1502	...	1532	1601	1625
52	Port Talbot **132** d.	...	...	...	...	...	...	0623	0722	...	0758	0825	0937	1036	1114	|	...	1211	1311	...	1350	1418	1515	...	1549	1614	1641
61	Neath **132** d.	...	...	...	...	...	...	0634	0733	...	0809	0835	0944	1043	1121	|	...	1218	1318	...	1401	1425	1522	...	1559	1621	1649
73	**Swansea** **132** a.	...	...	...	...	...	...	0651	0749	...	0828	0852	0956	1055	1135	|	...	1235	1334	...	1420	1434	1535	...	1615	1635	1702
73	**Swansea** **146** d.	...	...	...	...	...	0545	0653	0752	0814	...	0901	1002	1100	1138	|	1200	1240	1337	1400	*1435*	1437	1537	1600	1620	1640	1705
91	Llanelli **146** d.	...	...	...	...	...	0604	0711	0810	0831	...	0920	1021	1118	1154	1210a	1219	1259	1356	1416	*1451*	1456	1556	1618	1638	1659	1724
124	**Carmarthen** a.	...	...	...	...	...	0638	0743	0841	|	...	0950	1053	1144	1227	|	1248	1324	1430	1445	...	1522	1630	1647	...	1728	1755
124	**Carmarthen** d.	0450	0530	0550	0558	...	0639	0746	0843	|	...	0959	*1058*	1148	...	|	1251	1330	...	1451	...	1528	...	1651	...	1731	1757
147	Whitland d.	0503	0547	0605	0613	...	0656	0800	0902	0910	...	1014	*1113*	1201	...	1245	1306	1345	...	1506	...	1543	...	1706	...	1746	1813
172	Tenby a.	|	0614	|	|	...	0724	|	0930	|	...	|	*1141*	|	...	|	1334	|	...	1534	...	|	...	1734	...	|	|
191	**Pembroke Dock** a.	|	0654	|	|	...	0803	|	1018	|	...	|	*1223*	|	...	|	1419	|	...	1619	...	|	...	1819	...	|	|
166	Clarbeston Road d.	0518x	...	0620x	0627x	0720	...	0814x	...	0925x	...	1028x	...	1215x	...	|	...	1359x	...	...	...	1557x	...	...	...	1800x	1827x
174	Haverfordwest d.	0529	...	|	0635	|	...	0823	...	|	...	1036	...	1223	...	|	...	1408	...	...	...	1606	...	...	...	1808	|
189	**Milford Haven** a.	0552	...	|	0658	|	...	0843	...	|	...	1057	...	1248	...	|	...	1431	...	...	...	1629	...	...	...	1831	|
191	**Fishguard** Harbour a.	...	...	0644	...	0744	...	...	...	0950	...	...	...	...	...	1327	...	...	...	...	...	...	...	...	...	...	1856

	Ⓐ 🍷	Ⓐ 🍷	Ⓐ	Ⓐ 🍷	Ⓐ	Ⓐ A	Ⓐ 🍷		①–④	⑤	Ⓐ	Ⓐ	⑥	⑥	⑥	⑥	⑥	⑥	⑥	⑥ 🍷	⑥ b	⑥ c	⑥	⑥ 🍷	⑥ 🍷	⑥	⑥ 🍷	⑥ 🍷
Manchester Picc. **149** d.	1330	1430	...	1530	...	...	1630	...	1830	1832	...	1930		...	...	...	...	...	...	...	...	...	...	...	...	...	0630	...
Cardiff Central **149 132** d.	1704	1739	1806	1904	...	1929	1946	2104	2215	2208	...	2315		...	...	...	...	...	...	0533	0642	0642	0714	0758	0904	0914	1000	1059
Bridgend **132** d.	1727	1800	1830	1923	...	1950	2005	2127	2241	2235	...	2345		...	...	...	...	...	...	0603	0702	0703	0738	0817	0923	0934	1019	1119
Port Talbot **132** d.	1742	1818	1847	1938	...	2003	2021	2145	2254	2247	...	0001		...	...	...	...	...	...	0620	0718	0719	0754	0830	0936	0952	1031	|
Neath **132** d.	1752	1826	1858	1948	...	2010	2028	2152	|	2254	...	0013		...	...	...	...	...	...	0631	0729	0730	0805	0837	0943	1003	1038	|
Swansea **132** a.	1807	1839	1914	2004	...	2021	2042	2205	|	2307	...	0028		...	...	...	...	...	...	0647	0745	0746	0822	0851	0955	1021	1054	|
Swansea **146** d.	1814	1842	*1934*	2011	...	2034	2048	2227	|	2311	2345	0045		...	...	...	...	...	0545	0653	0750	0750	▬	0900	1004	▬	1100	|
Llanelli **146** d.	1833	1901	*1954*	2030	...	2051	2111	2246	2324	2331	0002	0102s		...	...	...	...	...	0604	0711	0808	0808	...	0919	1022	⑥	1118	1202
Carmarthen a.	1902	1928	*2029*	2100	...	2123	2139	2315	2359	0007	0033	0140		...	...	...	...	...	0637	0743	0840	0840	⑥	0948	1051		1145	|
Carmarthen d.	1905	1930	▬	...	2110	...	2141	2320	...	...	0035	...		0450	0530	0550	0558	...	0638	0746	0845	0843	c	0957	...	1056	1148	|
Whitland d.	1921	1946	...	...	2125	...	2156	2335	...	...	0051	...		0503	0546	0606	0613	...	0656	0800	0901	0902	0907	1014	...	1111	1203	1238
Tenby a.	1955	|	Ⓐ	...	2152	...	|	|	...	...	|	...		|	0614	|	|	...	0724	|	|	0930	|	|	...	1139	|	|
Pembroke Dock a.	*2036*	|		...	2226	...	|	|	...	...	|	...		|	0659	|	|	...	0807	|	|	1017	|	|	...	1220	|	|
Clarbeston Road d.	...	2000x	2005	...	...	...	2210x	2350x	...	...	0104x	...		0518x	...	0621x	0627x	0720	...	0815x	0915x	...	0922x	1028x	...	...	1217x	|
Haverfordwest d.	...	2009	|	...	...	...	2223	2358	...	...	|	...		0530	...	|	0635	|	...	0823	|	...	|	1036	...	...	1225	|
Milford Haven a.	...	2032	|	...	...	...	2246	0021	...	...	|	...		0553	...	|	0658	|	...	0848	|	...	|	1058	...	...	1248	|
Fishguard Harbour a.	...	...	2029	...	...	...	...	...	...	...	0135	...		...	...	0646	...	0744	...	...	0943	...	0947	...	...	...	...	1323

	⑥ Ab	⑥ c	⑥ 🍷	⑥	⑥ 🍷 c	⑥ 🍷 b	⑥ b	⑥ c	⑥ 🍷	⑥	⑥ 🍷	⑥ 🍷	⑥ c	⑥ b	⑥	⑥ 🍷	⑥ 🍷 B	⑥ 🍷	⑥	⑥ 🍷	⑥	⑥ 🍷	⑥ A	⑥ 🍷	⑥	⑥ 🍷	⑥	⑥
Manchester Picc. **149** d.	...	...	0730	...	0830	0830	...	...	0930	...	1030	1130	...	...	...	1230	...	1330	...	1430	...	1530	...	1630	...	1830	...	...
Cardiff Central **132** d.	1050	...	1105	1114	1204	1204	...	...	1304	1310	1404	1504	...	...	1514	1540	1600	1704	1738	1804	...	1904	1950	2001	2104	2208	...	2235
Bridgend **132** d.	1110	...	1124	1134	1223	1223	...	...	1323	1332	1423	1523	...	...	1534	1559	1622	1725	1758	1825	...	1924	2010	2020	2123	2235	...	2302
Port Talbot **132** d.	1123	...	1138	1150	1236	1236	...	...	1336	1348	1436	1536	...	...	1550	1612t	1638	1740	1814	1841	...	1939	2023	2033	2139	2247	...	2319
Neath **132** d.	1131	...	1146	1201	1243	1243	...	...	1343	1359	1443	1543	...	...	1601	1619t	1646	1750	1825	1849	...	1949	2031	|	2146	2254	...	2331
Swansea **132** a.	1143	...	1159	1220	1255	1255	...	...	1400	1418	1455	1555	...	...	1617	1631t	1701	1805	1844	1902	...	2005	2043	|	2157	2307	...	2347
Swansea **146** d.	1150	1150	1205	...	1302	1302	1335	1350	1405	...	1500	1600	1609	1609	1623	1635t	1706	1809	...	1904	1934	2013	2100	|	2225	2310	2347	0008
Llanelli **146** d.	1209	1211	1224	...	1322	1322	1351	1406	1424	...	1520	1619	1628	1632	1641	1654t	1724	1828	...	1924	1954	2032	2117	2106	2244	2329	0004	0027s
Carmarthen a.	1240	1240	1253	...	1347	1347	1420	1440	1453	...	1545	1653	1657	1709	...	1723t	1755	1905	...	1951	2029	2057	2148	2134	2318	0003	0035	0104
Carmarthen d.	1247	1258	...	...	1351	1351	1438	1458	...	...	1549	...	1659	1717	...	1731	1757	1905	...	1955	▬	2100	...	2205	...	...	0037	...
Whitland d.	1306	1312	...	...	1406	1415	1454	1512	...	...	1604	...	1714	1732	...	1746	1813	1921	...	2010	...	2115	...	2220	...	...	0053	...
Tenby a.	1334	1340	...	...	|	|	1522	1540	...	...	|	...	1741	1800	...	|	|	1957f	...	|	⑥	2142	...	|	...	...	|	...
Pembroke Dock a.	1414	1419	...	...	|	|	1609	1619	...	...	|	...	1818	1840	...	|	|	2029f	...	|		2218	...	|	...	...	|	...
Clarbeston Road d.	...	...	...	...	1420x	1429x	...	...	...	...	1618x	...	...	...	...	1800x	1827x	...	...	2025x	2030	...	...	2234x	...	...	0106x	...
Haverfordwest d.	...	...	...	...	1429	1437	...	...	...	...	1626	...	...	...	...	1808	|	...	...	2033	|	...	...	2242	...	...	|	...
Milford Haven a.	...	...	...	...	1452	1500	...	...	...	...	1649	...	...	...	...	1827	|	...	...	2056	|	...	...	2305	...	...	|	...
Fishguard Harbour a.	...	...	...	...	...	...	...	...	...	...	...	...	...	...	...	...	1856	...	...	...	2054	...	...	...	...	...	0135	...

⑦	⑦ d	⑦ 🍷 d	⑦	⑦	⑦ 🍷	⑦	⑦ A	⑦ 🍷 e	⑦ 🍷 d	⑦ g	⑦ h	⑦ Ah	⑦ Ag	⑦ 🍷 k	⑦ 🍷 n	⑦	⑦ Ag	⑦ 🍷 g	⑦ 🍷 h	⑦ Ah	⑦	⑦ 🍷 g	⑦ 🍷 h	⑦	⑦ 🍷 g	⑦ 🍷 h	⑦
Manchester Picc. **149** d.	...	...	...	...	...	...	...	...	...	...	...	...	...	1031	1031	...	...	1233	1233	...	...	1430	1430	...	...	...	...
Cardiff Central **132** d.	...	0710	...	...	0956	1119	1150	1200r	1205	...	...	1322	1401	1405	1405	...	1601	1614	1614	1634	...	1810	1810	...	2013	2013	2230
Bridgend **132** d.	...	0732	...	...	1025	1139	1213	1230r	1235	...	...	1344	1421	1435	1433	...	1621	1643	1643	1658	...	1839	1838	...	2033	2033	2251
Port Talbot **132** d.	...	0746	...	...	1040	1153	1226	1246r	1254	...	...	1401	1434	1452	1450	...	1634	1659	1659	1712	...	1855	1855	...	2049	2049	2305
Neath **132** d.	...	0754	...	...	1048	1201	1234	|	|	...	...	1409	1441	1500	1458	...	1641	1707	1707	1719	...	1903	1903	...	2057	2057	2313
Swansea **132** a.	...	0807	...	...	1100	1214	1248	|	|	...	...	1421	1457	1512	1511	...	1657	1722	1720	1731	...	1917	1916	...	2111	2110	2325
Swansea **146** d.	...	0815	...	...	1104	1216	1253	|	|	1402	1427	1441	1502	1536	1542	1638	1708	1725	1743	1737	1837	1922	1939	2050	2118	2137	2338
Llanelli **146** d.	...	0835	...	...	1124	1235	1310	1316r	1326	1422	1447	1503	1519	1555	1601	1658	1726	1744	1801	1754	1857	1941	1957	2110	2137	2156	2358
Carmarthen a.	...	0907	...	...	1156	1306	1341	1349r	1359	1455	1520	1532	1548	1624	1633	1730	1755	1815	1832	1823	1929	2009	2024	2142	2206	2225	0030
Carmarthen d.	0820	0910	0955	1019	1206	1308	...	1355	1405	1457	1522	...	...	1627	1634	1732	...	1820	1835	...	1932	2010	2024	...	2210	2227	0034
Whitland d.	0836	0926	1011	1034	1222	1324	...	1411	1421	1512	1537	...	...	1644	1651	1752p	...	1837	1852	...	1948	2030	2047	...	2226	2243	0050
Tenby a.	|	0954	|	1101	|	|	...	|	|	1540	1605	...	...	|	|	1820p	...	|	|	...	|	*2102*	*2119*	...	|	|	|
Pembroke Dock a.	|	1027	|	1141	|	|	...	|	|	1617	1642	...	...	|	|	1859p	...	|	|	...	|	*2136*	*2153*	...	|	|	|
Clarbeston Road d.	0852x	...	1027x	...	1239x	|	...	1427x	1437x	...	...	...	...	1700x	1707x	...	...	1853x	1908x	...	2004x	2046x	2102x	...	2242x	2259x	0103x
Haverfordwest d.	0900	...	1035	...	1247	|	...	1435	1445	...	...	...	...	1708	1715	...	...	1901	1916	...	2012	2054	2110	...	2250	2307	|
Milford Haven a.	0920	...	1055	...	1307	|	...	1455	1509	...	...	...	...	1729	1737	...	...	1925	1940	...	...	2120	2135	...	2310	2327	|
Fishguard Harbour a.	...	...	...	...	...	1400	...	...	...	...	...	...	...	...	...	...	...	...	...	...	...	...	...	...	...	...	0132

Ⓐ	②–⑤	Ⓐ	Ⓐ 🍷	Ⓐ 🍷	Ⓐ 🍷	Ⓐ 🍷	Ⓐ	Ⓐ 🍷	Ⓐ 🍷	Ⓐ 🍷	Ⓐ 🍷	Ⓐ 🍷	Ⓐ	Ⓐ 🍷	Ⓐ 🍷	Ⓐ	Ⓐ	Ⓐ 🍷	Ⓐ 🍷	Ⓐ 🍷	Ⓐ 🍷	Ⓐ 🍷	Ⓐ D	Ⓐ 🍷	Ⓐ 🍷 D	Ⓐ	Ⓐ 🍷
Fishguard Harbour d.	...	0150	...	...	...	...	0650	...	...	0750	...	...	0954	...	...	...	...	...	...	1329	...	...	...	...	...	...	...
Milford Haven d.	0018	|	...	...	...	0555	|	0705	...	|	0908	...	|	...	1108	...	...	...	1308	|	...	...	...	1508	...	...	...
Haverfordwest d.	0033	|	...	...	...	0610	|	0720	...	|	0923	...	|	...	1123	...	...	...	1323	|	...	...	...	1523	...	...	...
Clarbeston Road d.	0041x	0212x	...	...	...	0618x	0714	0728x	...	0811x	0931x	...	1017x	...	1131x	...	...	...	1331x	|	...	...	...	1531x	...	...	...
Pembroke Dock d.	|	|	...	...	...	|	▬	|	0659	|	|	0909	|	...	|	...	1109	...	|	|	1309	...	...	|	...	1509	...
Tenby d.	|	|	...	...	...	|	...	|	0729	|	|	0938	|	...	|	...	1143	...	|	|	1341	...	...	|	...	1541	...
Whitland d.	0054	0224	...	...	...	0631	Ⓐ	0741	0756	0824	0944	1007	1032	...	1144	...	1211	...	1344	1404	1409	...	...	1544	...	1609	...
Carmarthen a.	0116	0241	...	...	...	0647	A	0755	0815	0843	1003	1024	1049	...	1200	...	1229	...	1400	1421	1430	...	...	1600	...	1627	...
Carmarthen d.	...	0303	0503	0547	0615	0650	0730	0801	0818	0900	1006	1031	...	1103	1205	...	1233	1302	1405	1426	1438	1503	...	1605	...	1631	1658
Llanelli d.	...	0325	0528	0615	0644	0719	0805	0830	0848	0925	1032	1056	...	1131	1230	1245	1259	1330	1430	1448	1503	1532	...	1630	1645	1657	1726
Swansea a.	...	0346	|	0635	0704	0738	0821	0849	0907	0951	1049	1123	...	1150	1249	1304	1322	1351	1449	|	1523	1551	...	1649	1702	1722	1746
Swansea **132** d.	...	*0352*	|	0640	0706	0742	0829	0853	0910	0955	1055	...	...	1155	1254	1310	...	1355	1455	|	...	1555	1510	1655	1712	...	1749
Neath **132** d.	...	*0404*	|	0653	0717	0753	0841	0904	0925	1006	1106	...	...	1206	1305	1325	...	1406	1506	|	...	1606	1525	1706	1727	...	1803
Port Talbot **132** d.	...	*0412*	0601	0704	0724	0800	0849	0911	0936	1013	1113	...	...	1213	1312	1336	...	1413	1513	|	...	1613	1536	1713	1738	...	1814
Bridgend **132** d.	...	*0425*	0616	0720	0740	0815	0902	0924	0953	1026	1126	...	...	1226	1325	1353	...	1426	1526	1535	...	1626	1553	1726	1755	...	1829
Cardiff Central **132** a.	...	*0501*	0645	0748	0803	0838	0923	0945	1018	1048	1148	...	...	1248	1348	1415	...	1447	1547	1559	...	1647	1614	1746	1815	...	1850
Manchester Picc. **149** a.	...	...	1015	...	1115	1215	...	1315	...	1415	1515	...	...	1615	1715	...	...	1815	1915	...	...	2019	...	2106	...	...	2215

A – From/to London (operated by GW, see Table **132**). Conveys [12] and 🍷.
B – From Gloucester (Table **121**).
C – From Holyhead (Tables **149** and **160**).
D – To Chester (Tables **149** and **160**).

a – Arrives 10 minutes earlier.

b – May 27 - Sept. 9.
c – From Sept. 16.
d – May 21 - Sept. 10.
e – From Sept. 17.
f – Arrives 4 minutes earlier from Sept. 16.
g – May 21 - Sept. 10 and from Oct. 29.
h – Sept. 17 - Oct. 22.

k – From Oct. 29.
n – May 21 - Oct. 22.
p – 4 minutes earlier May 21 - Sept. 10.
r – 5 minutes later from Oct. 29.
s – Calls to set down only.
t – 5 minutes later May 27 - Sept. 9 and from Oct. 28.
x – Calls on request.

	Ⓐ	Ⓐ	Ⓐ	Ⓐ	Ⓐ	Ⓐ	Ⓐ	Ⓐ	Ⓐ	Ⓐ	Ⓐ		⑥	⑥	⑥	⑥	⑥	⑥	⑥	⑥	⑥	⑥	⑥	⑥	⑥	⑥	⑥	⑥	⑥	⑥
												⑥			🍷	🍷	🍷	🍷		🍷		a	🍷	🍷d	Ac	Ab	🍷			
Fishguard Hbr d.	...	...	1908	...	...	...	2050	...	...	...	...		...	0150	...	...	...	...	0650	...	...	...	0750	...	...	...	...	...	...	0953
Milford Haven d.	1708	...	|	1912	...	2036	|	...	...	...	2318		0018	|	...	...	...	0555	|	0705	...	...	|	...	...	...	0908	...	...	|
Haverfordwest d.	1723	...	|	1927	...	2051	|	...	...	...	2333		0033	|	...	...	...	0610	|	0720	...	...	|	...	...	...	0923	...	...	|
Clarbeston Road d.	1731x	...	1930	1935x	...	2059x	2112x	...	...	...	2341x		0041x	0212x	...	...	...	0618x	0714	0728x	...	...	0811x	...	...	...	0931x	...	...	1014x
Pembroke Dock d.	|	1709	▬	|	*1919*	|	|	...	2109	2228	|		|	|	...	...	...	|	...	|	0659	...	|	0835	...	...	|	...	0909a	|
Tenby d.	|	1738	...	|	1957	|	|	...	2153	2255	|		|	|	...	...	...	|	...	|	0729	...	|	0908	...	...	|	...	0937a	|
Whitland d.	1745	1807	Ⓐ	1948	2027	2112	2126	...	2221	2325	2354		0054	0224	...	...	...	0631	...	0741	0756	...	0824	0938	...	...	0944	...	1005	1029
Carmarthen a.	1802	1824		2004	2045	2134	2149	...	2239	2344	0016		0116	0241	...	...	...	0647	...	0755	0815	...	0843	...	...	...	1002	...	1025	1046
Carmarthen d.	1806	1831	1850	2009	2047	...	...	...	2244	...	...		...	0244	0504	0555	0620	0650	...	0801	0818	...	0900	...	0938	0950	1004	...	1027	...
Llanelli d.	1835	1857	1921	2033	2117	...	...	2201	2314	...	...		...	0306	0529	0624	0648	0719	...	0830	0848	0855	0928	...	1006	1018	1031	...	1053	...
Swansea a.	1855	1922	1943	2055	2142	...	...	2222	2343	...	...		...	0329	|	0643	0708	0738	...	0849	0907	0922	0950	...	1022	1034	1049	...	1119	...
Swansea 132 d.	1858	...	1951	2058	2145	...	...	2232	...	...	...		...	...	|	0647	0711	0744	...	0855	0910	0933	0954	...	1029	1043	1055	1110	...	...
Neath 132 d.	1913	...	2002	2109	2200	...	...	2247	...	...	...		...	...	|	0658	0726	0755	...	0906	0925	0945	1006	...	1041	1055	1106	1125	...	...
Port Talbot 132 d.	1924	...	2009	2116	2211	...	...	2258	...	...	...		...	...	0602	0705	0737	0802	...	0913	0936	0952	1013	...	1049	1103	1113	1136	...	...
Bridgend 132 d.	1940	...	2023	2131	2227	...	...	2315	...	...	...		...	...	0617	0720	0753	0817	...	0928	0953	1010	1028	...	1102	1116	1128	1152	...	...
Cardiff Central 132 a.	2003	...	2045	2200	2255	...	...	2340	...	...	...		...	...	0644	0743	0836f	0844	...	0953	1016	1033	1048	...	1123	1137	1148	1215	...	...
Manchester P 149 a.	...	...	...	...	...	...	...	...	...	...	...		...	...	1016	1115	...	1215	...	1315	...	...	1415	...	...	...	1515	...	...	...

	⑥	⑥	⑥	⑥	⑥	⑥	⑥	⑥	⑥	⑥	⑥	⑥	⑥	⑥	⑥	⑥	⑥	⑥	⑥	⑥	⑥	⑥	⑥	⑥	⑥	⑥	⑥	⑥		⑦
	🍷	Ad	🍷	🍷		🍷	🍷	🍷			🍷	🍷		Ad	b	🍷		d	a										⑦	
Fishguard Hbr d.	...	...	...	...	...	...	...	1328	...	...	...	...	...	...	...	...	...	...	...	1900	...	...	...	2100	...	...	...	...		0150
Milford Haven d.	...	...	1108	...	...	...	1308	|	...	...	...	1508	...	...	...	...	1708	...	...	|	1908	...	...	|	2116	...	...	2318		|
Haverfordwest d.	...	...	1123	...	...	...	1323	|	...	...	...	1523	...	...	...	...	1723	...	...	|	1923	...	...	|	2131	...	...	2333		|
Clarbeston Road d.	...	...	1131x	...	...	...	1331x	|	...	...	...	1531x	...	...	...	...	1731x	...	...	1922	1931x	...	...	2122x	2139x	...	...	2341x		|
Pembroke Dock d.	...	1001	|	...	1109a	...	|	|	...	1309	...	|	...	1455	1509	...	|	1625	1712	▬	|	1909t	...	|	|	2109	2218	|		|
Tenby d.	...	1037	|	...	1141	...	|	|	...	1340	...	|	...	1536	1544	...	|	1655	1743	...	|	1951t	...	|	|	2142	2245	|		|
Whitland d.	...	1108	1144	...	1209	...	1344	1403	...	1409	...	1544	...	1609	1612	...	1745	1726	1811	...	1944	2021t	...	2136	2152	2211	2315	2354		0224s
Carmarthen a.	...	1126	1200	...	1227	...	1400	1419	...	1428	...	1600	...	1627	1630	...	1803	1744	1833	⑥	2004	2039t	...	2159	2214	2228	2334	0016		0242
Carmarthen d.	1109	1135	1205	...	1233	1302	1405	1422	...	1431	1503	1605	...	1633	1632	1702	1807	1833	1837	1854	2007	2047	...	...	...	2235	...	...		0245
Llanelli d.	1137	1203	1230	1242	1259	1330	1430	1445	...	1456	1532	1630	1647	1705	1658	1730	1836	1859	1859	1925	2031	2117	*2138*	...	...	2305	...	...		0308s
Swansea a.	1156	1219	1249	1301	1319	1349	1449	|	...	1520	1551	1649	1704	1721	1720	1749	1856	1921	1920	1947	2051	2142	*2206*	...	...	2330	...	...		|
Swansea 132 d.	1200	1229	1253	1307	...	1400	1455	|	1510	...	1555	1658	1710	1729	...	1754	1900	...	...	1952	2055	2143	2220	...	...	...	...	...		|
Neath 132 d.	1211	1241	1304	1322	...	1411	1506	|	1525	...	1606	1709	1725	1741	...	1805	1911	...	...	2003	2106	2159	2235	...	...	...	...	...		|
Port Talbot 132 d.	1218	1249	1311	1333	...	1418	1513	|	1536	...	1613	1716	1736	1749	...	1812	1919	...	...	2010	2113	2210	2246	...	...	...	...	...		|
Bridgend 132 d.	1231	1302	1326	1352	...	1431	1526	1531	1553	...	1628	1731	1752	1802	...	1827	1933	...	...	2024	2126	2226	2302	...	...	...	...	...		|
Cardiff Central 132 a.	1252	1323	1348	1413	...	1452	1551r	1558	1616	...	1649	1752	1820	1823	...	1847	1956	...	...	2047	2147	2250	2326	...	...	...	...	...		0408
Manchester P 149 a.	1615	...	1714	...	...	1815	1915	...	...	...	2015	2115	...	...	...	2214	*2349*	...	...	...	...	...	...	...	...	...	...	...		...

	⑦	⑦	⑦	⑦	⑦	⑦	⑦	⑦	⑦	⑦	⑦	⑦	⑦	⑦	⑦	⑦	⑦	⑦	⑦	⑦	⑦	⑦	⑦	⑦	⑦	⑦	⑦	⑦	⑦	⑦
	🚌	🍷g		🍷	n	k	g	🍷		🍷	A	🍷n	🍷k	An	🍷	Ak	k	p	qm	A			k	n		k	k	n	k	n
Fishguard Hbr d.	...		...	...	...	...	...	...	...	...	...	1422	1422	...	...	...	...	...	...	...	...	...	...	...	...		...	...	...	...
Milford Haven d.	...	...	...	0928g	...	...	...	1123	...	1318	...	|	|	...	1507	...	...	1732	1740	...	...	...	1938	1953	...	2135	...	...	2315	2344
Haverfordwest d.	...	...	...	0943g	...	...	...	1138	...	1331	...	|	|	...	1522	...	...	1747	1755	...	...	...	1953	2012	...	2151	...	...	2330	2359
Clarbeston Road d.	...	...	...	0952h	...	...	...	1147x	...	1340x	...	|	|	...	1531x	...	...	1755x	1803x	...	...	...	2001x	2020x	...	2159x	...	...	2339x	0015x
Pembroke Dock d.	...	...	...	|	...	...	1040	|	1155j	|	...	|	|	...	|	...	1625	|	|	...	...	1901	|	|	...	|	2145	2201	|	|
Tenby d.	...	...	...	|	...	...	1116	|	1223j	|	...	|	|	...	|	...	1653	|	|	...	...	1928	|	|	...	|	2213	2229	|	|
Whitland d.	...	...	...	1006g	...	...	1145	1203	1254j	1357	...	1457	1457	...	1548	...	1724	1810	1816	...	...	1959	2017	2036	...	2214	2244	2300	2353	0022
Carmarthen a.	...	...	...	1024g	...	...	1201	1221	1317	1415	...	1514	1514	...	1611	...	1744	1829	1835	...	...	2019	2036	2055	...	2231	2306	2321	0014	0043
Carmarthen d.	0250	0845	0940	1030	1046	1053	...	1224	1320	1425	1458	1523	1540	1615	1616e	1655	1747	...	...	1903	...	2019	...	...	2115	2234	...	...	...	...
Llanelli d.	|	0912	1010	1056	1116	1123	...	1250	1350	1451	1527	1553	1610	1642	1646e	1722	1818	...	...	1930	1959	2051	...	...	2141	2304	...	...	...	...
Swansea a.	0350	0930	1036	1118	1139	1147	...	1313	1416	1517	1543	1618	1635	1659	1724v	1739	1846	...	...	1949	2025	2124	...	...	2204	2327	...	...	...	...
Swansea 132 d.	*0808*	0934	...	1131	*1144*	*1224*	...	1340	...	1534	1551	*1623*	*1651*	1715	1730	1751	*1851*	...	...	1953	2040	...	...	...	2210	2331	...	...	...	...
Neath 132 d.	*0820*	0945	...	1142	*1156*	*1236*	...	1351	...	1545	1603	*1635*	*1703*	1728	1741	1803	*1903*	...	...	2005	2051	...	...	...	2221	2343	...	...	...	...
Port Talbot 132 d.	*0827*	0952	...	1149	*1203*	*1243*	...	1358	...	1552	1610	*1642*	*1710*	1735	1748	1810	*1910*	...	...	2012	2058	...	...	...	2228	2350	...	...	...	...
Bridgend 132 d.	*0840*	1007	...	1204	*1216*	*1256*	...	1414	...	1607	1623	*1655*	*1723*	1748	1803	1823	*1923*	...	...	2026	2112	...	...	...	2245	0006	...	...	...	...
Cardiff Central 132 a.	*0904*	1031	...	1234	*1237*	*1317*	...	1453	...	1637	1647	*1715*	*1747*	1810	1832	1848	*1948*	...	...	2050	2137	...	...	...	2310	0035	...	...	...	...
Manchester P 149 a.	...	1420	...	1615	...	...	...	1818	...	2016	...	...	...	...	2219	...	...	...	...	...	...	...	...	...	...	...	...	...	...	...

A – To London (operated by GW, see Table **132**). Conveys [12] and 🍷.

a – From Sept. 16.
b – Sept. 16 - Oct. 21.
c – May 27 - Sept. 9 and from Oct. 28.
d – May 27 - Sept. 9.
e – Departs 13–16 minutes later Sept. 9 - Oct. 22.
f – Arrives 0825 Sept. 16 - Oct. 21.
g – May 21 - Sept. 10.
h – Calls on request May 21 - Sept. 10.
j – 5 minutes later from Oct. 29.
k – May 21 - Sept. 10 and from Oct. 29.
m – Runs 7 minutes later Sept. 17 - Oct. 22.
n – Sept. 17 - Oct. 22.
p – From Oct. 29.
q – May 21 - Oct. 22.
r – Arrives 5 minutes earlier May 27 - Sept. 9.
s – Calls to set down only.
t – 4 minutes later May 27 - Sept. 9.
v – Arrives 1708 May 21 - Sept. 10; 1715 from Oct. 29.
x – Calls on request.

GW 2nd class **CARDIFF - BRISTOL** 136

Not valid on ⑥⑦ Sept. 16 - Oct. 22 (See page 30 for service on these dates)

km			Ⓐ	Ⓐ	Ⓐ	Ⓐ	Ⓐ	Ⓐ	Ⓐ		Ⓐ	Ⓐ	Ⓐ	Ⓐ	Ⓐ		Ⓐ	Ⓐ	Ⓐ		⑥	⑥	⑥	⑥	⑥
		Ⓐ	A	B	A	C	A	G	A		A	G	A	D						⑥	E	A	B	A	G
0	**Cardiff** Central ‡ d.		0628	0700	0730	0759	0830	0900	0930	and at the same	1930	2000	2030	2100	2130	...	2204	2236	2327		0456	0630	0700	0730	0800
19	Newport ‡ d.		0642	0715	0744	0815	0844	0916	0944	minutes past	1944	2016	2044	2115	2143	...	2219	2252	2345		0510	0644	0715	0744	0815
61	**Bristol** T Meads a.		0717	0751	0819	0851	0919	0954	1019	each hour until ▽ **H**	2018	2053	2119	2151	2226	...	2307	2337	0033		0555	0719	0751	0819	0854

		⑥	⑥	⑥	⑥	⑥	⑥		⑦	⑦	⑦	⑦	⑦	⑦	⑦	⑦	⑦	⑦	⑦	⑦	⑦	⑦	⑦	⑦	⑦
		G	A		A	F		⑦	A	A	A	A	A	A	A	A	A	J	A	A	A	A	A		K
Cardiff Central ‡ d.	and at the same	1900	1930	1954	2030	2100	2200		0805c	0913	1008	1108	1208	1308	1408	1508	1608	1635	1708	1740	1808	1908	2018	2118	2210
Newport ‡ d.	minutes past	1915	1944	2010	2044	2115	2215		0828c	0931	1026	1129	1226	1327	1428	1528	1627	1653	1728	1758	1826	1929	2032d	2137	2228c
Bristol T Meads a.	each hour until ▽	1952	2019	2049	2117	2151	2301		0908	1013	1100	1203	1302	1403	1503	1604	1703	1725	1802	1839	1904	2007	2113	2229	2313

		②–⑤	Ⓐ	Ⓐ	Ⓐ	Ⓐ	Ⓐ	Ⓐ	Ⓐ	Ⓐ	Ⓐ		Ⓐ	Ⓐ	Ⓐ	Ⓐ	Ⓐ	Ⓐ	Ⓐ		⑥	⑥	⑥	⑥	⑥
	Ⓐ	E			D	E	G	M		A			G	A	B	A		A	A	⑥	E				
Bristol T Meads d.		0137	0554	0619	0650	0717	0720	0754	0824	0854	0921	and at the same	1921	1954	2015	2054	2119	2154	2254		0137	0650	0721	0754	0823
Newport ‡ a.		0210s	0629	0659	0725	0748	0807	0827	0902	0924	0958	minutes past	2001	2027	2047	2126	2159	2235b	2334		0203s	0726	0758	0828	0901
Cardiff Central ‡ a.		0231	0648	0718	0743	0803	0823	0846	0925	0945	1018	each hour until ▽	2020	2049	2103	2145	2223b	2259a	2357		0220	0744	0817	0843	0923

	⑥	⑥		⑥	⑥	⑥	⑥	⑥	⑥	⑥		⑦	⑦	⑦	⑦	⑦	⑦	⑦	⑦	⑦	⑦	⑦		⑦	⑦
	A			G	A	B	A	G	A	A	⑦			M	A	A	A		J	A		A		A	A
Bristol T Meads d.	0854	0921	and at the same	1921	1954	2010	2054	2129	2157	2255		0848	0948	1048	1147	1248	1347	1416	1448	1548	1612	1648	and	2148	2248
Newport ‡ a.	0924	0958	minutes past	1956	2023	2044	2123	2210	2238	2335		0918	1025e	1122	1221	1319	1419	1447	1521	1619	1644	1722	hourly	2225	2320
Cardiff Central ‡ a.	0942	1018	each hour until ▽	2015	2042	2100	2141	2231	2300	2356		0939	1046e	1144	1241	1340	1443	1508	1543	1645	1706	1744	until ▲	2251	2343

A – To/from Portsmouth Harbour (Table **140**).
B – To/from Manchester Piccadilly (Tables **121/122**).
C – To/from Paignton (Table **115**).
D – To/from Westbury (Table **140**).
E – To/from London Paddington (Table **132**).
F – To Exeter St Davids (Table **115**).
G – To/from Taunton (Table **120a**).
H – 0900 from Cardiff extended to Plymouth;
1300 from Cardiff extended to Exeter St Davids (Table **115**).
J – To/from Brighton (Table **140**).
K – To Warminster (Table **140**).
M – From Frome (Table **140**).

a – Arrives 2251 on ⑤.
b – Arrives 6–7 minutes earlier on ⑤.
c – Departs 5 minutes later from Oct. 29.
d – Departs 6 minutes later May 21 - Sept. 10.
e – Arrives 6 minutes earlier May 21 - June 18 and from Oct. 29.
s – Calls to set down only.

▽ – Timings may vary by up to 6 minutes.
▲ – Timings may vary by up to 3 minutes.
‡ – For additional services see Tables **121, 132** and **149**.

138 WORCESTER - GLOUCESTER - BRISTOL

2nd class GW

km		Ⓐ	ⒶA	ⒶB	Ⓐ	ⒶB	ⒶB	ⒶB	ⒶB	Ⓐ	ⒶB	ⒶB	ⒶB	ⒶB	ⒶB	ⒶB	ⒶB	Ⓐ	Ⓐ	Ⓐ	Ⓐ	Ⓐ	⑥A
	Great Malvern d.	...	...	...	...	...	...	0850	...	1048	...	1251	...	1450	...	1648	...	1850	...	...	...	...	...
0	**Worcester** Shrub Hill d.	0528	...	...	...	0649	*0708*	0906	...	1106	...	1306	...	1506	...	1706	...	1907	...	...	2146	2228	...
24	Ashchurch for Tewkesbury d.	0544	...	...	*0627*	0705	|	0924	...	1124	...	1324	...	1524	...	1724	...	1924	...	...	2202	2251	...
36	Cheltenham Spa ◧ d.	0554	...	0624	*0643*	0716	*0731*	0933	...	1133	...	1333	...	1533	...	1733	...	1934	2019	2133	2212	2305	...
46	**Gloucester** ◧ a.	0603	...	0634	*0653*	0726	*0740*	0942	...	1145	...	1344	...	1544	...	1744	...	1943	2029	2142	2223	2317	...
46	**Gloucester** d.	...	0616	0642	0705	0741	0841	0944	1041	1147	1241	1346	1441	1546	1640	1746	1841	1945	2040	2148	2228	...	0619
97	**Bristol** Parkway d.	...	0657	0724	0749	0820	0919	1022	1120	1223	1319	1423	1520	1624	1720	1823	1922	2027	2119	2224	2305	...	0700
108	**Bristol** Temple Meads a.	...	0713	0740	0800	0836	0935	1039	1135	1235	1335	1439	1538	1639	1735	1839	1938	2038	2133	2240	2319	...	0714

	⑥	⑥B	⑥B	⑥B	⑥B	⑥	⑥B	⑥B	⑥B	⑥B	⑥B	⑥B	⑥B	⑥	⑥	⑥	⑥	⑦A	⑦	⑦	⑦	⑦	⑦	⑦
Great Malvern d.	...	...	...	...	...	1046	...	...	...	1450	...	1650	...	1850	...	2115	...	...	...	...	...	...	...	...
Worcester Shrub Hill d.	...	0647	...	0908	...	1106	...	1254	...	1506	...	1706	...	1906	...	2131	2225	...	1138	1436	1640	1840	2038	...
Ashchurch for Tewkesbury d.	*0633*	0703	...	0927	...	1124	...	1310	...	1524	...	1724	...	1924	...	2151	2241	...	1153	1451	1656	1856	2054	...
Cheltenham Spa ◧ d.	0648	0713	...	0936	...	1134	...	1320	...	1534	...	1734	...	1934	2102	2201	2251	1004	1203	1501	1706	1906	2103	2201
Gloucester ◧ a.	0658	0725	...	0945	...	1145	...	1332	...	1544	...	1745	...	1945	2112	2211	2301	1014	1214	1511	1716	1917	2113	2211
Gloucester d.	0702	0740	0842	0948	1041	1147	1242	1343	1442	1547	1642	1747	1842	1947	2114	...	...	1016	1218	1513	1719	1919	2115	...
Bristol Parkway d.	0740	0820	0920	1025	1121	1225	1320	1422	1520	1624	1720	1825	1920	2025	2152	...	...	1055	1258	1555	1757	1958	2155	...
Bristol Temple Meads a.	0755	0834	0936	1039	1135	1239	1334	1437	1534	1639	1734	1839	1935	2039	2204	...	...	1107	1309	1608	1809	2010	2207	...

	Ⓐ	Ⓐ	ⒶB	ⒶB	Ⓐ	Ⓐ	Ⓐ	Ⓐ	Ⓐ	ⒶB	ⒶB	ⒶB	ⒶB	ⒶB	Ⓐ	Ⓐ	Ⓐ	Ⓐ	Ⓐ	⑥	⑥	⑥B	⑥B
Bristol Temple Meads d.	...	...	0734	0841	0940	1041	1141	1241	1340	1441	1541	1641	1741	1834	1941	2041	...	2144	2242	...	...	0741	0841
Bristol Parkway d.	...	...	0746	0852	0952	1055	1152	1252	1352	1452	1552	1652	1753	1846	1952	2052	...	2155	2253	...	...	0752	0852
Gloucester a.	...	...	0832	0933	1032	1134	1233	1334	1432	1534	1633	1734	1833	1928	2032	2132	...	2236	2333	...	...	0833	0933
Gloucester ◧ d.	0600	0714	...	0937	...	1136	...	1337	...	1536	...	1737	...	1948	2035	2133	2152	*2247*	...	0550	0715	...	0938
Cheltenham Spa ◧ a.	0611	0724	...	0946	...	1146	...	1346	...	1546	...	1747	...	2001	2048	2144	2202	*2256*	...	0559	0724	...	0947
Ashchurch for Tewkesbury a.	0619	0733	...	0955	...	1156	...	1355	...	1556	...	1756	...	2010	...	2153	|	...	...	0608	0733	...	0956
Worcester Shrub Hill a.	0641	0754	...	1014	...	1213	...	1414	...	1614	...	1816	...	2030	...	2214	2224	...	...	0633	0752	...	1014
Great Malvern a.	...	0812	...	1033	...	1233	...	1435	...	1632	...	1836	...	...	...	...	...	...	...	...	...	...	1032

	⑥B	⑥	⑥B	⑥	⑥B	⑥	⑥B	⑥B	⑥B	⑥B	⑥B	⑥	⑥		⑦	⑦		⑦	⑦	⑦	⑦		⑦	⑦
Bristol Temple Meads d.	0941	1041	1141	1241	1341	1441	1541	1641	1741	1841	1941	2043	2206	...	0920	1211	...	1441	1641	1837	2041	...	2230	...
Bristol Parkway d.	0952	1052	1153	1252	1352	1452	1552	1652	1753	1852	1952	2054	2218	...	0929	1222	...	1451	1651	1846	2051	...	2239	...
Gloucester a.	1032	1132	1234	1335	1435	1533	1633	1733	1833	1933	2033	2134	2301	...	1010	1304	...	1533	1733	1930	2134	...	2321	...
Gloucester ◧ d.	...	1136	...	1338	...	1538	...	1738	...	1938	2038	2138	...	...	1012	1305	...	1534	1735	1934	2138	...	...	2356
Cheltenham Spa ◧ a.	...	1147	...	1347	...	1547	...	1747	...	1948	2049	2148	...	...	1021	1316	...	1545	1745	1946	2147	...	...	0007
Ashchurch for Tewkesbury a.	...	1157	...	1357	...	1556	...	1756	...	1956	...	2157	...	...	1030	1325	...	1555	1755	1955	...	...	...	...
Worcester Shrub Hill a.	...	1215	...	1415	...	1614	...	1815	...	2015	...	2218	...	...	1051	1344	...	1612	1815	2022	...	...	...	...
Great Malvern a.	...	...	...	1432	...	1632	...	1836	...	2040	...	...	...	...	...	...	...	...	...	...	...	...	...	...

A – To Taunton (Table **137**). **B** – To/from Weymouth, Westbury or Frome (see Table **140**). ◧ – See also Tables **121** and **133.**

140 BRISTOL - WESTBURY - SOUTHAMPTON, PORTSMOUTH and WEYMOUTH

GW, SW

km		⚒	Ⓐ	⑥	ⒶP	Ⓐ	⑥	⚒	⚒C	⚒	⚒A	⚒	⑥A	ⒶA	⚒W	⑥g	⚒	⚒A	⚒	⚒A	⚒	⚒A	⚒	ⒶA	⑥A	⚒W	⚒	⚒A
	Cardiff Cent **136** d.	...	...	...	...	...	...	...	...	0628a	...	0730a	...	...	...	...	0830a	...	0930a	...	1030a	...	1130a	...	...	...	1230a	...
0	**Bristol** Temple M d.	...	...	...	0518	0544	0549	...	...	0721	0747	0822	0839	0841	0851	0906	0922	0949	1022	1049	1122	1149	1222	1239	1243	1249	1322	1349
19	Bath Spa d.	...	...	...	|	0603	0607	...	...	0735	0807	0836	0857	0859	0907	0927	0936	1007	1036	1107	1136	1207	1236	1256	1301	1307	1336	1407
34	Bradford on Avon d.	...	...	...	0542	0619	0623	...	...	0747	0823	0848	0913	0915	0921	0941	0948	1023	1048	1123	1148	1223	1248	1312	1313	1319	1348	1423
39	Trowbridge **132a** d.	...	...	...	0549	0626	0629	...	0648t	0752	0829	0854	0919	0921	0927	0948	0954	1029	1054	1129	1154	1229	1254	1318	1320	1327	1354	1429
46	**Westbury** **132a** a.	...	...	...	0557	0633	0636	...	0655t	0800	0836	0901	0926	0928	0935	0955	1001	1036	1101	1136	1201	1236	1301	1325	1327	1334	1401	1436
46	**Westbury** d.	0524	0549	0602	...	0640	0643	0646	0701	0800	...	0902	0927	0932	0939	1003	1002	1037	1102	...	1202	1237	1302	1330	1328	1339	1402	1437
	Frome d.	|	|	|	...	|	|	0655	|	|	...	|	0936	0941	|	1015	|	1046	|	...	|	1247	|	|	|	|	|	1451
	Castle Cary d.	|	|	|	...	|	|	0714	|	|	...	|	0953	1000	|	1036	|	1103	|	...	|	1304	|	|	|	|	|	...
	Yeovil Pen Mill d.	|	|	|	...	|	|	0735r	|	|	...	|	1007	1014	|	1053	|	1117	|	...	|	1317	|	|	|	|	|	...
	Dorchester West d.	|	|	|	...	|	|	0809r	|	|	...	|	1040	1048	|	1132	|	1154	|	...	|	1354	|	|	|	|	|	...
	Weymouth a.	|	|	|	...	|	|	0824r	|	|	...	|	1057	1103	|	1145	|	1209	|	...	|	1409	|	|	|	|	|	...
53	Warminster d.	0532	0557	0610	...	0648	0651	...	0712	0808	...	0910	...	...	0946	...	1010	...	1110	...	1210	...	1310	1339	1337	1346	1410	...
85	**Salisbury** d.	0558	0619	0632	...	0711	0724b	...	0736	0833	...	0932	...	...	1009	...	1033	...	1133	...	1233	...	1333	1402	1400	1412	1433	...
112	Romsey d.	...	0638	0651	...	0730	0745	...	0755	0851	...	0951	...	...	...	...	1051	...	1151	...	1251	...	1351	1421	1420	...	1451	...
123	**Southampton** C a.	...	0649	0702	...	0740	0802	...	0809	0904	...	1004	...	...	...	...	1104	...	1204	...	1304	...	1404	1432	1432	...	1504	...
147	Fareham a.	...	0715	0727	...	0805	0827	...	...	0927	...	1027	...	...	...	...	1128	...	1227	...	1327	...	1427	1458	1454	...	1527	...
164	**Portsmouth** & S a.	...	0738	0746	...	0824	0846	...	...	0947	...	1047	...	...	...	...	1147	...	1247	...	1347	...	1447	B	B	...	1547	...
165	**Portsmouth** Hbr a.	...	0744	0752	...	0830	0852	...	...	0954	...	1054	...	...	...	...	1154	...	1254	...	1354	...	1454	...	...	...	1554	...

	ⒶE	⚒	⚒A	⚒	⑥A	ⒶA	⚒W	⚒	⚒A	⑥	ⒶG	⚒	⚒A	⚒	⑥	ⒶD		⚒A	⚒	ⒶG	⚒A	⑥	Ⓐ	⚒	⑥D	⚒	ⒶG	⚒	⚒
Cardiff Cent **136** d.	...	1330a	...	1430a	...	...	...	1530a	c	g	W	1630a	...	1730a	...	...	...	...	1830a	...	...	1930a	1930	...	...	2030a	...	2100t	...
Bristol Temple M d.	...	1422	1448	1522	1538	1544	1551	1622	1649	1649	...	1722	1749	1822	...	...	...	1849	1922	...	1949	2022	2022	2049	...	2122	...	2201	2223
Bath Spa d.	...	1436	1506	1536	1557	1602	1607	1636	1707	1707	...	1736	1807	1836	...	...	...	1907	1936	...	2007	2036	2036	2107	...	2136	...	2219	2236
Bradford on Avon d.	...	1448	1522	1548	1613	1618	1624	1648	1724	1723	...	1748	1823	1848	...	...	...	1923	1948	...	2023	2048	2048	2123	...	2148	...	2235	2247
Trowbridge **132a** d.	...	1454	1528	1554	1619	1624	1630	1654	1731	1730	...	1754	1829	1854	...	1924	...	1929	1954	...	2029	2054	2054	2129	2144	2154	...	2241	2253
Westbury **132a** a.	...	1501	1536	1601	1626	1633	1637	1701	1736	1736	...	1801	1836	1901	...	1931	...	1939	2001	...	2036	2101	2101	2136	2152	2201	...	2250	2300
Westbury d.	1457	1502	1537	1602	...	...	1639	1702	1739	1740	1745	1802v	1840	1902	1918	1940	...	...	2002	2011	2037	2102	2102	2139	...	2201	2218	...	2305
Frome d.	1507	|	1546	|	...	...	|	|	1749	1750	|	|	1849	|	|	|	...	...	|	|	2048	|	|	2150	...	|	|	...	|
Castle Cary d.	1524	|	1602	|	...	...	|	|	1806	1809	|	|	1906	|	|	|	...	...	|	|	...	|	|	2208	...	|	|	...	|
Yeovil Pen Mill d.	1539	|	1617	|	...	...	|	|	1822	1825	|	|	1919	|	|	|	...	...	|	|	...	|	|	2223	...	|	|	...	|
Dorchester West d.	...	|	1658	|	...	...	|	|	1854d	1911	|	|	1954	|	|	|	...	...	|	|	...	|	|	2258	...	|	|	...	|
Weymouth a.	...	|	1710	|	...	...	|	|	1912	1927	|	|	2010	|	|	|	...	...	|	|	...	|	|	2313	...	|	|	...	|
Warminster d.	...	1510	...	1610	...	...	1647	1710	...	...	1752	1810v	...	1910	1928	1950	...	...	2010	2019	...	2110	2110	...	...	2212	2226	...	2312
Salisbury d.	...	1533	...	1633	...	...	1709	1733	...	...	1817	1833v	...	1933	1950	2011	...	...	2033	2042	...	2133	2133	...	...	2233	2246	...	2338
Romsey d.	...	1551	...	1651	...	...	...	1751	...	...	...	1851v	...	1951	2011	2030	...	...	2051	...	...	2151	2151	...	...	2251	...	...	...
Southampton C a.	...	1604	...	1704	...	...	...	1804	...	...	...	1904	...	2004	2021	2044	...	...	2104	...	...	2203	2204	...	...	2304	...	...	...
Fareham a.	...	1627	...	1727	...	...	...	1828	...	...	...	1927	...	2027	...	...	...	...	2127	...	...	2227	2242	...	...	2327	...	...	...
Portsmouth & S a.	...	1648	...	1747	...	...	...	1852r	...	...	...	1947	...	2047	...	...	...	...	2146	...	...	2246	2259	...	...	2347	...	...	...
Portsmouth Hbr a.	...	1654	...	1754	...	...	...	1900r	...	...	...	1955	...	2054	...	...	...	...	2154	...	...	2252	2304	...	...	2354	...	...	...

	⑥	Ⓐ	⑦	⑦	⑦	⑦	⑦B	⑦	⑦B	⑦	⑦		⑦	⑦W	⑦	⑦	⑦W	⑦B	⑦	⑦	⑦	⑦	⑦	⑦	⑦	⑦	⑦	⑦e
Cardiff Cent **136** d.	...	...	...	0805a	...	0913a	1008a	1108a	1208a	...	1308a	...	1408a	...	1508a	1608a	...	1635a	...	1708a	1740a	1808a	1908a	...	2018a	...	...	2208a
Bristol Temple M d.	2309	2320	0823	0910	0925	1015	1110	1210	1310	...	1410	...	1510	1604	1610	1710	...	1740	1743	1810	1847	1910	2015	2048	2125	2135	2215	2315
Bath Spa d.	2327	2338	0842	0926	0944	1028	1126	1222	1327	...	1425	...	1527	1620	1624	1727	...	1751	1801	1827	1901	1926	2027	2106	2138	2149	2233	2328
Bradford on Avon d.	2342	2354	0856	0939	1000	1045	1139	1239	1340	...	1442	...	1540	1631	1641	1740	...	1804	1817	1839	1913	1938	2044	2123	2150	2200	2250	2340
Trowbridge **132a** d.	2349	2359	0902	0947	1007	1051	1147	1246	1347	...	1449	...	1547	1637	1646	1747	...	1811	1824	1847	1919	1946	2051	2130	2157	2206	2256	2347
Westbury **132a** a.	2356	0007	0908	0956	1013	1058	1159	1254	1355	...	1457	...	1554	1644	1650	1754	...	1819	1831	1854	1929	1953	2058	2137	2204	2213	2303	2354
Westbury d.	2356	0008	0912	0959	1018	1102	1201	1301	1401	1425	1501	...	1603	1646	1701	1801	1816	1821	1831	1901	1930	1959	2101	2138	2205	2215	...	2355
Frome d.	0007	0019	0922	|	1031	|	|	|	|	1433	|	...	|	|	|	|	1804f	|	1839	|	|	|	|	2148	|	|	...	0004
Castle Cary d.	...	...	0940	|	1048	|	|	|	|	1450	|	...	|	|	|	|	|	|	1858	|	|	|	|	2205	|	|	...	...
Yeovil Pen Mill d.	...	...	0954	|	1103	|	|	|	|	1505	|	...	|	|	|	|	|	|	1912	|	|	|	|	2221	|	|	...	...
Dorchester West d.	...	...	1029	|	1141	|	|	|	|	1540	|	...	|	|	|	|	|	|	1947	|	|	|	|	2255	|	|	...	...
Weymouth a.	...	...	1042	|	1154	|	|	|	|	1554	|	...	|	|	|	|	|	|	2001	|	|	|	|	2307	|	|	...	...
Warminster d.	...	...	...	1008	...	1109	1210	1308	1410	—	1508	...	1612	1653	1710	1808	1823	1830	...	1908	1937	2008	2108	...	2213	2222	...	...
Salisbury d.	...	...	...	1032	...	1132	1232	1332	1436	...	1532	...	1632	1716	1732	1832	1843	1856	...	1932	2000	2032	2132	...	2236	2246	...	...
Romsey d.	...	...	...	1050	...	1150	1250	1350	1454	...	1550	...	1650	...	1750	1850	...	1915	...	1950	2019	2050	2150	...	2254	...	...	...
Southampton C a.	...	...	...	1103	...	1203	1303	1403	1503	⑦	1603	...	1703	...	1803	1903	...	1925	...	2003	2030	2103	2203	...	2305	...	...	...
Fareham a.	...	...	...	1126	...	1226	1329	1426	1527	1544	1626	...	1726	...	1826	1924	...	1949	...	2026	2055	2126	2226	...	2330	...	...	...
Portsmouth & S a.	...	...	...	1144	...	1244	*1408*	1444	B	1608	1644	...	1744	...	1844	1945	...	B	...	2047	2115	2143	2243	...	2346	...	...	...
Portsmouth Hbr a.	...	...	...	1152	...	1252	*1413*	1452	...	1613	1652	...	1752	...	1854	1952	...	...	...	2052	2125	2151	2251	...	2354	...	...	...

A – From Gloucester, Cheltenham Spa, Worcester or Great Malvern (see Table **138**).
B – To Brighton (journey time from Fareham: 1 hr 16 m - 1 hr 29 m), also calling at Havant, Chichester, Worthing and Hove.
C – From Gloucester on Ⓐ (Table **132a**).
D – From Cheltenham Spa (Table **132a**).
E – From London Waterloo (see other direction of table).
G – From Yeovil (see other direction of table).
P – To London Paddington (Table **115**).
W – To London Waterloo (Table **113**).

a – Not ⑥⑦ Sept. 16 - Oct. 22.
b – Arrives 0712.
c – Not ⑥ May 27 - Sept. 9.
d – 1858 on Ⓐ.
e – Runs 5 minutes earlier Sept. 17 - Oct. 22.
f – Calls at Frome before Westbury.
g – May 27 - Sept. 9.
h – Arrives 1604.
r – 6 minutes earlier on ⑥.
t – Ⓐ only.
v – 4 minutes later on Ⓐ.

GW, SW 2nd class — PORTSMOUTH, SOUTHAMPTON and WEYMOUTH - WESTBURY - BRISTOL 140

km		Ⓐ	⚒	⚒A	Ⓐ	⚒	Ⓐ	⚒A	Ⓐ	⑥	⚒	⑥A	ⒶA	Ⓐ	⑥	⚒A	⚒	⑥A	Ⓐ	⚒	⚒W	ⒶA	⑥A	⚒	⚒w	⚒	ⒶA	⑥A	⚒
	Portsmouth Hbr .... d.	...	...	...	...	...	...	...	0600	0600	...	...	...	0705	0723	...	0823	...	...	0923	...	...	...	1023	...	1123	...	...	1223
	Portsmouth & S .... d.	...	...	...	...	...	...	...	0604	0604	...	...	...	0709	0727	...	0827	...	...	0927	...	B	B	1027	...	1127	...	...	1227
	Fareham .... d.	...	...	...	...	...	...	...	0624	0628	...	...	...	0729	0747	...	0847	...	...	0947	...	1013	1016	1047	...	1147	...	...	1247
	Southampton C .... d.	...	...	...	...	...	...	...	0646	0653	...	...	...	0753	0810	0823t	0910	...	...	1010	...	1042	1042	1110	...	1210	1227	1227	1309
	Romsey .... d.	...	...	...	...	...	...	...	0700	0711	...	...	...	0811	0821	0835t	0921	...	...	1021	...	1054	1053	1121	...	1221	1239	1238	1320
	Salisbury .... d.	...	0602	...	...	0640	...	...	0719	0730	...	...	...	0830	0840	0901	0940	...	...	1040	1052	1113	1113	1140	...	1240	1306	1303r	1340
	Warminster .... d.	...	0624	...	...	0700	...	0723	0739	0750	...	...	...	0853	0901	0923	1001	...	...	1101	1112	1132	1135	1201	...	1301	1334	1325	1400
0	**Weymouth** .... d.	...	|	...	...	|	0533	|	|	|	0638	...	...	|	|	|	|	0846	0853	|	|	|	|	|	1110	|	|	|	|
11	Dorchester West . d.	...	|	...	...	|	0545	|	|	|	0651	...	...	|	|	|	|	0859	0906	|	|	|	|	|	1123	|	|	|	|
44	Yeovil Pen Mill .... d.	...	|	...	...	|	0620	|	|	|	0730	...	...	|	|	|	|	0934	0941	|	|	|	|	|	1205	|	|	|	|
63	Castle Cary .... d.	...	|	...	...	|	0644e	|	|	|	0744	...	...	|	|	|	|	0948	0955	|	|	|	|	|	1221	|	|	|	|
86	Frome .... d.	...	|	...	0645	|	0703	|	|	|	0802	...	...	|	|	|	|	1007	1015	|	|	|	|	|	1239	|	|	|	|
95	**Westbury** .... a.	...	0633	...	0654	0708	0711	0732	0749	0759	0811	...	...	0901	0909	0935	1009	1016	1024	1109	1120	1140	1144	1209	1250j	1309	1342	1333	1409
95	**Westbury** .... **132a** d.	0558	...	0638	0655	0709	0717	0738	0754	0802	0817	0838	0845	0910	0910	0935	1010	1038	1038	1110	1121	1141	1147	1210	1252j	1310	1344	1338	1410
105	Trowbridge .... **132a** d.	0604	...	0644	0702	0715	0723	0744	0800	0808	0823	0844	0851	0916	0916	0941	1016	1044	1044	1116	1127	1148	1153	1216	1256	1316	1350	1344	1416
110	Bradford on Avon .... d.	0610	...	0650	0708	0721	0729	0750	0806	0814	0829	0850	0857	0922	0922	0947	1022	1050	1050	1122	1133	1154	1159	1222	1302	1322	1356	1350	1422
125	Bath Spa .... a.	0626	...	0706	0724	0733	0745	0807	0821	0831	0846	0905	0913	0934	0934	1005	1034	1106	1106	1134	1146	1210	1215	1234	1320	1334	1412	1406	1434
144	**Bristol** Temple M .... a.	0646	...	0727	0746	0752	0805	0829	0842	0844	0906	0927	0935	0951	0950	1028	1049	1127	1128	1148	1205	1228	1235	1248	1343	1348	1435	1429	1448
	Cardiff Cent **136** .... a.	0743a	...	...	0846a	...	...	...	0945	0942a	...	...	...	1045	1041a	...	1145a	...	...	1245a	...	...	...	1345a	...	1443a	...	...	1545a

	⚒W	⚒A	ⒶD	⚒	⚒A	⚒	ⒶA	⑥A	⑥A	⚒	ⒶC	ⒶA	⑥A	⑥A	⚒	⚒w	⚒	⑥c	⑥b	Ⓐ	Ⓐ	⑥	⑥b	ⒶW	⚒	⚒	⚒	⚒W	⚒	⚒
Portsmouth Hbr .... d.	...	...	W	1323	...	1423	...	b	c	1523	...	...	c	b	1623	...	1723	...	...	...	...	...	...	s	1823	...	1923	...	...	2023
Portsmouth & S .... d.	...	...	...	1327	...	1427	...	...	...	1527	...	...	...	...	1627	...	1727	...	...	...	B	B	...	...	1827	...	1927	...	...	2027
Fareham .... d.	...	...	...	1347	...	1447	...	...	...	1547	...	...	...	...	1647	...	1747	...	...	...	1814	1815	...	...	1847	...	1947	...	...	2047
Southampton C .... d.	...	...	...	1410	...	1510	...	...	...	1610	...	...	...	...	1710	...	1810	...	...	...	1842	1845	...	...	1910	...	2010	...	...	2110
Romsey .... d.	...	...	...	1421	...	1521	...	...	...	1621	...	...	...	...	1721	...	1821	...	...	...	1853	1856	...	...	1921	...	2021	...	...	2121
Salisbury .... d.	1352	...	1424	1440	...	1540	...	...	...	1640	...	...	...	...	1740	...	1840	...	...	...	1913	1915	...	1823	1940	...	2040	2057	...	2140
Warminster .... d.	1412	...	1444	1501	1528	1601	...	1628	...	1701	...	1728	1728	...	1801	...	1901	...	...	...	1932	1936	...	|	2001	...	2101	2117	...	2201
Weymouth .... d.	|	1310	|	|	|	|	1508	|	1508	|	...	|	|	1608	|	...	|	1728	1728	1730	|	|	1828	|	|	...	|	|	2021	|
Dorchester West .. d.	|	1323	|	|	|	|	1521	|	1521	|	...	|	|	1621	|	...	|	1741	1740	1743	|	|	1841	|	|	...	|	|	2034	|
Yeovil Pen Mill .... d.	|	1406	|	|	|	|	1556	|	1556	|	1653	|	|	1705	|	...	|	1818	1822	1823	|	|	1920	1927	|	...	|	|	2106t	|
Castle Cary .... d.	|	1420	|	|	|	|	1610	|	1610	|	1707	|	|	1719	|	...	|	1832	1843d	1837	|	|	1934	1940	|	...	|	|	2118t	|
Frome .... d.	|	1439	|	|	|	|	1629	|	1629	|	1724	|	|	1738	|	...	|	1857	1905	1906	|	|	1955	1957	|	...	|	|	2138t	|
Westbury .... a.	1420	1450j	1451	1509	1536	1609	1638	1636	1638	1709	1733	1736	1736	1747	1809	...	1909	1906	1916	1915	1940	1945	2008	2006	2009	...	2109	2125	2151	2210
Westbury .... **132a** d.	1421	1451j	...	1510	1538	1610	1642	1638	1638	1710	...	1738	1746	1748	1809	1838	1910	1917	1918	1921	1941	1946	2017	...	2010	2038	2110	2125	2155	2210
Trowbridge .... **132a** d.	1427	1455	...	1516	1544	1616	1647	1644	1644	1716	...	1744	1752	1754	1816	1844	1916	1923	1925	1927	1948	1952	2023	...	2016	2044	2116	2131	2202	2216
Bradford on Avon .... d.	1433	1501	...	1522	1550	1622	1653	1650	1650	1722	...	1750	1758	1800	1822	1850	1922	1929	1932	1933	1954	1958	2029	...	2022	2050	2122	2137	2208	2222
Bath Spa .... a.	1446	1519	...	1534	1606	1634	1709	1706	1706	1734	...	1806	1814	1816	1834	1906	1934	1945	1947	1949	2006	2014	2045	...	2034	2106	2136	2150	2226	2234
Bristol Temple M .... a.	1505	1537	...	1548	1629	1648	1731	1727	1727	1748	...	1828	1838	1837	1848	1929	1948	2005	2009	2009	2028	2033	2105	...	2048	2129	2150	2206	2245	2250
Cardiff Cent **136** .... a.	...	...	...	1643a	...	1745a	...	...	...	1845a	...	...	...	...	1945a	...	2049a	...	...	...	...	...	...	...	2145a	...	2300a	...	...	2357a

	ⒶW	Ⓐ	⑥	Ⓐ	⑦	⑦	⑦	⑦	⑦	⑦	⑦	⑦W	⑦	⑦	⑦	⑦	⑦	⑦	⑦	⑦	⑦	⑦	⑦	⑦W	⑦	⑦	⑦	⑦	⑦
Portsmouth Hbr .... d.	s	...	...	2123	...	...	0908	...	...	1108	...	...	1308	...	1408	1508	...	...	1608	...	1708	...	1808	...	...	1908	...	2008	2205
Portsmouth & S .... d.	...	...	...	2127	...	...	0912	...	...	1112	B	...	1312	...	1412	1512	...	...	1612	B	1712	...	1812	...	B	1912	...	2012	2212
Fareham .... d.	...	...	...	2147	...	...	0932	...	...	1132	1232	...	1332	...	1432	1532	...	...	1632	1703	1732	...	1832	...	1905	1932	...	2032	2232
Southampton C .... d.	...	2120	2127	2222	...	...	0954	...	...	1154	1254	...	1354	...	1454	1554	...	...	1654	1726	1754	...	1854	...	1928	1954	...	2054	2257
Romsey .... d.	...	2131	2138	2234	...	...	1006	...	...	1206	1306	...	1406	...	1506	1606	...	...	1706	1739	1806	...	1906	...	1940	2006	...	2106	2308
Salisbury .... d.	2025	2153	2204	2300	...	...	1025	...	...	1225	1325	1355	1425	...	1525	1625	...	1710	1723	1801	1825	...	1925	1955	2001	2025	...	2125	2328
Warminster .... d.	|	2215	2226	2320	...	...	1049	...	...	1242	1344	1415	1444	...	1544	1644	...	1736	1744	1821	1844	...	1946	2015	2021	2044	...	2144	2350
Weymouth .... d.	|	|	|	|	...	...	|	...	1105	|	|	|	|	1415	|	|	1610	|	|	|	|	1756	|	|	|	|	2009	|	|
Dorchester West .. d.	|	|	|	|	...	...	|	...	1118	|	|	|	|	1428	|	|	1623	|	|	|	|	1809	|	|	|	|	2022	|	|
Yeovil Pen Mill .... d.	2127r	|	|	|	...	...	|	...	1154	|	|	|	|	1504	|	|	1658	|	|	|	|	1844	|	|	|	|	2057	|	|
Castle Cary .... d.	2141	|	|	|	...	...	|	...	1207	|	|	|	|	1518	|	|	1713	|	|	|	|	1859	|	|	|	|	2110	|	|
Frome .... d.	2158	|	|	|	...	0932	|	1140	1227	|	|	|	|	1537	|	|	1731	1757f	|	|	|	1918	|	|	|	|	2129	|	|
Westbury .... a.	2212	2226	2234	2331	...	0944	1058	1149	1236	1254	1356	1423	1456	1546	1556	1656	1740	1744	1756	1829	1856	1927	1957	2023	2030	2056	2139	2156	2359
Westbury .... **132a** d.	...	2232	2238	...	0905	0950	1058	1150	...	1256	1356	1424	1500	1547	1604	1700	1741	...	1800	1832	1857	1934	2000	2023	2039	2100	2147	2200	...
Trowbridge .... **132a** d.	...	2238	2244	...	0911	0956	1105	1156	...	1302	1402	1430	1506	1553	1610	1706	1748	...	1806	1838	1902	1940	2006	2029	2045	2106	2155	2206	...
Bradford on Avon .... d.	...	2244	2250	...	0917	1002	1111	1202	...	1308	1408	1436	1512	1559	1616	1712	1754	...	1812	1844	1908	1948	2012	2035	2051	2112	2201	2212	...
Bath Spa .... a.	...	2300	2307	...	0934	1021	1124	1219	...	1325	1424	1450	1524	1616	1628	1724	1806	...	1829	1855	1925	2007	2025	2049	2109	2125	2218	2225	...
Bristol Temple M .... a.	...	2323	2328	...	0953	1040	1144	1238	...	1344	1444	1506	1540	1635	1643	1744	1832	...	1844	1917	1939	2029	2039	2105	2128	2141	2237	2241	...
Cardiff Centl **136** ... a.	...	...	...	...	...	1144a	1241a	...	...	1443a	1543a	...	1645a	...	1744a	1844a	...	...	1945a	...	2045a	...	2142a	...	...	2251a	...	2343a	...

A – To Gloucester, Cheltenham Spa, Worcester or Great Malvern (see Table **138**).
B – From Brighton (journey time to Fareham 1hr 14m - 1hr 22m), also calling at Hove, Worthing, Chichester and Havant.
C – From Yeovil Junction (dep.1646). To London (see other direction of table).
D – To Yeovil (see other direction of table).
W – From London Waterloo (Table **113**).
a – Not ⑥⑦ Sept. 16 - Oct. 22.
b – May 27 - Sept 9.
c – From Sept. 16.
d – Arrives 1836.
e – Arrives 0633.
f – Arrival time. Calls after Westbury.
j – 2 minutes earlier on ⑥.
r – Arrives 4 – 6 minutes earlier.
s – To Salisbury (see other direction of table).
t – 3 – 5 minutes later on ⑥.
v – 2251 on ⑤.
w – Note **A** applies on ⑥.

SN — EAST CROYDON - MILTON KEYNES 141

km		Ⓐ	Ⓐ	Ⓐ	Ⓐ	Ⓐ	Ⓐ	Ⓐ	Ⓐ	Ⓐ	Ⓐ		Ⓐ	Ⓐ	Ⓐ	Ⓐ	Ⓐ	Ⓐ		⑥	⑥
0	**East Croydon** .... d.	...	...	...	...	...	...	0750	0808	0910	1010		1710	1811	1912	...	...	...	...	...	...
12	Clapham Junction .... ▶ d.	0503	0530	0555	0620	0638	0739	0819	0839	0939	1039	and at	1739	1839	1939	2039	2139	2239	...	0508	0538
18	Kensington Olympia ⊙ .... ▶ d.	0514	0544	0607	0630	0649	0750	0831	0850	0950	1050	the same	1750	1850	1950	2050	2150	2250	...	0519	0549
27	Wembley Central .... d.	|	0602	0624	0647	0707	0808	0847	0908	1008	1109	minutes	1809	1909	2009	2108	|	|	...	|	0607
40	Watford Junction .... **142** d.	0540	0614	0636	0657	0719	0820	0901	0920	1020	1121	past each	1821	1921	2021	2120	2223	2332	...	0547	0620
76	Leighton Buzzard .... **142** d.	...	0642	...	...	0751	0848	...	0948	1048	1148	hour until	1848	1948	2048	2150	...	...	...	...	0647
87	Bletchley .... **142** d.	...	0649	...	...	0758	0855	..	0955	1057	1155		1855	1955	2055	2158	...	...	...	...	0655
92	**Milton Keynes** .... **142** a.	...	0656	...	...	0803	0901	...	1001	1102	1200	✣	1900	2000	2100	2205	...	...	...	...	0700

	⑥	⑥	⑥		⑥	⑥	⑥	⑥	⑥	⑥	⑦	⑦	⑦	⑦	⑦	⑦		⑦	⑦	⑦	⑦
East Croydon .... d.	...	0610	0710		1710	1810	1910	...	...	...	...	...	...	...	...	...		...	...	...	...
Clapham Junction .... ▶ d.	0609	0636	0739	and at	1739	1839	1938	2025	2150	2241	0815	0915	1015	1115	1205	1305	and at	1905	2005	2115	2215
Kensington Olympia ⊙ .... ▶ d.	0620	0647	0750	the same	1750	1852	1948	2036	2201	2251	0826	0926	1026	1126	1216	1316	the same	1916	2016	2125	2226
Wembley Central .... d.	0638	0709	0809	minutes	1809	1909	|	|	|	|	|	|	|	|	|	|	minutes	|	|	|	|
Watford Junction .... **142** d.	0650	0721	0821	past each	1821	1921	2015	2109	2230	2319	0855	0957	1055	1154	1242	1342	past each	1942	2042	2153	2256
Leighton Buzzard .... **142** d.	...	0748	0848	hour until	1848	...	...	...	...	...	...	...	...	...	...	...	hour until	...	...	...	...
Bletchley .... **142** d.	...	0755	0855		1855	...	...	...	...	...	...	...	...	...	...	...		...	...	...	...
Milton Keynes .... **142** a.	...	0800	0900	✣	1900	...	...	...	...	...	...	...	...	...	...	...	✣	...	...	...	...

	Ⓐ	Ⓐ	Ⓐ	Ⓐ	Ⓐ	Ⓐ	Ⓐ	Ⓐ		Ⓐ	Ⓐ	Ⓐ	Ⓐ	Ⓐ	Ⓐ	Ⓐ	Ⓐ		⑥	⑥	
Milton Keynes .... **142** d.	...	...	...	0701	0813	...	0913	1013		1713	1813	1915	2013	2113	...	2211	...	...	...	...	...
Bletchley .... **142** d.	...	...	...	0706	0817	...	0917	1017	and at	1717	1817	1920	2017	2117	...	2215	...	...	...	...	...
Leighton Buzzard .... **142** d.	...	...	...	0713	0824	...	0924	1024	the same	1724	1824	1927	2024	2124	...	2222	...	...	...	...	...
Watford Junction .... **142** d.	0554	0653	0725	0738	0852	0915	0952	1052	minutes	1752	1851	1954	2051	2151	2227	2253	2336	...	0552	0655	...
Wembley Central .... d.	0605	0705	0737	0750	0904	0927	1004	1104	past each	1804	1905	2006	2104	|	|	|	|	...	0603	0706	...
Kensington Olympia ⊡ .... ▶ d.	0622	0722	0758	0807	0922	0947	1022	1122	hour until	1822	1920	2023	2122	2222	2251	2323	0007	...	0623	0724	...
Clapham Junction .... ▶ a.	0632	0732	0809	0817	0932	0957	1032	1132		1832	1930	2033	2132	2233	2301	2333	0017	...	0633	0734	...
East Croydon .... a.	...	...	...	0904	1001	...	1101	1201	✣	1903	...	...	...	...	...	2359	...	...	0656	0801	...

	⑥		⑥	⑥	⑥	⑥	⑥	⑥	⑥	⑥		⑦	⑦	⑦	⑦		⑦	⑦	⑦	⑦	⑦
Milton Keynes .... **142** d.	0713		1713	1813	...	1914	...	...	...	...	...	...	...	...	...		...	...	...	...	...
Bletchley .... **142** d.	0717	and at	1717	1817	...	1918	...	...	...	...	...	...	...	...	...	and at	...	...	...	...	...
Leighton Buzzard .... **142** d.	0724	the same	1724	1824	...	1925	...	...	...	...	...	...	...	...	...	the same	...	...	...	...	...
Watford Junction .... **142** d.	0752	minutes	1752	1851	1931	1951	2043	2144	2248	2325	...	0917	1017	1122	1222	minutes	1922	2022	2117	2217	2317
Wembley Central .... d.	0804	past each	1804	1903	1942	|	|	|	|	|	...	|	|	|	|	past each	|	|	|	|	|
Kensington Olympia ⊡ .... ▶ d.	0822	hour until	1822	1921	2001	2022	2111	2212	2316	2353	...	0947	1047	1149	1250	hour until	1950	2049	2147	2247	2347
Clapham Junction .... ▶ a.	0832		1832	1931	2010	2032	2121	2221	2326	0002	...	0958	1058	1159	1259		1959	2059	2200	2257	2357
East Croydon .... a.	0901	✣	1901	2001	...	2101	...	...	...	...	...	...	...	...	...	✣	...	...	...	...	0023

⊙ – All trains call at Shepherd's Bush, 2 – 3 minutes after Kensington Olympia.
⊡ – All trains call at Shepherd's Bush, 2 – 3 minutes before Kensington Olympia.
✣ – Timings may vary by up to 2 minutes.
▶ – Additional local services run between Clapham Junction and Shepherd's Bush.

① – Mondays ② – Tuesdays ③ – Wednesdays ④ – Thursdays ⑤ – Fridays ⑥ – Saturdays ⑦ – Sundays Ⓐ – Monday to Fridays, not holidays 43

km			Ⓐ	Ⓐ	Ⓐ	Ⓐ	Ⓐ	Ⓐ	Ⓐ	Ⓐ	Ⓐ	Ⓐ	Ⓐ	Ⓐ	Ⓐ	Ⓐ		Ⓐ	Ⓐ	Ⓐ	Ⓐ	Ⓐ	Ⓐ	Ⓐ	Ⓐ
0	**London** Euston . **143** ‡ d.	Ⓐ	...	...	...	0534	...	0624	0634	0713	0749	0754	0813	0849	0854	0913	and	1449	1454	1513	1549	1554	1613	1650	1713
28	Watford Junction **143** ‡ d.		...	...	...	0555	...	0641	0654	|	0803	0811	|	0903	0911	|	at	1503	1511	|	1603	1611	|	|	|
64	Leighton Buzzard .... d.		...	...	...	0628	...	0709	0725	0742	|	0836	0842	|	0936	0942	the	|	1536	1542	|	1636	1642	1720	|
75	Bletchley .... d.		...	...	...	0635	...	0716	0732	0750	|	0843	0850	0924**y**	0943	0950	same	|	1543	1550	|	1643	1650	1727	|
80	Milton Keynes .... **143** ‡ d.		...	0537	...	0640	...	0724	0737	0754	0825	0849	0854	0929**y**	0949	0954	minutes	1525	1549	1554	1625	1649	1654	1732	1748
106	**Northampton** ..... **143** a.		...	0553	...	0656	...	0740	0753	0810	0840	0906	0911	0944**y**	1006	1010	past	1544	1606	1610	1640	1706	1713	1748	1810
106	**Northampton** ..... **143** d.		0516	0555	0616	0658	0716	0745	0755	0813	0855	0916	*0925*	0955	...	1016	each	1555	...	1616	1655	1716	...	1755	1819
136	Rugby .... **143** ‡ d.		0538	0617	0638	0720	0738	0804	0817	0835	0917	0938	*0947*	1017	...	1038	hour	1617	...	1638	1717	1738	...	1817	1841
154	Coventry .... ‡ d.		0550	0630	0650	0732	0750	...	0830	0850	0930	0950	*1011*r	1030	...	1050	until	1630	...	1650	1730	1750	...	1830	1853
171	**Birmingham** Int'l ✈. ‡ d.		0605	0646	0705	0748	0805	...	0846	0905	0946	1005	*1029*	1046	...	1105	△	1646	...	1705	1746	1805	...	1846	1908
185	**Birmingham** New St ‡ a.		0617	0701	0717	0805	0817	...	0902	0918	1001	1017	*1042*	1101	...	1117		1702	...	1717	1801	1817	...	1901	1920

	Ⓐ	Ⓐ	Ⓐ	Ⓐ	Ⓐ	Ⓐ	Ⓐ	Ⓐ	Ⓐ	Ⓐ	Ⓐ	Ⓐ	Ⓐ	Ⓐ	Ⓐ	Ⓐ	Ⓐ	Ⓐ	Ⓐ		⑥	⑥	⑥	⑥	⑥	⑥
London Euston . **143** ‡ d.	1724	1749	1752	1813	1816	1849	1852	1913	1949	1954	2013	2049	2054	2113	2149	2154	2224	2304	2324	⑥	...	...	0534	...	...	0624
Watford Junction **143** ‡ d.	1744	|	1811	|	|	|	|	|	|	2011	|	|	2111	|	|	2215	2241	2328	2341		...	...	0553	...	...	0641
Leighton Buzzard .... d.	1809	1820	|	|	1844	|	1920	1942	2018	2036	2042	2118	2136	2144	2218	2247	2307	0001	0007		...	...	0625	...	...	0709
Bletchley .... d.	1816	|	1841	|	|	|	1927	|	|	2043	2049	|	2143	2152	|	2254	2314	0008	0014		0522	...	0632	...	...	0719
Milton Keynes .... **143** ‡ d.	1822	1831	1846	1846	1854	1923	1932	1956	2029	2049	2054	2129	2149	2157	2232	2302	2323	0017	0022		0537	...	0637	...	...	0724
Northampton ...... **143** a.	1838	1848	1908	1904	1915	1937	1953	2011	2045	2106	2111	2146	2209	2215	2250	2320	2340	0034	0040		0553	...	0653	...	...	0741
Northampton ...... **143** d.	1839	1857	...	1919	1931	1946	1955	2019	2055	...	2116	2155	...	2219	2255	...	...	...	...		0555	0616	0655	0716	0737	*0755*
Rugby .... **143** ‡ d.	1901	1919	...	1941	1956	2005	2017	2041	2117	...	2138	2217	...	2241	2317	...	...	...	...		0617	0638	0717	0738	0759	*0817*
Coventry .... ‡ d.	1911	1932	...	1953	2011	...	2030	2053	2130	...	2150	2230	...	2253	2330	...	...	...	...		0630	0650	0730	0750	0811	*0830*
Birmingham Int'l ✈. ‡ d.	1929	1948	...	2008	2029	...	2046	2108	2146	...	2205	2246	...	2311	2348	...	...	...	...		0646	0705	0746	0805	0829	*0846*
Birmingham New St ‡ a.	1942	2003	...	2020	2042	...	2102	2120	2202	...	2218	2302	...	2322	0004	...	...	...	...		0701	0717	0801	0817	0842	*0901*

	⑥	⑥	⑥	⑥	⑥	⑥	⑥	⑥	⑥		⑥	⑥	⑥	⑥	⑥	⑥	⑥	⑥	⑥	⑥	⑥	⑥	⑥	⑥	⑥
London Euston . **143** ‡ d.	...	0705	0749	0754	...	0849	0854	0913	0949	and	1754	1813	1849	1854	1913	...	1946	2034	2040	2107	2128	2154	2234	2304	2340
Watford Junction **143** ‡ d.	...	0726	0803	0811	...	0903	0911	|	1003	at	1811	|	1903	1911	|	...	2002	2050	2101	2124	2144	2214	2250	2324	2359
Leighton Buzzard .... d.	...	0758	|	0836	...	|	0936	0942	|	the	1836	1844	|	1936	1942	...	2034	2118	|	2150	2208	2247	2316	2356	0032
Bletchley .... d.	...	0805	|	0843	...	0924	0943	0950	1024**x**	same	1843	1852	|	1943	1950	...	2041	2125	2131	2157	2215	2254	2323	0003	0039
Milton Keynes .... **143** ‡ d.	...	0810	0825	0849	...	0929	0949	0954	1029**x**	minutes	1849	1856	1925	1949	1954	...	2049	2133	2140	2206	2224	2303	2331	0011	0047
Northampton ...... **143** a.	...	0826	0840	0905	...	0944	1006	1013	1045**x**	past	1906	1913	1944	2006	2011	...	2106	2150	2156	2223	2243	2320	2348	0028	0104
Northampton ...... **143** d.	0816	0837	0855	0916	0937	0955	...	1016	1055	each	...	1916	1955	...	2022	2055	2116	2159	2216	...	2255	...	...	...	...
Rugby .... **143** ‡ d.	0838	0859	0917	0938	0959	1017	...	1038	1117	hour	...	1938	2017	...	2044	2117	2138	2221	2238	...	2317	...	...	...	...
Coventry .... ‡ d.	0850	0911	0930	0950	1011	1030	...	1050	1130	until	...	1950	2030	...	2056	2130	2150	2233	2250	...	2330	...	...	...	...
Birmingham Int'l ✈. ‡ d.	0905	0929	0946	1005	1029	1046	...	1105	1146	△	...	2005	2046	...	2114	2146	2205	2249	2305	...	2349	...	...	...	...
Birmingham New St ‡ a.	0917	0942	1001	1017	1042	1101	...	1117	1201		...	2017	2102	...	2125	2201	2217	2304	2317	...	0004	...	...	...	...

		⑦	⑦	⑦	⑦	⑦	⑦	⑦	⑦	⑦	⑦	⑦	⑦	⑦	⑦	⑦		⑦	⑦	⑦	⑦	⑦	⑦	⑦	⑦
London Euston . **143** ‡ d.	⑦	0654	0724	0752	0824	0855	0924	0954	1001	1024	1028	1054	1124	1154	1234	1250	and	1950	2034	2106	2130	2200	2228	2258	2334
Watford Junction **143** ‡ d.		0713	0745	0810	0845	0914	0945	1010	1019	1040	1046	1114	1142	1214	1250	1306	at	2006	2050	2123	2150	2219	2249	2317	2355
Leighton Buzzard .... d.		0741	0814	0839	0914	0941	1014	1035	1047	1105	1115	1143	1212	1243	1315	1327	the	2027	2115	2149	2219	2247	2318	2350	0028
Bletchley .... d.		0748	0821	0845	0921	0948	1021	1042	|	1112	|	1150	1219	1250	1322	|	same	|	2122	2156	2226	2254	2325	2357	0035
Milton Keynes .... **143** ‡ d.		0758	0830	0851	0927	0957	1027	1050	1058	1120	1128	1158	1228	1258	1328	1337	minutes	2037	2128	2204	2234	2303	2333	0005	0043
Northampton ...... **143** a.		0815	0847	0909	0944	1014	1044	1106	1116	1138	1145	1215	1244	1315	1344	1351	past	2054	2146	2221	2250	2319	2350	0023	0100
Northampton ...... **143** d.		...	...	0926	1000	...	1100	1108	...	1140	1158	...	1255	...	1355	1402	each	2106	2155	...	2252	2332	...	...	...
Rugby .... **143** ‡ d.		...	...	0948	1022	...	1122	1130	...	1203	1220	...	1317	...	1417	1426	hour	2130	2217	...	2314	2354	...	...	...
Coventry .... ‡ d.		...	...	1000	1034	...	1134	...	...	...	1232	...	1330	...	1430	...	until	...	2230	...	2338	0007	...	...	...
Birmingham Int'l ✈. ‡ d.		...	...	1009	1052	...	1152	...	...	...	1250	...	1348	...	1448	...	△	...	2248	...	2356	...	...	...	...
Birmingham New St ‡ a.		...	...	1026	1103	...	1203	...	...	...	1301	...	1359	...	1459	...		...	2259	...	0007	...	...	...	...

		Ⓐ	Ⓐ	Ⓐ	Ⓐ	Ⓐ	Ⓐ	Ⓐ	Ⓐ	Ⓐ	Ⓐ	Ⓐ	Ⓐ	Ⓐ	Ⓐ	Ⓐ	Ⓐ	Ⓐ	Ⓐ	Ⓐ	Ⓐ	Ⓐ		Ⓐ	Ⓐ
Birmingham New St ‡ d.	Ⓐ	...	...	...	...	...	...	...	0553	0633	...	0614	0654	0714	0733	0754	*0814*	0833	0854	0914	0933	0954	and	1554	...
Birmingham Int'l ✈. ‡ d.		...	...	...	...	...	...	...	0605	0645	...	0630	0705	0730	0745	0805	*0830*	0845	0905	0930	0945	1005	at	1605	...
Coventry .... ‡ d.		...	...	...	...	...	0557	...	0621	0700	...	0648	0721	0742	0804	0821	*0848*	0900	0925	0948	1000	1021	the	1621	...
Rugby .... **143** ‡ d.		...	...	...	0516	...	0612	...	0632	0712	*0647*	0659	0732	0753	0815	0839	*0859*	0912	0938	0959	1012	1032	same	1632	...
Northampton ...... **143** a.		...	...	...	0537	...	0633	...	0654	0735	*0709*	0724	0754	0816	0837	0900	*0920*	0933	0959	1020	1033	1054	minutes	1657	...
Northampton ...... **143** d.		0415	0448	0505	0546	0618	0638	0700	0710	0742	0732	0738	0805	0825	0847	0905	0925	0950	1005	1025	1050	1105	past	1705	1725
Milton Keynes .... **143** ‡ d.		0430	0504	0521	0603	0635	0655	0718	0731	|	0747	0755	0822	0841	0905	0922	0941	1007	1022	1041	1107	1122	each	1722	1741
Bletchley .... d.		0435	0509	0526	0608	0640	0700	|	|	|	0752	0800	0827	0846	|	0927	0946	|	1027	1046	|	1127	hour	1727	1746
Leighton Buzzard .... d.		0442	0515	0533	0615	0647	0707	0727	0740	|	0759	0807	0833	0853	|	0933	0953	|	1033	1053	|	1133	until	1733	1753
Watford Junction **143** ‡ d.		0511	0550	0602	0635	0705	|	|	|	|	0827	|	|	|	0928	0959	|	1031	1059	|	1131	1159	△	1759	|
London Euston . **143** ‡ a.		0534	0611	0620	0651	0722	0739	0802	0812	0828	0848	0839	0910	0927	0946	1018	1023	1046	1117	1127	1146	1217		1818	1827

	Ⓐ	Ⓐ	Ⓐ	Ⓐ	Ⓐ	Ⓐ	Ⓐ	Ⓐ	Ⓐ	Ⓐ	Ⓐ	Ⓐ	Ⓐ	Ⓐ	Ⓐ	Ⓐ	Ⓐ	Ⓐ		⑥	⑥	⑥	⑥	⑥	⑥	⑥
Birmingham New St ‡ d.	1633	1654	1714	1733	1754	1814	1833	1854	1914	1933	1954	2033	2054	2134	2154	...	2254	2310	⑥	...	...	...	0614	0654	0714	0733
Birmingham Int'l ✈. ‡ d.	1645	1705	1726	1745	1805	1830	1845	1905	1930	1945	2005	2045	2105	2145	2205	...	2305	2320		...	...	...	0630	0705	0730	0745
Coventry .... ‡ d.	1700	1721	1742	1800	1821	1848	1900	1921	1948	2000	2021	2100	2121	2200	2221	...	2321	2331		...	...	...	0648	0721	0748	0800
Rugby .... **143** ‡ d.	1716	1732	1756	1812	1832	1859	1918	1932	1959	2015	2032	2114	2132	2212	2232	...	2332	2344		...	...	...	0659	0732	0759	0812
Northampton ...... **143** a.	1738	1756	1817	1837	1853	1921	1941	1954	2023	2038	2053	2135	2154	2235	2253	...	2355	0005**s**		...	...	...	0720	0754	0820	0836
Northampton ...... **143** d.	1750	1805	1825	1850	1905	1925	1950	2005	2025	...	2105	2137	2205	...	2255	2335	...	|		0515	0605	0705	0735	0805	0825	0850
Milton Keynes .... **143** ‡ d.	1807	1822	1841	1907	1922	1941	2007	2025	2041	...	2122	2153	2222	...	2313	2353	...	0024		0531	0621	0721	0752	0822	0841	0907
Bletchley .... d.	|	1827	1846	|	1927	1946	|	2030	2046	...	2127	2158	2227	...	2318	2358	...	|		0536	0627	0727	0757	0827	0846	|
Leighton Buzzard .... d.	|	1833	1853	|	1933	1953	|	2037	2053	...	2133	2204	2233	...	2324	0004	...	|		0543	0633	0733	0803	0833	0853	|
Watford Junction **143** ‡ d.	1831	1859	|	1931	1959	|	2031	2101	|	...	2159	2233	2303	...	2359	0033	...	0052**s**		0616	0701	0759	0828	0859	|	0934
London Euston . **143** ‡ a.	1846	1918	1928	1947	2020	2027	2048	2120	2128	...	2222	2252	2321	...	0021	0055	...	0115		0638	0720	0818	0846	0917	0927	0949

	⑥	⑥	⑥	⑥		⑥	⑥	⑥	⑥	⑥	⑥	⑥	⑥	⑥	⑥	⑥	⑥	⑥	⑥	⑥	⑥	⑥	⑥	⑥	⑥
Birmingham New St ‡ d.	0754	0814	0833	0854	and	1554	1614	1633	1654	1714	1733	1754	1814	1833	1854	1914	1933	1954	...	2033	2054	2134	2154	2214	2254
Birmingham Int'l ✈. ‡ d.	0805	0830	0845	0905	at	1605	1630	1645	1705	1731	1745	1805	1830	1845	1905	1930	1945	2005	...	2045	2105	2145	2205	2230	2305
Coventry .... ‡ d.	0821	0848	0900	0921	the	1621	1648	1700	1721	1749	1800	1821	1848	1900	1921	1948	2000	2021	...	2100	2121	2200	2221	2248	2321
Rugby .... **143** ‡ d.	0832	0859	0912	0932	same	1632	1659	1712	1732	1759	1812	1832	1859	1912	1932	1959	2012	2032	2047	2112	2132	2212	2232	2259	2332
Northampton ...... **143** a.	0857	0920	0934	0954	minutes	1654	1720	1734	1753	1821	1834	1854	1920	1934	1953	2020	2035	2053	2106	2135	2153	2233	2253	2321	2355
Northampton ...... **143** d.	0905	0925	0950	1005	past	1705	1725	1750	1805	1831	1850	1905	1931	...	2002	2032	...	2102	2120	...	2205	2243	...	2330	...
Milton Keynes .... **143** ‡ d.	0922	0941	1007	1022	each	1722	1741	1807	1822	1847	1907	1922	1947	...	2018	2047	...	2118	2134	...	2221	2259	...	2346	...
Bletchley .... d.	0927	0946	|	1027	hour	1727	1746	|	1827	1852	|	1927	1952	...	2023	|	...	|	2139	...	2226	2304	...	2351	...
Leighton Buzzard .... d.	0933	0953	|	1033	until	1733	1753	|	1833	1859	|	1933	1959	...	2030	2056	...	|	2146	...	2232	2311	...	2358	...
Watford Junction **143** ‡ d.	0959	|	1031	1059	△	1759	|	1831	1859	1927	1931	1959	2027	...	2052	2126	...	2152	2219	...	2307	2346	...	0020	...
London Euston . **143** ‡ a.	1017	1027	1046	1117		1817	1827	1846	1917	1946	1946	2018	2046	...	2112	2146	...	2212	2237	...	2327	0006	...	0040	...

		⑦	⑦	⑦	⑦	⑦	⑦	⑦	⑦	⑦	⑦	⑦	⑦		⑦	⑦	⑦	⑦	⑦	⑦		⑦	⑦	⑦	⑦
Birmingham New St ‡ d.	⑦	...	...	...	...	...	...	...	0914	...	1014	...	1114	and	...	1914	...	...	2014	...	...	2114	...	2214	2300
Birmingham Int'l ✈. ‡ d.		...	...	...	...	...	...	...	0925	...	1025	...	1125	at	...	1925	...	...	2025	...	...	2125	...	2225	2310
Coventry .... ‡ d.		...	...	...	...	...	...	...	0944	...	1044	...	1144	the	...	1944	...	...	2044	...	...	2144	...	2244	2321
Rugby .... **143** ‡ d.		...	...	...	...	...	...	...	0955	...	1055	1120	1155	same	1920	1955	2017	...	2055	2120	...	2155	...	2255	2335
Northampton ...... **143** a.		...	...	...	...	...	...	...	1017	...	1117	1141	1217	minutes	1941	2017	2038	...	2117	2141	...	2217	...	2319	2354**s**
Northampton ...... **143** d.		...	0620*	0753	0823	0853	0930	1009	1037	1108	1126	1150	1226	past	1950	2025	2051	...	2129	2155	...	2226	2300	...	|
Milton Keynes .... **143** ‡ d.		0642	0711	0809	0839	0909	0946	1026	1055	1124	1142	1207	1242	each	2007	2041	2107	2115	2145	2211	...	2242	2316	...	0013**s**
Bletchley .... d.		0647	0716	0814	0844	0914	0951	1031	1100	1129	1147	|	1247	hour	|	2046	|	2120	2150	2216	...	2246	2321	...	|
Leighton Buzzard .... d.		0653	0723	0821	0851	0921	0958	1037	1106	1136	1153	1215	1253	until	2015	2052	2115	2126	2156	2222	...	2253	2327	...	|
Watford Junction **143** ‡ d.		0725	0754	0853	0922	0952	1029	1105	1137	1206	1218	1240	1318	△	2035	2122	2140	2156	2226	2253	...	2323	2359	...	0043**s**
London Euston . **143** ‡ a.		0745	0814	0913	0945	1013	1051	1126	1159	1226	1238	1301	1338		2054	2142	2158	2219	2248	2315	...	2343	0021	...	0105

r – Arrives 0958.
s – Stops to set down only.
x – Trains 11xx and hourly to 17xx do not call at Bletchley and then run 4 minutes earlier to Northampton.
y – Trains 11xx and hourly to 14xx do not call at Bletchley and then run 4 minutes earlier to Northampton.

* – Connection by 🚌.
△ – Timings may vary by up to 3 minutes.
‡ – For faster journeys between these stations see Table **150**.

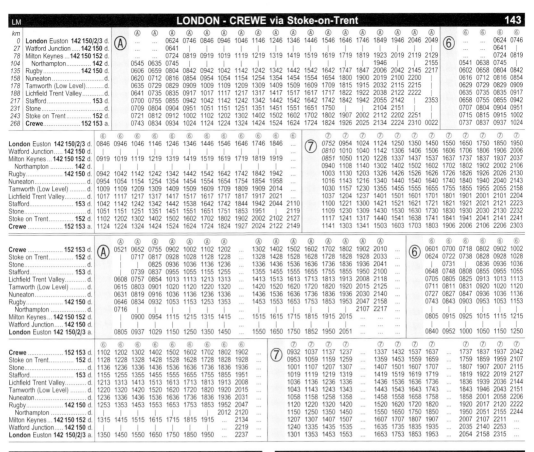

LM LONDON - CREWE via Stoke-on-Trent 143

km		Ⓐ	Ⓐ	Ⓐ	Ⓐ	Ⓐ	Ⓐ	Ⓐ	Ⓐ	Ⓐ	Ⓐ	Ⓐ	Ⓐ	Ⓐ	Ⓐ	Ⓐ	Ⓐ	Ⓐ	Ⓐ	Ⓐ	⑥	⑥	⑥	⑥	⑥
0	**London** Euston **142 150/2/3** d.		...	...	0624	0746	0846	0946	1046	1146	1246	1346	1446	1546	1646	1746	1849	1946	2046	2049		...	...	0624	0746
27	Watford Junction ..... **142 150** d.		...	...	0641	|	|	|	|	|	|	|	|	|	|	|	|	|	|	|		...	...	0641	|
78	Milton Keynes ... **142 150 152** d.		...	...	0724	0819	0919	1019	1119	1219	1319	1419	1519	1619	1719	1819	1923	2019	2119	2129		...	...	0724	0819
104	Northampton .... **142** d.		0545	0635	0745	|	|	|	|	|	|	|	|	|	|	|	1946	|	|	2155		0541	0638	0745	|
135	Rugby .... **142 150** d.		0606	0659	0804	0842	0942	1042	1142	1242	1342	1442	1542	1642	1747	1847	2006	2042	2145	2217		0602	0658	0804	0842
158	Nuneaton .... d.		0620	0712	0816	0854	0954	1054	1154	1254	1354	1454	1554	1654	1800	1900	2019	2100	2200	|		0616	0712	0816	0854
178	Tamworth (Low Level) .... d.		0635	0729	0829	0909	1009	1109	1209	1309	1409	1509	1609	1709	1815	1915	2032	2115	2215	|		0629	0729	0829	0909
188	Lichfield Trent Valley .... d.		0641	0735	0835	0917	1017	1117	1217	1317	1417	1517	1617	1717	1822	1922	2038	2122	2222	|		0635	0735	0835	0917
217	Stafford .... **153** d.		0700	0755	0855	0942	1042	1142	1242	1342	1442	1542	1642	1742	1842	1942	2055	2142	|	2353		0658	0755	0855	0942
231	Stone .... d.		0709	0804	0904	0951	1051	1151	1251	1351	1451	1551	1651	1750	|	|	2104	2151	|	|		0707	0804	0904	0951
243	Stoke on Trent .... **152** d.		0721	0812	0912	1002	1102	1202	1302	1402	1502	1602	1702	1802	1907	2002	2112	2202	2251	|		0715	0815	0915	1002
268	**Crewe** .... **152 153** a.		0743	0834	0934	1024	1124	1224	1324	1424	1524	1624	1724	1824	1926	2025	2134	2224	2310	0022		0737	0837	0937	1024

	⑥	⑥	⑥	⑥	⑥	⑥	⑥	⑥	⑥	⑥	⑥	⑥	⑦	⑦	⑦	⑦	⑦	⑦	⑦	⑦	⑦	⑦	⑦	⑦	⑦
London Euston **142 150/2/3** d.	0846	0946	1046	1146	1246	1346	1446	1546	1646	1746	1846	...		*0752*	0954	1024	1124	1250	1350	1450	1550	1650	1750	1850	1950
Watford Junction ..... **142 150** d.	|	|	|	|	|	|	|	|	|	|	|	...		*0810*	1010	1040	1142	1306	1406	1506	1606	1706	1806	1906	2006
Milton Keynes ... **142 150 152** d.	0919	1019	1119	1219	1319	1419	1519	1619	1719	1819	1919	...		*0851*	1050	1120	1228	1337	1437	1537	1637	1737	1837	1937	2037
Northampton .... **142** d.	|	|	|	|	|	|	|	|	|	|	|	...		0940	1108	1140	1302	1402	1502	1602	1702	1802	1902	2002	2106
Rugby .... **142 150** d.	0942	1042	1142	1242	1342	1442	1542	1642	1742	1842	1942	...		1003	1130	1203	1326	1426	1526	1626	1726	1826	1926	2026	2130
Nuneaton .... d.	0954	1054	1154	1254	1354	1454	1554	1654	1754	1854	1958	...		1016	1143	1216	1340	1440	1540	1640	1740	1840	1940	2040	2143
Tamworth (Low Level) .... d.	1009	1109	1209	1309	1409	1509	1609	1709	1809	1909	2014	...		1030	1157	1230	1355	1455	1555	1655	1755	1855	1955	2055	2158
Lichfield Trent Valley .... d.	1017	1117	1217	1317	1417	1517	1617	1717	1817	1917	2021	...		1037	1204	1237	1401	1501	1601	1701	1801	1901	2001	2101	2204
Stafford .... **153** d.	1042	1142	1242	1342	1442	1538	1642	1742	1844	1942	2044	2110		1100	1221	1300	1421	1521	1621	1721	1821	1921	2021	2121	2223
Stone .... d.	1051	1151	1251	1351	1451	1551	1651	1751	1853	1951	|	2119		1109	1230	1309	1430	1530	1630	1730	1830	1930	2030	2130	2232
Stoke on Trent .... **152** d.	1102	1202	1302	1402	1502	1602	1702	1802	1902	2002	2102	2127		1117	1241	1317	1440	1541	1638	1741	1841	1941	2041	2141	2241
Crewe .... **152 153** a.	1124	1224	1324	1424	1524	1624	1724	1824	1927	2024	2122	2149		1141	1303	1341	1503	1603	1703	1803	1906	2006	2106	2206	2303

	Ⓐ	Ⓐ	Ⓐ	Ⓐ	Ⓐ	Ⓐ	Ⓐ	Ⓐ		Ⓐ	Ⓐ	Ⓐ	Ⓐ	Ⓐ	Ⓐ	Ⓐ	Ⓐ		⑥	⑥	⑥	⑥	⑥	⑥	⑥
Crewe .... **152 153** d.		0521	0652	0755	0902	1002	1102	1202	...	1302	1402	1502	1602	1702	1802	1902	2010	...		0601	0700	0718	0802	0902	1002
Stoke on Trent .... **152** d.		|	0717	0817	0928	1028	1128	1228	...	1328	1428	1528	1628	1728	1828	1928	2033	...		0624	0722	0738	0828	0928	1028
Stone .... d.		|	|	0825	0936	1036	1136	1236	...	1336	1436	1536	1636	1736	1836	1936	2041	...		|	0731	|	0836	0936	1036
Stafford .... **153** d.		|	0739	0837	0955	1055	1155	1255	...	1355	1455	1555	1655	1755	1855	1950	2100	...		0648	0748	0808	0855	0955	1055
Lichfield Trent Valley .... d.		0608	0757	0854	1013	1113	1213	1313	...	1413	1513	1613	1713	1813	1913	2008	2118	...		0705	0805	0825	0913	1013	1113
Tamworth (Low Level) .... d.		0615	0803	0901	1020	1120	1220	1320	...	1420	1520	1620	1720	1820	1920	2015	2125	...		0711	0811	0831	0920	1020	1120
Nuneaton .... d.		0631	0819	0916	1036	1136	1236	1336	...	1436	1536	1636	1736	1836	1936	2030	2140	...		0727	0827	0847	0936	1036	1136
Rugby .... **142 150** d.		0646	0834	0932	1053	1153	1253	1353	...	1453	1553	1653	1753	1853	1953	2047	2158	...		0743	0843	0903	0953	1053	1153
Northampton .... d.		0716	|	|	|	|	|	|	...	|	|	|	|	|	|	2107	2217	...		|	|	|	|	|	|
Milton Keynes ... **142 150 152** d.		|	0900	0954	1115	1215	1315	1415	...	1515	1615	1715	1815	1915	2015	...	...	...		0805	0915	0925	1015	1115	1215
Watford Junction ..... **142 150** d.		|	|	|	|	|	|	|	...	|	|	|	|	|	|	...	...	...		|	|	|	|	|	|
London Euston **142 150/2/3** a.		0805	0937	1029	1150	1250	1350	1450	...	1550	1650	1750	1852	1950	2051	...	...	...		0840	0952	1000	1050	1150	1250

	⑥	⑥	⑥	⑥	⑥	⑥	⑥	⑥	⑥		⑦	⑦	⑦	⑦	⑦		⑦	⑦	⑦	⑦		⑦	⑦	⑦	⑦
Crewe .... **152 153** d.	1102	1202	1302	1402	1502	1602	1702	1802	1902	...		0932	1037	1137	1237	...	1337	1432	1537	1637	...	1737	1837	1937	2042
Stoke on Trent .... **152** d.	1128	1228	1328	1428	1528	1628	1728	1828	1928	...		0953	1059	1159	1259	...	1359	1453	1559	1659	...	1759	1859	1959	2107
Stone .... d.	1136	1236	1336	1436	1536	1636	1736	1836	1936	...		1001	1107	1207	1307	...	1407	1501	1607	1707	...	1807	1907	2007	2115
Stafford .... **153** d.	1155	1255	1355	1455	1555	1655	1755	1855	1951	...		1019	1119	1219	1319	...	1419	1519	1619	1719	...	1819	1922	2019	2127
Lichfield Trent Valley .... d.	1213	1313	1413	1513	1613	1713	1813	1913	2008	...		1036	1136	1236	1336	...	1436	1536	1636	1736	...	1836	1939	2036	2144
Tamworth (Low Level) .... d.	1220	1320	1420	1520	1620	1720	1820	1920	2015	...		1043	1143	1243	1343	...	1443	1543	1643	1743	...	1843	1946	2043	2151
Nuneaton .... d.	1236	1336	1436	1536	1636	1736	1836	1936	2031	...		1058	1158	1258	1358	...	1458	1558	1658	1758	...	1858	2001	2058	2206
Rugby .... **142 150** d.	1253	1353	1453	1553	1653	1753	1853	1952	2047	...		1120	1220	1320	1420	...	1520	1620	1720	1820	...	1920	2017	2120	2222
Northampton .... d.	|	|	|	|	|	|	|	2012	2120	...		1150	1250	1350	1450	...	1550	1650	1750	1850	...	1950	2051	2155	2244
Milton Keynes ... **142 150 152** d.	1315	1415	1515	1615	1715	1815	1915	...	2134	...		1207	1307	1407	1507	...	1607	1707	1807	1907	...	2007	2107	2211	...
Watford Junction ..... **142 150** d.	|	|	|	|	|	|	|	...	2219	...		1240	1335	1435	1535	...	1635	1735	1835	1935	...	2035	2140	2253	...
London Euston **142 150/2/3** a.	1350	1450	1550	1650	1750	1850	1950	...	2237	...		1301	1353	1453	1553	...	1653	1753	1853	1953	...	2054	2158	2315	...

LM NUNEATON - COVENTRY 143a

From Nuneaton: 2nd class only Journey ± 20 minutes *16 km*

Ⓐ: 0633, 0737, 0833, 1014 and hourly until 2014, 2114, 2220.
⑥: 0644, 0814, 0914, 1014 and hourly until 1814, 1944, 2114, 2220.
⑦: 1236, 1411, 1511, 1611, 1711, 1811, 2011, 2200.

From Coventry:

Ⓐ: 0604, 0704, 0804, 0904, 1042 and hourly until 1842, 1942, 2042, 2142.
⑥: 0615, 0715, 0842, 0942, 1042 and hourly until 1742, 1842, 2015, 2142.
⑦: 1146, 1339, 1439, 1539, 1639, 1739, 1939, 2132.

LM BEDFORD - BLETCHLEY 143b

From Bedford: 2nd class only Journey ± 44 minutes *26 km*

Trains call at **Woburn Sands** 30 minutes later:

0610Ⓐ, 0629⑥, 0729⚒, 0829⚒, 0929⚒, 1055⚒, 1155⚒, 1255⚒, 1355⚒, 1455⚒, 1555⚒, 1640Ⓐ, 1700⑥, 1740Ⓐ, 1755⑥, 1826Ⓐ, 1839⑥, 1929Ⓐ, 1936⑥, 2100⚒, 2200⚒.

From Bletchley:

Trains call at **Woburn Sands** 11 minutes later:

0516Ⓐ, 0534⑥, 0624Ⓐ, 0634⑥, 0731⚒, 0822Ⓐ, 0834⑥, 1001⚒, 1101⚒, 1201⚒, 1301⚒, 1401⚒, 1501⚒, 1551Ⓐ, 1601⑥, 1651Ⓐ, 1701⑥, 1736Ⓐ, 1750⑥, 1831Ⓐ, 1847⑥, 2001Ⓐ, 2004⑥, 2101⚒.

LM BIRMINGHAM - CREWE - LIVERPOOL 144

km		Ⓐ	Ⓐ	Ⓐ	Ⓐ	Ⓐ	Ⓐ	Ⓐ	Ⓐ		Ⓐ	Ⓐ	Ⓐ	Ⓐ	Ⓐ	Ⓐ	Ⓐ	Ⓐ	Ⓐ	Ⓐ	⑥	⑥	⑥	⑥	⑥
0	**Birmingham** New St **122** d.		...	...	...	0601	0636	0701	0736	and at	1701	1736	1801	1836	1901	1936	2036	2136	2239	2309		...	...	...	0601
19	Wolverhampton .... **122** d.		...	...	...	0621	0654	0720	0754	the same	1720	1754	1820	1854	1920	1954	2054	2154	2305	2336		...	...	...	0620
43	Stafford .... **122 143 153** d.		...	...	...	0637	0710	0736	0810	minutes	1736	1810	1836	1910	1945	2010	2110	2210	2321	2353		...	...	...	0636
82	**Crewe** .... **143 153** d.		0540	0603	0633	0659	0733	0757	0832	past each	1757	1832	1859	1933	2032	2033	2133	2242**a**	2358	0022		0548	0614	0633	0659
118	Runcorn .... **153** d.		0601	0630	0700	0725	0800	0825	0852	hour until	1825	1857	1922	1956	...	2056	2156	2307	...	...		0608	0633	0700	0725
131	**Liverpool** SP ‡ .... d.		0609	0639	0709	0733	0809	0833	0901	★	1833	1906	1931	2005	...	2105	2205	2316	...	...		0617	0642	0709	0733
140	**Liverpool** Lime St.... **153** a.		0621	0651	0721	0746	0821	0844	0911		1844	1917	1942	2017	...	2118	2216	2330	...	...		0627	0654	0721	0744

	⑥	⑥	⑥	⑥	⑥		⑥	⑥	⑥	⑥	⑥	⑥	⑥	⑥	⑥	⑦	⑦	⑦	⑦	⑦		⑦	⑦	⑦
Birmingham New St **122** d.	0636	0701	0736	0801	0836	and at	1701	1736	1801	1836	1901	2001	2036	2136	2239		0942	1042	1142	1235	and at	1835	1935	2142
Wolverhampton .... **122** d.	0654	0720	0754	0820	0854	the same	1720	1754	1820	1854	1920	2022	2054	2159	2306		1000	1100	1200	1253	the same	1853	1953	2200
Stafford .... **122 143 153** d.	0710	0736	0810	0836	0910	minutes	1736	1810	1836	1910	1936	2038	2110	2216	2322		1017	1117	1217	1309	minutes	1909	2009	2217
Crewe .... **143 153** d.	0733	0759	0832	0857	0932	past each	1757	1832	1857	1930	1957	2059	2149	2236	2342		1038	1138	1238	1331	past each	1931	2031	2238
Runcorn .... **153** d.	0800	0825	0852	0922	0952	hour until	1825	1852	1922	...	2025	2121	*2224*	...	...		1101	1201	1301	1354	hour until	1954	2054	2300
Liverpool SP ‡ .... d.	0809	0833	0901	0931	1001	★	1833	1901	1931	...	2033	2130	|	...	...		1110	1210	1310	1403		2003	2103	2310
Liverpool Lime St .... **153** a.	0821	0844	0911	0942	1011		1844	1911	1942	...	2044	2140	*2246*	...	...		1121	1221	1321	1414		2014	2114	2324

	Ⓐ	Ⓐ	Ⓐ	Ⓐ	Ⓐ	Ⓐ	Ⓐ	Ⓐ		Ⓐ	Ⓐ	Ⓐ	Ⓐ	Ⓐ	Ⓐ	Ⓐ	Ⓐ	Ⓐ	Ⓐ	Ⓐ	⑥	⑥	⑥	⑥	⑥
Liverpool Lime St .... **153** d.		...	...	0630	0704	0734	0804	0834	and at	1704	1734	1804	1834	1912	1934	2004	2034	2134	2234	2334		...	...	0632	0704
Liverpool SP ‡ .... d.		...	...	0640	0715	0744	0815	0844	the same	1716	1744	1815	1844	1922	1944	2015	2044	2144	2246	2346		...	...	0642	0715
Runcorn .... **153** d.		...	...	0648	0723	0752	0823	0852	minutes	1725	1752	1825	1852	1930	1952	2025	2052	2152	2255	2355		...	...	0650	0723
Crewe .... **143 153** d.		0619	0649	0716	0749	0817	0849	0919	past each	1749	1819	1849	1919	1955	2019	2047	2119	2219	2324	0026		0611	0649	0719**b**	0749
Stafford .... **122 143 153** d.		0641	0710	0740	0810	0840	0910	0940	hour until	1810	1843	1910	1939	2016	2039	2110	2139	2240	...	...		0631	0710	0740	0810
Wolverhampton .... **122** a.		0658	0726	0758	0827	0858	0927	0957	★	1827	1859	1928	1957	2032	2056	2127	2157	2259	...	...		0647	0727	0756	0827
Birmingham New St **122** a.		0720	0750	0818	0848	0918	0948	1018		1848	1918	1948	2018	2050	2118	2148	2218	2326	...	...		0715	0750	0818	0848

	⑥	⑥	⑥		⑥	⑥	⑥	⑥	⑥	⑥	⑥	⑥	⑥**d**	⑥**c**	⑥**e**	⑦	⑦	⑦	⑦		⑦	⑦	⑦	⑦
Liverpool Lime St .... **153** d.	0734	0804	0834	and at	1704	1734	1804	1834	1904	1934	2034	2134	2148	2204	2204		...	1134	1234	and at	1934	2034	2134	2330
Liverpool SP ‡ .... d.	0744	0815	0844	the same	1716	1744	1815	1844	1915	1944	2044	2144	2158	2215	2229		...	1144	1244	the same	1944	2044	2144	2342
Runcorn .... **153** d.	0752	0825	0852	minutes	1725	1752	1824	1852	1925	1952	2052	2152	2206	2223	2249		...	1152	1252	minutes	1952	2052	2152	2352
Crewe .... **143 153** d.	0819	0849	0919	past each	1749	1822	1849	1919	1951	2019	2119	2224	2231	2247	2356		1021	1219	1319	past each	2019	2119	2222	0020
Stafford .... **122 143 153** d.	0840	0910	0940	hour until	1810	1843	1910	1940	2012	2040	2140	2245	...	...	...		1042	1240	1340	hour until	2040	2140	2242	...
Wolverhampton .... **122** a.	0858	0927	0958	★	1828	1859	1928	1957	2028	2057	2158	2302	...	...	...		1101	1256	1357		2057	2157	2259	...
Birmingham New St **122** a.	0918	0948	1018		1848	1918	1948	2018	2048	2118	2218	2320	...	...	...		1119	1315	1415		2115	2215	2317	...

a – Arrives 2236.
b – Arrives 0715.
c – June 24 - Oct. 21.
d – May 27 - June 17 and from Oct. 28.
e – By 🚌 May 27 - June 17 and from Oct. 28.
‡ – Liverpool South Parkway. 🚌 connections available to / from Liverpool John Lennon Airport.
★ – Timings may vary by ± 3 minutes.

145 BIRMINGHAM - SHREWSBURY - CHESTER

2nd class AW

km		⚒	⑥	Ⓐ	⚒ A	⑥ 🍷	Ⓐ B	Ⓐ	⑥ 🍷	Ⓐ 🍷	⚒	Ⓐ 🍷	⑥ 🍷	⑥ 🍷	Ⓐ 🍷	⚒	⑥ 🍷	Ⓐ 🍷	⚒	⚒ 🍷	⚒ 🍷	Ⓐ C	⚒	⚒ 🍷	⑥ C	Ⓐ 🍷
	London Euston **150** d.		...	...	...	M	...	...	...	L	...	L	...	...	...	...	...	...	...	...	...	1023	...	...	1123	...
0	**Birmingham** Int'l ✈ d.		...	...	...	...	...	...	...	...	...	0709	0709	...	...	0809	0910	0910	1009	...	1110	1133	1209	...	1233	1308
13	**Birmingham** New St. d.		...	...	0530	...	...	...	...	...	0625	0723	0724	...	...	0825	0925	0925	1025	...	1125	1153	1225	...	1253	1325
34	Wolverhampton d.		...	...	0548	...	...	...	...	...	0643	0742	0742	...	...	0843	0943	0943	1043	...	1142	1211	1243	...	1311	1343
59	Telford Central d.		...	...	|	...	...	...	...	...	0659	0759	0759	...	...	0900	1000	0959	1059	...	1159	1228	1259	...	1328	1400
65	Wellington d.		...	...	|	...	...	...	...	...	0706	0805	0805	...	...	0907	1006	1005	1106	...	1205	1235	1306	...	1335	1406
81	**Shrewsbury** a.		...	...	|	...	...	...	...	...	0722	0819	0820	...	...	0920	1018	1021	1119	...	1221	1251	1320	...	1354	1420
	Aberystwyth **147** a.		...	...	|	...	...	...	...	...	0923	|	|	...	...	1120	|	|	1320	...	|	...	1520	...	...	|
	Cardiff Central **149** d.		...	...	|	...	...	...	0520	0508	...	|	|	0721	0721	...	|	|	...	0921	|	...	...	1121	...	|
81	**Shrewsbury** d.		0520	0520	|	0610	*0610*	0700	0722	0724	...	0821	0822	0925	0924	...	1022	1023	...	1125	1225	...	...	1325	...	1425
110	Gobowen d.		0539	0539	|	0630	*0630*	0720	0743	0743	...	0840	0841	0944	0943	...	1042	1044	...	1144	1243	...	...	1344	...	1445
122	Ruabon d.		0551	0551	|	0642	*0642*	0732	0754	0754	...	0852	0853	0955	0954	...	1054	1056	...	1155	1255	...	...	1355	...	1457
129	Wrexham General d.		0558	0604	|	0650	0700	0740	0801	0802	...	0900	0901	1002	1002	...	1101	1102	...	1202	1301	...	...	1402	...	1503
149	**Chester** **160** a.		0617	0625	0643	0710	0716	...	0819	0821	...	0919	0918	1020	1020	...	1120	1121	...	1220	1322	...	...	1420	...	1521
	Holyhead **160** a.		...	...	0823	...	...	...	1014	...	...	...	1105	1209	1222	...	1312	1317	...	1414	1508	...	...	1614	...	1716

	⑥ 🍷	⚒	⚒ 🍷	⚒ 🍷	⚒	⚒ 🍷	Ⓐ E	Ⓐ 🍷	⑥ 🍷	Ⓐ 🍴	⚒	⑥	Ⓐ	Ⓐ 🍷	⚒ 🍷	⚒ C	⑥	Ⓐ	Ⓐ	⑥ J	Ⓐ M	⑥	⑥	Ⓐ	⑥
London Euston **150** d.	...	...	...	...	...	...	...	L	...	...	...	...	...	F	...	1823	...	...	...	...	...	...	...	...	...
Birmingham International ✈ d.	1310	1409	...	1509	1609	...	...	1709	1709	...	1809	...	...	...	1904e	1933	2009	2004	...	...	2104	2109	...	...	...
Birmingham New Street d.	1325	1425	...	1525	1625	...	...	1725	1725	...	1825	...	...	...	1925	1950	2025	2025	...	...	2125	2125	...	2214	2235
Wolverhampton d.	1342	1443	...	1542	1643	...	...	1742	1743	...	1843	...	...	...	1943	2019	2043	2043	...	...	2142	2143	...	2244	2253
Telford Central d.	1359	1459	...	1558	1659	...	...	1801	1800	...	1859	...	...	...	2000	2036	2059	2059	...	...	2158	2200	...	2310	2309
Wellington d.	1406	1506	...	1605	1706	...	...	1806	1807	...	1906	...	...	...	2006	2043	2106	2105	...	...	2206	2206	...	2318	2316
Shrewsbury a.	1419	1520	...	1620	1719	...	...	1820	1820	...	1919	...	...	...	2020	2055	2120	2118	...	...	2218	2223	...	2330	2328
Aberystwyth **147** a.	|	1720	...	|	1921	...	...	|	|	...	2123	...	...	...	|	...	2330	2337	...	...	|	|	...	...	...
Cardiff Central **149** d.	|	...	1321	|	...	1521	1621	|	|	1716	...	1721	...	1821	|	...	...	...	1934	1934	|	|	2055	...	...
Shrewsbury d.	1422	...	1526	1624	...	1724	1810	1825	1822	1909	...	1924	1924	2013	2024	...	...	...	2139	2137	2224	2225	2306	...	...
Gobowen d.	1442	...	1545	1644	...	1743	|	1844	1842	|	...	1943	1943	|	2043	...	...	...	2158	2156	2243	2244	|	...	...
Ruabon d.	1454	...	1556	1656	...	1754	a	1856	1854	|	...	1954	1955	a	2055	...	...	...	2209	2207	2255	2256	a	...	...
Wrexham General d.	1500	...	1604	1703	...	1802	|	1905	1902	1943	...	2002	2002	|	2102	...	...	...	2214	2213	2303	2303	|	...	...
Chester **160** a.	1521	...	1624	1721	...	1822	1910	1924	1921	2002	...	2022	2024	2108	2121	...	...	...	2234	2232	2320	2322	0020	...	...
Holyhead **160** a.	1714	...	1821	1917c	...	2020	...	...	2131	2145	...	2225	...	...	...	...	...	...	0048	...	...	...	...	...	...

	Ⓐ	Ⓐ	⑥	Ⓐ	⑦	⑦ 🍷	⑦	⑦	⑦ 🍷	⑦ 🍷	⑦ 🍷	⑦ 🍷	⑦ 🍷	⑦ 🍷	⑦	⑦ 🍷	⑦ 🍷	⑦ 🍷	⑦	⑦ C	⑦	⑦	⑦	⑦	⑦
London Euston **150** d.	...	...	...	...		...	...	...	...	...	...	...	...	...	...	...	...	...	...	1900	...	...	...	...	...
Birmingham International ✈ d.	...	...	...	...		...	0951	1048	1207	1307	...	1407	1507	1607	...	1707	1807	1907	2008	2013	2108	...	2211	2240	2308
Birmingham New Street d.	...	2332	2335	2252		...	1004	1105	1224	1324	...	1424	1524	1624	...	1724	1824	1924	2024	2027	2124	...	2224	2255	2324
Wolverhampton d.	...	0002	2354	2327		...	1022	1127	1242	1342	...	1443	1543	1643	...	1743	1843	1943	2043	2056	2143	...	2242	2315	2346
Telford Central d.	...	0029	0022	|		...	1049	1154	1259	1358	...	1459	1559	1659	...	1759	1859	1959	2059	2113	2210	...	2309	|	0013
Wellington d.	...	0036	0030	|		...	1057	1201	1305	1404	...	1506	1606	1706	...	1805	1906	2006	2106	2120	2217	...	2316	|	0020
Shrewsbury a.	...	0052	0045	|		...	1110	1215	1324	1418	...	1520	1622	1719	...	1819	1919	2019	2119	2135	2230	...	2332	|	0036
Aberystwyth **147** a.	...	▬	▬	|		...	1320	|	1523	|	...	1721	|	1922	...	|	2120	|	2315	...	|	...	...	|	...
Cardiff Central **149** d.	2117	⑥	Ⓐ	|		...	...	|	...	|	1313	...	|	...	1513	|	...	|	▬	...	|	2101	...	|	...
Shrewsbury d.	2318	2333	2337	|		1016	...	1217	...	1420	1524	...	1624	...	1730	1820	...	2023	...	...	2232	2319	...	|	...
Gobowen d.	|	2352	2357	|		1035	...	1237	...	1439	1544	...	1643	...	1749	1840	...	2043	⑦	...	|	|	...	|	...
Ruabon d.	a	0004	0009	|		1047	...	1249	...	1451	1556	...	1655	...	1801	1851	...	2055		...	a	a	...	|	...
Wrexham General d.	|	0014	0015	|		1054	...	1256	...	1458	1602	...	1706	...	1808	1858	...	2102	2235	...	|	|	...	|	...
Chester **160** a.	0031	0033	0035	0037		1114	...	1320	...	1518	1622	...	1726	...	1825	1925	...	2120	2255	...	2331	0033	...	0022	...
Holyhead **160** a.	...	...	...	0224		...	...	...	...	...	1837	...	...	...	2018	2134	...	...	...	...	...	...	...	0220	...

	⚒	⑥	Ⓐ	Ⓐ	⑥	Ⓐ	⑥	Ⓐ	⑥ 🍷	Ⓐ 🍷	⚒	⑥ C	⑥ 🍷	Ⓐ 🍴	Ⓐ 🍷	Ⓐ 🍷	⑥ 🍷	⚒	⑥ 🍷	Ⓐ 🍷	Ⓐ 🍷	Ⓐ 🍷	⑥ 🍷	⚒	⚒ 🍷
Holyhead **160** d.		...	...	...	...	...	...	...	0425b	0425	...	...	0522	0533	...	0628	0635	...	0715	L	...	0805	0820	...	0923
Chester **160** d.		0422	0422	...	...	0530	0537	0545	0612	0618	...	...	0721	0714	...	0819	0819	...	0930	0926	...	1020	1019	...	1130
Wrexham General d.		|	|	...	...	0546	0555	0603	0638	0637	...	...	0737	0732	0747	0834	0834	...	0946	0942	...	1036	1035	...	1145
Ruabon d.		|	|	...	...	0553	▬	▬	0644	0643	...	...	0744	|	0755	0841	0841	...	0953	0949	...	1042	1042	...	1153
Gobowen d.		|	|	...	...	0605	...	...	0656	0655	...	...	0756	|	0807	0852	0852	...	1004	1001	...	1053	1053	...	1205
Shrewsbury a.		|	|	...	...	0627	...	...	0717	0716	...	...	0820	0807	0828	0913	0913	...	1029	1022	...	1114	1114	...	1229
Cardiff Central **149** a.		|	|	...	...	|	...	...	0922	0920	...	...	|	0958	|	1115	1120	...	|	1210	...	1322	1317	...	|
Aberystwyth **147** d.		|	|	...	...	|	⑥	Ⓐ C	...	...	0530	...	|	...	|	...	...	0730	|	...	...	...	...	0930	|
Shrewsbury d.		|	|	0518	0522	0633	0633	0639	...	...	0733	0818	0833	...	0832	...	...	0933	1033	...	1032	...	...	1133	1233
Wellington d.		|	|	0531	0535	0646	0646	0653	...	...	0746	0832	0846	...	0845	...	...	0946	1046	...	1046	...	...	1146	1246
Telford Central d.		|	|	0538	0542	0653	0653	0700	...	...	0753	0839	0853	...	0852	...	...	0953	1053	...	1052	...	...	1153	1253
Wolverhampton a.		0539	0539	0558	0601	0711	0711	0717	...	...	0811	0900	0911	...	0910	...	...	1010	1111	...	1109	...	...	1212	1310
Birmingham New Street a.		0558	0610	0615	0619	0730	0730	0747	...	...	0829	0921	0927	...	0929	...	...	1030	1128	...	1130	...	...	1232	1329
Birmingham International ✈ a.		...	...	0649	0649	0749	0749	0759	...	...	0849	0939	0950	...	0949	...	...	1050	1150	...	1149	...	...	1250	1350
London Euston a.		...	...	...	...	...	...	0915	...	...	...	1056	...	...	...	...	...	...	...	...	...	...	...	...	...

	⑥ 🍷	Ⓐ 🍷 F	⚒	⑥ 🍷	Ⓐ 🍷	Ⓐ 🍷	⑥ 🍷	⚒ C	⚒	Ⓐ 🍷	⑥ 🍷	⑥ 🍷	Ⓐ 🍷	⚒	⑥ 🍷	Ⓐ 🍷	⚒ 🍷	⚒	Ⓐ 🍷	⑥ 🍷	Ⓐ B	⑥	⑥	Ⓐ	Ⓐ D
Holyhead **160** d.	1033	1040	...	1123	1127	1232	1238	...	...	1324	1328	1425	1434	...	1523	1544	1650	...	1730	1730	...	...	...	...	...
Chester **160** d.	1219	1219	...	1330	1330	1419	1419	...	...	1530	1530	1619	1619	...	1728	1730	1828	...	1917	1928	2022	2026	...	...	2135
Wrexham General d.	1234	1234	...	1346	1346	1434	1434	...	...	1546	1546	1635	1635	...	1744	1748	1845	...	1933	1944	2038	2042	...	...	|
Ruabon d.	1241	1241	...	1353	1353	1441	1441	...	...	1553	1553	1642	1642	...	1751	1754	1851	...	1940	1951	*2056*	2049	...	...	|
Gobowen d.	1252	1253	...	1405	1405	1452	1452	...	...	1605	1605	1653	1653	...	1803	1806	1903	...	1952	2002	*2107*	2101	...	...	|
Shrewsbury a.	1313	1314	...	1428	1427	1513	1513	...	...	1629	1629	1714	1714	...	1824	1827	1924	...	2014	2026	*2128*	2121	...	...	|
Cardiff Central **149** a.	1524	1510	...	|	|	1716	1708	...	...	|	|	1915	1918	...	|	|	2138h	...	...	...	...	...	...	...	|
Aberystwyth **147** d.	...	...	1130	|	|	...	...	...	1330	|	|	...	...	1530	|	|	...	1730	...	...	...	...	1930	1930	|
Shrewsbury d.	...	...	1334	1433	1433	...	...	1524	1533	1633	1633	...	...	1733	1833	1833	...	1932	...	...	...	...	2133	2133	|
Wellington d.	...	...	1348	1446	1446	...	...	1538	1546	1647	1647	...	...	1746	1846	1846	...	1946	...	...	...	...	2146	2147	|
Telford Central d.	...	...	1354	1453	1453	...	...	1544	1553	1654	1653	...	...	1753	1853	1853	...	1953	...	...	...	...	2153	2153	|
Wolverhampton a.	...	...	1412	1511	1511	...	...	1601	1610	1709	1708	...	...	1811	1911	1911	...	2011	...	...	...	...	2209	2211	2227
Birmingham New Street a.	...	...	1432	1528	1530	...	...	1622	1630	1730	1728	...	...	1830	1928	1930	...	2029	...	...	...	...	2231	2231	2250
Birmingham International ✈ a.	...	...	1449	1550	1549	...	...	1639	1649	1749	1750	...	...	1849	1949	1949	...	2049	...	...	...	...	...	...	...
London Euston a.	...	...	...	...	...	...	...	1756	...	...	...	...	...	...	...	...	...	...	...	...	...	...	...	...	...

	Ⓐ	⑥	⚒	⑦	⑦	⑦	⑦	⑦	⑦ 🍷	⑦	⑦ 🍷	⑦	⑦ C	⑦ 🍷	⑦ 🍷	⑦ 🍷	⑦	⑦	⑦ 🍷	⑦	⑦ 🍷	⑦	⑦	⑦	⑦
Holyhead **160** d.	1921	1921	...		...	...	...	...	...	1020	...	...	...	...	...	...	...	1625	...	...	1825	...	1915d	...	...
Chester **160** d.	2121	2120	2228		0808	...	0922	...	1131	1221	...	1331	...	...	1531	...	1731	1824	...	1926	2027	...	2126	2204	2300
Wrexham General d.	2137	2137	2244		0828	...	0938	...	1148	1238	...	1348	...	...	1548	...	1748	1841	...	1942	|	...	2144	2223	|
Ruabon d.	2144	2143	2251		▬	...	0945	...	1155	1245	...	1354	...	...	1554	...	1754	1847	...	1949	|	...	2150	...	|
Gobowen d.	2155	2156	2302		...	...	0957	...	1206	1257	...	1406	...	...	1606	...	1806	1859	...	2000	|	...	2202	...	|
Shrewsbury a.	2216	2217	2323		...	...	1018	...	1227	1318	...	1427	...	...	1627	...	1827	1920	...	2021	|	...	2223	...	0014
Cardiff Central **149** a.	|	|	|		...	...	|	...	|	1541	...	|	...	...	|	...	|	2137	...	|	|	...	|	...	...
Aberystwyth **147** d.	|	|	|		⑦	...	|	0930	|	...	1130	|	...	1330	|	1530	|	...	1730	|	|	1930	|	...	...
Shrewsbury d.	2218	2231	2326		0810	0909	1020	1140	1231	...	1331	1431	1524	1533	1640	1733	1831	...	1931	2023	|	2131	2223	...	...
Wellington d.	2232	2245	2340		0824	0923	1034	1154	1245	...	1345	1445	1538	1547	1654	1747	1845	...	1945	2037	|	2145	2237	...	...
Telford Central d.	2238	2251	2347		0831	0930	1040	1200	1251	...	1351	1451	1544	1553	1700	1753	1851	...	1951	2044	|	2151	2245	...	...
Wolverhampton a.	2255	2308	0017		0859	0958	1056	1216	1307	...	1407	1507	1601	1609	1715	1809	1907	...	2008	2111	2129	2207	2314	...	...
Birmingham New Street a.	2328	2330	...		0915	1014	1113	1233	1323	...	1423	1524	1620	1625	1737	1827	1926	...	2025	2129	2153	2227	...	...	...
Birmingham International ✈ a.	...	...	...		0932	1032	1131	1302	1357	...	1500	1557	1639	1700	1757	1900	1957	...	2101	2157	2208	2301	...	...	...
London Euston a.	...	...	...		...	...	...	...	...	...	...	...	1757	...	...	...	...	...	...	...	...	...	...	...	...

A – (12) and 🍷 Birmingham New Street - Crewe - Holyhead (Table **151**).
B – (12) and 🍷 Wrexham - London Euston and v.v. (Table **151**).
C – (12) and 🍷 Shrewsbury - London Euston and v.v. (Table **150**).
D – (12) and 🍷 Bangor - Crewe - Birmingham New Street (Table **151**).
E – From Swansea (Table **135**).
F – To/from Llanelli (Table **135**).
J – To/from Llandudno Junction (Table **165**).
L – To/from Llandudno (Table **165**).
M – To/from Manchester Piccadilly (Table **160**).

a – Via Crewe (Table **149**).
b – From Sept. 16.
c – Arrives 1913 on ⑥.
d – May 21 - Sept. 10.
e – Departs 1909 on ⑥.
h – Arrives 2135 on ⑥.

AW 2nd class SHREWSBURY - SWANSEA 146

km		Ⓐ	⑥	Ⓐ	⑥	Ⓐ	⑦	⑥	Ⓐ	⑦	⑥	Ⓐ
0	**Shrewsbury** .... **149** d.	0445	0516	0556	0900	1009	1204	1358	1405	1618	1801	1824
20	Church Stretton **149** d.	0503	0533	0614	0918	1027	1222	1416	1423	1636	1821	1842
32	Craven Arms .... **149** d.	0514	0547	0624	0928	1037	1233	1426	1434	1647	1832	1854
52	Knighton .... d.	0536	0612	0656	0952	1101	1257	1455	1458	1711	1856	1918
84	**Llandrindod** .... a.	0610	0646	0734	1030	1139	1335	1533	1536	1749	1934	1956
84	**Llandrindod** .... d.	▬	0654	0735	1033	1200	1341	1540	1541	1758	1934	1956
110	Llanwrtyd .... d.	Ⓐ	0723	0809	1107	1231	1412	1611	1623	1829	2008	2030
128	Llandovery .... d.	0642	0747	0834	1132	1256	1437	1636	1648	1855	2034	2056
146	Llandeilo .... d.	0703	0808	0856	1154	1318	1459	1658	1710	1916	2055	2117
159	Pantyffynnon .... d.	0721	0825	0913	1211	1335	1516	1715	1727	1934	2113	2135
178	Llanelli .... **135** a.	0741	0848	0933	1235	1358	1537	1735	1747	1959	2133	2155
196	**Swansea** .... **135** a.	0808	0922	1002	1301	1425	1603	1809	1814	2025	2206	2222

	⑥	Ⓐ	Ⓐ	⑥	Ⓐ	⑦	⑥	Ⓐ	⑦	⑥	Ⓐ
Swansea .... **135** d.	0431	...	0604	0915	0933	1112	1312	1435	1526	1817	1821
Llanelli .... **135** d.	0450	0520	0625	0934	0954	1132	1332	1453	1549	1840	1842
Pantyffynnon .... d.	0510	0539	0644	0955	1013	1153	1353	1512	1609	1859	1901
Llandeilo .... d.	0529	0559	0706	1015	1033	1213	1413	1532	1632	1919	1921
Llandovery .... d.	0551	0623	0728	1037	1055	1235	1435	1554	1654	1941	1943
Llanwrtyd .... d.	0616	▬	0808	1105	1120	1300	1501	1624	1720	2008	2031
Llandrindod .... a.	0644	Ⓐ	0838	1136	1151	1331	1531	1654	1750	2038	2102
Llandrindod .... d.	0655	0618	0845	1140	1201	1343	1542	1659	1801	2042	2119
Knighton .... d.	0732	0703	0923	1218	1240	1422	1621	1737	1840	2118	2158
Craven Arms .... **149** a.	0753	0727	0946	1240	1302	1444	1642	1759	1902	2140	2220
Church Stretton **149** a.	0806	0742	0958	1253	1317	1457	1655	1812	1917	2153	2235
Shrewsbury .... **149** a.	0822	0757	1014	1309	1332	1512	1711	1828	1933	2209	2254

AW 2nd class SHREWSBURY - ABERYSTWYTH 147

km			⚒	Ⓐ	⑥	⚒	⚒	⚒	⚒	⚒	⚒	Ⓐ	⑥	⚒	Ⓐ	⑥	⑥	Ⓐ		⑦a	⑦b	⑦	⑦	⑦	⑦	⑦	⑦	⑦	⑦
	B'mingham NS **145** d.		...	0625	0625	0825	...	1025	1225	1425	1625	...	...	1825	...	...	2025	2025		...	🚌	1004	1224	1424	...	1624	...	1824	2024
0	**Shrewsbury** .... d.	⚒	0625	0727	0729	0930	1029	1127	1329	1530	1727	1831	1827	1930	2030	2039	2143	2150	⑦	0830	0830	1128	1328	1527	1629	1727	1828	1927	2127
32	Welshpool .... d.		0648	0749	0752	0952	1051	1149	1351	1552	1749	1853	1849	1952	2055	2101	2205	2212		0852	0905	1150	1350	1551	1651	1749	1850	1949	2149
54	Newtown .... d.		0703	0803	0806	1006	1106	1203	1405	1606	1803	1907	1903	2006	2110	2116	2220	2227		0906	0930	1204	1404	1605	1705	1803	1904	2003	2203
63	Caersws .... d.		0710	0810	0813	1013	1113	1210	1412	1613	1810	1914	1910	2013	2117	2123	2227	2234		0913	0945	1211	1412	1612	1712	1811	1911	2010	2210
98	**Machynlleth** .... a.		0742	0841	0844	1045	1141	1243	1443	1644	1841	1945	1942	2047	2145	2151	2255	2302		0945	1025	1245	1443	1643	1742	1842	1940	2041	2239
98	**Machynlleth** .... d.		0746	0848	0849	1050	1141**r**	1247	1449	1650	1849	1948	1946	2049**r**	2149	2151	2302	2307		0947	1025	1250	1448	1648	1745	1848	1942	2047	2245
104	Dovey Junction ‡ ...... d.		0755	0855	0856	1056	1154	1254	1455	1656	1858	1957	1955	2057**r**	2157	2159	2308	2313		0955	|	1258	1458	1654	1755	1856	1956	2055	2251
118	Borth .... d.		0805	0905	0906	1106	1203	1304	1505	1706	1908	2007	2005	2107**r**	2208	2209	2318	2323		1005	1050	1308	1508	1704	1805	1906	2006	2105	2301
131	**Aberystwyth** .... a.		0820	0922	0923	1120	1220	1320	1520	1720	1922	2020	2020	2120**r**	2224	2223	2330	2337		1021	1110	1320	1523	1721	1820	1922	2021	2120	2315

		⚒	⚒	Ⓐ	⑥	Ⓐ	⑥	⚒	Ⓐ	⑥	⚒	⚒	⚒	⑥	Ⓐ	Ⓐ	⑥	⑥	Ⓐ		⑦	⑦	⑦	⑦	⑦	⑦		⑦	⑦
Aberystwyth .... d.		0530	0630	0730	0730	0830	0830	0930	1130	1130	1230	1330	1530	1730	1730	1832	1833	1930	1930		0930	1030	1130	1330	1434	1530	...	1730	1930
Borth .... d.	⚒	0543	0643	0743	0743	0843	0843	0943	1143	1143	1243	1343	1543	1743	1743	1845	1845	1943	1943	⑦	0943	1043	1143	1343	1447	1543	...	1743	1943
Dovey Junction ‡ .... d.		0553	0653	0753	0754	0858	0859	0953	1153	1155	1257	1353	1553	1753	1753	1856	1856	1959	1959		0953	1056	1153	1356	1457	1553	...	1753	1953
Machynlleth .... a.		0601	0701	0800	0801	0905	0906	1000	1201	1200	1305	1400	1600	1800	1800	1903	1901	2004	2006		1000	1103	1200	1403	1504	1601	...	1800	2000
Machynlleth .... d.		0601	0703	0805	0808	0906	0908	1008	1204	1207	1306	1407	1608	1805	1805	1909	1905	2011	2011		1008	1105	1206	1406	1508	1605	...	1805	2005
Caersws .... d.		0628	0730	0828	0931	0933	0935	1035	1232	1234	1333	1434	1631	1828	1830	1932	1928	2034	2034		1031	1128	1229	1429	1531	1630	...	1828	2028
Newtown .... d.		0635	0737	0839	0842	0940	0942	1042	1239	1241	1340	1441	1642	1839	1841	1943	1939	2044	2044		1041	1138	1240	1440	1541	1641	...	1839	2039
Welshpool .... d.		0650	0752	0854	0856	0955	0956	1056	1254	1255	1354	1455	1656	1853	1856	1957	2000	2102	2059		1057	1154	1254	1455	1556	1655	...	1854	2053
Shrewsbury .... a.		0713	0814	0916	0918	1017	1018	1118	1316	1317	1418	1519	1720	1915	1918	2022	2022	2124	2121		1119	1217	1316	1517	1620	1717	...	1916	2116
B'mingham N S **145** .a.		0829	...	1030	1030	...	...	1232	1430	1432	...	1630	1830	2029	2029	...	...	2231	2231		1233	...	1423	1625	...	1827	...	2025	2227

a – May 21 - Sept 10.
b – From Sept. 17.
r – On ⑥ runs 3 minutes later.
‡ – Trains call on request.
▷ – Additional journeys Machynlleth - Aberystwyth and v.v.:
From Machynlleth at 0453⚒, 0545Ⓐ, 0547⑥, 0647⚒, 0850⑦, 0947⑦**b**, 1049⑦, 1349⑦, 1801⚒.
From Aberystwyth at 1830⑦, 2030Ⓑ, 2036⑥, 2130Ⓑ, 2135⑥, 2230⚒, 2320⑦, 2335⑥, 2340Ⓐ.

AW 2nd class MACHYNLLETH - PWLLHELI 148

km			Ⓐ	Ⓐ	Ⓐ	Ⓐ	Ⓐ	Ⓐ	Ⓐ	Ⓐ	Ⓐ		⑥	⑥	⑥	⑥		⑥	⑥	⑥	⑥	⑥		⑦a	⑦a	⑦
	Birmingham New Str. **145** .. d.		...	...	*0625*	0825	1025	1225	1425	1625	*1825*		...	...	*0625*	0825	...	1025	1225	1425	1625	*1825*		...	*1224*	1624
	Shrewsbury **147** .... d.	Ⓐ	...	...	*0727*	0930	1127	1329	1530	1729	*1930*	⑥	...	...	*0729*	0931	...	1129	1329	1530	1727	*1930*	⑦	...	*1328*	1727
0	**Machynlleth** .... d.		0507	0643	0852	1055	1251	1456	1655	1904	2143		0507	0643	0853	1055	...	1252	1456	1655	1904	2130		1010	1452	1855
6	Dovey Junction ‡ .... d.		0513	0649	0858	1101	1257	1502	1701	1910	2149		0513	0649	0859	1101	...	1258	1502	1701	1910	2136		1016	1458	1901
16	Aberdovey .... d.		0526	0702	0911	1114	1310	1515	1714	1923	2202		0526	0702	0912	1114	...	1311	1515	1714	1923	2202		1029	1511	1914
22	Tywyn .... a.		0533	0711	0920	1123	1319	1524	1724	1932	2211		0533	0711	0921	1123	...	1319	1524	1724	1932	2158		1035	1517	1920
22	Tywyn .... d.		0533	0716	0929	1130	1325	1526	1729	1933	2216		0533	0714	0929	1132	...	1324	1525	1729	1933	2215		1036	1531	1925
37	Fairbourne .... d.		0552	0734	0948	1149	1344	1545	1747	1951	2234		0552	0732	0948	1150	...	1343	1544	1747	1951	2234		1054	1549	1944
41	**Barmouth** .... a.		0604	0745	0959	1159	1355	1556	1758	2003	2245		0604	0745	0959	1201	...	1354	1555	1758	1959	2245		1103	1557	1952
41	**Barmouth** .... d.		...	0747	1001	1201	1357	1558	1800	2004	2247		...	0747	1001	1202	...	1356	1557	1800	2001	2247		1104	1559	1954
58	Harlech .... a.		...	0811	1025	1225	1421	1622	1824	2030	2312		...	0811	1025	1226	...	1420	1621	1824	2025	2311		1130	1625	2020
58	Harlech .... d.		...	0825	1027	1227	1431	1629	1833	2030	2314		...	0825	1027	1229	...	1431	1629	1833	2027	2313		1132	1625	2022
67	Penrhyndeudraeth .... d.		...	0838	1040	1240	1444	1642	1846	2043	2327		...	0838	1040	1242	...	1444	1642	1846	2040	2326		1146	1639	2036
69	Minffordd .... **160** d.		...	0842	1044	1244	1448	1645	1849	2047	2330		...	0842	1044	1245	...	1448	1645	1849	2044	2330		1149	1642	2039
72	**Porthmadog** .... **160** d.		...	0850	1052	1252	1456	1653	1857	2055	2338		...	0850	1052	1253	...	1456	1653	1857	2052	2338		1157	1648	2045
80	Criccieth .... d.		...	0857	1059	1259	1503	1700	1904	2103	2346		...	0857	1059	1301	...	1503	1700	1904	2100	2345		1205	1655	2053
93	**Pwllheli** .... a.		...	0912	1114	1315	1521	1718	1920	2118	0001		...	0913	1114	1316	...	1520	1716	1919	2116	0001		1221	1714	2112

		Ⓐ	Ⓐ	Ⓐ	Ⓐ		Ⓐ	Ⓐ	Ⓐ	Ⓐ	Ⓐ		⑥	⑥	⑥	⑥		⑥	⑥	⑥	⑥	⑥		⑦a	⑦	⑦a
Pwllheli .... d.		...	0629	0724	0934	...	1137	1338	1537	1742	2026		...	0629	0724	0934	...	1137	1338	1537	1742	2012		1128	1348	1736
Criccieth .... d.	Ⓐ	...	0643	0738	0948	...	1151	1352	1551	1756	2040	⑥	...	0643	0738	0948	...	1151	1352	1551	1756	2026	⑦	1141	1402	1750
Porthmadog .... **160** d.		...	0653	0747	0957	...	1201	1402	1601	1806	2055**b**		...	0653	0747	0958	...	1201	1402	1601	1806	2053**e**		1157	1412	1800
Minffordd .... **160** d.		...	0657	0752	1001	...	1205	1406	1605	1810	2059		...	0657	0752	1002	...	1205	1406	1605	1810	2058		1202	1416	1805
Penrhyndeudraeth .... d.		...	0701	0756	1005	...	1209	1410	1609	1814	2103		...	0701	0756	1006	...	1209	1410	1609	1814	2101		1206	1420	1809
Harlech .... a.		...	0715	0809	1020	...	1224	1425	1624	1827	2117		...	0715	0809	1021	...	1224	1425	1624	1827	2115		1218	1432	1821
Harlech .... d.		...	0717	0821	1029	...	1228	1428	1629	1830	2119		...	0717	0821	1028	...	1228	1428	1629	1830	2118		1219	1434	1822
Barmouth .... a.		...	0742	0845	1054	...	1253	1453	1654	1855	2144		...	0742	0845	1053	...	1253	1453	1654	1855	2143		1245	1459	1848
Barmouth .... d.		0645	0746	0852	1059	...	1255	1455	1656	1857	2146		0645	0746	0852	1101	...	1255	1455	1656	1857	2145		1248	1501	1850
Fairbourne .... d.		0653	0754	0900	1107	...	1303	1503	1704	1905	2154		0653	0754	0900	1109	...	1303	1503	1704	1905	2153		1256	1509	1857
Tywyn .... a.		0713	0812	0920	1127	...	1323	1524	1724	1925	2214		0713	0812	0920	1129	...	1323	1524	1724	1925	2213		1316	1527	1919
Tywyn .... d.		0714	0816	0927	1130	...	1325	1526	1727	1934	2217		0714	0816	0927	1130	...	1325	1526	1727	1935	2215		1316	1528	1924
Aberdovey .... d.		0720	0822	0933	1136	...	1331	1532	1733	1940	2223		0720	0822	0933	1136	...	1331	1532	1733	1941	2221		1322	1535	1930
Dovey Junction ‡ .... d.		0735	0838	0947	1149	...	1345	1546	1747	1956	2238		0735	0838	0947	1151	...	1345	1546	1747	1956	2237		1336	1549	1946
Machynlleth .... a.		0743	0845	0954	1157	...	1352	1554	1755	2004	2245		0743	0845	0955	1158	...	1353	1555	1755	2003	2244		1346	1559	1954
Shrewsbury **147** .... a.		0916	*1017*	1118	1316	...	1519	1720	*1918*	2121**c**	...		0918	*1018*	1118	1317	...	1517	1719**d**	*1915*	2124	...		*1517*	1717**d**	*2116*
Birmingham New Str. **145** ... a.		1030	...	1230	1430	...	1630	1830	*2029*	2231**c**	...		1030	...	1232	1432	...	1630	1830**d**	*2029*	2231	...		*1625*	1827**d**	*2227*

a – May 21 - Sept. 10.
b – Arrives 2048.
c – On ⑤ change at Machynlleth.
d – From Sept. 16 change at Machynlleth.
e – Arrives 2034.
f – Arrives 1148.
‡ – Trains call on request.

AW 2nd class Most trains convey 🍷 CARDIFF - HEREFORD - CREWE - MANCHESTER 149

Most Manchester trains continue to / from destinations on Table **135**

km			Ⓐ	Ⓐ J	Ⓐ	Ⓐ	Ⓐ	Ⓐ	Ⓐ	Ⓐ	Ⓐ	Ⓐ	Ⓐ	Ⓐ	Ⓐ	Ⓐ	Ⓐ	Ⓐ	Ⓐ	Ⓐ	Ⓐ	Ⓐ	Ⓐ	Ⓐ	Ⓐ	Ⓐ ✕	Ⓐ
0	**Cardiff** Central ..... **132** d.	Ⓐ	0435	0508	0538	...	0650	0721	0805	...	0850	0921	1005	1050	1121	1205	1250	1321	1405	1450	1521	1550	1621	...	1650	1716	1750
19	Newport .... **132** d.		0453	0527	0557	...	0704	0736	0819	...	0905	0935	1019	1104	1136	1219	1304	1335	1419	1504	1536	1604	1635	...	1704	1731	1804
30	Cwmbrân .... d.		0505	0539	0608	...	0714	0746	0829	...	0915	0946	1029	1114	1146	1229	1314	1346	1429	1514	1546	1614	1644	...	1714	1742	1815
35	Pontypool & New Inn .. d.		0511	0545	0614	...	|	0752	|	...	|	0951	|	|	1152	|	|	1351	|	|	1552	1619	|	...	|	1749	1820
50	Abergavenny .... d.		0522	0554	0623	...	0727	0801	0842	...	0928	1001	1042	1127	1201	1242	1326	1401	1443	1527	1601	1629	1657	...	1727	1800	1829
89	**Hereford** .... d.		0547	0625**g**	0649	...	0753	0827	0908	...	0954	1027	1108	1153	1227	1308	1355	1425	1508	1553	1627	1654	1724	...	1753	1825	1855
109	Leominster .... d.		0600	0638	0702	...	0806	|	0921	...	1007	|	1121	1206	|	1321	1408	|	1521	1606	1640	1707	|	...	1806	|	1908
127	Ludlow .... d.		0611	0649	0713	...	0817	0848	0932	...	1018	1048	1132	1217	1248	1332	1419	1446	1532	1617	1651	1718	|	...	1817	|	1919
138	Craven Arms .... **146** d.		0620	0657	0721	0728	0825	0856	|	0947	1026	1057	|	1225	1256	|	1427	1455	|	1625	|	1727	|	1800	1825	|	1927
150	Church Stretton .... **146** d.		0629	0708	0730	0742	0834	0905	|	0959	1039	1106	|	1238	1305	|	1436	1504	|	|	1708	1736	|	1813	1841	|	1936
170	**Shrewsbury** .... **146** a.		0643	0722	0744	0757	0848	0919	0958	1014	1052	1121	1158	1252	1321	1358	1450	1523	1558	1648	1724	1750	1809	1828	1855	1908	1950
170	**Shrewsbury** ....¶ d.		0644	0724	0746	0800	0851	0924	1000	1018	1054	1125	1159	1254	1325	1359	1452	1526	1559	1650	1725	1753	1810	1830	1856	1909	1952
200	Whitchurch ....¶ d.		0704	|	0806	0828	0908	|	|	1046	1112	|	|	1310	|	|	1509	|	|	1710	|	1809	|	1857	1913	|	|
223	**Crewe** ....¶ a.		0724	|	0824	0853	0927	|	1028	1110	1128	|	1228	1328	|	1428	1528	|	1628	1727	|	1827	1843	1920	1933	|	2022
	Chester **145, 160** ...... a.		|	0821	|	...	|	1020	|	...	|	1220	|	|	1420	|	|	1624	|	|	1821	|	1910	...	|	2002	|
	Holyhead **145, 160** ... a.		|	...	|	...	|	1222	|	...	|	1414	|	|	1614	|	|	1821	|	|	2020	|	...	...	|	2145	|
263	Stockport .... a.		0753	...	0859	...	0957	...	1058	...	1158	...	1258	1358	...	1458	1558	...	1659	1758	...	1858	...	...	2003	...	2050
273	**Manchester** Piccadilly . a.		0808	...	0915	...	1015	...	1115	...	1215	...	1315	1415	...	1515	1615	...	1715	1815	...	1915	...	...	2019	...	2106

J – To / from Llandudno (Tables **145** / **160**).
L – To Llandudno Junction (Tables **145** / **160**).

For continuation of Table and additional footnotes see next page ▶ ▶ ▶

① – Mondays ② – Tuesdays ③ – Wednesdays ④ – Thursdays ⑤ – Fridays ⑥ – Saturdays ⑦ – Sundays Ⓐ – Monday to Fridays, not holidays 47

Most Manchester trains continue to / from destinations on Table **135**

	Ⓐ	Ⓐ	Ⓐ	Ⓐ	Ⓐ	Ⓐ		⑥	⑥	⑥	⑥	⑥	⑥	⑥	⑥	⑥	⑥	⑥	⑥	⑥	⑥	⑥	⑥	⑥	⑥	⑥	⑥
Cardiff Central ... **132** d.	1821	1855	1934	2017	2117	2155	⑥	0435	0520	0537	0650	0721	0750	0850	0921	0955	1055	1121	1155	1255	1321	1355	1455	1521	1555	1618	1655
Newport .... **132** d.	1835	1909	1948	2031	2132	2212		0452	0535	0556	0704	0736	0804	0904	0935	1009	1109	1135	1209	1309	1335	1409	1509	1536	1609	1634	1709
Cwmbrân .... d.	1845	1919	1958	2041	2143	2224		0503	0545	0608	0714	0746	0814	0914	0946	1019	1119	1146	1219	1319	1346	1419	1519	1546	1619	1644	1719
Pontypool & New Inn . d.	|	1924	2003	2047	|	2230		0509	0551	0613	|	0751	|	|	0952	|	|	1150	|	|	1350	|	|	1552	1624	1650	|
Abergavenny .... d.	1859	1934	2012	2056	2156	2240		0518	0600	0623	0727	0801	0827	0927	1001	1032	1132	1200	1232	1332	1401	1432	1532	1601	1634	1702	1732
Hereford .... d.	1924	1959	2039	2122	2221	2308		0547	0625	0649	0753	0827	0853	0953	1026	1058	1158	1228	1258	1358	1427	1458	1558	1629**d**	1700	...	1758
Leominster .... d.	|	2012	2052	2135	2234	2321		0600	0638	0702	0806	|	0906	1006	|	1111	1211	|	1311	1411	|	1511	1611	1642	1713	...	1811
Ludlow .... d.	1945	2023	2103	2146	2245	2332		0611	0649	0713	0817	0848	0917	1017	1048	1122	1222	1249	1322	1422	1448	1522	1622	1654	1724	...	1822
Craven Arms ...... **146** d.	|	2032	2112	2154	2254	2342		0620	0657	0721	0825	0856	|	1025	1057	|	1230	1257	|	1430	1456	|	1630	|	|	...	1830
Church Stretton .. **146** d.	|	2041	2121	2204	2303	2351		0629	0706	0730	0834	0905	|	1034	1107	|	1239	1306	|	1440	1505	|	1639	1708	|	...	1839
Shrewsbury .... **146** a.	2011	2055	2137	2218	2317	0007		0643	0722	0744	0851	0923	0943	1048	1123	1148	1252	1320	1348	1453	1524	1548	1653	1722	1750	...	1853
Shrewsbury ..... **145** ¶ d.	2013	2056	2139	2220	2318	0012		0646	0722	0746	0852	0925	0947	1050	1125	1149	1254	1325	1349	1455	1528	1549	1655	1724	1752	...	1855
Whitchurch .... ¶ d.	|	2113	|	2243	2344	0038		0706	|	0806	0909	|	1004	1107	|	1206	|	|	1406	|	|	1606	|	|	1808	...	|
Crewe .... ¶ a.	2043	2133	|	2304	0005	0103		0725	|	0824	0927	|	1023	1125	|	1224	1326	|	1424	1525	|	1624	1726	|	1827	...	1926
Chester **145, 160** .... a.	2108	|	2234	|	0031	...		|	0819	|	|	1020	|	|	1219	|	|	1419	|	|	1624	|	|	1822	|	...	|
Holyhead **145, 160** .. a.	...	|	0048	|	...	...		|	1014	|	|	1209	|	|	1413	|	|	1613	|	|	1819	|	|	2018	|	...	|
Stockport .... a.	...	2201	...	2332	...	...		0754	...	0858	0958	...	1058	1158	...	1258	1358	...	1458	1558	...	1659	1758	...	1858	...	1958
Manchester P'dilly ..... a.	...	2215	...	2350	...	...		0810	...	0915	1016	...	1115	1215	...	1315	1415	...	1515	1615	...	1714	1815	...	1915	...	2015

	⑥	⑥	⑥	⑥ L	⑥	⑥	⑥		⑦	⑦	⑦	⑦	⑦		⑦	⑦	⑦	⑦	⑦	⑦		⑦	⑦	⑦	⑦	⑦	⑦
Cardiff Central ... **132** d.	1721	1755	1850	1934	2010	2055	2154	⑦	...	0830	0917	1034	1135	...	1236	1313	1340	1456	1513	1556	...	1640	1735	1836	1940	2101	2315
Newport .... **132** d.	1735	1809	1904	1948	2026	2110	2212		...	0849	0941	1054	1154	...	1254	1335	1358	1514	1533	1614	...	1658	1753	1858	1959	2119	2338
Cwmbrân .... d.	1746	1820	1915	1958	2037	2121	2224		...	0859	0951	1105	1207	...	1309	1347	1409	1524	1544	1624	...	1709	1804	1909	2010	2130	2348
Pontypool & New Inn . d.	1752	1825	1920	2003	2042	|	2229		...	0905	0957	1111	1213	...	1315	|	|	|	1550	|	...	1715	1810	|	2016	2136	2354
Abergavenny .... d.	1801	1835	1930	2012	2052	2134	2239		...	0914	1008	1121	1224	...	1325	1400	1422	1538	1559	1637	...	1725	1820	1922	2026	2146	0004
Hereford .... d.	1827	1900	1955	2039	2120	2200	2306		...	0941	1036	1150	1254**d**	...	1355**d**	1426	1448	1604	1628**d**	1704	...	1753**d**	1849**d**	1949	2054	2214	0032
Leominster .... d.	|	1913	2008	2052	2133	2214	▬		...	0955	1050	1203	1308	...	1408	|	1501	|	1641	|	...	1807	1903	2003	2108	2227	...
Ludlow .... d.	1848	1924	2019	2103	2144	2225	...		...	1006	1101	1214	1319	...	1419	1448	1512	1625	1652	1726	...	1818	1914	2014	2119	2238	...
Craven Arms ...... **146** d.	1856	|	2028	2112	2154	2233	...		...	1014	|	1224	|	...	1428	|	|	|	1700	|	...	1826	|	2022	2129	2248	...
Church Stretton .. **146** d.	1905	|	2037	2121	2203	2242	⑥		...	1023	|	1233	|	...	1437	|	|	|	1709	|	...	1835	|	2031	2138	2257	...
Shrewsbury .... **146** a.	1919	1950	2053	2135	2217	2257			...	1037	1130	1248	1348	...	1451	1521	1538	1651	1723	1752	...	1849	1941	2045	2156	2314	...
Shrewsbury ..... **145** ¶ d.	1924	1952	2057	2137	2219	2306	2330		0955	1039	1131	1251	1350	...	1453	1524	1540	1653	1730	1754	...	1854	1942	2048	*2232*	2319	...
Whitchurch .... ¶ d.	|	2008	|	|	2244	2332	2355		|	1100	1158	|	|	...	|	|	1606	|	|	|	...	|	2007	|	|	2346	...
Crewe .... ¶ a.	|	2027	2128	|	2304	2354	0016		1025	1122	1222	1326	1425	...	1525	|	1627	1725	|	1825	...	1924	2028	2121	*2303*	0009	...
Chester **145, 160** .... a.	2022	|	|	2232	|	0022	...		|	|	*1320*t	|	*1518*t	...	|	1622	|	|	1825	*1925*t	...	|	*2120*t	|	*2331*	0033	...
Holyhead **145, 160** .. a.	2225	|	|	...	|	...	...		|	|	|	|	|	...	|	1837	|	|	2018	*2134*t	...	|	|	|	...	...	...
Stockport .... a.	...	2059	2158	...	2332	...	...		1058	|	1258	1400	1500	...	1558	...	1658	1758	...	1858	...	1958	2057	2158	...	...	...
Manchester P'dilly ..... a.	...	2115	2214	...	2349	...	...		1117	1202	1313	1420	1515	...	1615	...	1714	1818	...	1915	...	2016	2115	2219	...	...	...

		Ⓐ	Ⓐ	Ⓐ	Ⓐ	Ⓐ	Ⓐ	Ⓐ ✕	Ⓐ	Ⓐ	Ⓐ	Ⓐ	Ⓐ J	Ⓐ	Ⓐ	Ⓐ	Ⓐ	Ⓐ	Ⓐ	Ⓐ	Ⓐ	Ⓐ	Ⓐ	Ⓐ	Ⓐ	Ⓐ	Ⓐ
Manchester P'dilly ..... d.	Ⓐ	...	...	...	...	...	0630	...	0730	...	0830	...	...	0930	...	1030	1130	...	1230	1330	...	1430	1530	...	1630	1730	...
Stockport .... d.		...	...	...	...	...	0639	...	0739	...	0839	...	...	0939	...	1040	1140	...	1240	1340	...	1440	1540	...	1640	1740	...
Holyhead **145, 160** .. d.		...	...	...	...	0425	|	0533	|	0628	|	...	...	|	0805	|	|	1040	|	|	1232	|	|	1434	|	|	1650
Chester **145, 160** .... d.		...	...	...	...	0618	|	0714	|	0819	|	...	0926	|	1020	|	|	1219	|	|	1419	|	|	1619	|	|	1828
Crewe .... ¶ d.		...	0449	...	0558	|	0708	|	0808	|	0908	0914	|	1008	|	1108	1208	|	1308	1408	|	1508	1608	|	1708	1809	|
Whitchurch .... ¶ d.		...	0508	...	0619	|	|	|	|	|	|	0937	|	|	|	|	|	|	|	1428	|	|	1628	|	|	1829	|
Shrewsbury ..... **145** ¶ a.		...	0528	...	0645	0716	0742	0807	0837	0913	0937	1006	1022	1037	1114	1137	1237	1314	1337	1445	1513	1537	1647	1714	1737	1848	1924
Shrewsbury .... **146** d.		0445	0530	0610	0647	0718	0744	0810	0840	0914	0940	1009	1024	1039	1116	1139	1239	1315	1340	1450	1515	1540	1650	1716	1740	1850	1925
Church Stretton .. **146** d.		0503	0545	0626	0702	|	0759	|	|	0930	|	1027	|	1054	|	1154	|	1330	|	1505	1530	|	1706	1731	|	1905	1940
Craven Arms ...... **146** d.		0513	0553	0634	0710	|	0807	|	|	0938	|	1037	|	|	1137	|	|	1338	|	1513	1538	|	1714	1739	|	1913	1948
Ludlow .... d.		▬	0601	0643	0717	0744	0815	|	0906	0945	1006	...	|	1108	1144	1208	1305	1345	1406	1520	1546	1606	1721	1746	1806	1920	1956
Leominster .... d.		Ⓐ	0611	0654	0728	0754	0826	|	0916	|	1016	...	|	1118	|	1218	1315	|	1416	1531	|	1616	1732	1757	1816	1931	|
Hereford .... d.		0526	0641**e**	0710	0745	0811	0842	0858	0933	1010	1033	...	|	1135	1208	1235	1332	1411	1433	1551	1611	1633	1751	1814	1833	1948	2022
Abergavenny .... d.		0551	0704	0734	0808	0834	0905	|	0958	1033	1056	...	|	1158	1231	1258	1355	1433	1456	1614	1634	1656	1814	1837	1856	2011	2045
Pontypool & New Inn . d.		0602	0714	0745	0818	0844	|	|	|	1043	|	...	|	|	1242	|	1405	|	|	1623	1644	|	1824	|	|	2021	|
Cwmbrân .... d.		0607	0719	0750	0823	0849	0917	|	1011	1048	1109	...	|	1211	1247	1311	1410	|	1509	1628	1649	1709	1829	1849	1909	2026	2057
Newport .... **132** a.		0619	0729	0800	0837	0900	0934	0940	1022	1101	1120	...	1153	1222	1256	1322	1420	1454	1521	1639	1659	1721	1839	1900	1922	2037	2115
Cardiff Central ...... **132** a.		0642	0749	0818	0855	0920	0959	0958	1039	1115	1138	...	1210	1237	1322	1340	1437	1510	1539	1657	1716	1738	1855	1918	1943	2103	2138

	Ⓐ	Ⓐ	Ⓐ	Ⓐ	Ⓐ	Ⓐ		⑥	⑥	⑥	⑥	⑥	⑥	⑥	⑥	⑥	⑥	⑥	⑥	⑥	⑥	⑥	⑥	⑥	⑥	⑥	⑥
Manchester P'dilly ..... d.	1830	1930	2030	2136	...	2236	⑥	...	...	...	...	...	0630	0730	...	0830	0930	...	1030	1130	...	1230	1330	...	1430	1530	...
Stockport .... d.	1839	1939	2040	2145	...	2244		...	...	...	...	...	0639	0739	...	0839	0939	...	1039	1140	...	1240	1340	...	1440	1540	...
Holyhead **145, 160** .. d.	|	|	|	|	...	|		...	...	...	...	0425**a**	|	|	0635	|	|	0820	|	|	1033	|	|	1238	|	|	1425
Chester **145, 160** .... d.	|	|	|	|	...	|		...	...	...	...	0612	|	|	0819	|	|	1019	|	|	1219	|	|	1419	|	|	1619
Crewe .... ¶ d.	1908	2010	2121	2212	...	2314		...	0454	...	0555	|	0708	0808	|	0908	1008	|	1108	1208	|	1308	1408	|	1509	1608	|
Whitchurch .... ¶ d.	1929	2029	2142	2233	...	2334		...	0513	...	0616	|	0728	0827	|	|	|	|	|	1228	|	|	1427	|	|	1627	|
Shrewsbury ..... **145** ¶ a.	1955	2048	2208	2301	...	0004		...	0533	...	0642	0717	0747	0845	0913	0937	1036	1114	1137	1245	1313	1337	1445	1513	1538	1645	1714
Shrewsbury .... **146** d.	1956	2050	2209	...	2308	...		0516	0540	0613	0644	0719	0750	0850	0915	0940	1038	1115	1140	1250	1315	1340	1446	1515	1540	1646	1716
Church Stretton .. **146** d.	2011	2105	2224	...	2324	...		0533	0555	0628	0659	|	0805	0905	|	0955	1054	|	1155	1305	1330	|	1501	|	1555	1701	|
Craven Arms ...... **146** d.	2019	2113	2232	...	2332	...		0547	0603	0636	0707	|	0813	0913	|	1003	1102	|	1203	1313	1338	|	1509	|	1603	1709	|
Ludlow .... d.	2027	2120	2240	...	2341	...		▬	0610	0644	0714	0745	0820	0920	0944	1010	1109	1141	1210	1320	1344	1406	1517	1541	1610	1717	1742
Leominster .... d.	2037	2131	2250	...	2352	...		⑥	0621	0655	0725	0755	0831	0931	|	1021	1120	|	1221	1331	|	1416	1527	|	1621	1727	|
Hereford .... d.	2054	2150**d**	2311	...	0009	...		0542	0642**d**	0711	0744**d**	0812	0851	0950	1009	1038	1140**h**	1206	1238	1351	1410	1433	1546	1606	1638	1746	1807
Abergavenny .... d.	2122	2216	2334	...	0033	...		0607	0705	0734	0807	0835	0914	1013	1032	1101	1203	1229	1301	1414	1432	1456	1609	1629	1701	1809	1830
Pontypool & New Inn . d.	2132	|	2343	...	|	...		0618	0715	0744	0817	0845	|	|	1042	|	|	1239	|	|	1443	|	|	1639	|	|	1840
Cwmbrân .... d.	2137	2228	2348	...	0046	...		0623	0720	0749	0822	0850	0926	1025	1047	1113	1215	1244	1313	1426	1448	1509	1621	1644	1713	1821	1845
Newport .... **132** a.	2151	2241	2359	...	0057	...		0634	0737	0800	0831	0901	0937	1038	1058	1127	1227	1254	1328	1436	1504	1521	1635	1654	1733	1836	1855
Cardiff Central ... **132** a.	2211**f**	2304	0023	...	0121	...		0654	0754	0819	0850	0922	0959	1102	1120	1157	1257	1317	1353	1453	1524	1537	1654	1708	1753	1855	1915

	⑥	⑥	⑥	⑥	⑥	⑥	⑥	⑥		⑦ 🚌	⑦	⑦	⑦	⑦	⑦	⑦	⑦	⑦	⑦	⑦	⑦	⑦	⑦	⑦	⑦	⑦
Manchester P'dilly ..... d.	...	1630	1730	...	1830	1930	2030	2133	2235	⑦	...	...	0930	1031	1124	...	1233	1330	1430	1530	1630	1730	...	1830	1930	2030	...
Stockport .... d.	...	1640	1740	...	1839	1939	2039	2143	2244		...	...	0940	1040	1140	...	1243	1340	1440	1539	1639	1739	...	1839	1939	2039	...
Holyhead **145, 160** .. d.	...	|	|	1650	|	|	|	|	|		...	...	|	|	|	1020	|	|	|	|	|	|	1625	|	|	|	...
Chester **145, 160** .... d.	...	|	|	1829	|	|	|	|	|		...	...	|	|	*1131*t	1221	|	*1331*t	|	*1531*t	|	*1731*t	1824	|	*1926*t	|	2300
Crewe .... ¶ d.	...	1708	1809	|	1910	2009	2109	2212	2314		...	...	1013	1111	1213	|	1313	1413	1510	1613	1713	1813	|	1913	2010	2113	2323
Whitchurch .... ¶ d.	...	1727	1828	|	1931	2028	2130	2233	2334		...	...	1035	|	|	|	1334	|	|	|	1734	|	|	1934	|	2135	2345
Shrewsbury ..... **145** ¶ a.	...	1744	1846	1924	1956	2047	2153	2301	0005		...	...	1101	1141	1243	1318	1359	1443	1544	1643	1800	1843	1920	2000	2044	2203	0014
Shrewsbury .... **146** d.	...	1746	1850	1926	1958	2048	2155	...	▬		0750	...	1103	1145	1244	1319	1401	1444	1547	1644	1801	1844	1921	2001	2045	2204	...
Church Stretton .. **146** d.	...	1801	1905	1941	2013	2103	2210	...	...		0815	...	1119	|	|	1335	|	1500	|	1700	|	|	1937	|	2101	2220	...
Craven Arms ...... **146** d.	...	1809	1913	1949	2021	2111	2218	...	...		0835	...	1127	|	|	1343	|	1508	|	1708	|	|	1945	|	2110	2229	...
Ludlow .... d.	...	1816	1920	1955	2028	2119	2226	...	⑥		0855	...	1136	1213	1313	1351	1428	1516	1617	1716	1829	1912	1953	2029	2118	2237	...
Leominster .... d.	...	1827	1931	|	2039	2129	2237	...			0920	...	1147	1223	1324	1402	1439	1526	1628	1726	1839	|	2004	2039	2130	2249	...
Hereford .... d.	...	1844	1951	2021	2056	2146	2253	...	2315		0950	1007	1203	1239	1340	1419	1456	1543	1644	1743	1857	1936	2021	2055	2146	2305	...
Abergavenny .... d.	...	1907	2014	2044	2119	2209	2316	...	2338		...	1031	1227	1302	1403	1442	1519	1606	1708	1806	1920	1959	2046	2118	2210	2329	...
Pontypool & New Inn . d.	...	|	2023	|	2128	|	2326	...	|		...	1041	|	1312	|	1452	|	1616	|	1816	|	|	2056	|	2221	2339	...
Cwmbrân .... d.	...	1919	2028	2057	2133	2222	2331	...	2350		...	1046	1240	1317	1416	1457	1531	1621	1721	1821	1933	2011	2101	2131	2226	2344	...
Newport .... **132** a.	...	1934	2040	2113	2144	2235	2344	...	0007		...	1057	1253	1329	1426	1510	1546	1632	1735	1834	1943	2026	2110	2144	2235	2354	...
Cardiff Central ... **132** a.	...	1958	2100	2135	2205	2301	0010	...	0034		...	1118	1318	1355	1449	1541	1611	1656	1806**b**	1857	2008	2051	2137	2210	2258	0018	...

◄◄◄ For additional notes see previous page.

a – From Sept. 16.
b – Arrives 1756 from Oct. 29.
d – Arrives 4–6 minutes earlier.
e – Arrives 0630.

f – Arrives 2205 on ⑤.
g – Arrives 0618.
h – Arrives 1136.
n – Arrives 1344.
t – Change at Shrewsbury.

¶ – Additional journeys Shrewsbury - Whitchurch - Crewe and v.v.:
From Shrewsbury at 0531Ⓐ, 0544⑥, 0757⑥, 1018⑥, 1224⚒, 1424⚒, 1624⚒, 1825⑥, 2032⚒, 2330⑥.
From Crewe at 0640Ⓐ, 0720⑥, 0734Ⓐ, 0920⑥, 1120⚒, 1320⚒, 1520⑥, 1522Ⓐ, 1720⚒.

VT Most trains convey 🍸 LONDON - BIRMINGHAM - WOLVERHAMPTON 150

Certain services continue to/from destinations in Table **154**. For trains via Northampton see Table **142**.

km	Ⓐ	Ⓐ	Ⓐ	Ⓐ	Ⓐ	Ⓐ	C	Ⓐ	Ⓐ	Ⓐ	Ⓐ	ⒶD		Ⓐ	Ⓐ	Ⓐ	Ⓐ	Ⓐ	Ⓐ		Ⓐ	Ⓐ	Ⓐ
0	**London** Euston ...... **151/2/3** d.	0620	0643	0703	0723	0743	and	1703	1723	1743	1803	1823	...	1843	1903	1923	1943	2003	2023	...	2043	2103	2143
28	Watford Junction ...... △ d.	0634	|	|	0737	|	at the	|	1737	|	|	1837	...	|	|	1937	|	|	2037	...	|	|	2158
80	Milton Keynes ...... **151/2/3** d.	|	0713	|	|	0813	same	|	|	1813u	|	|	...	1913	|	|	2013	|	|	...	2113	2135	2217
133	Rugby ...... a.	0712	|	0751	|	|	minutes	1751	|	|	1851	|	...	|	1951	|	|	2051	|	...	|	2156	|
151	Coventry ...... **119** a.	0722	0742	0802	0822	0842	past	1802	1822	1842	1902	1922	...	1942	2002	2022	2042	2102	2124	...	2142	2207	2246
168	Birmingham Int'l ✈ ...... **119** a.	0733	0753	0813	0833	0853	each	1813	1833	1853	1913	1933	...	1953	2013	2033	2053	2113	2134	...	2153	2218	2300
182	**Birmingham** NS ..... **119 122** a.	0745	0808	0827	0845	0908	hour	1827	1845	1908	1927	1945	...	2008	2027	2045	2108	2127	2146	...	2205	2230	2316
190	Sandwell & Dudley ...... a.	...	0824	...	...	0924	until	...	...	1924	|	1958	...	2024	...	2058	2124	|	2159	...	2216	2241	2333
202	**Wolverhampton** ...... **122** a.	...	0837	...	...	0937		...	...	1937	2000	2011	...	2037	...	2112	2137	2158	2212	...	2230	2256	2347

	Ⓐ	①–④	⑤	⑥	⑥	⑥	⑥	⑥	⑥	⑥	E	⑥	⑥	⑥	⑥	⑥D	⑥	⑥	⑥	⑥	⑥	⑥	⑥
London Euston ...... **151/2/3** d.	2230	2330	2330	0623	0703	0723	0743	0803	0823	0843	and	1703	1723	1743	1803	1823	1843	1903	1923	1943	2025	2103	2143
Watford Junction ...... △ d.	2245	|	|	0637	|	0737	|	|	0837	|	at the	|	1737	|	|	1837	|	|	1937	|	2040	2118	2158
Milton Keynes ...... **151/2/3** d.	2329	0029	0028	|	|	|	0813	|	|	0913	same	|	|	1813	|	|	1913	|	|	2020	|	2150	2230
Rugby ...... a.	2358	0100	0105	|	0751	|	|	0851	|	|	minutes	1751	|	|	1851	|	|	1951	|	|	|	2211	2252
Coventry ...... **119** a.	0010	0113	0118	0722	0802	0822	0842	0902	0922	0942	past	1802	1822	1842	1902	1922	1942	2002	2022	2050	2136	2222	2302
Birmingham Int'l ✈ ...... **119** a.	0021	0124	0129	0733	0813	0833	0853	0913	0933	0953	each	1813	1833	1853	1913	1933	1953	2013	2033	2101	2150	2233	2313
Birmingham NS ...... **119 122** a.	0032	0136	0141	0745	0827	0845	0908	0927	0945	1008	hour	1827	1845	1908	1927	1945	2008	2027	2045	2113	2204	2245	2325
Sandwell & Dudley ...... a.	|	|	|	...	...	...	0924	...	...	1024	until	...	1858	1924	1943	1958	2024	2053	2058	|	2224	2256	2336
Wolverhampton ...... **122** a.	0103	0207	0210	...	...	...	0937	...	...	1037		...	1911	1937	1955	2011	2037	2109	2112	2138	2238	2310	2350

	⑦	⑦	⑦	⑦	⑦	⑦	⑦	⑦		⑦	⑦	⑦	⑦	⑦D	⑦	⑦	⑦	⑦	⑦	⑦	⑦	⑦	⑦
London Euston ...... **151/2/3** d.	0850	0950	1050	1150	1220	1240	1300	1320	and	1740	1800	1820	1840	1900	1920	1940	2000	2018	2038	2054	2155	2225	2325
Watford Junction ...... △ d.	0907	1005	1105	1205	1234	|	|	1334	at the	|	|	1834	|	|	1934	|	|	2032	|	2110	2209	2239	2339
Milton Keynes ...... **151/2/3** d.	0939	1038	1138	1230	|	1313	|	|	same	1813	|	|	1913	|	|	2013	|	|	2116	2143	2245	2312	0012
Rugby ...... a.	1013	1113	1213	1249	|	|	1351	|	minutes	|	1851	|	|	1952	|	|	2051	|	|	2205	2322	2346	0046**s**
Coventry ...... **119** a.	1024	1123	1223	1259	1322	1342	1402	1422	past	1844	1902	1922	1942	2003	2022	2042	2103	2120	2146	2216	2333	2357	0058**s**
Birmingham Int'l ✈ ...... **119** a.	1035	1134	1234	1310	1333	1353	1413	1433	each	1854	1913	1933	1953	2013	2033	2053	2113	2131	2157	2227	2344	0008	0109**s**
Birmingham NS ...... **119 122** a.	1047	1147	1247	1325	1346	1408	1425	1445	hour	1908	1925	1945	2008	2025	2045	2108	2125	2145	2209	2239	2356	0021	0122**s**
Sandwell & Dudley ...... a.	1058	1158	1258	...	1356	1425	...	...	until	1925	1948	...	2024	2035	2056	2124	...	2156	2224	2251	|	|	|
Wolverhampton ...... **122** a.	1111	1211	1310	...	1408	1437	...	...	☆	1937	2000	...	2037	2047	2111	2137	...	2208	2236	2303	0015	0041	0142

	Ⓐ	Ⓐ	Ⓐ	Ⓐ	Ⓐ	Ⓐ	Ⓐ	Ⓐ	ⒶD	ⒶK	Ⓐ	Ⓐ	Ⓐ	Ⓐ	F	Ⓐ	Ⓐ	Ⓐ	Ⓐ	Ⓐ	Ⓐ	Ⓐ	Ⓐ
Wolverhampton ...... **122** d.	0500	0524	0545	0604	0627	0645	0705	...	0724	0745	...	...	0845	...	and	...	1845	...	1945	...	2047	2145	2242
Sandwell & Dudley ...... d.	|	0534	0555	0615	0638	0656	0715	...	|	0757	...	...	0855	...	at the	...	1855	...	1955	...	2057	2155	2255
Birmingham NS ...... **119 122** d.	0529	0550	0610	0630	0650	0710	0730	...	0750	0810	0830	0850	0910	0930	same	1850	1910	1930	2010	2050	2110	2210	2310
Birmingham Int'l ✈ ...... **119** d.	0540	0600	0620	0640	0700	0720	|	0741	0800	0821	0840	0900	0920	0940	minutes	1900	1920	1940	2020	2100	2120	2220	2320
Coventry ...... **119** d.	0551	0611	0631	0651	0711	0731	|	0752	0811	0831	0851	0911	0931	0951	past	1911	1931	1951	2031	2111	2131	2231	2331
Rugby ...... d.	0603	|	|	|	|	|	|	|	0823	|	|	0923	|	|	each	1923	|	2003	|	2123	|	2245	2344
Milton Keynes ...... **151/2/3** d.	0626	0638	0659	|	0740**s**	|	|	|	|	|	0920	|	1000	|	hour	|	2000	|	2100	|	2159	2308	0024
Watford Junction ...... ▽ a.	0647	|	|	0737	|	|	|	|	|	0916	|	|	|	1039	until	|	|	2041	2119	|	2220	2339	0052
London Euston ...... **151/2/3** a.	0705	0713	0734	0753	0815	0831	0843	0850	0915	0934	0955	1015	1032	1056	☆	2015	2034	2058	2139	2213	2243	0006	0115

	⑥	⑥	⑥	⑥	⑥	⑥	⑥	⑥		⑥	⑥	⑥	⑥D	⑥	⑥	⑥	F	⑥	⑥	⑥	⑥	⑥	⑥
Wolverhampton ...... **122** d.	...	0545	0606	0627	0645	0705	0725	0745	...	...	...	...	0905	...	0945	...	and	...	...	1845	1945	2045	2109
Sandwell & Dudley ...... d.	...	0555	0617	0637	0656	0715	|	0755	...	...	...	...	|	...	0955	...	at the	...	...	1855	1955	2055	2119
Birmingham NS ...... **119 122** d.	0550	0610	0630	0650	0710	0730	0750	0810	...	0830	0850	0910	0930	0950	1010	1030	same	1830	1850	1910	2010	2110	2130
Birmingham Int'l ✈ ...... **119** d.	0600	0620	0640	0700	0720	0740	0800	0820	...	0840	0900	0920	0940	1000	1020	1040	minutes	1840	1900	1920	2020	2120	2140
Coventry ...... **119** d.	0611	0631	0651	0711	0731	0751	0811	0831	...	0851	0911	0931	0951	1011	1031	1051	past	1851	1911	1931	2031	2131	2151
Rugby ...... d.	0624	|	|	0723	|	|	0823	|	...	|	0923	|	|	1023	|	|	each	|	1923	1943	2043	2143	2203
Milton Keynes ...... **151/2/3** d.	|	0659	|	|	0759	|	|	0859	...	|	|	0959	|	|	1059	|	hour	|	|	2007	2105	2205	2226
Watford Junction ...... ▽ a.	|	0719	0736	|	|	0837	|	|	...	0939	|	|	1039	|	|	1139	until	1939	|	2034	2135	2234	2312
London Euston ...... **151/2/3** a.	0717	0738	0755	0817	0835	0856	0915	0935	...	0959	1015	1034	1056	1115	1133	1155	☆	1956	2023	2055	2157	2255	2331

	⑦	⑦	⑦	⑦	⑦	⑦	⑦	F	⑦	⑦	⑦	⑦	⑦	⑦	⑦	⑦	⑦	⑦	⑦		⑦	⑦	⑦
Wolverhampton ...... **122** d.	0805	0905	1005	1105	...	1145	...	and	...	1645	...	...	1745	...	...	1845	...	1945	...	...	2105	2205	2237
Sandwell & Dudley ...... d.	0815	0915	1015	1115	...	1155	...	at the	...	1655	...	...	1755	...	...	1855	...	1955	...	...	2117	2216	2248
Birmingham NS ...... **119 122** d.	0830	0930	1030	1130	1150	1210	1230	same	1650	1710	1730	1750	1810	1830	1850	1910	1930	2010	2030	...	2130	2230	2300
Birmingham Int'l ✈ ...... **119** d.	0840	0940	1040	1140	1200	1220	1240	minutes	1700	1720	1740	1800	1820	1840	1900	1920	1940	2020	2040	...	2140	2240	2310
Coventry ...... **119** d.	0851	0951	1051	1151	1211	1231	1251	past	1711	1730	1751	1811	1831	1851	1911	1931	1951	2031	2051	...	2151	2251	2321
Rugby ...... d.	0904	1004	1104	1205	1225	|	|	each	1725	|	|	1825	|	|	1926	|	|	|	2105	...	2204	2304	2335
Milton Keynes ...... **151/2/3** d.	0939	1039	1139	1227	|	1301	|	hour	|	1759	|	|	1859	|	|	2000	|	2101	2128	...	2237	2337	0013**s**
Watford Junction ...... ▽ a.	1007	1111	1208	|	|	|	1338	until	|	|	1838	|	|	1938	|	|	2039	|	2202	...	2305	0006	0043
London Euston ...... **151/2/3** a.	1027	1131	1227	1306	1320	1338	1357	☆	1818	1838	1857	1917	1939	1957	2018	2039	2057	2148	2223	...	2325	0027	0105

C – The 1023 from London continues to Shrewsbury (Table **145**) calling at Wolverhampton (a. 1210).
D – To/from Shrewsbury (Table **145**).
E – The 1123 from London continues to Shrewsbury (Table **145**) calling at Wolverhampton (a. 1310).
F – The 1630 from Birmingham New Street starts from Shrewsbury (Table **145**) calling at Wolverhampton (d. 1604).
K – From Manchester Piccadilly (Table **152**).

s – Calls to set down only.
u – Calls to pick up only.

☆ – Timings may vary by up to 3 minutes.
△ – Trains call here to pick up only.
▽ – Trains call here to set down only.

VT Most trains convey 🍸 LONDON - CHESTER (- HOLYHEAD) 151

km		ⒶA	Ⓐ	Ⓐ	Ⓐ		Ⓐ	Ⓐ	Ⓐ	Ⓐ	Ⓐ	Ⓐ	Ⓐ		Ⓐ	ⒶG	Ⓐ	Ⓐ		⑥A	⑥
0	**London** Euston ...... **150 152 153** d.	...	0710	0810	0910	...	1010	1110	1210	1310	1410	1510	1610	...	1710	1810	1910	2010	...	...	0810
80	Milton Keynes ...... **150 152 153** d.	...	0741	0843	0941	...	1041	1141	1241	1341	1441	1541	1641**u**	...	1741**u**	1841**u**	1941	2041	...	...	0841
254	Crewe ...... **152 153** d.	0623	0849	0953	1049	...	1149	1249	1352	1449	1549	1649	1749	...	1857	1956	2055	2149	...	0623	0949
288	**Chester** ...... a.	0643	0913	1013	1113	...	1213	1313	1413	1513	1613	1713	1808	...	1916	2015	2120	2213	...	0643	1013
	Bangor **160** ...... a.	0749	*1051*	1124	1216	...	*1331*	*1435*	*1530*	*1642*	*1738*	*1846*	1921	...	2028	2125	2229	*0013*	...	0749	*1135*
	Holyhead **160** ...... a.	0823	*1122*	1158	1250	...	*1414*	*1508*	*1614*	*1716*	*1821*	*1917*	*2020*	...	2059	2159	2303	*0048*	...	0823	*1209*

	⑥	⑥	⑥	⑥	⑥	⑥	⑥	⑥	⑥	⑥		⑦	⑦	⑦	⑦	⑦	⑦	⑦	⑦	⑦		⑦
London Euston ...... **150 152 153** d.	0910	1010	1110	1210	1310	1410	1510	1610	1710	1810	...	*0815*	*0945*	*1115*	*1337*	*1437*	1508	1608	1708	1808	...	1908
Milton Keynes ...... **150 152 153** d.	0941	1041	1141	1241	1341	1441	1541	1641	1740	1841	...	|	*1033*	*1204*	|	|	1542	1642	1742	1842	...	1942
Crewe ...... **152 153** d.	1049	1156	1249	1352	1449	1549	1649	1749	1852	1949	...	1042	1227	1327	1527	1627	1652	1752	1901	1952	...	2055
Chester ...... a.	1113	1217	1313	1416	1513	1610	1713	1810	1911	2013	...	1102	1252	1351	1549	1649	1713	1813	1919	2013	...	2113
Bangor **160** ...... a.	1216	*1332*	*1438*	*1532*	*1636*	1717	*1841*	1921	2023	*2142*	...	1209	1417	1512	1712	1817	*1914***f**	*1947*	2034	2123	...	2222
Holyhead **160** ...... a.	1250	*1413*	*1508*	*1613*	*1714*	1751	*1913*	1955	2058	*2225*	...	1240	1453	1555	1757	1854	*1954***f**	*2018*	2103	2154	...	2253

	ⒶH	Ⓐ	ⒶG	Ⓐ	Ⓐ		Ⓐ	Ⓐ	Ⓐ	Ⓐ	Ⓐ	Ⓐ	Ⓐ	Ⓐ	Ⓐ	ⒶB	⑥H	⑥	⑥	⑥	⑥
Holyhead **160** ...... d.	...	0448	0551	0655	*0715*	...	0855	*0923*	*1040*	*1127*	1252	1358	*1434*	*1544*	*1730*	*1921*	...	*0425*	0652	0755	0855
Bangor **160** ...... d.	...	0514	0618	0722	*0802*	...	0922	*1002*	*1107*	*1200*	1320	1425	*1504*	*1623*	*1809*	2020	...	*0456*	0720	0822	0922
Chester ...... d.	0422	0626	0735	0835	0935	...	1035	1135	1235	1335	1435	1535	1635	1735	1935	2135	0422	0717	0835	0935	1035
Crewe ...... **152 153** a.	0444	0647	0754	0854	0954	...	1054	1154	1254	1354	1454	1554	1654	1754	1954	2154	0443	0736	0854	0954	1054
Milton Keynes ...... **150 152 153** a.	*0651*	|	|	1002	1102	...	1202	1302	1402	1502	1602	1702	1802	1901	2104	...	*0711*	0852	1002	1102	1202
London Euston ...... **150 152 153** a.	*0729*	0834	0941	1039	1139	...	1239	1339	1439	1539	1639	1739	1839	1939	2143	...	*0753*	0930	1039	1138	1239

	⑥	⑥	⑥		⑥	⑥	⑥		⑥	⑥		⑦	⑦	⑦	⑦	⑦	⑦		⑦	⑦	⑦	⑦
Holyhead **160** ...... d.	*0923*	*1033*	*1123*	...	238	1358	*1425*	...	*1523*	*1823*	...	0845	*0845*	1055	1150	1250	1355	...	*1530*	*1625*	*1730*	*1825*
Bangor **160** ...... d.	*1002*	*1105*	*1202*	...	1307	1425	*1453*	...	*1602*	*1902*	...	0912	*0912*	1122	1217	1318	1422	...	*1558*	*1704*	*1759*	*1904*
Chester ...... d.	1135	1235	1335	...	1435	1535	1635	...	1735	2035	...	1039	1128	1233	1330	1433	1533	...	1735	1835	1935	2037
Crewe ...... **152 153** a.	1154	1254	1354	...	1454	1554	1654	...	1754	2054	...	1103	1147	1253	1350	1454	1552	...	1753	1853	1956	2056
Milton Keynes ...... **150 152 153** a.	1302	1402	1502	...	1602	1702	1802	...	|	...	...	|	1304	1403	1503	1603	1703	...	1904	2003	*2136*	*2304*
London Euston ...... **150 152 153** a.	1339	1439	1539	...	1639	1739	1839	...	*2005*	...	...	*1313*	1346	1444	1545	1644	1744	...	1944	2046	*2228*	*2354*

A – From Birmingham New Street (d. 0530), Wolverhampton (d. 0548) and Stafford (d. 0601).
B – To Wolverhampton (a. 2227) and Birmingham New Street (a. 2250).
G – Conveys 🛏 London Euston - Wrexham and v.v. (Table **145**).
H – To Stafford (a. 0524), Wolverhampton (a. 0539), and Birmingham New Street (a. 0558⑥, 0610Ⓐ).

f – From Sept. 17.
u – Calls to pick up only.

152 LONDON - MANCHESTER VT

km		Ⓐ	Ⓐ	Ⓐ	Ⓐ	Ⓐ	Ⓐ	Ⓐ	Ⓐ	Ⓐ	Ⓐ	Ⓐ		Ⓐ	Ⓐ	Ⓐ	④-⑤2	Ⓐ		Ⓐ	Ⓐ	Ⓐ	Ⓐ
0	**London** Euston **150/1/3/4** d.	0616	0636	0655	0720	0735	0800	0820	0840	0900	0920	0940	and at	1800	1820	1840	1857	1900	...	1920	1940	2000	2040
80	Milton Keynes ...... **150/1/4** d.	0646	│	0727	0750	0806	│	0850	│	│	0950	│	the same	│	1850**u**	│	│	│	...	1950	│	│	│
235	Stoke on Trent .... **122** d.	0745	│	0825	0848	│	0925	0948	│	1025	1048	│	minutes	1925	1948	│	│	2025	...	2050	│	2126	│
267	Macclesfield .... **122** d.	0802	│	0841	│	│	0941	│	│	1041	│	│	past each	1941	│	│	│	│	...	2107	│	2142	│
	Crewe .... **154** d.	│	0811	│	│	0911	│	│	1011	│	│	1111	hour until	│	│	2018	2033**s**	│	...	│	2123	│	2213
	Wilmslow .... d.	│	0827	│	│	0927	│	│	1027	│	│	1127		│	│	2033	│	│	...	│	2138	│	2229
287	Stockport .... **122** d.	0817	0837	0856	0917	0937	0955	1017	1037	1056	1117	1137	♡	1956	2017	2043	│	2053	...	2120	│	2155	2239
296	**Manchester** Piccadilly **122** a.	0828	0849	0907	0928	0949	1007	1028	1049	1107	1128	1149		2007	2028	2053	2110	2108	...	2131	2157	2207	2248

	Ⓐ	Ⓐ		Ⓐ	Ⓐ	⑥	⑥	⑥	⑥	⑥		⑥	⑥	⑥	⑥	⑥		⑥	⑥	⑥	⑥		⑥
London Euston . **150/1/3/4** d.	2100	2140	...	2200	2300	0636	0655	0720	0735	0800	...	0820	0840	0900	0920	0940	and at	1900	1920	1940	2020	...	2100
Milton Keynes .... **150/1/4** d.	2131	│	...	2240	│	│	0727	0750	0806	│	...	0850	│	│	0950	│	the same	│	1950	│	2105	...	2145
Stoke on Trent .... **122** d.	2228	2305	...	│	0118**s**	│	0825	0848	│	0925	...	0948	│	1025	1048	│	minutes	2025	2048	│	2205	...	│
Macclesfield .... **122** d.	2244	2321	...	│	0134**s**	│	0841	│	│	0941	...	│	│	1041	│	│	past each	2041	│	│	2221	...	│
Crewe .... **154** d.	│	│	...	0017	│	0811	│	│	0911	│	...	│	1011	│	│	1111	hour until	│	│	2119	│	...	2259
Wilmslow .... d.	│	│	...	...	│	0827	│	│	0927	│	...	│	1027	│	│	1127		│	│	2134	│	...	2315
Stockport .... **122** d.	2259	2339	...	...	0148**s**	0837	0856	0917	0937	0955	...	1017	1037	1056	1117	1137		2056	2120	2145	2236	...	2327
Manchester Piccadilly **122** a.	2311	2350	...	...	0159	0849	0907	0928	0949	1007	...	1028	1049	1107	1128	1149		2107	2130	2153	2251	...	2339

	⑦	⑦	⑦	⑦		⑦	⑦	⑦	⑦	⑦	⑦	⑦		⑦	⑦	⑦	⑦	⑦	⑦	⑦	⑦	⑦	⑦
London Euston . **150/1/3/4** d.	0810	0820	0920	1020	...	1120	1217	1237	1257	1317	1337	1357	and at	1817	1837	1857	1917	1937	1957	2015	2035	2125	2151
Milton Keynes .... **150/1/4** d.	0856	0906	1007	1107	...	1208	1250	│	│	1350	│	│	the same	1850	│	│	1950	│	│	2048	│	2214	2239
Stoke on Trent .... **122** d.	│	1021	1123	1225	...	1311	1350	│	1426	1450	│	1526	minutes	1950	│	2026	2050	│	2126	2150	│	2329	│
Macclesfield .... **122** d.	│	1038	1139	1242	...	1328	│	│	1442	│	│	1542	past each	│	│	2042	│	│	2142	│	│	2346	│
Crewe .... **154** d.	1019	│	│	│	...	│	│	1413	│	│	1513	│	until	│	2013	│	│	2113	│	│	2221	│	0016**s**
Wilmslow .... d.	1034	│	│	│	...	│	│	1429	│	│	1529	│		│	2029	│	│	2129	│	│	2236	│	│
Stockport .... **122** d.	1044	1052	1153	1256	...	1342	1421	1439	1456	1520	1539	1556	☆	2021	2039	2057	2119	2139	2159	2220	2246	0001	0038**s**
Manchester Piccadilly **122** a.	1054	1102	1204	1305	...	1350	1431	1448	1506	1531	1548	1605		2030	2048	2106	2131	2149	2209	2229	2254	0009	0048

km		Ⓐ	Ⓐ	Ⓐ	Ⓐ	Ⓐ	Ⓐ	Ⓐ	Ⓐ	Ⓐ	Ⓐ	Ⓐ	Ⓐ	Ⓐ	Ⓐ	Ⓐ	Ⓐ		Ⓐ	Ⓐ	Ⓐ	Ⓐ	Ⓐ
0	**Manchester** Piccadilly **122** d.	0505	0555	0610	0635	0643	0700	0715	0627	0735	0755	0815	0835	0855	0915	0935	0955	and at	1655	1715	1735	1755	1815
9	Stockport .... **122** d.	0513	0603	0618	0643	0651	0707**u**	0723	0635	0743	0804	0823	0843	0904	0923	0943	1004	the same	1704	1723	1743	1804	1823
30	Wilmslow .... d.	│	0611	│	│	0659	│	│	│	│	0811	│	│	0911	│	│	1011	minutes	1711	│	│	1811	│
50	Crewe .... **154** d.	0536	0628	│	│	0717	│	│	│	│	0829	│	│	0929	│	│	1029	past each	1729	│	│	1829	│
	Macclesfield .... **122** d.	│	│	0631	0656	│	│	│	0648	0756	│	│	0856	│	│	0956	│	until	│	│	1756	│	│
	Stoke on Trent .... **122** d.	│	│	0648	0712	│	│	0750	0706	0812	│	0850	0912	│	0950	1012	│		│	1750	1812	│	1850
	Milton Keynes ...... **150/1/4** a.	0651	│	│	│	│	│	0846	**b**	│	│	0949	│	│	1046	│	│	♧	│	1848	│	1933	1946
304	**London** Euston **150/1/3/4** a.	0729	0808	0823	0846	0854	0900	0924	0934	0952	1019	1026	1053	1108	1124	1143	1205		1909	1924	1943	2008	2024

	Ⓐ	Ⓐ	Ⓐ	Ⓐ	Ⓐ	Ⓐ	⑥	⑥	⑥	⑥	⑥	⑥	⑥	⑥	⑥	⑥	⑥	⑥	⑥	⑥		⑥	⑥
Manchester Piccadilly **122** d.	1835	1855	1915	1955	2015	2115	0525	0555	0610	0635	0655	0715	0735	0755	0815	0835	0855	0915	0935	0955	and at	1715	1735
Stockport .... **122** d.	1843	1903	1923	2004	2023	2123	0534	0603	0618	0643	0704	0723	0743	0804	0823	0843	0904	0923	0943	1004	the same	1723	1743
Wilmslow .... d.	│	1911	│	2011	│	│	0541	0611	│	│	0711	│	│	0811	│	│	0911	│	│	1011	minutes	│	│
Crewe .... **154** d.	│	1929	│	2029	│	│	0600	0629	│	│	0729	│	│	0829	│	│	0930	│	│	1029	past each	│	│
Macclesfield .... **122** d.	1856	│	1936	│	2036	2136	│	│	0631	0656	│	│	0756	│	│	0856	│	│	0956	│	until	│	1756
Stoke on Trent .... **122** d.	1912	│	1952	│	2052	2153	│	│	0648	0712	│	0750	0812	│	0850	0912	│	0950	1012	│		1750	1812
Milton Keynes .... **150/1/4** a.	│	2031	2048	2135	2151	2300	0711	0731	│	│	│	0846	│	│	0946	│	│	1046	│	│	♧	1848	│
London Euston . **150/1/3/4** a.	2042	2106	2126	2213	2228	2351	0753	0810	0828	0846	0905	0924	0943	1011	1024	1043	1108	1124	1143	1205		1925	1943

	⑥	⑥	⑥	⑥	⑥	⑥	⑦	⑦	⑦	⑦	⑦	⑦	⑦	⑦	⑦		⑦	⑦	⑦	⑦	⑦	⑦	⑦
Manchester Piccadilly **122** d.	1755	1815	1835	1855	1935	2035	0805	0820	0920	1020	1035	1115	1135	1155	1215	and at	1815	1835	1855	1915	1935	2021	2055
Stockport .... **122** d.	1804	1823	1843	1904	1943	2043	0814	0828	0928	1029	1046	1124	1144	1205	1223	the same	1822	1842	1904	1922	1941	2027	2103
Wilmslow .... d.	1811	│	│	1911	│	│	0822	│	│	1037	│	│	│	1212	│	minutes	│	│	1911	│	│	│	│
Crewe .... **154** d.	1829	│	│	1929	│	│	0843	│	│	1055	│	│	│	1230	│	past each	│	│	1929	│	│	│	│
Macclesfield .... **122** d.	│	│	1856	│	1956	2056	│	0841	0940	│	1057	│	1157	│	│	until	│	1855	│	│	1954	2040	2116
Stoke on Trent .... **122** d.	│	1849	1912	│	2012	2112	│	0857	1000	│	1115	1152	1214	│	1251		1850	1912	│	1950	2011	2057	2133
Milton Keynes .... **150/1/4** a.	│	1945	│	│	2110	2210	│	│	1116	│	1221	1250	│	│	1347	☆	1948	│	│	2046	│	2203	2246
London Euston . **150/1/3/4** a.	2005	2034	2059	2120	2201	2302	1058	1102	1209	1257	1300	1328	1348	1410	1428		2027	2048	2110	2131	2159	2257	2349

b – Via Birmingham New Street (Table **150**).
s – Calls to set down only.

☆ – Timings may vary by up to 3 minutes.
♡ – The 1720 Ⓐ from London calls at Milton Keynes to pick up only.
♧ – The 1255 from Manchester Piccadilly arrives London Euston 1509; the 1315 from Manchester Piccadilly arrives London Euston 1530.

153 LONDON - LIVERPOOL 🍷 conveyed on most services VT

km		Ⓐ	⚒	⑥	Ⓐ	Ⓐ	⑥	⚒	⚒		⚒	⚒	⚒	⚒	⚒	⑥	Ⓐ	⑥	Ⓐ	⚒	⑥	Ⓐ
0	**London** Euston ..... **142/3 150/1/2/4** d.	0527	0707	0807	0807	0907	0907	1007	1107	...	1207	1307	1407	1507	1607	1633	1707	1707	1733	1807	1833	1833
80	Milton Keynes .... **142/3 150/1/2/4** d.	0615	│	│	0838	│	│	│	│	...	│	│	│	│	│	│	│	│	│	│	│	│
135	Rugby .... **142/3 150** d.	│	│	│	│	│	│	│	│	...	│	│	│	│	│	│	│	│	1823	│	│	1923
155	Nuneaton .... **143** d.	0645	│	│	│	│	│	│	│	...	│	│	│	│	│	│	│	1803	│	│	│	│
215	Stafford .... **143 144** d.	0708	0823	0924	0927	1024	1026	1124	1224	...	1324	1424	1524	1624	1724	1759	1824	1827	1856	1924	1959	1954
254	Crewe .... **143 144 151 152 154** d.	0728	0843	0943	│	1043	1046	1143	1243	...	1343	1443	1543	1643	1743	│	1844	1847	1916	1943	│	2016
290	Runcorn .... **144** a.	0745	0900	1000	1000	1100	1103	1200	1300	...	1400	1500	1600	1700	1800	1832	1900	1904	1933	2000	2031	2033
312	**Liverpool** Lime Street .... **144** a.	0805	0921	1021	1021	1121	1121	1221	1321	...	1421	1521	1621	1721	1821	1852	1921	1925	1952	2021	2053	2053

	Ⓐ	⑥	Ⓐ	⑥	Ⓐ	⑦	⑦	⑦	⑦		⑦	⑦	⑦	⑦	⑦	⑦		⑦	⑦	⑦	⑦	⑦
London Euston ...... **142/3 150/1/2/4** d.	1907	1907	2007	2011	2107	0815	0914	1015	1115	...	1205	1305	1405	1505	1605	1705	...	1805	1905	2005	2008	2121
Milton Keynes .... **142/3 150/1/2/4** d.	│	│	│	│	2139	│	│	│	1204	...	│	│	│	│	│	│	...	│	│	│	2041	│
Rugby .... **142 143 150** d.	│	│	│	2115	│	│	│	│	│	...	│	│	│	│	│	│	...	│	│	│	│	│
Nuneaton .... **143** d.	│	2003	2103	│	2208	0944	1045	1147	│	...	│	│	│	│	│	1804	...	│	2004	2104	│	2253
Stafford .... **143 144** d.	│	2027	2127	2146	│	1008	1114	1214	1253	...	1325	1425	1525	1625	1726	│	...	1925	2029	│	2133	2318
Crewe .... **143 144 151 152 154** d.	│	2047	2148	2206	2251	1030	1136	1234	1315	...	1345	1445	1545	1645	1746	1846	...	1945	2049	2146	2155	2344
Runcorn .... **144** a.	2050	2105	2205	2224	2309	1047	1153	1251	1332	...	1402	1502	1602	1702	1802	1902	...	2002	2106	2203	2212	0004
Liverpool Lime Street .... **144** a.	2108	2125	2225	2246	2334	1105	1211	1308	1351	...	1420	1520	1623	1721	1821	1921	...	2020	2123	2220	2229	0027

	Ⓐ	⑥	Ⓐ	⑥	Ⓐ	⑥	Ⓐ	⑥	Ⓐ		⑥	⚒	⚒	⚒	⚒	⚒	⚒	⚒	Ⓐ	⑥	⑥	Ⓐ
Liverpool Lime Street .... **144** d.	0526	0547	0605	0645	0700	0720	0747	0747	0847	...	0847	0947	1047	1147	1247	1347	1447	1547	1647	1647	1747	1747
Runcorn .... **144** d.	0543	0603	0621	0701	0715**u**	0737	0803	0803	0903	...	0903	1003	1103	1203	1303	1403	1503	1603	1703	1703	1803	1803
Crewe .... **143 144 151 152 154** d.	0602	│	│	0720	│	0757	0823	0822	0925	...	0924	1022	1122	1222	1324	1422	1522	1622	│	1723	│	1824
Stafford .... **143 144** d.	0622	0636	0654	0739	│	0816	0843	0842	0944	...	0943	1042	1142	1242	1343	1442	1542	1642	1736	1743	1836	1843
Nuneaton .... **143** d.	│	0659	│	│	│	│	│	0905	│	...	│	│	│	│	│	│	│	│	│	│	│	│
Rugby .... **142 143 150** d.	0654	│	│	│	│	│	│	│	│	...	│	│	│	│	│	│	│	│	│	│	│	│
Milton Keynes .... **142/3 150/1/2/4** d.	0714	│	│	│	│	│	│	│	│	...	│	│	│	│	│	│	│	│	1824	│	│	│
London Euston ...... **142/3 150/1/2/4** a.	0751	0805	0823	0900	0904	0947	1001	1006	1105	...	1105	1159	1259	1400	1505	1559	1659	1759	1903	1907	1959	2007

	Ⓐ	⑥	Ⓐ	⑥	Ⓐ	⑦	⑦	⑦		⑦	⑦	⑦	⑦	⑦	⑦	⑦		⑦	⑦	⑦	⑦	⑦
Liverpool Lime Street .... **144** d.	1847	1847	1947	1948	2048	0818	0838	0938	...	1038	1147	1247	1347	1447	1547	1618	...	1647	1747	1847	1947	2047
Runcorn .... **144** d.	1903	1903	2003	2004	2104	0835	0854	0954	...	1054	1203	1303	1403	1503	1603	1634	...	1703	1803	1903	2003	2103
Crewe .... **143 144 151 152 154** d.	1922	1923	2024	2023	2124	0853	0913	1014	...	1114	1223	1323	1423	1523	1623	1654	...	1723	1823	1923	2024	2124
Stafford .... **143 144** d.	1942	1942	│	2043	2144	│	0933	1034	...	1136	1244	1344	1444	1544	1644	│	...	1744	1844	1944	2043	2144
Nuneaton .... **143** d.	│	│	2103	│	2218	│	0956	1057	...	1159	│	│	│	│	│	│	...	│	│	│	│	2219
Rugby .... **142 143 150** d.	│	│	│	│	2232	│	│	│	...	│	│	│	│	│	│	│	...	│	│	│	│	2233
Milton Keynes .... **142/3 150/1/2/4** d.	│	│	│	│	2255	1021	│	1147	...	│	│	│	│	│	│	1805	...	│	│	│	2137	2306
London Euston ...... **142/3 150/1/2/4** a.	2104	2117	2209	2215	2346	1108	1137	1232	...	1313	1404	1504	1604	1705	1803	1844	...	1904	2005	2103	2228	2354

u – Calls to pick up only.

km			Ⓐ	⚒	⚒	⚒	Ⓐ	⑥	Ⓐ	⚒	⑥	Ⓐ	⑥	⑥	⚒	Ⓐ	⑥	⚒	⚒	Ⓐ	⚒	⚒	⚒	⑥	Ⓐ
														W		◐				W	◐			◐	◐
0	**London Euston** .... **150/1/2/3** d.	⚒	...	...	...	...	...	...	0531	...	0605	...	...	...	0730	0643	...	...	0830	...	0743	...	0930	0843	0843
80	Milton Keynes .... **150/1/2/3** d.		...	...	...	...	...	...	0623	...	0641	...	...	...	|	0713	...	...	|	...	0813	...	|	0913	0913
	Birmingham New St **144 150** d.		...	...	...	0615	...	...	|	...	|	0715	0715	...	|	0815	0815	...	|	...	0915	...	|	1015	1015
	Wolverhampton .... **144 150** d.		...	...	...	0637	...	...	|	...	|	0737	0737	...	|	0837	0837	...	|	...	0937	...	|	1037	1037
253	Crewe............ **144 151 152 153** d.		...	0557	...	0709	...	...	0732	...	0755	0809	0809	...	|	0909	0909	...	|	...	1009	...	|	1109	1109
291	Warrington Bank Quay..............d.		...	0615	...	0727	...	...	0749	...	0812	0827	0827	...	0914	0927	0927	...	1014	...	1027	...	1114	1127	1127
	Manchester Airport ✈**156 157** d.		...	|	0558	|	0700	0700	|	0729	|	|	|	0829	|	|	|	0900	|	...	|	1000	|	|	|
	Manchester Piccadilly **156 157** d.		0457	|	0615	|	0715	0715	|	0744	|	|	|	0846	|	|	|	0915	|	...	|	1015	|	|	|
310	Wigan North Western .... d.		|	0625	0643	0738	0743	0743	0800	0810	0823	0838	0838	|	0925	0938	0938	0943	1025	...	1038	1043	1125	1138	1138
334	**Preston** .... **156 157 158** d.		0542f	0640	0658	0753	0758	0758	0815	0825	0837	0853	0853	0932	0941	0954	0953	0958	1041	1029	1053	1058	1141	1153	1153
368	Lancaster.................. **157 158** d.		0558	0654	0714	0808	0814	0814	0830	0841	0852	0908	0913	0948	0955	1008	1008	1014	1055	1100	1108	1114	1155	1208	1208
398	Oxenholme....................... **158** d.		0612	0709	0729	0822	|	0829	0843	0855	0906	|	|	1004	|	1022	1022	1029	1108	1120	|	|	|	1221	1221
450	Penrith .... d.		|	0734	0754	|	0852	0854	|	0920	0932	0944	0948	...	1031	|	|	1054	|	...	1145	|	1230	|	|
478	Carlisle............................... **214** d.		0652	0751	0811	0901	0910	0911	0922	0937	0948	1001	1003	...	1047	1101	1101	1111	1147	...	1202	1206	1247	1301	1301
519	Lockerbie .... d.		0711	0810	0830	|	0929	0930	|	0956	|	|	|	...	|	|	|	1130	|	...	|	|	|	|	|
	Haymarket .... a.		|	|	0930s	1013	|	|	|	1057s	|	|	|	...	|	1216	1217	|	|	...	|	1320s	|	1412	1412
641	**Edinburgh** Waverley .... a.		|	|	0937	1022	|	|	|	1103	|	|	|	...	|	1222	1222	|	|	...	|	1326	|	1417	1422
643	**Glasgow** Central..............**214** a.		0819	0913	...	...	1029	1029	1036	...	1059	1116	1115	...	1201	...	...	1229	1301	...	1317	...	1401	...	...

	⚒	Ⓐ	⑥	⑥	Ⓐ	⑥	⚒	⚒	⚒	Ⓐ	⑥	⚒	⚒	⚒	Ⓐ	⑥	⚒	Ⓐ	⑥	⑥	Ⓐ	⑥	Ⓐ	⚒	⚒
				W	◐	◐			◐				◐				◐					◐	◐		
London Euston ....**150/1/2/3** d.	...	1030	1030	...	0943	0943	...	1130	1043	...	...	1230	1143	...	1330	1330	1243	...	...	1430	1430	1343	1343	...	1530
Milton Keynes............**150/1/2/3** d.	...	|	|	...	1013	1013	...	|	1113	...	...	|	1213	...	|	|	1313	...	...	|	|	1413	1413	...	|
Birmingham New St**144 150** d.	...	|	|	...	1115	1115	...	|	1215	...	...	|	1315	...	|	|	1415	...	...	|	|	1515	1515	...	|
Wolverhampton .... **144 150** d.	...	|	|	...	1137	1137	...	|	1237	...	...	|	1337	...	|	|	1437	...	...	|	|	1537	1537	...	|
Crewe............**144 151 152 153** d.	...	|	|	...	1209	1209	...	|	1309	...	...	|	1409	...	|	|	1509	...	...	|	|	1609	1609	...	|
Warrington Bank Quay..............d.	...	1214	1214	...	1227	1227	...	1314	1327	...	...	1414	1427	...	1514	1514	1527	...	...	1614	1614	1627	1627	...	1714
Manchester Airport ✈**156 157** d.	1100	|	|	1129	|	|	1200	|	|	1300	1300	|	|	1400	|	|	|	1500	1500	|	|	|	|	1600	|
Manchester Piccadilly **156 157** d.	1115	|	|	1146	|	|	1215	|	|	1315	1315	|	|	1415	|	|	|	1515	1515	|	|	|	|	1615	|
Wigan North Western................d.	1143	1225	1225	|	1238	1238	1242	1325	1338	1343	1343	1425	1438	1443	1525	1525	1538	1543	1543	1625	1625	1638	1638	1643	1725
Preston................**156 157 158** d.	1158	1241	1241	1248	1253	1255	1258	1341	1353	1358	1402	1441	1453	1458	1541	1541	1553	1558	1558	1641	1641	1653	1653	1658	1741
Lancaster................... **157 158** d.	1214	|	1255	1304	1308	1310	1314	1355	1408	1414	|	1455	1508	1514	|	1555	1608	1614	1614	1655	1655	1708	1708	1714	1755
Oxenholme .... **158** d.	1229	|	1308	1319	1322	1325	1329	1408	|	|	|	|	1522	1529	1606	1610	|	1629	1629	|	1709	1722	1722	1729	1808
Penrith.....................................d.	|	1328	|	...	|	|	1354	|	1443	1451	|	1530	|	1554	1631	|	1645	|	1654	1730	1735	|	1747	1754	|
Carlisle .... **214** d.	1308	1345	1347	...	1401	1403	1411	1447	1459	1508	1508	1546	1602	1611	1647	1648	1701	1711	1711	1747	1751	1802	1806	1811	1847
Lockerbie.................................d.	1327	|	|	...	|	|	1430	|	|	1527	1527	|	|	1630	|	|	|	1730	1730	|	|	|	|	1830	|
Haymarket...........................a.	|	|	|	...	|	|	1534s	|	1616	|	|	|	|	1729s	|	|	1814	|	|	|	|	|	|	1931s	|
Edinburgh Waverley............a.	|	|	|	...	|	|	1540	|	1622	|	|	|	|	1736	|	|	1822	|	|	|	|	|	|	1940	|
Glasgow Central .... **214** a.	1429	1501	1501	...	1517	1517	...	1601	...	1627	1627	1701	1717	...	1801	1801	...	1829	1829	1901	1915	1916	1923	...	2001

	⚒	Ⓐ	⑥	Ⓐ	⑥	⚒	⚒	Ⓐ	Ⓐ	Ⓐ	⑥	Ⓐ	⑥	Ⓐ	⚒	Ⓐ	⑥	⑥	Ⓐ	⑤	Ⓐ	⑥	⚒	Ⓐ	⑥a
	◐					◐		A				◐	◐			◐	◐						◐		
London Euston ....**150/1/2/3** d.	1443	...	...	1630	1630	1543	...	1633	1657	1730	1730	1643	1643	1757	1830	1743	1743	...	...	1846	1930	1930	1843	2030	2031
Milton Keynes............**150/1/2/3** d.	1513	...	...	|	|	1613	...	|	|	|	|	1713	1713	|	|	1813u	1813	...	...	1919	|	|	1913	|	|
Birmingham New St**144 150** d.	1615	...	...	|	|	1715	...	|	|	|	|	1815	1815	|	|	1915	1915	...	...	|	|	|	2015	|	|
Wolverhampton .... **144 150** d.	1637	...	...	|	|	1737	...	|	|	|	|	1837	1837	|	|	1937	1937	...	...	|	|	|	2037	|	|
Crewe............**144 151 152 153** d.	1709	...	...	|	|	1809	...	1820	|	|	|	1909	1909	|	|	2009	2009	...	...	2042s	|	2105	2116	2219	2231
Warrington Bank Quay..............d.	1727	...	...	1815	1814	1827	...	1837	1850	1914	1914	1927	1927	1950	2014	2027	2027	...	...	2101s	2116	2123	...	2236	2248
Manchester Airport ✈**156 157** d.	|	1700	1700	|	|	|	1800	|	|	|	|	|	|	|	|	|	|	2000	2000	|	|	|	...	|	|
Manchester Piccadilly **156 157** d.	|	1715	1715	|	|	|	1815	|	|	|	|	|	|	|	|	|	|	2016	2015	|	|	|	...	|	|
Wigan North Western................d.	1738	|	1743	1826	1825	1838	1843	1848	1901	1925	1925	1938	1938	2001	2025	2038	2038	|	2043	2112s	2127	2133	...	2247	2302
Preston................**156 157 158** d.	1753	1758	1758	1843	1841	1853	1858	1902	1915	1941	1941	1953	1954	2015	2041	2053	2057	2058	2058	2131	2142	2149	...	2305	2317
Lancaster................... **157 158** d.	1808	1814	1814	1858	1855	1908	1914	...	1930	1955	1955	2008	...	2031	2055	2108	...	2114	2114	...	2157	...	...	...	...
Oxenholme .... **158** d.	1823	1829	1829	|	1908	1921	1929	...	1945	2008	2008	|	...	...	2110	2123	...	...	2129	...	2210	...	...	...	...
Penrith.....................................d.	1848	1854	1854	1932	1934	|	1954	...	2010	|	2034	2045	...	...	2135	|	...	...	2154	...	2235	...	...	...	...
Carlisle .... **214** d.	1904	1911	1911	1948	1951	2001	2011	...	2025	2047	2051	2102	...	...	2150	2202	...	...	2211	...	2251	...	...	...	...
Lockerbie.................................d.	|	1930	1930	|	|	|	|	...	2044	|	|	|	...	...	2209	|	...	...	2230	...	|	...	...	...	...
Haymarket...........................a.	2013	|	|	|	|	|	2130s	...	|	|	|	2213	...	...	|	|	...	...	2328s	...	|	...	...	...	...
Edinburgh Waverley............a.	2023	|	|	|	|	|	2138	...	|	|	|	2222	...	...	|	|	...	...	2337	...	|	...	...	...	...
Glasgow Central .... **214** a.	...	2033	2034	2101	2101	2117	...	...	2148	2202	2201	...	...	...	2311	2317	...	...	...	...	0005	...	...	...	...

	Ⓐ	Ⓐ	Ⓐ		⑦	⑦	⑦	⑦	⑦	⑦	⑦	⑦	⑦	⑦	⑦	⑦		⑦	⑦	⑦	⑦	⑦	⑦	⑦	⑦
	◐				b		c	d	g	b	g				g										
London Euston ....**150/1/2/3** d.	1943	...	2110	⑦	...	...	...	...	...	...	...	...	0845	...	...	0945	...	...	...	1045	...	...	1228	...	...
Milton Keynes............**150/1/2/3** d.	2013	...	|		...	...	...	...	...	...	...	...	0933	...	...	1033	...	...	...	1133	...	...	|	...	...
Birmingham New St**144 150** d.	2115	...	|		...	0845	0920	0920	0920	...	...	...	|	1020	...	|	...	1120	...	|	1220	...	|	1320	...
Wolverhampton .... **144 150** d.	2137	...	|		...	0904	0937	0937	0937	...	...	...	|	1037	...	|	...	1137	...	|	1237	...	|	1337	...
Crewe............**144 151 152 153** d.	2216	...	2259		...	0937	1009	1009	1009	...	...	1027	1057	1109	...	1157	...	1209	...	1258	1309	...	|	1409	...
Warrington Bank Quay..............d.	...	...	2321		...	0954	1027	1027	1027	...	...	1043	1113	1127	...	1214	...	1227	...	1315	1327	...	1416	1427	...
Manchester Airport ✈**156 157** d.	...	2200	|		0900	|	|	|	|	1000	1000	|	|	|	1100	|	...	|	1200	|	|	1300	|	|	1400
Manchester Piccadilly **156 157** d.	...	2216	|		0915	|	|	|	|	1015	1015	|	|	|	1115	|	...	|	1215	|	|	1315	|	|	1415
Wigan North Western................d.	...	2255	2332		0944	1006	1038	1038	1038	1043	1042	1054	1124	1138	1143	1225	...	1238	1243	1326	1338	1343	1427	1438	1443
Preston................**156 157 158** d.	...	2313	2350		1002	1019	1051	1054	1102e	1058	1106e	1119f	1139	1153	1158	1240	...	1253	1258	1342	1353	1358	1442	1453	1457
Lancaster................... **157 158** d.	...	2328	...		1018	...	1109	1109	1118	1114	1123	1136	1154	1208	1214	1255	...	1308	1314	1357	1408	1414	1458	1509	1514
Oxenholme .... **158** d.	...	...	...		1032	...	1122	1122	1133	1128	1138	...	1208	1224	1229	1308	...	1322	1329	1410	|	1429	|	1524	1528
Penrith.....................................d.	...	...	...		1056	...	|	|	|	|	1202	...	1234	|	|	1334	...	|	1354	1436	1445	1454	1532	|	1553
Carlisle .... **214** d.	...	...	...		1115	...	1201	1201	1212	1217e	1223	...	1249	1303	1309	1350	...	1402	1411	1452	1503	1511	1548	1603	1611
Lockerbie.................................d.	...	...	...		1133	...	|	|	|	1235	1242	...	|	|	1327	|	...	|	1430	|	|	|	|	|	1629
Haymarket...........................a.	...	...	...		1231s	...	|	|	|	|	1343s	...	|	1415	|	|	...	|	1528s	|	1614	|	|	|	1728s
Edinburgh Waverley............a.	...	...	...		1238	...	|	|	|	|	1348	...	|	1420	|	|	...	|	1535	|	1620	|	|	|	1735
Glasgow Central .... **214** a.	...	...	...		...	...	1316	1326	1327	1337	...	...	1403	...	1430	1502	...	1515	...	1604	...	1628	1701	1714	...

	⑦	⑦	⑦	⑦	⑦	⑦	⑦	⑦	⑦	⑦	⑦	⑦	⑦	⑦	⑦	⑦	⑦	⑦	⑦	⑦	⑦	⑦	⑦	⑦	⑦
		◐			◐			◐			◐			◐	h	k	◐m	◐n	◐p	m	q	◐		◐	
London Euston ....**150/1/2/3** d.	1328	1240	...	1428	1340	...	1528	1440	...	1628	1540	...	1728	1640	1828	1828	1740	1740	1740	1928	1928	1840	2025	1940	2050
Milton Keynes............**150/1/2/3** d.	|	1313	...	|	1413	...	|	1513	...	|	1613	...	|	1713	|	|	1813	1813	1813	|	|	1913	|	2013	2137
Birmingham New St**144 150** d.	|	1415	...	|	1515	...	|	1615	...	|	1715	...	|	1815	|	|	1915	1915	1915	|	|	2015	|	2115	|
Wolverhampton .... **144 150** d.	|	1437	...	|	1537	...	|	1637	...	|	1737	...	|	1837	|	|	1937	1937	1937	|	|	2037	|	2137	|
Crewe............**144 151 152 153** d.	|	1509	...	|	1609	...	|	1709	...	|	1809	...	|	1909	|	|	2009	2009	2009	|	|	2110	2213	2217	2251
Warrington Bank Quay..............d.	1516	1527	...	1616	1627	...	1716	1727	...	1816	1827	...	1917	1927	2016	2016	2027	2027	2027	2116	2116	...	2230	2236	2308
Manchester Airport ✈**156 157** d.	|	|	1500	|	|	1600	|	|	1700	|	|	1800	|	|	|	|	|	|	|	|	|	...	|	|	|
Manchester Piccadilly **156 157** d.	|	|	1515	|	|	1616	|	|	1715	|	|	1815	|	|	|	|	|	|	|	|	|	...	|	|	|
Wigan North Western................d.	1527	1538	1543	1627	1638	1643	1727	1738	1743	1827	1838	1843	1928	1938	2027	2027	2038	2038	2038	2127	2127	...	2241	2247	2319
Preston................**156 157 158** d.	1542	1553	1558	1642	1653	1658	1742	1753	1758	1842	1853	1858	1942	1953	2042	2042	2053	2053	2053	2142	2142	...	2255	2301	2339
Lancaster................... **157 158** d.	1558	1608	1614	1657	1708	1714	1757	1809	1814	1857	1908	1914	1957	2008	2057	2057	2108	2108	2108	2157	2157	...	...	...	...
Oxenholme .... **158** d.	1611	|	1629	|	1723	1729	1811	1823	1829	1911	1922	1929	2012	|	2111	2111	2123	2123	2123	2211	2211	...	...	...	...
Penrith.....................................d.	|	1645	|	1732	|	1754	|	1848	1854	1936	|	1954	2037	2045	2136	2136	|	|	|	2236	2236	...	...	...	...
Carlisle .... **214** d.	1649	1702	1708	1748	1803	1811	1849	1904	1917f	1953	2001	2011	2051	2102	2152	2152	2202	2202	2202	2252	2252	...	...	...	...
Lockerbie.................................d.	|	|	1727	|	|	1830	|	|	1936	|	|	2030	|	|	|	|	2221	2221	2221	|	|	...	...	...	...
Haymarket...........................a.	|	1811	|	|	|	1929s	|	2014	|	|	|	2128s	|	2214	|	|	|	|	|	|	|	...	...	...	...
Edinburgh Waverley............a.	|	1818	|	|	|	1937	|	2022	|	|	|	2134	|	2220	|	|	|	|	|	|	|	...	...	...	...
Glasgow Central .... **214** a.	1801	...	1828	1900	1912	...	1959	...	2038	2103	2111	...	2201	...	2305	2328	2320	2338	2347	0001	0026	...	...	...	...

A – To Blackpool North (a. 1931).
W – To Windermere (Table **158**).

a – June 24 - Sept. 9.
b – From June 25.
c – From Sept. 17.
d – June 25 - Sept. 10.
e – Arrives 10 – 11 minutes earlier.
f – Arrives 7 minutes earlier.
g – May 21 - June 18.
h – May 21 - Oct. 8.
k – From Oct. 15.
m – May 21 - June 25.
n – July 2 - Aug. 27.
p – From Sept. 3.
q – From July 2.
s – Calls to set down only.

◐ – Via Table **150**.

km			Ⓐ	⑥	Ⓐ	Ⓐ	Ⓐ	⑥	⑥	Ⓐ	⑥	⚒	Ⓐ	⑥	⑥	Ⓐ	⚒	⚒	⚒	⚒	⚒	⑤2	⚒
					B				◐				◐		◐	◐			◐				◐
	Glasgow Central ... **214** d.	⚒	...	...	...	...	0428	0426	...	0422	...	0540	...	...	0550	0550	...	0630	...	0709	0735	...	0800
	Edinburgh Waverley ... d.		...	...	...	...	|	|	...	|	...	|	...	...	|	|	0615	|	0652	|	|	...	|
	Haymarket ... d.		...	...	...	...	|	|	...	|	...	|	...	...	|	|	0619u	|	0656	|	|	..	|
	Lockerbie ... d.		...	...	...	...	|	|	...	0550	...	|	...	...	|	|	|	0725	|	0808	|	...	|
	Carlisle ... **214** d.		...	...	...	...	0544	0544	...	0622	...	0649	...	...	0702	0703	0733	0746	0806	0833	0849	...	0910
	Penrith ... d.		...	...	...	...	0558	0558	...	0642	...	|	...	...	0717	0718	0748	0800	0820	0848	|	...	|
	Oxenholme ... **158** d.		...	...	...	...	0621	0621	...	0709	...	0724	...	...	0741	0742	0812	0823	|	0912	0923	...	|
	Lancaster ... **157 158** d.		0513	0538	...	...	0636	0636	...	0724	0724	0738	0658	0658	0756	0757	0827	0838	0857	0927	0938	...	0956
0	**Preston** ... **156 157 158** d.		0533	0558	0600	0617	0657	0657	0617	0744	0744	0758	0717	0717	0817	0817	0847	0858	0917	0947	0958	0952	1017
24	Wigan North Western ... d.		0545	0609	0611	0628	0709	0709	0628	0756	0756	0809	0728	0728	0828	0828	0858	0909	0928	0959	1009	1004	1028
57	**Manchester** Piccadilly ... **156 157** a.		|	|	|	|	|	|	|	0827	0827	|	|	|	|	|	0928	|	|	1028	|	|	|
73	**Manchester** Airport ✈ .. **156 157** a.		|	|	|	|	|	|	|	0847	0848	|	|	|	|	|	0947	|	|	1047	|	|	|
—	Warrington Bank Quay ... d.		0556	0620	0622	0639	0719	0719	0639	...	...	0820	0739	0739	0839	0839	...	0920	0939	...	1020	1016	1039
0	Crewe ... **144 151 152 153** a.		|	|	0642	0659	|	|	0657	...	...	|	0757	0757	0857	0857	...	|	0958	...	|	1038	1057
63	Wolverhampton ... **144 150** a.		|	|	|	0735	|	|	0732	...	...	|	0833	0833	0933	0932	...	|	1033	...	|	|	1133
82	**Birmingham** New St ... **144 150** a.		|	|	|	0801	|	|	0805	...	...	|	0905	0905	1005	1005	...	|	1105	...	|	|	1205
	Milton Keynes ... **150/1/2/3** a.		|	0738	|	...	|	|	0858	...	...	|	0958	|	1058	1058	...	|	1158	...	|	|	1258
	London Euston ... **150/1/2/3** a.		0758	0817	0834	...	0907	0913	0935	...	...	1013	1032	1056	1133	1134	...	1116	1233	...	1213	1231	1334

	⚒	⚒	Ⓐ	⑥	⑥	⑥	Ⓐ	Ⓐ	⚒	⚒	⚒	⚒	⚒	Ⓐ	⑥	⚒	⚒	Ⓐ	⑥	⚒	⚒	⚒	⚒
			◐	◐	W			W		◐			◐				◐				◐		
Glasgow Central ... **214** d.	...	0840	...	...	...	0906	0906	...	0940	1000	...	1040	...	1109	1109	1140	1200	...	...	1240	...	1309	1340
Edinburgh Waverley ... d.	0812	|	0851	0852	...	|	|	...	|	|	1011	|	1051	|	|	|	|	1212	1212	|	1252	|	|
Haymarket ... d.	0816u	|	0857	0857	...	|	|	...	|	|	1016u	|	1057	|	|	|	|	1216u	1216u	|	1257	|	|
Lockerbie ... d.	0911	|	|	|	...	1007	1012	...	|	|	1110	|	|	1207	1207	|	|	1311	1311	|	|	1408	|
Carlisle ... **214** d.	0933	0949	1008	1009	...	1030	1033	...	1049	1111	1133	1149	1208	1231	1231	1249	1311	1333	1333	1349	1408	1430	1449
Penrith ... d.	0948	1003	|	|	...	1045	1048	...	|	1125	1148	|	|	1247	1247	1303	|	|	1348	|	1422	1445	|
Oxenholme ... **158** d.	1012	|	1042	1043	1101	1109	|	1114	1123	|	1212	1223	1243	1312	|	|	|	1410	1412	1424	|	1509	1523
Lancaster ... **157 158** d.	1027	1038	1057	1057	1117	1124	1124	1132	1138	|	1227	1238	1257	1327	1327	1338	1356	1425	1427	1439	1456	1525	1538
Preston ... **156 157 158** d.	1047	1058	1117	1117	1137	1147	1147	1151	1158	1217	1247	1258	1317	1347	1347	1358	1417	1447	1447	1458	1517	1547	1558
Wigan North Western ... d.	1059	1109	1128	1128	...	|	1159	...	1209	1228	1259	1309	1328	1359	1359	1409	1428	1459	1459	1509	1528	1559	1609
Manchester Piccadilly ... **156 157** a.	1128	|	|	|	...	1228	1228	...	|	|	1328	|	|	1428	1428	|	|	1528	1528	|	|	1628	|
Manchester Airport ✈ ... **156 157** a.	1147	|	|	|	...	1247	1247	...	|	|	1347	|	|	1447	1447	|	|	1547	1547	|	|	1647	|
Warrington Bank Quay ... d.	...	1120	1139	1139	...	...	...	...	1220	1239	...	1320	1339	...	...	1420	1439	...	...	1520	1539	...	1620
Crewe ... **144 151 152 153** a.	...	|	1157	1157	...	...	...	...	|	1257	...	|	1357	...	...	|	1457	...	...	|	1557	...	|
Wolverhampton ... **144 150** a.	...	|	1232	1233	...	...	...	...	|	1333	...	|	1433	...	...	|	1533	...	...	|	1633	...	|
Birmingham New St ... **144 150** a.	...	|	1305	1305	...	...	...	...	|	1405	...	|	1505	...	...	|	1605	...	...	|	1705	...	|
Milton Keynes ... **150/1/2/3** a.	...	|	1358	1358	...	...	...	...	|	1458	...	|	1558	...	...	|	1658	...	...	|	1758	...	|
London Euston ... **150/1/2/3** a.	...	1313	1433	1433	...	...	...	...	1413	1534	...	1514	1634	...	...	1613	1733	...	...	1713	1834	...	1813

	⚒	⚒	⚒	Ⓐ	⑥	Ⓐ	⑥	Ⓐ	⑥	Ⓐ	⑥	⚒	Ⓐ	⑥	⑥	Ⓐ	Ⓐ	⑥	⚒	Ⓐ	⑥	Ⓐ	⑥
	◐			◐	◐					◐	◐				W	W	◐	◐					
Glasgow Central ... **214** d.	1400	...	1440	...	...	1509	1509	1540	1540	1600	1600	...	1640	1640	...	...	...	...	1709	1730	1740	1740	1800
Edinburgh Waverley ... d.	|	1418	|	1452	1452	|	|	|	|	|	|	1612	|	|	...	...	1652	1652	|	|	|	|	|
Haymarket ... d.	|	1422u	|	1458	1457	|	|	|	|	|	|	1616u	|	|	...	...	1657	1657	|	|	|	|	|
Lockerbie ... d.	|	1517	|	|	|	1608	1608	|	|	|	|	1710	|	|	...	...	|	|	1808	|	1832	1835	|
Carlisle ... **214** d.	1510	1540	1549	1608	1608	1631	1631	1648	1649	1710	1710	1733	1753	1752	...	...	1808	1807	1830	1846	1852	1857	1910
Penrith ... d.	|	|	|	1621	1622	1646	1646	1703	1703	|	|	1748	1807	|	...	...	|	|	1845	1900	1906	|	|
Oxenholme ... **158** d.	1544	1616	1624	|	|	1714	1710	|	|	1744	1744	1812	1831	1826	1831	1834	1842	1843	1909	1924	1929	1933	|
Lancaster ... **157 158** d.	|	1631	1638	1657	1657	1729	1725	1737	1738	|	|	1827	1845	1841	1847	1903a	1859	1858	1925	1938	1944	1947	1957
Preston ... **156 157 158** d.	1617	1650	1658	1717	1717	1747	1747	1758	1758	1817b	1819	1847	1905	1901	1906	1926	1917	1918	1947	1958	2004	2008	2017
Wigan North Western ... d.	1628	|	1709	1728	1728	1759	1759	1809	1809	1828	1830	1859	1916	1912	...	...	1931	1929	1959	2009	2015	2019	2028
Manchester Piccadilly ... **156 157** a.	|	1730	|	|	|	1828	1828	|	|	|	|	1929	|	|	...	...	|	|	2029	|	|	|	|
Manchester Airport ✈ ... **156 157** a.	|	1748	|	|	|	1847	1847	|	|	|	|	1947	|	|	...	...	|	|	2047	|	|	|	|
Warrington Bank Quay ... d.	1639	...	1720	1739	1739	...	...	1820	1820	1839	1841	...	1927	1923	...	...	1941	1940	...	2020	2026	2032	2039
Crewe ... **144 151 152 153** a.	1657	...	|	1757	1757	...	...	|	|	1857	1900	...	|	|	...	...	2000	1959	...	2039	2045	2051	2059
Wolverhampton ... **144 150** a.	1733	...	|	1833	1832	...	...	|	|	1933	1934	...	|	|	...	...	2038	2032	...	|	|	2130	2132
Birmingham New St ... **144 150** a.	1805	...	|	1905	1905	...	...	|	|	2005	2005	...	|	|	...	...	2105	2105	...	|	|	2154	2155
Milton Keynes ... **150/1/2/3** a.	1858	...	|	1958	2005	...	...	|	|	2058	2104	...	2045	2042	...	...	2158	2204	...	2148	2151	...	...
London Euston ... **150/1/2/3** a.	1933	...	1915	2034	2055	...	...	2012	2019	2139	2157	...	2125	2138	...	...	2243	2255	...	2225	2245	...	...

	⚒	Ⓐ	⑥	Ⓐ	⑥	Ⓐ	Ⓐ		⑦	⑦	⑦	⑦	⑦	⑦	⑦	⑦	⑦	⑦	⑦	⑦	⑦	⑦	⑦
												c					◐			◐			◐
Glasgow Central ... **214** d.	...	1840	1840	...	...	2010	...	⑦	...	...	...	...	...	...	...	0938	...	...	1038	...	1116	1138	1155
Edinburgh Waverley ... d.	1813	|	|	1852	1852	|	2014		...	...	...	...	...	...	...	|	...	1012	|	1051	|	|	|
Haymarket ... d.	1817u	|	|	1856	1856	|	2018u		...	...	...	...	...	...	...	|	...	1016u	|	1055	|	|	|
Lockerbie ... d.	1912	|	|	|	|	2105	2112		...	...	...	...	...	...	...	|	...	1110	|	|	|	|	|
Carlisle ... **214** d.	1934	1949	1948	2007	2009	2126	2135		...	...	...	...	...	...	...	1050	...	1133	1151	1207	1233	1249	1307
Penrith ... d.	1949	|	2002	|	2023	2139	|		...	...	...	...	...	...	...	1104	...	1148	1205	|	1248	|	|
Oxenholme ... **158** d.	2013	2024	2025	2042	2047	2203	2212		...	...	...	...	...	...	...	1127	...	1212	1229	1243	1312	1323	|
Lancaster ... **157 158** d.	2028	2038	2040	2056	2102	2218	2227		...	...	...	1022	...	...	1124	1142	1158	1227	1243	1257	1327	1338	1353
Preston ... **156 157 158** d.	2048	2058	2100	2117	2122	2240	2247		0900	1000	1017	1047b	1058	1117	1147	1202	1217	1247	1304	1317	1347	1358	1417
Wigan North Western ... d.	2101	2109	2111	2128	2133	2252	2259		0911	1012	1028	|	1109	1128	|	1213	1228	1259	1315	1328	1359	1409	1428
Manchester Piccadilly ... **156 157** a.	2130	|	|	|	|	|	2328		|	|	|	1127	|	|	1227	|	|	1328	|	|	1429	|	|
Manchester Airport ✈ ... **156 157** a.	2147	|	|	|	|	|	2347		|	|	|	1147	|	|	1247	|	|	1347	|	|	1447	|	|
Warrington Bank Quay ... d.	...	2120	2122	2139	2144	2303	...		0922	1022	1039	...	1120	1139	...	1224	1239	...	1326	1339	...	1420	1439
Crewe ... **144 151 152 153** a.	...	|	2141	2159	2204	2326	...		0941	1041	1059	...	|	1159	...	|	1259	...	|	1359	...	|	1458
Wolverhampton ... **144 150** a.	...	|	2222	2232	2239	...	...		|	|	1131	...	|	1232	...	|	1332	...	|	1432	...	|	1534
Birmingham New St ... **144 150** a.	...	|	2248	2257	2259	...	...		|	|	1150	...	|	1250	...	|	1406	...	|	1506	...	|	1606
Milton Keynes ... **150/1/2/3** a.	...	2240	...	...	...	...	...		1107	1207	...	...	|	...	...	|	1458	...	|	1558	...	|	1658
London Euston ... **150/1/2/3** a.	...	2339	...	...	...	...	...		1206	1247	...	...	1322	...	...	1416	1539	...	1521	1639	...	1613	1738

	⑦	⑦	⑦	⑦	⑦	⑦	⑦	⑦	⑦	⑦	⑦	⑦	⑦	⑦	⑦	⑦	⑦	⑦	⑦	⑦	⑦	⑦	⑦
			◐			◐			◐			◐									W		
Glasgow Central ... **214** d.	...	1238	...	1316	1338	1355	...	1438	...	1516	1538	1557	...	1638	...	1716	1738	...	1838	...	...	...	2008
Edinburgh Waverley ... d.	1212	|	1251	|	|	|	1412	|	1451	|	|	|	1612	|	1651	|	|	1812	|	1851	...	1957	|
Haymarket ... d.	1216u	|	1255	|	|	|	1416u	|	1455	|	|	|	1616u	|	1655	|	|	1816u	|	1856	...	2001u	|
Lockerbie ... d.	1310	|	|	|	|	|	1510	|	|	1615	|	|	1710	|	|	|	1832	1910	|	|	...	2055	2103
Carlisle ... **214** d.	1333	1349	1407	1436	1449	1511	1533	1549	1607	1636	1649	1709	1733	1751	1807	1833	1852	1933	1946	2007	...	2117	2124
Penrith ... d.	1348	|	1422	|	|	|	1548	|	1622	|	1703	|	1748	1805	|	1848	1906	1948	|	2022	...	|	2139
Oxenholme ... **158** d.	1412	1423	|	1512	1523	1545	1612	1623	|	1712	|	1744	1812	1828	1842	1912	1929	2012	2023	|	2112	2153	2203
Lancaster ... **157 158** d.	1427	1438	1457	1527	1538	|	1627	1638	1657	1727	1738	|	1827	1843	1857	1927	1944	2027	2036	2057	2132	2208	2218
Preston ... **156 157 158** d.	1447	1458	1517	1547	1558	1617	1647	1658	1717	1747	1758	1817	1847	1903	1917	1947	2004	2047	2057	2117	2153	2228	2238
Wigan North Western ... d.	1459	1509	1528	1559	1609	1629	1659	1709	1729	1759	1809	1828	1859	1914	1928	2001	2015	2059	2108	2129	...	2240	2252
Manchester Piccadilly ... **156 157** a.	1528	|	|	1629	|	|	1728	|	|	1830	|	|	1928	|	|	2030	|	2128	|	|	...	2309	|
Manchester Airport ✈ ... **156 157** a.	1547	|	|	1647	|	|	1748	|	|	1847	|	|	1947	|	|	2047	|	2147	|	|	...	2326	|
Warrington Bank Quay ... d.	...	1520	1539	...	1620	1640	...	1720	1740	...	1820	1839	...	1925	1939	...	2026	...	2119	2139	...	...	2303
Crewe ... **144 151 152 153** a.	...	|	1559	...	|	1659	...	|	1759	...	|	1858	...	|	1959	...	2045	...	2138	2159	...	...	2321
Wolverhampton ... **144 150** a.	...	|	1632	...	|	1732	...	|	1833	...	|	1934	...	|	2033	...	|	...	2214	2232	...	...	...
Birmingham New St ... **144 150** a.	...	|	1706	...	|	1805	...	|	1906	...	|	2006	...	|	2051	...	|	...	2232	2255	...	...	...
Milton Keynes ... **150/1/2/3** a.	...	|	1758	...	|	1858	...	|	1958	...	|	2059	...	|	...	...	2152	...	...	...	...	...	...
London Euston ... **150/1/2/3** a.	...	1711	1838	...	1814	1939	...	1911	2039	...	2013	2148	...	2122	...	...	2255	...	...	...	...	...	...

B – From Blackpool North (connection d. 0457, by 🚌).
W – From Windermere (Table **158**).

a – Arrives 9 minutes earlier.
b – Arrives 5 minutes earlier.
c – From June 25.

u – Calls to pick up only.
◐ – Via Table **150**.

EM 2nd class — CREWE - STOKE - DERBY — 155

km		Ⓐ	Ⓐ	Ⓐ		Ⓐ	Ⓐ		⑥	⑥	⑥		⑥	⑥		⑦	⑦	⑦	⑦	⑦	⑦	⑦	⑦
0	**Crewe** .... **143** d.	0607	0658	0807	and at	1907	2045	...	0607	0707	0807	and at	1907	2045	...	1404	1505	1608	1708	1808	1908	2015	2116
24	Stoke on Trent .... **143** d.	0633	0724	0833	the same	1933	2118	...	0633	0733	0833	the same	1933	2119	...	1429	1532	1635	1735	1835	1935	2040	2142
33	Blythe Bridge .... d.	0646	0736	0845	minutes	1945	2130	...	0645	0745	0845	minutes	1945	2131	...	1441	1544	1647	1747	1847	1947	2052	2154
51	Uttoxeter .... d.	0658	0749	0858	past each	1958	2142	...	0658	0758	0858	past each	1958	2144	...	1454	1557	1659	1759	1859	1959	2105	2206
82	**Derby** .... a.	0726	0818	0928	hour until	2027	2209	...	0728	0828	0928	hour until	2024	2213		1519	1624	1727	1828	1928	2028	2134	2236

	Ⓐ	Ⓐ	Ⓐ		Ⓐ	Ⓐ		⑥	⑥	⑥		⑥	⑥		⑦	⑦	⑦	⑦	⑦	⑦	⑦
Derby .... d.	0640	0740	0842	and at	1942	2042	...	0640	0740	0842	and at	1942	2042	...	1438	1538	1638	1741	1841	1941	2040
Uttoxeter .... d.	0705	0807	0907	the same	2007	2107	...	0707	0807	0907	the same	2007	2107	...	1503	1603	1703	1806	1906	2006	2105
Blythe Bridge .... d.	0719	0821	0921	minutes	2021	2121	...	0721	0821	0921	minutes	2021	2121	...	1517	1617	1717	1820	1920	2020	2119
Stoke on Trent .... **143** a.	0732	0832	0933	past each	2033	2133	...	0734	0832	0933	past each	2033	2133	...	1530	1631	1730	1833	1934	2034	2133
Crewe .... **143** a.	0800	0902	1004	hour until	2104	2204	...	0800	0902	1004	hour until	2101	2204	...	1600	1700	1802	1901	2001	2100	2200

NT 2nd Class only — MANCHESTER - PRESTON - BLACKPOOL — 156

For other trains Manchester - Preston and v.v. see Tables **154** and **157**

km		Ⓐ	Ⓐ	Ⓐ	Ⓐ	Ⓐ	Ⓐ	Ⓐ		Ⓐ	Ⓐ	Ⓐ	Ⓐ	Ⓐ	⑤	①–④	⑤	①–④	①–④	⑤	①-④	⑥	⑥	⑥	⑥
0	**Manchester** Airport ... d.	0527	0618	0757	0825	0929	1029	1129	and at	1629	1729	1829	1929	2029	2129	2129	2229	2229	2330	2330	🚌	0527	0629	0757	0929
16	**Manchester** Piccadilly d.	0544	0633	0816	0846	0946	1046	1146	the same	1646	1746	1846	1946	2046	2146	2146	2246	2246	2346	2346	2355	0544	0646	0816	0946
34	Bolton .... d.	0603	0653	0833	0907	1007	1107	1207	minutes	1706	1808	1907	2007	2107	2207	2207	2307	|	|	2359**s**	0020**s**	0603	0707	0833	1007
66	**Preston** .... a.	0632	0722	0903	0937	1033	1136	1237	past each	1733	1838	1939	2036	2136	2233	2238	2337	2336	0031	0036	0055	0633	0739	0902	1035
66	**Preston** .... d.	0635	0725	0905	0939	1038	1138	1238	hour until	1735	1842	1941	2038	2138	2238	...	2341	...	...	0038	0055	0635	0741	0904	1038
94	**Blackpool** North .... a.	0703	0754	0934	1009	1109	1209	1309	♧	1806	1911	2007	2109	2204	2303	...	0009	...	...	0104	0135	0704	0809	0933	1104

	⑥	⑥	⑥	⑥	⑥	⑥	⑥	⑥	⑥	⑥	⑥	⑥	⑥	⑦🚌	⑦🚌	⑦	⑦	⑦	⑦	⑦		⑦	⑦	⑦	⑦	⑦
Manchester Airport .... d.	1029	1129	1229	1329	1429	1529	1629	1729	1829	1929	2029	2129	2229	0005	0530	0848	0929	1029	1129	1229	and at	1929	2029	2129	2229	2330
Manchester Piccadilly d.	1046	1146	1246	1346	1446	1546	1646	1746	1846	1946	2046	2147	2246	0030	0555	0904	0947	1046	1146	1246	the same	1946	2046	2146	2246	2346
Bolton .... d.	1107	1207	1307	1407	1507	1607	1707	1807	1907	2007	2107	2207	2307	0055**s**	0620**s**	0924	1007	1106	1207	1307	minutes	2007	2107	2208	|	|
Preston .... a.	1136	1235	1336	1436	1536	1636	1733	1839	1937	2036	2133	2236	2338	0130**s**	0655**s**	0956	1037	1136	1237	1333	past each	2037	2134	2243	2336	0036
Preston .... d.	1138	1238	1340	1438	1538	1637	1738	1842	1939	2038	2138	2238	...	|	|	...	1039	1138	1239	1338	hour until	2039	*2220*	*2324*	*0033*	...
Blackpool North .... a.	1204	1305	1407	1508	1608	1706	1806	1912	2004	2104	2203	2304	...	0210	0735	...	1102	1204	1304	1403	♧	2104	*2247*	*0029*	*0133*	...

	Ⓐ	Ⓐ🚌	Ⓐ	Ⓐ	Ⓐ	Ⓐ	Ⓐ		Ⓐ	Ⓐ	Ⓐ	Ⓐ	Ⓐ	Ⓐ	Ⓐ	Ⓐ	Ⓐ	⑥	⑥	⑥	⑥	⑥	⑥	⑥	⑥
Blackpool North .... d.	...	0337	...	...	0635	0753	0840	and at	1540	1635	1712	1753	1840	1940	2040	2140	2245	0337	0446	0638	0740	0830	0940	1040	1140
Preston .... a.	...	|	...	...	0703	0818	0904	the same	1604	1704	1742	1819	1904	2005	2103	2204	2309	|	0509	0705	0807	0854	1004	1104	1204
Preston .... d.	0402	0417**u**	0512	0641	0705	0820	0905	minutes	1609	1705	1743	1821	1909	2010	2105	2205	2310	0402**u**	0512	0707	0809	0905	1012	1105	1205
Bolton .... d.	|	0452**u**	|	0708	0734	0856	0934	past each	1635	1734	1813	1855	1934	2036	2134	2234**b**	2339**b**	0435**u**	0540	0734	0834	0934	1035	1134	1234
Manchester Piccadilly a.	0444	0517	0600	0727	0757	0919	0957	hour until	1656	1757	1837	1920	1957	2058	2157	2259	2358	0452	0601	0756	0857	0957	1056	1157	1257
Manchester Airport .... a.	0503	...	0617	0747	0818	*0947*	1023	♧	1717	1817	1855	*1947*	2022	2117	2215	2316	0024	0508	0618	0817	0923	1022	1123	1223	1322

	⑥	⑥	⑥	⑥	⑥	⑥	⑥	⑥	⑥	⑥	⑥	⑦🚌	⑦🚌	⑦	⑦	⑦	⑦	⑦	⑦	⑦	⑦	⑦		⑦	⑦	⑦
Blackpool North .... d.	1239	1340	1440	1540	1635	1735	1840	1940	2040	2140	2245	0320	0520	...	...	1044	1140	1236	1340	1435	1533	1640	and at	2040	2140	...
Preston .... a.	1303	1404	1504	1604	1704	1804	1904	2003	2104	2204	2309	|	|	...	...	1108	1204	1304	1404	1459	1557	1704	the same	2104	2204	...
Preston .... d.	1305	1412	1509	1605	1705	1805	1912	2005	2105	2205	2310	0400**u**	0600**u**	0905	1005	1109	1205	1305	1405	1509	1605	1705	minutes	2105	2205	2335
Bolton .... d.	1334	1435	1535	1634	1734	1834	1935	2034	2134	2234	2339	0435**u**	0635**u**	0934	1034	1135	1234	1334	1434	1535	1634	1734	past each	2134	|	|
Manchester Piccadilly a.	1357	1458	1556	1657	1757	1859	1957	2057	2157	2257	2358	0500**u**	0700**u**	0957	1057	1156	1257	1357	1457	1556	1657	1757	hour until	2157	2257	0024
Manchester Airport .... a.	1423	1523	1623	1723	1823	1917	2018	2116	2215	2316	0024	0525	0725	1016	1115	1215	1317	1415	1515	1615	1715	1815	♧	2215	2315	0043

b – ⑤ only.
s – Calls to set down only.
u – Calls to pick up only.
♧ – Timings may vary by up to 5 minutes.

NT — MANCHESTER - PRESTON - BARROW IN FURNESS — 157

For other trains Manchester - Preston / Lancaster and v.v. see Tables **154** and **156**.

km		Ⓐ2	Ⓐ2	Ⓐ2**D**	Ⓐ2	Ⓐ2	Ⓐ	Ⓐ2**A**	Ⓐ	Ⓐ2	Ⓐ2**A**	Ⓐ	Ⓐ2	Ⓐ2	Ⓐ2	Ⓐ2	Ⓐ	Ⓐ2**E**	Ⓐ2	Ⓐ	Ⓐ	⑥	⑥2**A**	⑥
0	**Manchester** Airport ✈ d.	...	*0558*	...	*0802*	...	0929	...	...	...	...	...	...	...	*1603*	1629	1729	...	...	...	2200	*0558*	...	...
16	**Manchester** Piccadilly d.	...	*0615*	...	0831**f**	...	0946	...	...	...	...	...	...	...	1627	1646	1746	...	...	...	2216	*0615*	...	...
34	Bolton .... d.	...	|	...	0852	...	1007	...	...	...	...		...	...	1649	1706	1808	...	...	...	|	|	...	...
66	**Preston** .... d.	0519	*0658*	...	0927	1004	1048**j**	...	...	...	...	1546	...	...	1728	1805**r**	1847**t**	2006	2109	2147	2313	*0658*	0842	0945
100	Lancaster .... d.	0542	0733	0848	0947	1025	1105	1219	1320	1437	1533	1602	1648	1720	1748	1826	1903	2026	2129	2203	2329	0733	0902	1001
110	Carnforth .... d.	0552	0742	0857	0957	1035	1113	1229	1328	1447	1543	1610	1658	1730	1758	1838	1911	2038	2139	2211	2337	0742	0912	1009
119	Arnside .... d.	0602	0752	0908	1008	1047	1123	1239	1338	1457	1554	1620	1709	1741	1809	1848	1921	2048	2150	2221	2347	0752	0922	1019
124	Grange over Sands .... d.	0608	0758	0914	1014	1053	1129	1245	1344	1503	1600	1626	1715	1747	1815	1854	1927	2054	2156	2227	2352	0758	0928	1025
140	Ulverston .... d.	0625	0815	0931	1030	1112	1143	1302	1400	1520	1615	1642	1732	1803	1831	1911	1943	2111	2212	2243	0008	0815	0944	1041
156	**Barrow in Furness** .... a.	0646	0838	0950	1054	1133	1205	1323	1423	1542	1637	1705	1756	1825	1856	1934	2006	2132	2236	2306	0030	0838	1006	1104

	⑥2**A**	⑥	⑥2**A**	⑥	⑥2	⑥	⑥2**E**	⑥2	⑥	⑥	⑥2**E**	⑥	⑥**a**	⑥**b**	⑦**c**	⑦**d**	⑦	⑦2	⑦2	⑦2		⑦	⑦2	⑦2	⑦
Manchester Airport ✈ . d.	...	...	...	...	...	...	...	...	1629	...	...	2000	2200	...	*0848*	...	...	...	...	...	...	1629	...	...	2029
Manchester Piccadilly . d.	...	...	...	...	...	...	...	...	1646	...	...	2016	2216	...	*0904*	...	...	...	...	...	...	1646	...	...	2046
Bolton .... d.	...	...	...	...	...	...	...	...	1707	...	...	2034	2234	...	*0924*	...	...	...	...	...	...	1707	...	...	2107
Preston .... d.	...	...	...	1407	...	1546	...	...	1745**r**	1908	2003	2058	2258	...	1017	1123	1204	1402	1608	...	...	1747**r**	2004	...	2147**e**
Lancaster .... d.	1119	1223	1332	1423	1520	1602	1700	1731	1801	1929	2023	2114	2314	2314	1037	1143	1220	1422	1628	1720	...	1803	2024	2103	2203
Carnforth .... d.	1128	1231	1341	1431	1530	1610	1710	1740	1810	1939	2033	2122	2322	2322	1047	1153	1228	1432	1638	1730	...	1811	2034	2128	2211
Arnside .... d.	1139	1241	1352	1440	1540	1620	1721	1752	1820	1949	2044	2132	2334	2334	1058	1203	1238	1443	1649	1741	...	1821	2044	2138	2226
Grange over Sands...... d.	1145	1247	1358	1445	1546	1626	1727	1758	1825	1955	2050	2138	2339	2339	1104	1209	1244	1449	1655	1747	...	1827	2050	2144	2231
Ulverston .... d.	1201	1303	1414	1458	1603	1642	1744	1816	1842	2012	2106	2154	2355	2355	1120	1225	1300	1505	1711	1802	...	1843	2107	2200	2247
Barrow in Furness ..... a.	1223	1326	1436	1518	1624	1705	1806	1840	1905	2035	2128	2217	0017	0017	1142	1249	1323	1529	1735	1826	...	1906	2130	2224	2311

	Ⓐ	Ⓐ2	Ⓐ2	Ⓐ		Ⓐ2	Ⓐ2**A**	Ⓐ2	Ⓐ2	Ⓐ2	Ⓐ2	Ⓐ2**A**	Ⓐ2	Ⓐ2**A**		Ⓐ2	Ⓐ**B**	Ⓐ2	Ⓐ	Ⓐ2		⑥2	⑥	⑥
Barrow in Furness ..... d.	0435	0523	0615	0648	...	0713	0804	0850	1009	1113	1213	1331	1441	1524	...	1610	1720	1803	2015	2143	...	0435	0532	0615
Ulverston .... d.	0451	0539	0634	0707	...	0731	0827	0908	1028	1132	1232	1349	1457	1543	...	1628	1737	1821	2034	2201	...	0451	0547	0634
Grange over Sands...... d.	0503	0551	0650	0723	...	0745	0845	0924	1044	1148	1247	1405	1509	1559	...	1644	1752	1837	2050	2217	...	0504	0600	0650
Arnside .... d.	0509	0557	0656	0729	...	0751	0851	0930	1050	1154	1253	1411	1515	1605	...	1650	1758	1843	2056	2223	...	0510	0606	0656
Carnforth .... d.	0519	0608	0708	0740	...	0803	0905	0942	1108	1206	1305	1423	1525	1617	...	1702	1809	1856	2107	2236	...	0520	0616	0707
Lancaster .... a.	0531	0616	0718	0748	...	0813	0913	0952**h**	1118	1215	1314	1433	1533	1628	...	1714	1818	1904	2115	2245	...	0531	0623	0718
Preston .... a.	...	0639	...	0807	...	...	0937	1024	...	1240	...	...	...	...	...	...	...	1932	2135	2311	...	...	0642	...
Bolton .... a.	...	0707	...	0834	...	...	...	...	...	...	...	...	...	...	...	...	...	...	...	...	...	...	0708	...
Manchester Piccadilly . a.	...	0727	...	0856	...	...	...	...	...	...	...	...	...	...	...	...	...	...	...	...	...	...	0727	...
Manchester Airport ✈ . a.	...	0747	...	0916	...	...	...	...	...	...	...	...	...	...	...	...	...	...	...	...	...	...	0747	...

	⑥2	⑥2	⑥	⑥2**C**	⑥	⑥2**A**	⑥	⑥2**A**	⑥	⑥2	⑥🍸**B**	⑥2**A**	⑥	⑥2		⑦**c**	⑦**d**	⑦**Dg**	⑦	⑦2	⑦2	⑦	⑦2	⑦2	⑦2**D**
Barrow in Furness ..... d.	0707	0808	0850	1009	1120	1211	1333	1455	1525	1629	1720	1803	1917	2135	...	0922	0922	1005	1023	1210	1310	1348	1612	1815	1911
Ulverston .... d.	0726	0826	0907	1028	1137	1229	1352	1515	1541	1647	1737	1821	1936	2153	...	0941	0941	1020	1042	1229	1329	1405	1631	1834	1929
Grange over Sands...... d.	0742	0842	0922	1044	1152	1245	1408	1532	1553	1703	1752	1837	1952	2209	...	0957	0957	1033	1058	1245	1345	1419	1647	1850	1945
Arnside .... d.	0748	0848	0928	1050	1158	1251	1414	1539	1559	1709	1758	1843	1958	2215	...	1003	1003	1039	1104	1251	1351	1425	1653	1856	1951
Carnforth .... d.	0800	0900	0939	1102	1209	1303	1425	1556	1609	1721	1809	1856	2009	2228	...	1014	1014	1049	1115	1304	1404	1437	1706	1909	2004
Lancaster .... a.	0808**h**	0909	0947	1111	1219	1315	1433	1608	1617	1736	1818	1905	2017	2239	...	1022	1024	1101	1123	1312	1415	1444	1715	1917	2014
Preston .... a.	0841	...	1007	...	...	...	1452	...	1637	...	...	1931	2037	2303**a**	...	1041	...	...	1143	1337	...	1504	1740	1942	...
Bolton .... a.	...	...	...	...	...	...	...	...	...	...	...	...	...	...	...	1108	...	...	1208	...	...	...	...	...	...
Manchester Piccadilly . a.	...	...	...	...	...	...	...	...	...	...	...	...	...	...	...	1127	...	...	1227	...	...	...	...	...	...
Manchester Airport ✈ . a.	...	...	...	...	...	...	...	...	...	...	...	...	...	...	...	1147	...	...	1247	...	...	...	...	...	...

A – From / to Carlisle (Table **159**).
B – To Windermere (Table **158**).
C – From Sellafield (Table **159**).
D – To / from Morcambe (Table **174**).
E – To Millom (Table **159**).
a – June 24 - Sept. 9.
b – May 27 - June 17 and from Sept. 16.
c – From June 25.
d – May 27 - June 18.
e – Arrives 2134.
f – Manchester **Oxford Road.**
g – May 21 - Sept. 10.
h – Departs 10 minutes later.
j – Arrives 1033.
r – Arrives 1733.
t – Arrives 1838.

158 PRESTON - OXENHOLME - WINDERMERE

2nd Class NT

km		Ⓐ	Ⓐ	Ⓐ	Ⓐ	Ⓐ	Ⓐ	Ⓐ	Ⓐ	Ⓐ	Ⓐ	Ⓐ	Ⓐ	Ⓐ	Ⓐ	Ⓐ	Ⓐ	Ⓐ	⑥	⑥	⑥	⑥	⑥	⑥
														B									M	
	Preston ... 154 d.	...	...	...	...	...	1029	...	...	...	...	...	...	...	...	...	...	...	...	...	...	...	0932	1044
	Lancaster ... 154 d.	0546	...	...	...	...	1100	...	...	...	...	...	...	1821	...	...	...	...	0602	...	...	...	0948	|
0	Oxenholme ... 154 d.	0623	0733	0826	0911	1033	1120	1226	1333	1422	1534	1622	1734	1838	1934	2022	2115	2218	0622	0721	0826	0911	1004	1120
4	Kendal ... d.	0628	0737	0830	0915	1037	1125	1230	1337	1426	1538	1626	1738	1843	1938	2026	2119	2222	0627	0725	0830	0915	1009	1125
16	Windermere ... a.	0641	0752	0846	0931	1050	1142	1243	1354	1443	1555	1643	1755	1858	1953	2041	2132	2237	0641	0742	0846	0931	1026	1142

	⑥	⑥	⑥	⑥	⑥	⑥	⑥	⑥	⑥	⑥	⑥ b	⑦	⑦ d	⑦	⑦	⑦	⑦	⑦	⑦	⑦	⑦	⑦	⑦	⑦
		M					🍷 B			a	🚌	c	🚌	c	d									
Preston ... 154 d.	...	1248	...	1430	...	1704	...	...	...	...	...	1010	0905	...	...	...	...	...	...	...	...	...	...	...
Lancaster ... 154 d.	...	1304	...	1500	...	1720	1825	...	...	...	...	1026	0955	...	1129	...	...	...	...	...	...	...	...	...
Oxenholme ... 154 d.	1226	1321	1417	1519	1634	1737	1842	1934	2022	2115	2120	1042	1040	1136	1145	1227	1335	1421	1535	1621	1733	1841	1927	2016
Kendal ... d.	1230	1325	1421	1524	1638	1741	1846	1938	2026	2119	2130	1046	1050	1140	1149	1231	1339	1425	1539	1625	1737	1845	1931	2020
Windermere ... a.	1243	1341	1436	1541	1655	1756	1901	1953	2041	2134	2205	1059	1125	1155	1202	1246	1354	1440	1554	1640	1752	1901	1944	2036

	Ⓐ	Ⓐ	Ⓐ	Ⓐ	Ⓐ	Ⓐ	Ⓐ	Ⓐ	Ⓐ	Ⓐ	Ⓐ	Ⓐ	Ⓐ	Ⓐ	Ⓐ	Ⓐ	Ⓐ	⑥	⑥	⑥	⑥	⑥	⑥
Windermere ... d.	0645	0756	0850	0947	1056	1147	1247	1358	1458	1600	1649	1803	1906	1958	2050	2140	2245	0657	0747	0850	0937	1040	1147
Kendal ... d.	0659	0811	0902	1001	1108	1202	1302	1413	1513	1613	1704	1818	1918	2012	2104	2154	2259	0712	0802	0902	0952	1054	1202
Oxenholme ... 154 a.	0704	0816	0907	1006	1113	1207	1307	1418	1518	1618	1709	1823	1923	2017	2109	2159	2304	0717	0807	0907	0957	1059	1207
Lancaster ... 154 a.	...	...	...	...	1131	...	...	...	...	...	...	1854	...	...	...	...	2322	...	...	...	|	1117	...
Preston ... 154 a.	...	...	...	...	1151	...	...	...	...	...	...	1926	...	...	...	...	2342	...	...	...	1039	1137	...

	⑥	⑥	⑥	⑥	⑥	⑥	⑥	⑥	⑥	⑥	⑥	⑥ b	⑦ d	⑦	⑦	⑦	⑦	⑦	⑦	⑦	⑦	⑦	⑦	⑦
									a	b	a	🚌	🚌	c										
Windermere ... d.	1251	1345	1441	1550	1707	1803	1906	1958	2045	2045	2140	2140	1043	1104	1206	1250	1358	1447	1558	1648	1802	1905	1948	2040
Kendal ... d.	1306	1359	1455	1605	1722	1817	1918	2012	2056	2056	2154	2215	1108	1116	1220	1302	1412	1501	1612	1702	1816	1918	2002	2055
Oxenholme ... 154 a.	1311	1404	1500	1610	1727	1822	1923	2017	2102	2102	2159	2225	1118	1121	1225	1307	1417	1506	1617	1707	1821	1923	2007	2100
Lancaster ... 154 a.	1333	...	1517	...	1748	1846	...	...	...	2117	2216	2310	...	...	...	...	...	...	...	...	1838	...	...	2131
Preston ... 154 a.	1406	...	1537	...	1811	1906	...	...	...	...	2237	2350	...	...	...	...	...	...	...	...	1858	...	...	2153

B – From Barrow in Furness (Table **157**).
M – From Manchester Airport (Table **154**).
a – June 24 - Sept. 9.
b – May 27 - June 17 and from Sept 16.
c – June 25 - Sept. 10.
d – May 21 - June 18 and from Sept. 17.

159 BARROW - WHITEHAVEN - CARLISLE

2nd class NT

km		Ⓐ	Ⓐ	Ⓐ	Ⓐ	Ⓐ	Ⓐ	Ⓐ	Ⓐ	Ⓐ	Ⓐ	Ⓐ	Ⓐ	Ⓐ	Ⓐ	Ⓐ	Ⓐ	Ⓐ	Ⓐ		⑥	⑥
																		B				
	Lancaster 154 157 ... d.	...	...	...	...	...	...	...	...	...	1219	...	1533	...	...	...	...	2026	...	...	...	...
0	Barrow in Furness ... 157 d.	...	0546	0651	0744	...	0920	1010	1140	1236	1331	1437	1643	1731	1830	1940	...	2134	...	...	...	0546
26	Millom ... d.	...	0621	0719	0812	...	0948	1038	1214	1304	1359	1512	1711	1805	1858	2010	...	2204	...	...	...	0621
47	Ravenglass for Eskdale ... 🚂 d.	...	0642	0737	0829	...	1005	1055	1235	1321	1416	1533	1728	1826	1915	...	...	...	...	...	...	0642
56	Sellafield ... d.	...	0656	0751	0840	...	1019	1108	1248	1336	1428	1547	1740	1840	1925	...	...	...	...	...	...	0656
74	Whitehaven ... d.	0624	0718	0812	...	0904	1037	1128	1310	1356	1454	1612	1800	1915	1946	...	2030	...	2151	...	0622	0718
85	Workington ... d.	0642	0739	0831	...	0922	1055	1146	1332	1414	1513	1634	1818	1936	2004	...	2048	...	2211	...	0640	0739
92	Maryport ... d.	0650	0749	0839	...	0930	1104	1154	1342	1422	1522	1644	1826	1946	2013	...	2056	...	...	...	0648	0749
119	Wigton ... d.	0711	0812	0900	...	0951	1126	1216	1405	1443	1544	1707	1847	2010	2034	...	2117	...	...	...	0709	0812
138	Carlisle ... a.	0733	0833	0925	...	1013	1149	1238	1426	1506	1604	1728	1910	2031	2056	...	2139	...	...	...	0731	0833

	⑥	⑥	⑥	⑥		⑥	⑥	⑥	⑥		⑥	⑥	⑥	⑥	⑥	⑥	⑥	⑥		⑦	⑦	⑦	⑦
						B												B					
Lancaster 154 157 ... d.	...	...	...	...	...	0902	...	1119	...	...	1332	...	...	1700	...	...	...	2023	...	...	...	...	...
Barrow in Furness ... 157 d.	0655	0741	...	0845	...	1010	1138	1239	1350	...	1452	1533	1732	1810	...	1940	...	2130	...	...	...	...	...
Millom ... d.	0724	0809	...	0919	...	1038	1212	1307	1418	...	1520	1601	1806	1840	...	2010	...	2200	...	...	...	...	...
Ravenglass for Eskdale ... 🚂 d.	0742	0826	...	0940	...	1055	1233	1324	1435	...	1537	1618	1827	...	...	...	...	...	...	...	...	...	...
Sellafield ... d.	0756	0839	...	0954	...	1108	1246	1336	1447	...	1550	1630	1841	...	...	...	...	...	...	...	...	...	...
Whitehaven ... d.	0816	...	0906	1019	...	1128	1308	1355	1507	...	1612	1656	1913	...	1943	...	2030	...	...	1233	1433	1633	1933
Workington ... d.	0834	...	0924	1040	...	1146	1329	1413	1525	...	1630	1714	1934	...	2001	...	2048	...	...	1251	1451	1651	1951
Maryport ... d.	0842	...	0932	1051	...	1154	1340	1421	1533	...	1638	1722	1944	...	2009	...	2056	...	...	1259	1459	1659	1959
Wigton ... d.	0904	...	0953	1114	...	1216	1403	1442	1555	...	1659	1744	2008	...	2030	...	2117	...	...	1318	1518	1718	2018
Carlisle ... a.	0926	...	1015	1137	...	1238	1426	1505	1617	...	1720	1806	2029	...	2053	...	2139	...	...	1341	1541	1741	2041

	Ⓐ	Ⓐ	Ⓐ	Ⓐ	Ⓐ	Ⓐ	Ⓐ	Ⓐ	Ⓐ	Ⓐ	Ⓐ	Ⓐ	Ⓐ	Ⓐ	Ⓐ	Ⓐ	Ⓐ	Ⓐ	Ⓐ	Ⓐ		⑥
		B													A							
Carlisle ... d.	...	0515	...	0737	...	0842	0938	1054	1208	1252	1435	1513	1631	1737	1814	...	1915	2037	...	2200	...	...
Wigton ... d.	...	0534	...	0755	...	0901	0956	1112	1226	1310	1454	1531	1649	1756	1832	...	1933	2055	...	2218	...	...
Maryport ... d.	...	0558	0646	0816	...	0925	1017	1133	1247	1331	1517	1552	1710	1820	1853	...	1954	2116	...	2239	...	...
Workington ... d.	...	0609	0704	0827	...	0935	1028	1144	1258	1342	1528	1604	1721	1831	1904	...	2005	2127	...	2250	...	...
Whitehaven ... d.	...	0631	0724	0847	...	0956	1048	1205	1318	1403	1549	1623	1741	1852	1925	...	2025	2147	...	2310	...	...
Sellafield ... d.	...	0652	0742	...	0900	1018	1108	1225	1335	1421	1611	1644	1804	1917	...	...	...	...	...	...	...	...
Ravenglass for Eskdale ... 🚂 d.	...	0706	0753	...	0910	1031	1118	1235	1345	1431	1624	1655	1814	1930	...	...	...	...	...	...	...	...
Millom ... d.	0609	0727	0812	...	0929	1052	1136	1254	1404	1450	1645	1715	1835	1951	...	2016	...	...	2209	...	...	0609
Barrow in Furness ... 157 a.	0642	0803	0845	...	1000	1130	1208	1326	1436	1522	1723	1749	1910	2031	...	2049	...	...	2242	...	...	0641
Lancaster 154 157 ... a.	...	0913	...	...	...	...	...	1433	...	1628	...	...	...	...	...	...	...	...	...	...	...	...

	⑥	⑥	⑥	⑥	⑥	⑥	⑥	⑥	⑥	⑥	⑥	⑥	⑥	⑥	⑥	⑥	⑥	⑥		⑦	⑦	⑦	⑦
										B			A										
Carlisle ... d.	0515	0735	...	0842	0938	1054	1156	1252	1433	1525	1636	1740	1814	1900	...	2015	...	2145	...	1410	1710	1910	2110
Wigton ... d.	0534	0753	...	0901	0956	1112	1215	1310	1452	1543	1654	1758	1832	1918	...	2032	...	2203	...	1427	1727	1927	2127
Maryport ... d.	0557	0814	...	0925	1017	1133	1239	1331	1515	1604	1715	1819	1853	1939	...	2052	...	2224	...	1447	1747	1947	2147
Workington ... d.	0608	0825	...	0935	1028	1144	1251	1342	1526	1616	1726	1830	1904	1950	...	2104	...	2235	...	1459	1759	1959	2159
Whitehaven ... d.	0630	0845	...	0956	1048	1204	1315	1402	1547	1636	1748	1850	1925	2010	...	2125	...	2255	...	1520	1820	2020	2220
Sellafield ... d.	0651	...	0905	1018	1108	1222	1336	1419	1612	1656	1808	1911	...	...	...	...	...	...	...	...	...	...	...
Ravenglass for Eskdale ... 🚂 d.	0705	...	0915	1031	1118	1232	1350	1429	1625	1706	1818	1921	...	...	...	...	...	...	...	...	...	...	...
Millom ... d.	0725	...	0934	1052	1136	1251	1411	1448	1646	1725	1837	1939	...	...	2016	...	2208	...	...	...	...	...	...
Barrow in Furness ... 157 a.	0803	...	1005	1130	1208	1325	1449	1520	1723	1757	1911	2013	...	...	2049	...	2241	...	...	...	...	...	...
Lancaster 154 157 ... a.	...	...	1111	...	1315	...	1608	...	...	1905	...	...	...	...	...	...	...	...	...	...	...	...	...

A – From Newcastle (Table **213**).
B – To / from Preston (Table **157**).
🚂 – Ravenglass and Eskdale Railway. ✆ 01229 717171. www.ravenglass-railway.co.uk

191 BLACKPOOL - PRESTON - CLITHEROE - HELLIFIELD

2nd class NT

TABLE TEMPORARILY RELOCATED FROM PAGE 149

km			⑦ A		⑦ B		⑦ A	
0	Blackpool North ... 156 190 d.	...	...	...	...	...	*1240*	...
29	Preston ... 156 190 d.	...	0839	...	0901	...	1319	...
48	Blackburn ... 163 190 d.	...	0904	...	0927	...	1339	...
63	Clitheroe ... 163 d.	...	0927	...	0951	...	1402	...
85	Hellifield ... a.	...	0952	...	1014	...	1427	...
	Carlisle 173 ... a.	...	*1155*	...	1217	...	*1642*	...

		⑦ A		⑦ A		⑦ B	
Carlisle 173 ... d.	...	...	...	*1339*	...	1757	...
Hellifield ... d.	...	1030	...	1455	...	1948	...
Clitheroe ... 163 d.	...	1055	...	1518	...	2013	...
Blackburn ... 163 190 d.	...	1125	...	1545	...	2040	...
Preston ... 156 190 a.	...	1147	...	1605	...	2101	...
Blackpool North ... 156 190 a.	...	...	...	1633	...	2130	...

A – From Sept. 17.
B – May 21 - Sept. 10.

54 *For explanation of standard symbols see page 1*

AW, VT 2nd class

HOLYHEAD - CHESTER - MANCHESTER 160

km		Ⓐ	Ⓐ	Ⓐ	Ⓐ 🍷C	Ⓐ 🍷A	Ⓐ	Ⓐ 🍷	Ⓐ ✕C	Ⓐ ✕A	Ⓐ	Ⓐ	Ⓐ 🍷C	Ⓐ ✕A	Ⓐ 🍷		Ⓐ 🍷	Ⓐ 🍷C	Ⓐ 🍷	Ⓐ 🍷C	Ⓐ ✕A	Ⓐ 🍷	Ⓐ 🍷B	Ⓐ 🍷	Ⓐ 🍷C	Ⓐ 🍷	Ⓐ 🍷B
0	**Holyhead** d. (Ⓐ)	...	...	...	0425	0448	...	0514	0533	0551	...	...	0628	0655	...	...	0715	...	...	0805	0855	...	0923	...	1040	...	1127
40	Bangor d.	...	...	...	0457	0514	...	0543	0601	0618	...	...	0706	0722	...	...	0802**d**	...	...	0902**c**	0922	...	1002	...	1107	...	1200
	Llandudno ‡ d.	...	...	...	|	|	...	|	|	|	...	0646	|	|	0745	...	|	0830	...	|	|	0945	|	1044	|	1144	|
64	Llandudno Junction ‡ d.	...	0438	...	0515	0532	0546	0607	0619	0636	...	0656	0725	0740	0754	...	0825	0839	0854	0925	0940	0954	1025	1053	1125	1153	1223
71	Colwyn Bay d.	...	0444	...	0521	0538	0552	0613	0627	0642	...	0702	0731	0747	0800	...	0831	0845	0900	0931	0947	1000	1031	1059	1131	1159	1229
88	Rhyl d.	...	0457	...	0531	0549	0602	0626	0638	0653	...	0715	0741	0758	0813	...	0841	0856	0913	0941	0958	1013	1041	1112	1141	1212	1240
94	Prestatyn d.	...	0502	...	0537	|	0608	0631	|	0658	...	0721	0747	0804	0819	...	0847	|	0919	0947	1004	1019	1047	1118	1147	1218	1245
116	Flint d.	...	0516	...	0550	|	0621	0645	0655	0712	...	0735	0800	0817	0832	...	0900	|	0932	1000	1017	1032	1100	1131	1200	1231	1259
136	**Chester** a.	...	0534	...	0605	0617	0638	0702	0709	0726	...	0753	0815	0831	0850	...	0914	0923	0950	1015	1031	1050	1115	1149	1214	1249	1313
136	**Chester 151** ♥ d.	0334	0537	0538	...	0626	0640	0712	...	0735	0738	0755	...	0835	0852	...	0916	...	0952	...	1035	1052	...	1152	...	1252	...
170	**Crewe 151** ♥ a.	|	0558	|	...	0647	|	|	...	0754	|	0818	...	0854	|	...	0937	...	|	...	1054	|	...	|	...	|	...
165	Warrington Bank Quay a.	|	...	0605	...	...	0709	0739	...	...	0808	...	...	...	0918	...	...	...	1018	...	...	1118	...	1220	...	1318	...
201	**Manchester** Piccadilly a.	0446	...	0644	...	...	0751	0814	...	...	0854	...	...	...	0952	...	...	...	1052	...	...	1152	...	1252	...	1352	...
217	**Manchester** Airport a.	0504	...	...	...	...	...	...	...	...	...	...	...	...	1020	...	...	...	1120	...	...	1220	...	1320	...	1420	...

	Ⓐ 🍷	Ⓐ 🍷C	Ⓐ 🍷A	Ⓐ 🍷	Ⓐ 🍷B	Ⓐ 🍷A	Ⓐ 🍷	Ⓐ 🍷	Ⓐ 🍷C	Ⓐ	Ⓐ 🍷	Ⓐ 🍷B	Ⓐ 🍷	Ⓐ 🍷C	Ⓐ	Ⓐ 🍷D	Ⓐ	Ⓐ	Ⓐ		Ⓐ	Ⓐ	Ⓐ B	Ⓐ 🍷B	Ⓐ	Ⓐ	Ⓐ	Ⓐ K
Holyhead d.	...	1232	1252	1305	1324	1358	...	...	1434	...	...	1544	...	1650	...	1730	...	...	1823	...	...	...	1921	...	...	2032	...	...
Bangor d.	...	1307	1320	1332	1404	1425	...	...	1504	...	...	1623	...	1718	...	1809	...	...	1902	...	...	...	2000	2020	...	2101	...	...
Llandudno ‡ d.	...	|	|	|	|	|	1440	1508	|	...	1607	|	1705	|	...	|	...	1844	|	...	1934	...	|	|	2043	|	2145	...
Llandudno Junction ‡ d.	1253	1325	1339	1350	1429	1443	1449	1517	1527	1618	1625	1646	1715	1737	...	1832	1839	1853	1926	...	1946	...	2023	2038	2052	2128	2155	...
Colwyn Bay d.	1259	1331	1345	1358	1435	1450	1455	1523	1533	1624	1631	|	1721	1743	...	|	1845	1859	1932	...	1954	...	2029	2044	2058	2134	2201	...
Rhyl d.	1312	1341	1356	1412	1445	1500	1508	1536	1544	1634	1644	|	1733	1753	...	|	1855	1912	1942	...	2009	...	2039	2055	2111	2147	2216	...
Prestatyn d.	1318	1347	1401	1418	1451	|	1514	1542	1549	1640	1649	|	1739	1759	...	|	1901	1918	1948	...	2016	...	2045	2101	2117	2152	2222	...
Flint d.	1331	1400	1415	1431	1504	|	1527	1555	1603	1653	1703	|	1752	1812	...	|	1914	1931	2001	...	2030	...	2058	2114	2130	2206	2237	...
Chester a.	1349	1415	1428	1445	1525	1528	1544	1613	1617	1707	1720	1726	1811	1826	...	1911	1930	1949	2016	...	2044	...	2116	2128	2147	2222	2255	...
Chester 151 ♥ d.	1350	...	1435	1447	...	1535	1549	1622	...	...	1722	...	1816	...	1850	...	...	1952	2018	...	2046	2052	...	2135	2151	2224	2301	2322
Crewe 151 ♥ a.	|	...	1454	|	...	1554	|	|	...	...	|	...	|	...	|	...	...	|	2041	...	2106	|	...	2154	|	2252	2326	|
Warrington Bank Quay a.	1418	...	...	1517	...	...	1618	1651	...	...	1749	...	1845	...	1918	...	...	2018	...	...	...	2119	...	...	2217	...	...	2351
Manchester Piccadilly a.	1452	...	...	1554	...	...	1654	1727	...	...	1825	...	1927	...	1952	...	...	2052	...	...	...	2153	...	...	2255	...	...	0025
Manchester Airport a.	1520	...	...	...	...	...	...	...	...	...	...	...	...	...	2020	...	...	2119	...	...	...	...	...	...	...	...	...	...

⑥	⑥	⑥	⑥	⑥ a	⑥e 🍷C	⑥ e	⑥	⑥ 🍷D	⑥ 🍷B	⑥ 🍷	⑥ 🍷C	⑥ 🍷A	⑥ 🍷	⑥ 🍷B	⑥ 🍷A	⑥ 🍷	⑥ C🍷	⑥ 🍷A	⑥ 🍷	⑥ 🍷B	⑥ 🍷	⑥ 🍷C	⑥ 🍷	⑥ 🍷B	⑥ 🍷	⑥ 🍷C	⑥ 🍷
Holyhead d.	...	...	...	0425	0425	...	...	...	0522	...	0635	0652	...	0715	0755	...	0820	0855	...	0923	...	1033	...	1123	...	1238	...
Bangor d.	...	...	...	0457	0457	...	...	...	0601	...	0707	0720	...	0802	0822	...	0902	0922	...	1002	...	1105	...	1202	...	1307	1331
Llandudno ‡ d.	...	...	...	|	|	...	...	...	|	0634	|	|	0745	|	|	0845	|	|	0945	|	1044	|	1144	|	1236	|	|
Llandudno Junction ‡ d.	...	0438	...	0515	0515	...	0537	...	0624	0644	0725	0738	0754	0825	0840	0854	0925	0940	0954	1025	1053	1125	1153	1225	1253	1325	1356
Colwyn Bay d.	...	0444	...	0521	0521	...	0543	...	0630	0650	0731	0744	0800	0831	0847	0900	0931	0947	1000	1031	1059	1131	1159	1231	1259	1331	1402
Rhyl d.	...	0457	...	0531	0531	...	0556	...	0640	0703	0741	0755	0813	0841	0858	0913	0941	0958	1013	1041	1112	1141	1212	1241	1312	1341	1415
Prestatyn d.	...	0502	...	0537	0537	...	0601	...	0646	0708	0747	0801	0819	0847	0904	0919	0947	1003	1019	1047	1118	1147	1218	1247	1318	1347	1421
Flint d.	...	0516	...	0550	0550	...	0615	...	0659	0721	0800	0815	0832	0900	0917	0932	1000	|	1032	1100	1131	1200	1231	1300	1331	1400	1434
Chester a.	...	0533	...	0604	0604	...	0633	...	0715	0738	0815	0828	0850	0915	0931	0950	1014	1028	1050	1116	1149	1216	1249	1315	1349	1414	1452
Chester 151 ♥ d.	0336	0537	0538	0613	...	0613	0635	0712	...	0740	...	0835	0852	...	0935	0952	...	1035	1052	...	1152	...	1251	...	1352	...	1453
Crewe 151 ♥ a.	|	0558	|	|	...	|	0659	|	...	|	...	0854	|	...	0954	|	...	1054	|	...	|	...	|	...	|	...	|
Warrington Bank Quay a.	|	...	0605	0639	...	0639	...	0738	...	0806	...	...	0918	...	...	1018	...	...	1118	...	1220	...	1318	...	1420	...	1520
Manchester Piccadilly a.	0441	...	0643	0719	...	0714	...	0818	...	0852	...	...	0952	...	...	1052	...	...	1152	...	1252	...	1352	...	1452	...	1552
Manchester Airport a.	0504	...	...	...	...	...	...	...	...	0920	...	...	1020	...	...	1120	...	...	1220	...	1320	...	1420	...	1520	...	1620

	⑥ 🍷B	⑥ 🍷A	⑥ 🍷	⑥ 🍷C	⑥ 🍷	⑥ 🍷B	⑥ 🍷	⑥ 🍷C	⑥ 🍷	⑥ 🍷D	⑥	⑥	⑥	⑥ B	⑥	⑥	⑥	⑥	⑥	⑦ ¶	⑦ g	⑦ g	⑦ h¶	⑦	⑦ 🍷¶	⑦ 🍷A	⑦ 🍷¶
Holyhead d.	1328	1358	...	1425	...	1523	...	1650	...	1730	...	1823	...	1921	...	...	2037	...	...	...	0716	0750	...	0845	...	...	...
Bangor d.	1407	1425	...	1453	...	1602	...	1718	...	1809	...	1903	...	2000	...	...	2106	...	...	...	0743	0828	...	0913	...	...	...
Llandudno ‡ d.	|	|	1442	|	1544	|	1644	|	1744	|	1844	|	1942	|	2043	...	|	2145	...	...	|	|	...	|	...	...	...
Llandudno Junction ‡ d.	1425	1443	1451	1516	1553	1625	1653	1736	1753	1832	1853	1926	1951	2023	2052	...	2129	2155	...	...	0800	0851	...	0935	...	...	...
Colwyn Bay d.	1431	1450	1457	1522	1559	1631	1659	1742	1759	1838	1859	1932	1957	2029	2058	...	2135	2201	...	...	0807	0857	...	0941	...	...	...
Rhyl d.	1441	1500	1510	1533	1612	1641	1712	1752	1812	1848	1912	1942	2010	2039	2111	...	2148	2216	...	...	0820	0908	...	0954	...	...	...
Prestatyn d.	1447	|	1516	1538	1618	1647	1718	1758	1818	1854	1918	1948	2016	2045	2117	...	2154	2222	...	...	0825	|	...	0959	...	...	...
Flint d.	1500	|	1529	1552	1631	1700	1731	1811	1831	1907	1931	2001	2029	2058	2130	...	2207	2237	...	...	0839	|	...	1013	...	...	...
Chester a.	1517	1527	1546	1605	1648	1715	1749	1825	1849	1924	1949	2016	2047	2113	2148	...	2223	2255	...	...	0856	0939	...	1030	...	...	...
Chester 151 ♥ d.	...	1535	1548	...	1652	...	1750	...	1852	...	1950	2018	2050	...	...	2153	2226	2301	2322	0839	0857	0942	0942	1039	1036	1128	1136
Crewe 151 ♥ a.	...	1554	|	...	|	...	|	...	|	...	|	2041	|	...	...	|	2250	2326	|	|	0922	|	|	1103	|	1147	|
Warrington Bank Quay a.	...	...	1617	...	1719	...	1818	...	1920	...	2018	...	2119	...	...	2220	...	...	2350	0907	...	1009	1009	...	1103	...	1203
Manchester Piccadilly a.	...	...	1652	...	1752	...	1852	...	1952	...	2056	...	2156	...	...	2254	...	...	0022	0945	...	1049	1049	...	1141	...	1240
Manchester Airport a.	...	...	1720	...	1820	...	...	...	2020	...	...	...	...	...	...	...	...	...	...	...	...	...	...	...	...	...	...

	⑦ 🍷C	⑦ 🍷A	⑦ 🍷¶	⑦ 🍷A	⑦ 🍷¶	⑦ 🍷A	⑦ 🍷¶	⑦ 🍷A	⑦ ¶	⑦ 🍷¶	⑦	⑦ h	⑦ 🍷A	⑦ g	⑦ h¶	⑦ 🍷C	⑦ 🍷A	⑦ ¶	⑦	⑦ ¶	⑦ 🍷K	⑦ ¶	⑦ Lg	⑦ h	⑦ ¶	⑦ ¶	⑦	⑦
Holyhead d.	1020	1055	...	1150	...	1250	...	1355	...	1430	...	1530	...	1544	...	1625	...	...	1730	...	1825	...	1915	1940	...	...	2035	2140
Bangor d.	1059	1122	...	1217	...	1318	...	1422	...	1508	...	1558	...	1612	...	1704	...	...	1800	...	1901	...	1954	2009	...	...	2114	2200
Llandudno ‡ d.	|	|	...	|	...	|	...	|	...	|	...	|	...	|	...	|	...	...	|	...	|	...	|	|	...	...	|	|
Llandudno Junction ‡ d.	1122	1140	...	1235	...	1336	...	1440	...	1526	...	1625	...	1635	...	1725	...	...	1824	...	1924	...	2021	2037	...	...	2137	2227
Colwyn Bay d.	1128	1146	...	1242	...	1342	...	1446	...	1532	...	1631	...	1641	...	1731	...	...	1830	...	1930	...	2027	2043	...	...	2143	2233
Rhyl d.	1141	1157	...	1253	...	1353	...	1457	...	1545	...	1644	...	1654	...	1744	...	...	1843	...	1943	...	2040	2056	...	...	2156	2243
Prestatyn d.	1146	1203	...	1259	...	1359	...	1503	...	1551	...	1649	...	1659	...	1749	...	...	1848	...	1948	...	2046	2102	...	...	2201	2249
Flint d.	1200	1216	...	|	...	1413	...	|	...	1604	...	1703	...	1713	...	1803	...	...	1902	...	2002	...	2100	2116	...	...	2215	2302
Chester a.	1218	1230	...	1324	...	1426	...	1531	...	1622	...	1720	...	1734	...	1821	...	...	1921	...	2019	...	2122	2134	...	...	2232	2316
Chester 151 ♥ d.	...	1233	1236	1330	1336	1433	1436	1533	1536	1636	1627	1722	1735	1736	1736	...	1835	1836	1924	1936	2027	2036	...	2135	2143	2206	2235	...
Crewe 151 ♥ a.	...	1253	|	1350	|	1454	|	1552	|	|	1651	1742	1753	|	|	...	1853	|	1948	|	2048	|	...	2200	|	|	2300	...
Warrington Bank Quay a.	...	...	1303	...	1403	...	1503	...	1603	1703	...	...	...	1803	1803	...	...	1903	...	2003	...	2103	...	...	2210	2233	...	...
Manchester Piccadilly a.	...	...	1340	...	1441	...	1540	...	1640	1740	...	...	...	1840	1835	...	...	1940	...	2040	...	2140	...	..	2249	2310	...	...
Manchester Airport a.	...	...	...	...	...	...	...	...	...	...	...	...	...	...	...	...	...	...	...	...	...	...	...	...	...	...	...	...

CAERNARFON - PORTHMADOG - BLAENAU FFESTINIOG △ §

km		🚂 H	🚂 G	🚂 EF	🚂 H		🚂 G	🚂 F	🚂 H	🚂 EF	🚂 F
0	**Blaenau Ffestiniog** d.	...	...	1135	...	...	...	1340	...	1505**b**	1720
19	Minffordd d.	...	...	1230	...	...	...	1435	...	1555**b**	1815
22	**Porthmadog** Harbour d.	0940	1045	1245	1255	...	1410	1450	1540	1610**b**	1830
35	Beddgelert d.	1025	1125	...	1335	...	1450	...	1620	...	...
42	Rhyd Ddu d.	1100	1155	...	1400	...	1515	...	1645	...	...
50	Waunfawr d.	1125	1220	...	1430	...	1545	...	1715	...	...
61	**Caernarfon** a.	1205	1300	...	1510	...	1615	...	1750	...	...

	🚂 EF	🚂 F	🚂 GH	🚂 EF		🚂 H	🚂 F	🚂 G	🚂 H	
Caernarfon d.	...	...	1000	...	...	1300	...	1415	1545	...
Waunfawr d.	...	...	1030	...	...	1330	...	1445	1615	...
Rhyd Ddu d.	...	...	1055	...	...	1400	...	1515	1645	...
Beddgelert d.	...	...	1125	...	...	1430	...	1540	1710	...
Porthmadog Harbour d.	1005	1125	1210	1335	...	1510	1545	1625	1755	...
Minffordd d.	1015	1135	...	1345	...	...	1555	...	...	...
Blaenau Ffestiniog d.	1120	1240	...	1445	...	...	1700	...	...	...

A – Conveys 🛏(12) to / from London Euston (Table **151**).
B – To / from Birmingham New Street (Table **145** or **151**).
C – To / from Cardiff Central (Tables **145** and **149**).
D – To / from Shrewsbury (Table **145**).
E – FR Pink service: May 5–8, 12–15, 19, 22, 26, June 5, 9, 12, 16, 19, 23, 26, Sept. 18, 22, 25, 29, Oct. 1, 2, 6–9, 13–16, 20, Nov. 3, 4, 5.
F – FR Blue service: May 1–4, 9–11, 16–18, 20, 21, 23–25, 27–31, June 1–4, 6–8, 10, 11, 13–15, 17, 18, 20–22, 24, 25, 27–30, July 1 - Sept. 17, Sept. 19–21, 23, 24, 26–28, 30, Oct. 3–5, 10–12, 17–19, 21–31, Nov. 1, 2.
G – WHR Yellow service: May 2–4, 6, 7, 9–11, 14, 16–18, 21–27, June 3–8, 10–15, 17–22, 24–26, 30, July 1–3, 7–9, 14–17, 21–23, 28, Sept. 2–4, 8–30, Oct. 1, 3–5, 7, 8, 10–12, 14, 15, 17–19, 21–31, Nov. 1–4.
H – WHR Red service: May 1, 19, 20, 28–31, June 1, 2, 27–29, July 4–6, 11–13, 18–20, 24–27, 29–31, Aug. 1–31, Sept. 1, 5–7.
K – To / from Birmingham International (Table **145**).

L – To Wolverhampton (Table **145**).

a – May 27 - Sept. 9.
b – Runs 15 minutes later on certain dates (check with operator for details).

* – Connection by 🚌.
¶ – Subject to alteration from Oct. 29.
‡ – For full service Llandudno - Llandudno Junction and v.v. see next page.
♥ – For full service Chester - Crewe and v.v. see next page.
§ – Additional trains operate ②–④ June 26 - Sept. 13 and ① July 24 - Aug. 28 Blaenau Ffestiniog - Porthmadog and v.v.
△ – Operators: Ffestiniog Railway and Welsh Highland Railways. www.festrail.co.uk Ffestiniog Railway ✆ 01766 516024. Welsh Highland Railway ✆ 01286 677018.

c – Arrives 20 minutes earlier.
d – Arrives 10 minutes earlier.
e – From Sept. 16.
g – May 21 - Sept. 10.
h – From Sept. 17.

MANCHESTER - CHESTER - HOLYHEAD

2nd class AW, VT

	Ⓐ	① K	②–⑤ B	Ⓐ 🍷B	Ⓐ 🍷	Ⓐ 🍷	Ⓐ 🍷	Ⓐ 🍷C	Ⓐ 🍷	Ⓐ 🍷B	Ⓐ 🍷	Ⓐ 🍷	Ⓐ 🍷A		Ⓐ 🍷C	Ⓐ 🍷	Ⓐ 🍷A	Ⓐ 🍷B	Ⓐ 🍷	Ⓐ 🍷C	Ⓐ 🍷	Ⓐ 🍷B	Ⓐ 🍷	Ⓐ 🍷C	Ⓐ 🍷	Ⓐ 🍷B	Ⓐ 🍷
Manchester Airport d.		...	...	...	0533	...	...	...	...	...	...	...	...	...	...	...	...	...	1036	...	1136	...	1236	...	1336	...	1436
Manchester Piccadilly d.		...	...	...	0548	...	0650	...	0750	...	0850	...	...	...	...	0950	...	...	1052	...	1152	...	1252	...	1352	...	1452
Warrington Bank Quay d.		...	...	...	0621	...	0725	...	0824	...	0926	...	...	...	...	1027	...	...	1126	...	1227	...	1326	...	1426	...	1526
Crewe 151 ♥ d.		0001	0015	0623	|	0654	|	...	|	...	|	...	0953	...	...	|	1049	...	|	...	|	...	|	...	|	...	|
Chester 151 ♥ a.		0022	0037	0643	0649	0717	0752	...	0853	...	0953	...	1013	...	...	1058	1113	...	1153	...	1255	...	1353	...	1454	...	1553
Chester d.		0038	0040	0644	0655	0719	0755	0822	0855	0923	0958	1002	1016	...	1024	1100	1116	1125	1155	1224	1256	1324	1355	1424	1455	1525	1555
Flint d.		0051	0053	0657	0708	0734	0810	0838	0908	0938	|	1018	1029	...	1039	|	|	1138	1210	1237	1311	1337	1410	1437	1510	1538	1610
Prestatyn d.		0104	0106	0710	0721	0747	0823	0852	0921	0951	|	1031	1042	...	1053	1124	|	1151	1223	1250	1325	1350	1423	1450	1524	1552	1623
Rhyl d.		0110	0112	0716	0727	0753	0829	0858	0927	0957	|	1037	1048	...	1059	1131	1143	1157	1229	1256	1331	1356	1429	1456	1530	1558	1629
Colwyn Bay d.		0121	0123	0727	0738	0807	0843	0912	0938	1011	|	1051	1059	...	1109	|	1154	1211	1243	1307	1345	1407	1443	1507	1544	1608	1643
Llandudno Junction ‡ d.		0128	0129	0733	0744	0816	0851	0918	0944	1018	1036	1058	1106	...	1116	1146	1201	1218	1250	1313	1351	1413	1450	1513	1550	1620	1650
Llandudno ‡ a.		|	|	|	0756	|	...	0927	|	1031	|	1109	|	...	|	|	|	|	...	|	1403	|	1502	|	1602	|	1702
Bangor d.		0144	0146	0750	...	0838	...	...	1008	...	1053	...	1125	...	1139	1202	1217	1236	...	1331	...	1437	...	1531	...	1644	...
Holyhead ▽ a.		0220	0215	0823	...	0922	...	...	1036	...	1122	...	1158	...	1222	1239	1250	1317	...	1414	...	1508	...	1614	...	1716	...

	Ⓐ 🍷C	Ⓐ 🍷	Ⓐ 🍷B	Ⓐ 🍷	Ⓐ 🍷A	Ⓐ 🍷C	Ⓐ 🍷	Ⓐ 🍷		Ⓐ 🍷A	Ⓐ 🍷B	Ⓐ	Ⓐ C🍴	Ⓐ 🍷A	Ⓐ	Ⓐ	Ⓐ 🍷A	Ⓐ	Ⓐ	Ⓐ	Ⓐ C	Ⓐ	Ⓐ	⑥	⑥ B	⑥ 🍷B	⑥ 🍷
Manchester Airport d.	...	1536	...	...	...	...	...	...	...	...	...	...	...	...	...	...	...	2032	...	2132	...	...	...		...	...	0533
Manchester Piccadilly d.	...	1552	...	1650	...	...	1719	1750	...	...	...	1850	...	...	...	1950	...	2050	...	2150	...	2212	2314		...	...	0548
Warrington Bank Quay d.	...	1626	...	1728	...	...	1752	1824	...	...	...	1922	...	...	...	2026	...	2126	...	2224	...	2257	2348		...	...	0621
Crewe 151 ♥ d.	...	|	...	|	1749	...	|	|	...	1857	...	|	...	1956	...	|	2055	|	2136	|	...	|	|		0015	0623	|
Chester 151 ♥ a.	...	1654	...	1801	1808	...	1822	1853	...	1916	...	1950	...	2015	...	2053	2120	2155	2159	2251	...	2325	0015		0037	0643	0649
Chester d.	1627	1655	1725	1803	1810	1824	...	1855	...	1923	1932	...	2006	2026	2034	...	2124	...	2204	...	2256	...	...		0040	0644	0655
Flint d.	1640	1710	1740	|	1823	1839	...	1910	...	1936	1947	...	2018	|	2049	...	2137	...	2219	...	2311	...	...		0053	0657	0710
Prestatyn d.	1654	1723	1753	1826	1836	1853	...	1923	...	1949	2000	...	|	|	2102	...	2150	...	2232	...	2324	...	...		0106	0710	0723
Rhyl d.	1700	1729	1759	1833	1842	1859	...	1929	...	1955	2006	...	2035	2053	2108	...	2157	...	2238	...	2330	...	...		0112	0716	0729
Colwyn Bay d.	1710	1743	1813	1845	1853	1913	...	1940	...	2006	2020	...	2047	2104	2122	...	2208	...	2252	...	2344	...	...		0123	0727	0743
Llandudno Junction ‡ d.	1716	1750	1825	1852	1900	1919	...	1950	...	2013	2030	...	2054	2110	2129	...	2214	...	2259	...	2352	...	...		0129	0733	0750
Llandudno ‡ a.	|	1802	|	1904	|	|	...	|	...	|	2042	...	|	|	|	...	|	...	|	...	|	...	...		|	|	0802
Bangor d.	1739	...	1847	...	1921	1935	...	2015	...	2029	...	...	2111	2127	2152	...	2231	...	2322	...	0014	...	...		0146	0750	...
Holyhead ▽ a.	1821	...	1917	...	...	2020	...	2045	...	2059	...	...	2145	2159	2235	...	2303	...	0005	...	0048	...	...		0215	0823	...

	⑥ 🍷	⑥ 🍷	⑥ 🍷C	⑥ 🍷	⑥ 🍷B	⑥ 🍷	⑥ 🍷C	⑥ 🍷	⑥ 🍷A	⑥ 🍷B	⑥ 🍷	⑥	⑥ 🍷C	⑥ 🍷	⑥ 🍷B	⑥ 🍷	⑥ 🍷C	⑥ 🍷	⑥ 🍷B	⑥ 🍷	⑥ 🍷A		⑥ 🍷C	⑥ 🍷	⑥ 🍷B	⑥ 🍷	⑥ 🍷A
Manchester Airport d.	...	...	...	...	...	...	...	0936	...	...	1036	...	...	1136	...	1236	...	1336	...	1436	...	...	...	1536	...	1636	...
Manchester Piccadilly d.	...	0650	...	0750	...	0850	...	0952	...	...	1052	...	...	1152	...	1252	...	1352	...	1452	...	...	...	1552	...	1652	...
Warrington Bank Quay d.	...	0723	...	0825	...	0926	...	1026	...	...	1126	...	...	1227	...	1326	...	1426	...	1527	...	...	...	1626	...	1726	...
Crewe 151 ♥ d.	0703	|	...	|	...	|	...	|	1049	...	|	...	...	|	...	|	...	|	...	|	1549	...	...	|	...	|	1749
Chester 151 ♥ a.	0723	0750	...	0854	...	0953	...	1053	1113	...	1153	...	...	1255	...	1353	...	1453	...	1554	1610	...	...	1654	...	1753	1810
Chester d.	0725	0755	0822	0856	0924	0955	1023	1055	1116	1124	1155	...	1223	1256	1326	1355	1423	1455	1522	1556	1612	...	1627	1655	1724	1755	1816
Flint d.	0739	0810	0836	0911	0937	1010	1036	1110	|	1139	1210	...	1236	1311	1339	1410	1436	1510	1537	1611	1625	...	1642	1710	1739	1810	1829
Prestatyn d.	0752	0823	0849	0924	0950	1023	1050	1123	|	1152	1223	...	1250	1325	1352	1423	1450	1523	1550	1624	1638	...	1655	1724	1752	1823	1842
Rhyl d.	0758	0829	0855	0930	0956	1029	1056	1129	1143	1158	1229	...	1257	1331	1358	1429	1457	1529	1556	1630	1645	...	1701	1730	1758	1829	1849
Colwyn Bay d.	0809	0843	0906	0944	1007	1043	1106	1143	1154	1209	1243	...	1309	1345	1409	1443	1509	1543	1607	1644	1656	...	1712	1744	1812	1843	1900
Llandudno Junction ‡ d.	0815	0850	0912	0951	1013	1050	1113	1150	1201	1215	1250	1257	1315	1351	1415	1450	1515	1550	1614	1651	1702	...	1717	1750	1819	1850	1906
Llandudno ‡ a.	|	0902	|	1003	|	1102	|	1202	|	|	|	1307	|	1403	|	1502	|	1602	|	1702	|	...	|	1803	|	1902	|
Bangor d.	0838	...	0936	...	1031	...	1136	...	1217	1233	1315	...	1333	...	1440	...	1532	...	1637	...	1719	...	1741	...	1843	...	1923
Holyhead ▽ a.	0921	...	1014	...	1105	...	1209	...	1250	1312	...	...	1413	...	1508	...	1613	...	1714	...	1751	...	1819	...	1913	...	1955

	⑥ 🍷C	⑥ 🍷	⑥ 🍷A	⑥ 🍷B	⑥	⑥ C	⑥	⑥	⑥	⑥ C	⑥ 🚌	⑥	⑥	⑥	⑦	⑦ g	⑦ g	⑦ 🚌	⑦	⑦ ¶	⑦ 🍷A	⑦ ¶	⑦	⑦ 🍷¶	⑦ 🍷	⑦ 🍷¶	⑦ 🍷
Manchester Airport d.	...	1736	...	...	1836	...	...	...	2032	...	...	...	...	...		...	...	...	...	...	...	...	...	...	...	...	...
Manchester Piccadilly d.	...	1752	...	...	1852	...	1951	...	2050	...	...	2151	2226	2314		...	...	0718	...	0956	...	1052	...	1156	...	1256	...
Warrington Bank Quay d.	...	1826	...	...	1926	...	2030	...	|	...	...	2224	2256	2348		...	...	0838	...	1028	...	1126	...	1227	...	1329	...
Crewe 151 ♥ d.	...	|	1852	...	|	...	|	2100	2128	...	...	|	|	|		...	0827	|	0925	|	1042	|	1127	|	1227	|	1327
Chester 151 ♥ a.	...	1853	1911	...	1954	...	2057	2121	2158	...	...	2254	2325	0015		...	0849	0938	0947	1059	1102	1154	1150	1255	1252	1357	1351
Chester d.	1824	1855	1918	1932	...	2032	...	2126	...	2236	...	...	...	...		0620	0900	...	0948	...	1107	...	1203	...	1302	...	1402
Flint d.	1839	1910	1931	1947	...	2047	...	2141	...	2251	...	...	...	...		0633	0913	...	1003	...	|	...	1218	...	1317	...	1417
Prestatyn d.	1852	1923	1944	2000	...	2100	...	2154	...	2305	...	...	...	...		0647	0926	...	1017	...	1130	...	1231	...	1330	...	1430
Rhyl d.	1858	1929	1951	2006	...	2106	...	2200	...	2311	...	...	...	...		0653	0932	...	1023	...	1137	...	1237	...	1336	...	1436
Colwyn Bay d.	1909	1943	2002	2020	...	2119	...	2214	...	2325	...	...	...	...		0703	0943	...	1037	...	1148	...	1248	...	1350	...	1450
Llandudno Junction ‡ d.	1916	1950	2008	2027	...	2126	...	2221	...	2338	2348	...	...	...		0710	0954	...	1043	...	1154	...	1254	...	1357	...	1457
Llandudno ‡ a.	|	2002	|	|	...	|	...	|	...	...	|	...	...	...		|	|	...	|	...	|	...	|	...	|	...	|
Bangor d.	1933	...	2025	2048	...	2143	...	2245	...	...	0013	...	...	...		0726	1012	...	1106	...	1211	...	1311	...	1419	...	1514
Holyhead ▽ a.	2018	...	2058	2131	...	2225	...	2318	...	...	0048	...	...	...		0800	1048	...	1149	...	1240	...	1342	...	1453	...	1555

	⑦ 🍷¶	⑦ 🍷	⑦ 🍷¶	⑦	⑦ 🍷C	⑦ 🍷¶	⑦	⑦ 🍷A	⑦ ¶	⑦ h	⑦ 🍷A	⑦ 🍷C		⑦	⑦ 🍷¶	⑦ 🍷A	⑦ 🍷B	⑦ ¶	⑦ 🍷A	⑦ ¶	⑦ 🍷A	⑦ ¶	⑦	⑦ ¶	⑦	⑦ ¶	⑦ ¶
Manchester Airport d.	...	...	...	...	...	...	...	...	...	...	...	...	...	...	...	...	...	...	...	...	...	...	...	...	...	...	...
Manchester Piccadilly d.	1356	...	1456	...	...	1556	...	...	1656	...	...	...	...	...	1756	...	...	1856	...	1956	...	2056	...	2156	...	2256	2325
Warrington Bank Quay d.	1427	...	1528	...	...	1627	...	...	1727	...	...	...	...	...	1827	...	...	1930	...	2031	...	2128	...	2226	...	2330	2354
Crewe 151 ♥ d.	|	1427	|	1527	...	|	1627	1652	|	1727	1752	...	...	1827	|	1901	...	|	1952	|	2055	|	2128	|	2229	|	|
Chester 151 ♥ a.	1455	1451	1556	1549	...	1655	1649	1713	1755	1749	1813	...	...	1849	1855	1919	...	1958	2013	2059	2113	2156	2151	2254	2252	2357	0024
Chester d.	...	1502	...	1602	1636	...	1702	...	...	1802	...	1829	...	1852	...	1929	1938	...	2018	...	2117	...	2201	...	2300	...	...
Flint d.	...	1517	...	1617	1651	...	1717	...	...	1817	...	1844	...	1907	...	1942	1955	...	2031	...	2130	...	2216	...	2315	...	...
Prestatyn d.	...	1530	...	1630	1704	...	1730	...	...	1830	...	1857	...	1921	...	1955	2011	...	2044	...	2143	...	2229	...	2328	...	...
Rhyl d.	...	1536	...	1636	1710	...	1736	...	...	1836	...	1903	...	1927	...	2002	2017	...	2051	...	2150	...	2235	...	2334	...	...
Colwyn Bay d.	...	1550	...	1650	1724	...	1750	...	...	1850	...	1917	...	1941	...	2013	2031	...	2102	...	2201	...	2249	...	2345	...	...
Llandudno Junction ‡ d.	...	1557	...	1657	1731	...	1757	...	...	1857	...	1924	...	1947	...	2019	2037	...	2108	...	2207	...	2256	...	2351	...	...
Llandudno ‡ a.	...	|	...	|	|	...	|	...	...	|	...	|	...	|	...	|	|	...	|	...	|	...	|	...	|	...	...
Bangor d.	...	1619	...	1714	1754	...	1819	...	...	1914	...	1948	...	2009	...	2036	2059	...	2125	...	2224	...	2313	...	0014	...	...
Holyhead ▽ a.	...	1653	...	1757	1837	...	1854	...	...	1954	...	2018	...	2044	...	2103	2134	...	2154	...	2253	...	2355	...	0051	...	...

LLANDUDNO - BLAENAU FFESTINIOG

km		⚒	⚒	Ⓐ	⑥	⚒	⚒		⑥	Ⓐ	
0	**Llandudno** d.	...	*0708*	1008	1022	1308	1620	...	1903	1905	...
5	**Llandudno** Junction d.	0530	0726	1028	1034	1330	1633	...	1918	1920	...
18	Llanrwst d.	0548	0749	1050	1056	1352	1655	...	1940	1942	...
24	Betws y Coed d.	0554	0755	1056	1102	1358	1701	...	1946	1948	...
44	**Blaenau Ffestiniog** d.	0624	0829	1130	1136	1432	1735	...	2020	2020	...

	⚒	Ⓐ	⑥	⚒	⑥	Ⓐ	Ⓐ	⑥	⚒	
Blaenau Ffestiniog d.	0624	0835	0846	1135	1457	1457	1736	1737	2023	...
Betws y Coed d.	0650	0902	0913	1202	1524	1524	1803	1804	2050	...
Llanrwst d.	0656	0908	0919	1208	1530	1530	1809	1810	2056	...
Llandudno Junction a.	0720	0933	0944	1233	1555	1555	1834	1835	2121	...
Llandudno a.	*0741*	0956	1013	1245	1609	1617	1853	1853	2144	...

♥ – All trains **Chester** - **Crewe**. Journey time ± 23 minutes:
On ⚒: 0422, 0455, 0537, 0551, 0626Ⓐ, 0635⑥, 0645Ⓐ, 0717⑥, 0735Ⓐ, 0755, 0835, 0855, 0916Ⓐ, 0935, 0955, 1035, 1055 and at the same minutes past each hour until 1735, 1755, 1855, 1935Ⓐ, 1935⑥**a**, 1955, 2018, 2035⑥, 2046Ⓐ, 2055, 2135Ⓐ, 2224Ⓐ, 2226⑥, 2301.
On ⑦: 0756**g**, 0827**g**, 0840**h**, 0857**g**, 0927**g**, 0939**h**, 0957**g**, 1039, 1057**g**, 1128, 1157**g**, 1221, 1233, 1257**g**, 1320**h**, 1330, 1357**g**, 1423**h**, 1433, 1457**g**, 1533, 1557**g**, 1627, 1657**g**, 1722**h**, 1735, 1759**g**, 1835, 1859, 1924, 1935, 1950**h**, 1957**g**, 2027, 2037, 2050**h**, 2157**g**, 2127**g**, 2135, 2150**h**, 2157**g** 2235, 2300.

‡ – All trains **Llandudno Junction** - **Llandudno**. Journey time ± 10 minutes:
On ⚒: 0540Ⓐ, 0613, 0651, 0731, 0744Ⓐ, 0750⑥, 0817Ⓐ, 0828⑥, 0850⑥, 0918Ⓐ, 0928⑥, 0948Ⓐ, 0951⑥, 1003⑥, 1018Ⓐ, 1028⑥, 1050⑥, 1058Ⓐ, 1126⑥, 1128Ⓐ, 1150⑥, 1224⑥, 1235, 1257, 1351, 1428, 1450, 1530⑥, 1550, 1559⑥, 1605Ⓐ, 1626⑥, 1650, 1728⑥, 1750, 1826, 1841, 1850⑥, 1852Ⓐ, 1928⑥, 1950⑥, 1955Ⓐ, 2030, 2058Ⓐ, 2132.
On ⑦ May 21 - Sept. 10: 1000, 1050, 1125, 1200, 1242, 1258, 1339, 1402, 1500, 1530, 1604, 1639, 1705, 1740, 1831.

← FOR OTHER NOTES SEE PREVIOUS PAGE

♥ – All trains **Crewe** - **Chester**. Journey time ± 23 minutes:
On ⚒: 0001①, 0007②–⑥, 0010① 0015②–⑥, 0623, 0654Ⓐ, 0703⑥, 0711Ⓐ, 0723⑥, 0823, 0849Ⓐ, 0923, 0940Ⓐ, 0949⑥, 0953Ⓐ, 1023, 1049, 1123, 1149Ⓐ,1156⑥, 1223, 1249 and at the same minutes past each hour until 1823, 1845Ⓐ, 1852⑥, 1857Ⓐ, 1923, 1949⑥, 1956Ⓐ, 2023, 2048Ⓐ, 2055Ⓐ, 2100⑥, 2136, 2149Ⓐ, 2223, 2321⑥, 2330Ⓐ, 2357⑥.
On ⑦: 0827**g**, 0925, 0957**g**, 1007**h**, 1042, 1057**g**, 1105**h**, 1127, 1155, 1227, 1254**h**, 1257**g**, 1327, 1357, 1427, 1457, 1527, 1557**g**, 1627, 1652, 1727, 1752, 1827, 1901, 1924, 1952, 2027, 2055, 2128, 2157**g**, 2203**h**, 2229, 2306, 2338.

‡ – All trains **Llandudno** - **Llandudno Junction**. Journey time ± 10 minutes:
On ⚒: 0554Ⓐ, 0634⑥, 0646Ⓐ, 0708, 0745, 0802Ⓐ, 0808⑥, 0830Ⓐ, 0845⑥, 0908⑥, 0945, 1008, 1022⑥, 1044, 1108⑥, 1112Ⓐ, 1144, 1208⑥, 1236⑥, 1246, 1308, 1408, 1440Ⓐ, 1442⑥, 1508, 1544⑥, 1607, 1620, 1644⑥, 1705Ⓐ, 1708⑥, 1744⑥, 1808, 1844, 1903⑥, 1905Ⓐ, 1913⑥, 1934Ⓐ, 1942⑥, 2008, 2043, 2111Ⓐ, 2145.
On ⑦ May 21 - Sept. 10: 1022, 1107, 1140, 1218, 1319, 1330, 1350, 1420, 1511, 1544, 1616, 1652, 1720, 1805, 1855.

All trains in this table convey 🛏 1, 2 cl., 🚻 (reservation compulsory) ✗ and ⚑. Only available for overnight journeys.

	⑦	⑦	⑦	Ⓐ	Ⓐ	Ⓐ	⑦	Ⓐ	⑦	Ⓐ			⑦	⑦	Ⓐ	Ⓐ	Ⓐ	Ⓐ	Ⓐ	⑦	⑦	⑦
							✪	✪	✪	✪												
London Euston 151/2/3......d.	2057	2057	2057	2115	2115	2115	2328	2328	2350	2350		Fort William 218........d.	...	...	...	...	1950	...	1900	...	...	...
Watford Junction.............d.	2117	2117	2117	2133	2133	2133	2349	2349	0010	0010		Inverness 223............d.	...	...	...	2044		2026		...	...	...
Crewe 151 152 153 154...d.	2336	2336	2336	2356	2356	2356						Perth 223................d.	...	...	...	2330		2306		...	...	...
Preston 154..................d.	0035	0035	0035	0100	0100	0100						Aberdeen 222............d.	...	...	...					2143		2143
Carlisle 154...............a.							0441	0441	0516	0516		Dundee 222..............d.	...	...	...					2306		2306
Motherwell....................							0652		0655			Edinburgh Waverley 154. d.	2315		2340					...	...	...
Glasgow Central 154... ▯ a.							0720		0720			Glasgow Central 154.... d.		2315		2340				...	...	...
Edinburgh Waverley 154 ▯ a.							0721		0721	...		Motherwell..................d.		2330		0001				...	...	...
Dundee 222..............a.	0611		0611		...		...		...	...		Carlisle 154..............d.	0144	0144	0146	0146				...	...	...
Aberdeen 222............ ▯ a.	0739		0739		...		...		...	...		Preston 154...............a.					0436	0436	0436	0444	0444	0444
Perth 223................a.	...	0539		0539	...		...		...	...		Crewe 151 152 153 154 ... a.					0538	0538	0538	0538	0538	0538
Inverness 223............a.	...	0838		0838	...		...		...	...		Watford Junction............a.	0643	0643	0643	0643				...	...	...
Fort William 218.........a.	...		0955		0955		...		...	...		London Euston 151/2/3 ▯ a.	0707	0707	0707	0707	0747	0747	0747	0747	0747	0747

✪ – Sleeping-car passengers may occupy their cabins from 2200.
▯ – Sleeping-car passengers may occupy their cabins until 0800 following arrival at these stations.

| NT   2nd class | | | | | | | **PRESTON - LIVERPOOL** | | | | | | | | | **162** | | | | | | |

km		✗	✗	⑥	Ⓐ	✗			✗	✗	✗	✗	...	✗	✗	✗		⑦	⑦	⑦		⑦	⑦	⑦
0	Preston.............d.	✗✗	0730	0830	0930	0930	1030	and	1630	1730	1830	1930	...	2030	2140	2242	⑦	...	0925	1025	and	2125	2225	2310
24	Wigan North Western..d.		0750	0851	0950	0950	1050	hourly	1650	1750	1850	1950	...	2050	2202	2304		0847	0946	1046	hourly	2146	2247	2331
38	St Helens Central.....d.		0807	0907	1006	1006	1106	until	1706	1806	1906	2006	...	2106	2220	2323		0903	1003	1103	until	2203	2304	2348
57	Liverpool Lime Street a.		0836	0929	1027	1031	1128	★	1731	1828	1929	2028	...	2128	2254	2354		0934	1035	1135	★	2235	2336	0020

		✗	✗	⑥	Ⓐ	✗			✗	✗	✗	✗	⑥	✗	✗	✗		⑦	⑦	⑦		⑦	⑦	⑦
	Liverpool Lime Street ...d.	✗✗	0657	0757	0828	0928	and	1628	1716	1732	1800	1930	2030	2147	2147	2302	⑦	0847	0947	1047	and	2047	2147	2247
	St Helens Central ....d.		0717	0815	0849	0949	hourly	1649	1745	1801	1829	1949	2049	2216	2216	2331		0914	1014	1114	hourly	2114	2214	2314
	Wigan North Western.......d.		0731	0831	0903	1003	until	1703	1804	1820	1851	2003	2103	2234	2238	2348		0930	1030	1130	until	2131	2230	2330
	Preston............a.		0755	0858	0927	1027	★	1727	1830	1851a	1917	2027	2132	2258	2302	0013		0953	1053	1154	★	2155	2253	2353

a – On ⑥ arr. 1845.   ★ – Timings may vary by up to 3 minutes.

| ME, NT   2nd class | **MANCHESTER and LIVERPOOL local services** | **163** |

MANCHESTER - CLITHEROE
Journey time: ± 76 – 80 minutes   57 km   NT

From Manchester Victoria:
Ⓐ: Trains call at Bolton ± 19 and Blackburn ± 48 minutes later: 0555, 0700, 0752p, 0903, 1003, 1103, 1203, 1303, 1403, 1503, 1603, 1635, 1703, 1803, 1903, 2003, 2103, 2203.

⑥: Trains call at Bolton ± 19 and Blackburn ± 48 minutes later: 0555, 0700, 0752p, 0903, 1003, 1103, 1203, 1303, 1403, 1503, 1603, 1635, 1703, 1803, 1903, 2003, 2103, 2203.

⑦: Trains call at Bolton ± 19 and Blackburn ± 48 minutes later: 0802, 0903 and hourly until 2103.

From Clitheroe:
Ⓐ: Trains call at Blackburn ± 23 and Bolton ± 54 minutes later: 0645, 0705, 0745, 0825, 0946, 1046, 1146, 1246, 1346, 1446, 1528, 1646, 1745, 1810, 1846, 1946, 2046, 2144, 2244⑤.

⑥: Trains call at Blackburn ± 24 and Bolton ± 51 minutes later: 0705, 0745, 0825, 0946, 1046, 1146, 1246, 1346, 1446, 1528, 1645, 1745, 1803, 1845, 1946, 2045, 2144, 2248.

⑦: Trains call at Blackburn ± 24 and Bolton ± 53 minutes later: 0946, 1044 and hourly until 2044.

MANCHESTER - BUXTON
Journey time: ± 60 – 70 minutes   41 km   NT

From Manchester Piccadilly:
Trains call at Stockport ± 11, Hazel Grove ± 22 and New Mills Newtown ± 38 minutes later.
Ⓐ: 0649, 0749, 0849, 0949, 1049, 1149, 1249, 1349, 1449, 1549, 1621, 1649, 1722, 1749, 1821, 1849, 1949, 2049, 2149, 2310.

⑥: 0649, 0749, 0849, and hourly until 1649, 1721, 1749, 1849, 1949, 2049, 2154, 2310.

⑦: 0856, 0950, 1051, 1149 and hourly until 1949, 2049, 2149, 2249.

From Buxton:
Trains call at New Mills Newtown ± 21, Hazel Grove ± 34 and at Stockport ± 46 minutes later.
Ⓐ: 0559, 0621, 0648, 0719, 0744, 0822, 0922, 1024, 1124, 1224, 1324, 1424, 1524, 1624, 1657, 1728, 1757, 1824, 1927, 2024, 2126, 2252.

⑥: 0559, 0622, 0723, 0758, 0822, 0925, 1024 and hourly until 1926, 2024, 2127, 2252.

⑦: 0820, 0915, 1022, 1122 and hourly until 1922, 2022, 2124, 2222.

MANCHESTER - NORTHWICH - CHESTER
Journey time: ± 90 – 95 minutes   73 km   NT

From Manchester Piccadilly:
Trains call at Stockport ± 13, Altrincham ± 29 and Northwich ± 57 minutes later.
✗: 0618, 0717, 0817, 0917, 1017, 1117, 1217, 1317, 1417, 1517, 1617, 1709Ⓐ, 1717⑥, 1817, 1917, 2017, 2117⑥, 2122Ⓐ, 2217, 2317.

⑦: 0923, 1122, 1322, 1522, 1722, 1922, 2122.

From Chester:
Trains call at Northwich ± 30, Altrincham ± 55 and Stockport ± 74 minutes later.
✗: 0600, 0658, 0802, 0857, 0957, 1057, 1157, 1257, 1357, 1459, 1557, 1657, 1804, 1904, 2002, 2133, 2248.

⑦: 0902, 1102, 1302, 1502, 1702, 1902, 2102.

MANCHESTER - ST HELENS - LIVERPOOL
Journey time: ± 65 minutes   57 km   NT

From Manchester Victoria:
Trains call at St Helens Junction ± 30 minutes later.
✗: 0539, 0602, 0702, 0738, 0802, 0838, 0902 and hourly until 1702, 1738, 1802, 1902, 2002, 2109, 2209, 2309.

⑦: 0859p, 1001p, 1101p, and hourly (note p applies to all trains) until 2301p.

From Liverpool Lime Street:
Trains call at St Helens Junction ± 28 minutes later.
✗: 0520, 0620, 0720, 0742, 0820 and hourly until 1620, 1642, 1721, 1739, 1820, 1920, 2020⑥, 2022Ⓐ, 2120⑥, 2122Ⓐ, 2220, 2319.

⑦: 0812p 0915p, and hourly (note p applies to all trains) until 2315p.

MANCHESTER - WIGAN - SOUTHPORT
Journey time: ± 75 minutes   62 km   NT

From Manchester Piccadilly:
Trains call at Wigan Wallgate ± 35 minutes later.
Ⓐ: 0641v, 0703v, 0738v, 0810v, 0822 and hourly until 1822, 1923, 2020, 2122, 2238.

⑥: 0641v, 0703v, 0822 and hourly until 1822, 1923, 2020, 2122, 2236.

⑦: 0835, 0935, 1031, 1133, 1231, 1335 and hourly until 2035.

From Southport:
Trains call at Wigan Wallgate ± 30 minutes later.
Ⓐ: 0618, 0649v, 0719, 0757v, 0822 and hourly until 1620, 1729, 1812, 1917, 2017, 2218.

⑥: 0618, 0719, 0822, 0920 and hourly until 1620, 1729, 1812, 1917, 2017, 2122v, 2214.

⑦: 0910, 1001 and hourly until 2201.

MANCHESTER AIRPORT - CREWE
Journey time: ± 33 minutes   37 km   NT

From Manchester Airport:
✗: 0634, 0730⑥, 0831, 0934, 1034, 1134 and hourly until 1533, 1634, 1733, 1834.
    Additional later services (and all day on ⑦) available by changing at Wilmslow.

From Crewe:
✗: 0547, 0711, 0811, 0911 and hourly until 1611, 1711⑥, 1713Ⓐ, 1811.
    Additional later services (and all day on ⑦) available by changing at Wilmslow.

LIVERPOOL - BIRKENHEAD - CHESTER
Journey time: ± 42 minutes   29 km   ME

From Liverpool Lime Street:
Trains call at Liverpool Central ± 2 minutes and Birkenhead Central ± 9 minutes later.
✗: 0538, 0608, 0643, 0713, 0743, 0755Ⓐ, 0813, 0820Ⓐ, 0843, 0858⑥, 0913, 0928, 0943, 0958 and every 15 minutes until 1858, 1913 and every 30 minutes until 2343.

⑦: 0813, 0843 and every 30 minutes until 2313, 2343.

From Chester:
Trains call at Birkenhead Central ± 33 minutes and Liverpool Central ± 44* minutes later.
✗: 0555, 0630, 0700, 0722Ⓐ, 0730⑥, 0737Ⓐ, 0752Ⓐ, 0800⑥, 0807Ⓐ, 0815⑥, 0831, 0845 and every 15 minutes until 1830, 1900 and every 30 minutes until 2300.

⑦: 0800, 0830 and every 30 minutes until 2300.

LIVERPOOL - SOUTHPORT
Journey time: ± 44 minutes   30 km   ME

From Liverpool Central:
✗: 0608, 0623, 0638, 0653, 0708 and every 15 minutes until 2308, 2323, 2338.

⑦: 0808, 0823, 0853, 0923, 0953 and every 30 minutes until 2253, 2323, 2338.

From Southport:
✗: 0538, 0553, 0608, 0623, 0643, 0658, 0713, 0728, 0738Ⓐ, 0743⑥, 0748Ⓐ, 0758, 0803Ⓐ, 0813 and every 15 minutes until 2258, 2316.

⑦: 0758, 0828, 0858, 0928, 0958 and every 30 minutes until 2258, 2316.

p – Starts / terminates at Manchester **Piccadilly**, not Victoria.
v – Starts / terminates at Manchester **Victoria**, not Piccadilly.
* – Trains FROM Chester call at Liverpool Lime Street, then Liverpool Central.

170 LONDON - LEICESTER - NOTTINGHAM, DERBY and SHEFFIELD

Most trains convey 🍷 EM

km			②–⑥	⚒	Ⓐ	⑥	Ⓐ	⑥S	⚒	Ⓐ	⑥	Ⓐ	⑥	⑥	Ⓐ	⚒	Ⓐ	⚒	⚒	⚒		⚒	⚒	⚒	ⒶF	⚒	⚒
0	**London** St Pancras d.	⚒	0015	...	0545	0545	0632	0637	...	0652	0652	0655	0701	...	0724	0729	...	0757	0801	0815	...	0826	0829	0856	...	0900	0915
47	Luton ✈ Parkway d.		0043	...	|	|	|	|	...	0713	0713	|	|	...	|	0749	...	|	|	|	...	|	0849	|	...	|	|
49	Luton d.		0047	...	0612	0612	0654	0659	...	|	|	0718	0722	...	|	|	...	|	0822	|	...	|	|	|	...	0922	|
80	Bedford d.		0111	...	0627	0627	0709	|	...	|	|	0733	0736	...	|	0804	...	|	0837	|	...	|	0904	|	...	0937	|
105	Wellingborough d.		0131	...	0639	0639	0721	|	...	|	|	0746	0748	...	|	0817	...	|	0849	|	...	|	0917	|	...	0949	|
116	Kettering d.		0143	...	0647	0647	0729	0727	0738	|	|	0756	0758	...	|	0823	0832	|	0900	|	...	|	0923	|	...	1000	|
128	**Corby** a.		|	...	|	|	|	|	0747	|	|	|	|	...	|	|	0841	|	0911	|	...	|	|	|	0926	1011	|
133	Market Harborough d.		0155	...	0657	0657	0739	0737	...	|	|	0807	0808	...	0816	0834	...	|	...	0910	...	|	0934	|	|	...	1010
159	**Leicester** d.		0210	...	0712	0712	0752	0753	...	0758	0800	0823	0823	0830	0830	0848	...	0901	...	0925	...	0930	0948	1001	|	...	1025
180	Loughborough d.		▬	...	0722	0723	0802	0803	...	0808	0809	0834	0833	0840	0840	0858	...	|	...	|	...	0940	0958	|	|	...	|
191	E. Midlands Parkway d.		...	...	0729	|	|	0811	...	0816	|	0842	0841	0848	0848	|	...	|	...	0942	...	0948	|	|	1031	...	1042
204	**Nottingham** a.		⚒	...	|	|	|	|	...	0832	0831	0854	0854	|	|	0918	...	|	...	0955	...	|	1018	|	|	...	1055
207	**Derby** a.		0627	0721	0745	0743	0817	0823	...	...	...	...	...	0903	0903	...	...	0923	...	...	...	1003	...	1023	1045	...	...
246	Chesterfield d.		0646	0743	0810	0810	0838	0844	...	...	...	...	...	0927	0927	...	...	0943	...	...	...	1027	...	1043	...	...	...
265	**Sheffield** a.		0713	0800	0827	0826	0855	0858	...	...	...	...	...	0940	0941	...	...	0958	...	...	...	1041	...	1100	...	...	...

	⚒	⚒	⚒	⚒	⚒	⚒	⚒	⚒	⚒	⚒	⚒	⚒		⚒	⚒	⚒	⚒	⚒	⚒	⚒	⚒	⚒	⚒	⚒	⚒	⚒	⚒
London St Pancras d.	0926	0929	0958	1001	1015	1026	1029	1058	1101	1115	1126	1129	...	1158	1201	1215	1226	1229	1258	1301	1315	1326	1329	1358	1401	1415	1426
Luton ✈ Parkway d.	|	0949	|	|	|	|	1049	|	|	|	|	1149	...	|	|	|	|	1249	|	|	|	|	1349	|	|	|	|
Luton d.	|	|	|	1022	|	|	|	|	1122	|	|	|	...	|	1222	|	|	|	|	1322	|	|	|	|	1422	|	|
Bedford d.	|	1004	|	1037	|	|	1104	|	1137	|	|	1204	...	|	1237	|	|	1304	|	1337	|	|	1404	|	1437	|	|
Wellingborough d.	|	1017	|	1049	|	|	1117	|	1149	|	|	1217	...	|	1249	|	|	1317	|	1349	|	|	1417	|	1449	|	|
Kettering d.	|	1023	|	1100	|	|	1123	|	1200	|	|	1223	...	|	1300	|	|	1323	|	1400	|	|	1423	|	1500	|	|
Corby a.	|	|	|	1111	|	|	|	|	1212	|	|	|	...	|	1311	|	|	|	|	1412	|	|	|	|	1512	|	|
Market Harborough d.	|	1034	|	...	1110	|	1134	|	...	1210	|	1234	...	|	...	1310	|	1334	|	...	1410	|	1434	|	...	1510	|
Leicester d.	1030	1048	1101	...	1125	1130	1148	1201	...	1225	1230	1248	...	1301	...	1325	1330	1348	1401	...	1425	1430	1448	1501	...	1525	1530
Loughborough d.	1040	1058	|	...	|	1140	1158	|	...	|	1240	1258	...	|	...	|	1340	1358	|	...	|	1440	1458	|	...	|	1540
E. Midlands Parkway d.	1048	|	|	...	1142	1148	|	|	...	1242	1248	|	...	|	...	1342	1348	|	|	...	1442	1448	|	|	...	1542	1548
Nottingham a.	|	1118	|	...	1155	|	1218	|	...	1255	|	1318	...	|	...	1355	|	1418	|	...	1455	|	1518	|	...	1555	|
Derby a.	1103	...	1123	...	...	1203	...	1223	...	...	1303	...	...	1323	...	...	1403	...	1423	...	...	1503	...	1523	...	...	1603
Chesterfield d.	1127	...	1143	...	...	1227	...	1243	...	...	1327	...	...	1343	...	...	1427	...	1443	...	...	1527	...	1543	...	...	1627
Sheffield a.	1141	...	1159	...	...	1241	...	1259	...	...	1341	...	...	1402	...	...	1441	...	1500	...	...	1541	...	1559	...	...	1641

	⚒	⚒	⚒	⚒	⑥	Ⓐ	⚒	⚒	⚒	⚒	⚒	⑥	Ⓐ	⚒	⑥	Ⓐ	Ⓐ	⑥	Ⓐ	⑥	⑥B	Ⓐ	⚒	Ⓐ	⑥	ⒶC	⑥
London St Pancras d.	1429	1458	1501	1515	1526	1526	1529	1558	1601	1615	1626	1629	1629	1657	1701	1700	1700	1715	1715	1726	1729	1730	1757	1745	1801	1800	1826
Luton ✈ Parkway d.	1449	|	|	|	|	|	1549	|	|	|	|	1649	1649	|	|	|	|	|	|	|	1749	|	|	1808	|	|	|
Luton d.	|	|	1522	|	|	|	|	|	1622	|	|	|	1653	|	1722	|	|	|	1740	|	|	|	|	|	1822	1822	|
Bedford d.	1504	|	1537	|	|	|	1604	|	1637	|	|	1704	1707	|	1737	1737	1737	|	|	|	1804	1804	|	|	1837	1837	|
Wellingborough d.	1517	|	1549	|	|	|	1617	|	1649	|	|	1717	1719	|	1749	1749	1749	|	|	|	1817	1817	|	1832	1849	1849	|
Kettering d.	1523	|	1600	|	|	|	1623	|	1700	|	|	1723	1726	|	1800	1806g	1814g	|	|	|	1823	1823	|	1844	1900	1906	|
Corby a.	|	|	1611	|	|	|	|	|	1711	|	|	|	|	|	1811	1815	|	|	|	|	|	|	|	|	1911	1916	|
Market Harborough d.	1534	|	...	1610	|	|	1634	|	...	1710	|	1734	1736	|	...	...	|	1810	1816	|	1834	1834	|	1856	...	...	|
Leicester d.	1548	1601	...	1625	1630	1630	1648	1701	...	1725	1730	1748	1751	1801	...	...	1837	1825	1832	1830	1848	1848	1901	1914	...	...	1930
Loughborough d.	1558	|	...	|	1640	1640	1658	|	...	|	1740	1758	1801	|	...	...	1847	|	|	1840	1858	1858	|	1926	...	...	1940
E. Midlands Parkway d.	|	|	...	1642	1648	1648	|	|	...	1742	1748	|	|	|	...	...	1856	1842	1850	1848	|	1905	|	1934	...	...	1948
Nottingham a.	1618	|	...	1655	|	|	1718	|	...	1755	|	1818	1821	|	...	...	|	1855	1909	|	1918	1920	|	1947	...	...	|
Derby a.	...	1623	...	...	1703	1703r	...	1723	...	...	1803	...	...	1823	...	...	1913	...	...	1903	...	...	1923	2031	...	...	2003
Chesterfield d.	...	1643	...	...	1727	1734	...	1743	...	...	1827	...	...	1843	...	...	1934	...	...	1927	...	...	1943	...	...	...	2027
Sheffield a.	...	1659	...	...	1742	1748	...	1800	...	...	1841	...	...	1900	...	...	1950	...	...	1941	...	...	1959	...	...	...	2041

	Ⓐ	⑥L	ⒶL	⑥	ⒶB	⑥	Ⓐ	⑥	Ⓐ	Ⓐ	⑥	⑥	Ⓐ	⑥	ⒶL	⑥L	ⒶL	Ⓐ	⑥	Ⓐ	⑥	⚒	Ⓐ	⑥	⑥	Ⓐ	Ⓐ
London St Pancras d.	1825	1815	1815	1829	1830	1858	1857	1901	1900	1915	1915	1926	1928	1929	1955	1958	1932	2000	2001	2015	2015	2026	2030	2030	2056	2055	2100
Luton ✈ Parkway d.	|	|	|	1849	1850	|	|	|	|	|	|	|	|	1949	|	|	1953	|	|	|	|	|	2049	2050	|	|	|
Luton d.	1850	|	|	|	|	|	|	1922	1924	|	|	|	|	|	|	|	|	2022	2025	|	|	|	|	|	|	|	2123
Bedford d.	|	|	|	1904	1907	|	|	1937	1940	|	|	|	|	2004	|	|	2009	2037	2039	|	|	|	2104	2104	|	|	2138
Wellingborough d.	|	|	1903	1917	1920	|	|	1949	1954	|	|	|	|	2017	|	|	2022	2049	2051	|	|	|	2118	2117	|	|	2150
Kettering d.	|	|	1911	1923	1926	|	|	2000	2006	|	|	|	2019	2023	|	|	|	2101	2100	|	|	|	2123	2124	|	|	2157
Corby a.	|	|	|	|	|	|	|	2011	2017	|	|	|	|	|	|	|	|	2112	2111	|	|	|	|	|	|	|	|
Market Harborough d.	1927	1910	|	1934	|	|	1949	...	...	2010	2010	|	2029	2034	|	|	2038	...	...	2109	2110	|	2134	2134	|	|	2207
Leicester d.	1942	1925	1934	1948	1952	2001	2002	...	...	2025	2025	2030	2045	2048	2102	2105	2053	...	...	2122	2125	2130	2148	2148	2201	2203	2222
Loughborough d.	1953	|	1945	1958	|	|	2013	...	...	|	|	2040	2055	2058	|	|	2103	...	...	|	|	2140	2158	2158	|	|	2232
E. Midlands Parkway d.	|	1942	1954	|	2009	|	2021	...	...	2038	2042	2051	2102	|	|	|	|	...	...	2136	2138	2148	|	2207	|	|	2239
Nottingham a.	|	1955c	2008a	2018	2023	|	|	...	...	2051	2055	|	|	2118	|	|	2128b	...	...	2149	2150	|	2218	2221	|	|	|
Derby a.	2015	|	|	...	...	2023	2034	...	...	...	...	2108	2119	...	2129	2131d	|	...	...	...	...	2205	...	...	2223	2225	2254
Chesterfield d.	2039	2052	2109	...	...	2043	2054	...	...	...	...	...	...	...	2153	2203	2222	...	...	...	...	...	...	...	2247	2245	...
Sheffield a.	2055	2105	2123	...	...	2059	2109	...	...	...	...	...	...	...	2208	2217	2236	...	...	...	...	...	...	...	2300	2301	...

	⑥	⑥	Ⓐ	⚒	⚒	⚒	⑥	Ⓐ	⑥	Ⓐ	Ⓐ		⑦Y	⑦	⑦	⑦	⑦	⑦	⑦	⑦	⑦	⑦	⑦	⑦	⑦	⑦	⑦
London St Pancras d.	2101	...	...	2125	2130	2200	...	...	2226	2225	2315	⑦	...	0900	0930	1000	1030	1100	1130	1210	1237	1250	1310	1337	1355	1410	1440
Luton ✈ Parkway d.	|	...	...	|	2151	|	...	...	2247	2248	|		...	0928	|	1029	|	1129	1159	1231	1258	|	1331	1358	|	1431	|
Luton d.	2124	...	...	|	|	2224	...	...	|	|	2346		...	|	0959	|	1102	1133	1203	1234	1300	|	1334	1400	|	|	1502
Bedford d.	2139	...	...	|	2205	2239	...	...	2303	2303	0012	✥	...	0950	1019	1054	1125	1154	1223	1249	1316	|	1349	1416	|	1446	1516
Wellingborough d.	2152	...	...	|	2218	2252	...	...	2315	2317	0024		...	1003	1031	1108	1136	1207	1235	1302	1328	|	1402	1428	|	1459	1528
Kettering d.	2202	2206	2211	|	2225	2300	2305	2311	2322	2326	0042		...	1010	1038	1116	1143	1215	1242	1309	1340	1339	1409	1437	|	1506	1539
Corby a.	|	2221	2226	|	|	|	2319	2326	|	|	|		...	|	|	|	|	|	|	|	1350	|	|	1447	|	|	1549
Market Harborough d.	2213	...	...	2218	2235	2311	...	...	2332	2337	0052		...	1020	1049	1127	1153	1225	1252	1319	...	1350	1419	...	1451	1516	...
Leicester d.	2229	...	...	2233	2249	2327	...	...	2346	2353	0107		1020	1036	1105	1145	1210	1241	1309	1336	...	1408	1436	...	1509	1533	...
Loughborough d.	|	...	...	2243	2259	2338	...	...	2356	0004	0119		1030	1046	1115	1156	1220	1251	1319	1346	...	1419	1446	...	1520	1543	...
E. Midlands Parkway d.	2245	...	...	2250	2307	2347	...	...	0004	0012	0130		1037	1053	1123	1205	1227	1259	1326	1353	...	1427	1453	...	1527	1550	...
Nottingham a.	|	...	...	2304	|	0006	...	...	|	|	0145		|	1108	|	1216	|	1312	|	1407	...	|	1507	...	|	1605	...
Derby a.	2259	...	...	...	2325	...	...	...	0019	0026	0210		1054	...	1143t	...	1243t	...	1342t	...	...	1444	...	...	1545	...	...
Chesterfield d.	...	...	...	...	...	...	...	...	...	0048	...		1114	...	1210	...	1312	...	1411	...	...	1508	...	...	1608	...	...
Sheffield a.	...	...	...	...	...	...	...	...	...	0104	...		1128	...	1228	...	1328	...	1425	...	...	1529	...	...	1628	...	...

	⑦L	⑦	⑦	⑦	⑦	⑦	⑦	⑦	⑦	⑦	⑦	⑦	⑦	⑦	⑦	⑦	⑦	⑦	⑦	⑦	⑦	⑦	⑦L	⑦	⑦	⑦	⑦
London St Pancras d.	1455	1510	1540	1555	1610	1635	1640	1705	1710	1735	1740	1805	1810	1835	1840	1905	1910	1935	1940	2000	2010	2035	2040	2110	2130	2230	2300
Luton ✈ Parkway d.	|	1533	|	|	1631	|	|	|	1731	|	|	|	1831	|	|	|	1931	|	|	|	2031	|	|	2131	|	2251	2327
Luton d.	|	|	1602	|	|	|	1702	|	|	|	1802	|	|	|	1902	|	|	|	2002	|	|	|	2104	|	2152	|	|
Bedford d.	|	1548	1616	|	1646	|	1716	|	1746	|	1816	|	1846	|	1916	|	1946	|	2016	|	2047	|	2120	2146	2206	2313	2351
Wellingborough d.	|	1602	1629	|	1659	|	1729	|	1758	|	1829	|	1858	|	1929	|	1958	|	2029	|	2058	|	2133	2159	2219	2326	0004
Kettering d.	|	1611	1637	|	1706	|	1737	|	1806	|	1837	|	1905	|	1937	|	2005	|	2037	|	2106	|	2141	2206	2227	2333	0012
Corby a.	|	|	|	|	|	|	|	|	|	|	|	|	|	|	|	|	|	|	|	|	|	|	|	|	|	|	|
Market Harborough d.	1551	1622	|	1651	1716	|	1747	|	1815	|	1847	|	1915	|	1947	|	2015	|	2047	|	2116	|	2152	2216	2237	2343	0022
Leicester d.	1608	1638	1702	1709	1733	1744	1803	1811	1833	1841	1903	1910	1932	1945	2003	2022	2033	2041	2103	2110	2133	2141	2210	2233	2254	0004	0042
Loughborough d.	1619	1651	1712	|	1743	|	1813	|	1843	|	1913	|	1942	|	2013	|	2043	|	2113	2121	2143	2151	|	2247	2304	0014	0052
E. Midlands Parkway d.	1626	1659	1718	1724	1750	1800	1821	1825	1850	1855	1921	1925	1949	2001	2021	2039	2050	2055	2121	2129	2150	2159	2226	2258	2316	0026	0104
Nottingham a.	|	1714	|	|	1805	|	|	1836	1905	|	|	1936	2005	|	|	2051	2105	|	|	2145	2205	|	|	2311	|	0042	|
Derby a.	1647	...	1735	1744	...	1814	1836	...	...	1908t	1937	...	...	2013	2037	...	...	2107	2136	...	...	2211	2240t	...	2335	...	0119
Chesterfield d.	1712	...	...	1808	...	1837	...	...	...	1934	...	...	...	2037	...	...	...	2129	...	...	...	...	2309	...	2355	...	...
Sheffield a.	1728	...	...	1825	...	1851	...	...	...	1950	...	...	...	2051	...	...	...	2143	...	...	...	...	2323	...	0008	...	...

B – To/from Lincoln (Table **187**).
C – To/from Melton Mowbray (see panel on page 137).
D – To/from London St. Pancras (Table **170**).
E – 🚌12 Derby - Corby - London St Pancras.
F – Via Melton Mowbray (see panel on page 137).
L – To/from Leeds (Table **171**).
R – From York (d. 1750) and Doncaster (d. 1813).
S – To Doncaster (a. 0953) and York (a. 1017).
V – From York (d. 1750) and Doncaster (d. 1813⑦, 1819⑥).

Y – To Doncaster (a. 1152) and York (a. 1215).

a – Departs 2033.
b – Departs 2146.
c – Departs 2016.
d – Departs 2142.
e – Arrives 1121.
f – Arrives Kettering 9 minutes after Corby.
g – Arrives 1800.
h – Also calls at Doncaster (d. 0557).

k – Arrives 7–9 minutes earlier.
n – Arrives 0919.
p – On Ⓐ Chesterfield d.0002, Nottingham a. 0040.
r – Departs 1715.
t – Departs 7–10 minutes later.
v – On ⑥ Bedford d. 0544, Luton Airport Parkway d. 0601, London St Pancras a. 0628.

✥ – For additional Kettering - Corby services on ⑦, see next page.

EM Most trains 🍷 SHEFFIELD, DERBY and NOTTINGHAM - LEICESTER - LONDON 170

	⚒	Ⓐ	Ⓐ	⑥	⑥	Ⓐ	Ⓐ C	⑥	Ⓐ		⑥	⚒	⑥	Ⓐ	Ⓐ	⑥	Ⓐ	Ⓐ L h	⑥	⑥	Ⓐ	Ⓐ	Ⓐ	⑥	Ⓐ	⑥
Sheffield d.	...	...	...	...	0529	...	...	...	0530	...	...	...	...	...	0600	0629	...	0629	...	...	...	...	0649	...	...	...
Chesterfield d.	...	...	...	...	0541	...	...	...	0542	...	...	...	...	...	0613	0641	...	0640	...	...	...	...	0701	...	...	...
Derby d.	...	0500	0519	0521	0601	...	...	...	0604	...	...	...	0621	...	0633	0701	...	0705	...	0721	...	...	0722	...	...	...
Nottingham d.	...	|	|	|	|	0532	...	0605	|	...	0632	...	|	0630	|	|	0652	|	0705	|	0710	...	|	0730	0755	...
E. Midlands Parkway d.	...	0511	|	0535	|	0543	...	|	0617	...	0643	...	0635	0642	|	|	0704	|	|	0735	0725	...	0733	0743	0804	...
Loughborough d.	...	0518	|	0542	|	0552	...	0621	0626	...	|	...	0642	|	0653	|	|	0722	0721	0742	|	...	0741	|	|	...
Leicester d.	0445	0529	0543	0553	0624	0604	...	0632	0639	...	0700	...	0653	0659	0706	0724	0719	0736	0732	0753	0742	...	0756	0801	0819	...
Market Harborough d.	|	0543	0558	0607	|	0620	...	0646	0654	...	0714	...	|	0713	|	|	0733	|	0746	|	0757	...	|	0815	|	...
Corby d.	|	|	|	|	|	|	0635	|	|	...	|	0706	|	|	|	|	|	|	|	|	|	0802	|	|	|	0816
Kettering d.	0505	0554	0608	0617	|	0631	0645	0656	0706	...	|	0717	0726	0724	0730	|	0743	0759	0756	|	0809	0811	0817	|	|	0826
Wellingborough d.	0517	0602	0616	0624	|	0640	0654	0703	0714	...	|	...	0734	0732	0738	|	0751	0807	0803	|	|	...	0825	|	|	0834
Bedford d.	0538**v**	|	0630	0638	|	|	0709	0717	|	...	|	...	0747	|	0755	|	|	|	0817	|	0829	...	|	|	|	0847
Luton d.	|	0625	|	0653	|	|	0724	|	|	...	|	...	0803	0757	|	|	0815	|	|	|	|	...	|	|	|	0903
Luton ✈ Parkway d.	0556**v**	|	|	|	|	0704	|	0732	0739	...	|	...	|	|	0811	|	|	|	0832	|	|	...	|	|	|	|
London St Pancras a.	0619**v**	0649	0708	0718	0729	0731	0748	0756	0807	...	0814	...	0827	0823	0839	0831	0842	0856	0856	0900	0906	...	0910	0914	0926	0926

	⚒	Ⓐ	⚒ B	⑥	Ⓐ	Ⓐ L	⑥ L	⚒	⚒	⚒	⚒	Ⓐ	⑥ L	⚒	⚒	⚒		⚒	⚒	⚒	⚒	⚒	⚒	⚒	⚒	⚒	⚒
Sheffield d.	0729	...	...	...	0746	0724	0737	...	0829	...	0849	...	0834	...	0929	...	...	0949	...	...	1029	...	1049	...	...	1129	...
Chesterfield d.	0741	...	...	...	0759	0737	0750	...	0841	...	0901	...	0847	...	0941	...	...	1001	...	...	1041	...	1101	...	...	1141	...
Derby d.	0801	0736	...	0821	0819	|	|	...	0901	...	0921	...	|	...	1001	...	...	1021	...	...	1101	...	1121	...	...	1201	...
Nottingham d.	|	|	0805	|	|	0832**k**	0832**k**	...	|	0905	|	0932	0932**n**	...	|	1005	...	|	1032	...	|	1105	|	1132	...	|	1205
E. Midlands Parkway d.	|	|	|	0835	0835	0843	0843	...	|	|	0935	0943	0943	...	|	|	...	1035	1043	...	|	|	1135	1143	...	|	|
Loughborough d.	|	0754	0821	0842	0842	|	|	...	|	0921	0942	|	|	...	|	1021	...	1042	|	...	|	1121	1142	|	...	|	1221
Leicester d.	0824	0805	0832	0853	0856	0900	0900	...	0924	0932	0953	1000	1000	...	1024	1032	...	1053	1100	...	1124	1132	1153	1200	...	1224	1232
Market Harborough d.	|	0819	0846	|	|	0914	0914	...	|	0946	|	1014	1014	...	|	1046	...	|	1114	...	|	1146	|	1214	...	|	1246
Corby d.	|	|	|	|	|	|	|	0916	|	|	|	|	|	1016	|	|	...	|	|	1116	|	|	|	|	1216	|	|
Kettering d.	|	0829	0856	|	|	|	|	0926	|	0956	|	|	|	1026	|	1056	...	|	|	1126	|	1156	|	|	1226	|	1256
Wellingborough d.	|	0842	0903	|	|	|	|	0934	|	1003	|	|	|	1034	|	1103	...	|	|	1134	|	1203	|	|	1234	|	1303
Bedford d.	|	0905	0917	|	|	|	|	0947	|	1017	|	|	|	1047	|	1117	...	|	|	1147	|	1217	|	|	1247	|	1317
Luton d.	|	0919	|	|	|	|	|	1003	|	|	|	|	|	1103	|	|	...	|	|	1203	|	|	|	|	1303	|	|
Luton ✈ Parkway d.	|	|	0932	|	|	|	|	|	|	1032	|	|	|	|	|	1132	...	|	|	|	|	1232	|	|	|	|	1332
London St Pancras a.	0933	0945	0956	0959	1006	1017	1014	1026	1030	1056	1100	1114	1114	1126	1130	1156	...	1201	1214	1226	1231	1256	1300	1314	1326	1331	1357

	⚒	⚒	⚒	⚒	⚒	⚒	⚒	⚒	⚒	⚒	⚒	⚒	⚒	⚒	⚒	⚒	⚒	⚒	⚒	⚒	⑥	Ⓐ	⑥	Ⓐ	⚒	⑥	Ⓐ
Sheffield d.	1149	...	...	1229	...	1249	...	...	1329	...	1349	...	...	1429	...	1449	...	...	1529	...	1549	1549	...	...	...	1629	1629
Chesterfield d.	1201	...	...	1241	...	1301	...	...	1341	...	1401	...	...	1441	...	1501	...	...	1541	...	1601	1601	...	...	...	1641	1641
Derby d.	1221	...	...	1301	...	1321	...	...	1401	...	1421	...	...	1501	...	1521	...	...	1601	...	1621	1621	...	...	...	1701	1701
Nottingham d.	|	1232	...	|	1305	|	1332	...	|	1405	|	1432	...	|	1505	|	1532	...	|	1605	|	|	1632	1630	...	|	|
E. Midlands Parkway d.	1235	1243	...	|	|	1335	1343	...	|	|	1435	1443	...	|	|	1535	1543	...	|	|	1635	1635	1643	1641	...	|	|
Loughborough d.	1242	|	...	|	1321	1342	|	...	|	1421	1442	|	...	|	1521	1542	|	...	|	1621	1642	1642	|	|	...	|	|
Leicester d.	1253	1300	...	1324	1332	1353	1400	...	1424	1432	1453	1500	...	1524	1532	1553	1600	...	1624	1632	1653	1653	1700	1658	...	1726	1724
Market Harborough d.	|	1314	...	|	1346	|	1414	...	|	1446	|	1514	...	|	1546	|	1614	...	|	1646	|	|	1714	1712	...	|	|
Corby d.	|	|	1316	|	|	|	|	1416	|	|	|	|	1516	|	|	|	|	1616	|	|	|	|	|	|	1716	|	|
Kettering d.	|	|	1326	|	1356	|	|	1426	|	1456	|	|	1526	|	1556	|	|	1626	|	1656	|	1714	|	|	1726	|	|
Wellingborough d.	|	|	1334	|	1403	|	|	1434	|	1503	|	|	1534	|	1603	|	|	1634	|	1703	|	|	|	|	1734	|	|
Bedford d.	|	|	1347	|	1417	|	|	1447	|	1517	|	|	1547	|	1617	|	|	1647	|	1717	|	|	|	|	1747	|	|
Luton d.	|	|	1403	|	|	|	|	1503	|	|	|	|	1603	|	|	|	|	1703	|	|	|	|	|	1749	1803	|	1811
Luton ✈ Parkway d.	|	|	|	|	1431	|	|	|	|	1532	|	|	|	|	1632	|	|	|	|	1732	|	|	|	|	|	|	|
London St Pancras a.	1400	1414	1427	1430	1456	1459	1514	1527	1531	1556	1559	1614	1627	1632	1656	1700	1715	1726	1730	1756	1800	1807	1814	1815	1826	1829	1836

	⚒	⑥	Ⓐ	⚒	Ⓐ E	⑥	⚒	⚒	Ⓐ	⑥	⚒	Ⓐ	⑥	⚒	⚒	Ⓐ	⑥	⑥ V	⚒	Ⓐ	⚒	⑥	⑥	Ⓐ	Ⓐ	Ⓐ	⑥
Sheffield d.	...	1649	1649	...	...	...	1729	...	1738	1749	...	...	...	1829	...	1849	...	1849	...	...	1929	...	...	...	...	...	2029
Chesterfield d.	...	1701	1701	...	...	...	1741	...	1754	1801	...	...	...	1841	...	1901	...	1901	...	...	1941	...	...	...	...	...	2040
Derby d.	...	1721	1721	...	1636	...	1801	...	1821	1821	...	...	...	1901	...	1921	...	1921	...	...	2001	...	...	...	...	...	2100
Nottingham d.	1705	|	|	1732	|	...	|	1805	|	|	1832	...	...	|	1905	|	...	|	1932	...	|	...	2005	2002	...	2102	|
E. Midlands Parkway d.	|	1735	1735	1743	1648	...	|	|	1835	1835	1843	...	...	|	|	1935	...	1935	1943	...	|	...	2017	2015	...	2114	2113
Loughborough d.	1721	1742	1742	|	|	...	|	1821	1842	1842	|	...	...	|	1921	1942	...	1942	|	...	|	...	2025	2022	...	2122	2120
Leicester d.	1732	1753	1753	1800	|	...	1824	1832	1853	1853	1900	...	...	1924	1932	1953	...	1953	2000	...	2024	...	2036	2033	...	2133	2131
Market Harborough d.	1746	|	|	1814	|	...	|	1846	|	|	1914	...	...	|	1946	|	...	|	2014	...	|	...	2049	2047	...	2147	...
Corby d.	|	|	|	|	1751	1816	|	|	|	|	|	1856	1916	|	|	|	1950	|	|	1953	|	2043	|	|	2051	|	...
Kettering d.	1756	|	1814	|	1823**f**	1826	|	1856	|	|	|	1926**f**	1926	|	1956	|	2026**f**	2014	|	2026**f**	|	2126**f**	2058	2057	2118**f**	2157	...
Wellingborough d.	1803	|	|	|	1834	1834	|	1903	|	|	|	1934	1934	|	2003	|	2034	|	|	2034	|	2134	2107	2104	2127	2204	...
Bedford d.	1817	|	|	|	1847	1847	|	1917	|	|	|	1947	1947	|	2017	|	2047	|	|	2047	|	2147	2121	2118	2142	2218	...
Luton d.	|	|	|	|	1903	1903	|	|	|	|	|	2003	2003	|	|	|	2103	|	|	2103	|	2203	|	|	2159	2235	...
Luton ✈ Parkway d.	1832	|	|	|	|	|	|	1932	|	|	|	|	|	|	2032	|	|	|	|	|	|	|	2136	2132	|	2239	...
London St Pancras a.	1856	1900	1903	1915	1926	1926	1933	1958	2002	2000	2016	2027	2027	2033	2056	2101	2126	2103	2116	2126	2134	2226	2159	2157	2224	2305	...

	⑥	Ⓐ	⑥	⑥	Ⓐ	⚒	Ⓐ	⑥	⑥	Ⓐ	⚒		⑦	⑦	⑦	⑦	⑦	⑦	⑦	⑦	⑦	⑦ L	⑦ L	⑦	⑦	⑦	⑦
Sheffield d.	...	2049	...	...	...	2137	2201	2242	2320	2321	2337	⑦	...	...	...	...	0818	...	0925	...	1025	1035	1143	...	...	1249	...
Chesterfield d.	...	2101	...	...	...	2154	2213	2256	2332	2345	2353**p**		...	...	...	...	0831	...	0938	...	1037	1048	1155	...	...	1301	...
Derby d.	...	2121	...	...	...	|	2234	|	0006	0005	|		0650	...	0751	...	0851	...	0959	...	1057	|	1217	...	...	1322	...
Nottingham d.	...	|	2105	2132	2132	2235	—	2328	...	...	0030**p**	✥	|	0729	|	0822	|	0920	|	1030	|	1139**e**	|	...	1249	|	...
E. Midlands Parkway d.	...	2135	2117	|	|	*2323*	...	...	...	...	...		0702	0739	0805	0835	0905	0931	1013	1045	1111	1150	1234	...	1303	1336	...
Loughborough d.	...	2142	2125	2147	2147	*2331*	...	...	...	...	...		|	|	0813	0843	0912	0940	1020	1053	1119	1159	1242	...	1312	1344	...
Leicester d.	...	2153	2137	2158	2158	*2356*	...	...	...	...	...		0720	0755	0825	0855	0924	0954	1032	1108	1130	1213	1256	...	1326	1355	...
Market Harborough d.	...	|	2150	2212	2212	...	⚒	...	...	...	...		0738	0811	0841	0911	0940	1011	1045	1122	1143	1227	1310	...	1340	1408	...
Corby d.	2143	|	|	|	|	...	2243	...	...	...	...		|	|	|	|	|	|	|	|	|	|	|	1310	|	|	1410
Kettering d.	2152	|	2158	2223	2223	...	2252	...	...	...	...		0749	0821	0851	0921	0950	1022	1055	1133	1153	1238	|	1320	1351	|	1420
Wellingborough d.	...	|	2207	2230	2230	...	...	...	...	...	...		0801	0832	0902	0932	1002	1030	1102	1141	1201	1246	|	1329	1359	|	1428
Bedford d.	...	|	2221	2243	2245	...	...	...	...	...	...		0815	0845	0915	0945	1015	1045	1116	1157	1215	1302	|	1341	1415	|	1443
Luton d.	...	|	2236	2301	2302	...	...	...	...	...	...		0834	|	0935	|	1035	|	1136	|	1230	|	|	1357	|	|	1457
Luton ✈ Parkway d.	...	|	2240	|	|	...	...	...	...	...	...		|	0907	|	1007	|	1106	|	1213	|	1318	|	|	1431	|	|
London St Pancras a.	...	2301	2315	2340	2338	...	...	...	...	...	...		0915	0945	1015	1048	1117	1148	1214	1241	1254	1344	1409	1421	1459	1504	1521

	⑦	⑦	⑦	⑦	⑦	⑦	⑦	⑦ L	⑦	⑦	⑦		⑦	⑦	⑦	⑦	⑦	⑦	⑦	⑦	⑦ V	⑦	⑦	⑦	⑦	⑦	⑦
Sheffield d.	...	1343	...	...	1449	...	...	1529	1550	...	...	...	...	1649	...	...	...	1750	...	...	1847	...	1928	2026	...	2236	2330
Chesterfield d.	...	1356	...	...	1501	...	...	1542	1602	...	...	...	...	1700	...	...	...	1802	...	...	1900	...	1941	2039	...	2248	2344
Derby d.	...	1417	...	...	1522	...	...	1602	1626	...	...	...	1657	1723	...	...	1806	1826	...	...	1919	...	2003	2101	...	2323	|
Nottingham d.	1349	|	...	1452	|	1543	1552	|	|	1645	1650	...	|	|	1745	1752	|	|	1845	1852	|	1951	|	|	2121	...	0023
E. Midlands Parkway d.	1403	1431	...	1504	1536	1553	1605	1616	1637	1655	1703	...	1711	1736	1755	1804	1820	1837	1855	1905	1934	2004	2018	2113	2131	...	...
Loughborough d.	1412	1439	...	1512	1543	|	1612	1625	|	|	1711	...	1719	|	|	1812	1828	|	1902	1912	1942	2011	2027	|	2139	...	...
Leicester d.	1426	1455	...	1524	1555	1612	1624	1639	1655	1710	1723	...	1731	1754	1814	1825	1840	1854	1914	1925	1955	2023	2041	2132	2154	...	...
Market Harborough d.	1440	1508	...	1537	|	|	1637	1653	|	|	1736	...	1744	|	|	1838	1853	|	1927	1938	2008	2036	2055	2146	2208	...	...
Corby d.	|	|	1510	|	|	|	|	|	|	|	|	...	|	|	|	|	|	|	|	|	|	|	|	|	|	...	...
Kettering d.	1451	|	1520	1547	|	|	1647	1703	|	|	1746	...	1755	|	|	1848	1905	|	1937	1948	2015	2046	2106	2157	2218	...	...
Wellingborough d.	1459	|	1528	1554	|	|	1655	1712	|	|	1754	...	1802	|	|	1855	1912	|	1945	1955	2025	2053	2114	2205	2225	...	...
Bedford d.	1515	|	1543	1609	|	|	1709	1728	|	|	1808	...	1817	|	|	1909	1928	|	1959	2009	2040	2109	2131	2221	2239	...	...
Luton d.	|	|	1557	|	1642	|	|	1745	|	|	|	...	1831	|	|	|	1944	|	2015	|	2054	2123	2146	2237	2254	...	...
Luton ✈ Parkway d.	1531	|	|	1624	|	|	1725	|	|	|	1824	...	|	|	|	1924	|	|	|	2024	2058	|	|	|	|	...	...
London St Pancras a.	1557	1605	1621	1648	1709	1723	1748	1810	1802	1817	1847	...	1855	1909	1925	1948	2007	2000	2039	2049	2121	2148	2213	2303	2324	...	...

✥ – **Kettering - Corby** and v.v. additional trains on ⑦. Journey time: 10 minutes.
From Kettering at 0955, 1055, 1155, 1250, 1650, 1750, 1855, 1950, 2050, 2155.
From Corby at 0930, 1025, 1125, 1220, 1620, 1720, 1820, 1920, 2020, 2125.

← FOR OTHER NOTES SEE PREVIOUS PAGE

CORBY - MELTON MOWBRAY - DERBY

km		Ⓐ	Ⓐ D			Ⓐ D	Ⓐ E	
0	**Corby** d.	0926	1916	...	**Derby** d.	...	1636	...
23	Oakham d.	0947	1936	...	East Mids Parkway d.	...	1648	...
43	**Melton Mowbray** d.	1000	1948	...	**Melton Mowbray** d.	0600	1714	...
81	East Mids Parkway d.	1031	...	...	Oakham d.	0612	1727	...
97	**Derby** a.	1045	...	...	**Corby** a.	0635	1751	...

171 NOTTINGHAM - SHEFFIELD - HUDDERSFIELD and LEEDS

2nd class NT

NOTTINGHAM - SHEFFIELD - LEEDS

km			Ⓐ	⚒	⚒	Ⓐ	⚒	Ⓐ	⚒	Ⓐ	⑥	⚒	⚒	⚒	⚒		⚒	⚒	⑥	Ⓐ	⚒	⚒	⚒	⚒	⑥A
0	**Nottingham** .. 170 206 d.	⚒	...	...	0520	...	...	0621	*0639*	0712	0711	*0746*	0817	*0847*	0917	and	*1644*	1717	*1744*	*1747*	1817	*1847*	1917	...	2016
18	Langley Mill d.		...	...	|	...	...	0640	|	0731	0730	|	0836	|	0936	at	|	1736	*1800*	*1803*	1836	|	1936	...	2033
29	Alfreton 206 d.		...	...	|	...	...	0648	*0700*	0739	0738	*0809*	0844	*0908*	0944	the	*1705*	1744	*1808*	*1811*	1844	*1908*	1944	...	2041
45	Chesterfield ... 170 206 d.		...	...	0549	0626	...	0658	*0710*	0749	0748	*0820*	0855	*0920*	0955	same	*1715*	1755	*1818*	*1820*	1855	*1920*	1955	...	2052
64	**Sheffield** ...... 170 206 a.		...	...	0615	0646	...	0716	*0728*	0804	0811	*0837*	0914	*0937*	1014	minutes	*1737*	1814	*1834*	*1838*	1914	*1937*	2014	...	2105
64	**Sheffield** ...... 192 193 d.		0550	0606	...	0649	0706	0718	0751	0818	0818	0850	0918	0950	1018	past	1750	1818	1850	1850	1916f	1952	2018	2106	2126
70	Meadowhall ... 192 193 d.		0556	0612	...	0655	0712	0724	0757	0825	0825	0856	0924	0956	1024	each	1756	1824	1856	1856	1922f	1958	2024	2112	|
90	Barnsley d.		0610	0634	...	0712	0734	0741	0812	0842	0842	0912	0942	1012	1042	hour	1813	1842	1915	1915	1943	2013	2043	2134	|
107	Wakefield Kirkgate ..... d.		0628	0651	...	0728	0751	0758	0828	0858	0858	0928	0958	1028	1058	until	1828	1858	1932	1931	1959	2028	2059	2152	2202e
130	**Leeds** a.		0649	0729	...	0751	0826	0819	0849	0919	0919	0949	1017	1049	1118	◇	1851	1926	1951	1952	2018	2049	2120	2228	2217

	ⒶA	⚒A	Ⓐ	⑥	⑥	Ⓐ	ⒶA		⑦	⑦B	⑦	⑦	⑦	⑦	⑦	⑦	⑦	⑦	⑦A	⑦	⑦	⑦	⑦	⑦	⑦	⑦A
Nottingham .. 170 206 d.	2033	...	...	2117	...	2114	2146	⑦	...	...	...	1008	1117	1217	1317	1417	1512	1617	...	1717	1817	1917	*1943*	*2015*	2133	...
Langley Mill d.	2050	...	...	2136	...	2141	2203		...	...	...	1032	1136	1236	1336	1436	1536	1636	...	1736	1836	1936	|	*2034*	2157	...
Alfreton 206 d.	2058	...	...	2144	...	2149	2211		...	...	...	1040	1144	1244	1344	1444	1544	1644	...	1744	1844	1944	*2004*	*2042*	2205	...
Chesterfield .. 170 206 d.	2109	...	...	2155	...	2201	2222		...	...	...	1051	1154	1254	1354	1454	1556	1654	...	1754	1854	1954	*2014*	*2052*	2216	...
Sheffield ...... 170 206 a.	2123	...	...	2214	...	2220	2236		...	...	...	1110	1215	1315	1415	1515	1615	1715	...	1815	1915	2015	*2031*	*2117*	2236	...
Sheffield ...... 192 193 d.	2126	2217	2206	...	2224	...	2253		0839	1017	1039	1117	1217	1317	1417	1517	1617	1717	1734	1817	1917	2017	2039	2136	2239	2326
Meadowhall .. 192 193 d.	|	|	2212	...	2231	...	|		0845	1023	1045	1123	1223	1323	1423	1523	1623	1723	|	1823	1923	2023	2045	2142	2245	|
Barnsley d.	|	|	2234	...	|	...	|		0910	1037	1110	1137	1237	1337	1437	1537	1637	1737	|	1837	1937	2037	2110	|	2310	|
Wakefield Kirkgate ..... d.	2201e	2247e	2255	...	2320e	...	2323e		0930	1056	1130	1156	1259	1356	1456	1556	1656	1756	1806e	1856	1956	2056	2130	2228e	2330	2352e
Leeds a.	2218	2305	2330	...	2340	...	2342		1005	1116	1205	1216	1318	1416	1516	1616	1716	1816	1823	1916	2016	2116	2205	2250	0005	0007

		Ⓐ	⑥	Ⓐ	ⒶA	Ⓐ	⑥	Ⓐ	ⒶA	⑥A	⚒	⚒	⑥A	⚒	⚒	⚒		⚒	⚒	⚒	⑥	Ⓐ	⚒	⚒	⚒
Leeds d.	⚒	...	...	...	0525	...	...	0605	0634	0634	0638	0705	0738	0740	0805	0840	and	1706	1740	1806	1840	1840	1906	1945	2030
Wakefield Kirkgate ..... d.		...	...	...	0538e	0604	...	0622	0647e	0646e	0709	0725	0751e	0758	0825	0858	at	1725	1758	1825	1858	1858	1925	2002	2049
Barnsley d.		...	...	*0523*	|	0622	0622	0638	|	|	0727	0742	|	0814	0840	0914	the	1740	1814	1840	1914	1918	1940	2019	2105
Meadowhall .. 192 193 d.		...	...	*0545*	|	0643	0643	0652	|	|	0749	0755	|	0830	0854	0930	same	1754	1829	1854	1932	1935	1954	2036	2122
Sheffield ...... 192 193 a.		...	...	*0554*	0620	0653	0652	0700	0722	0722	0758	0805	0822	0840	0902	0937	minutes	1803	1838	1903	1939	1942	2002	2044	2130
Sheffield ...... 170 206 d.		0505	0554	0603	...	...	0703	0703	0724	0737	...	0808	0834	...	0905	...	past	1805	...	1905	...	...	2005	...	*2137*
Chesterfield .. 170 206 d.		0520	0619	0619	...	...	0719	0720	0737	0750	...	0824	0847	...	0922	...	each	1822	...	1922	...	...	2022	...	*2154*
Alfreton 206 d.		|	0629	0630	...	...	0729	0731	0748	0801	...	0834	0857	...	0932	...	hour	1832	...	1932	...	...	2032	...	*2205*
Langley Mill d.		|	0637	0637	...	...	0737	0739	0757	0809	...	0842	|	...	0940	...	until	1840	...	1940	...	...	2040	...	*2213*
Nottingham .. 170 206 a.		0607	0702	0701	...	...	0755	0757	0823	0825	...	0902	0919	...	1000	...	◇	1900	...	2000	...	...	2100	...	*2235*

	⚒	⚒	Ⓐ	⑥	Ⓐ	⑥		⑦	⑦	⑦	⑦A	⑦	⑦A	⑦	⑦	⑦	⑦	⑦A	⑦	⑦	⑦	⑦B	⑦	⑦	⑦	⑦
Leeds d.	2037	2137	...	...	2237	2244	⑦	...	0832	0905	0950	1002	1050	1105	1205	1305	1405	1434	1505	1605	1705	1803	1905	2022	2145	2217
Wakefield Kirkgate ..... d.	2108	2208	...	...	2310	2300e		...	0903	0922	1003e	1019	1103e	1121	1222	1322	1422	1447e	1521	1622	1722	1822	1922	2052	2200e	2248
Barnsley d.	2126	2229	...	...	2331	|		...	0924	0941	|	1038	|	1141	1241	1341	1441	|	1541	1641	1741	1841	1941	2113	|	2312
Meadowhall .. 192 193 d.	2148	2250	...	...	2352	2345		...	0945	0957	|	1053	|	1156	1254	1356	1457	|	1557	1657	1758	1857	1954	2136	2246	2336
Sheffield ...... 192 193 a.	2157	2301	...	...	0002	2358		...	0955	1004	1030	1102	1131	1203	1304	1405	1506	1517	1605	1705	1805	1904	2004	2143	2256	2343
Sheffield ...... 170 206 d.	...	...	2337	2338	...	...		0905	...	1007	1035	1103	...	1207	1306	1407	1507	...	1607	1707	1807	1907	2007	...	*2330*	...
Chesterfield .. 170 206 d.	...	...	0002	2353	...	...		0921	...	1023	1048	1120	...	1223	1323	1423	1523	...	1623	1723	1823	1923	2023	...	*2344*	...
Alfreton 206 d.	...	...	|	|	...	...		0932	...	1033	|	1130	...	1233	1333	1433	1533	...	1633	1733	1833	1933	2033	...	*2355*	...
Langley Mill d.	...	...	|	|	...	...		0940	...	1041	|	1138	...	1241	1341	1441	1541	...	1641	1741	1841	1941	2041	...	*0002*	...
Nottingham .. 170 206 a.	...	...	0040	0030	...	...		1000	...	1101	1121	1158	...	1301	1401	1501	1601	...	1701	1801	1901	1959	2101	...	*0023*	...

SHEFFIELD - HUDDERSFIELD *'The Penistone Line'*

km			Ⓐ	⚒	⚒		⚒	Ⓐ	⑥	⑥	Ⓐ	⚒	⚒	⚒	⚒	⚒		⑦	⑦	⑦	⑦	⑦	⑦	⑦	⑦
0	**Sheffield** ...... 192 193 d.	⚒	0536	0636	0736	and at	1536	1633	1636	1737	1737	1836	1937	2042	2140	2241	⑦	0939	1149	1236	1339	1539	1654	1740	1939
6	Meadowhall ... 192 193 d.		0542	0642	0742	the same	1542	1639	1642	1743	1743	1842	1943	2048	2146	2247		0945	1155	1242	1345	1545	1700	1747	1945
26	Barnsley d.		0601	0701	0801	minutes	1601	1700	1703	1804	1804	1903	2008	2108	2208	2308		1006	1216	1306	1406	1606	1715	1810	2006
38	Penistone d.		0618	0718	0818	past each hour until	1618	1717	1720	1821	1824	1920	2025	2125	2225	2325		1023	1233	1323	1423	1623	1732	1827	2023
59	**Huddersfield** a.		0654	0754t	0854t	◇	1654t	1749	1755t	1856t	1857	1957t	2100	2201t	2301t	0001t		1057	1307t	1357t	1457t	1657	1807t	1900	2057t

		⚒	⚒	⚒	⚒		⚒	Ⓐ	⑥	Ⓐ	⚒	⚒	⚒	⚒			⑦	⑦	⑦	⑦	⑦	⑦	⑦	⑦
Huddersfield d.	⚒	0606r	0706r	0806	0908r	and at	1708r	1751	1808r	1818	1913r	2013r	2113r	2213r	...	⑦	0915r	1011r	1115r	1315r	1411r	1515r	1719r	1915r
Penistone d.		0642	0742	0842	0944	the same	1744	1831	1844	1849	1950	2052	2149	2249	...		0950	1046	1150	1350	1446	1550	1755	1950
Barnsley d.		0658	0758	0858	1001	minutes past each	1801	1848	1901	1906	2007	2112	2206	2306	...		1012	1103	1207	1412	1503	1612	1812	2012
Meadowhall 192 193 d.		0722	0822	0921	1021	hour until	1822	1906	1920	1925	2028	2131	2225	2327	...		1035	1121	1230	1435	1521	1636	1836	2035
Sheffield 192 193 a.		0729	0829	0928	1030	◇	1831	1914	1930	1933	2036	2140	2236	2336	...		1044	1128	1238	1443	1528	1644	1844	2043

A – From/to London St. Pancras (Table **170**).
B – To/from Carlisle (Table **173**).
e – Wakefield Westgate.
f – Departs 6 minutes later on Ⓐ.
r – Until Oct. 7 departs 4–5 minutes later.
t – Until Oct. 7 arrives 4–5 minutes earlier.
◇ – Timings may vary by up to 2 minutes.

172 NOTTINGHAM - WORKSOP and MATLOCK

2nd class EM

NOTTINGHAM - WORKSOP *'The Robin Hood Line'*

km			⚒	⑥	Ⓐ	⑥	Ⓐ	⚒	⚒		⚒	⚒	⚒	⚒	⚒	⚒	⑥		⑦	⑦	⑦	⑦	⑦	⑦	⑦	⑦
0	**Nottingham** ..... d.	⚒	0540	0605	0605	0703	0701	0826	0926	and	1726	1755	1855	1955	2055	2205	2305	⑦	0807	0942	1128	1328	1525	1653	1829	2025
28	Mansfield .... d.		0613	0638	0638	0740	0740	0900	0957	hourly	1803	1836	1929	2036	2136	2242	2343		0840	1016	1202	1401	1558	1726	1902	2058
50	**Worksop** .... a.		0649	0719	0723	0814	0818	0933	1033	until	1837	1908	2005	2109	2208	2314	...		...	...	...	...	...	...	...	...

		⚒	⚒	⚒	⚒	⚒		⚒	⚒	⚒	⚒	⚒	⚒	⚒	⚒			⑦	⑦	⑦	⑦	⑦	⑦	⑦	⑦
Worksop d.	⚒	0550	0656	0738	0838	0938	and	1538	1642	1746	1841	1922	2022	2122	2222	...	⑦	...	...	...	...	...	...	...	...
Mansfield d.		0621	0729	0810	0910	1010	hourly	1610	1714	1818	1913	1953	2053	2153	2253	...		0855	1033	1217	1415	1612	1739	1921	2110
Nottingham a.		0656	0805	0845	0943	1043	until	1643	1746	1852	1948	2030	2125	2226	2326	...		0931	1107	1251	1450	1646	1813	1955	2144

NOTTINGHAM - DERBY - MATLOCK

km			⚒	Ⓐ	⑥	⚒	⚒	⚒		⚒	⚒	Ⓐ	⑥			⑦	⑦	⑦	⑦	⑦		⑦	⑦A
0	**Nottingham** 123 d.	⚒	...	0617	0620	0720	0820	0920		1920	2020	*2139*	*2139*	...	⑦	0926	1127	1323	1528	1722	...	1922	2124
26	**Derby** 123 a.		...	0650	0650	0750	0850	0950	and	1950	2050	*2208*	*2208*	...		0954	1155	1351	1556	1751	...	1950	2152
26	**Derby** d.		0542	0651	0652	0752	0852	0952	hourly	1952	2052	2215	2216	...		0956	1156	1356	1558	1756	...	1952	2155
34	Duffield ◧ d.		0549	0658	0659	0759	0859	0959	until	1959	2059	2222	2223	...		1003	1204	1403	1605	1803	...	1959	2202
46	Whatstandwell ◧ d.		0604	0713	0714	0814	0914	1014		2014	2114	2237	2238	...		1018	1219	1418	1620	1818	...	2014	2217
50	Cromford d.		0610	0719	0720	0820	0920	1020	★	2020	2120	2243	2244	...		1024	1224	1424	1626	1824	...	2020	2223
52	Matlock Bath ◧ d.		0612	0721	0722	0822	0922	1022		2022	2122	2245	2246	...		1026	1227	1426	1628	1826	...	2022	2225
53	**Matlock** ◧ a.		0615	0726	0727	0827	0927	1027		2027	2127	2250	2250	...		1030	1230	1430	1632	1830	...	2026	2229

		⚒		⚒	⚒	⚒	⚒		⚒	⚒	⚒	⚒			⑦	⑦		⑦	⑦	⑦		⑦	⑦
Matlock ◧ d.	⚒	0620	...	0736	0836	0936	1036		1936	2036	2140	2254	...	⑦	1038	1238	...	1441	1638	1838	...	2038	2244
Matlock Bath ◧ d.		0622	...	0738	0838	0938	1038	and	1938	2038	2142	2256	...		1040	1240	...	1443	1640	1840	...	2040	2246
Cromford d.		0625	...	0741	0841	0941	1041	hourly	1941	2041	2145	2259	...		1043	1243	...	1446	1643	1843	...	2043	2249
Whatstandwell ◧ d.		0630	...	0746	0846	0946	1046	until	1946	2046	2150	2304	...		1048	1248	...	1451	1648	1848	...	2048	2254
Duffield ◧ d.		0646	...	0803	0903	1003	1103		2003	2103	2203	2321	...		1105	1305	...	1507	1705	1905	...	2105	2311
Derby d.		0655	...	0811	0911	1011	1111	★	2011	2111	2216	2328	...		1112	1312	...	1515	1712	1912	...	2112	2318
Derby 123 d.		*0708*	...	0813	0913	1013	1113		2013	2113	*2259*	2330	...		1114	1314	...	1516	1714	1914	...	2114	...
Nottingham 123 a.		*0738*	...	0846	0942	1041	1141		2043	2141	*2327*	0002	...		1141	1341	...	1543	1744	1944	...	2141	...

A – From Liverpool Lime Street (Table **206**).

★ – Timings may vary by up to 2 minutes.

◧ – Visitor attractions near these stations:
Duffield: Ecclesbourne Valley Railway (shares National Rail station). ✆ 01629 823076.
Whatstandwell: Crich National Tramway Museum (1.6 km walk). ✆ 01773 854321.
Matlock Bath: Heights of Abraham (short walk to cable car). ✆ 01629 582365.
Matlock: Peak Rail (shares National Rail station). ✆ 01629 580381.

NT 2nd class — LEEDS - SETTLE - CARLISLE — 173

km			Ⓐ		⑥	⚒	⑦	⑦E	⚒	⚒	⑦C		⚒	⑦		⚒	⑦	⑥	Ⓐ	⚒		ⒶA	⑥A	⑦A
	London Kings Cross **180** d.	...	...	...	...	...	...	...	...	...	...	...	...	...	...	...	...	...	...	...	...	1803	1835	1835
0	**Leeds** **176** d.	...	0529	...	0619	0849	0900	...	0947	1049	1120	...	1249	1357	...	1449	1741	1750	1806	1919	...	2039	2055	2101
27	Keighley **176** d.	...	0556	...	0642	0912	0929	...	1012	1112	1142	...	1312	1421	...	1512	1802	1813	1829	1942	...	2057**s**	2114**s**	2121**s**
42	Skipton **176** d.	...	0616	...	0656	0926	0948	...	1026	1126	1155	...	1326	1435	...	1526	1815	1835	1846	2000	...	2113	2131	2139
58	Hellifield **191** d.	...	0627	...	0708	0940	1002	1015	|	1137	|	...	1340	1449	...	1537	1828	1849	1900	2015	...	...	...	...
66	**Settle** d.	...	0636	...	0715	0950	1011	1035	1044	1146	1214	...	1348	1458	...	1545	1835	1857	1908	2024	...	...	...	...
76	Horton in Ribblesdale d.	...	|	...	0724	0958	1020	1044	|	1154	|	...	1357	1507	...	1553	1844	1906	1917	2032	...	...	...	...
84	Ribblehead d.	...	0651	...	0732	1006	1028	1052	|	1202	|	...	1405	1515	...	1601	1851	1914	1925	2042	...	...	...	...
93	Dent d.	...	|	...	0741	1016	1038	1102	|	1212	|	...	1414	1525	...	1611	1901	1923	1934	...	...	...	...	...
99	Garsdale d.	...	0706	...	0747	1021	1043	1107	|	1217	|	...	1420	1530	...	1616	1907	1929	1940	...	...	...	...	...
115	Kirkby Stephen d.	...	0718	...	0759	1034	1056	1120	1122	1230	1251	...	1432	1543	...	1629	1919	1941	1952	...	...	...	...	...
132	Appleby d.	...	0732	...	0812	1047	1110	1134	1136	1243	1305	...	1445	1556	...	1641	1931	1954	2005	...	...	...	...	...
149	Langwathby d.	...	0746	...	0826	1101	1124	1148	|	1257	|	...	1459	1610	...	1655	1945	2008	2019	...	...	...	...	...
166	Armathwaite d.	...	0759	...	0839	1115	1138	1202	|	1311	|	...	1512	1624	...	1709	1959	2021	2032	...	...	...	...	...
182	**Carlisle** a.	...	0817	...	0858	1134	1155	1217	1217	1329	1347	...	1533**t**	1642	...	1728	2014	2040	2052	...	...	...	...	...

	⑥A	ⒶA	⑥	Ⓐ	⑥	Ⓐ	⑦	⑥	⑥	Ⓐ	⑦	Ⓐ		⑥	Ⓐ	⑦D	⑥	⚒	⑦	⑦B	⑥	Ⓐ	Ⓐ	⑥
Carlisle d.	...	...	...	0550	0752	0853	0925	0924	1151	1155	1259	1404	...	1421	1506	1520	1549	1618	1700	1757	1807	1814	...	...
Armathwaite d.	...	...	...	0604	0806	0907	0939	0938	1205	1209	1313	1418	...	1435	|	|	|	1632	1714	1811	1821	1828	...	...
Langwathby d.	...	...	...	0618	0819	0920	0953	0951	1218	1222	1327	1431	...	1448	|	|	|	1645	1728	1825	1834	1841	...	...
Appleby d.	...	...	...	0632	0834	0935	1007	1006	1233	1236	1341	1447	...	1504	1543	1557	1626	1701	1743	1840	1849	1856	...	...
Kirkby Stephen d.	...	...	...	0646	0847	0948	1021	1019	1246	1250	1355	1500	...	1517	1556	1610	1639	1714	1757	1854	1902	1909	...	...
Garsdale d.	...	...	...	0659	0900	1002	1034	1033	1259	1302	1408	1513	...	1530	|	|	|	1727	1810	1907	1915	1922	...	...
Dent d.	...	...	...	|	0905	1007	1040	1038	1304	1308	1414	1518	...	1535	|	|	|	1732	1816	1913	1920	1927	...	...
Ribblehead d.	...	...	0714	0714	0915	1017	1049	1047	1314	1317	1423	1529	...	1545	|	|	|	1742	1825	1922	1930	1937	2100	2100
Horton in Ribblesdale d.	...	...	0720	0720	0921	1024	1056	1054	1320	1324	1430	1536	...	1551	|	|	|	1748	1832	1929	1936	1943	2106	2106
Settle d.	...	...	0728	0728	0929	1032	1104	1102	1328	1332	1438	1545	...	1559	1634	1646	1717	1757	1841	1937	1944	1951	2114	2114
Hellifield **191** d.	...	...	0737	0737	0937	1039	1113	1109	1337	1339	1447	1553	...	1607	|	|	|	1806	1851	1950	1952	1959	2123	2123
Skipton **176** a.	0655	0655	0753	0753	0952	1054	1129	1124	1355	1356	1504	1610	...	1623	1654	1707	1738	1823	1907	...	2007	2014	2138**d**	2140
Keighley **176** a.	0709**u**	0707**u**	0808	0807	1008	1107	1140	1137	1407	1407	1516	1622	...	1637	1707	1720	1751	1837	1918	...	2018	2025	2202	*2203*
Leeds **176** a.	0733	0731	0836	0837	1035	1136	1205	1207	1436	1437	1545	1653	...	1707	1738	1746	1817	1907	1948	...	2045	2050	2234	*2234*
London Kings Cross **180** a.	0951	0957	...	...	...	...	...	...	...	...	...	...	...	...	...	...	...	...	...	...	...	...	...	...

A – (12) and 🍸 London Kings Cross - Skipton and v.v. (Table **180**).
B – May 21 - Sept 10. To Blackpool North (Table **191**).
C – From Sheffield (Table **171**).
D – To Nottingham (Table **171**).
E – May 21 - Sept 10. From Preston (Table **191**).
d – Departs 2146
s – Calls to set down only.
t – On ⑥ arrives 1527.
u – Calls to pick up only.

NT 2nd class — LEEDS - LANCASTER - HEYSHAM — 174

km	km		Ⓐ	⑥		⑥	Ⓐ		⑦	Ⓐ		⑥	⑦		Ⓐ	⑥		⑦	⑥		Ⓐ	⑦		
0	0	**Leeds** **173 176** d.	...	0554	...	0819	0818	...	0840	1017	...	1019	1100	...	1316	1350	...	1459	1646	...	1645	1720	...	...
27	27	Keighley **173 176** d.	...	0621	...	0843	0841	...	0907	1043	...	1042	1123	...	1340	1413	...	1522	1710	...	1709	1747	...	...
42	42	Skipton **173 176** d.	0541	0638	...	0900	0855	...	0926	1100	...	1100	1140	...	1401	1433	...	1538	1725	...	1725	1803	...	...
58	58	Hellifield **173** d.	0556	0652	...	0914	0910	...	0940	1114	...	1114	1154	...	1415	1448	...	1552	1740	...	1739	1818	...	...
66	66	Giggleswick d.	0607	0703	...	0925	0920	...	0952	1124	...	1125	1204	...	1425	1459	...	1602	1750	...	1750	1828	...	...
82	82	Bentham d.	0621	0717	...	0939	0934	...	1006	1139	...	1139	1218	...	1440	1513	...	1617	1805	...	1804	1842	...	...
103	103	Carnforth d.	0643	0739	...	1002	0956	...	1029	1202	...	1202	1240	...	1502	1536	...	1638	1826	...	1827	1904	...	...
113		**Lancaster** a.	0652	0750	...	1013	1008	...	1038	1211	...	1211	1251	...	1516	1545	...	1647	1838	...	1838	1912	...	...
120	112	Morecambe a.	*0736*	*0838*	...	1031	1032	...	1055	1243	...	1236	1316	...	1535	1602	...	1714	1858	...	1901	1935	...	...
127	119	**Heysham** Port a.	...	...	...	...	...	...	...	1301	...	1254	...	...	...	...	...	...	...	...	...	...	...	...

		Ⓐ	⑥		⑥	Ⓐ		⑦	⑥		Ⓐ	⑦		Ⓐ	⑥		⑦	Ⓐ		⑥	⑦		
Heysham Port d.	...	...	...	...	...	...	...	...	1315	...	1317	...	...	...	...	...	...	...	...	...	...	...	...
Morecambe d.	...	*0610*	*0736*	...	1034	1034	...	1222	1331	...	1333	1446**d**	...	1619**d**	1616	...	1723	1908	...	1909	1946	...	...
Lancaster d.	...	0707	0823	...	1049	1049	...	1248	1348	...	1349	1429**d**	...	1605**d**	1640	...	1737	1924	...	1925	2002	...	...
Carnforth d.	...	0718	0833	...	1107	1107	...	1258	1358	...	1359	1500	...	1632	1650	...	1754	1934	...	1935	2012	...	...
Bentham d.	...	0737	0852	...	1126	1126	...	1317	1418	...	1418	1520	...	1652	1709	...	1813	1953	...	1954	2032	...	...
Giggleswick d.	...	0752	0907	...	1142	1142	...	1332	1433	...	1434	1535	...	1708	1725	...	1829	2009	...	2010	2047	...	...
Hellifield **173** d.	...	0803	0919	...	1153	1153	...	1344	1446	...	1444	1546	...	1720	1736	...	1840	2020	...	2020	2058	...	...
Skipton **173 176** a.	...	0821	0936	...	1210	1210	...	1401	1503	...	1503	1603	...	1737	1753	...	1857	2038	...	2037	2115	...	...
Keighley **173 176** a.	...	0837	0951	...	1222	1223	...	1416	1520	...	1520	1617	...	1750	1807	...	1910	2050	...	2048	2126	...	...
Leeds **173 176** a.	...	0905	1020	...	1250	1254	...	1444	1548	...	1547	1646	...	1815	1836	...	1944	2115	...	2116	2154	...	...

d – Calls at Lancaster, then Morecambe.

NT 2nd class — LEEDS - HARROGATE - YORK — 175

km		⚒	Ⓐ	⑥	Ⓐ	⑥	⑥	Ⓐ	⑥	Ⓐ	⑥	Ⓐ	⚒	⚒		⚒	⚒	Ⓐ	⑥	⚒	⚒	⚒	Ⓐ
0	**Leeds** **124 188** d.		0609	0610	0631	0636	0713	0714	0741	0743	0755	0801	0829	0859	and at	1529	1559	1629	1629	1659	1713	1729	1743
29	**Harrogate** d.		0646	0647	0708	0713	0749	0751	0818	0820	0832	0838	0906	0936	the same	1606	1636	1707	1706	1736	1750	1806	1820
36	Knaresborough d.		0654	0657	0718	0723	0759	0759	0826	0829	0843	0849	0915	0947	minutes past each	1615	1647	1715	1714	1747	1801	1815	1837**t**
62	**York** **124 188** a.		0725	0726	0747	0750	0827	0832	0859	0858	...	...	0946	...	hour until	1645	...	1745	1744	...	...	1846	1904

	⚒	⚒	Ⓐ	⚒	⚒	⑥	Ⓐ		⑦	⑦	⑦	⑦		⑦	⑦	⑦		⑦	⑦	⑦		⑦	⑦	⑦
Leeds **124 188** d.	1759	1829	1859	1930	2029	2120	2129	...		0954	1054	1154	...	1254	1354	1454	...	1554	1654	1754	...	1855	1954	2119
Harrogate d.	1836	1906	1936	2007	2106	2157	2206	...		1048**r**	1130	1233	...	1333	1430	1533	...	1633	1733	1833	...	1933	2033	2156
Knaresborough d.	1847	1916	1947	2016	2115	2208	2216	...		1057	1141	1245	...	1347	1445**t**	1544	...	1644	1745	1844	...	1945	2044	2205
York **124 188** a.	...	1945	...	2045	2144	...	...	...		1125	1204	1310	...	1413	1509	1609	...	1707	1810	1908	...	2008	2107	...

	⚒	⑥	Ⓐ	⑥	Ⓐ	Ⓐ	⑥	Ⓐ	Ⓐ	⑥	⑥	Ⓐ	⑥	Ⓐ	⚒	⚒	⚒		⚒	⚒	⚒	⚒	Ⓐ
York **124 188** d.		...	...	0652	0649	...	...	...	0754	0756	...	...	0843	0847	0911	...	1011	and at the same	...	1611	...	1704	1729
Knaresborough d.		0647	0657	0720	0716	0742	0750	0757	0819	0821	0850	0855	0908	0911	0936	1005	1036	minutes	1605	1636	1706	1734	1757
Harrogate d.		0656	0707	0729	0740**s**	0751	0759	0806	0829	0830	0859	0904	0918	0921	0945	1014	1045	past each	1614	1645	1715	1744	1807
Leeds **124 188** a.		0733	0746	0806	0816	0830	0836	0840	0908	0907	0936	0937	0955	0957	1022	1052	1122	hour until	1652	1722	1752	1822	1841

	⑥	⑥	Ⓐ	Ⓐ	⑥	Ⓐ	⚒	⚒	⚒	⑥	Ⓐ	⑦	⑦	⑦	⑦	⑦	⑦	⑦	⑦	⑦		⑦	⑦	⑦
York **124 188** d.	1728	...	...	1805	1812	...	1913	2011	2112	2157	2211		1114	1217	1320	1418	1517	1617	1718	1817	...	1918	2017	2127
Knaresborough d.	1756	1808	1810	1834	1837	1906	1938	2036	2137	2222	2237		1142	1242	1344	1442	1542	1641	1743	1842	...	1942	2042	2151
Harrogate d.	1805	1817	1824	1843	1846	1915	1947	2045	2146	2236	2248		1153	1253	1354	1452	1553	1652	1753	1853	...	1952	2053	2202
Leeds **124 188** a.	1842	1854	1901	1924	1923	1952	2024	2123	2223	2313	2326		1228	1330	1430	1529	1630	1730	1830	1930	...	2029	2130	2239

Additional trains	⚒A	⑦A	⑦	Ⓐ	⑥	⑥	⑦	Ⓐ	
Leeds d.	1959	2034	2230	2238	2233	2322	2323	2332	...
Harrogate a.	2025	2100	2307	2317	2311	0001	2359	0011	...

Additional trains	⚒	Ⓐ	ⒶA	⑥A	Ⓐ	⑦	⑦	⑦A	⑦
Harrogate d.	0605	0625	0734	0811	0815	0953	1053	1707	2312
Leeds a.	0644	0701	0806	0838	0852	1031	1129	1733	2349

A – (12) and 🍸 Harrogate - Leeds - London Kings Cross and v.v. (Table **180**).
r – Arrives 1031.
s – Arrives 0726.
t – Arrives 7 – 8 minutes earlier.

NT 2nd class — WEST YORKSHIRE LOCAL SERVICES — 176

BRADFORD FORSTER SQUARE - SKIPTON

Journey: ± 38 minutes *30 km*

From Bradford Forster Square: Trains call at **Keighley** ± 22 minutes later.

Ⓐ: 0603, 0638, 0715, 0741, 0811, 0841, 0911 and every 30 minutes until 1541, 1612, 1638, 1711, 1738, 1816, 1841, 1908, 1936, 2009, 2109, 2209, 2309.

⑥: 0609, 0709, 0811, 0842, 0911 and every 30 minutes until 1541, 1612, 1638, 1711, 1738, 1811, 1841, 1908, 1936, 2009, 2112, 2202, 2309.

⑦: 1055, 1255, 1455, 1655, 1855, 2055, 2255.

From Skipton: Trains call at **Keighley** ± 14 minutes later.

Ⓐ: 0556, 0626, 0700, 0724, 0800, 0831, 0900 and every 30 minutes until 1330, 1402, 1430, 1458, 1530, 1558, 1630, 1700, 1724, 1800, 1830, 1900, 1931, 1954, 2054, 2154.

⑥: 0600, 0704, 0730, 0800, 0831, 0900 and every 30 minutes until 1330, 1401, 1430, 1458, 1530, 1600, 1630, 1700, 1728, 1800, 1830, 1900, 1930, 1954, 2057, 2155.

⑦: 0932, 1142, 1342, 1542, 1742, 1942, 2142.

Table continues on next page ▶ ▶ ▶

176 WEST YORKSHIRE local services

2nd class NT

Stopping trains. For faster trains see Table 180.

LEEDS - DONCASTER

Journey: ± 50 minutes *48 km*

From Leeds:
Ⓐ: 0620, 0721, 0821 and hourly until 1621, 1657, 1721, 1821, 1921, 2022, 2121, 2240.
⑥: 0621, 0721, 0821 and hourly until 1921, 2022, 2121, 2219.
⑦: 1021, 1221, 1421, 1621, 1821, 2021, 2121.

From Doncaster:
Ⓐ: 0626, 0708, 0726, 0756, 0826 and hourly until 1826, 1922, 2026, 2127, 2227.
⑥: 0626, 0726, 0827, 0926 and hourly until 1826, 1922, 2026, 2122, 2226.
⑦: 0912, 1112, 1312, 1512, 1712, 1927, 2152.

See also Tables 173/174

LEEDS - SKIPTON

Journey: ± 45 minutes *42 km*

From Leeds: Trains call at **Keighley** ± 24 minutes later.
Ⓐ: 0529, 0616, 0657, 0725, 0751, 0825, 0856, 0926, 0956 and every 30 minutes until 1726, 1740, 1756, 1826, 1856, 1926, 1956, 2022, 2055, 2126, 2156, 2226, 2256, 2319.
⑥: 0554, 0650, 0750, 0825, 0856, 0926, 0956 and every 30 minutes until 1956, 2026, 2100, 2126, 2204, 2226, 2256, 2319.
⑦: 0840, 0900, 1009, 1109, 1216 and hourly until 2116, 2220, 2320.

From Skipton: Trains call at **Keighley** ± 13 minutes later.
Ⓐ: 0545, 0614, 0640, 0706, 0718, 0730, 0745, 0813, 0837, 0917, 0947 and every 30 minutes until 1617, 1647, 1715, 1747, 1817, 1847, 1915, 1947, 2022, 2045, 2117, 2217.
⑥: 0545, 0644, 0745, 0816, 0847, 0917, 0947, and every 30 minutes until 1917, 1947, 2022, 2050, 2117, 2149, 2217.
⑦: 0832, 0912, 1012 and hourly until 1612, 1714, 1812, 1922, 2012, 2122, 2212, 2312.

For Leeds - Bradford Interchange see Table 190

LEEDS - BRADFORD FORSTER SQUARE

Journey: ± 21 minutes *22 km*

From Leeds:
Ⓐ: 0645, 0739, 0810, 0832, 0841, 0910, 0942, 1012, 1040, and every 30 minutes until 1540, 1607, 1638, 1709, 1736, 1810, 1837, 1908, 2101.
⑥: 0710, 0810, 0841, 0910, 0939, 1010, 1040, and every 30 minutes until 1540, 1607, 1638, 1708, 1736, 1810, 1837, 1910, 2158.
⑦: 0831, 0941 and hourly until 1641, 1745, 1841, 1942, 2041, 2141, 2241.

From Bradford Forster Square:
Ⓐ: 0558, 0630, 0654, 0757, 0826, 0902, 0930, 1000 and every 30 minutes until 1600, 1630, 1701, 1730, 1800, 1830, 1900, 1930.
⑥: 0600, 0658, 0733, 0758, 0826, 0901, 0930, 1000 and every 30 minutes until 1600, 1630, 1701, 1730, 1800, 1831, 1900, 1930.
⑦: 0901, 1003, 1113 and hourly until 1713, 1815, 1913, 2013, 2113, 2213, 2313.

LEEDS - ILKLEY

Journey: ± 30 minutes *26 km*

From Leeds:
Ⓐ: 0600, 0634, 0704, 0729, 0733, 0758, 0835, 0902 and every 30 minutes until 1602, 1632, 1702, 1716, 1732, 1746, 1802, 1832, 1902, 1933, 2007, 2107, 2207, 2315.
⑥: 0602, 0702, 0758, 0832, 0902, 0932, 1004, 1032 and every 30 minutes until 1832, 1903, 1933, 2007, 2107, 2208, 2315.
⑦: 0905 and hourly until 2005, 2108, 2215, 2310.

From Ilkley:
Ⓐ: 0602, 0633, 0710, 0737, 0756, 0805, 0816, 0838, 0910, 0938 and at the same minutes past each hour until 1438, 1510, 1536, 1612, 1638, 1712, 1743, 1804, 1812, 1842, 1910, 1938, 2028, 2118, 2218, 2318.
⑥: 0610, 0710, 0810, 0838, 0910, 0940, 1010, 1038 and at the same minutes past each hour until 1538, 1612, 1638, 1712, 1738, 1812, 1842, 1910, 1938, 2028, 2118, 2224, 2318.
⑦: 0905 and hourly until 2105, 2215, 2315.

HUDDERSFIELD - WAKEFIELD WESTGATE

Journey: ± 38 minutes *25 km*

From Huddersfield: Trains call at **Wakefield Kirkgate** ± 30 minutes later.
Ⓐ: 0531, 0631, 0735, 0831, 0931 and hourly until 1931, 2031, 2135.
⑥: 0640, 0735, 0831, 0931, and hourly until 1931, 2031, 2135.

From Wakefield Westgate: Trains call at **Wakefield Kirkgate** ± 5 minutes later.
Ⓐ: 0643, 0744, 0844, and hourly until 1844, 1946, 2050, 2142, 2248.
⑥: 0730, 0844, 0944, and hourly until 1844, 1944, 2050, 2144, 2248.

BRADFORD FORSTER SQUARE - ILKLEY

Journey: ± 31 minutes *22 km*

From Bradford Forster Square:
Ⓐ: 0615, 0642 0711, 0745, 0816, 0846 and every 30 minutes until 1246, 1315, 1346, 1416, 1446, 1516, 1546, 1616, 1643, 1716, 1748, 1811, 1846, 1941 2038, 2140, 2240, 2326.
⑥: 0615, 0716, 0816, 0846 and every 30 minutes until 1716, 1743, 1816, 1846, 1946, 2038, 2140, 2240, 2320.
⑦: 1027, 1227, 1426, 1627, 1827, 2027, 2237.

From Ilkley:
Ⓐ: 0617, 0652, 0720, 0748, 0824, 0852, 0921, 0951 and every 30 minutes until 1651, 1720, 1751, 1821, 1851, 1921, 2009, 2043, 2143, 2243.
⑥: 0621, 0721, 0821, 0852, 0921, 0951 and every 30 minutes until 1851, 1921, 2009, 2048, 2143, 2243.
⑦: 0925, 1125, 1325, 1525, 1725, 1925, 2130.

177 HULL - BRIDLINGTON - SCARBOROUGH

2nd class NT

km		⚒	⚒	⚒	⚒A		⚒A	⚒	⑥A		ⒶA	⚒	ⒶA	⑥A		⑦	⑦A	⑦A	⑦A		⑦A	⑦A	⑦A
0	**Hull** △ d.	0653	0814	0947	1114	...	1314	1444	1614	...	1618	1738	1915	1922	...	0925	1025	1205	1405	...	1605	1800	1859
13	Beverley △ d.	0707	0828	1001	1128	...	1328	1458	1628	...	1632	1752	1929	1936	...	0939	1039	1219	1419	...	1619	1814	1913
31	Driffield △ d.	0724	0842	1015	1140	...	1340	1512	1643	...	1647	1809	1943	1951	...	0956	1054	1234	1434	...	1634	1826	1928
50	**Bridlington** △ a.	0739	0857	1030	1156	...	1354	1527	1658	...	1702	1825	1958	2006	...	1011	1109	1249	1449	...	1649	1839	1946
50	**Bridlington** d.	0741	0900	1038	1206	...	1406	1535	1704	...	1704	1835	2003	2019	...	1014	1111	1255	1455	...	1655	1844	...
71	Filey d.	0803	0922	1100	1228	...	1428	1557	1726	...	1726	1857	2025	2041	...	1036	1133	1317	1517	...	1717	1906	...
87	**Scarborough** a.	0821	0940	1118	1246	...	1446	1615	1744	...	1744	1915	2043	2059	...	1054	1151	1335	1535	...	1735	1924	...

		⚒	⚒	⚒	⚒A		⚒A	⚒	⚒A		⚒		⑥	Ⓐ		⑦A	⑦A	⑦A	⑦A	⑦A	⑦A	⑦A	⑦
Scarborough d.	...	0650	0902	1000	1128	...	1328	1457	1625	...	1757	...	1940	2004	...	...	1111	1206	1406	1606	...	1806	1937
Filey d.	...	0705	0917	1015	1143	...	1343	1512	1640	...	1812	...	1955	2019	...	...	1126	1221	1421	1621	...	1821	1952
Bridlington a.	...	0727	0939	1037	1205	...	1405	1534	1702	...	1834	...	2017	2041	...	...	1148	1243	1443	1643	...	1843	2014
Bridlington △ d.	...	0730	0941	1041	1211	...	1411	1536	1705	...	1841	...	2023	2044	...	0951	1150	1246	1446	1646	1746	1856	2016
Driffield △ d.	...	0747	0957	1057	1224	...	1424	1552	1719	...	1857	...	2039	2100	...	1007	1206	1259	1459	1659	1759	1912	2029
Beverley △ d.	...	0806	1012	1112	1237	...	1437	1607	1731	...	1912	...	2054	2115	...	1022	1221	1312	1512	1712	1812	1929	2042
Hull △ a.	...	0822	1028	1128	1253	...	1454	1623	1748	...	1930	...	2110	2131	...	1038	1237	1328	1528	1728	1828	1946	2058

A – From/to Sheffield (Table **192**).
B – From Doncaster (Table **192**).
△ – All trains Hull - Bridlington and v.v.:
From Hull on ⚒ at 0556, 0620, 0653, 0714, 0752, 0814, 0916 **A**, 0947, 1014 **A**, 1044, 1114 **A**, 1140, 1215 **A**, 1244, 1314 **A**, 1344, 1414 **A**, 1444, 1514 **A**, 1544, 1614⑥**A**, 1618Ⓐ**A**, 1644, 1714 **A**, 1738, 1814 **A**, 1915Ⓐ**A**, 1922⑥**A**, 2015⑥**A**, 2148 **A**; on ⑦ at 0900, 0925, 1025 **A**, 1125 **B**, 1205 **A**, 1255, 1405 **A**, 1500 **A**, 1605 **A**, 1655 **A**, 1715, 1800 **A**, 1859 **A**.
From Bridlington on ⚒ at 0644, 0712 **A**, 0730, 0808 **A**, 0905 **A**, 0941, 1011 **A**, 1041 and at the same minutes past each hour until 1511 **A**, 1536, 1611 **A**, 1641, 1705⑥**A**, 1706Ⓐ**A**, 1736, 1815, 1841, 1908Ⓐ**A**, 1911⑥**A**, 2023⑥, 2044Ⓐ, 2128⑥ **A**, 2128Ⓐ, 2242; on ⑦ at 0951 **A**, 1150 **A**, 1246 **A**, 1346 **A**, 1446 **A**, 1545 **A**, 1646 **A**, 1720, 1746 **A**, 1816, 1856 **A**, 1956, 2016.

178 HULL - YORK

2nd class NT

km		⚒	⑦	Ⓐ	⑥	⚒	⑥	⑦	⚒	⑥	Ⓐ	⑦	⑥	⑦	Ⓐ	⑥	Ⓐ	⑦	Ⓐ	⑥	⑥	Ⓐ	⑦	⚒	⑦	⑦	⑥
0	**Hull** .... **181 189** d.	0707	0854	0902	0903	1012	1107	1146	1204	1308	1315	1317	1415	1420	1422	1503	1503	1606	1610	1610	1711	1717	1725	1918	1925	2030	2102
50	Selby .. **181 189** d.	0748	0928	0942	0939	1049	1141	1220	1239	1349	1358	1351	1449	1454	1458	1537	1541	1640	1649	1649	1800	1804	1759	1954	2000	2104	2137
84	**York** a.	0822	0952	1016	1011	1120	1205	1252	1304	1422	1427	1417	1522	1526	1528	1602	1606	1706	1713	1715	1823	1828	1825	2025	2025	2128	2159

	Ⓐ	⑥	⚒	⑥	Ⓐ	⑦	⑥	⚒	⑦	⚒	⚒	⑦	⑥	⑦	Ⓐ	⑦	⑥	Ⓐ	⑦	⚒	⑥	Ⓐ	⑦	⑥	⑦	⑥	Ⓐ
York d.	0730	0740	0843	0951	1019	1040	1047	1145	1205	1247	1344	1354	1447	1452	1502	1606	1606	1611	1714	1725	1809	1844	1916	1950	2150	2212	2229
Selby .. **181 189** d.	0750	0759	0906	1009	1039	1058	1106	1204	1224	1306	1408	1423	1506	1511	1521	1635	1632	1637	1733	1750	1838	1913	1935	2008	2210	2230	2247
Hull .... **181 189** a.	0846	0856	0948	1053	1123	1136	1153	1251	1306	1351	1451	1504	1551	1552	1602	1716	1722	1728	1814	1834	1927	2002	2016	2048	2250	2316	2335

179 LINCOLN - SHEFFIELD

2nd class NT

km		⚒	⚒	⚒	⚒		⚒	⑥	⚒		⚒	⑥	⚒	⚒	⚒	⚒	⑥	⚒	⚒	⚒	⚒	⑦	⑦	⑦	⑦	⑦	⑦
0	**Lincoln** d.	...	...	0700	0825		1125	...	1227		1523	...	1625	1722	...	1825	...	1943	2027	2127	...	...	1515	1715	1915	2108	...
26	Gainsborough ‡ d.	...	...	0721	0845	and	1144	1211f	1246	and	1543	1617f	1646	1741	...	1844	1932f	2004	2048	2148	...	...	1536	1736	1936	2129	...
40	Retford d.	...	0701	0739	0901	hourly	1200	1231	1302	hourly	1559	1636	1701	1757	1814	1900	1954	2019	2103	2203	2245	1450	1551	1751	1951	2144	2224
52	Worksop ▽ d.	0630	0713	0751	0913	until	1211	1243	1314	until	1611	1648	1713	1809	1825	1912	2005	2031	2115	2215	2258	1502	1603	1803	2003	2156	2236
78	**Sheffield** ▽ a.	0703	0749	0825	0948	▲	1248	1317	1348	▲	1648	1723	1748	1834	1858	1953b	2040	2105	2146	2250	2332	1535	1635	1835	2035	2228	2308

	⚒	⚒	⚒	⚒	⑥	⚒		⚒	⑥	⚒		⚒	⑥	⚒	⚒	⚒		⚒	⚒	⚒	⑦	⑦	⑦	⑦	⑦	⑦
Sheffield ▽ d.	0539	0546	0644	0730	0803	0844		1144	1203	1244		1544	1601	1644	1723	1744	...	1844	1949	2142	1342	1355	1543	1743	1932	2106
Worksop ▽ d.	0603	0623	0715	0801	0834	0915	and	1215	1237	1315	and	1615	1637	1716	1754	1815	...	1915	2020	2214	1403	1426	1614	1814	2003	2137
Retford d.	0613	0637	0725	0811	0845	0925	hourly	1225	1247	1325	hourly	1625	1646	1727	1808	1825	...	1925	2030	2229	1413	1438	1624	1824	2013	2148
Gainsborough ‡ d.	0628	...	0740	0825	0902f	0943	until	1240	1304f	1340	until	1640	1702f	1742	...	1840	...	1940	2045	...	1428	...	1639	1839	2028	...
Lincoln a.	0656	...	0807	0853	...	1007	▲	1306	...	1406	▲	1707	...	1806	...	1906	...	2007	2110	...	1454	...	1703	1903	2053	...

b – Arrives 1946 on ⑥.
f – Gainsborough Central.
‡ – Gainsborough Lea Road.
▲ – Timings may vary ± 4 minutes.
▽ – Additional journeys Worksop - Sheffield and v.v: **From Worksop** at 0813Ⓐ, 2126⑥, 2130Ⓐ and 2328⚒. **From Sheffield** at 2045⚒ and 2244⚒.

For additional services see Tables **124**, **181**, **182**, **183**, **184** and **188**.

Ⓐ

km		Ⓐ	Ⓐ	Ⓐ	Ⓐ	Ⓐ	Ⓐ	Ⓐ	Ⓐ	Ⓐ	Ⓐ	Ⓐ	Ⓐ	Ⓐ	Ⓐ	Ⓐ	Ⓐ	Ⓐ	Ⓐ	Ⓐ	Ⓐ	Ⓐ	Ⓐ	Ⓐ	Ⓐ	Ⓐ
				A																		A				
0	**London** Kings Cross d.	...	...	...	0550	0615	0630	0700	0705	0708	0730	0735	0800	0806	0830	0835	0900	0903	0908	0930	0935	1000	1003	1008	1030	1035
44	Stevenage d.	...	...	...	0611	0635	0650	|	|	0728	|	0755	|	|	|	0855	|	|	0929	|	0955	|	|	1029	|	1055
123	Peterborough d.	...	...	...	0642	0706	0721	0746	0752	0759	0816	|	|	0853	0916	|	0946	0952	1000	1016	|	|	1051	1101	1116	|
170	Grantham d.	...	...	...	0702	0726	0740	|	|	0819	|	0840	|	|	|	0940	|	|	1021	|	1040	|	|	1121	|	1140
193	Newark North Gate d.	...	...	...	0714	0738	|	|	|	0831	0844	|	|	|	0944	|	|	|	1033	1044	|	|	|	1135	1144	|
223	Retford d.	...	...	...	0729	0754	|	|	|	0846	|	|	|	|	|	|	|	|	1049	|	|	|	|	...	|	|
251	Doncaster d.	...	0615	...	0745	0811	0813	|	0842	0901	0910	0914	|	0942	1010	1014	|	1043	1105	1111	1114	|	1142	...	1210	1214
283	Wakefield Westgate a.	...	|	...	0802	|	0832	|	0900	|	|	0931	|	1000	|	1031	|	1100	|	|	1131	|	1200	...	|	1231
299	**Leeds** a.	...	|	0710	0818	|	0848	|	0917	|	|	0946	|	1015	|	1048	|	1116	|	|	1147	|	1216	...	|	1248
303	**York** d.	...	0639	0737	...	0835	...	0855	...	0925	0935	...	0953	...	1035	...	1055	...	1130	1136	...	1154	...	...	1235	...
351	Northallerton d.	...	|	|	...	0855	...	|	...	...	|	...	|	...	1055	...	|	...	...	|	...	|	...	...	1255	...
374	Darlington d.	...	0707	0806	...	0908	...	0923	...	...	1004	...	1022	...	1108	...	1123	...	...	1205	...	1222	...	...	1308	...
409	Durham d.	...	0724	0824	...	0925	...	|	...	...	1022	...	|	...	1125	...	|	...	...	1223	...	|	...	...	1325	...
432	**Newcastle** a.	0622	0739	0838	...	0940	...	0951	...	...	1037	...	1050	...	1142	...	1151	...	...	1239	...	1250	...	...	1342	...
488	Alnmouth a.	0653	0808	|	...	|	...	|	...	...	1107	...	|	...	...	...	|	...	...	1310	...	|	...	...	|	...
540	Berwick upon Tweed a.	0717	0832	0929	...	|	...	1038	...	...	|	...	1136	...	...	...	1238	...	...	|	...	1337	...	...	1429	...
632	**Edinburgh** Waverley a.	0807	0921	1020	...	1112	...	1120	...	...	1209	...	1219	...	...	...	1320	...	...	1413	...	1420	...	...	1514	...

	Ⓐ	Ⓐ	Ⓐ	Ⓐ	Ⓐ	Ⓐ	Ⓐ	Ⓐ	Ⓐ	Ⓐ	Ⓐ	Ⓐ	Ⓐ	Ⓐ	Ⓐ	Ⓐ	Ⓐ	Ⓐ	Ⓐ	Ⓐ	Ⓐ	Ⓐ	Ⓐ	Ⓐ	Ⓐ	Ⓐ	Ⓐ
						B										A					K			C		A	
London Kings Cross d.	1100	1105	1108	1130	1135	1200	1203	1208	1230	1235	1300	1305	1308	1330	1335	1400	1405	1408	1430	1435	1500	1505	1508	1530	1535	1600	1606
Stevenage d.	|	|	1129	|	1156	|	|	1229	|	1255	|	|	1329	|	1355	|	|	1428	|	1455	|	|	1529	|	1555	|	|
Peterborough d.	|	1152	1159	1216	|	|	1251	1300	1316	|	1346	1352	1400	1416	|	|	1451	1500	1516	|	|	1551	1600	1616	|	|	1654
Grantham d.	|	|	1219	|	1241	|	|	1322	|	1340	|	|	1421	|	1440	|	|	1520	|	1540	|	|	1621	|	1641	|	|
Newark North Gate d.	|	|	1231	1244	|	|	|	1334	1344	|	|	|	1434	1444	|	|	|	1534	1544	|	|	|	1633	1644	|	|	|
Retford d.	|	|	1246	|	|	|	|	...	|	|	|	|	1449	|	|	|	|	...	|	|	|	|	1649	|	|	|	|
Doncaster d.	|	1242	1305	1310	1314	|	1342	...	1410	1414	|	1442	1504	1511	1514	|	1542	...	1610	1614	|	1641	1705	1710	1714	|	1745
Wakefield Westgate a.	|	1300	|	|	1332	|	1400	...	|	1431	|	1459	|	|	1531	|	1559	...	|	1631	|	1659	|	|	1731	|	1805
Leeds a.	|	1316	|	|	1348	|	1416	...	|	1448	|	1516	|	|	1548	|	1616	...	|	1648	|	1716	|	|	1747	|	1820
York d.	1253	...	1329	1336	...	1355	...	...	1435	...	1454	...	1530	1535	...	1555	...	...	1635	...	1654	...	1729	1736	...	1754	...
Northallerton d.	|	...	...	|	...	|	...	...	1455	...	|	...	...	1555	...	|	...	...	1655	...	|	...	...	1756	...	|	...
Darlington d.	1321	...	...	1406	...	1423	...	...	1508	...	1522	...	...	1608	...	1623	...	...	1708	...	1722	...	...	1809	...	1823	...
Durham d.	|	...	...	1423	...	|	...	...	1525	...	|	...	...	1625	...	|	...	...	1725	...	|	...	...	1826	...	|	...
Newcastle a.	1349	...	...	1439	...	1452	...	...	1540	...	1550	...	...	1640	...	1651	...	...	1740	...	1750	...	...	1841	...	1851	...
Alnmouth a.	|	...	...	1509	...	|	...	...	...	...	|	...	...	1710	...	|	...	...	...	...	|	...	...	1909	...	|	...
Berwick upon Tweed a.	|	...	...	|	...	1539	...	...	...	...	1638	...	...	|	...	1739	...	...	...	...	1837	...	...	|	...	1939	...
Edinburgh Waverley a.	1517	...	...	1613	...	1622	...	...	...	...	1721	...	...	1813	...	1822	...	...	...	...	1920	...	...	2013	...	2022	...

	Ⓐ	Ⓐ	Ⓐ	Ⓐ	Ⓐ	Ⓐ	Ⓐ	Ⓐ	Ⓐ	Ⓐ	Ⓐ	Ⓐ	Ⓐ	Ⓐ	Ⓐ	Ⓐ	Ⓐ	Ⓐ	Ⓐ	Ⓐ	Ⓐ	Ⓐ	Ⓐ	Ⓐ	Ⓐ	Ⓐ	Ⓐ
						D		E			F			G			H			J							
London Kings Cross d.	1609	1630	1633	1700	1703	1719	1730	1733	1749	1800	1803	1819	1830	1833	1900	1903	1906	1930	1933	2000	2005	2035	2100	2135	2200	2257	2330
Stevenage d.	1630	|	1653	|	|	|	|	1755	|	|	|	|	|	1853	|	|	1928	|	1953	|	|	2055	2121	2157	|	|	|
Peterborough d.	1701	1716	|	|	1750	1808	1817	|	1837	|	1851	1907	1918	|	|	1953	2000	2016	|	|	2051	2126	2151	2228	2247	2345s	0017s
Grantham d.	1722	|	1740	|	|	1829	|	1842	1906	|	|	1927	|	1942	|	|	2021	|	2040	|	|	2146	|	2249	2309	0007s	0045s
Newark North Gate d.	1736	1744	|	|	|	1841	1846	|	|	|	1922	|	1946	|	|	|	2036	2044	|	|	2120	2159	2219	2302	2321	0019s	0057s
Retford d.	...	|	1802	|	|	|	|	|	1928	|	|	|	|	2005	|	|	...	|	|	|	|	|	|	2319	|	|	|
Doncaster d.	...	1810	1818	|	1841	1910	|	1915	1944	|	1950	|	2012	2021	|	2041	...	2110	2114	|	2145	2223	2248	2335	2352	0055s	0124s
Wakefield Westgate a.	...	|	1835	|	1859	...	|	1933	2002	|	2007	|	|	2038	|	2100	...	|	2131	|	2207	2240	|	2352	|	|	|
Leeds a.	...	|	1851	|	1917	...	|	1948	2020	|	2021	|	|	2053	|	2117	...	|	2149	|	2223	2257	|	0008	|	|	0234
York d.	...	1836	...	1853	...	...	1929	...	...	1951	...	2020	2036	...	2053	...	...	2134	...	2153	...	...	2313	...	0042	0130	...
Northallerton d.	...	1857	...	|	...	...	|	...	...	|	...	2040	|	...	|	...	...	2154	...	|	...	...	2344	...	0110s	...	...
Darlington d.	...	1910	...	1922	...	...	1957	...	...	2019	...	2053	2105	...	2121	...	...	2207	...	2221	...	...	2357	...	0124s	...	...
Durham d.	...	1927	...	|	...	...	2014	...	...	|	...	2110	2122	...	|	...	...	2224	...	2239	...	...	0014	...	0143s	...	...
Newcastle a.	...	1942	...	1950	...	...	2029	...	...	2047	...	2125	2137	...	2149	...	...	2239	...	2254	...	...	0041	...	0214	...	...
Alnmouth a.	...	|	...	|	...	...	2058	...	...	|	...	...	2209	...	|	...	...	2311f	...	...	...	...	...	...	...	...	...
Berwick upon Tweed a.	...	|	...	2037	...	...	|	...	...	2135	...	...	|	...	2238	...	...	2336f	...	...	...	...	...	...	...	...	...
Edinburgh Waverley a.	...	2112	...	2122	...	...	2208	...	...	2220	...	...	2315	...	2328	...	...	0026f	...	...	...	...	...	...	...	...	...

⑥

	⑥	⑥	⑥	⑥	⑥	⑥	⑥	⑥	⑥	⑥	⑥	⑥	⑥	⑥	⑥	⑥	⑥	⑥	⑥	⑥	⑥	⑥	⑥	⑥	⑥	⑥
			A														A							B		
London Kings Cross d.	...	...	...	0615	0630	0700	0705	0730	0800	0803	0830	0833	0900	0905	0930	0935	1000	1003	1030	1100	1103	1130	1134	1200	1203	1230
Stevenage d.	...	...	...	0635	0650	0720	|	|	|	|	|	0854	|	|	|	0955	|	|	|	|	|	|	1154	|	|	|
Peterborough d.	...	...	...	0706	0721	|	0753	0816	|	0849	0916	|	|	0951	1016	|	|	1050	1116	|	1149	1216	|	|	1250	1316
Grantham d.	...	...	...	0726	0741	|	0813	|	|	|	|	0941	|	1012	|	1040	|	|	|	|	1209	|	1240	|	|	|
Newark North Gate d.	...	...	...	0738	|	|	0825	|	|	0917	0944	|	|	1024	|	|	|	1118	1146	|	1221	|	|	|	1319	1344
Retford d.	...	...	...	0754	|	|	|	0855	|	|	|	|	|	|	1054	|	|	|	|	|	|	1254	|	|	|	|
Doncaster d.	...	0610	...	0810	0814	|	|	0912	|	0943	1010	1015	|	|	1110	1114	|	1144	1211	|	|	1311	1317	|	1344	1410
Wakefield Westgate a.	...	|	...	|	0831	|	0901	|	|	1000	|	1032	|	1102	|	1132	|	1201	|	|	1304	|	1334	|	1401	|
Leeds a.	...	|	0710	|	0849	|	0918	|	|	1018	|	1049	|	1119	|	1148	|	1218	|	|	1320	|	1350	|	1418	|
York d.	...	0634	0737	0835	...	0855	...	0935	0953	...	1036	...	1053	...	1135	...	1154	...	1235	1253	...	1336	...	1354	...	1435
Northallerton d.	...	0654	|	0853	...	|	...	|	|	...	1055	...	|	...	|	...	|	...	1255	|	...	|	...	|	...	1455
Darlington d.	...	0707	0806	0908	...	0923	...	1005	1024	...	1108	...	1121	...	1204	...	1222	...	1308	1321	...	1404	...	1423	...	1508
Durham d.	...	0724	0824	0925	...	|	...	1022	|	...	1126	...	|	...	1222	...	|	...	1325	|	...	1422	...	|	...	1525
Newcastle a.	0618	0739	0837	0940	...	0952	...	1037	1052	...	1141	...	1149	...	1237	...	1251	...	1340	1349	...	1437	...	1451	...	1540
Alnmouth a.	0648	0808	|	|	...	|	...	1105	|	...	|	...	|	...	1306	...	|	...	|	|	...	1505	...	|	...	|
Berwick upon Tweed a.	0712	0832	0931	|	...	1039	...	|	1139	...	|	...	1239	...	|	...	1339	...	|	1439	...	|	...	1539	...	|
Edinburgh Waverley a.	0803	0920	1024	1110	...	1127	...	1212	1227	...	1310	...	1326	...	1413	...	1425	...	1510	1527	...	1610	...	1624	...	1712

	⑥	⑥	⑥	⑥	⑥	⑥	⑥	⑥	⑥	⑥	⑥	⑥	⑥	⑥	⑥	⑥	⑥	⑥	⑥	⑥	⑥	⑥	⑥	⑥	⑥	⑥	⑥
						A														D		E			H		F
London Kings Cross d.	1234	1300	1305	1330	1335	1400	1403	1430	1434	1500	1503	1530	1535	1600	1603	1630	1633	1700	1703	1710	1730	1735	1800	1803	1808	1830	1835
Stevenage d.	1255	|	|	|	1355	|	|	|	1455	|	|	|	1555	|	|	|	|	|	1724	|	|	|	|	|	1829	|	|
Peterborough d.	|	|	1352	1416	|	|	1450	1516	|	|	1551	1616	|	|	1651	1716	1720	|	1754	1800	1816	1823	|	1850	1900	1916	1924
Grantham d.	1341	1403	1412	|	1440	|	|	|	1540	|	1612	|	1640	|	|	|	1740	|	1814	1821	|	|	|	|	1921	|	|
Newark North Gate d.	|	|	1424	|	|	|	1518	1544	|	|	1624	|	|	|	1719	1744	|	|	1826	|	1844	|	|	1918	1933	1944	|
Retford d.	|	|	|	1455	|	|	|	|	|	|	|	1654	|	|	|	|	|	|	|	|	|	|	|	1933	...	|	|
Doncaster d.	1416	|	|	1512	1517	|	1543	1611	1616	|	|	1710	1716	|	1744	1809	1815	|	1851	1854	1911	1915	|	1950	...	2011	2015
Wakefield Westgate a.	1433	|	1502	|	1534	|	1602	|	1633	|	1702	|	1733	|	1801	|	1832	|	1908	...	|	1932	|	2007	...	|	2032
Leeds a.	1450	|	1519	|	1550	|	1618	|	1650	|	1719	|	1749	|	1818	|	1849	|	1924	...	|	1948	|	2023	...	|	2047
York d.	...	1456	...	1536	...	1553	...	1635	...	1654	...	1735	...	1752	...	1837	...	1853	...	...	1936	...	1954	...	...	2035	...
Northallerton d.	...	|	...	|	...	|	...	1655	...	|	...	|	...	|	...	1857	...	|	...	...	|	...	|	...	...	2055	...
Darlington d.	...	1524	...	1605	...	1622	...	1708	...	1722	...	1803	...	1821	...	1910	...	1922	...	...	2005	...	2022	...	...	2108	...
Durham a.	...	|	...	1622	...	|	...	1725	...	|	...	1820	...	|	...	1927	...	|	...	...	2022	...	|	...	...	2125	...
Newcastle a.	...	1552	...	1637	...	1650	...	1740	...	1750	...	1835	...	1849	...	1942	...	1950	...	...	2039	...	2050	...	...	2142	...
Alnmouth a.	...	|	...	1705	...	|	...	|	...	|	...	1906	...	|	...	|	...	|	...	...	...	...	2124	...	...	...	...
Berwick upon Tweed a.	...	1641	...	|	...	1739	...	|	...	1843	...	|	...	1939	...	|	...	2037	...	...	...	...	2149	...	...	...	...
Edinburgh Waverley a.	...	1728	...	1810	...	1825	...	1911	...	1928	...	2012	...	2024	...	2114	...	2122	...	...	...	...	2237	...	...	...	...

A – To / from Aberdeen (Table **222**).
B – To / from Inverness (Table **223**).
C – To / from Glasgow Central (Table **220**).
D – To / from Hull (Table **181**).
E – To / from Harrogate (Table **175**).

F – To / from Skipton (Table **173**).
G – To / from Bradford Forster Square (Table **182**).
H – To / from Lincoln (Table **186**).
J – To / from Sunderland (Table **210**).
K – To / from Stirling (Table **222**).

f – ⑤ only.
s – Calls to set down only.
u – Calls to pick up only.

For additional services see Tables **124, 181, 182, 183, 184** and **188**.

Block 1

| | ⑥ | ⑥ | ⑥ | ⑥ | ⑥ | ⑥ | ⑥ | ⑥ | ⑦ | ⑦ | ⑦ | ⑦ | ⑦ | ⑦ | ⑦ | ⑦ | ⑦ | ⑦ | ⑦ | ⑦ | ⑦ | ⑦ | ⑦ | ⑦ | ⑦ | ⑦ |
		G							⑦					A									B			
London Kings Cross . d.	1900	1904	1930	2000	2005	2030	2100	2200			0845	0900	0903	0930	1000	1003	1010	1030	1100	1103	1120	1130	1200	1203	1220
Stevenage d.		1950										0923								1123				
Peterborough d.	1957	2021	2048	2054	2116	2148	2247				0954	1016		1050	1056	1116		1154		1216		1250	1309
Grantham d.		2041		2115	2136		2307				1014			1117		1214	1225		1310
Newark North Gate d.		2053	2116		2148		2319				1026			1129	1144	1226		1322
Retford d.					2203		2334					1055				1255
Doncaster d.	2046	2118	2141	2150	2219		2349			0937	1051	1111		1140	1155	1211	1251	1311	1347	1358
Wakefield Westgate a.	2103	2134		2207	2236		0007				1108		1212		1308		1404
Leeds a.	2119	2150		2225	2252		0023			0830	1126		1229		1325		1421
York d.	2053		2206			2258			0900	1001	1037	1049	1135	1152	1208	1235	1251	1317	1335	1352	1423
Northallerton d.					2319				0921					1255		1337
Darlington d.	2121		2235			2332			0935	1029	1105	1117	1203	1221	1238	1308	1319	1350	1403	1421	1451
Durham d.			2252			2350			0953	1046	1123		1220	1256	1325	1407	1420	1508
Newcastle a.	2151		2309			0007		0845	0915	1006	1101	1138	1145	1235	1249	1311	1340	1347	1422	1435	1449	1525
Alnmouth a.								0914	1042		1309		1508
Berwick upon Tweed a.								0939	0959	1107	1148	1233	1337	1434	1537
Edinburgh Waverley a.								1028	1045	1158	1232	1310	1318	1419	1420	1445	1508	1518	1558	1618	1620

Block 2

| | ⑦ | ⑦ | ⑦ | ⑦ | ⑦ | ⑦ | ⑦ | ⑦ | ⑦ | ⑦ | ⑦ | ⑦ | ⑦ | ⑦ | ⑦ | ⑦ | ⑦ | ⑦ | ⑦ | ⑦ | ⑦ | ⑦ | ⑦ | ⑦ |
			A								C			D				E		F				
London Kings Cross d.	1230	1233	1300	1303	1330	1400	1403	1430	1500	1503	1530	1600	1605	1630	1635	1700	1703	1730	1735	1800	1803	1827	1830	1835	1900	1903
Stevenage d.		1255		1323			1523			1655			1755				1855
Peterborough d.	1316		1354	1416		1452	1516		1554	1617		1653	1716		1751		1817		1846	1851		1950
Grantham d.		1342		1414		1512		1614	1638		1713	1740	1826	1838	1843		1941
Newark North Gate d.	1344		1426		1524	1544		1626		1725	1744	1819	1838		1920		1945		2018
Retford d.			1455		1550	1611		1642			1803			2004
Doncaster d.	1411	1420	1451	1511				1658	1712	1751	1810	1820	1844	1903	1912	1916	1948	2010	2020	2043
Wakefield Westgate a.		1437	1508		1607		1715		1810	1839	1901	1933	2005	2037	2100
Leeds a.		1454	1525		1625		1731		1828	1856	1918	1951	2023	2052	2118
York d.	1435		1453		1535	1552		1635	1652		1736	1749		1835		1851		1938		1959		2026	2036		2053
Northallerton d.	1455					1655				1855			2056
Darlington d.	1508		1521		1603	1621		1708	1720		1805	1817	1908	1919	2006	2027	2054	2109	2122
Durham d.	1525				1620		1725		1823		1925		2023		2112	2126
Newcastle a.	1540		1549		1635	1649		1740	1748		1838	1845	1940	1947	2038	2055	2129	2141	2150
Alnmouth a.				1703			1906			2110		2223
Berwick upon Tweed a.			1636		1737		1835		1936		2035		2143		2228	2248
Edinburgh Waverley a.	1709		1720		1809	1820		1908	1920		2013	2020	2114	2120	2218	2228	2313	2340

Block 3

| | ⑦ | ⑦ | ⑦ | ⑦ | ⑦ | ⑦ | ⑦ | ⑦ | ⑦ | ⑦ | ⑦ | ⑦ | | | Ⓐ | Ⓐ | Ⓐ | Ⓐ | | Ⓐ | Ⓐ | Ⓐ |
	H																					G
London Kings Cross d.	1908	1930	1935	2000	2005	2035	2100	2105	2135	2200	2204	2235		Edinburgh Waverley d.								
Stevenage d.	1929		1955			2055			2156					Berwick upon Tweed d.								
Peterborough d.	2001	2018	2026	2046	2052	2126	2146	2152	2227	2247	2251	2323s		Alnmouth d.								
Grantham d.	2022		2046			2146			2248		2315	2344s		Newcastle d.				0445			0525	
Newark North Gate d.	2034	2047			2158		2220	2300		2327	2355s		Durham d.				0500			0539	
Retford d.				2132			2252	2316				Darlington d.				0518			0558	
Doncaster d.		2115	2119		2148	2223		2309	2340	2343	0002	0024s		Northallerton d.				0529			0609	
Wakefield Westgate a.		2136		2206	2239		2329	2357			York d.				0600			0631	
Leeds a.		2152		2222	2257			0014		0130		York d.		0505	0530			0605		0640 0700
York d.		2140		2157			2302		0035		Leeds d.		0518	0544			0618		0653 0713
Northallerton d.					2338		0106s		Wakefield Westgate d.								
Darlington d.		2219	2239		2351		0120s		Doncaster d.	0507	0536	0603	0624		0636	0654 0712
Durham d.		2237	2256		0008		0138s		Retford d.			0551			0651		
Newcastle a.		2308	2327		0039		0210		Newark North Gate d.	0536	0606	0629	0647		0707		0737
Alnmouth a.								Grantham d.	0548	0618	0641	0700		0720 0726		
Berwick upon Tweed a.								Peterborough d.	0610	0639	0701	0721		0741 0750		
Edinburgh Waverley a.								Stevenage d.								
								London Kings Cross a.	0700	0729	0752	0812		0833	0843	0850 0859

Block 4

| | Ⓐ | Ⓐ | Ⓐ | Ⓐ | Ⓐ | Ⓐ | Ⓐ | Ⓐ | Ⓐ | Ⓐ | Ⓐ | Ⓐ | Ⓐ | Ⓐ | Ⓐ | Ⓐ | Ⓐ | Ⓐ | Ⓐ | Ⓐ |
	J	H			D	F		E					K			C				
Edinburgh Waverley d.				0540				0548	0626			0655	0730		0800	0830			0900	0930
Berwick upon Tweed d.				0600				0634	0710				0812			0912				1012
Alnmouth d.				0621				0655				0900								
Newcastle d.	0559		0630	0655	0704			0729	0757		0825	0859		0930	1000		1026	1059
Durham d.	0612		0644	0708		←		0742			0838		0943		1039	
Darlington d.	0632		0703	0731		0731	0801	0828		0857	0928		1001	1029		1058	1128
Northallerton d.			0715	→						0908			1109	
York d.	0701		0737			0802	0831	0857		0931	0958	1003	1031	1059		1131	1157
Leeds d.		0715			0740	0817		0845	0916		0945		1015		1045		1115		1145
Wakefield Westgate d.		0728			0753	0830		0858	0929		0958		1028		1058		1128		1158
Doncaster d.		0746		0757	0813		0848	0855	0917	0947	0955	1017	1025	1046	1058	1117	1146	1155	1217
Retford d.					0836					1039	
Newark North Gate d.		0757		0822	0838		0919		1019		1054	1121		1154	1219
Grantham d.		0818		0835		0921		1018		1106	1118		1207	1218
Peterborough d.	0812	0827		0843	0902	0907		0950	1009	1051	1108	1128	1152	1209	1228	1250	1307
Stevenage d.		0858	0903			1009		1102		1157	1202		1258	1303
London Kings Cross a.	0906	0924	0929	0937		0940	0955	0957	1002	1035	1042	1051	1100	1128	1142	1151	1159	1223	1228	1242	1250	1300	1324	1328	1341	1349	1358

Block 5

| | Ⓐ | Ⓐ | Ⓐ | Ⓐ | Ⓐ | Ⓐ | Ⓐ | Ⓐ | Ⓐ | Ⓐ | Ⓐ | Ⓐ | Ⓐ | Ⓐ | Ⓐ | Ⓐ | Ⓐ | Ⓐ | Ⓐ | Ⓐ |
			A					B			A									
Edinburgh Waverley d.			1000	1030				1130			1200	1230			1300	1330			1400	1430
Berwick upon Tweed d.				1112					1312			1412				1512	
Alnmouth d.			1100					1300				1500	
Newcastle d.			1130	1200			1225	1257		1330	1400		1426	1500		1533	1559
Durham d.			1143				1238		1343		1439		1546	
Darlington d.			1201	1229			1257	1328		1401	1429		1458	1527		1605	1628
Northallerton d.							1308				1509	
York d.	1203		1231	1259			1331	1357		1402		1431	1459		1531	1557		1602		1635	1657
Leeds d.		1215			1245	1315		1345	1415		1445	1515		1545	1615		1645		1715
Wakefield Westgate d.		1228			1258	1328		1358	1428		1458	1528		1558	1628		1658		1728
Doncaster d.	1225	1246	1255		1317		1346	1354	1417	1425	1446	1455	1517		1546	1554	1617	1625	1646	1658	1717		1746
Retford d.	1240					1441			1641		1800
Newark North Gate d.	1255		1319		1354		1417	1456		1519		1552	1620		1656		1721		1754
Grantham d.	1307	1318		1406	1418		1508	1517		1604	1619		1708	1718		1806	1824
Peterborough d.	1328		1351		1409	1427		1452		1509	1529		1608	1625		1650		1709	1730		1751		1809	1828
Stevenage d.	1358	1403			1457	1502		1558	1602		1656	1703		1800	1805		1858	1908
London Kings Cross a.	1425	1428	1442	1451	1459	1524	1527	1544	1551	1600	1625	1628	1642	1651	1659	1721	1728	1742	1753	1800	1827	1830	1844	1850	1902	1925	1935

← **FOR NOTES SEE PREVIOUS PAGE**

180a 🚌 PETERBOROUGH - KINGS LYNN 🚌
First Excel service **X1**

From **Peterborough** railway station : Journey 75 minutes. Buses call at **Wisbech** bus station ± 39 minutes later.

Ⓐ : 0704, 0734, 0809 and every 30 minutes until 1109, 1149, 1219 and every 30 minutes until 1449, 1520, 1550, 1620, 1650, 1720, 1755, 1833, 1903, 1933, 2033, 2233.

⑥ : 0739, 0809 and every 30 minutes until 1109, 1149, 1219 and every 30 minutes until 1719, 1754, 1833, 1903, 1933, 2033, 2233.

⑦ : 0909, 1009 and hourly until 2009.

Table **180a** continues on the next page.

For additional services see Tables **124, 181, 182, 183, 184** and **188**.

	Ⓐ	Ⓐ	Ⓐ	Ⓐ	Ⓐ	Ⓐ	Ⓐ	Ⓐ	Ⓐ	Ⓐ	Ⓐ	Ⓐ A	Ⓐ	Ⓐ	Ⓐ	Ⓐ A	⑤		⑥	⑥	⑥	⑥	⑥	⑥	⑥	⑥ D	⑥	⑥ F
Edinburgh Waverley . d.	...	1530	...	...	...	1600	1630	...	...	1700	...	1731	...	1830	1935	2100	2201	⑥	...	...	...	...	...	...	...	...	...	...
Berwick upon Tweed.. d.	...	1612	...	...	...	|	1712	...	...	|	...	1818	...	1916	2017	2148	2247		...	...	...	...	...	...	...	...	...	...
Alnmouth d.	...	|	...	...	...	|	|	...	...	1800	...	|	...	1939	2040	2211	2310		...	...	...	...	...	...	...	...	...	...
Newcastle d.	1625	1659	...	...	...	1726	1759	...	...	1830	...	1906	...	2016	2115	2246	2356		...	...	0445	...	0559	...	...	...	0630	...
Durham d.	1638	|	...	...	...	1739	|	...	...	1843	...	|	...	2029	2128	2300	...		...	...	0500	...	0612	...	...	...	0643	...
Darlington d.	1657	1727	...	...	...	1758	1828	...	...	1901	...	1935	...	2048	2147	2322	...		...	...	0518	...	0632	...	...	...	0702	...
Northallerton d.	1709	|	...	...	...	1809	|	...	...	|	...	|	...	|	2158	2348s	...		...	...	0529	...	|	...	...	...	0713	...
York d.	1731	1757	...	1802	...	1831	1857	...	...	1931	...	2005	...	2117	2220	0018	...		...	...	0600	...	0701	...	...	...	0735	...
Leeds d.	|	|	1745	|	1815	|	|	1845	1916	|	1945	|	2045	|	|	0045	...		0505	0530	|	0605	|	0640	0705	...	|	0738
Wakefield Westgate d.	|	|	1758	|	1828	|	|	1858	1929	|	1958	|	2058	|	|	...	...		0518	0543	|	0618	|	0653	0718	...	|	|
Doncaster d.	1755	|	1817	1826	1846	1855	|	1917	1947	1955	2017	2028	2116	2140	2243	...	...		0536	0601	0624	0636	0725	0711	0736	0745	0758	0811
Retford d.	|	|	|	1840	|	|	|	|	|	|	|	|	2131	|	|	...	...		0550	|	|	0650	|	|	|	|	|	|
Newark North Gate d.	1819	|	|	1855	|	1918	|	|	|	2019	|	|	|	2204	2307	...	...		0605	0625	|	0705	|	|	0800	|	0822	|
Grantham d.	|	|	|	1907	1918	|	|	|	2018	|	|	|	2154	2216	2319	...	...		0617	0639	|	0717	|	|	0812	0818	|	0843
Peterborough d.	1849	|	1908	1929	|	1951	|	2008	|	2049	2105	2117	2215	2237	2347	...	...		0639	0701	0713	0738	0814	|	0833	0840	0851	|
Stevenage d.	|	|	|	1959	2004	2020	2026	|	2103	2118	|	2150	2246	2306	0028s	...	...		0708	|	|	0807	|	|	0902	|	|	|
London Kings Cross . a.	1943	1950	2000	2025	2028	2046	2052	2059	2128	2142	2156	2213	2311	2332	0103	...	...		0734	0753	0804	0835	0906	0844	0928	0935	0942	0951

	⑥	⑥ G	⑥	⑥	⑥ E	⑥ H	⑥		⑥	⑥	⑥	⑥	⑥ C	⑥	⑥	⑥	⑥	⑥	⑥	⑥	⑥	⑥ A	⑥	⑥	⑥	⑥ B	⑥	⑥
Edinburgh Waverley . d.	...	...	...	0620	...	...	...	...	0655	0730	...	...	0800	0830	...	...	0900	0930	...	...	1000	1030	...	...	1100	1130	...	...
Berwick upon Tweed.. d.	...	...	...	0706	...	...	...	...	|	0813	...	...	|	0913	...	...	|	1013	...	...	|	1113	...	...	|	|	...	...
Alnmouth d.	...	...	...	0727	...	...	...	...	|	|	...	...	0900	|	...	...	|	|	...	...	1100	|	...	...	|	|	...	...
Newcastle d.	0655	...	0725	0801	...	...	...	...	0825	0900	...	...	0930	1000	...	...	1026	1100	...	...	1130	1200	...	...	1226	1301	...	...
Durham d.	0708	...	0738	|	...	...	...	...	0838	|	...	...	0943	|	...	...	1039	|	...	...	1143	|	...	...	1239	|	...	...
Darlington d.	0727	...	0757	0829	...	...	...	...	0857	0929	...	...	1001	1029	...	...	1057	1129	...	...	1201	1229	...	...	1257	1329	...	...
Northallerton d.	|	...	0808	|	...	...	...	...	0908	|	...	...	|	|	...	...	1109	|	...	...	|	|	...	...	1309	|	...	...
York d.	0757	...	0830	0859	...	...	...	...	0930	0959	...	...	1031	1059	...	...	1131	1159	...	...	1231	1259	...	...	1331	1400	...	...
Leeds d.	|	0805	|	|	0845	...	0915	...	|	|	0945	1015	|	|	1045	1115	|	|	1145	1215	|	|	1245	1315	|	|	1345	1415
Wakefield Westgate d.	|	0818	|	|	0858	...	0928	...	|	|	0958	1028	|	|	1058	1128	|	|	1158	1228	|	|	1258	1328	|	|	1358	1428
Doncaster d.	0820	0838	0854	|	0919	...	0946	...	0953	|	|	1046	1055	|	|	1146	1156	|	1219	1246	1255	|	1320	1346	1355	|	1421	1446
Retford d.	|	0854	|	|	|	...	|	...	1007	|	|	|	|	|	|	|	1210	|	|	|	|	|	|	|	1409	|	|	|
Newark North Gate d.	|	0909	0918	|	|	0954	1009	...	|	|	|	1109	1119	|	|	1209	|	|	1244	|	1319	|	1345	|	|	|	1446	|
Grantham d.	|	|	0930	|	|	1006	1021	...	1030	|	|	1121	|	|	|	1221	|	|	1256	1316	|	|	|	1417	|	|	|	1517
Peterborough d.	|	0938	0953	1006	|	1029	1043	...	1052	|	1101	|	1151	|	1201	1243	1251	|	1322	|	1351	|	1415	|	1451	|	1515	|
Stevenage d.	|	|	|	|	|	1101	|	...	|	|	|	1208	|	|	|	1317	|	|	|	1403	|	|	|	1503	|	|	|	1602
London Kings Cross . a.	0954	1030	1044	1057	1101	1126	1136	...	1143	1152	1155	1235	1242	1253	1256	1342	1345	1354	1416	1428	1442	1452	1512	1530	1542	1555	1607	1628

	⑥	⑥ A	⑥	⑥	⑥	⑥	⑥	⑥	⑥		⑥	⑥	⑥	⑥	⑥	⑥	⑥	⑥	⑥	⑥	⑥	⑥	⑥	⑥ A	⑥	⑥	⑥	⑥
Edinburgh Waverley . d.	1200	1230	...	...	1300	1330	...	...	1400	...	1430	...	...	1500	1530	...	...	1600	1630	...	...	1700	...	1730	...	1830	1900	2000
Berwick upon Tweed.. d.	|	1313	...	...	|	1412	...	...	|	...	1512	...	...	|	1612	...	...	|	1712	...	...	|	...	1816	...	1912	1945	2043
Alnmouth d.	1300	|	...	...	|	|	...	...	1500	...	|	...	...	|	|	...	...	|	|	...	...	1800	...	|	...	|	2008	2109
Newcastle d.	1330	1400	...	...	1426	1500	...	...	1530	...	1559	...	...	1626	1659	...	...	1726	1759	...	...	1830	...	1904	...	1959	2043	2143
Durham d.	1343	|	...	...	1439	|	...	...	1544	...	|	...	...	1639	|	...	...	1739	|	...	...	1843	...	|	...	...	2056	...
Darlington d.	1401	1429	...	...	1457	1529	...	...	1603	...	1628	...	...	1657	1728	...	...	1757	1828	...	...	1902	...	1933	...	...	2115	...
Northallerton d.	|	|	...	...	1509	|	...	...	|	...	|	...	...	1709	|	...	...	1809	|	...	...	|	...	|	...	...	2128	...
York d.	1431	1459	...	...	1531	1558	...	...	1633	...	1657	...	...	1731	1758	...	...	1831	1857	...	...	1931	...	2003	...	...	2150	...
Leeds d.	|	|	1445	1515	|	|	1545	1615	|	...	|	1645	1715	|	|	1745	1815	|	|	1845	1915	|	1945	|	2015	...	|	...
Wakefield Westgate d.	|	|	1458	1528	|	|	1558	1628	|	...	|	1658	1728	|	|	1758	1828	|	|	1858	1928	|	1958	|	2028	...	|	...
Doncaster d.	1455	|	1520	1546	1555	|	1618	1646	1656	...	|	1719	1746	1755	|	1818	1846	1855	|	1919	1946	1955	2017	2026	2046	...	2215	...
Retford d.	|	|	|	|	1609	|	|	|	|	...	|	|	|	1809	|	|	|	|	|	|	|	|	|	|	2100	...	...	...
Newark North Gate d.	1519	|	1545	|	|	|	1643	|	1720	...	|	1747	|	|	|	1844	|	1919	|	1949	2010	|	|	|	2115	...	...	...
Grantham d.	|	|	|	1617	|	|	|	1716	|	...	|	|	1818	|	|	1856	1918	|	|	|	2022	2027	|	2058	2127	...	...	...
Peterborough d.	1551	|	1615	|	1651	|	1712	|	1751	...	|	1816	|	1851	|	1919	|	1951	|	2019	2043	2051	2105	2121	2151	...	...	...
Stevenage d.	|	|	|	1702	|	|	|	1803	|	...	|	|	1904	|	|	|	2002	2020	|	|	2117	|	|	2151	|	...	...	...
London Kings Cross . a.	1642	1656	1713	1728	1744	1751	1805	1828	1842	...	1852	1911	1931	1942	1952	2013	2029	2046	2051	2113	2142	2145	2156	2218	2242	...	...	...

		⑦	⑦	⑦	⑦	⑦	⑦	⑦	⑦	⑦	⑦	⑦	⑦	⑦	⑦	⑦	⑦	⑦	⑦	⑦	⑦	⑦	⑦	⑦	⑦	⑦ A	⑦	⑦
Edinburgh Waverley . d.	⑦	...	...	...	...	...	...	...	...	...	...	...	0900	0930	...	1000	1030	...	1100	1120	1130	...	...	1200	1220	1230	...	...
Berwick upon Tweed.. d.		...	...	...	...	...	...	...	...	...	...	...	|	1013	...	|	1112	...	|	|	1213	...	...	|	|	1313	...	...
Alnmouth d.		...	...	...	...	...	...	...	...	...	...	...	|	|	...	1100	|	...	|	|	|	...	...	1300	|	|	...	...
Newcastle d.		...	...	0755	...	...	0855	...	...	0925	1000	...	1029	1100	...	1130	1200	...	1226	1251	1301	...	1315	1330	1352	1400	...	1420
Durham d.		...	...	0809	...	...	0908	...	...	0938	|	...	1042	|	...	1143	|	...	1239	1304	|	...	1328	1343	1405	|	...	1433
Darlington d.		...	...	0827	...	...	0928	...	...	0957	1028	...	1101	1130	...	1202	1229	...	1258	1323	1329	...	1348	1401	|	1430	...	1453
Northallerton d.		...	...	|	...	...	|	...	...	1008	|	...	1112	|	...	|	|	...	1310	|	|	...	1401	|	|	|	...	|
York d.		0800	...	0858	...	...	0958	...	...	1031	1058	...	1134	1159	...	1232	1258	...	1332	1356	1400	...	1424	1431	1449	1459	...	1523
Leeds d.		|	0805	|	0843	0905	|	0940	1005	|	|	1105	|	|	1205	|	|	1305	|	|	|	1405	|	|	|	|	1505	|
Wakefield Westgate d.		|	0818	|	0856	0918	|	0953	1018	|	|	1118	|	|	1218	|	|	1318	|	|	|	1418	|	|	|	|	1518	|
Doncaster d.		0823	0836	|	0920	0937	|	|	1036	1055	|	1136	1157	|	1236	1255	|	1336	1355	|	|	1436	1448	1455	|	|	1537	1546
Retford d.		|	0850	|	|	|	|	1019	1051	|	|	|	1211	|	|	|	|	|	1409	|	|	|	|	|	|	|	|	|
Newark North Gate d.		|	0905	|	|	1000	|	1039	1106	1119	|	1200	|	|	1259	1319	|	1400	|	|	|	1459	|	1519	|	|	1600	1609
Grantham d.		|	0917	|	|	1012	|	|	1119	|	|	1212	|	|	1311	|	|	1412	|	|	|	1511	|	|	1540	|	1612	|
Peterborough d.		0911	0941	1005	1011	1034	1104	1108	1141	1151	1204	1234	1251	|	1333	1351	|	1434	1451	|	|	1533	1540	1551	|	|	1634	1642
Stevenage d.		0940	|	|	|	1105	|	|	|	|	|	1308	|	|	|	|	|	1504	|	|	|	|	|	|	|	|	1705	|
London Kings Cross . a.		1007	1033	1057	1108	1132	1156	1159	1233	1242	1255	1333	1342	1352	1424	1442	1450	1532	1542	1550	1556	1624	1632	1642	1646	1652	1732	1735

	⑦	⑦	⑦ B	⑦	⑦	⑦ A	⑦	⑦	⑦	⑦	⑦	⑦	⑦ E	⑦	⑦	⑦	⑦ A	⑦	⑦	⑦	⑦	⑦	⑦	⑦	⑦	⑦	⑦	⑦
Edinburgh Waverley . d.	1300	1319	1330	...	1400	1430	...	...	1447	...	1500	1530	...	...	1600	1620	1630	...	...	1700	1730	...	1800	...	1830	1900	2000	2100
Berwick upon Tweed.. d.	1343	|	1413	...	|	|	...	...	1532	...	|	1612	...	...	|	|	1713	...	...	|	1816	...	|	...	1912	1946	2047	2147
Alnmouth d.	|	|	|	...	1501	|	...	...	|	...	|	|	...	...	1700	|	|	...	...	|	|	...	1900	...	|	|	2110	2210
Newcastle d.	1431	1445	1500	...	1531	1558	...	1552	1621	...	1627	1701	...	...	1730	1750	1800	...	...	1829	1903	...	1930	...	2001	2033	2145	2239
Durham d.	|	1459	|	...	1544	|	...	|	1634	...	1640	|	...	...	1743	|	|	...	...	1842	|	...	1944	...	|	2046	2159	...
Darlington d.	1500	1517	1531	...	1603	|	...	1630	1653	...	1659	1729	...	...	1801	1817	1830	...	...	1901	1932	...	2003	...	2029	2105	2219	...
Northallerton d.	|	1532	|	...	|	|	...	1641	|	...	|	|	...	...	|	1829	|	...	...	1912	|	...	|	...	|	|	2232	...
York d.	1530	1557	1601	...	1633	1659	...	1707	1722	...	1731	1759	...	...	1831	1853	1859	...	...	1933	2001	...	2032	...	2059	2135	2306	...
Leeds d.	|	|	|	1616	|	|	1645	|	|	1716	|	|	1745	1815	|	|	|	1845	1916	|	|	1945	|	2045	|	|	2336	...
Wakefield Westgate d.	|	|	|	1629	|	|	1659	|	|	1729	|	|	1759	1828	|	|	|	1859	1929	|	|	1959	|	2058	|	|	...	...
Doncaster d.	1553	|	|	1647	1656	|	1720	1736	|	1747	1757	|	1819	1846	1855	|	|	1920	1947	1957	|	2020	2055	2116	2125	2158	...	...
Retford d.	1608	|	|	|	|	|	|	|	|	1801	|	|	|	|	|	|	|	|	2001	|	|	|	|	2130	|	|	...	...
Newark North Gate d.	|	|	|	|	1719	|	1745	|	1803	|	|	|	1844	|	1919	|	|	1945	|	2021	|	2046	2119	|	2149	2221	...	...
Grantham d.	|	|	|	1718	|	|	|	1808	|	1824	1830	|	|	1917	|	1943	|	|	2024	|	2050	|	|	2153	2201	2233	...	...
Peterborough d.	1651	|	|	|	1751	|	1814	|	1834	|	1852	|	1914	|	1950	|	|	2014	|	2051	2110	2115	2151	2214	2223	2255	...	...
Stevenage d.	|	|	|	1802	|	|	|	|	|	1909	|	|	|	2002	|	|	|	|	2109	|	|	|	|	2245	2254	2333s	...	...
London Kings Cross . a.	1743	1750	1755	1830	1842	1852	1906	1919	1925	1935	1944	1949	2007	2027	2042	2048	2055	2107	2134	2142	2202	2207	2243	2310	2318	2359	...	...

FOR NOTES SEE PAGE 141

First Excel service **X1** 🚌 KINGS LYNN - PETERBOROUGH 🚌 **180a**

From **Kings Lynn** bus station: Journey 80 minutes. Buses call at **Wisbech** bus station ± 32 minutes later.

Ⓐ: 0534, 0604, 0634, 0704, 0734, 0805, 0835, 0905, 0935, 1015 and every 30 minutes until 1615, 1655, 1725, 1755, 1900, 2110.

⑥: 0604, 0634, 0704, 0734, 0805, 0835, 0905, 0935, 1015 and every 30 minutes until 1615, 1655, 1725, 1755, 1900, 2110.

⑦: 0740 and hourly until 1840.

Table **180a** continues on the previous page.

181   LONDON - HULL   All trains ⚹   HT

km		Ⓐ	Ⓐ	Ⓐ	Ⓐ	Ⓐ	Ⓐ△	Ⓐ	Ⓐ	⑥	⑥	⑥	⑥	⑥	⑥	⑥	⑦	⑦	⑦	⑦△	⑦	⑦
0	London Kings Cross 180 d. Ⓐ	0722	0948	1148	1348	1548	1719	1850	2030 ⑥	0713	0948	1148	1448	1710	1748	1948 ⑦	1048	1248	1448	1720	1744	1950
170	Grantham 180 d.	0825	1049	1249	1449	1649	1829	1952	2132	0820	1049	1249	1549	1821	1849	2052	1147	1347	1547	1826	1848	2051
223	Retford 180 d.	0851	1110	1310	1511	1711		2013	2153	0843	1110	1310	1609		1911	2113	1208	1408	1608		1908	2112
251	Doncaster 180 d.	0905	1123	1324	1525	1724	1906	2026	2206	0857	1123	1323	1623	1854	1924	2126	1222	1422	1625	1903	1923	2126
280	Selby a.	0922	1139	1339	1540	1740	1925	2047	2222	0914	1139	1339	1640	1911	1940	2142	1243	1444	1645	1921	1945	2142
330	Hull a.	1001	1214	1414	1615	1818	2005	2123	2300	1001	1218	1414	1725	1953	2015	2217	1320	1521	1722	2002	2020	2217
330	Hull 177 a.	...	...	...	...	...	2135	...		...	...	...	...	...	2025		...	...	...	2030		
343	Beverley 177 a.	...	...	...	...	...	2145			...	...	...	...	...	2038		...	...	...	2043		

		Ⓐ	Ⓐ△	Ⓐ	Ⓐ	Ⓐ	Ⓐ	Ⓐ	Ⓐ	⑥	⑥△	⑥	⑥	⑥	⑥	⑥	⑦	⑦	⑦	⑦	⑦	⑦
	Beverley 177 d. Ⓐ	0600	...							⑥ 0559	...						⑦ ...	1051	...			
	Hull 177 d.	0613	...							0612	...						...	1104	...			
	Hull d.	0626	0700	0823	1030	...	1233	1512	1710 1911	0620	0650	0823	1031	1331	1530	1836	0906	1112	1436	...	1632	1848
	Selby d.	0700	0737	0901	1106	...	1306	1546	1744 1945	0658	0725	0903	1106	1405	1605	1910	0940	1146	1510	...	1706	1922
	Doncaster 180 d.	0721	0757	0925	1125	...	1325	1605	1803 2003	0715	0745	0925	1126	1426	1624	1929	1000	1204	1528	...	1727	1940
	Retford 180 d.	0740		0939	1139	...	1339	1619	1817 2017			0939	1140	1440	1638	1943	1014	1218	1542	...	1741	1954
	Grantham 180 d.	0803	0835	1001	1201	...	1401	1640	1839 2040	0746	0818	0959	1201	1502	1700	2006	1035	1239	1605	...	1802	2016
	London Kings Cross 180 a.	0913	0955	1105	1305	...	1507	1746	1945 2146	0852	0935	1108	1309	1611	1806	2114	1140	1344	1714	...	1915	2119

△ – Operated by GR (Table 180).

---

182   LONDON - BRADFORD   All trains ⚹   GC

km		Ⓐ	Ⓐ	Ⓐ	Ⓐ△	Ⓐ	⑥	⑥	⑥	⑥	⑥	⑦	⑦	⑦	⑦
0	London Kings Cross 180 d. Ⓐ	1048	1448	1603	1833	1952	⑥ 1048	1548	1636	1923	1930	⑦ 1150	1550	1845	1922
251	Doncaster 180 d.	1222	1622	1735	2020	2119	1216	1718	1819	2051	2116	1319	1717	2024	2057
278	Pontefract Monkhill a.	1247	1647							2114					
292	Wakefield Kirkgate a.	1304	1704	1804	2038e	2145	1243	1742	1844	2131	2134e	1347	1746	2054	2120
	Mirfield a.	1316	1716	1820		2159	1255	1755	1856	2142		1359	1759	2112	2135
313	Brighouse a.	1324	1724	1828		2207	1308	1809	1910	2151		1408	1808	2123	2143
322	Halifax 190 a.	1339	1739	1840		2223	1320	1821	1922	2203		1420	1820	2136	2155
335	Bradford Interchange 190 a.	1354	1754	1855	2123f	2238	1337	1838	1938	2219	2220f	1436	1835	2152	2210

		Ⓐ	Ⓐ	Ⓐ	Ⓐ	Ⓐ	⑥	⑥△	⑥	⑥	⑥	⑦ a	⑦ 🚌	⑦ b	⑦	⑦	⑦	⑦
	Bradford Interchange 190 d. Ⓐ	0630f	0655	0754	1021	1433	⑥ 0655	0733f	0851	1021	1521	⑦ 0755	b	0810	1205	1505	1559
	Halifax 190 d.		0708	0807	1034	1447	0709		0905	1035	1535	0810	0737		1219	1520	1613
	Brighouse d.		0719	0817	1048	1503	0720		0915	1048	1549	0821	0757		1230	1535	1623
	Mirfield d.		0727	0825	1057	1513	0728		0924	1057	1557	0830	0812		1238	1543	1631
	Wakefield Kirkgate d.	0713e	0744	0855	1113	1535	0743	0818e	0940	1114	1614	0846	0837	0846	1255	1602	1648
	Pontefract Monkhill d.		0801		1136	1554	0800		0957	1133	1634						
	Doncaster 180 d.		0831	0931	1207	1621	0832	0838	1025	1206	1711	0911		0911	1321	1627	1713
	London Kings Cross 180 a.	0859	1010	1113	1343	1809	1005	1030	1156	1346	1844	1040		1040	1452	1757	1845

a – May 21 - Oct. 22.
b – From Oct. 29.
e – Wakefield Westgate.
f – Bradford Forster Square.
△ – Operated by GR (Table 180).

---

183   LONDON - YORK - SUNDERLAND   All trains ⚹   GC

km		Ⓐ	Ⓐ	Ⓐ	Ⓐ	Ⓐ	⑥	⑥	⑥	⑥	⑥	⑦	⑦	⑦	⑦
0	London Kings Cross 180 d. Ⓐ	0803	1121	1253	1650	1918	⑥ 0811	1120	1320	1647	1911	⑦ 0948	1348	1647	1822
303	York 180 d.	0958	1321	1451	1841	2119	1019	1319	1519	1842	2101	1139	1539	1842	2014
339	Thirsk d.	1015	1337	1514	1858	2136	1036	1336	1536	1858	2118	1155	1556	1901	2030
351	Northallerton 180 d.	1024	1346	1524	1907	2146	1045	1345	1546	1907	2128	1204	1606	1912	2040
375	Eaglescliffe a.	1042	1403	1541	1924	2203	1104	1403	1604	1925	2146	1222	1623	1929	2057
399	Hartlepool a.	1108	1423	1607	1944	2223	1123	1423	1623	1944	2206	1241	1652	1952	2117
428	Sunderland a.	1138	1451	1638	2021	2251	1150	1450	1650	2021	2236	1308	1720	2020	2151

		Ⓐ	Ⓐ	Ⓐ	Ⓐ	Ⓐ	⑥	⑥	⑥	⑥	⑥	⑦	⑦	⑦	⑦
	Sunderland d. Ⓐ	0645	0842	1228	1518	1731	⑥ 0643	0830	1218	1529	1729	⑦ 0920	1212	1412	1812
	Hartlepool d.	0710	0908	1252	1550	1757	0710	0855	1242	1553	1754	0945	1236	1440	1840
	Eaglescliffe d.	0732	0928	1312	1611	1822	0731	0917	1302	1612	1814	1005	1304	1504	1904
	Northallerton 180 d.	0753	0947	1331	1631	1842	0752	0943	1320	1631	1832	1024	1324	1524	1924
	Thirsk d.	0801	0959	1344	1643	1851	0801	0952	1330	1643	1843	1033	1333	1533	1933
	York 180 d.	0821	1027	1406	1702	1911	0820	1012	1356	1702	1902	1052	1352	1552	1953
	London Kings Cross 180 a.	1020	1230	1605	1905	2105	1014	1205	1546	1853	2057	1243	1544	1744	2143

---

184   LONDON - PETERBOROUGH   TL

km		Ⓐ	Ⓐ	Ⓐ	Ⓐ	Ⓐ	Ⓐ	Ⓐ	Ⓐ	Ⓐ	Ⓐ	and at	Ⓐ	Ⓐ	Ⓐ	Ⓐ	Ⓐ	Ⓐ	Ⓐ	Ⓐ	Ⓐ	Ⓐ
0	London Kings Cross 180 d. Ⓐ	0034	0134	0522	0622	0634	0722	0734	0809	0822	0834	the same	1522	1534	1622	1640	1650	1707	1712	1737	1742	1807
4	Finsbury Park d.	0040	0140	0528	0628	0640	0728	0740		0828	0840	minutes	1528	1540	1628		1656		1719		1749	
44	Stevenage 180 d.	0112	0221	0638	0647	0712	0747	0812		0847	0912	past each	1547	1613	1649		1717		1740		1809	
95	Huntingdon d.	0151s	0258s	0638	0723	0750	0823	0850	0854	0922	0950	hour until	1623	1650	1732	1727	1755	1800	1818	1830	1846	1858
123	Peterborough 180 a.	0212	0316	0654	0739	0806	0839	0906	0912	0938	1006	▽	1639	1706	...	1743	1811	1818	1838	1853	1903	1921

		Ⓐ	Ⓐ	Ⓐ	Ⓐ	Ⓐ	Ⓐ	Ⓐ	Ⓐ	Ⓐ	Ⓐ	Ⓐ	Ⓐ	Ⓐ	Ⓐ	⑥	⑥	⑥		⑥	⑥	⑥	⑥	⑥
	London Kings Cross 180 d.	1812	1837	1842	1910	1922	1952	2010	2022	2107	2122	2207	2222	2301	2322 ⑥	0001	0034	0136	...	0522	0622	0634	0722	0740
	Finsbury Park d.	1819		1849		1928	1958		2028		2128		2228		2328		0040	0140	...	0528	0628	0640	0728	0740
	Stevenage 180 d.	1839		1910		1948	2019		2047		2147		2247		2347	0022	0112	0221	...	0559	0647	0712	0747	0812
	Huntingdon d.	1916	1927	1947	2000		2053	2123	2154	2223	2254	2323	2348	0023	0057s	0151s	0255s	...	0638	0723	0750	0823		
	Peterborough 180 a.	1932	1943	2003	2019	2041	2114	2111	2139	2210	2240	2310	2343	0014	0042	0113	0212	0316	...	0654	0739	0806	0839	0906

		⑥	⑥	and at	⑥	⑥	⑥	⑥	⑥	⑥	⑥	⑥	⑥	⑥	⑥	⑥	⑥		⑥	⑥	⑥	⑥	⑥	⑥
	London Kings Cross 180 d. ⑥	0822	0834	the same	1622	1634	1640	1722	1734	1740	1822	1834	1840	1922	1934	2022	2034	...	2122	2134	2222	2252	2322	2352
	Finsbury Park d.	0828	0840	minutes	1628	1640		1728	1740		1828	1840		1928	1940	2028	2040	...	2128	2140	2228	2258	2328	2358
	Stevenage 180 d.	0847	0912	past each	1647	1713		1747	1813		1847	1912		1947	2012	2047	2112	...	2147	2212	2247	2317	2347	0017
	Huntingdon d.	0923	0950	hour until	1723	1750	1727	1823	1850	1827	1923	1950	1927	2023	2050	2123	2150	...	2222	2250	2323	2353	0023	0103s
	Peterborough 180 a.	0939	1008	▽	1739	1806	1743	1839	1906	1844	1939	2006	1939	2039	2106	2139	2206	...	2238	2306	2341	0014	0044	0124

		⑦r	⑦r	⑦	⑦	⑦	⑦	⑦	⑦	⑦	⑦	⑦	⑦	⑦	⑦	⑦	⑦	⑦	⑦	⑦	⑦	⑦	⑦	⑦
	London Kings Cross 180 d. ⑦	0022	0054	0704	0822	0922	1022	1122	1222	1322	1422	1522	1622	1710	1722	1810	1822	1840	1922	2022	2122	2222	2233	2322
	Finsbury Park d.	0028	0100	0710	0828	0928	1028	1128	1228	1328	1428	1528	1628		1728		1828		1928	2028	2128	2228	2239	2328
	Stevenage 180 d.	0057	0133	0750	0847	0947	1047	1147	1247	1347	1447	1528	1647		1747		1847		1947	2047	2147	2247	2313	2347
	Huntingdon d.	0134s	0211s	0828	0923	1023	1123	1223	1323	1423	1522	1623	1723	1757	1823	1855	1923	1932	2023	2123	2223	2323	2349	0023
	Peterborough 180 a.	0156	0233	0844	0939	1039	1139	1240	1339	1439	1539	1640	1739	1819	1839	1913	1939	1951	2040	2139	2239	2343	0007	0043

For return service and footnotes see next page ▷ ▷ ▷

TL PETERBOROUGH - LONDON 184

		Ⓐ	Ⓐ	Ⓐ	Ⓐ	Ⓐ	Ⓐ	Ⓐ	Ⓐ	Ⓐ	Ⓐ	Ⓐ	Ⓐ	Ⓐ	Ⓐ	Ⓐ	Ⓐ	Ⓐ	Ⓐ	Ⓐ	Ⓐ	and at	Ⓐ
Peterborough 180 d.	Ⓐ	0325	0410	0510	0540	0547	0615	0632	0656	0715	0707	0726	0733	0746	0816	0846	0919	0930	0946	1018	1046	the same	1616
Huntingdon d.		0339	0425	0524	0555	0601	0630	0646	0710	0733	0722	0740	0748	0801	0830	0900	0934	0944	1000	1034	1100	minutes	1630
Stevenage 180 d.		0415	0504	0603	|	0639	0658	0724	0736	0758	0801	|	0827	0832	0907	0937	1003	1021	1036	1111	1136	past each	1708
Finsbury Park d.		0452**s**	0537	0623	|	0706	|	0744	|	|	0821	|	0848	|	0928	1000	|	|	1056	1143	1156	hour until	1728
London Kings Cross 180 a.		0501	0546	0629	0642	0712	0722	0750	0800	0821	0829	0828	0856	0855	0934	1006	1027	1047	1103	1149	1202	▽	1735

	Ⓐ	Ⓐ	Ⓐ	Ⓐ	Ⓐ	Ⓐ	Ⓐ	Ⓐ	Ⓐ	Ⓐ	Ⓐ	Ⓐ	Ⓐ			⑥	⑥	⑥	⑥	⑥	⑥	⑥	⑥	⑥
Peterborough 180 d.	1646	1722	1754	1822	1846	1916	1946	2016	2044	2121	2146	2222	2244	...	⑥	0325	0419	0519	0546	0619	0646	0719	0746	0809
Huntingdon d.	1700	1737	1812	1840	1901	1936	2000	2033	2058	2136	2200	2236	2258	...		0339	0434	0534	0600	0634	0700	0734	0800	0824
Stevenage 180 d.	1736	1816	1850	1918	1936	2014	2036	2111	2136	2213	2236	2317	2336	...		0415	0511	0611	0636	0711	0736	0811	0836	|
Finsbury Park d.	1756	1851	1911	1950	1956	2045	2056	2144	2156	2244	2256	2348	2356	...		0453**s**	0543	0643	0656	0743	0756	0844	0856	|
London Kings Cross 180 a.	1802	1857	1917	1956	2002	2051	2103	2149	2202	2250	2302	2354	0003	...		0459	0549	0649	0702	0749	0802	0850	0902	0912

	⑥	⑥	⑥	⑥	⑥	⑥	⑥	⑥	and at	⑥	⑥	⑥	⑥	⑥		⑥	⑥	⑥	⑥		⑥	⑥	⑥
Peterborough 180 d.	0819	0846	0908	...	0946	1013	1019	1046	the same	1719	1746	1819	1846	1916	...	1946	2016	2046	2116	...	2146	2219	2246
Huntingdon d.	0834	0900	0923	0934	1000	1027	1033	1100	minutes	1734	1800	1834	1900	1934	...	2000	2034	2100	2134	...	2200	2234	2300
Stevenage 180 d.	0911	0936	|	1011	1036	|	1111	1136	past each	1811	1836	1911	1936	2011	...	2036	2111	2136	2211	...	2236	2311	2336
Finsbury Park d.	0945	0956	|	1043	1056	|	1145	1156	hour until	1843	1856	1943	1956	2043	...	2056	2143	2156	2243	...	2256	2343	2359**s**
London Kings Cross 180 a.	0951	1001	1012	1049	1102	1116	1151	1202	▽	1849	1902	1949	2002	2049	...	2102	2149	2202	2249	...	2302	2349	0009

		⑦**r**	⑦**r**	⑦	⑦	⑦	⑦	⑦	⑦	⑦	⑦	⑦	⑦		⑦	⑦	⑦	⑦		⑦	⑦	⑦	⑦	⑦
Peterborough 180 d.	⑦	0546	0646	0746	0846	0915	0946	1015	1046	1115	1146	1246	1346	...	1446	1546	1646	1746	...	1846	1946	2046	2146	2301
Huntingdon d.		0600	0700	0800	0900	0930	1000	1030	1100	1130	1200	1300	1400	...	1500	1600	1700	1800	...	1900	2000	2100	2200	2315
Stevenage 180 d.		0641	0739	0836	0936	|	1036	|	1136	|	1236	1336	1436	...	1536	1636	1736	1836	...	1936	2036	2136	2236	2352
Finsbury Park d.		0714	0802	0900	0956	|	1057	|	1157	|	1257	1357	1456	...	1557	1656	1756	1857	...	1957	2057	2157	2257	0017**s**
London Kings Cross 180 a.		0723	0810	0906	1002	1017	1103	1116	1203	1216	1303	1403	1502	...	1603	1702	1802	1903	...	2003	2103	2203	2303	0026

r – Subject to alteration from Sept. 17. Check locally for details. **s** – Calls to set down only. ▽ – Timings may vary by up to 2 minutes.

EM 2nd class PETERBOROUGH - LINCOLN - DONCASTER 185

km		⑥	Ⓐ	⚒**T**	⚒	⚒	Ⓐ**D**	⚒	⑥	Ⓐ	Ⓐ		⚒**E**	⚒	Ⓐ	⚒	⚒	⑥	Ⓐ**D**	⚒	⚒**D**	⚒	Ⓐ	⑥	⚒
0	**Peterborough** d.	...	...	0630	...	0730	...	0833	0932	0935	1040	...	1150	1241	1341	1511	1625	...	...	1732	...	1836	...	...	2030
27	Spalding d.	...	...	0653	...	0753	...	0854	0953	0956	1101	...	1213	1302	1404	1532	1646	...	...	1755	...	1859	...	...	2053
57	Sleaford d.	0650	0653	...	0743	...	0840	0918	1020	1021	1125	...	1241	1326	1429	1614	1718	1754	1756	...	1900	...	2005	2010	...
91	**Lincoln** a.	0722	0726	...	0815	...	0913	0956	1053	1053	1201	...	1314	1403	1503	1647	1751	1827	1829	...	1932	...	2039	2044	...

	Ⓐ	⚒	Ⓐ	⑥	⚒	⚒**N**	Ⓐ	Ⓐ	⑥	⚒	Ⓐ	Ⓐ**R**	⑥**R**	⚒	Ⓐ	Ⓐ**R**	⑥**R**	⚒	⑥	Ⓐ	⚒	⚒	⑥	Ⓐ	⚒**L**	⑥**T**	Ⓐ**T**
Lincoln d.	0617	...	...	...	0705	0800	0910	1018	1018	1110	1210	1330	1330	1441	1512	1600	1601	...	1715	1718	1810	...	1905	1915	2048	...	...
Sleaford d.	0645	...	...	...	0737	0834	0942	1051	1051	1142	1242	1403	1403	1516	1544	1634	1634	...	1747	1753	1842	...	1937	1947	2120	...	...
Spalding d.	...	0700	0800	0805	...	0900	1006	1113	1119	1204	1307	1425	1427	1538	...	1656	1657	1808	...	...	...	1959	...	...	...	2103	2105
Peterborough a.	...	0722	0822	0827	...	0924	1030	1134	1141	1228	1330	1446	1451	1602	...	1718	1723	1831	...	...	...	2022	...	...	...	2125	2127

km		Ⓐ	Ⓐ**S**	⑥	⚒	Ⓐ**P**	⑥	⑥	Ⓐ**S**	⚒**S**
0	**Lincoln** d.	0700	0915	0915	1154	1315	1410	1511	1831	1932
26	Gainsborough Lea Road d.	0721	0935	0935	1215	1335	1430	1531	1855	1952
60	**Doncaster** a.	*0808*r	1002	1005	1245	1407	1458	1600	1925	2023

	⑥	Ⓐ	Ⓐ	⑥	Ⓐ	⑥	⑥	Ⓐ	⚒
Doncaster d.	1024	1024	1301	1305	1427	1507	1627	1937	2033
Gainsborough Lea Road d.	1048	1053	1329	1329	1452	1531	1652	2001	2056
Lincoln a.	1110	1116	1354	1354	1515	1557	1719	2023	2125

D – To / from Doncaster (lower panel).
E – To / from Doncaster on Ⓐ (lower panel).
L – To Boston (Table **194**).
N – From Nottingham (Table **186**).
P – To / from Peterborough (upper panel).
R – From Newark North Gate (Table **186**).
S – To / from Sleaford (upper panel).
T – To Nottingham (Table **206**).
r – Change trains at Retford (a. 0736, d. 0754).

EM 2nd class GRIMSBY - LINCOLN - NOTTINGHAM 186

km			Ⓐ	Ⓐ	Ⓐ	Ⓐ**A**	Ⓐ**B**	Ⓐ	Ⓐ	Ⓐ	Ⓐ	Ⓐ	Ⓐ	Ⓐ	Ⓐ	Ⓐ	Ⓐ	Ⓐ	Ⓐ	Ⓐ	Ⓐ	Ⓐ	Ⓐ	Ⓐ	Ⓐ	Ⓐ
0	**Grimsby** Town d.	Ⓐ	...	...	0556	...	...	...	0703	...	...	...	0920	...	...	...	1128	...	...	...	1349	...	...	...	1545	...
47	Market Rasen d.		...	...	0632	...	...	...	0739	...	...	...	0955	...	...	...	1203	...	...	...	1425	...	...	...	1621	...
71	**Lincoln** a.		...	...	0651	...	...	...	0757	...	...	...	1014	...	...	...	1222	...	...	...	1444	...	...	...	1640	...
71	**Lincoln** d.		0526	0646	0654	0704	0730	0736	0759	0836	0907	0937	1016	1036	1135	1140	1223	1234	1337	1436	1446	1536	1542	1634	1643	1726
97	Newark North Gate a.		0556	|	0722	|	0755	|	0824	|	0932	|	1040	|	1200	|	1250	|	|	|	1511	|	1611	|	1711	|
98	Newark Castle ♧ d.		0609	0714	...	0729	...	0806	...	0907	...	1007	...	1107	...	1207	...	1305	1407	1506	...	1608	...	1705	...	1756
126	**Nottingham** ♧ a.		0647	0742	...	0756	...	0834	...	0932	...	1032	...	1132	...	1230	...	1332	1432	1532	...	1632	...	1732	..	1832

	Ⓐ	Ⓐ	Ⓐ	Ⓐ	Ⓐ	Ⓐ	Ⓐ		⑥	⑥**A**	⑥	⑥	⑥	⑥	⑥**B**	⑥	⑥	⑥	⑥	⑥	⑥	⑥	⑥	⑥	⑥
Grimsby Town d.	...	...	1828	...	...	2124	...	⑥	...	...	...	0650	...	...	...	...	0920	...	...	...	1128	...	...	...	1349
Market Rasen d.	...	...	1904	...	...	2200	...		...	...	...	0726	...	...	...	...	0955	...	...	...	1203	...	...	...	1425
Lincoln a.	...	...	1923	...	...	2219	...		...	...	...	0744	...	...	...	...	1014	...	...	...	1222	...	...	...	1444
Lincoln d.	1818	1835	1925	2031	2140	...	2226		0526	0704	0726	0746	0835	0901	0930	0936	1015	1036	1130	1140	1223	1236	1337	1432	1446
Newark North Gate a.	1846	|	1953	|	|	...	|		0556	|	|	0812	|	0925	0953	|	1044	|	1152	|	1252	|	|	|	1511
Newark Castle ♧ d.	...	1903	...	2058	2207	...	2255		0610	0729	0755	...	0904	...	...	1007	...	1104	...	1204	...	1306	1405	1501	...
Nottingham ♧ a.	...	1932	...	2129	2239	...	2330		0648	0757	0825	...	0933	...	...	1032	...	1132	...	1229	...	1331	1431	1527	...

	⑥	⑥	⑥	⑥	⑥	⑥	⑥	⑥	⑥		⑦	⑦	⑦**b**	⑦**c**	⑦**b**	⑦**b**	⑦	⑦	⑦	⑦**b**	⑦	⑦	⑦**b**	⑦**c**	⑦
Grimsby Town d.	...	...	1600	...	...	1828	...	1945	...	⑦	...	...	1403	...	...	...	...	...	...	1825	...	...	2022	...	...
Market Rasen d.	...	...	1635	...	...	1902	...	2020	...		...	...	1437	...	...	...	...	...	...	1859	...	...	2057	...	...
Lincoln a.	...	...	1653	...	...	1921	...	2039	...		...	...	1456	...	1544	...	...	...	...	1918	...	...	2115	...	...
Lincoln d.	1526	1635	1655	1725	1830	1924	1939	...	2045		1105	1245	1508	1508	1609	1656	1709	1805	1903	1922	2005	2100	2123	2126	2210
Newark North Gate d.	|	|	1722	|	|	1953	|	...	|		1130	1310	1536	1536	...	|	1734	|	|	1946	|	2127	2152	2155	|
Newark Castle ♧ d.	1557	1705	...	1754	1859	...	2004	...	2110		...	...	1550	1550	...	1724	...	1834	1933	...	2035	2140	...	...	2239
Nottingham ♧ a.	1629	1732	...	1831	1926	...	2033	...	2137		...	...	1620	1620	...	1802	...	1911	2005	...	2103	2209	...	...	2316

		Ⓐ	Ⓐ	Ⓐ**P**	Ⓐ	Ⓐ	Ⓐ	Ⓐ	Ⓐ	Ⓐ	Ⓐ	Ⓐ	Ⓐ	Ⓐ	Ⓐ**P**	Ⓐ	Ⓐ	Ⓐ	Ⓐ**P**	Ⓐ	Ⓐ	Ⓐ	Ⓐ	Ⓐ	Ⓐ
Nottingham ♧ d.	Ⓐ	...	0554	0653	...	...	0812	0925	...	...	1029	1129	...	1229	...	1329	...	1429	...	1529	...	1627	...	1721	1750
Newark Castle ♧ d.		...	0630	0727	...	...	0840	0952	...	...	1051	1153	...	1253	...	1352	...	1453	...	1553	...	1653	...	1752	1818
Newark North Gate d.		...	|	|	0742	0831	|	|	0957	1050	|	|	1206	|	1302	|	...	|	1528	|	1646	|	1728	|	|
Lincoln a.		...	0704	0756	0812	0902	0908	1019	1023	1114	1130	1223	1236	1325	1330	1425	...	1524	1555	1625	1713	1718	1800	1826	1851
Lincoln d.		0557	...	...	0815	...	...	...	1025	...	...	...	1237	...	...	...	1437	...	...	...	1722	...	...	...	...
Market Rasen d.		0613	...	...	0832	...	...	...	1042	...	...	...	1254	...	...	...	1454	...	...	...	1739	...	...	...	...
Grimsby Town a.		0655	...	...	0912	...	...	...	1122	...	...	...	1335	...	...	...	1534	...	...	...	1818	...	...	...	...

	Ⓐ	Ⓐ	Ⓐ	Ⓐ	Ⓐ**B**	Ⓐ**A**	Ⓐ	Ⓐ		⑥	⑥	⑥**P**	⑥	⑥	⑥	⑥	⑥	⑥	⑥	⑥	⑥	⑥**P**	⑥	⑥	⑥**P**
Nottingham ♧ d.	1817	...	1919	...	...	2030	2120	2226	⑥	...	0555	0653	...	0811	...	0922	...	1029	1129	...	1229	...	1329	1419	...
Newark Castle ♧ d.	1853	...	1954	...	...	2054	2155	2257		...	0630	0726	...	0842	...	0950	...	1051	1155	...	1250	...	1350	1444	...
Newark North Gate d.	|	1935	|	2003	2036	|	|	2310		...	|	|	0820	|	0935	|	1049	|	|	1205	|	1302	|	|	1529
Lincoln a.	1924	2001	2023	2027	2102	2122	2224	2340		...	0703	0758	0855	0909	0959	1019	1117	1127	1228	1236	1321	1330	1424	1513	1556
Lincoln d.	...	2002	...	...	...	...	...	...		0538	...	*0808*	...	...	1006	...	...	...	...	1236	...	...	*1452*	...	...
Market Rasen d.	...	2019	...	...	...	...	...	...		0554	...	*0825*	...	...	1023	...	...	...	...	1254	...	...	*1510*	...	...
Grimsby Town a.	...	2056	...	...	...	...	...	...		0636	...	*0912*	...	...	1102	...	...	...	...	1334	...	...	*1550*	...	...

	⑥	⑥	⑥	⑥	⑥	⑥**B**	⑥**A**	⑥	⑥	⑥		⑦	⑦	⑦**b**	⑦**b**	⑦	⑦	⑦	⑦	⑦**b**	⑦	⑦**B**	⑦	⑦	⑦
Nottingham ♧ d.	1528	1621	1729	...	1823	...	1929	...	2030	2124	⑦	...	...	1529	...	1633	...	1726	1836	...	1935	...	2039	...	2228
Newark Castle ♧ d.	1550	1652	1750	...	1850	...	1953	...	2104	2157		...	...	1559	...	1659	...	1801	1859	...	1958	...	2103	...	2303
Newark North Gate d.	|	|	|	1807	|	1935	|	2032	|	2209		1135	1335	|	1645	|	1755	|	1928**a**	1953	|	2036	|	2210	2317
Lincoln a.	1624	1710	1825	1834	1925	2001	2026	2056	2133	2242		1202	1402	1626	1716	1731	1820	1833	1957	2019	2030	2102	2135	2237	2348
Lincoln d.	...	*1722*	...	1835	...	...	...	2057	...	...		1202**b**	...	1627	...	...	1822**b**	...	...	...	...	...	...	...	...
Market Rasen d.	...	*1738*	...	1852	...	...	...	2115	...	...		1218**b**	...	1643	...	...	1838**b**	...	...	...	...	...	...	...	...
Grimsby Town a.	...	*1818*	...	1934	...	...	...	...	...	...		1253**b**	...	1718	...	...	1913**b**	...	...	...	...	...	...	...	...

A – (12) 🍸 Lincoln - London St Pancras and v.v. (Table **170**).
B – (12) 🍸 Lincoln - London Kings Cross and v.v. (Table **180**).
P – To Peterborough (Table **185**).
a – Arrives 1909.
b – May 21 - Sept. 10.
c – From Sept. 17.

♧ – Additional journeys Newark Castle - Nottingham and v.v. Journey time: 28 – 36 minutes.
From Newark Castle at 0642Ⓐ, 0739Ⓐ, 0741⑥, 0841Ⓐ, 0843⑥, 0938⚒, 1047⚒, 1139⚒, 1247⚒, 1347Ⓐ, 1349⑥, 1439⚒, 1547⚒, 1638⑥, 1639Ⓐ, 1739⚒, 1847⑥, 1947⚒. **From Nottingham** at 0756Ⓐ, 0758⑥, 0854⚒, 0949Ⓐ, 0951⑥, 1049Ⓐ, 1052⑥, 1153⚒, 1249⚒, 1349⚒, 1452⑥, 1453Ⓐ, 1549⚒, 1649⚒, 1749⑥, 1852Ⓐ, 1857⑥.

From July 8 to July 30 no trains will operate between Leeds and Liverpool via Manchester Victoria. Please call National Rail Enquiries for details ☎ 03457 48 49 50.

km			②–⑤	①	⑥	②–⑤	①	⑥	②–⑥	①	Ⓐ	⚒	⚒	⚒	Ⓐ	⚒ f	⚒	⑥	Ⓐ	⚒	⚒	⚒	⚒	⚒	⚒	⚒	⚒	⚒	Ⓐ
0	**Newcastle** d.	⚒	...	...	...	...	...	...	...	...	...	...	...	...	...	...	...	...	0533	...	...	0602	...	...	...	...	0708	...	...
23	Durham d.		...	...	...	...	...	...	...	...	...	...	...	...	...	...	...	...	0546	...	...	0620	...	...	...	...	0721	...	...
34	**Middlesbrough** d.		...	...	...	...	...	...	...	...	...	...	...	...	...	...	...	...	|	0554	...	|	...	0631	...	...	|	0715	...
58	Darlington d.		...	...	...	...	...	...	...	...	...	...	...	...	...	...	...	...	0603	|	...	0637	...	|	...	...	0738	|	...
81	Northallerton d.		...	...	...	...	...	...	...	...	...	...	...	...	...	...	...	...	|	0622	...	0649	...	0659	...	...	|	0743	...
93	Thirsk d.		...	...	...	...	...	...	...	...	...	...	...	...	...	...	...	...	|	0630	...	|	...	0710	...	...	|	0755	...
◧	**Scarborough** d.		...	...	...	...	...	...	...	...	...	...	...	...	...	...	...	...	|	|	...	|	0630	|	0700	...	|	|	0738
◧	Malton d.		...	...	...	...	...	...	...	...	...	...	...	...	...	...	...	...	|	|	...	|	0653	|	0723	...	|	|	0801
129	**York** a.		...	...	...	...	...	...	...	...	...	...	...	...	...	...	...	...	0636	0648	...	0712	0718	0728	0747	...	0810	0813	0826
129	**York** d.		0138	0138	0138	0252	0252	0252	0400	0420	...	0521	...	0555	...	0616	...	0640	0645	0651	...	0714	0723	0737	0750	...	0814	0823	0840
◧	**Hull** d.		|	|	|	|	|	|	|	|	...	|	...	|	...	|	0548	|	|	|	0637	|	|	|	|	0735	|	|	|
◧	Selby d.		|	|	|	|	|	|	|	|	...	|	...	|	...	|	0623	|	|	|	0709	|	|	|	|	0808	|	|	|
170	**Leeds** a.		0220	0204	0219	0333	0318	0333	0441	0446	...	0547	...	0618	...	0640	0647	0705	0708	0717	0733	0741	0750	0804	0820	0832	0841	0851	0904
170	**Leeds** d.		0220	0205	0220	0335	0320	0335	0449	0449	...	0550	...	0620	0635	0644	0652	0711	0710	0720	0735	0744f	0753	0809	0824	0836	0844f	0854	0909
185	Dewsbury d.		|	|	|	|	|	|	|	|	...	0601	...	0631	0646	|	|	0722	0721	|	0746	|	|	0820	|	0847	|	|	0920
198	Huddersfield d.		0243	0243	0256	0358	0358	0411	0526	0526	...	0611	...	0640	0655	0702	0710	0731	0731	0739	0756	0802f	0811	0830	0842	0856	0902f	0912	0930
227	Stalybridge d.		|	|	|	|	|	|	|	|	...	0630	...	0659	0714	|	0728	0750	0750	0759	0817	|	|	0850	|	0915	|	|	0950
	Manchester Victoria d.		|	|	|	|	|	|	|	|	...	|	...	|	|	0735	|	|	|	|	|	0835f	|	|	|	|	0935f	|	|
239	**Manchester** Piccadilly a.		0343	0343	0329	0458	0458	0443	0557	0557	0607	0645	0707	0714	0730	|	0743	0806	0805	0816	0833	|	0845	0905	0913	0932	|	0945	1005
255	**Manchester** Airport ✈ a.		0400	0400	0349	0515	0515	0505	0619	0619	|	0710	|	0742	...	|	0810	|	|	0840	...	|	0911	|	0939	...	|	1010	|
265	Warrington Central a.		...	...	...	...	...	...	...	...	0628	...	0728	...	...	|	...	0831	0830	...	...	|	...	0930	...	...	|	...	1030
286	**Liverpool** South Parkway a.		...	...	...	...	...	...	...	...	|	...	|	...	...	|	...	0847	0847	...	...	|	...	0947	...	...	|	...	1046
295	**Liverpool** Lime Street a.		...	...	...	...	...	...	...	...	0656	...	0753	...	...	0810	...	0859	0859	...	...	0909f	...	0959	...	...	1008f	...	1059

	⑥	⚒	⚒	⚒	⚒	⚒	⚒	⚒	⚒	⚒	⚒	⚒	⚒	⚒	⑥ e	⚒	⚒	⚒	⚒	⚒	⚒	⚒	⚒	⚒	⚒	⑥ e	⚒	⚒	⚒
Newcastle d.	...	0748r	...	0806	...	...	...	...	0910	...	...	...	...	1003g	...	...	...	1048t	...	1110	...	...	...	...	1206	...	...	...	1248t
Durham d.	...	0801r	...	0822	...	...	...	...	0923	...	...	...	...	1020	...	...	...	1101r	...	1123	...	...	...	...	1222	...	...	...	1301r
Middlesbrough d.	...	|	...	|	0827	...	...	...	|	0927	...	...	...	|	...	1027	...	|	...	|	1127	...	...	...	|	...	1227	...	|
Darlington d.	...	0818r	...	0839	|	...	...	...	0940	|	...	...	...	1037	...	|	...	1118	...	1140	|	...	...	...	1239	...	|	...	1318
Northallerton d.	...	|	...	0850	0856	...	...	...	0951	0956	...	...	...	1049	...	1056	...	|	...	1151	1156	...	...	...	1250	...	1256	...	|
Thirsk d.	...	|	...	|	0904	...	...	...	|	1004	...	...	...	|	...	1104	...	|	...	|	1204	...	...	...	|	...	1304	...	|
Scarborough d.	0750	|	...	|	|	0850	...	...	|	|	0950	...	...	|	1030	|	1050	|	...	|	|	1150	...	...	|	1230	|	1250	|
Malton d.	0813	|	...	|	|	0913	...	...	|	|	1013	...	...	|	|	|	1113	|	...	|	|	1213	...	...	|	|	|	1313	|
York a.	0838	0850r	...	0915	0922	0938	...	...	1014	1022	1038	...	...	1113	1116	1122	1138	1151	...	1214	1222	1238	...	...	1313	1316	1322	1338	1351
York d.	0840	0853	...	0915	0923	0940	0953	...	1015	1023	1040	1053	...	1115	...	1123	1140	1153	...	1215	1223	1240	1253	...	1315	...	1323	1340	1353
Hull d.	|	|	0838	|	|	|	|	0938	|	|	|	|	1038	|	...	|	|	|	1138	|	|	|	|	1238	|	...	|	|	|
Selby d.	|	|	0910	|	|	|	|	1010	|	|	|	|	1110	|	...	|	|	|	1210	|	|	|	|	1310	|	...	|	|	|
Leeds a.	0904	0916	0934	0941	0949	1004	1017	1034	1041	1049	1104	1116	1134	1141	...	1150	1204	1216	1234	1241	1249	1304	1316	1334	1341	...	1349	1404	1416
Leeds d.	0909	0920	0936	0944f	0953	1009	1020	1036	1044f	1053	1109	1120	1136	1144f	...	1153	1209	1220	1236	1244f	1253	1309	1320	1336	1344f	...	1351	1409	1420
Dewsbury d.	0920	|	0947	|	|	1020	|	1047	|	|	1120	|	1147	|	...	|	1220	|	1247	|	|	1320	|	1347	|	...	|	1420	|
Huddersfield d.	0930	0940	0956	1002f	1011	1030	1040	1056	1102f	1111	1130	1140	1156	1202f	...	1211	1230	1240	1256	1302f	1311	1330	1340	1356	1402f	...	1409	1430	1440
Stalybridge d.	0950	|	1015	|	|	1050	|	1115	|	|	1150	|	1215	|	...	|	1250	|	1315	|	|	1350	|	1415	|	...	|	1450	|
Manchester Victoria d.	|	|	|	1035f	|	|	|	|	1135f	|	|	|	|	1235f	...	|	|	|	|	1335f	|	|	|	|	1435f	...	|	|	|
Manchester Piccadilly a.	1005	1013	1032	|	1044	1105	1113	1132	|	1144	1205	1213	1232	|	...	1244	1305	1313	1332	|	1342	1405	1413	1432	|	...	1444	1505	1513
Manchester Airport ✈ a.	|	1039	...	|	1110	|	1139	...	|	1210	|	1239	...	|	...	1310	|	1339	...	|	1410	|	1439	...	|	...	1510	|	1539
Warrington Central a.	1030	...	...	|	...	1130	...	...	|	...	1230	...	...	|	...	...	1330	...	...	|	...	1430	...	...	|	...	...	1530	...
Liverpool South Parkway a.	1046	...	...	|	...	1147	...	...	|	...	1247	...	...	|	...	...	1347	...	...	|	...	1447	...	...	|	...	...	1547	...
Liverpool Lime Street a.	1059	...	...	1108f	...	1159	...	...	1208f	...	1259	...	...	1308f	...	...	1359	...	...	1409f	...	1459	...	...	1508f	...	...	1559	...

	⚒	⚒	⚒	⚒	⚒	⚒	Ⓐ	⑥	⚒	⚒	Ⓐ	⑥	⚒	⚒	⚒	⚒	⚒	⚒	⚒	⚒	⚒	⑥	Ⓐ	⚒	Ⓐ	⑥	⚒	⚒	⚒ d
Newcastle d.	...	1310	...	...	...	...	1403	1406	...	...	1447	1452	...	1508	...	...	...	...	1606	...	...	1651	...	...	1703	1706	...	...	...
Durham d.	...	1323	...	...	...	...	1420	1422	...	...	1501	|	...	1523	...	...	...	...	1622	...	...	|	...	...	1719	1722	...	...	...
Middlesbrough d.	...	|	1327	...	...	...	|	|	1427	...	|	|	...	|	1527	...	...	...	|	1626	...	|	...	...	|	|	1726	...	...
Darlington d.	...	1340	|	...	...	...	1437	1439	|	...	1518	1519	...	1540	|	...	...	...	1639	|	...	1718	...	...	1736	1739	|	...	...
Northallerton d.	...	1351	1356	...	...	...	1448	1450	1456	...	|	|	...	1551	1556	...	...	...	1650	1654	...	|	...	...	1747	1750	1754	...	...
Thirsk d.	...	|	1404	...	...	...	|	|	1504	...	|	|	...	|	1604	...	...	...	|	1702	...	|	...	...	|	|	1802	...	...
Scarborough d.	...	|	|	1350	...	...	|	|	|	1450	|	|	...	|	|	1550	...	...	|	|	1650	|	...	...	|	|	|	1750	...
Malton d.	...	|	|	1413	...	...	|	|	|	1513	|	|	...	|	|	1613	...	...	|	|	1713	|	...	...	|	|	|	1813	...
York a.	...	1415	1422	1438	...	...	1511	1513	1522	1538	1550	1551	...	1615	1622	1638	...	...	1713	1720	1738	1751	...	...	1810	1815	1820	1838	...
York d.	...	1415	1423	1440	1453	...	1515	1515	1523	1540	1553	1553	...	1615	1623	1640	1653	...	1715	1722	1740	1753	1753	...	1815	1815	1822	1840	1853
Hull d.	1338	|	|	|	|	1438	|	|	|	|	|	|	1538	|	|	|	|	1638	|	|	|	|	|	1738	|	|	|	|	|
Selby d.	1410	|	|	|	|	1510	|	|	|	|	|	|	1610	|	|	|	|	1710	|	|	|	|	|	1810	|	|	|	|	|
Leeds a.	1434	1441	1449	1504	1516	1534	1541	1541	1549	1606	1616	1616	1634	1641	1649	1706	1716	1735	1741	1749	1804	1816	1816	1834	1841	1841	1849	1904	1916
Leeds d.	1436	1444f	1453	1509	1520	1536	1544f	1544f	1553	1609	1620	1620	1636	1644f	1653	1709	1720	1737	1744f	1753	1809	1820	1820	1836	1844f	1844f	1853	1909	1920
Dewsbury d.	1447	|	|	1520	|	1547	|	|	|	1620	|	|	1647	|	|	1720	1731	1748	|	|	1820	|	|	1847	|	|	|	1920	|
Huddersfield d.	1456	1502f	1511	1530	1540	1556	1602f	1602f	1611	1630	1640	1640	1656	1702f	1711	1730	1740	1757	1802f	1811	1830	1840	1840	1856	1902f	1902f	1911	1930	1940
Stalybridge d.	1515	|	|	1550	|	1615	|	|	|	1650	|	|	1715	|	|	1750	|	1816	|	|	1850	|	|	1915	|	|	|	1950	|
Manchester Victoria d.	|	1535f	|	|	|	|	1635f	1635f	|	|	|	|	|	1735f	|	|	|	|	1835f	|	|	|	|	|	1935f	1935f	|	|	|
Manchester Piccadilly a.	1532	|	1542	1605	1613	1634	|	|	1644	1705	1716	1713	1732	|	1746	1805	1818	1833	|	1842	1905	1914	1916	1932	|	|	1942	2005	2014
Manchester Airport ✈ a.	...	|	1610	|	1639	...	|	|	1712	|	...	1739	...	|	1810	|	1839	...	|	1916j	|	1940	...	...	|	|	2010	|	...
Warrington Central a.	...	|	...	1630	...	...	|	|	...	1730	...	...	...	|	...	1830	...	...	|	...	1930	...	...	...	|	|	...	2030	...
Liverpool South Parkway a.	...	|	...	1647	...	...	|	|	...	1747	...	...	...	|	...	1847	...	...	|	...	1947	...	...	...	|	|	...	2047	...
Liverpool Lime Street a.	...	1608f	...	1659	...	...	1710f	1710f	...	1802	...	...	...	1808f	...	1859	...	...	1909f	...	1959	...	...	...	2011f	2011f	...	2059	...

	⑥ e	⚒	⚒	⚒	⚒	⚒	⚒	⚒	⚒	⚒	Ⓐ	Ⓐ	⑥	Ⓐ	⑥	⚒	⚒	⚒	⚒	⑥	①–④	⑤		⑦		⑦	⑦		⑦
Newcastle d.	...	1804	...	...	...	1910	...	...	...	...	...	2027	...	...	...	...	...	...	...	2155	2155	2155	⑦	...	...	...	...	...	...
Durham d.	...	1822	...	...	...	1923	...	...	...	...	...	2045	...	...	...	...	...	...	...	2210	2210	2210		...	...	...	...	...	...
Middlesbrough d.	...	|	...	1827	...	|	...	1930	...	...	...	|	...	2052	2052	...	...	...	2150	|	|	|		...	...	...	...	...	...
Darlington d.	...	1839	...	|	...	1940	...	|	...	...	...	2102	...	|	|	...	...	...	2219	2227	2227	2227		...	...	...	...	...	...
Northallerton d.	...	1850	...	1856	...	1951	...	1958	...	...	...	2113	...	2120	2120	...	...	...	2230	2238	2238	2238		...	...	...	...	...	...
Thirsk d.	...	|	...	1904	...	|	...	2006	...	...	...	|	...	2128	2128	...	...	...	2238	|	|	|		...	...	...	...	...	...
Scarborough d.	1807	|	...	|	1850	|	...	|	1950	...	2045	|	2050	|	|	...	...	2207	|	|	|	|		...	...	...	...	...	...
Malton d.	|	|	...	|	1913	|	...	|	2013	...	2109	|	2113	|	|	...	...	2230	|	|	|	|		...	...	...	...	...	...
York a.	1851	1913	...	1922	1938	2014	...	2025	2038	...	2133	2136	2138	2146	2152	...	...	2255	2257	2302	2302	2302		...	...	...	...	...	...
York d.	1853	1915	...	1923	1940	2016	...	...	2040	2116	...	2140	2140	2148	...	...	2228	...	...	2305	2305	2305		0230	...	0400	0512	...	0612
Hull d.	|	|	1849	|	|	|	1959	...	|	|	...	|	|	|	...	2138	|	...	...	|	|	|		|	...	|	|	...	|
Selby d.	|	|	1920	|	|	|	2030	...	|	|	...	|	|	|	...	2212	|	...	...	|	|	|		|	...	|	|	...	|
Leeds a.	1916	1941	1943	1951	2004	2039	2059	...	2104	2139	...	2205	2205	2213	...	2240	2305	...	...	2332	2332	2332		0256	...	0426	0538	...	0638
Leeds d.	1920	1941f	...	1953	2009	2041	...	...	2109	2141	...	2209	2209	...	...	2241	2309	...	...	2335	2335	2335		0300	...	0430	0540	...	0640
Dewsbury d.	|	1952f	...	|	2020	2052	...	...	2120	2152	...	2220	2220	...	...	2252	2320	...	...	2346	2346	2346		|	...	|	|	...	0651
Huddersfield d.	1940	2002f	...	2011	2030	2102	...	...	2130	2202	...	2230	2230	...	...	2302	2330	...	...	2355	2355	2355		0318	...	0448	0558	...	0701
Stalybridge d.	|	|	...	|	2050	|	...	...	2150	|	...	2250	2250	...	...	|	|	...	...	|	|	|		|	...	|	|	...	0719
Manchester Victoria d.	|	2035f	...	|	|	|	...	...	|	|	...	|	|	...	...	|	|	...	...	|	|	|		|	...	|	|	...	|
Manchester Piccadilly a.	2014	|	...	2042	2106	2133	...	...	2205	2233	...	2305	2305	...	...	2337	0004	...	...	0027	0028	0041		0349	...	0519	0630	...	0734
Manchester Airport ✈ a.	...	|	...	2111	|	2154	...	...	|	2256	...	|	|	...	...	...	...	...	...	0046	0050	0056		0408	...	0538	0650	...	0754
Warrington Central a.	...	|	...	...	2130	...	...	...	2230	...	...	2330	2330	...	...	...	...	...	...	...	...	...		...	...	...	...	...	...
Liverpool South Parkway a.	...	|	...	...	2147	...	...	...	2245	...	...	2345	2345	...	...	...	...	...	...	...	...	...		...	...	...	...	...	...
Liverpool Lime Street a.	...	2114n	...	...	2159	...	...	...	2256	...	...	2356	2356	...	...	...	...	...	...	...	...	...		...	...	...	...	...	...

c – Runs 8 minutes later on ⑥.
d – Not ⑥ June 24 - Aug. 26.
e – June 24 - Aug. 26.
f – Not July 8 – 29.
g – Departs 3 minutes later on ⑥.
j – Arrives 3 minutes earlier on ⑥.
n – On ⑥ arrives 2108. Also does not run July 10 – 29.
r – ⑥ only.
t – Departs 3 minutes later on Ⓐ.
◧ – Distances: York (*0 km*) - Malton (*33 km*) - Scarborough (*67 km*). Hull (*0 km*) - Selby (*34 km*) - Leeds (*83 km*).

TP THE NORTH EAST and YORKSHIRE - MANCHESTER and LIVERPOOL 188

From July 8 to July 30 no trains will operate between Leeds and Liverpool via Manchester Victoria. Please call National Rail Enquiries for details ✆ 03457 48 49 50.

	⑦	⑦	⑦	⑦	⑦	⑦	⑦	⑦	⑦	⑦	⑦	⑦ c	⑦ a	⑦	⑦	⑦	⑦	⑦	⑦	⑦	⑦	⑦	⑦	⑦	⑦	⑦	⑦	⑦	⑦
Newcastle d.	...	...	...	...	0800	...	...	...	...	0906	...	...	...	1004	...	...	...	1110	1120	...	...	1206	...	...	...	1306	1310	...	...
Durham d.	...	...	...	...	0813	...	...	...	...	0919	...	...	...	1020	...	...	...	1123	1133	...	...	1222	...	...	...	1319	|	...	...
Middlesbrough d.	...	...	...	...	|	...	...	...	...	|	...	...	...	|	1027	...	...	|	|	...	...	|	1227	...	...	|	|	...	...
Darlington d.	...	...	...	...	0831	...	...	...	...	0936	...	...	...	1039	|	...	...	1140	1150	...	...	1240	|	...	...	1336	1341	...	...
Northallerton d.	...	...	...	...	0842	...	...	...	...	0947	...	...	...	1050	1056	...	...	1151	|	...	...	1251	1256	...	...	|	1353	...	...
Thirsk d.	...	...	...	...	0850	...	...	...	...	|	...	...	...	|	1104	...	...	|	|	...	...	|	1304	...	...	|	|	...	...
Scarborough d.	...	...	...	...	|	...	...	0853	...	|	...	...	0953	|	|	1053	...	|	|	1153	...	|	|	1253	...	|	|	1353	...
Malton d.	...	...	...	...	|	...	...	0916	...	|	...	...	1016	|	|	1116	...	|	|	1216	...	|	|	1316	...	|	|	1416	...
York a.	...	...	...	...	0909	...	...	0941	...	1010	...	...	1041	1113	1122	1141	...	1214	1222	1241	...	1314	1322	1341	...	1408	1416	1441	...
York d.	0712	...	0809	0850	0911	...	0928	0944	...	1012	1028	1045	1045	1115	1123	1145	...	1216	1223	1245	...	1315	1323	1345	...	1416	1423	1445	...
Hull d.	|	...	|	|	|	0835	|	|	0934	|	|	|	|	|	|	|	1137	|	|	|	1237	|	|	|	1339	|	|	|	1429
Selby d.	|	...	|	|	|	0910	|	|	1006	|	|	|	|	|	|	|	1208	|	|	|	1308	|	|	|	1410	|	|	|	1500
Leeds a.	0738	...	0835	0913	0934	0938	0953	1008	1032	1036	1051	1108	1108	1138	1147	1208	1234	1240	1247	1308	1334	1339	1347	1408	1434	1439	1447	1508	1527
Leeds d.	0740	...	0840	0916	0944f	...	0953	1010	1036	1044f	1053	1110	1110	1144f	1153	1210	1236	1244f	1253	1310	1336	1344f	1353	1410	1436	1444f	1453	1510	1536
Dewsbury d.	0751	...	0851	0927	|	...	|	1021	1047	|	|	1121	1121	|	|	1221	1247	|	|	1321	1347	|	|	1421	1447	|	|	1521	1547
Huddersfield d.	0801	...	0901	0936	1002f	...	1011	1030	1056	1102f	1111	1130	1131	1202f	1211	1230	1256	1302f	1311	1330	1356	1402f	1411	1430	1456	1502f	1511	1530	1556
Stalybridge d.	0819	...	0919	0955	|	...	|	1050	1115	|	|	1150	1150	|	|	1250	1315	|	|	1350	|	|	|	1450	1516	|	|	1550	1615
Manchester Victoria d.	|	...	|	|	1035f	...	|	|	|	1135f	|	|	|	1235f	|	|	|	1335f	|	|	|	1435f	|	|	|	1535f	|	|	|
Manchester Piccadilly a.	0834	0912	0934	1010	|	...	1047	1106	1131	|	1142	1206	1206	|	1242	1306	1331	|	1344	1406	1431	|	1442	1506	1531	|	1542	1606	1631
Manchester Airport ✈ a.	0854	|	0954	|	|	...	1118	|	...	|	1209	|	|	|	1311	|	...	|	1405	|	...	|	1508	|	...	|	1605	|	...
Warrington Central d.	...	0933	...	1033	|	...	...	1130	...	|	...	1230	1230	|	...	1330	...	|	...	1430	...	|	...	1530	...	|	...	1630	...
Liverpool South Parkway a.	...	0949	...	1049	|	...	...	1147	...	|	...	1247	1247	|	...	1347	...	|	...	1447	...	|	...	1547	...	|	...	1647	...
Liverpool Lime Street a.	...	1001	...	1101	1108r	...	...	1159	...	1208r	...	1258	1258	1308r	...	1359	...	1408r	...	1458	...	1508r	...	1559	...	1608r	...	1658	...

	⑦	⑦	⑦	⑦	⑦	⑦	⑦	⑦	⑦	⑦	⑦	⑦	⑦	⑦	⑦	⑦	⑦	⑦	⑦	⑦	⑦	⑦	⑦	⑦	⑦	⑦	⑦	⑦	⑦
Newcastle d.	1405	...	...	...	1510	1517	...	...	1604	...	1643	...	...	1710	1719	...	1804	...	...	...	1910	...	2010	...	...	...	...	...	2200
Durham d.	1421	...	...	...	1523	1530	...	...	1620	...	1657	...	...	1723	|	...	1822	...	...	...	1923	...	2023	...	...	...	...	...	2214
Middlesbrough d.	|	1423	...	...	|	|	...	...	|	1623	|	...	...	|	|	...	|	...	1819	...	|	...	|	...	2041	...	...	2208	|
Darlington d.	1438	|	...	...	1540	1547	...	...	1638	|	|	...	...	1741	1746	...	1840	...	|	...	1940	...	2040	...	|	...	...	|	2231
Northallerton d.	|	1451	...	...	1551	|	...	...	|	1652	|	...	...	1753	1758	...	|	...	1847	...	1951	...	2051	...	2109	...	...	2237	2243
Thirsk d.	|	1459	...	...	|	|	...	...	|	1700	|	...	...	|	|	...	|	...	1859	...	|	...	|	...	2117	...	...	2245	|
Scarborough d.	|	|	1453	...	|	|	1553	...	|	|	|	1703	...	|	|	1753	|	...	|	1853	|	1953	|	...	|	2138	...	|	|
Malton d.	|	|	1516	...	|	|	1616	...	|	|	|	1727	...	|	|	1816	|	...	|	1916	|	2016	|	...	|	2201	...	|	|
York a.	1512	1522	1541	...	1614	1619	1641	...	1711	1722	1744	1751	...	1815	1821	1841	1913	...	1917	1941	2014	2041	2114	...	2143	2226	...	2309	2315
York d.	1515	1523	1545	...	1616	1623	1645	...	1715	1723	1746	1753	...	1816	1823	1845	1915	...	1923	1945	2015	2045	2115	...	2145	2228	...	...	2317
Hull d.	|	|	|	1539	|	|	|	1643	|	|	|	|	1739	|	|	|	|	1842	|	|	|	|	|	2049	|	|	2207	...	|
Selby d.	|	|	|	1610	|	|	|	1714	|	|	|	|	1810	|	|	|	|	1914	|	|	|	|	|	2120	|	|	2238	...	|
Leeds a.	1539	1548	1608	1634	1640	1647	1708	1738	1742	1748	1808	1818	1834	1839	1848	1908	1938	1942	1947	2008	2039	2108	2139	2147	2208	2251	2302	...	2343
Leeds d.	1544f	1553	1610	1636	1644f	1653	1710	1738	1744f	1753	1810	...	1836	1844f	1853	1910	1941f	...	1953	2010	2041	2110	2141	...	2210	2253	...	...	2345
Dewsbury d.	|	|	1621	1647	|	|	1721	|	|	|	1821	...	1847	|	|	1921	1952f	...	|	2021	2052	2121	2152	...	2221	2304	...	...	2356
Huddersfield d.	1602f	1611	1630	1656	1702f	1711	1730	1756	1802f	1811	1830	...	1856	1902f	1911	1930	2002f	...	2011	2030	2102	2130	2202	...	2230	2313	...	...	0005
Stalybridge d.	|	|	1650	1715	|	|	1750	|	|	|	1850	...	1915	|	|	1950	|	...	|	2050	|	2150	|	...	2250	2332	...	...	|
Manchester Victoria d.	1635f	|	|	|	1735f	|	|	|	1835f	|	|	...	|	1935f	|	|	2033f	...	|	|	|	|	|	...	|	|	...	...	|
Manchester Piccadilly a.	|	1643	1706	1731	|	1746	1806	1831	|	1842	1906	...	1931	|	1944	2006	|	...	2045	2106	2135	2206	2233	...	2305	2349	...	...	0037
Manchester Airport ✈ a.	|	1708	|	...	|	1805	|	...	|	1908	|	...	...	|	2006	|	|	...	2108	|	...	|	2254	...	|	...	...	...	0058
Warrington Central d.	|	...	1730	...	|	...	1830	...	|	...	1930	...	...	|	...	2030	|	...	...	2130	...	2230	...	...	2330	...	...	...	...
Liverpool South Parkway a.	|	...	1747	...	|	...	1847	...	|	...	1947	...	...	|	...	2047	|	...	...	2147	...	2246	...	...	2346	...	...	...	...
Liverpool Lime Street a.	1708r	...	1759	...	1808r	...	1859	...	1908r	...	1959	...	...	2008r	...	2059	2108r	...	...	2159	...	2259	...	...	2359	...	...	...	...

		②–⑤	⑥	①	⚒	Ⓐ	⑥	⚒	⚒	⚒	⚒		⚒	⚒	⚒	⚒	⚒	⚒	⚒	⚒	⑥ b	⚒	Ⓐ	⑥	⚒	⚒	⚒	⚒	⚒
Liverpool Lime Street d.	⚒	...	...	...	...	...	...	...	...	...	...	...	...	0612t	...	0622	...	...	0712t	...	...	0715	...	...	...	0812t	...	0822	...
Liverpool South Parkway d.		...	...	...	...	...	...	...	...	...	...	...	...	|	...	0632	...	...	|	...	...	0725	...	...	...	|	...	0832	...
Warrington Central d.		...	...	...	...	...	...	...	...	...	...	...	...	|	...	0645	...	...	|	...	...	0741	...	...	...	|	...	0845	...
Manchester Airport d.		0038	0038	0045	...	0422	0425	...	0530	...	...	...	...	|	0634	|	0706	...	|	0732	...	|	0806	0806	...	|	0834	|	0906
Manchester Piccadilly d.		0053	0055	0100	...	0437	0440	...	0547	...	0615	...	0626	|	0657	0712	0726	0740	|	0757	...	0811	0826	0826	0841	|	0857	0911	0926
Manchester Victoria d.		|	|	|	...	|	|	...	|	...	|	...	|	0646t	|	|	|	|	0751t	|	...	|	|	|	|	0851t	|	|	|
Stalybridge d.		|	|	|	...	|	|	...	0600	...	0627	...	|	0658t	|	0725	|	0752	|	|	...	0825	|	|	0854	|	|	0925	|
Huddersfield d.		|	0125	|	...	0540	0540	...	0618	...	0646	...	0655	0717t	0727	0746	0755	0812	0821t	0827	...	0846	0855	0855	0913	0921t	0927	0946	0955
Dewsbury d.		|	|	|	...	|	|	...	0627	...	0655	...	0705	0726t	|	0755	0804	0823	|	|	...	0855	|	|	0923	|	|	0955	|
Leeds a.		0159	0202	0209	...	0559	0559	...	0642	...	0708	...	0718	0739t	0747	0810	0817	0836	0840t	0846	...	0909	0915	0915	0936	0940t	0946	1008	1015
Leeds d.		0205	0205	0215	...	0601	0601	...	0643	...	0714	...	0722	0743	0749	0812	0820	0838	0843	0848	...	0912	0917	0917	0938	0943	0948	1012	1017
Selby d.		|	|	|	...	|	|	...	|	...	|	...	0742	|	|	|	|	0858	|	|	...	|	|	|	0958	|	|	|	|
Hull a.		|	|	|	...	|	|	...	|	...	|	...	0820	|	|	|	|	0932	|	|	...	|	|	|	1034	|	|	|	|
York a.		0245	0244	0244	...	0624	0624	...	0706	...	0737	...	...	0806	0812	0838	0843	...	0906	0914	...	0936	0940	0940	...	1006	1013	1036	1040
York d.		...	...	...	0600	0626	0626	0640	0708	0718	0740	...	...	0808	0815	0840	...	...	0908	0915	0920	0940	0942	0942	...	1008	1015	1040	...
Malton d.		...	...	...	|	|	|	0704	|	|	0804	...	...	|	|	0904	...	...	|	|	0943	1004	|	|	...	|	|	1104	...
Scarborough a.		...	...	...	|	|	|	0729	|	|	0829	...	...	|	|	0930	...	...	|	|	1009	1029	|	|	...	|	|	1129	...
Thirsk d.		...	...	...	0616	|	|	...	0725	0734	...	...	...	|	0831	...	...	...	|	0931	...	...	|	|	...	|	1031	...	...
Northallerton d.		...	...	...	0624	0647	0647	...	0733	0742	...	...	...	0829	0840	...	...	...	0929	0940	...	...	|	|	...	1029	1040	...	...
Darlington d.		...	...	...	0640	0700	0700	...	0745	|	...	...	...	0841	|	...	...	...	0941	|	...	...	|	1012	...	1041	|	...	...
Middlesbrough a.		...	...	...	0707	|	|	...	|	0817	...	...	...	|	0912	...	...	...	|	1012	...	...	|	|	...	|	1112	...	...
Durham d.		...	...	...	...	0717	0717	...	0801	...	...	...	...	0857	...	...	...	...	0957	...	...	...	1027	1029	...	1057	...	...	...
Newcastle a.		...	...	...	...	0735	0735	...	0819	...	...	...	...	0914	...	...	...	...	1015	...	...	...	1042	1044	...	1112	...	...	...

	⚒	⚒	⚒	⑥ b	⚒	⚒	⚒	⚒	⚒	⚒	⚒	⚒	⚒	⚒	⑥ b	⚒	⚒	⚒	⚒	⚒	⚒	⚒	⚒	⚒	⚒	⚒	Ⓐ	⑥	⚒
Liverpool Lime Street d.	...	0912t	...	...	0922	...	...	1012t	...	1022	...	...	1111t	...	...	1122	...	...	1212t	...	1222	...	...	1312t	...	1322	...	...	...
Liverpool South Parkway d.	...	|	...	...	0932	...	...	|	...	1032	...	...	|	...	...	1132	...	...	|	...	1232	...	...	|	...	1332	...	...	...
Warrington Central d.	...	|	...	...	0945	...	...	|	...	1045	...	...	|	...	...	1145	...	...	|	...	1245	...	...	|	...	1345	...	...	...
Manchester Airport d.	...	|	0933	...	|	1006	...	|	1033	|	1106	...	|	1133	...	|	1206	...	|	1233	|	1306	...	|	1333	|	1406	1406	...
Manchester Piccadilly d.	0941	|	0957	...	1011	1026	1041	|	1057	1111	1126	1141	|	1157	...	1211	1226	1241	|	1257	1311	1326	1341	|	1357	1411	1426	1426	1441
Manchester Victoria d.	|	0951t	|	...	|	|	|	1051t	|	|	|	|	1151t	|	...	|	|	|	1251t	|	|	|	|	1351t	|	|	|	|	|
Stalybridge d.	0954	|	|	...	1025	|	1054	|	|	1125	|	1154	|	|	...	1225	|	1254	|	|	1325	|	1354	|	|	1425	|	|	1454
Huddersfield d.	1013	1021t	1027	...	1046	1055	1113	1121t	1127	1146	1155	1213	1221t	1227	...	1246	1255	1313	1321t	1327	1346	1355	1413	1421t	1427	1446	1455	1455	1513
Dewsbury d.	1023	|	|	...	1055	|	1123	|	|	1155	|	1223	|	|	...	1255	|	1323	|	|	1355	|	1423	|	|	1455	|	|	1523
Leeds a.	1036	1040t	1046	...	1108	1114	1136	1140t	1146	1208	1215	1236	1240t	1246	...	1308	1315	1336	1340t	1346	1408	1415	1436	1440t	1446	1508	1515	1515	1536
Leeds d.	1038	1043	1048	...	1112	1117	1138	1143	1148	1212	1217	1238	1243	1248	...	1312	1317	1338	1343	1348	1412	1417	1438	1443	1448	1512	1517	1517	1538
Selby d.	1058	|	|	...	|	|	1158	|	|	|	|	1258	|	|	...	|	|	1358	|	|	|	|	1458	|	|	|	|	|	1558
Hull a.	1135	|	|	...	|	|	1235	|	|	|	|	1335	|	|	...	|	|	1435	|	|	|	|	1535	|	|	|	|	|	1635
York a.	...	1106	1113	...	1136	1140	...	1206	1213	1236	1240	...	1306	1313	...	1336	1340	...	1406	1413	1436	1440	...	1506	1513	1536	1540	1540	...
York d.	...	1108	1115	1130	1140	1142	...	1208	1215	1240	...	...	1308	1315	1330	1340	1342	...	1408	1415	1440	...	...	1508	1515	1540	...	1542	...
Malton d.	...	|	|	|	1204	|	...	|	|	1304	...	...	|	|	|	1404	|	...	|	|	1504	...	...	|	|	1604	...	|	...
Scarborough a.	...	|	|	1216	1229	|	...	|	|	1329	...	...	|	|	1416	1429	|	...	|	|	1529	...	...	|	|	1629	...	|	...
Thirsk a.	...	|	1131	...	...	|	...	|	1231	...	...	...	|	1331	...	...	|	...	|	1431	...	...	...	|	1531	...	...	|	...
Northallerton a.	...	1129	1140	...	...	|	...	1229	1240	...	...	...	1329	1340	...	...	|	...	1429	1440	...	...	...	1529	1540	...	...	|	...
Darlington a.	...	1141	|	...	...	|	...	1241	|	...	...	...	1341	|	...	...	|	...	1441	|	...	...	...	1541	|	...	...	|	...
Middlesbrough a.	...	|	1212	...	...	|	...	|	1312	...	...	...	|	1412	...	...	|	...	|	1512	...	...	...	|	1612	...	...	|	...
Durham a.	...	1157	...	...	...	1227	...	1257	...	...	...	...	1357	...	...	...	1427	...	1457	...	...	...	...	1557	...	...	...	1627	...
Newcastle a.	...	1215	...	...	...	1242	...	1316	...	...	...	...	1415	...	...	...	1443	...	1512	...	...	...	...	1615	...	...	...	1642	...

a – June 25 - Sept. 10.
b – June 24 - Aug. 26.
c – May 21 - June 18 and from Sept. 17.
f – May 21 - July 2 and from Aug. 6.
r – From Aug. 6.
t – Not July 8 – 29.

① – Mondays ② – Tuesdays ③ – Wednesdays ④ – Thursdays ⑤ – Fridays ⑥ – Saturdays ⑦ – Sundays Ⓐ – Monday to Fridays, not holidays

From July 8 to July 30 no trains will operate between Liverpool and Leeds via Manchester Victoria. Please call National Rail Enquiries for details ✆ 03457 48 49 50.

	⚒	⚒	⚒		⚒	⚒	⚒	⚒	⚒	⚒	⚒	⚒		⚒	⚒	Ⓐ	⑥	⚒		⚒	⚒	⚒	⚒	⚒	⚒	⚒	⚒	Ⓐ
Liverpool Lime Street d.	1412t	...	1422	...	...	...	1511t	...	1522	...	...	1612t	...	...	1622	...	...	...	...	1710t	...	1722	...	...	1812t	...	1822	...
Liverpool South Parkway d.	|	...	1432	...	...	...	|	...	1532	...	...	|	...	...	1632	...	...	...	...	|	...	1732	...	...	|	...	1832	...
Warrington Central d.	|	...	1445	...	...	...	|	...	1545	...	...	|	...	...	1645	...	...	...	...	|	...	1745	...	...	|	...	1845	...
Manchester Airport d.	|	1433	|	...	1506	...	|	1533	|	1606	...	|	...	1633	|	1703j	1706	...	...	|	1733	|	1806v	...	|	1833	|	...
Manchester Piccadilly d.	|	1457	1511	...	1526	1541	|	1557	1611	1626	1641	|	...	1656	1711	1725	1725	1741	...	|	1754	1811	1826	1841	|	1857	1911	1926
Manchester Victoria d.	1451t	|	|	...	|	|	1551t	|	|	|	|	1651t	...	|	|	|	|	|	...	1751t	|	|	|	|	1851t	|	|	|
Stalybridge d.	|	|	1525	...	|	1554	|	|	1625	|	1654	|	...	|	1725	1738	1738	1756	...	|	|	1825	|	1854	|	|	1925	|
Huddersfield d.	1521t	1527	1546	...	1555	1613	1621t	1627	1646	1655	1713	1721t	...	1727	1746	1757	1757	1816	...	1821t	1827	1846	1855	1914	1921t	1927	1946	1956
Dewsbury d.	|	|	1555	...	|	1623	|	|	1655	|	1723	|	...	|	1755	|	|	1825	...	|	|	1855	|	1924	|	|	1956	|
Leeds a.	1540t	1546	1608	...	1615	1636	1640t	1646	1708	1715	1736	1742t	...	1746	1808	1816	1816	1838	...	1842t	1846	1909	1916	1937	1942t	1946	2009	2017
Leeds d.	1543	1548	1612	...	1617	1638	1643	1648	1712	1717	1740	1744	...	1749	1812	1818	1818	1841	...	1845	1849	1912	1917	1939	1943	1949	2012	2020
Selby d.	|	|	|	...	|	1658	|	|	|	|	1801	|	...	|	|	|	|	1904	...	|	|	|	|	2001	|	|	|	2055
Hull a.	|	|	|	...	|	1735	|	|	|	|	1838	|	...	|	|	|	|	1939	...	|	|	|	|	2041	|	|	|	2135
York a.	1606	1613	1636	...	1640	...	1706	1713	1736	1743	...	1807	...	1814	1836	1845	1845	...	...	1908	1913	1936	1940	...	2006	2012	2035	...
York d.	1608	1615	1640	...	...	...	1708	1715	1740	...	...	1809	...	1816	1840	1857	1857	...	...	1910	1916	1940	...	...	2008	2016	2040	...
Malton d.	|	|	1704	...	...	...	|	|	1804	...	...	|	...	|	1904	|	|	...	...	|	|	2004	...	...	|	|	2104	...
Scarborough a.	|	|	1729	...	...	...	|	|	1829	...	...	|	...	|	1929	|	|	...	...	|	|	2029	...	...	|	|	2129	...
Thirsk a.	|	1631	...	...	...	...	|	1731	...	...	...	|	...	1832	...	|	|	...	...	|	1933	...	...	...	|	2035	...	...
Northallerton a.	1629	1640	...	...	...	...	1729	1740	...	...	...	1830	...	1840	...	|	|	...	...	1931	1941	...	...	...	2029	2043	...	...
Darlington a.	1641	|	...	...	...	...	1741	|	...	...	...	1842	...	|	...	|	1927	...	...	1943	|	...	...	...	2041	|	...	...
Middlesbrough a.	|	1712	...	...	...	...	|	1812	...	...	...	|	...	1914	...	|	|	...	...	|	2014	...	...	...	|	2115	...	...
Durham a.	1657	...	...	...	...	...	1757	...	...	...	...	1858	...	...	...	1943	1944	...	...	2001	...	...	...	...	2057	...	...	...
Newcastle a.	1712	...	...	...	...	...	1815	...	...	...	...	1914	...	...	...	1957	1958	...	...	2019	...	...	...	...	2113	...	...	...
	⚒	⚒	⑥	⚒	Ⓐ	Ⓐ	⑥	⑥	Ⓐ	Ⓐ	⑥	⚒	⚒	⚒	⚒	⑥	Ⓐ	⑥		⑤	①-④			⑦	⑦	⑦	⑦	⑦ a
Liverpool Lime Street d.	...	1912t	...	1922	...	...	...	...	2022	...	2022	...	...	2130	...	2230	2230	...	...	...	...	...	⑦	...	...	...	...	...
Liverpool South Parkway d.	...	|	...	1932	...	...	...	...	2032	...	2032	...	...	2140	...	2240	2240	...	...	...	...	...		...	...	...	...	...
Warrington Central d.	...	|	...	1945	...	...	...	...	2045	...	2045	...	...	2153	...	2253	2253	...	...	...	...	...		...	...	...	...	...
Manchester Airport d.	1924	|	...	|	...	2024	2024	...	|	...	|	...	2124	|	2224	|	|	2320	...	2320	2320	...		0100	0425	0630	...	...
Manchester Piccadilly d.	1942	|	...	2011	...	2042	2042	...	2111	...	2111	...	2142	2219	2242	2321	2321	2335	...	2335	2335	...		0117	0442	0647	...	...
Manchester Victoria d.	|	1951t	...	|	...	|	|	...	|	...	|	...	|	|	|	|	|	2351	...	2351	2351	...		|	|	|	...	...
Stalybridge d.	|	|	...	2025	...	|	|	...	2125	...	2125	...	|	2231	2254	2334	2334	|	...	|	|	...		|	|	0700	...	...
Huddersfield d.	2012	2021t	...	2046	...	2112	2112	...	2146	...	2146	...	2211	2250	2313	2352	2352	0021	...	0021	0052	...		0147	0512	0718	...	...
Dewsbury d.	|	|	...	2055	...	|	|	...	2155	...	2155	...	|	2259	2322	|	|	0030	...	0030s	0102s	...		|	|	0727	...	...
Leeds a.	2031	2042t	...	2108	...	2131	2131	...	2208	...	2208	...	2230	2312	2335	0011	0031	0043	...	0044	0115	...		0206	0531	0740	...	...
Leeds d.	2033	2043	2105	2112	2121	2133	2133	...	2211	...	2211	2221	2233	2316	2337	0015	0034	0045	...	0047	0123	...		0208	0533	0743	...	...
Selby d.	|	|	2128	|	2145	|	|	...	|	...	|	2243	|	|	|	|	|	|	...	|	|	...		|	|	|	...	...
Hull a.	|	|	2207	|	2223	|	|	...	|	...	|	2319	|	|	|	|	|	|	...	|	|	...		|	|	|	...	...
York a.	2058	2107	...	2137	...	2157	2158	...	2234	...	2236	...	2258	2342	0003	0043	0113	0113	...	0129	0207	...		0236	0601	0811	...	...
York d.	...	2109	...	...	...	2200	...	2212	2235	2242	...	...	...	...	...	...	...	...	...	...	...	...		...	...	...	0847	0857
Malton d.	...	|	...	...	...	2224	...	2236	|	2306	...	...	...	...	...	...	...	...	...	...	...	...		...	...	...	|	0921
Scarborough a.	...	|	...	...	...	2249	...	2301	|	2331	...	...	...	...	...	...	...	...	...	...	...	...		...	...	...	|	0946
Thirsk a.	...	2126	...	...	...	...	...	...	2258	...	...	...	...	...	...	...	...	...	...	...	...	...		...	...	...	0903	...
Northallerton a.	...	2134	...	...	...	...	...	...	2306	...	...	...	...	...	...	...	...	...	...	...	...	...		...	...	...	0911	...
Darlington a.	...	2146	...	...	...	...	...	...	2318	...	...	...	...	...	...	...	...	...	...	...	...	...		...	...	...	0925	...
Middlesbrough a.	...	|	...	...	...	...	...	...	|	...	...	...	...	...	...	...	...	...	...	...	...	...		...	...	...	0952	...
Durham a.	...	2202	...	...	...	...	...	...	2334	...	...	...	...	...	...	...	...	...	...	...	...	...		...	...	...	...	...
Newcastle a.	...	2219	...	...	...	...	...	...	0008	...	...	...	...	...	...	...	...	...	...	...	...	...		...	...	...	...	...
	⑦	⑦ b	⑦ c	⑦ c	⑦ b	⑦	⑦	⑦	⑦	⑦	⑦	⑦	⑦	⑦	⑦	⑦	⑦	⑦	⑦	⑦	⑦	⑦	⑦	⑦	⑦	⑦	⑦	⑦
Liverpool Lime Street d.	...	...	...	...	...	...	0822	...	0912r	...	0922	1010r	...	1022	...	1112r	...	1122	1122	1210r	...	1222	...	1312r	...	1322	1405r	...
Liverpool South Parkway d.	...	...	...	...	...	...	0832	...	|	...	0932	|	...	1032	...	|	...	1132	1132	|	...	1232	...	|	...	1332	|	...
Warrington Central d.	...	...	...	...	...	...	0844	...	|	...	0944	|	...	1044	...	|	...	1145	1145	|	...	1245	...	|	...	1345	|	...
Manchester Airport d.	0729	0802	...	0824	...	...	|	...	|	0935	|	|	1033	|	...	|	1133	|	|	|	1233	|	...	|	1333	|	|	...
Manchester Piccadilly d.	0747	0820	...	0847	...	...	0911	0928	|	1003	1011	|	1057	1111	1143	|	1157	1211	1211	|	1257	1311	1343	|	1357	1411	|	1443
Manchester Victoria d.	|	|	...	|	...	...	|	|	0951f	|	|	1046f	|	|	|	1151f	|	|	|	1244f	|	|	|	1351f	|	|	1440f	|
Stalybridge d.	0800	0833	...	0900	...	...	0924	|	|	|	1025	|	|	1125	1155	|	|	1225	1225	|	|	1325	1355	|	|	1425	|	1456
Huddersfield d.	0818	0852	...	0918	...	...	0946	1005	1021f	1032	1046	1115f	1127	1146	1214	1221f	1227	1246	1246	1314f	1327	1346	1414	1421f	1427	1446	1509f	1515
Dewsbury d.	0827	0901	...	0927	...	...	0955	1015	|	|	1055	|	|	1155	1223	|	|	1255	1255	|	|	1355	1423	|	|	1455	|	1525
Leeds a.	0840	0914	...	0940	...	...	1008	1030	1040f	1051	1109	1134f	1146	1209	1236	1240f	1246	1309	1309	1333f	1346	1409	1436	1440f	1446	1509	1528f	1538
Leeds d.	0843	0915	0915	0943	0943	...	1012	1038	1043	1053	1112	1138	1148	1212	1238	1243	1248	1312	1312	1338	1348	1412	1438	1443	1449	1512	1536	1540
Selby d.	|	|	|	|	|	0952	|	1104	|	|	|	|	|	|	1301	|	|	|	|	|	|	|	1458	|	|	|	|	1603
Hull a.	|	|	|	|	|	1014	|	1140	|	|	|	|	|	|	1336	|	|	|	|	|	|	|	1532	|	|	|	|	1637
York a.	0906	0938	0938	1008	1006	1049	1038	...	1106	1116	1139	1201	1211	1235	...	1306	1311	1336	1336	1402	1411	1439	...	1506	1511	1540	1603	...
York d.	0908	0942	0942	1008	1008	...	1042	...	1108	1117	1142	1203	1212	1242	...	1308	1314	1340	1343	1404	1413	1442	...	1508	1514	1542	1607	...
Malton d.	|	1006	1005	|	|	...	1106	...	|	|	1206	|	|	1306	...	|	|	|	1407	|	|	1506	...	|	|	1606	|	...
Scarborough a.	|	1031	1031	|	|	...	1131	...	|	|	1231	|	|	1331	...	|	|	|	1432	|	|	1531	...	|	|	1631	|	...
Thirsk a.	|	...	...	|	|	...	...	...	|	1134	...	|	|	...	...	|	1331	|	...	|	|	...	...	|	1531	...	|	...
Northallerton a.	0929	...	...	1029	1029	...	...	...	1129	1142	...	|	1233	...	...	1329	1340	|	...	1425	|	...	...	1529	1540	...	|	...
Darlington a.	0941	...	...	1041	1041	...	...	...	1141	|	...	|	1245	...	...	1341	|	1411	...	1436	1443	...	...	1541	|	...	1637	...
Middlesbrough a.	|	...	...	|	|	...	...	...	|	1214	...	|	|	...	...	|	1412	|	...	|	|	...	...	|	1612	...	|	...
Durham a.	0957	...	...	1057	1057	...	...	...	1157	...	...	|	1302	...	...	1357	...	1428	...	|	1500	...	...	1557	...	...	1654	...
Newcastle a.	1015	...	...	1114	1114	...	...	...	1215	...	...	1300	1317	...	...	1416	...	1442	...	1506	1515	...	...	1615	...	...	1709	...
	⑦	⑦	⑦	⑦	⑦	⑦	⑦	⑦	⑦	⑦	⑦	⑦	⑦	⑦	⑦	⑦	⑦	⑦	⑦	⑦	⑦	⑦	⑦	⑦	⑦	⑦	⑦	⑦
Liverpool Lime Street d.	...	1422	...	1512r	...	1522	...	1612r	...	1622	...	1712r	...	1722	1812r	...	1822	...	...	1912r	1922	...	2012r	2022	...	...	2152	...
Liverpool South Parkway d.	...	1432	...	|	...	1532	...	|	...	1632	...	|	...	1732	|	...	1832	...	...	|	1932	...	|	2032	...	...	2202	...
Warrington Central d.	...	1445	...	|	...	1545	...	|	...	1645	...	|	...	1745	|	...	1845	...	...	|	1945	...	|	2045	...	...	2215	...
Manchester Airport d.	1433	|	...	|	1533	|	...	|	1633	|	...	|	1733	|	|	1833	|	...	1920	|	|	2020	|	|	...	2120	|	2320
Manchester Piccadilly d.	1457	1511	1543	|	1557	1611	1643	|	1657	1711	1743	|	1757	1811	|	1857	1911	...	1942	|	2012	2042	|	2112	...	2142	2242	2346
Manchester Victoria d.	|	|	|	1551f	|	|	|	1652f	|	|	|	1751f	|	|	1851f	|	|	...	|	1951f	|	|	2051f	|	...	|	|	|
Stalybridge d.	|	1525	1555	|	|	1625	1655	|	|	1725	1754	|	|	1825	|	|	1925	...	|	|	2025	|	|	2125	...	|	2255	|
Huddersfield d.	1527	1546	1614	1621f	1630	1646	1714	1721f	1727	1746	1814	1821f	1827	1846	1921f	1927	1946	...	2011	2021f	2046	2111	2121f	2146	...	2211	2313	0021
Dewsbury d.	|	1555	1623	|	|	1655	1723	|	|	1755	1823	|	|	1855	|	|	1955	...	|	|	2055	|	|	2155	...	2220	2322	0030
Leeds a.	1546	1609	1636	1640f	1649	1709	1736	1741f	1746	1808	1836	1840f	1846	1909	1940f	1946	2008	...	2030	2040f	2108	2133	2140f	2208	...	2233	2335	0043
Leeds d.	1548	1612	1637	1643	1650	1712	1738	1744	1748	1812	1838	1843	1849	1912	1943	1949	2012	2018	2033	2043	2112	2138	2143	2211	2221	2236	2341	0045
Selby d.	|	|	1657	|	|	|	1800	|	|	|	1901	|	|	|	|	|	|	2051	|	|	|	2201	|	|	2243	|	|	|
Hull a.	|	|	1732	|	|	|	1835	|	|	|	1936	|	|	|	|	|	|	2127	|	|	|	2237	|	|	2319	|	|	|
York a.	1611	1635	...	1706	1713	1737	...	1807	1811	1835	...	1906	1912	1936	2006	2014	2035	...	2056	2106	2137	...	2206	2234	...	2304	0022	0113
York d.	1613	1642	...	1708	1715	1742	...	1809	1813	1842	...	1908	1915	1942	2008	...	2042	...	2100	2108	...	...	2208	2235	...	...	...	...
Malton d.	|	1706	...	|	|	1806	...	|	|	1906	...	|	|	2006	|	...	2106	...	|	|	...	...	2232	|	...	...	...	...
Scarborough a.	|	1731	...	|	|	1831	...	|	|	1931	...	|	|	2031	|	...	2131	...	|	|	...	...	2257	|	...	...	...	...
Thirsk a.	|	...	...	|	1731	...	...	|	|	...	...	|	1933	...	|	...	...	...	2116	|	...	...	...	2258	...	...	...	...
Northallerton a.	1634	...	...	1729	1740	...	...	|	1834	...	...	1929	1944	...	2029	...	...	...	2124	2129	...	...	...	2306	...	...	...	...
Darlington a.	1646	...	...	1741	|	...	...	1839	1846	...	...	1941	|	...	2041	...	...	...	|	2141	...	...	...	2318	...	...	...	...
Middlesbrough a.	|	...	...	|	1812	...	...	|	|	...	...	|	2016	...	|	...	...	...	2158	|	...	...	...	|	...	...	...	...
Durham a.	1702	...	...	1757	...	...	...	1856	1902	...	...	1957	...	...	2057	...	...	...	...	2157	...	...	...	2334	...	...	...	...
Newcastle a.	1717	...	...	1815	...	...	...	1913	1917	...	...	2014	...	...	2114	...	...	...	...	2214	...	...	...	0007	...	...	...	...

a – June 25 - Sept. 10.
b – May 21 - Sept. 10.
c – From Sept. 17.
f – May 21 - July 2 and from Aug. 6.
j – ①–④ only.
r – From Aug. 6.
t – Not July 8 – 29.
v – ⑥ only.

NT 2nd class — YORK - LEEDS - HALIFAX - BLACKPOOL and MANCHESTER — 190

km			Ⓐ	⑥	⚒	Ⓐ	⑥	Ⓐ	⚒	⚒	⚒	⚒	⚒	⚒	⚒	⚒	⚒		⚒	⚒	⚒	⚒	⚒	⚒	⚒
0	**York** 124 188 d.	⚒	...	...	...	...	...	0535	...	0620	...	...	...	0718a	...	...	...		1718	...	...	...	1827	...	...
41	**Leeds** 124 188 d.		0508	0535	0557	0608	0618	0623	0651	0708	0718	0723	0751	0805	0818	0826	0851		1805	1818	1823	1851	1905	1919	1951
56	Bradford Interchange d.		0531	0558	0617	0631	0641	│	0714	0728	0741	│	0814	0826	0841	│	0914	and	1826	1841	│	1914	1926	1942	2014
69	**Halifax** d.		0544	0611	0629	0644	0654	│	0727	0740	0754	│	0827	0839	0854	│	0927	at	1838	1854	│	1927	1939	1955	2027
	Dewsbury d.		│	│	│	│	│	0639	│	│	│	0739	│	│	│	0842	│	the	│	│	1841	│	│	│	│
	Brighouse d.		│	│	│	│	│	0659	│	│	│	0758	│	│	│	0859	│	same	│	│	1859	│	│	│	│
83	Hebden Bridge d.		0559	0627	0646	0659	0710	0717	0742	0752	0805	0817	0842	0852	0906	0918	0942	minutes	1852	1906	1917	1942	1952	2011	2042
90	Todmorden d.		0607	0634	│	0707	0717	0724	0750	│	0813	0824	0850	│	0913	0925	0950	past	│	1913	1925	1950	│	2018	2050
104	Rochdale d.		0623	0651	│	0720	0734	0741	0804	│	0825	0841	0900	│	0924	0942	1000	each	│	1924	1941	2000	│	2035	2100
120	**Manchester** Victoria a.		0647	0717	│	0737	0758	0803	0824	│	0847	0904	0917	│	0941	1004	1017	hour	│	1942	2006	2018	│	2100	2117
103	Burnley Manchester Road d.		...	...	0705	...	...	...	...	0812	...	...	...	0912	...	...	...	until	1912	...	...	...	2012	...	...
113	Accrington d.		...	...	0714	...	...	...	...	0821	...	...	...	0921	...	...	...		1921	...	...	...	2021	...	...
123	Blackburn 191 d.		...	...	0723	...	...	...	...	0829	...	...	...	0930	...	...	...	✣	1930	...	...	...	2030	...	...
142	Preston 156 191 a.		...	...	0746	...	...	...	...	0852	...	...	...	0947	...	...	...		1949	...	...	...	2047	...	...
171	**Blackpool** North 156 191 a.		...	...	0814	...	...	...	...	0923	...	...	...	1015	...	...	...		2017	...	...	...	2116	...	...

	⚒	⚒	⚒	⚒	⚒		⑦	⑦	⑦	⑦	⑦	⑦	⑦	⑦	⑦	⑦		⑦	⑦	⑦	⑦	⑦	⑦	⑦	⑦
York 124 188 d.	1918	...	...	...	...	⑦	...	0812	...	0905	...	1015	...	...	1118a	...		1827	...	1918	...	2027	...	...	...
Leeds 124 188 d.	2005	2035	2108	2135	2235		0818	0853	0908	0953	1008	1053	1108	1151	1208	1251		1908	1951	2008	2052	2108	2135	2208	2235
Bradford Interchange d.	2026	2058	2128	2158	2258		0841	0913	0933	1014	1033	1113	1133	1215	1228	1314	and	1928	2014	2028	2115	2128	2158	2231	2259
Halifax d.	2039	2111	2140	2211	2311		0854	0926	0945	1026	1045	1126	1145	1228	1240	1327	at	1940	2027	2040	2128	2140	2211	2246	2314
Dewsbury d.	│	│	│	│	│		│	│	│	│	│	│	│	│	│	│	the	│	│	│	│	│	│	│	│
Brighouse d.	│	│	│	│	│		│	│	│	│	│	│	│	│	│	│	same	│	│	│	│	│	│	2257	2325
Hebden Bridge d.	2052	2126	2154	2226	2326		0909	0940	1001	1041	1101	1140	1201	1244	1252	1342	minutes	1952	2042	2052	2144	2152	2226	...	...
Todmorden d.	│	2134	│	2234	2334		0917	│	1009	│	1109	│	1209	1251	│	1350	past	│	2050	│	2152	│	2234	...	...
Rochdale d.	│	2150	│	2250	2350		0929	│	1021	│	1121	│	1221	1304	│	1403	each	│	2103	│	*2222*	│	2250	...	...
Manchester Victoria a.	│	2215	│	2315	0008		0946	│	1039	│	1139	│	1239	1320	│	1420	hour	│	2120	│	*2245*	│	2313	...	...
Burnley Manchester Road d.	2112	...	2214	...	...		...	1001	...	1103	...	1201	...	...	1312	...	until	2012	...	2112	...	2212	...	...	...
Accrington d.	2121	...	2223	...	...		...	1010	...	1112	...	1210	...	...	1321	...		2021	...	2121	...	2221	...	...	...
Blackburn 191 d.	2130	...	2231	...	...		...	1019	...	1121	...	1220	...	...	1330	...	✣	2030	...	2130	...	2230	...	...	...
Preston 156 191 a.	2148	...	2251	...	...		...	1041	...	1140	...	1242	...	...	1348	...		2048	...	2147	...	2252	...	...	...
Blackpool North 156 191 a.	2212f	...	2321f	...	...		...	1108	...	1210	...	1315	...	...	1414	...		*2121*	...	2216	...	*0001*	...	...	...

		⚒	⚒	⑥	Ⓐ	⚒	⚒	⚒	⚒	⚒	⚒	⚒	⚒	⚒	⚒	⚒		⚒	⚒	⚒	⚒	⚒	⚒	⚒	⚒
Blackpool North 156 191 d.	⚒	...	0511b	...	...	...	0611b	...	...	...	...	0711	...	...	...	0811		...	...	...	1656	...	...	...	1811
Preston 156 191 d.		...	0537	...	...	...	0637	...	...	...	...	0737	...	...	...	0836		...	...	...	1725	...	...	...	1837
Blackburn 191 d.		...	0555	...	...	...	0655	...	...	...	...	0755	...	...	...	0855	and	...	...	...	1753	...	...	...	1856
Accrington d.		...	0603	...	...	...	0703	...	...	...	...	0803	...	...	...	0903	at	...	...	...	1801	...	...	...	1904
Burnley Manchester Road d.		...	0612	...	...	...	0712	...	...	...	...	0812	...	...	...	0912	the	...	...	...	1812	...	...	...	1913
Manchester Victoria d.		0547	│	0608	0612	0636	│	...	0712	0726	0748	│	0816	0826	0848	│	same	1708	1725	1745	│	1810	1826	1848	│
Rochdale d.		0602	│	0627	0626	0653	│	...	0726	0747	0802	│	0830	0847	0902	│	minutes	1727	1747	1803	│	1827	1847	1902	│
Todmorden d.		0612	│	0644	0643	0710	│	...	0743	0804	0813	│	0841	0904	0913	│	past	1743	1804	1816	│	1841	1904	1913	│
Hebden Bridge d.		0619	0634	0651	0650	0717	0734	0739	0750	0811	0820	0834	0848	0911	0920	0934	each	1750	1811	1822	1834	1848	1911	1920	1935
Brighouse d.		│	│	│	│	│	│	0756	│	0829	│	│	│	0929	│	│	hour	│	1829	│	│	│	1929	│	│
Dewsbury d.		│	│	│	│	│	│	0811	│	0842	│	│	│	0941	│	│	until	│	1841	│	│	│	1941	│	│
Halifax d.		0637	0648	0709	0707	0734	0748	│	0807	│	0833	0848	0906	│	0933	0947		1807	│	1835	1847	1906	│	1934	1949
Bradford Interchange d.		0652	0704	0724	0723	0750	0804	│	0823	│	0849	0904	0921	│	0949	1002	✣	1824	│	1852	1903	1922	│	1949	2004
Leeds 124 188 a.		0714	0722	0746	0746	0813	0822	0834	0845	0904	0910	0923	0944	1003	1012	1023		1844	1903	1915	1923	1944	2003	2011	2026
York 124 188 a.		...	0803	...	...	...	0904	...	...	...	...	1000	...	...	...	1103		...	...	...	2004	...	...	...	...

	⚒	⚒	⚒	⚒	⚒	⚒	Ⓐ	⑥	Ⓐ		⑦	⑦	⑦	⑦	⑦	⑦		⑦	⑦	⑦	⑦	⑦	⑦	⑦	⑦
Blackpool North 156 191 d.	...	...	1911	...	2029	...	...	...	...	⑦	...	...	...	...	...	1111		1811	...	1911	...	2011	...	2111	...
Preston 156 191 d.	...	...	1937	...	2056	...	...	...	...		...	0937	...	1038	...	1137		1837	...	1937	...	2037	...	2137	...
Blackburn 191 d.	...	...	1955	...	2124	...	...	...	...		...	0955	...	1055	...	1155	and	1855	...	1955	...	2055	...	2155	...
Accrington d.	...	...	2003	...	2132	...	...	...	...		...	1003	...	1103	...	1203	at	1903	...	2003	...	2103	...	2203	...
Burnley Manchester Road d.	...	...	2012	...	2141	...	...	...	...		...	1012	...	1112	...	1212	the	1912	...	2012	...	2112	...	2212	...
Manchester Victoria d.	1916	1926	│	2026	│	2126	2226	2254	2321		0915	│	1015	│	1115	│	same	│	1915	│	2015	│	2115	│	2210
Rochdale d.	1931	1947	│	2047	│	2147	2247	2308	2342		0929	│	1029	│	1129	│	minutes	│	1929	│	2029	│	2129	│	2231
Todmorden d.	1942	2004	│	2104	│	2204	2304	2325	2359		0942	│	1042	│	1142	│	past	│	1942	│	2042	│	2142	│	2248
Hebden Bridge d.	1949	2011	2034	2111	2203	2211	2311	2331	0006		0949	1034	1049	1134	1149	1234	each	1934	1949	2034	2049	2134	2149	2234	2255
Brighouse d.	│	2029	│	│	│	│	│	│	│		│	│	│	│	│	│	hour	│	│	│	│	│	│	│	│
Dewsbury d.	│	2041	│	│	│	│	│	│	│		│	│	│	│	│	│	until	│	│	│	│	│	│	│	│
Halifax d.	2007	│	2049	2129	2218	2229	2329	2349	0023		1007	1047	1107	1147	1207	1247		1947	2007	2049	2107	2149	2207	2249	2313
Bradford Interchange d.	2022	│	2104	2144	2233	2244	2345	0004	0039		1023	1103	1123	1203	1223	1303	✣	2003	2024	2105	2123	2205	2223	2305	2328
Leeds 124 188 a.	2044	2103	2126	2206	2253	2309	0006	0026	0057		1044	1122	1144	1224	1244	1322		2022	2044	2122	2144	2226	2246	2324	2351
York 124 188 a.	2130b	...	2230d	...	2340	...	...	...	...		...	1158	...	1303	...	1400		...	...	2203	...	...	...	...	...

a – Departs xx27 on the even hours except on ⑥ when departs 0818, 0918, 1027.
b – ⑥ only.
d – On ⑥ arrives 2218.
f – ⑤ only.
✣ – Timings may vary by ± 5 minutes.

NT 2nd class — BLACKPOOL - PRESTON - CLITHEROE - HELLIFIELD — 191

THIS TABLE HAS TEMPORARILY MOVED TO BELOW TABLE 159

NT 2nd classs — HULL - DONCASTER - SHEFFIELD — 192

km			Ⓐ	Ⓐ	Ⓐ A	Ⓐ A	Ⓐ A	Ⓐ A	Ⓐ A	Ⓐ B	Ⓐ A	Ⓐ B	Ⓐ A	Ⓐ A	Ⓐ	Ⓐ B	Ⓐ	Ⓐ A	Ⓐ	Ⓐ		⑥	⑥	⑥ A	⑥ A	⑥ A
0	**Hull** 181 d.	Ⓐ	0520	0641	0803	0857	0957	1057	1157	1257	1357	1457	1557	1657	1743	1757	1857	2003	2057	2220	⑥	0520	0640	0803	0857	0957
38	Goole d.		0547	0717	0830	0924	1024	1124	1224	1324	1424	1524	1624	1725	1821	│	1924	2036	2124	2254		0547	0716	0830	0924	1024
66	**Doncaster** 181 a.		0617	0747	0854	0949	1047	1148	1247	1348	1447	1548	1648	1747	1851	1848	1949	2106	2147	2324		0617	0746	0857	0948	1047
66	**Doncaster** 193 d.		0628	0748	0856	0950	1049	1148	1249	1349	1449	1549	1649	1749	1902	1850	1950	2107	2149	2325		0629	0748	0902	0949	1049
90	Meadowhall 193 d.		0657	0825	0916	1010	1110	1210	1310	1410	1510	1610	1710	1810	1929	1910	2010	2134	2212	2355		0658	0825	0924	1010	1110
96	**Sheffield** 193 a.		0706	0833	0926	1019	1120	1219	1319	1420	1519	1620	1720	1820	1940	1917	2017	2142	2221	0004		0707	0832	0931	1019	1120

	⑥ A	⑥ A	⑥ B	⑥ A	⑥ B	⑥ A	⑥ A	⑥	⑥ B	⑥	⑥ A	⑥	⑥ A		⑦	⑦	⑦ A	⑦ B	⑦ B	⑦ A	⑦ B	⑦ A	⑦ B	⑦ A	⑦ B	⑦
Hull 181 d.	1058	1157	1257	1357	1457	1557	1657	1743	1755	1857	2003	2057	2216	⑦	0840	0943	1050	1241	1330	1441	1532	1637	1732	1835	2001	2140
Goole d.	1124	1224	1324	1426	1524	1624	1725	1821	│	1924	2036	2124	2250		0909	1017	1118	1314	1402	1509	1602	1708	1802	1903	2034	2208
Doncaster 181 a.	1147	1247	1347	1447	1547	1648	1748	1851	1847	1947	2106	2147	2320		0931	1047	1146	1337	1426	1532	1627	1731	1831	1934	2059	2235
Doncaster 193 d.	1149	1249	1348	1449	1549	1649	1749	1901	1849	1950	2107	2149	2321		0939	*1130*	1148	1339	1429	1533	1629	1732	1834	1936	2101	2240
Meadowhall 193 d.	1210	1310	1410	1510	1610	1710	1810	1929	1910	2010	2134	2212	2350		1001	│	1208	1359	1452	1554	1654	1754	1853	1957	2128	2307
Sheffield 193 a.	1220	1320	1420	1520	1617	1720	1817	1939	1919	2017	2142	2222	2359		1008	*1154*	1218	1408	1503	1601	1701	1801	1904	2006	2138	2315

		Ⓐ	Ⓐ A	Ⓐ A	Ⓐ B	Ⓐ A	Ⓐ B	Ⓐ A	Ⓐ A	Ⓐ B	Ⓐ A	Ⓐ A	Ⓐ B	Ⓐ	Ⓐ A	Ⓐ	Ⓐ A	Ⓐ	Ⓐ		⑥	⑥ A	⑥ A	⑥ B	⑥ A	⑥ B
Sheffield 193 d.	Ⓐ	0529	0741	0841	0941	1041	1141	1241	1341	1441	1541	1641	1741	1753	1841	1946	2000	2115	2234	⑥	0529	0741	0841	0941	1041	1141
Meadowhall 193 d.		0535	0747	0847	0947	1047	1147	1247	1347	1447	1547	1647	1747	1800	1847	1953	2006	2121	2240		0535	0748	0847	0947	1047	1147
Doncaster 193 a.		0606	0819	0915	1015	1115	1215	1314	1415	1517	1615	1717	1812	1835	1911	2013	2037	2154	2312		0606	0819	0914	1015	1112	1214
Doncaster 181 d.		0610	0824	0919	1019	1119	1219	1319	1419	1519	1619	1719	1819	1839	1919	2017	2044	2156	2315		0612	0824	0919	1019	1118	1219
Goole d.		0636	0844	0938	1038	1138	1238	1338	1438	1537	1638	1742	1838	1912t	1938	2036	│	2222	2343		0638	0844	0938	1038	1137	1238
Hull 181 a.		0718	0913	1010	1110	1209	1308	1410	1511	1607	1709	1811	1908	1950	2010	2106	2144	2257	...		0720	0915	1010	1110	1209	1309

	⑥ A	⑥ A	⑥ B	⑥ A	⑥ A	⑥ B	⑥	⑥ A	⑥	⑥ A	⑥	⑥		⑦ B	⑦ A	⑦ B	⑦ B	⑦ A	⑦ B	⑦ A	⑦ B	⑦ A	⑦	⑦	⑦	⑦
Sheffield 193 d.	1241	1341	1441	1541	1641	1741	1753	1841	1946	2000	2115	2233	⑦	0845	...	1026	1228	1324	1428	1529	1628	1728	1828	2002	2128	2214
Meadowhall 193 d.	1247	1347	1447	1547	1647	1747	1759	1847	1953	2006	2121	2239		0851	...	1032	1235	1332	1434	1535	1635	1735	1835	2008	2134	2220
Doncaster 193 a.	1316	1416	1516	1616	1712	1813	1837	1912	2015	2036	2154	2309		0922	...	1052	1256	1403	1456	1556	1656	1755	1855	2030	2204	2240
Doncaster 181 d.	1319	1419	1519	1619	1719	1820	1841	1917	2017	2043	2156	2310		0926	1019	1057	1258	1405	1500	1558	1656	1758	1856	2030	2206	2245
Goole d.	1338	1438	1537	1638	1742	1839	1911	1937	2036	│	2222	2338		0947	1040	1116	1317	1425	1519	1619	1716	1817	1922	2049	2225	2306
Hull 181 a.	1410	1509	1609	1709	1811	1911	1951	2009	2106	2146	2259	...		1021	1118	1150	1354	1455	1557	1652	1748	1851	1956	2121	2257	2339

A – From / to Bridlington (Table **177**).
B – From / to Scarborough (Table **177**).
t – Arrives 1905.

193 CLEETHORPES - DONCASTER - SHEFFIELD - MANCHESTER TP

km			①	②–⑥	⚒	⚒	⑥	Ⓐ	⚒	⚒	⚒	⚒		⚒	⚒	⚒	⚒	⚒	⚒	⚒		⚒	⚒
0	**Cleethorpes** d.	⚒	...	...	...	...	0505	0507	0620	0726	0826	0926	...	1026	1126	1226	1326	1426	1526	1626	...	1726	1826
5	Grimsby Town d.		...	...	...	...	0513	0515	0628	0734	0834	0934	...	1034	1134	1234	1334	1434	1534	1634	...	1734	1834
48	Scunthorpe d.		...	...	...	...	0546	0546	0703	0809	0908	1008	...	1108	1208	1308	1408	1508	1608	1708	...	1808	1908
85	**Doncaster** a.		...	...	...	...	0623	0623	0733	0838	0938	1038	...	1138	1238	1338	1438	1538	1638	1738	...	1838	1938
85	**Doncaster** 192 d.		...	...	...	0540	0625	0625	0735	0842	0942	1042	...	1142	1242	1342	1442	1542	1642	1742	...	1840	1942
109	Meadowhall 192 d.		...	...	...	0601	0646	0646	0752	0901	1001	1101	...	1201	1301	1401	1501	1601	1701	1801	...	1901	2001
115	**Sheffield** 192 a.		...	...	...	0608	0655	0655	0801	0908	1008	1108	...	1208	1308	1408	1508	1608	1708	1808	...	1908	2008
115	**Sheffield** 206 d.		0325	0325	0511	0611	*0708*	0708	0804	0911	1011	1111	...	1211	1311	1411	1511	1611	1711	1811	...	1911	2011
175	Stockport 206 a.		|	|	|	0653	*0752*	0752	0852	0952	1052	1152	...	1252	1352	1452	1552	1652	1752	1852	...	1952	2052
184	**Manchester** Piccadilly 206 a.		0417	0451	0603	0703	*0802*	0802	0903	1002	1103	1203	...	1303	1403	1503	1603	1703	1803	1903	...	2003	2103
200	**Manchester** Airport a.		0442	0512	0628	0727	*0825*	0825	0927	1027	1133**a**	1227	...	1327	1429	1527	1633**a**	1729	1827	1925	...	2039	2132

	⚒	Ⓐ	⑥			⑦	⑦	⑦		⑦		⑦	⑦		⑦	⑦	⑦	⑦	⑦	⑦	⑦	⑦	⑦
Cleethorpes d.	1926	2026	2026	...	⑦	...	...	...	...	0926	...	1026	1126	...	...	1326	1426	1526	1626	1726	1826	1926	2026
Grimsby Town d.	1934	2034	2034	...		...	...	...	...	0934	...	1034	1134	...	...	1334	1434	1534	1634	1734	1834	1934	2034
Scunthorpe d.	2008	2108	2108	...		...	...	...	...	1010	...	1108	1211	...	...	1408	1508	1608	1708	1810	1908	2010	2111
Doncaster a.	2040	2140	2140	...		...	...	...	...	1040	...	1140	1240	...	...	1438	1535	1634	1738	1839	1939	2040	2141
Doncaster 192 d.	2042	2142	2142	...		...	...	...	...	1042	...	1142	1242	...	1342	1442	1542	1642	1742	1842	1942	2042	2142
Meadowhall 192 d.	2109	2159	2159	...		...	...	...	...	1101	...	1201	1301	...	1401	1501	1601	1701	1801	1901	2001	2101	2206
Sheffield 192 a.	2119	2208	2207	...		...	...	...	...	1108	...	1208	1308	...	1409	1508	1607	1708	1808	1908	2008	2108	2214
Sheffield 206 d.	...	2211	*2224*	...		0751	0911	1011	...	1110	...	1210	1310	...	1411	1511	1611	1711	1811	1911	2011	2111	...
Stockport 206 a.	...	2252	*2322*	...		0832	0953	|	...	1153	...	1251	1352	...	1453	1552	1652	1752	1852	1952	2052	2153	...
Manchester Piccadilly 206 a.	...	2302	*2337*	...		0841	1003	1103	...	1206	...	1303	1403	...	1503	1602	1702	1802	1903	2002	2103	2203	...
Manchester Airport a.	...	2323	...	...		0909	1029	1127	...	1229	...	1328	1429	...	1529	1628	1727	1829	1929	2029	2129	2229	...

		⑥	⑥	Ⓐ	⚒	⚒	⚒	⚒	⚒	⚒	⚒	⚒	⚒	⑥	Ⓐ		⚒	⚒	Ⓐ	⑥		⚒	Ⓐ
Manchester Airport d.	⚒	0550	...	0550	0655	0753	0855	0955	1055	1155	1255	1355	1455	1555	1555	...	1655	1755	1855	1855	...	1955	...
Manchester Piccadilly 206 d.		0613	...	0613	0720	0820	0920	1020	1120	1220	1320	1420	1520	1620	1620	...	1718	1820	1918	1918	...	2020	...
Stockport 206 d.		0621	...	0621	0728	0828	0928	1028	1128	1228	1328	1428	1528	1628	1628	...	1726	1828	1926	1926	...	2028	...
Sheffield 206 a.		0702	...	0702	0810	0908	1008	1109	1208	1308	1408	1508	1608	1709	1709	...	1810	1910	2009	2009	...	2112	...
Sheffield 192 d.		▬	0709	0712	0812	0910	1010	1110	1210	1310	1410	1510	1610	1710	1710	...	1812	1912	2011	2027	...	...	2134
Meadowhall 192 d.		...	0715	0718	0818	0916	1016	1116	1216	1316	1416	1516	1616	1716	1716	...	1818	1918	2017	2033	...	...	2140
Doncaster 192 a.		Ⓐ	0739	0738	0837	0935	1035	1135	1235	1335	1435	1535	1635	1737	1737	...	1845	1941	2045	2101	...	...	2202
Doncaster d.		0530	0743	0739	0839	0937	1037	1137	1237	1337	1437	1537	1637	1739	1747	...	1847	1948	2046	2107	...	...	2205
Scunthorpe d.		0600	0809	0805	0905	1003	1103	1203	1303	1403	1503	1603	1703	1805	1813	...	1915	2015	2112	2133	...	...	2231
Grimsby Town a.		0643	0847	0846	0940	1039	1137	1240	1337	1439	1537	1639	1737	1843	1849	...	1948	2048	2148	2209	...	...	2309
Cleethorpes a.		0654	0856	0855	0951	1051	1149	1251	1349	1451	1549	1651	1750	1856	1859	...	2000	2101	2200	2221	...	...	2320

	⚒	⑥	Ⓐ	⑥	⚒	Ⓐ			⑦	⑦	⑦	⑦	⑦	⑦	⑦	⑦	⑦	⑦	⑦	⑦	⑦	⑦	⑦
Manchester Airport d.	...	...	2047	2047	2147	2327	...	⑦	0838**b**	1054	1155	1255	1355	1455	1555	1655	1755	1855	1955	2055	...	2155	2255
Manchester Piccadilly 206 d.	2043	...	2120	2120	2222	2353	...		0858	1118	1218	1320	1420	1520	1620	1720	1820	1920	2018	2120	...	2216	2316
Stockport 206 d.	2054	...	2128	2128	|	|	...		0906	1127	1228	1328	1428	1529	1627	1727	1828	1928	2027	2127	...	2224	2324
Sheffield 206 a.	2135	...	2209	2211	2315	0121	...		0947	1207	1308	1408	1509	1609	1708	1808	1908	2008	2108	2211	...	2306	0006
Sheffield 192 d.	...	2152	2210	...	...	...	...		0951	1210	1310	1410	1510	1610	1710	1810	1910	2010	2110	...	2231	...	...
Meadowhall 192 d.	...	2158	2216	...	...	...	...		0958	1216	1316	1416	1516	1616	1716	1816	1916	2016	2116	...	2237	...	...
Doncaster 192 a.	...	2220	2243	...	...	...	...		1028	1235	1335	1435	1535	1635	1735	1835	1935	2035	2135	...	2256	...	...
Doncaster d.	...	2225	2245	...	...	...	...		1029	1237	...	1437	1537	1637	1737	1837	1937	2037	2137	...	2258	...	...
Scunthorpe d.	...	2259	2319	...	...	...	...		1055	1303	...	1503	1603	1703	1803	1903	2003	2103	2203	...	2324	...	...
Grimsby Town a.	...	2335	2355	...	...	...	...		1132	1337	...	1538	1639	1737	1839	1937	2037	2139	2239	...	2358	...	...
Cleethorpes a.	...	2347	0009	...	...	...	...		1142	1349	...	1549	1651	1749	1851	1949	2049	2151	2251	...	0010	...	...

km	*NT 2nd class only*		⚒	⚒	⑥	⚒	⚒	⑥	⚒	⑥	⚒	⑥	⚒	Ⓐ	⑥	⚒	⚒	⚒	⑥	Ⓐ		⑦	⑦	⑦	⑦	⑦	⑦	⑦
0	**Sheffield** ⊙ d.	⚒	0618	0712	0814	0914	1014	1114	1214	1314	1414	1514	1614	1714	1714	1814	1914	2035	2224	2248	⑦	0914	1114	1314	1514	1714	1914	2214
16	Grindleford d.		0634	0730	0828	0929	1028	1129	1229	1329	1429	1529	1628	1729	1728	1829	1928	2050	2238	2302		0929	1129	1329	1529	1729	1930	2229
18	Hathersage d.		0639	0733	0832	0932	1032	1133	1232	1332	1433	1532	1632	1732	1732	1833	1932	2054	2242	2306		0933	1133	1333	1533	1733	1934	2233
24	Hope d.		0647	0741	0839	0940	1039	1140	1240	1340	1440	1540	1639	1740	1739	1840	1939	2101	2249	2313		0940	1140	1340	1540	1740	1941	2240
32	Edale d.		0655	0749	0847	0948	1047	1148	1248	1348	1448	1548	1647	1748	1747	1848	1947	2109	2256	2322		0948	1148	1348	1548	1748	1949	2248
41	Chinley d.		0703	0757	0855	0956	1055	1156	1256	1356	1456	1556	1655	1756	1755	1856	1955	2117	2304	2330		0956	1156	1356	1556	1756	1957	2256
67	**Manchester** P'dilly ⊙ a.		0734	0835	0934	1034	1134	1234	1334	1434	1534	1634	1734	1831	1836	1935	2035	2205	2337	2359		1034	1233	1434	1634	1833	2034	2329

NT 2nd class only		⚒	⑥	Ⓐ	⑥	⚒	⑥	⚒	⑥	⚒	⑥	⚒	⚒	⚒	⚒	⚒	Ⓐ	⑥	⚒		⑦	⑦	⑦	⑦	⑦	⑦	⑦	⑦
Manchester P'dilly ⊙ d.	⚒	0546	0635	0708	0749	0849	0949	1049	1149	1249	1349	1449	1549	1649	1749	1849	2045	2049	2228	⑦	0744	0922	1140	1340	1540	1740	1940	2211
Chinley d.		0614	0714	0748	0823	0923	1025	1123	1225	1323	1425	1523	1623	1723	1823	1923	2120	2123	2253		0823	0959	1217	1417	1617	1817	2017	2243
Edale d.		0623	0723	0758	0833	0933	1034	1133	1234	1333	1434	1533	1633	1733	1833	1933	2129	2133	2301		0833	1008	1227	1427	1627	1827	2027	2251
Hope d.		0629	0729	0804	0839	0939	1040	1139	1240	1339	1440	1539	1639	1739	1839	1939	2135	2139	2307		0839	1014	1233	1433	1633	1833	2033	2257
Hathersage d.		0636	0736	0811	0845	0946	1046	1145	1246	1346	1446	1546	1646	1746	1846	1946	2142	2146	2315		0845	1021	1240	1440	1640	1840	2040	2303
Grindleford d.		0640	0740	0815	0849	0949	1050	1149	1250	1350	1450	1550	1650	1750	1850	1949	2146	2150	2319		0849	1025	1244	1444	1644	1844	2044	2312
Sheffield ⊙ a.		0657	0757	0832	0906	1006	1106	1206	1305	1406	1506	1606	1706	1808	1908	2007	2202	2207	2335		0906	1043	1300	1459	1700	1900	2100	2326

a – On Ⓐ arrives 7 minutes earlier.
b – May 27 - Oct. 22.

⊙ – Additional journeys on ⑦ May 27 - Nov. 5: From **Sheffield** at 1020, 1215, 1415, 1614, 1815. From **Manchester Piccadilly** at 0823, 1040, 1240, 1440, 1645.

194 SKEGNESS - NOTTINGHAM 2nd class EM

km			Ⓐ	Ⓐ	Ⓐ	Ⓐ	Ⓐ	Ⓐ		Ⓐ	Ⓐ	Ⓐ	Ⓐ	Ⓐ	Ⓐ	Ⓐ	Ⓐ	Ⓐ	Ⓐ	Ⓐ		⑥	⑥	⑥	⑥	⑥	⑥
0	**Skegness** d.	Ⓐ	...	...	0709	0810	0906	1015	...	1115	1215	1315	1415	1509	1611	1730	1814	1914	2015	2102	⑥	...	...	0709	0815	0915	1015
8	Wainfleet d.		...	...	0719	0818	0914	1023	...	1123	1223	1323	1423	1517	1621	1738	1822	1922	2023	2110		...	...	0719	0823	0923	1023
38	Boston d.		...	0613	0746	0845	0941	1050	...	1150	1250	1350	1450	1544	1648	1805	1848	1949	2050	2137		...	0613	0746	0850	0950	1050
66	Sleaford d.		...	0635	0811	0907	1003	1112	...	1212	1313	1413	1512	1610	1713	1827	1913	2013	2118	2200		...	0635	0811	0912	1014	1112
89	Grantham a.		...	0704	0842	0939	1031	1141	...	1241	1342	1442	1541	1641	1742	|	1941	2040	2145	|		...	0707	0842	0941	1043	1141
89	Grantham 206 d.		0610	0710	0845	0945	1036	1145	...	1245	1348	1445	1545	1645	1745	|	1945	2044	2149	|		0610	0710	0845	0945	1046	1145
126	**Nottingham** 206 a.		0654	0753	0920	1021	1114	1222		1323	1422	1523	1622	1720	1822	1922	2025	2120	2226	2253		0654	0752	0920	1021	1123	1222

	⑥	⑥**a**	⑥	⑥	⑥	⑥	⑥	⑥	⑥	⑥	⑥	⑥		⑦**c**	⑦**c**	⑦**c**	⑦	⑦**b**	⑦**c**	⑦	⑦	⑦**c**	⑦	⑦**c**	⑦	⑦	⑦**c**
Skegness d.	1115	1140	1215	1315	1415	1509	1611	1724	1814	1919	2015	2102	⑦	...	1014	1115	...	...	1227	...	1410	1515	1610	1622	1807	1915	2043
Wainfleet d.	1123	|	1223	1323	1423	1517	1621	1732	1822	1927	2023	2110		...	1022	1123	...	...	1235	...	1418	1523	1618	1630	1815	1923	2051
Boston d.	1150	1225	1250	1350	1450	1544	1648	1759	1849	1954	2050	2137		0906	1049	1149	...	1213	1302	...	1445	1552	1650	1657	1842	1950	2118
Sleaford d.	1212	1247	1312	1413	1512	1610	1713	1821	1913	2018	2112	2200		0928	1111	1211	...	1235	1324	...	1507	1620	1712	1719	1904	2012	2142
Grantham a.	1241	|	1341	1442	1541	1641	1742	|	1941	2045	2143	|		0957	1140	1241	...	1304	|	...	1535	1646	1741	|	1933	2041	2210
Grantham 206 d.	1245	|	1346	1445	1545	1645	1745	|	1945	2048	2147	|		1001	1146	1245	1252	...	|	1509	1540	1650	1745	|	1937	2045	2213
Nottingham 206 a.	1323	1343	1423	1523	1622	1720	1822	1922	2024	2125	2225	2254		1037	1225	1321	1330	...	1416	1539	1617	1722	1820	1811	2012	2120	2249

		Ⓐ	Ⓐ	Ⓐ	Ⓐ	Ⓐ	Ⓐ	Ⓐ	Ⓐ	Ⓐ	Ⓐ		Ⓐ	Ⓐ	Ⓐ	Ⓐ	Ⓐ	Ⓐ**A**	Ⓐ		⑥	⑥	⑥	⑥	⑥	⑥**a**	⑥
Nottingham 206 d.	Ⓐ	0507	0550	0641	0735	0845	0955	1045	1145	1245	1345	...	1445	1545	1645	1744	1844	...	2051	⑥	0507	...	0550	0641	0731	0824	0840
Grantham 206 a.		0546	0627	0719	0812	0926	|	1123	1219	1323	1423	...	1522	1625	1728	1825	1923	...	2132		0546	...	0627	0718	0809	|	0923
Grantham d.		▬	0631	0723	0816	0932	|	1127	1225	1327	1427	...	1526	1629	1732	1829	1926	...	2138		...	...	0631	0724	0817	|	0930
Sleaford d.		Ⓐ	0657	0751	0845	1003	1044	1153	1250	1355	1452	...	1552	1655	1801	1855	1955	2120	2203		...	...	0657	0751	0846	0917	0956
Boston d.		0625	0725	0818	0912	1026	1111	1219	1315	1421	1517	...	1620	1721	1826	1921	2019	2153	2229		...	0625	0725	0818	0912	0950	1022
Wainfleet d.		0649	0751	0843	0936	1050	1135	1244	1340	1447	1542	...	1645	1748	1851	1946	2044	...	...		...	0649	0751	0843	0936	|	1047
Skegness a.		0703	0805	0856	0949	1100	1150	1258	1354	1500	1556	...	1659	1800	1905	1959	2057	...	...		...	0703	0805	0856	0948	1031	1100

	⑥	⑥	⑥	⑥	⑥	⑥	⑥	⑥	⑥	⑥	⑥**A**	⑥		⑦**c**	⑦**c**	⑦**c**	⑦**c**	⑦	⑦	⑦	⑦**c**	⑦	⑦	⑦**c**	⑦**b**	⑦**c**	⑦
Nottingham 206 d.	0955	1045	1145	1245	1345	1445	1545	1645	1744	1845	...	2051	⑦	...	0900	0941	1109	1157	1240	...	1357	1456	1623	1816	1831	1948	2045
Grantham 206 a.	|	1123	1219	1325	1423	1522	1625	1728	1825	1923	...	2131		...	|	1015	1144	1229	1313	...	1431	1531	1703	1850	1908	2022	2118
Grantham d.	|	1127	1225	1329	1427	1526	1629	1732	1829	1926	...	2136		...	|	1020	1150	1233	...	1350	1435	1536	1707	1854	1913	2027	...
Sleaford d.	1044	1153	1250	1355	1452	1552	1655	1801	1855	1955	2121	2201		...	0949	1046	1215	1259	...	1416	1515	1602	1736	1927	1941	2053	...
Boston d.	1111	1219	1315	1421	1517	1620	1721	1826	1921	2019	2153	2229		0931	1016	1111	1241	1324	...	1445	1532	1629	1802	1950	2010	2117	...
Wainfleet d.	1135	1244	1340	1446	1542	1645	1748	1851	1946	2043	...	...		0955	1040	1136	1306	1349	...	1509	1557	1653	1827	2014	...	...	...
Skegness a.	1150	1258	1354	1500	1556	1659	1800	1905	1959	2057	...	...		1007	1055	1150	1320	1400	...	1524	1611	1708	1838	2026	...	...	...

A – From Lincoln (Table **185**). **B** – From Liverpool (Table **206**). **a** – July 29 - Sept. 9. **b** – From Sept. 17. **c** – May 21 - Sept. 10.

72 *For explanation of standard symbols see page 1*

LONDON - KINGS LYNN — 196

TL

km			Ⓐ	⑥	Ⓐ	⚒	Ⓐ	⑥	Ⓐ	Ⓐ	⚒	Ⓐ	⚒	⚒	⚒	⚒	⚒	⚒	⚒	⚒	⚒	⑥	Ⓐ	⚒	⑥	Ⓐ
0	**London** Kings Cross **197** d.	⚒	...	...	0542	0644	0714	0744	0744	0814	0844	0914	0944	1014	1044	1114	1144	1214	1244	1314	1344	1414	1414	1444	1514	1514
93	Cambridge **197** d.		0615	0635	0652	0733	0806	0835	0838	0909	0935	1015	1035	1104	1135	1204	1235	1304	1335	1404	1435	1504	1507	1535	1604	1606
117	Ely d.		0633	0651	0708	0751	0822	0851	0854	0928	0951	1037	1051	1121	1151	1222	1251	1321	1351	1421	1451	1521	1524	1551	1621	1623
142	Downham Market d.		0653	0707	0725	0807	0838	0907	0910	...	1007	...	1107	...	1207	...	1307	...	1407	...	1507	...	...	1607	...	...
160	**Kings Lynn** a.		0707	0721	0740	0821	0852	0921	0925	...	1021	...	1121	...	1221	...	1321	...	1421	...	1521	...	...	1621	...	...

	⑥	Ⓐ	Ⓐ	⚒	⑥	Ⓐ	Ⓐ	⚒	⑥		Ⓐ	⑥	Ⓐ	Ⓐ	⑥	Ⓐ	Ⓐ		⑥	Ⓐ	⑥	Ⓐ	⑥	Ⓐ	Ⓐ	Ⓐ
London Kings Cross **197** d.	1544	1544	1558r	1614	1644	1644	1707r	1714	1744	...	1744	1814	1814	1807r	1844	1844	1907r	...	1914	1914	1944	1944	2014	2014	2004	2044
Cambridge **197** d.	1635	1635	1721	1704	1735	1740	1817	1805	1835	...	1839	1905	1909	1919	1935	1939	2014	...	2007	2008	2035	2040	2107	2110	2128	2140
Ely d.	1651	1652	1742	1723	1751	1757	1833	1823	1851	...	1856	1919	1924	1935	1951	1956	2030	...	2023	2025	2051	2056	2123	2126	2146	2156
Downham Market d.	1707	1710	...	...	1807	1813	1850	...	1907	...	1912	1935	1939	1952	2007	2012	2047	...	2039	...	2108	2112	2139	2142	...	2212
Kings Lynn a.	1721	1724	...	...	1821	1827	1908	...	1921	...	1927	1951	1954	2010	2021	2026	2105	...	2053	...	2121	2126	2153	2156	...	2226

	⑥	⑥	Ⓐ	⑥	Ⓐ	⚒	Ⓐ	⚒		⑦	⑦	⑦	⑦	⑦	⑦	⑦		⑦	⑦	⑦	⑦	⑦	⑦	⑦	⑦	⑦
London Kings Cross **197** d.	2044	2114	2114	2144	2144	2214	2244	2314	⑦	0752	0915	1015	1115	1215	1315	1415	...	1515	1615	1715	1815	1915	2015	2115	2215	2315
Cambridge **197** d.	2140	2207	2210	2237	2240	2310	2340	0010		0906	1006	1106	1206	1306	1406	1506	...	1606	1706	1806	1906	2006	2106	2206	2306	0007
Ely d.	2159	2223	2228	2254	2300	2328	2359	0026		0922	1022	1122	1222	1322	1422	1522	...	1622	1722	1822	1922	2022	2122	2222	2322	0023
Downham Market d.	...	2239	2244	...	...	2344	...	0042		0938	1038	1138	1238	1338	1438	1538	...	1638	1738	1838	1938	2038	2138	2238	2338	0039
Kings Lynn a.	...	2253	2258	...	...	2358	...	0058		0953	1053	1153	1253	1353	1453	1553	...	1653	1753	1853	1953	2052	2153	2253	2353	0054

		Ⓐ	⑥	Ⓐ	Ⓐ	⑥	Ⓐ	Ⓐ	Ⓐ	⑥	Ⓐ	Ⓐ	Ⓐ	Ⓐ	⑥	Ⓐ	Ⓐ	⑥	⑥	Ⓐ	Ⓐ	⑥	Ⓐ	⚒	Ⓐ	⑥
Kings Lynn d.	⚒	0454	...	0517	0551	0554	0610	0617	0651	0654	...	0714	0725	...	0754	0754	0827	...	0854	0857	...	0925	0930	0954	...	1026
Downham Market d.		0508	...	0531	0605	0608	0622	0631	0705	0708	...	0728	0737	...	0808	0808	0841	...	0908	0911	...	0937	0949	1008	...	1038
Ely d.		0525	0526	0550	0622	0625	0647t	0650	0722	0726	0730	0748	0756	0800	0825	0826	0858	0859	0925	0928	0949	0956	1007	1025	1058	1058
Cambridge **197** a.		0544	0545	0610	0639	0644	0704	0710	0739	0742	0747	0804	0810	0820	0841	0843	0915	0915	0941	0945	1006	1013	1023	1041	1115	1115
London Kings Cross **197** a.		0636	0639	0725r	0737	0735	0806	0825r	0838	0836	0920r	0909	0909	0950r	0937	0944	1013	1006	1035	1043	1108	1106	1132	1137	1205	1208

	⚒	⚒	⚒	⚒	⚒	⚒	⚒	⚒	⚒	Ⓐ	⑥	Ⓐ	⚒	⚒	Ⓐ	⑥	Ⓐ	⚒	Ⓐ	⑥	Ⓐ	⑥	⚒	Ⓐ	⑥	Ⓐ
Kings Lynn d.	1054	...	1154	...	1254	...	1354	...	1454	...	...	...	1554	...	1636	1654	...	...	1736	1754	...	...	1835	...	1935	1937
Downham Market d.	1108	...	1208	...	1308	...	1408	...	1508	...	...	...	1608	...	1651	1708	1710	...	1750	1808	...	...	1849	...	1949	1953
Ely d.	1125	1158	1225	1258	1325	1358	1425	1458	1525	1532	1558	1605	1625	1658	1709	1725	1726	1754	1808	1825	1848	1859	1908	1959	2006	2010
Cambridge **197** a.	1141	1215	1241	1315	1342	1416	1441	1515	1541	1553	1615	1623s	1642	1715	1725	1741	1743	1812	1824	1841	1905	1916	1924	2016	2023	2026
London Kings Cross **197** a.	1238	1308	1335	1406	1435	1510	1535	1607	1636	1719	1707	1749	1738	1823p	1833	1835	1839	1908	1937	1936	2005	2006	2036	2107	2132	2133

	Ⓐ	Ⓐ	⚒	Ⓐ	Ⓐ	⚒	⑥	Ⓐ	⑥		⑦	⑦	⑦	⑦	⑦	⑦	⑦	⑦	⑦	⑦	⑦	⑦	⑦	⑦	⑦	⑦
Kings Lynn d.	...	...	2035	...	...	2135	2226	2231	2310	⑦	0827	0927	1027	1127	1227	1327	1427	1527	1627	1727	1757	1827	1927	2027	2127	2227
Downham Market d.	...	...	2049	...	...	2149	2240	2245	2324		0841	0941	1041	1141	1241	1341	1441	1541	1641	1741	1809	1841	1941	2041	2141	2241
Ely d.	2029	2059	2106	2126	2157	2206	2257	2302	2343		0858	0958	1058	1158	1258	1358	1458	1558	1658	1758	1826	1858	1958	2058	2158	2258
Cambridge **197** a.	2043	2116	2124	2143	2214	2225	2313	2321	0001		0915	1015	1115	1215	1315	1415	1515	1615	1715	1815	1840	1915	2015	2115	2215	2314
London Kings Cross **197** a.	2133	2205	2232	2238	2305	2335	0042	0050	...		1009	1108	1208	1308	1408	1508	1609	1709	1808	1909	1936	2009	2109	2210	2311	0042

p – Arrives 1809 on ⑥. **r** – London **Liverpool Street**. **s** – Stops to set down only. **t** – Arrives 5 minutes earlier.

LONDON KINGS CROSS - CAMBRIDGE — 197

TL

km			Ⓐ	Ⓐ	Ⓐ	Ⓐ	Ⓐ	Ⓐ	Ⓐ	Ⓐ	Ⓐ	Ⓐ	Ⓐ	and at the same	Ⓐ	Ⓐ	Ⓐ	Ⓐ	Ⓐ	Ⓐ	Ⓐ	Ⓐ	Ⓐ	Ⓐ
0	**London** Kings Cross . d.	Ⓐ	0004	0542	0608	0644	0714	0744	0814	0844	0914	0944	1014	minutes past each	1514	1544	1552	1614	1644	1714	1744	1814	1823	1844
93	**Cambridge** a.		0129	0650	0703	0731	0804	0833	0904	0930	1009	1030	1102	hour until ☆	1602	1630	1655	1702	1735	1804	1834	1908	1928	1934

	Ⓐ	Ⓐ	Ⓐ	Ⓐ	Ⓐ	Ⓐ	Ⓐ	Ⓐ	Ⓐ	Ⓐ		⑥	⑥	⑥	⑥	⑥	⑥	⑥	⑥	and at the same	⑥	⑥	⑥	⑥
London Kings Cross . d.	1914	1944	2014	2044	2114	2144	2214	2244	2314	2344	⑥	0004	0031	0544	0644	0716	0744	0752	0814	minutes past each	1944	1952	2014	2044
Cambridge a.	2005	2035	2105	2135	2205	2235	2305	2335	0005	0040		0124	0129	0655	0730	0810	0830	0855	0903	hour until	2030	2055	2101	2135

	⑥	⑥	⑥	⑥	⑥	⑥	⑥		⑦	⑦	⑦	⑦	⑦	⑦	⑦	⑦	and at the same	⑦	⑦	⑦	⑦	⑦	⑦	⑦
London Kings Cross . d.	2052	2114	2144	2152	2214	2244	2314	⑦	0014	0635	0752	0852	0915	0952	1015	1052	minutes past each	2015	2052	2115	2152	2215	2252	2315
Cambridge a.	2155	2202	2235	2255	2305	2337	0005		0122	0745	0855	0955	1001	1055	1101	1155	hour until	2101	2155	2201	2255	2301	2355	0006

		Ⓐ	Ⓐ	Ⓐ	Ⓐ	Ⓐ	Ⓐ	Ⓐ	Ⓐ	Ⓐ	Ⓐ	Ⓐ	Ⓐ	Ⓐ	Ⓐ	Ⓐ	and at the same	Ⓐ	Ⓐ	Ⓐ	Ⓐ	Ⓐ	Ⓐ	Ⓐ
Cambridge d.	Ⓐ	0514	0545	0614	0645	0715	0745	0815	0850	0920	0927	0950	1017	1047	1117	1147	minutes past each	1845	1915	1945	2017	2045	2117	2145
London Kings Cross . a.		0610	0636	0716	0737	0806	0838	0909	0944	1013	1033	1043	1108	1135	1205	1238	hour until ☆	1939	2005	2039	2107	2135	2205	2238

	Ⓐ	Ⓐ	⑤	Ⓐ		⑥	⑥	⑥	⑥	⑥	⑥	⑥	⑥	⑥	and at the same	⑥	⑥	⑥	⑥	⑥	⑥	⑥	⑥	⑥
Cambridge d.	2217	2231	2256	2322	⑥	0546	0615	0646	0717	0748	0817	0847	0917	0947	minutes past each	1915	1946	2017	2047	2117	2147	2217	2229	2315
London Kings Cross . a.	2305	2335	0007	0050		0639	0702	0735	0805	0836	0907	0937	1006	1035	hour until ☆	2006	2035	2107	2135	2205	2235	2304	2332	0042

		⑦a	⑦	⑦	⑦	⑦	⑦	⑦	⑦	⑦	and at the same	⑦	⑦	⑦	⑦	⑦	⑦		⑦	⑦	⑦	⑦	⑦	⑦
Cambridge d.	⑦	0628	0728	0828	0920	0928	1020	1028	1120	1128	minutes past each	1820	1828	1845	1920	1928	2020	...	2028	2120	2128	2220	2228	2316
London Kings Cross . a.		0739	0835	0935	1009	1030	1108	1130	1208	1230	hour until ☆	1909	1930	1936	2009	2030	2109	...	2130	2210	2230	2311	2330	0042

☆ – Timings may vary by up to 3 minutes. **a** – Until Oct. 22.

LONDON - SOUTHEND and CAMBRIDGE — 199

CC, LE

Typical off-peak journey time in hours and minutes
READ DOWN ↓ READ UP ↑

Journey times may be extended during peak hours on Ⓐ (0600 - 0900 and 1600 - 1900) and also at weekends.
The longest journey time by any train is noted in the table heading.

LONDON FENCHURCH STREET - SOUTHEND CENTRAL — Longest journey: 1 hour 08 minutes — CC

km	A				A
0	0h00	↓	d.**London** F Street....a.	↑	1h04
8	0h09		d.West Ham..............d.		0h56
12	0h14	↓	d.Barking ....d.	↑	0h50
39	0h34		d.Basildon.................d.		0h29
56	0h53	↓	a.**Southend** Central..d.	↑	0h10
63	1h03		a.Shoeburyness........d.		0h00

From London Fenchurch Street: 0500⚒/0634⑦ and at least every 30 minutes (every 10 - 20 minutes 0840Ⓐ - 2010Ⓐ) until 2341.

From Southend Central*: 0424⚒/0544⑦ and at least every 30 minutes (every 15 minutes 0424Ⓐ - 2020Ⓐ) until 2249⑦, 2335⚒.

A – During peak hours on Ⓐ (0600 - 0900 and 1600 - 1900) trains may not make all stops.

* – Trains depart Shoeburyness 10 minutes before Southend Central.

☛ On ⑦ passengers for Basildon and Shoeburyness should change at Barking.

LONDON LIVERPOOL STREET - SOUTHEND VICTORIA — Longest journey: 1 hour 14 minutes — LE

km					
0	0h00	↓	d.**London** L Street....a.	↑	0h58
6	0h07		d.Stratford.................d.		0h49
32	0h25	↓	d.Shenfield ....d.	↑	0h35
53	0h43		d.Rayleigh ....d.		0h16
64	0h54	↓	a.**Southend** Airport...d.	↑	0h05
66	1h01		a.**Southend** Victoria .d.		0h00

From London Liverpool Street: 0535⚒/0714⑦ and at least every 30 minutes (every 20 minutes 0635⚒ - 2213⚒) until 2344.

From Southend Victoria: 0400⚒/0615⑦ and at least every 30 minutes (every 20 minutes 0626⚒ - 2130⚒) until 2249⑦/2300⚒.

LONDON LIVERPOOL STREET - CAMBRIDGE — Longest journey: 1 hour 39 minutes — LE

km					
0	0h00	↓	d.**London** L Street....a.	↑	1h23
10	0h12		d.Tottenham Hale .....d.		0h57
36	0h29	↓	d.Harlow Town..........d.	↑	0h38
48	0h42		d.Bishops Stortford ...d.		0h28
67	0h54	↓	d.Audley End............d.	↑	0h15
89	1h23		a.**Cambridge**............d.		0h00

From London Liverpool Street: on Ⓐ at 0528, 0558 and every 30 minutes until 1528, 1558, 1628, 1643, 1707, 1713, 1737, 1743, 1807, 1813, 1837, 1843, 1907, 1911, 1928, 1958, 2028 and every 30 minutes until 2258, 2328, 2358⑤; on ⑥ at 0520, 0558, 0628, 0658 and every 30 minutes until 2328, 2358; on ⑦ at 0742, 0828, 0857 and at the same minutes past each hour until 2228, 2257.

From Cambridge: on Ⓐ at 0448, 0520, 0548, 0551, 0618, 0621, 0647, 0651, 0717, 0721, 0747, 0751, 0818, 0821, 0848, 0918, 1004, 1021 and at the same minutes past each hour until 1521, 1551 and every 30 minutes until 1921, 2004, 2021, 2102, 2121, 2204, 2221, 2251; on ⑥ at 0438, 0521, 0604, 0621 and at the same minutes past each hour until 2221, 2251; on ⑦ at 0732, 0751 and at the same minutes past each hour until 2132, 2232.

① – Mondays ② – Tuesdays ③ – Wednesdays ④ – Thursdays ⑤ – Fridays ⑥ – Saturdays ⑦ – Sundays Ⓐ – Monday to Fridays, not holidays 73

For Rail - Sea - Rail services London - Amsterdam and v.v. via Harwich and Hoek van Holland see Table **15a**.

km			Ⓐ	Ⓐ	Ⓐ	Ⓐ	Ⓐ	Ⓐ	Ⓐ	Ⓐ	Ⓐ	Ⓐ	Ⓐ	Ⓐ	Ⓐ	Ⓐ		Ⓐ	Ⓐ	Ⓐ	Ⓐ	Ⓐ	Ⓐ	Ⓐ	Ⓐ	Ⓐ	Ⓐ	Ⓐ	Ⓐ
			P						C																				
0	**London** L St ‡ d.	Ⓐ	...	...	...	0600	...	0625	...	0638	0700	0730	0755	...	0830	0900	and	1530	1600	...	*1602*	1630	1644	1700	1702	1730	...	1750	...
48	Chelmsford d.		...	...	...	0630	...	0658	...	0710	|	0803	|	...	0903	|	at	1600	|	...	*1635*	|	1715	|	1736	|	...	|	...
84	Colchester d.		0540	0610	...	0650	...	0723	...	0743	0751	0823	0847	...	0923	0947	the	1621	1647	...	*1705*	1717	1747t	|	1801	|	...	1843	...
97	Manningtree d.		0549	0618	...	0658	0724	0731	...	0751	0759	0831	0855	0900	0931	0955	same	1629	1655	1700	1724	|	1757	|	1809	1827	1835	1852	1902
112	**Harwich** Int'l d.		|	0636	...	|	0741	|	0750	0810	|	|	|	0917	|	|	minutes	|	|	1717	1741	|	1815	|	|	|	1852	|	1919
115	**Harwich** Town a.		|	0641	...	|	0746	|	|	0815	|	|	|	0922	|	|	past	|	|	1722	1746	|	1822	|	|	|	1857	|	1924
111	**Ipswich** 205 d.		0600	...	0639	0711	...	0744	0820	...	0812	0844	0908	...	0944	1008	each	1641	1708	...	...	1736	...	1800	1825	1839	...	1904	...
130	Stowmarket 205 d.		0611	...	0651	0722	...	0755	0834	...	0823	0855	|	...	0955	|	hour	1652	1719	...	...	1747	...	|	1836	1850	...	1916	...
153	Diss d.		...	...	0704	0735	...	0808	...	...	0836	0908	0929	...	1008	1029	until	1705	1732	...	...	1800	...	1821	1848	1903	...	1929	...
185	**Norwich** a.		...	...	0724	0754	...	0827	...	...	0855	0927	0948	...	1027	1050		1724	1753	...	...	1822	...	1842	1909	1925	...	1950	...

	Ⓐ	Ⓐ	Ⓐ	Ⓐ	Ⓐ	Ⓐ	Ⓐ	Ⓐ	Ⓐ	Ⓐ	Ⓐ	Ⓐ	Ⓐ	Ⓐ	Ⓐ	Ⓐ	Ⓐ	Ⓐ	Ⓐ	Ⓐ	Ⓐ	Ⓐ		⑥	⑥	⑥	⑥	⑥	⑥	⑥
													L											P					C	
London L St ‡ d.	1810	1830	...	1820	1900	...	1930	1932	...	2000	...	2030	...	2100	...	2102	2130	2200	...	2230	...	2330	⑥	...	...	0534	...	0630	...	0638
Chelmsford d.	|	|	...	1857	|	...	|	2002	...	|	...	2103	...	|	...	2134	2203	2228	...	2303	...	0003		...	...	0610	...	0703	...	0712
Colchester d.	1902	1923	...	1930	1947	...	2020	2025	...	2047	...	2123	...	2147	...	2204	2223	2247	...	2323	...	0023		0540	0553	0640	...	0723	...	0740
Manningtree d.	1911	1932	1938	1940	1955	2000	2028	2034	2038	2055	2100	2132	...	2156	2200	2212	2232	2255	2300	2332	2336	0032		0549	0601	0648	0700	0731	...	0748
Harwich Int'l d.	|	|	1955	2002	|	2017	|	2054	2055	|	2117	|	2138	|	2217	2228	|	|	2317	|	2353	|		|	0618	|	0717	|	0750	0809
Harwich Town a.	|	|	2000	...	|	2022	|	...	2100	|	2122	|	|	|	2222	...	|	|	2322	|	2358	|		|	0623	|	0722	|	|	...
Ipswich 205 d.	1923	1944	...	...	2008	...	2041	...	...	2108	...	2145	2204	2209	...	...	2245	2308	...	2345	...	0045		0600	...	0700	...	0744	0820	...
Stowmarket 205 d.	1934	1955	...	...	2019	...	2052	...	...	2119	...	2156	...	2220	...	...	2256	...	...	2356	...	0056		0611	...	*0721*	...	0755	0834	...
Diss d.	1947	2008	...	...	2032	...	2105	...	...	2132	...	2209	...	2233	...	...	2309	...	...	0009	...	0109		...	...	*0734*	...	0808	...	...
Norwich a.	2009	2030	...	...	2051	...	2124	...	...	2151	...	2229	...	2253	...	...	2329	...	...	0029	...	0135		...	...	*0753*	...	0827	...	...

	⑥	⑥	⑥	⑥	⑥		⑥	⑥	⑥	⑥	⑥	⑥	⑥	⑥	⑥	⑥	⑥	⑥	⑥	⑥	⑥	⑥	⑥		⑦	⑦	⑦	⑦	⑦
														L											C				
London L St ‡ d.	0700	...	0730	0800	...	and	1900	...	1930	1932	2000	...	2030	...	2100	...	2102	2130	2200	...	2230	...	2330	⑦	...	...	0755	0802	0830
Chelmsford d.	|	...	0803	|	...	at	|	...	2003	2007	|	...	2103	...	|	...	2134	2203	2228	...	2303	...	|		...	...	0836	0843	|
Colchester d.	0747	...	0823	0847	...	the	1947	...	2023	2032	2047	...	2123	...	2147	..	2204	2223	2248	...	2323	...	0026		...	0818	0859	0913	0925
Manningtree d.	0755	0800	0831	0855	0900	same	1955	2000	2031	2040	2055	2100	2132	...	2155	2200	2212	2232	2256	2300	2332	2336	0035		...	0826	0907	0921	0933
Harwich Int'l d.	|	0817	|	|	0917	minutes	|	2017	|	2056	|	2117	|	2138	|	2217	2228	|	|	2317	|	2353	|		0830	0843	0925	|	|
Harwich Town a.	|	0822	|	|	0922	past	|	2022	|	...	|	2122	|	|	|	2222	...	|	|	2322	|	2358	|		|	0848	*0948*	|	|
Ipswich 205 d.	0808	...	0844	0908	...	each	2008	...	2044	...	2108	...	2145	2203	2208	...	...	2245	2308	...	2345	...	0048		0902	...	...	0935	0946
Stowmarket 205 d.	|	...	0855	|	...	hour	|	...	2055	...	|	...	2156	...	...	...	...	2256	...	...	2356	...	0100		0917	...	...	...	0957
Diss d.	0829	...	0908	0929	...	until	2029	...	2108	...	2129	...	2209	...	...	...	...	2309	...	...	0009	...	0113		...	...	...	...	1010
Norwich a.	0850	...	0927	0950	...		2050	...	2127	...	2150	...	2229	...	...	...	...	2329	...	...	0035	...	0138		...	...	...	...	1031

	⑦	⑦	⑦	⑦		⑦	⑦	⑦	⑦	⑦	⑦	⑦	⑦	⑦	⑦	⑦	⑦	⑦	⑦	⑦	⑦	⑦	⑦	⑦	⑦	⑦	⑦	⑦
	P								a																			
London L St ‡ d.	...	0902	...	0930	and	1702	...	1730	1800	1802	...	1830	1900	1902	...	1930	1932	2002	...	...	2030	2102	...	2130	2202	2230	2302	2330	2332
Chelmsford d.	...	0943	...	|	at	1743	...	|	|	1843	...	|	|	1943	...	|	2011	2043	...	...	|	2143	...	|	2243	|	2343	|	0011
Colchester d.	0932	1013	...	1025	the	1813	...	1825	1855	1913	...	1925	1955	2013	...	2025	2046	2113	...	...	2125	2213	...	2225	2313	2325	0013	0025	0043
Manningtree d.	0940	1021	1026	1033	same	1821	1826	1833	|	1921	1926	1933	2003	2021	2026	2033	2055	2121	...	2126	2134	2221	2226	2234	2321	2334	0021	0034	...
Harwich Int'l d.	|	|	1043	|	minutes	|	1843	|	|	|	1943	|	|	|	2043	|	2114	|	2110	2143	|	|	2243	|	|	|	|	|	...
Harwich Town a.	|	|	1048	|	past	|	1848	|	|	|	1948	|	|	|	2048	|	...	|	|	2148	|	|	2248	|	|	|	|	|	...
Ipswich 205 d.	0955	1033	...	1046	each	1833	...	1846	1914	1933	...	1946	2016	2033	...	2046	...	2133	2137	...	2147	2233	...	2247	2333	2347	0039	0047	...
Stowmarket 205 d.	1006	...	...	1057	hour	...	...	1857	1925	...	...	1957	2027	...	...	2057	...	...	...	...	2158	...	...	2258	...	2358	...	0058	...
Diss d.	...	...	...	1110	until	...	...	1910	1937	...	...	2010	2040	...	...	2110	...	...	...	...	2211	...	...	2311	...	0011	...	0111	...
Norwich a.	...	...	...	1131		...	...	1931	1959	...	...	2031	2101	...	...	2131	...	...	...	...	2231	...	...	2331	...	0031	...	0136	...

		Ⓐ	Ⓐ	Ⓐ	Ⓐ	Ⓐ	Ⓐ	Ⓐ	Ⓐ	Ⓐ	Ⓐ	Ⓐ	Ⓐ	Ⓐ	Ⓐ	Ⓐ	Ⓐ	Ⓐ	Ⓐ	Ⓐ	Ⓐ	Ⓐ	Ⓐ	Ⓐ	Ⓐ		Ⓐ	Ⓐ	Ⓐ
				b	c	b	c		b	c		L																	
Norwich d.	Ⓐ	...	...	0455	0500	0525	0530	...	0555	0600	...	...	0622	0645	...	...	0703	0740	...	...	...	0800	0830	...	0900	and	1530	...	1600
Diss d.		...	...	0514	0518	0544	0548	...	0614	0618	...	...	0640	0704	...	...	0721	0758	...	...	...	0817	0847	...	0917	at	1547	...	1617
Stowmarket 205 d.		...	...	0527	0530	0557	0600	...	0627	0630	...	...	0652	0717	...	...	0734	|	...	0810	...	0829	|	...	0929	the	|	...	1629
Ipswich 205 d.		0514	...	0542	0544	0612	0614	...	0642	0644	...	0659	0707	0732	...	...	0749	0820	...	0826	...	0843	0909	...	0943	same	1609	...	1643
Harwich Town d.		|	0524	|	|	|	|	0624	|	|	0652	|	|	|	...	0716	|	|	0758	|	0828	|	|	0928	|	minutes	|	1628	|
Harwich Int'l d.		|	0529	|	|	|	|	0629	|	|	0657	0727	|	|	0715	0721	|	|	0803	|	0833	|	|	0933	|	past	|	1633	|
Manningtree d.		0525	0546	0553	0554	0623	0624	0646	0653	0654	0714	...	0718	0743	0731	0738	0759	|	0820	0836	0850	0853	0919	0950	0953	each	1619	1650	1653
Colchester d.		0535	...	0605	0605	0635	0635	...	0705	0705	...	...	0730	|	0742	0754t	0810	|	0837t	0845	...	0903	0930	...	1003	hour	1630	...	1703
Chelmsford d.		0558	...	|	|	|	|	...	|	|	...	...	|	|	0814	0819	|	|	0859	0904	...	0921	|	...	1021	until	|	...	1721
London L St ‡ a.		0634	...	0654	0654	0727	0727	...	0758	0758	...	...	0824	0842	0854	0858	0904	0924	0936	0939	...	0958	1019	...	1055		1719	...	1758

	Ⓐ	Ⓐ	Ⓐ	Ⓐ	Ⓐ	Ⓐ	Ⓐ	Ⓐ	Ⓐ	Ⓐ	Ⓐ	Ⓐ	Ⓐ	Ⓐ	Ⓐ	Ⓐ	Ⓐ	Ⓐ	Ⓐ	Ⓐ	Ⓐ	Ⓐ	Ⓐ	Ⓐ	Ⓐ	Ⓐ	Ⓐ		⑥	⑥
																		C		P					P					
Norwich d.	...	1630	...	1700	1730	...	...	1800	1830	...	...	1900	1930	...	...	2000	...	...	2030	...	...	2100	...	2200	...	...	2305	⑥	0500	0530
Diss d.	...	1647	...	1717	1747	...	...	1817	1847	...	...	1917	1947	...	...	2017	...	...	2047	...	...	2117	...	2217	...	...	2322		0517	0547
Stowmarket 205 d.	...	|	...	1729	1759	...	...	1829	|	...	...	1929	|	...	...	2029	...	2045	|	2114	...	2129	...	2229	2308	...	2334		0529	|
Ipswich 205 d.	...	1709	...	1743	1813	...	...	1843	1909	...	...	1943	2009	...	...	2043	...	2101	2109	2128	...	2143	...	2243	2322	...	2348		0543	0609
Harwich Town d.	1653	|	1728	|	|	1800	1826	|	|	1905	1928	|	|	2005	2028	|	...	|	|	|	2128	|	2228	|	|	2328	...		|	|
Harwich Int'l d.	1658	|	1733	|	|	1805	1831	|	|	1910	1933	|	|	2010	2033	|	2045	2129	|	|	2133	|	2233	|	|	2333	...		|	|
Manningtree d.	1715	1719	1750	1753	|	1822	1848	1853	1919	1927	1950	1953	2019	2027	2050	2053	2058	...	2119	2138	2150	2153	2250	2253	2332	2350	...		0553	0619
Colchester d.	...	1730	...	1803	1830	*1843*	...	1903	1930	*1946*	...	2003	2030	*2045*	...	2103	2112	...	2130	2151	...	2203	...	2303	2343	2359	...		0603	0630
Chelmsford d.	...	|	...	1821	|	*1909*	...	1921	|	...	...	2021	|	...	...	2121	2140	...	|	...	...	2221	...	2325	...	...	...		0621	|
London L St ‡ a.	...	1819	...	1855	1917	*1945*	...	1955	2020	...	...	2055	2119	...	...	2155	2214	...	2219	...	...	2255	...	0003	...	...	...		0655	0719

	⑥	⑥	⑥	⑥	⑥	⑥	⑥	⑥		⑥	⑥	⑥	⑥	⑥	⑥	⑥	⑥	⑥	⑥	⑥	⑥	⑥	⑥	⑥	⑥	⑥	⑥	⑥
																			C		P						P	
Norwich d.	...	0600	...	0630	...	...	0700	0730	and	1730	...	1800	1830	...	1900	...	...	2000	...	...	...	...	...	2100	...	...	2200	...	...
Diss d.	...	0617	...	0647	...	...	0717	0747	at	1747	...	1817	1847	...	1917	...	...	2017	...	...	...	...	...	2117	...	...	2217	...	...
Stowmarket 205 d.	...	0629	...	|	...	...	0729	|	the	1759	...	1829	|	...	1929	...	...	2029	...	2045	...	2114	...	2129	...	...	2229	2308	...
Ipswich 205 d.	...	0643	0659	0709	...	...	0743	0809	same	1813	...	1843	1909	...	1943	2009	...	2043	...	2101	2109	2128	...	2143	2223	...	2243	2322	...
Harwich Town d.	0628	|	|	|	...	0728	|	|	minutes	|	1828	|	|	1928	|	|	2028	|	...	|	|	|	2128	|	|	2228	|	|	2328
Harwich Int'l d.	0633	|	0727	|	0720	0733	|	|	past	|	1833	|	|	1933	|	|	2033	|	2045	2129	|	|	2133	|	|	2233	|	|	2333
Manningtree d.	0650	0653	...	0719	0733	0750	0753	0819	each	|	1850	1853	1919	1950	1953	2019	2050	2053	2058	...	2119	2138	2150	2153	2233	2250	2253	2332	2350
Colchester d.	...	0703	...	0730	0743	...	0803	0830	hour	1830	...	1903	1930	...	2003	2030	...	2103	2112	...	2130	2149	...	2203	2243	...	2303	2343	2359
Chelmsford d.	...	0721	...	|	0809	...	0821	|	until	|	...	1921	|	...	2021	|	...	2121	2140	...	|	...	...	2221	2309	...	2325	...	...
London L St ‡ a.	...	0755	...	0819	0846	...	0855	0919		1919	...	1955	2019	...	2055	2117	...	2155	2214	...	2217	...	...	2255	2351	...	0010	...	...

	⑥		⑦	⑦	⑦	⑦	⑦	⑦	⑦	⑦	⑦	⑦	⑦		⑦	⑦	⑦	⑦	⑦	⑦	⑦	⑦	⑦	⑦	⑦	⑦	⑦	⑦	⑦
								a						A					C				P						
Norwich d.	2305	⑦	...	0700	...	...	0800	0820	...	...	0900	...	...	and	1900	...	...	...	...	2000	...	...	...	2100	...	...	2200	...	2305
Diss d.	2322		...	0717	...	...	0817	0838	...	...	0917	...	...	at	1917	...	...	...	...	2017	...	...	...	2117	...	...	2217	...	2322
Stowmarket 205 d.	2336		...	0729	...	...	0829	0850	...	...	0929	...	...	the	1929	...	...	...	2018	2029	...	...	2111	2129	...	...	2229	...	2334
Ipswich 205 d.	2350		...	0743	0751	0809	0843	0905	...	0909	0943	...	1009	same	1943	...	2009	...	2036	2043	...	2109	2125	2143	...	2209	2243	...	2350
Harwich Town d.	...		...	|	|	|	|	|	0853	|	|	0953	|	minutes	1953	1953	|	...	|	|	2053	|	|	|	2153	|	|	2253	...
Harwich Int'l d.	...		0720	|	0816	|	|	|	0858	|	|	0958	|	past	|	1958	|	2035	2105	|	2058	|	|	|	2158	|	|	2258	...
Manningtree d.	...		0734	0753	...	0819	0853	|	0915	0919	0953	1015	1019	each	|	2015	2019	2048	...	2053	2115	2119	2135	2153	2215	2219	2253	2315	...
Colchester d.	...		0748r	0803	...	0830	0903	0923	...	0930	1003	...	1030	hour	2003	...	2030	2057	...	2103	...	2130	2146	2203	...	2230	2303	2324	...
Chelmsford d.	...		0810	|	...	0858	|	|	...	0958	|	...	1058	until	|	...	2058	2115	...	|	...	2158	...	|	...	2258	2325	...	...
London L St ‡ a.	...		0859	0904	...	0944	1003	1030	...	1044	1103	...	1144		2103	...	2144	2202	...	2204	...	2240	...	2303	...	2340	0007	...	...

A – Additional Norwich - London departures at 1520**a** and 1620. Calling at Diss xx38, Stowmarket xx50, Ipswich xx05, Colchester xx23 and London xx30.

C – To / from Cambridge (Table **205**).
P – To / from Peterborough (Table **205**).
L – To / from Lowestoft (Table **201**).

a – Until Sept. 10.
b – From Oct. 9.
c – Until Oct. 6.

r – Arrives 0743.
t – Arrives 7–8 minutes earlier.
‡ – **London** Liverpool Street.

LE — IPSWICH - LOWESTOFT — 201

km			Ⓐ 2	Ⓐ 2	⑥ 2	Ⓐ 2	⑥ 2	⚒ 2	and at	⚒ 2	Ⓐ 2	⑥ 2	⚒ 2	Ⓐ 2	⑥ 2	⚒ 2	⚒ 2	⚒ 2	⚒ H		⑦		⑦ 2	⑦ 2	⑦ 2	⑦
0	**Ipswich** d.	⚒	0620	...	0717	0735	0817	0917	the same	1517	1554	1617	1717	1813	1817	1917	2017	2117	2217	⑦	1002	and every	1802	1907	2002	2202
17	Woodbridge d.		0637	...	0732	0753	0832	0932	minutes	1532	1618	1632	1732	1830	1832	1932	2032	2132	2232		1019	**two** hours	1819	1924	2019	2219
36	Saxmundham d.		0658	0744	0754	0815	0854	0954	past each	1554	1640	1654	1754	1851	1854	1954	2054	2154	2254		1040	until	1840	1945	2040	2240
65	Beccles d.		...	0816	0825	0846	0925	1025	hour until	1625	1719	1725	1825	1925	1925	2025	2125	2225	2325		1112	☆	1912	2021	2112	2312
79	**Lowestoft** a.		...	0833	0843	0906	0943	1043	☆	1643	1736	1751	1843	1943	1943	2043	2143	2243	2343		1130		1930	2039	2130	2330

		Ⓐ H	⑥	Ⓐ	Ⓐ	⑥	Ⓐ 2	⑥ 2	⚒	and at	⚒	⑥ 2	Ⓐ 2	Ⓐ	⑥	⚒ 2	⚒ 2	⚒ 2	⚒ 2		⑦		⑦ 2	⑦ 2	⑦ 2	⑦
Lowestoft d.	⚒	0525	0607	0614	0641	0707	0727	0807	0907	the same	1507	1607	1607	1702	1707	1807	1907	2007	2107	⑦	0805	and every	1605	1705	1805	2005
Beccles d.		0541	0625	0630	0657	0725	0743	0825	0925	minutes	1525	1625	1625	1725	1725	1825	1925	2025	2125		0821	**two** hours	1621	1721	1821	2021
Saxmundham d.		0613	0657	0703	0729	0757	0817	0857	0957	past each	1557	1657	1707**t**	1757	1757	1857	1957	2057	2157		0853	until	1653	1753	1853	2053
Woodbridge d.		0635	0718	0725	0751	0818	0839	0918	1018	hour until	1618	1718	1728	1818	1818	1918	2018	2118	2218		0914	☆	1714	1814	1914	2114
Ipswich a.		0653	0736	0744	0809	0836	0857	0936	1036	☆	1636	1736	1746	1836	1836	1936	2037	2136	2236		0932		1732	1832	1932	2132

H – To / from Harwich International (Table **200**). **t** – Arrives 6 minutes earlier.

☆ – All trains are 2nd class only except the following which also convey 1st class: From Ipswich at 0917⑥, 1002⑦, 1117Ⓐ, 1317⑥, 1517Ⓐ, 1602⑦, 1717⑥, 1917Ⓐ, 2117⑥, 2202⑦, 2217⚒. From Lowestoft at 0525Ⓐ, 0607⑥, 0614Ⓐ, 0641Ⓐ, 0707⑥, 0805⑦, 0907Ⓐ, 1005⑦, 1107⑥, 1307Ⓐ, 1405⑦, 1507⑥, 1605⑦, 1702Ⓐ, 1907⑥, 2005⑦.

LE 2nd class — NORWICH and IPSWICH local services — 203

NORWICH - GREAT YARMOUTH
Journey time ± 32 minutes *30 km (33 km via Reedham)*

From Norwich: Trains noted '**r**' call at **Reedham** 18 – 21 minutes later.

Ⓐ: 0506, 0611, 0652, 0736**r**, 0809, 0836, 0906**b**, 0936, 1025**b**, 1036, 1136**r**, 1236, 1318**b**, 1336, 1425**b**, 1440, 1536, 1638, 1706, 1736, 1804, 1840, 1933, 2038, 2140, 2300.

⑥: 0530**r**, 0636, 0706, 0736**r**, 0809, 0836, 0906**a**, 0936, 0955**a**, 1025**a**, 1036, 1136**r**, 1236, 1318**a**, 1336, 1418**a**, 1436, 1518**a**, 1536, 1640, 1706, 1736, 1806, 1840, 1933, 2040, 2140, 2300.

⑦: 0736**r**, 0845, 0936**r**, 1045, 1136**r**, 1245, 1336**r**, 1445, 1536**r**, 1645, 1736**r**, 1845, 1936**r**, 2045, 2136**r**, 2236.

From Great Yarmouth: Trains noted '**r**' call at **Reedham** 12 – 14 minutes later.

Ⓐ: 0543, 0624, 0658, 0730, 0817, 0846, 0917, 0952**b**, 1017, 1113**b**, 1117, 1217, 1317, 1352**b**, 1417, 1517**r**, 1542**b**, 1617, 1717, 1747**r**, 1817, 1847**r**, 1917, 2017, 2117, 2217, 2334**r**.

⑥: 0615, 0717, 0745, 0817, 0847, 0917, 0947**a**, 1017, 1041**a**, 1115**a**, 1117, 1157**a**, 1217, 1255**a**, 1317, 1355**a**, 1417, 1455**a**, 1512**r**, 1555**a**, 1617, 1717, 1747**r**, 1817, 1847**r**, 1917, 2017, 2117, 2217, 2334**r**.

⑦: 0817**r**, 0922, 1017**r**, 1122, 1217**r**, 1322, 1417**r**, 1522, 1617**r**, 1722, 1817**r**, 1922, 2017**r**, 2122, 2217**r**, 2317**r**.

NORWICH - LOWESTOFT
Journey time ± 43 minutes *38 km*

From Norwich: Trains noted '**r**' call at **Reedham** 18 – 21 minutes later.

Ⓐ: 0536**r**, 0627**r**, 0645**r**, 0755**r**, 0855, 1005**r**, 1058, 1205**r**, 1258, 1405**r**, 1455**r**, 1550**r**, 1658**r**, 1750**r**, 1902**r**, 2005**r**, 2105**r**, 2205**r**, 2240**r**.

⑥: 0540**r**, 0650**r**, 0750**r**, 0855, 1005**r**, 1058, 1205**r**, 1258, 1405**r**, 1458**r**, 1550**r**, 1658**r**, 1750**r**, 1905**r**, 2005**r**, 2105**r**, 2205**r**, 2240**r**.

⑦: 0725, 0805**cr**, 0858**r**, 1005**cr**, 1058**r**, 1205**cr**, 1258**r**, 1405**cr**, 1458**r**, 1605**cr**, 1658**r**, 1805**cr**, 1858**r**, 2005**cr**, 2058**r**.

From Lowestoft: Trains noted '**r**' call at **Reedham** 20 – 23 minutes later.

Ⓐ: 0542**r**, 0635**r**, 0735**r**, 0747**r**, 0850**r**, 0948**r**, 1057, 1148**r**, 1257, 1348**r**, 1457, 1548**r**, 1648**r**, 1748**r**, 1848**r**, 1955**r**, 2057, 2148**r**, 2248**r**, 2330**r**.

⑥: 0638**r**, 0740**r**, 0848**r**, 0948**r**, 1057, 1148**r**, 1257, 1348**r**, 1457, 1548**r**, 1648**r**, 1748**r**, 1848**r**, 1955**r**, 2057, 2148**r**, 2248**r**, 2330**r**.

⑦: 0856**cr**, 0946**r**, 1056**cr**, 1146**r**, 1256**cr**, 1346**r**, 1456**cr**, 1546**r**, 1656**cr**, 1746**r**, 1856**cr**, 1946**r**, 2056**cr**, 2146**r**, 2335**r**.

NORWICH - SHERINGHAM (🚂)
Journey time ± 57 minutes *49 km*

From Norwich:
Trains call at **Hoveton and Wroxham** 🚂 ± 15 minutes, and **Cromer** ± 45 minutes later.

⚒: 0510Ⓐ, 0520⑥, 0540Ⓐ, 0545⑥, 0715, 0821, 0945, 1045, 1145, 1245, 1345, 1445, 1545, 1645, 1745, 1855, 1955, 2115, 2245①–④, 2305⑤⑥.

⑦: 0836, 0945, 1036, 1145, 1236, 1345, 1436, 1545, 1636, 1745, 1836, 1945, 2036.

From Sheringham:
Trains call at **Cromer** ± 11 minutes, and **Hoveton and Wroxham** 🚂 ± 39 minutes later.

⚒: 0007⑥, 0621⑥, 0631Ⓐ, 0716, 0822, 0944, 1047, 1144, 1247, 1344, 1447, 1546, 1649, 1749, 1852, 1956, 2110, 2217, 2347①–④ (also 0553Ⓐ from Cromer).

⑦: 0007, 0942, 1041, 1142, 1241, 1342, 1441, 1542, 1641, 1742, 1841, 1942, 2041, 2142.

IPSWICH - FELIXSTOWE
Journey time ± 25 minutes *25 km*

From Ipswich:

Ⓐ: 0504, 0604, 0714, 0825, 0857, 0958 and hourly until 2058, 2228.

⑥: 0558, 0658, 0758, 0858, 0958, 1058 and hourly until 2058, 2228.

⑦: 0955**c**, 1055 and hourly until 1955.

From Felixstowe:

Ⓐ: 0534, 0636, 0747, 0854, 0928 and hourly until 2128, 2301.

⑥: 0628, 0728, 0828, 0928, 1028 and hourly until 2128, 2258.

⑦: 1025**c**, 1125 and hourly until 2025.

a – May 27 - Sept. 9.
b – ①⑤ July 24 - Sept. 8.
c – May 21 - Sept 10.
r – Via Reedham.

🚂 – Heritage and Tourist railways:
NORTH NORFOLK RAILWAY: Sheringham - Holt and v.v. *8 km*. ✆ 01263 820800. www.nnrailway.co.uk
BURE VALLEY STEAM RAILWAY: Wroxham - Aylsham and v.v. ✆ 01253 833858. www.bvrw.co.uk

LE — IPSWICH - CAMBRIDGE and PETERBOROUGH — 205

km			⚒ 2	⚒ C	⚒	Ⓐ	⑥	⑥	Ⓐ	⚒ H	⚒	⚒	⚒	⚒	⚒	⚒	⚒	⚒	⚒	⚒	⚒	⚒	⚒	Ⓐ
0	**Ipswich** 200 d.	⚒	0510	0600	0616	0654	0720	0800	0803	0820	0920	0958	1020	1120	1158	1220	1320	1358	1420	1520	1558	1620	1720	1749
19	Stowmarket 200 d.		0526	0612	0631	0709	0735	0812	0816	0835	0935	1011	1035	1135	1211	1235	1335	1411	1435	1535	1611	1635	1735	1804
42	Bury St Edmunds d.		0549	0629	0654	0733	0757	0829	0832	0857	0957	1029	1057	1157	1229	1257	1357	1429	1457	1557	1629	1657	1757	1830**b**
65	Newmarket d.		0609	|	0714	0752	0817	|	|	0916	1017	|	1116	1217	|	1316	1417	|	1516	1617	|	1717	1817	|
88	**Cambridge** 208 a.		0633	|	0739	0819	0839	|	|	0939	1039	|	1139	1239	|	1339	1439	|	1539	1639	|	1739	1839	|
82	Ely 208 d.		...	0656	...	...	...	0858	0858	...	...	1058	...	...	1258	...	...	1458	...	...	1658	...	...	1858
108	March 208 d.		...	0714	...	...	...	0916	0916	...	...	1116	...	...	1316	...	...	1516	...	...	1716	...	...	1916
132	**Peterborough** 208 a.		...	0737	...	...	...	0939	0939	...	...	1139	...	...	1339	...	...	1539	...	...	1739	...	...	1939

	⑥	Ⓐ	⑥	Ⓐ	⑥	⚒	⚒	⚒ 2	⚒ 2		⑦ 2	⑦ a	⑦ H	⑦ C	⑦	⑦	⑦	⑦	⑦	⑦	⑦	⑦	⑦	⑦ 2
Ipswich 200 d.	1758	1817	1820	1913	1920	1958	2018	2117	2219	⑦	0732	0755	0902	0955	1102	1155	1302	1355	1502	1555	1702	1755	1902	2102
Stowmarket 200 d.	1811	1832	1835	1928	1935	2011	2035	2133	2235		0748	0807	0918	1007	1118	1207	1318	1407	1518	1607	1718	1807	1918	2118
Bury St Edmunds d.	1829	1857**b**	1857	1957**c**	1957	2029	2056	2156	2257		0811	0824	0941	1024	1141	1224	1341	1424	1541	1624	1741	1824	1941	2141
Newmarket d.	|	1916	1916	2017	2017	|	2116	2217	...		0831	|	1001	|	1201	|	1401	|	1601	|	1801	|	2001	2201
Cambridge 208 a.	|	1939	1939	2039	2039	|	2140	2240	...		0857	|	1025	|	1225	|	1425	|	1625	|	1825	|	2024	2224
Ely 208 d.	1858	...	...	...	...	2058	...	...	...		...	0852	...	1052	...	1252	...	1452	...	1652	...	1852	...	...
March 208 d.	1916	...	...	...	...	2116	...	...	...		...	0908	...	1108	...	1308	...	1508	...	1708	...	1908	...	...
Peterborough 208 a.	1939	...	...	...	...	2139	...	...	...		...	0931	...	1131	...	1331	...	1531	...	1731	...	1931	...	...

		Ⓐ	Ⓐ 2	⑥ 2	⚒ 2	⚒	⚒		⚒	⚒	⚒	⚒	⚒		⚒	⚒	⚒	⚒		⚒	⚒	⚒	⚒	⚒
Peterborough 208 d.	⚒	...	...	...	...	...	0750	...	...	...	0950	...	...	...	1150	...	...	1350	...	...	...	1550	...	...
March 208 d.		...	...	...	...	...	0809	...	...	...	1009	...	...	...	1209	...	...	1409	...	...	...	1609	...	...
Ely 208 d.		...	...	...	...	...	0832	...	...	...	1032	...	...	...	1232	...	...	1432	...	...	...	1632	...	...
Cambridge 208 d.		...	...	...	0642	0744	|	...	0844	0944	|	1044	1144	...	|	1244	1344	|	...	1444	1544	|	1644	1744
Newmarket d.		...	...	...	0702	0805	|	...	0904	1005	|	1104	1205	...	|	1304	1405	|	...	1504	1605	|	1705	1805
Bury St Edmunds d.		0531	0621	0623	0723	0824	0858	...	0924	1024	1058	1124	1224	...	1258	1324	1424	1458	...	1524	1624	1658	1725	1825
Stowmarket 200 d.		0552	0642	0644	0745	0845	0914	...	0945	1045	1114	1145	1245	...	1314	1345	1445	1514	...	1545	1645	1714	1745	1845
Ipswich 200 a.		0607	0700	0702	0802	0902	0928	...	1002	1102	1128	1202	1302	...	1328	1402	1502	1528	...	1602	1702	1728	1804	1902

	⚒	⚒	⚒ H	⚒ C	⚒	⚒	⚒ C	⚒ 2			⑦ 2	⑦ a	⑦	⑦	⑦	⑦	⑦	⑦	⑦	⑦	⑦ H	⑦ C	⑦	⑦ 2
Peterborough 208 d.	1750	...	...	1950	...	...	2145	...	...	⑦	...	0950	...	1150	...	1350	...	1547	...	1745	...	1947	...	...
March 208 d.	1809	...	...	2009	...	...	2204	...	...		...	1009	...	1209	...	1409	...	1606	...	1804	...	2006	...	...
Ely 208 d.	1832	...	...	2032	...	...	2226	...	...		...	1032	...	1232	...	1432	...	1629**b**	...	1829**b**	...	2029**b**	...	...
Cambridge 208 d.	|	1844	1944	|	2044	2144	|	2244	...		0912	|	1112	|	1312	|	1512	|	1712	|	1912	|	2112	2250
Newmarket d.	|	1904	2005	|	2104	2205	|	2306	...		0934	|	1134	|	1334	|	1534	|	1734	|	1934	|	2134	2312
Bury St Edmunds d.	1858	1924	2024	2058	2124	2224	2252	2327	...		0955	1058	1155	1258	1355	1458	1555	1655	1755	1855	1955	2055	2155	2333
Stowmarket 200 d.	1914	1945	2045	2114	2145	2245	2308	2348	...		1018	1114	1218	1314	1418	1514	1618	1711	1818	1911	2018	2111	2218	2355
Ipswich 200 a.	1928	2004	2100	2128	2202	2302	2322	0005	...		1036	1128	1236	1328	1436	1528	1636	1725	1836	1925	2036	2125	2236	0011

C – To / from Colchester (Table **200**). **H** – To / from Harwich International (Table **200**). **a** – May 21 - Sept. 10. **b** – Arrives 4 – 5 minutes earlier. **c** – Arrives 1948.

① – Mondays ② – Tuesdays ③ – Wednesdays ④ – Thursdays ⑤ – Fridays ⑥ – Saturdays ⑦ – Sundays Ⓐ – Monday to Fridays, not holidays 75

206 NORWICH - NOTTINGHAM - SHEFFIELD - MANCHESTER - LIVERPOOL   2nd class EM

km			Ⓐ	Ⓐ	Ⓐ	Ⓐ	Ⓐ	Ⓐ	Ⓐ	Ⓐ		Ⓐ	Ⓐ	Ⓐ	Ⓐ	Ⓐ	Ⓐ AD		⑥	⑥	⑥	⑥		⑥	⑥
0	**Norwich** 207 d.	Ⓐ	...	...	...	0550	0651	0757	0857	0957	**B**	1457	1548	1657	1754	1857	...	⑥	...	...	...	0550	...	0653	0757
49	Thetford 207 d.		...	...	...	0623	0719	0824	0924	1024		1524	1623	1727	1827	1924	...		...	...	...	0623	...	0722	0824
86	Ely 205 207 208 d.		...	...	...	0651	0744	0848	0946	1050	and	1547	1647	1752	1852	1952	...		...	...	...	0648	...	0748	0848
111	March 205 208 d.		...	...	...	0707	0800	0907	|	|	at	|	|	|	1908	|	...		...	...	...	0707	...	0804	0905
135	**Peterborough** 180 205 208 d.		...	...	...	0727	0824	0927	1028	1128	the	1627	1724	1826	1926	2027	2131		...	...	...	0727	...	0828	0925
181	Grantham 180 194 d.		...	...	...	0758	0855	0958	1100	1200	same	1658	1757	1857	1959	2059	|		...	...	...	0758	...	0859	0953
218	**Nottingham** 194 a.		...	...	...	0840	0926	1035	1134	1235	minutes	1735	1835	1935	2031	2133	2254		...	...	...	0839	...	0935	1035
218	**Nottingham** 171 d.		0521	0639	0746	0847	0947	1047	1147	1247	past	1747	1847	1941	*2047*	*2146*	...		0520	0640	0746	0847	...	0947	1047
247	Alfreton 171 d.		|	0659	0810	0908	1008	1108	1208	1310	each	1810	1908	2002	|	*2211*	...		|	0700	0809	0908	...	1008	1108
264	Chesterfield 171 d.		0549	0710	0820	0920	1020	1120	1220	1320	hour	1820	1920	2012	*2131*	*2222*	...		0549	0711	0819	0920	...	1020	1120
283	**Sheffield** 171 193 d.		0618	0732	0840	0940	1040	1140	1240	1340	until	1840	1940	2031	*2158*	*2236*	...		0620	0732	0840	0940	...	1040	1140
343	Stockport 193 a.		0722	0824	0924	1025	1125	1224	1325	1425	♤	1924	2025	2124	...	...	...		0722	0824	0925	1025	...	1125	1224
352	**Manchester** Piccadilly 193 a.		0734	0836	0937	1036	1136	1236	1336	1436		1936	2036	2136	...	...	...		0734	0836	0936	1036	...	1136	1236
378	Warrington Central 188 a.		0753	0857	0957	1057	1157	1257	1357	1457		1957	2057	...	...	...	...		0753	0857	0957	1057	...	1157	1257
399	**Liverpool** SP ▷ 188 a.		0818	0915	1015	1115	1215	1315	1415	1515		2018	2118	...	...	...	...		0818	0915	1015	1115	...	1215	1315
408	**Liverpool** Lime Street 188 a.		0832	0932	1031	1131	1231	1331	1431	1531		2035	2136	...	...	...	...		0831	0931	1031	1131	...	1231	1331

	⑥	⑥		⑥	⑥	⑥	⑥	⑥	⑥ D		⑦	⑦	⑦	⑦ e	⑦ h	⑦	⑦	⑦	⑦	⑦	⑦	⑦	⑦	⑦	⑦
Norwich 207 d.	0857	0957	**B**	1457	1552	1654	1750	1857	...	⑦	...	...	...	0947	...	1047	...	...	1347	1453	1554	1654	1754	1856	2052
Thetford 207 d.	0924	1024		1524	1623	1724	1823	1924	...		...	...	...	1015	...	1114	...	...	1414	1520	1621	1721	1821	1923	2119
Ely 205 207 208 d.	0946	1048	and	1547	1647	1747	1848	1948	...		...	...	...	1041	...	1139	...	...	1440	1546	|	1748	1848	1948	2144
March 205 208 d.	|	|	at	|	|	|	1905	|	...		...	...	...	|	...	|	...	...	|	1603	|	|	|	|	|
Peterborough 180 205 208 d.	1022	1123	the	1627	1725	1826	1930**c**	2026	2127		...	...	...	1114	...	1216	...	1431	1523**d**	1624	1723**a**	1826**c**	1926	2030**c**	2223**b**
Grantham 180 194 d.	1055	1156	same	1656	1759	1858	2003**c**	2058	2202		...	...	...	1156	...	1252**c**	...	1509	1555	1656	1755	1858	1957	2102	2255
Nottingham 194 a.	1136	1235	minutes	1735	1834	1933	2036	2132	2232		...	...	...	1230	...	1330	...	1539	1624	1731	1827	1933	2031	2134	2328
Nottingham 171 d.	1147	1247	past	1744	1847	1939	*2117*	...	...		0947	1048	1144	1240	1240	1342	1447	1547	1642	1739	1840	1943	*2133*	...	...
Alfreton 171 d.	1208	1310	each	1808	1908	2000	*2144*	...	...		1004	1108	1207	1304	1304	1405	1510	1607	1711	1804	1903	2003	*2205*	...	...
Chesterfield 171 d.	1220	1320	hour	1818	1920	2010	*2155*	...	...		1018	1119	1218	1317	1317	1416	1521	1618	1721	1815	1914	2013	*2216*	...	...
Sheffield 193 d.	1240	1340	until	1837	1940	2032	*2214*	...	...		1041	1139	1239	1338	1338	1437	1543	1639	1744	1836	1935	2035	*2236*	...	...
Stockport 193 a.	1325	1425	♤	1924	2025	2117	...	...	...		1126	1225	1325	1425	1425	1525	1625	1728	1825	1925	2025	2124	...	...	...
Manchester Piccadilly 193 a.	1336	1436		1936	2036	2128	...	...	...		1137	1237	1337	1437	1437	1537	1637	1738	1837	1937	2038	2137	...	...	...
Warrington Central 188 a.	1357	1457		1957	2057	...	...	...	...		1158	1258	1358	1458	1458	1558	1658	1758	1858	1958	...	...	...	...	...
Liverpool SP ▷ 188 a.	1415	1515		2015	2120	...	...	...	...		1216	1316	1416	1516	1516	1616	1716	1816	1916	2016	...	...	...	...	...
Liverpool Lime Street 188 a.	1431	1531		2031	2133	...	...	...	...		1230	1330	1430	1530	1530	1630	1730	1830	1930	2030	...	...	...	...	...

		Ⓐ A	Ⓐ D	Ⓐ A	Ⓐ	Ⓐ	Ⓐ	Ⓐ	Ⓐ		Ⓐ	Ⓐ	Ⓐ	Ⓐ	Ⓐ	Ⓐ	Ⓐ		⑥ A	⑥ D	⑥ A	⑥	⑥	⑥	⑥
Liverpool Lime Street 187 d.	Ⓐ	...	...	...	...	...	0647	0742	0852		1452	1552	1652	1752	1852	1952	2137	⑥	...	...	...	...	...	0649	0742
Liverpool SP ▷ 188 d.		...	...	...	...	...	0657	0753	0903		1503	1603	1703	1803	1903	2003	2147		...	...	...	...	...	0659	0752
Warrington Central 188 d.		...	...	...	...	...	0715	0813	0919	and	1519	1619	1719	1819	1919	2019	2203		...	...	...	...	...	0715	0813
Manchester Piccadilly 193 d.		...	...	...	...	...	0742	0843	0943	at	1543	1643	1743	1843	1943	2043	2228		...	...	...	...	...	0742	0843
Stockport 193 d.		...	...	...	...	...	0754	0854	0954	the	1554	1655	1754	1854	1954	2054	2238		...	...	...	...	...	0754	0854
Sheffield 171 d.		...	...	...	*0603*	*0724*	0837	0937	1037	same	1637	1745	1852	1937	2041**c**	2137	2337		...	...	...	*0554*	*0737*	0837	0937
Chesterfield 171 d.		...	...	...	*0619*	*0737*	0852	0952	1052	minutes	1653	1801	1907	1952	2056	2155	0002		...	...	...	*0619*	*0750*	0852	0952
Alfreton 171 d.		...	...	...	*0630*	*0748*	0903	1003	1103	past	1704	1811	1918	2003	2108	2205	|		...	...	...	*0629*	*0801*	0903	1003
Nottingham 171 a.		...	...	...	*0701*	*0823*	0927	1027	1127	each	1727	1831	1941	2027	2133	2235	0040		...	...	...	*0702*	*0825*	0927	1027
Nottingham 194 d.		0456	0507	0610	0752	0835	0934	1034	1134	hour	1734	1837	...	2034	...	...	...		0505	0507	0610	0745	0834	0934	1034
Grantham 180 194 d.		|	0551**c**	|	0828**c**	0912**c**	1011**c**	1110	1211	until	1811	1909	...	2107	...	...	...		|	0551**c**	|	0820**c**	0910	1009	1109
Peterborough 180 205 208 d.		0627**c**	0623	0736	0859	0940	1045**c**	1141	1242	♤	1845**c**	1942	...	2139	...	...	...		0627	0625	0735	0858	0943	1040	1141
March 205 208 a.		0642	...	0752	|	|	|	|	|		1859	|	...	|	...	...	...		0642	...	0750	|	|	|	|
Ely 205 207 208 a.		0701	...	0811	0942	1013	1118	1213	1314		1919	2015	...	2213	...	...	...		0701	...	0811	0931	1016	1113	1213
Thetford 207 a.		0728	...	0836	1006	1037	1143	1238	1339		1950	2038	...	2237	...	...	...		0730	...	0836	1006	1043	1137	1238
Norwich 207 a.		0813	...	0913	1044	1112	1215	1313	1413		2022	2113	...	2318	...	...	...		0813	...	0915	1043	1115	1213	1313

	⑥		⑥	⑥	⑥	⑥	⑥	⑥	⑥	⑥		⑦ e	⑦ e	⑦	⑦	⑦	⑦	⑦	⑦	⑦	⑦	⑦ C	⑦	⑦	⑦
Liverpool Lime Street 187 d.	0852		1452	1552	1652	1752	1852	1952	2052	2137	⑦	...	...	...	...	...	1252	1352	1452	1552	1654	1752	1852	1952	2121
Liverpool SP ▷ 188 d.	0903		1503	1603	1703	1803	1903	2003	2103	2147		...	...	...	...	...	1303	1403	1503	1603	1705	1803	1903	2003	2131
Warrington Central 188 d.	0919	and	1519	1619	1719	1819	1919	2019	2119	2203		...	...	...	...	...	1319	1419	1519	1619	1721	1819	1919	2019	2147
Manchester Piccadilly 193 d.	0943	at	1543	1643	1743	1843	1943	2043	2143	2228		...	...	...	...	1243	1344	1444	1544	1644	1746	1844	1944	2044	2211
Stockport 193 d.	0954	the	1554	1654	1754	1854	1954	2054	2152	2238		...	...	...	...	1255	1354	1454	1553	1654	1755	1854	1954	2054	2228
Sheffield 171 d.	1037	same	1637	1741	1840	1937	2039**c**	2138	2242**f**	2338		...	1048	*1103*	1243	1348**d**	1441	1539	1643**c**	1740**c**	1839	1940**c**	2040**c**	2140**c**	2330
Chesterfield 171 d.	1052	minutes	1653	1757	1857	1952	2054	2154	2256	2353		...	1104	*1120*	1257	1402	1455	1553	1657	1754	1854	1954	2054	2156	2344
Alfreton 171 d.	1103	past	1704	1808	1908	2003	2105	2205	2307	|		...	1114	*1130*	1308	1412	1508	1603	1707	1805	1905	2005	2105	2206	2355
Nottingham 171 a.	1127	each	1727	1829	1930	2027	2133	2234	2328	0030		...	1139	*1158*	1334	1435	1532	1628	1730	1834	1933	2030	2133	2236	0023
Nottingham 194 d.	1134	hour	1734	1837	...	2034	...	...	...	...		0952	1139	1240	1347	1445	1550	1645	1736	1846	...	2045	...	...	...
Grantham 180 194 d.	1207	until	1814	1909	...	2107	...	...	...	...		1029	1223**d**	1315	1422	1520	1622	1721**c**	1817	1924	...	2120	...	...	...
Peterborough 180 205 208 d.	1240	♤	1844	1941	...	2140	...	...	...	...		1109	1256	1343	1458**c**	1558**c**	1659**c**	1757**c**	1849	1959	...	2153	...	...	...
March 205 208 a.	|		1900	|	...	|	...	...	...	...		1125	|	|	|	|	|	1812	|	|	...	|	...	...	...
Ely 205 207 208 a.	1313		1919	2014	...	2213	...	...	...	...		1143	1331	1416	1531	1631	1732	1832	1922	2032	...	2226	...	...	...
Thetford 207 a.	1337		1943	2038	...	2237	...	...	...	...		1213	1355	1443	1555	1655	1756	1856	1949	2056	...	2250	...	...	...
Norwich 207 a.	1413		2016	2113	...	2319	...	...	...	...		1253	1428	1524	1635	1726	1830	1929	2026	2137	...	2324	...	...	...

A – Via Melton Mowbray (Table **208**).
B – The 1057 from Norwich also calls at March (d.1205⑥ / 1208Ⓐ).
C – Conveys [2] Liverpool - Nottingham - Matlock (Table **172**).
D – From / to Spalding (Table **185**).
a – Arrives 1712.
b – Arrives 2216.
c – Arrives 5 – 6 minutes earlier.
d – Arrives 10 minutes earlier.
e – May 21 - Sept 10.
f – Arrives 2231.
h – From Sept. 17.
♤ – Timings may vary by up to 6 minutes.
▷ – **Liverpool** South Parkway.

207 CAMBRIDGE - NORWICH   LE

km			Ⓐ	⑥	⑥	Ⓐ	⚒	Ⓐ	⑥	⚒		⚒	⚒	⑥	Ⓐ	⑥	Ⓐ	⑥	Ⓐ	⚒ 2	⚒			⑦	⑦	⑦
0	**Cambridge** d.	⚒	0602	0605	0700	0700	0810	0906	0910	1010	and at	1710	1810	1910	1922	2012	2019	2110	2115	*2140*	2255	...	⑦	0850	1050	1150
24	Ely 206 d.		0619	0622	0716	0719	0828	0926	0928	1028	the same	1728	1828	1928	1940	2028	2037	2128	2133	2216	2312	...		0907	1107	1207
63	Thetford 206 d.		0644	0647	0743	0747	0853	0951	0953	1053	minutes	1753	1853	1953	2004	2053	2101	2153	2157	2237	2337	...		0934	1134	1232
84	Attleborough d.		0703	0706	0803	0806	0908	1006	1008	1108	past each	1808	1908	2008	2019	2108	2116	2208	2212	2251	2352	...		0949	1149	1247
94	Wymondham d.		0711	0714	0813	0816	0915	1015	1015	1115	hour until	1815	1915	2015	2027	2115	2124	2215	2220	2258	2359	...		0957	1157	1254
110	**Norwich** 206 a.		0727	0728	0830	0830	0930	1030	1030	1130	△	1830	1930	2030	2041	2130	2138	2232	2235	2319	0013	...		1013	1213	1312

	⑦	⑦	⑦	⑦	⑦	⑦	⑦	⑦	⑦ 2	⑦	⑦ 2
Cambridge d.	1250	1350	1450	1550	1650	1750	1850	1950	*2006*	2150	*2206*
Ely 206 d.	1307	1407	1507	1607	1707	1807	1907	2007	2036	2207	2229
Thetford 206 d.	1334	1432	1532	1634	1732	1832	1932	2032	2057	2232	2250
Attleborough d.	1349	1447	1547	1649	1747	1847	1947	2047	2111	2247	2304
Wymondham d.	1357	1454	1554	1657	1754	1854	1954	2054	2118	2254	2311
Norwich 206 a.	1413	1513	1613	1713	1813	1910	2013	2110	2137	2313	2324

		Ⓐ	⑥	Ⓐ	⑥	Ⓐ	⑥	⚒		⚒
Norwich 206 d.	⚒	0533	0537	0633	0640	0737	0740	0840	and at the	1440
Wymondham d.		0545	0549	0645	0652	0749	0752	0852	same	1452
Attleborough d.		0552	0556	0652	0659	0756	0759	0859	minutes	1459
Thetford 206 d.		0606	0610	0706	0713	0810	0813	0913	past each	1513
Ely 206 a.		0631	0635	0731	0738	0837	0838	0938	hour until	1538
Cambridge a.		0652	0656	0753	0759	0859	0859	0959	△	1559

	⑥	Ⓐ	⚒	⚒	⑥	Ⓐ	Ⓐ	⑥	⑥	Ⓐ	⚒			⑦	⑦	⑦	⑦	⑦	⑦	⑦	⑦	⑦	⑦	⑦ 2	⑦	⑦ 2	⑦
Norwich 206 d.	1535	1540	1638	1735	1838	1840	1938	1940	2110	2115	2240	...	⑦	0903	1003	1103	1203	1303	1403	1503	1603	1703	1803	1856	2003	2052	2203
Wymondham d.	1547	1552	1650	1747	1850	1852	1950	1952	2122	2127	2252	...		0915	1015	1115	1215	1315	1415	1515	1615	1715	1815	|	2015	|	2215
Attleborough d.	1554	1559	1659	1754	1857	1859	1958	1959	2129	2134	2259	...		0922	1022	1122	1222	1322	1422	1522	1622	1722	1822	|	2022	|	2222
Thetford 206 d.	1613	1613	1713	1813	1911	1913	2012	2013	2143	2148	2313	...		0936	1036	1136	1236	1336	1436	1536	1636	1736	1836	1923	2036	2119	2236
Ely 206 a.	1638	1638	1738	1838	1938	1938	2039	2038	2210	2216	2338	...		1003	1101	1203	1301	1401	1501	1603	1701	1801	1901	1944	2101	2140	2301
Cambridge a.	1659	1659	1759	1901	1959	1959	2059	2059	2231	2235	2359	...		1022	1122	1222	1322	1422	1522	1622	1722	1822	1922	*2007*	2122	*2207*	2322

△ – Timings may vary by up to 2 minutes.

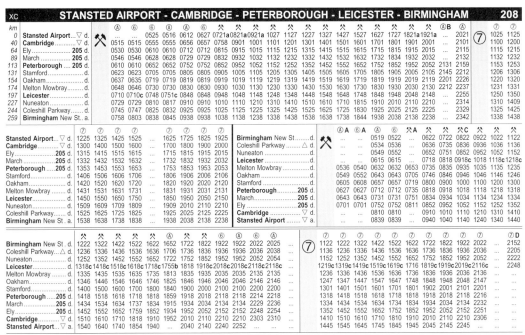

km		Ⓐ	⑥	⑥	Ⓐ	Ⓐ	⑥	⚒	⚒	⚒	⚒	⚒	⚒	⚒	⚒	⚒	⚒	⚒	⚒	⚒	ⒶB	Ⓐ	⑦	⑦
0	**Stansted Airport** ... ▽ d.	...	...	0525	0516	0612	0627	0721a	0821a	0921a	1027	1127	1227	1327	1427	1527	1627	1727	1821a	1921a	...	2021	1025	1125
40	**Cambridge** ▽ d.	0515	0515	0555	0555	0656	0657	0758	0901	1001	1101	1201	1301	1401	1501	1601	1701	1801	1901	2001	...	2101	1100	1200
64	Ely **205** d.	0530	0530	0610	0610	0712	0712	0815	0915	1015	1115	1215	1315	1415	1515	1615	1715	1815	1915	2015	...	2115	1115	1215
89	March **205** d.	0546	0546	0628	0628	0729	0729	0832	0932	1032	1132	1232	1332	1432	1532	1632	1732	1834	1932	2032	...	2132	1132	1232
113	**Peterborough** **205** d.	0610	0610	0652	0652	0752	0752	0852	0952	1052	1152	1252	1352	1452	1552	1652	1752	1852	1952	2052	2131	2159	1153	1253
131	Stamford d.	0623	0623	0705	0705	0805	0805	0905	1005	1105	1205	1305	1405	1505	1605	1705	1805	1905	2005	2105	2145	2212	1206	1306
154	Oakham d.	0637	0635	0719	0719	0819	0819	0919	1019	1119	1219	1319	1419	1519	1619	1719	1819	1919	2019	2119	2201	2226	1220	1320
174	Melton Mowbray d.	0648	0646	0730	0730	0830	0830	0930	1030	1130	1230	1330	1430	1530	1630	1730	1830	1930	2030	2130	2212	2237	1231	1331
197	**Leicester** d.	0710	0710c	0748	0751c	0848	0848	0948	1048	1148	1248	1348	1448	1548	1648	1748	1848	1948	2048	2148	...	2255	1250	1350
227	Nuneaton d.	0729	0729	0810	0817	0910	0910	1010	1110	1210	1310	1410	1510	1610	1710	1815	1910	2010	2110	2210	...	2314	1310	1409
244	Coleshill Parkway d.	0745	0747	0825	0832	0925	0925	1025	1125	1225	1325	1425	1525	1625	1725	1830	1925	2025	2125	2225	...	2329	1325	1425
259	**Birmingham** New St. a.	0758	0803	0838	0845	0938	0938	1038	1138	1238	1338	1438	1538	1638	1738	1844	1938	2038	2138	2238	...	2342	1338	1438

	⑦	⑦	⑦	⑦		⑦	⑦	⑦	⑦
Stansted Airport ... ▽ d.	1225	1325	1425	1525	...	1625	1725	1825	1925
Cambridge ▽ d.	1300	1400	1500	1600	...	1700	1800	1900	2000
Ely **205** d.	1315	1415	1515	1615	...	1715	1815	1915	2015
March **205** d.	1332	1432	1532	1632	...	1732	1832	1932	2032
Peterborough **205** d.	1353	1453	1553	1653	...	1753	1853	1953	2053
Stamford d.	1406	1506	1606	1706	...	1806	1906	2006	2106
Oakham d.	1420	1520	1620	1720	...	1820	1920	2020	2120
Melton Mowbray d.	1431	1531	1631	1731	...	1831	1931	2031	2131
Leicester d.	1450	1550	1650	1750	...	1850	1950	2050	2150
Nuneaton d.	1509	1609	1709	1809	...	1909	2010	2110	2210
Coleshill Parkway d.	1525	1625	1725	1825	...	1925	2025	2125	2225
Birmingham New St . a.	1538	1638	1738	1838	...	1938	2038	2138	2238

	ⒶA	⑥A	Ⓐ	⑥	⚒A	⚒	⚒	⚒C	⚒	⚒	⚒
Birmingham New St d.	...	...	0519	0522	...	0622	0722	0822	0922	1022	1122
Coleshill Parkway △ d.	...	...	0534	0536	...	0636	0735	0836	0936	1036	1136
Nuneaton d.	...	...	0549	0552	...	0652	0751	0852	0952	1052	1152
Leicester d.	...	...	0615	0615	...	0718	0818	0918c	1018	1118c	1218c
Melton Mowbray d.	0536	0540	0632	0632	0653	0735	0835	0935	1035	1135	1235
Oakham d.	0549	0552	0643	0643	0705	0746	0846	0946	1046	1146	1246
Stamford d.	0605	0608	0657	0657	0719	0800	0900	1000	1100	1200	1300
Peterborough **205** d.	0627	0627	0712	0712	0735	0818	0918	1018	1118	1218	1318
March **205** d.	0643	0643	0731	0731	0751	0834	0934	1034	1134	1234	1334
Ely **205** d.	0701	0701	0752	0752	0811	0852	0952	1052	1152	1252	1352
Cambridge ▽ d.	...	...	0810	0810	...	0910	1010	1110	1210	1310	1410
Stansted Airport ▽ a.	...	...	0839	0839	...	0940	1040	1140	1240	1340	1440

	⚒	⚒	⚒	⚒	⚒	Ⓐ	⚒	⚒	⑥	Ⓐ	⑥	Ⓐ		⑦	⑦	⑦	⑦	⑦	⑦	⑦	⑦	⑦	⑦		⑦D
Birmingham New St . d.	1222	1322	1422	1522	1622	1652	1722	1822	1922	1922	2022	2025	...	1122	1222	1322	1422	1522	1622	1722	1822	1922	2022	...	2152
Coleshill Parkway ... △ d.	1236	1336	1436	1536	1636	1706	1736	1836	1936	1936	2036	2038	...	1136	1236	1336	1436	1536	1636	1736	1836	1936	2036	...	2205
Nuneaton d.	1252	1352	1452	1552	1652	1722	1752	1852	1952	1952	2052	2054	...	1152	1252	1352	1452	1552	1652	1752	1852	1952	2052	...	2222
Leicester d.	1318c	1418c	1518c	1618c	1718c	1755b	1818	1918c	2018c	2018c	2118c	2118c	...	1219c	1319c	1419c	1519c	1619c	1716	1819c	1919c	2019c	2116c	...	2248
Melton Mowbray d.	1335	1435	1535	1635	1735	1813	1835	1935	2035	2035	2135	2135	...	1236	1336	1436	1536	1636	1736	1836	1936	2036	2136	...	...
Oakham d.	1346	1446	1546	1646	1746	1825	1846	1946	2046	2046	2146	2146	...	1247	1347	1447	1547	1647	1748	1848	1948	2048	2147	...	...
Stamford d.	1400	1500	1600	1700	1800	1840	1900	2000	2100	2100	2200	2200	...	1301	1401	1501	1601	1701	1801	1902	2001	2101	2201	...	...
Peterborough **205** d.	1418	1518	1618	1718	1818	1859	1918	2018	2118	2118	2214	2218	...	1318	1418	1518	1618	1718	1818	1918	2018	2118	2216	...	...
March **205** d.	1434	1534	1634	1737	1834	1915	1934	2034	2134	2134	2229	2236	...	1334	1434	1534	1634	1734	1834	1934	2034	2134	2232	...	...
Ely **205** d.	1452	1552	1652	1759	1852	1934	1952	2052	2152	2152	2248	2254	...	1352	1452	1552	1652	1752	1852	1952	2052	2152	2251	...	...
Cambridge ▽ d.	1510	1610	1710	1818	1910	1952	2010	2110	2210	2210	2303	2310	...	1410	1510	1610	1710	1810	1910	2010	2110	2210	2306	...	...
Stansted Airport ... ▽ a.	1540	1640	1740	1854	1940	...	2040	2140	2240	2252	...	...	...	1445	1545	1645	1745	1845	1945	2045	2145	2245	...	...	...

A – 🚆2 Nottingham - Norwich (Table **206**).
B – 🚆2 Spalding - Nottingham (Tables **185** and **206**).
C – 🚆12 Gloucester - Stansted Airport (Table **121**); 🍷 Birmingham - Peterborough.
D – 🚆12 Cardiff Central - Leicester (Table **121**).

a – Departs 6 minutes later on ⑥.
b – Arrives 9 minutes earlier.
c – Arrives 4 – 6 minutes earlier.

△ – 🚌 connections available to the National Exhibition Centre (NEC) and Birmingham International Airport.

☛ **Full service Leicester - Birmingham New Street and v.v.**

From Leicester:
On ⚒ at 0549⑥, 0617Ⓐ, 0643Ⓐ, 0649⑥, 0710, 0722Ⓐ, 0748⑥, 0751Ⓐ, 0816, 0848, 0918, 0948 and every 30 minutes until 2018, 2048, 2116Ⓐ, 2118⑥, 2148, 2216⑥, 2227Ⓐ, 2255Ⓐ.
On ⑦ at 1022, 1119, 1219, 1250 and then at 19 and 50 minutes past each hour until 2019, 2050, 2150, 2219.

From Birmingham New Street:
On ⚒ at 0519Ⓐ, 0522⑥, 0550Ⓐ, 0552⑥, 0622, 0652, 0722, 0752, 0822, 0852 and every 30 minutes until 1522, 1552, 1609Ⓐ, 1622, 1652, 1709Ⓐ, 1722, 1752, 1822, 1852, 1922, 1952, 2022⑥, 2025Ⓐ, 2052, 2222.
On ⑦ at 0952, 1052, 1122, 1152 and every 30 minutes until 2022, 2052, 2152.

▽ – **Full service Cambridge - Stansted Airport and v.v.**

From Cambridge:
On ⚒ at 0444Ⓐ, 0456⑥, 0517Ⓐ, 0542⑥, 0610⑥, 0632Ⓐ, 0640⑥, 0710⑥, 0740, 0810, 0826⑥, 0910, 0926⑥, 0931Ⓐ, 1010, 1026, 1110, 1126, 1210, 1226, 1310, 1326, 1410, 1426, 1510, 1526, 1610, 1626⑥, 1710, 1726⑥, 1817⑥, 1818Ⓐ, 1826⑥, 1910, 1926⑥, 2010, 2026⑥, 2110, 2126, 2210.

On ⑦ at 0739, 0824, 0915, 0924, 1015, 1024, 1115, 1124, 1215, 1224, 1315, 1324, 1410, 1424, 1510, 1524, 1610, 1624, 1710, 1724, 1810, 1824, 1910, 1924, 2010, 2024, 2110, 2124, 2210.

From Stansted Airport:
On ⚒ at 0516Ⓐ, 0525⑥, 0612Ⓐ, 0627⑥, 0648⑥, 0721Ⓐ, 0727⑥, 0748⑥, 0821Ⓐ, 0827⑥, 0905⑥, 0921Ⓐ, 0927⑥, 1005, 1027, 1105, 1127, 1205, 1227, 1305, 1327, 1405, 1427, 1505, 1527, 1605, 1627, 1705⑥, 1727, 1805⑥, 1821Ⓐ, 1827⑥, 1905⑥, 1921Ⓐ, 1927⑥, 2005⑥, 2021Ⓐ, 2027⑥, 2105⑥, 2127, 2205, 2227, 2257Ⓐ, 2327⑥.

On ⑦ at 0840, 0909, 1009, 1025, 1109, 1125, 1209, 1225, 1309, 1325, 1409, 1425, 1509, 1525, 1609, 1625, 1709, 1725, 1809, 1825, 1909, 1925, 2009, 2025, 2104, 2118, 2209, 2225, 2304.

NT 2nd class — MIDDLESBROUGH - NEWCASTLE — 210

km		ⒶA	⚒	⚒	⚒	⚒	⚒	and at	⚒	⚒	⚒	⚒	⚒	⑥Y	Ⓐ	⑦	⑦	and at	⑦	⑦	⑦	⑦Y
0	**Middlesbrough** d.	...	...	0655	0732	0832	0932	the same	1532	1632	1743	1832	1942	2047	2110	0931	1032	the same	1632	1742	1831	1934
9	Stockton d.	...	...	0706	0743	0843	0943	minutes	1543	1643	1754	1843	1954	2058	2121	0942	1043	minutes	1643	1753	1842	1945
28	Hartlepool **183** d.	...	0703	0725	0802	0902	1002	past each	1602	1702	1813	1902	2013	2117	2140	1001	1102	past each	1703	1815	1901	2004
57	Sunderland **183** d.	0540	0730	0755	0830	0930	1030	hour until	1630	1730	1843	1929	2039	2142	2211a	1028	1128	hour until	1730	1843	1928	2029
77	**Newcastle** a.	0556	0751	0816	0853	0952	1053	✣	1653	1752	1907	1955b	2104	2204	2232	1048	1148	✣	1748	1908	1952	2050

	Ⓐ	⑥	⚒	⚒	and at	⚒	⚒	⚒	⚒	⚒	Ⓐ	⑥	Ⓐ	⑥	ⒶA	⑦W	and at	⑦	⑦	⑦	⑦	⑦
Newcastle d.	0600	0600	0700	0730	the same	1630	1653	1730	1830	1930	2030	2033	2118	2130	2300	1000	the same	1600	1700	1800	1900	2000
Sunderland **183** d.	0620	0628a	0720	0750	minutes	1650	1715	1752	1851	1951	2051	2055	2138	2151	2320	1021	minutes	1621	1720	1821	1922	2021
Hartlepool **183** d.	0646	0653	0749	0815	past each	1715	1739	1818	1915	2017	2115	2122	2203	2215	...	1046	past each	1646	1746	1845	1946	2045
Stockton d.	...	...	0804	0833	hour until	1733	1758	1837	1933	2036	2133	2140	2221	2234	...	1104	hour until	1705	1805	1904	2005	2104
Middlesbrough a.	...	...	0825	0848	✣	1748	1816	1852	1948	2049	2148	2155	2236	2248	...	1118	✣c	1717	1825	1916	2021	2120

A – To/from London Kings Cross (Table **180**).
W – The 1000 departure continues to Whitby (Table **211**).
Y – From Whitby (Table **211**).

a – Arrives 8 minutes earlier.
b – Arrives 1951 on Ⓐ.
c – The 1100 departure arrives Middlesbrough at 1223.

✣ – Timings may vary by ± 3 minutes.

NT 2nd class — MIDDLESBROUGH and PICKERING - WHITBY — 211

km		⚒	⑦C	⚒	⑦B	⑦	⚒	⑦D	⚒	
0	**Middlesbrough** d.	0704	0905	1028	1121	1356	1403	1617	1740	...
18	Battersby d.	0734	0935	1058	1151	1433	1435	1655	1810	...
41	Glaisdale d.	0808	1009	1131	1225	1507	1509	1728	1843	...
46	Grosmont d.	0817	1017	1139	1233	1515	1517	1736	1851	...
56	**Whitby** a.	0837	1036	1159	1252	1534	1536	1756	1911	...

	⚒	⑦	⚒	⑦D	⑦C	⚒	⑦B	Ⓐ	⑥B
Whitby d.	0845	1044	1215	1301	1547	1559	1804	1918	1918
Grosmont d.	0902	1101	1232	1318	1604	1617	1821	1935	1935
Glaisdale d.	0913	1112	1243	1329	1615	1627	1832	1946	1946
Battersby d.	0947	1156	1318	1404	1650	1702	1906	2020	2020
Middlesbrough a.	1015	1223	1345	1433	1717	1729	1933	2047	2047

km		🚂	🚂		🚂	🚂	🚂		🚂	🚂
0	**Pickering** d.	...	0925	...	1100	1200	1300	...	1500	1610
29	Grosmont a.	...	1025	...	1205	1305	1405	...	1615	1710
29	Grosmont d.	0915	1040	...	...	1315	1430	...	...	1715
39	**Whitby** a.	0945	1110	...	...	1345	1500	...	...	1745

	🚂	🚂		🚂	🚂	🚂	🚂	🚂	
Whitby d.	1000	...	...	1245	1400	...	1640	1800	...
Grosmont a.	1025	...	...	1315	1425	...	1705	1825	...
Grosmont d.	1030	1130	...	1330	1430	1540	1715	...	...
Pickering a.	1140	1240	...	1440	1540	1650	1820	...	...

B – To/from Newcastle (Table **210**).
C – To/from Bishop Auckland (Table **212**).
D – To/from Darlington (Table **212**).

🚂 – Apr. 2 - Oct. 29, 2017. National rail tickets **not** valid. An amended service operates on most ⑦ and on certain other dates - please confirm with operator. The North Yorkshire Moors Railway (✆ 01751 472508. www.nymr.co.uk).

212 BISHOP AUCKLAND - DARLINGTON - MIDDLESBROUGH - SALTBURN
2nd class NT

km		✕	✕	Ⓐ	⑥	✕	✕	✕	✕	✕	Ⓐ	⑥	✕	⑦A	⑦	⑦	⑦	⑦A	⑦	⑦	⑦	⑦
0	**Bishop Auckland** d.	0717	0821	0926	0926	1125	1325	1525	1623	1805	1902	1920	2110	0812	1007	1207	1507	...	1708	1838	1907	...
4	Shildon d.	0722	0826	0931	0931	1130	1330	1530	1628	1810	1907	1925	2115	0817	1012	1212	1512	...	1713	1843	1912	...
8	Newton Aycliffe d.	0727	0831	0936	0936	1135	1335	1535	1633	1815	1912	1930	2120	0822	1017	1217	1517	...	1718	1848	1917	...
19	**Darlington** a.	0743	0847	0953	0953	1151	1351	1551	1650	1831	1928	1947	2136	0838	1033	1233	1533	...	1734	1904	1933	...
19	**Darlington** ▶ d.	0744	0900	0955	0955	1153	1353	1553	1653	1833	1930	1955	2138	0840	1035	1235	1535	1550	1736	...	1935	2245
43	**Middlesbrough** ▶ d.	0811	0927	1022	1024	1221	1421	1621	1720	1900	1957	2023	2206	0905	1103	1303	1603	1617	1803	...	2003	2310
55	Redcar Central ▶ d.	*0907*	0938	1034	1036	1233	1433	1633	1732	1910	2009	*2110*	2218	*1013*	1115	1315	1615	...	1815	...	2015	...
63	**Saltburn** ▶ a.	*0926*	0955	1051	1053	1250	1450	1650	1750	1926	2026	*2126*	2235	*1028*	1130	1330	1630	...	1830	...	2030	...

	✕	✕	⑥	Ⓐ	✕	✕	✕	✕	✕	✕	✕	✕	✕		⑦	⑦	⑦	⑦	⑦A	⑦	⑦A	⑦
Saltburn ▷ d.	...	...	0621	0624	...	0754	0958	1157	1357	1457	1630	1730	1930	...	...	...	1036	1336	...	1536	*1636*	1736
Redcar Central ▷ d.	...	...	0634	0637	...	0807	1011	1210	1410	1510	1643	1743	1943	...	...	...	1049	1349	...	1549	*1649*	1749
Middlesbrough ▷ d.	0544	...	0647	0650	...	0820	1023	1221	1421	1521	1657	1755	1955	...	...	0850	1102	1402	1434	1602	1719	1802
Darlington ▷ a.	0614	...	0719	0720	...	0851	1053	1252	1452	1552	1726	1825	2026	...	...	0920	1130	1431	1459	1631	1747	1831
Darlington d.	...	0648	...	...	0749	0851	1054	1254	1454	1554	1728	1832	2032	...	0743	0929	1132	1431	...	1631	1749	1834
Newton Aycliffe d.	...	0702	...	...	0804	0906	1108	1308	1508	1608	1742	1846	2046	...	0757	0943	1146	1445	...	1645	1803	1848
Shildon d.	...	0707	...	...	0808	0910	1113	1313	1513	1613	1747	1851	2051	...	0802	0948	1151	1450	...	1650	1808	1853
Bishop Auckland a.	...	0715	...	...	0816	0918	1120	1320	1520	1620	1754	1858	2058	...	0810	0955	1158	1457	...	1657	1815	1900

A – To/from Whitby (Table **211**).

▶ – All trains Darlington - Middlesbrough - Redcar - Saltburn:
✕: 0629, 0658, 0725Ⓐ, 0730⑥, 0823⑥, 0831Ⓐ, 0900, 0931, 0955, 1032, 1053, 1131, 1153, 1232, 1253, 1332, 1353, 1432, 1453, 1531, 1553, 1631, 1653, 1730, 1754Ⓐ, 1800⑥, 1833, 1930, 2030⑥, 2032Ⓐ, 2138.
⑦: 0835, 0933, 1035, 1135, 1235, 1333, 1434, 1535, 1635, 1736, 1836, 1935, 2035, 2145.

▷ – All trains Saltburn - Redcar - Middlesbrough - Darlington:
✕: 0621⑥, 0624Ⓐ, 0710, 0725Ⓐ, 0728⑥, 0754, 0830, 0930, 0958, 1030, 1057, 1130, 1157, 1230, 1257, 1330, 1357, 1430, 1457, 1530, 1555, 1630, 1655, 1730, 1757, 1829, 1857, 1930, 2030Ⓐ, 2034⑥, 2130, 2239.
⑦: 0936, 1036, 1136, 1236, 1336, 1436, 1536, 1636, 1736, 1836, 1936, 2042, 2136, 2243.

213 NEWCASTLE - CARLISLE
2nd class NT

km		⑥	Ⓐ	✕	✕	✕	✕	✕	✕	✕	✕	✕	✕	✕	✕	✕	✕	✕	Ⓐ	⑦	⑦	⑦	⑦
0	**Newcastle** ▶ d.	0630	0646	0824	0924	1022	1122	1222	1323	1424	1524	1622	1716	1754	1824	1925	2016	2118	2235	0910	1010	1110	1210
6	MetroCentre ▶ d.	0638	0654	0832	0932	1033	1132	1232	1333	1432	1532	1632	1724	1802	1833	1934	2024	2126	2243	0918	1018	1118	1218
19	Prudhoe ▶ d.	0650	0704	0844	0942	1043	1142	1242	1344	1442	1542	1644	1737	1814	1848	1947	2039	2138	2258	0930	1032	1130	1232
36	Hexham ▶ d.	0709	0717	0858	0955	1055	1155	1255	1357	1455	1555	1703	1750	1833	1906	2005	2100	2157	2319	0949	1051	1149	1251
62	Haltwhistle d.	0732	0740	0921	1014	1118	1214	1318	1416	1518	1616	1726	1813	1855	1925	2028	...	2220	...	1011	1114	1208	1314
99	**Carlisle** a.	0807	0815	0959	1048	1200	1250	1359	1451	1559	1653	1803	1852	1935	2000	2104	...	2258	...	1047	1152r	1243r	1352
	Glasgow Central **214** a.	1037	1037	...	...	...	...	...	1737	...	...	...	2140	...	...	...	...	...	...	...	...	...	...

	⑦	⑦	⑦	⑦	⑦		⑦	⑦
Newcastle ▶ d.	1310	1410	1510	1610	1710	...	1810	2015
MetroCentre ▶ d.	1318	1418	1518	1618	1718	...	1818	2024
Prudhoe ▶ d.	1330	1432	1530	1632	1730	...	1832	2038
Hexham ▶ d.	1349	1451	1549	1651	1749	...	1851	2057
Haltwhistle d.	1408	1510	1611	1710	1808	...	1914	2120
Carlisle a.	1443r	1545r	1647	1745r	1843r	...	1952r	2158r
Glasgow Central **214** a.	...	...	...	...	...	...	...	...

	✕	⑥	Ⓐ	✕	✕	✕	Ⓐ	⑥	✕
Glasgow Central **214** d.	...	...	...	...	...	0707	...	...	...
Carlisle d.	...	0625	0628	0718	0828	0943	1025	1025	1133
Haltwhistle d.	...	0657	0700	0750	0900	1011	1057	1057	1201
Hexham ▷ d.	0612	0719	0722	0812	0922	1029	1120	1122	1222
Prudhoe ▷ d.	0630	0737	0740	0829	0934	1041	1132	1134	1234
MetroCentre ▷ d.	0645	0750	0753	0846	0946	1053	1144	1146	1246
Newcastle ▷ a.	0655	0807	0807	0901	0959	1106	1157	1159	1259

	✕	✕	✕	✕	✕	✕	Ⓐ	⑥	✕	✕	✕	Ⓐ	⑦	⑦	⑦	⑦	⑦	⑦	⑦	⑦	⑦	⑦	⑦
Glasgow Central **214** d.	...	...	1213	...	...	...	1613	1613	...	...	...	...	...	...	...	...	...	...	...	...	...	...	...
Carlisle d.	1225	1332	1436	1528	1625	1728	1838	1841	1938	...	2125	...	0859t	1001t	1105t	1201t	1305t	1407t	1508	1601t	1705t	1801t	2012t
Haltwhistle d.	1257	1404	1505	1556	1657	1800	1910	1913	2007	...	2157	...	0933t	1036t	1136t	1236t	1333t	1435t	1536	1633t	1733t	1833t	2040t
Hexham ▷ d.	1322	1426	1523	1615	1722	1822	1932	1935	2028	2112	2222	2322	0956	1058	1156	1258	1356	1458	1556	1658	1756	1855t	2102
Prudhoe ▷ d.	1334	1438	1535	1626	1734	1840	1949	1952	2045	2130	2240	2340	1013	1115	1213	1315	1413	1515	1613	1715	1813	1912t	2119
MetroCentre ▷ d.	1346	1450	1547	1638	1746	1853	2003	2006	2059	2145	2253	2353	1029	1129	1229	1329	1429	1529	1629	1729	1829	1929	2135
Newcastle ▷ a.	1400	1503	1558	1650	1759	1907	2017	2017	2113	2158	2306	0004	1039	1139	1241	1341	1441	1541	1641	1741	1841	1942	2148

r – Arrives 2–3 minutes earlier May 21 - Oct. 1.
t – Departs 2–3 minutes later May 21 - Oct. 1.

▶ – Additional Trains Newcastle - Hexham. Journey time 43–45 minutes:
0625Ⓐ, 0753✕, 0854✕ and houly until 1454✕, 1554✕, 1654Ⓐ, 1656⑥ 1724✕.

▷ – Additional Trains Hexham - Newcastle. Journey time 42–47 minutes:
0742✕, 0845✕, 0943✕, 1045✕, 1143✕, 1245✕, 1342✕, 1445✕, 1543✕, 1645✕, 1743✕, 1843✕.

214 CARLISLE - DUMFRIES - GLASGOW
2nd class SR

km		✕	⑥	Ⓐ	✕	⑥	Ⓐ	⑥	✕	⑥	✕	⑦	⑥	✕	⑦	✕	⑦	⑥	✕	⑦	✕		⑥	✕	⑦	✕
	Newcastle **213** d.	...	...	...	...	0630	0646	...	...	...	...	...	...	1323	...	...	...	...	...	...	1716	...	...	...	...	...
0	**Carlisle** **154** d.	...	0525	0531	0608	0815	0815	0955	1115	1220	1312	1313	1422	1512	1515	1617	1712	1716	1757	1912	1917	...	2022	2112	2126	2310
16	Gretna Green d.	...	0536	0543	0619	0826	0826	1006	1126	1232	1323	1324	1433	1523	1526	1628	1723	1727	1808	1923	1928	...	2033	2123	2137	2321
28	Annan d.	...	0545	0552	0627	0834	0834	1014	1134	1240	1331	1332	1441	1531	1534	1636	1731	1735	1816	1931	1937	...	2041	2131	2145	2329
53	**Dumfries** d.	0546	0602	0609	0646	0853	0853	1032	1153	1258	1350	1351	1459	1550	1552	1654	1749	1753	1835	1950	1955	...	2059	2150	2203	2347
124	Auchinleck d.	0634	...	...	0735	0941	0941	...	1241	...	1438	1439	...	1638	...	...	...	...	1923	2038	2044	...	...	2238	...	...
146	**Kilmarnock** ▽ d.	0652	...	...	0755	0959	0959	...	1259	...	1458	1457	...	1657	...	...	...	...	1957a	2057	2101	...	...	2257	...	...
185	**Glasgow** Central **154** ▽ a.	0732	...	...	0838	1037	1037	...	1335	...	1538	1542	...	1737	...	...	...	...	2037	2135	2140	...	...	2336	...	...

	✕	✕	Ⓐ	⑥	✕	✕	⑥	✕	⑦	⑥	✕	✕	⑦	⑥	⑦	✕	✕	⑥	⑦	✕	✕	⑥	Ⓐ	⑦	⑥	Ⓐ
Glasgow Central . **154** ▽ d.	...	...	...	...	0707	0837	...	1013	...	...	1213	1313	...	...	1503	...	1613	...	...	1742	1913	...	2113	2212	2213	2313
Kilmarnock ▽ d.	...	...	...	...	0754	0918	...	1051	...	...	1250	1350	...	...	1550	...	1652	...	...	1825	1952	...	2153	2249	2253	0002
Auchinleck d.	...	...	...	...	0811	0935	...	1108	...	...	1307	1407	...	...	1607	...	1709	...	...	1842	2009	...	2210	2306	2309	0020
Dumfries d.	0458	0618	0743	0743	0901	1025	1102	1158	1300	1314	1357	1457	1501	1602	1700	1707	1759	1841	1901	1933	2100	2213	2300	2356	2359	0115
Annan d.	0513	0633	0758	0758	0916	1040	1117	1213	1315	1329	1413	1512	1516	1617	1715	1722	1814	1856	1916	1948	2115	2228	2315	0011	0014	...
Gretna Green d.	0522	0642	0807	0807	0925	1049	1126	1222	1324	1338	1421	1521	1525	1626	1724	1731	1823	1905	1925	1957	2124	2237	2324	0020	0023	...
Carlisle **154** a.	0535	0655	0820	0820	0941	1104	1139	1235	1337	1354	1435	1534	1538	1639	1737	1744	1836	1918	1938	2011	2143	2250	2337	0033	0036	...
Newcastle **213** a.	...	0901	0958	...	1106	...	...	...	...	...	1558	...	...	...	...	...	2017	...	...	...	...	...	...	...	...	...

a – Arrive 1940.

▽ – Frequent additional services are available (half-hourly on ✕, hourly on ⑦).

215 GLASGOW and KILMARNOCK - STRANRAER
2nd class SR

For ⛴ Cairnryan - Belfast and v.v. see Table 2002.

km		✕	✕	✕	✕	✕	✕	⑦	✕	✕	⑦	✕	✕	⑦	✕	✕	✕	⑦	✕	Ⓐ	⑥	⑦	✕	B	✕	A
0	**Glasgow** Central **216** d.	...	...	...	...	0807	...	...	...	...	...	...	...	...	1413	...	...	...	1713	1813	...	...	...	2013	...	2213
39	**Kilmarnock 214** a.	...	...	...	...	0849	...	...	...	...	...	...	...	...	1450	...	...	...	1752	1852	...	...	...	2052	...	2252
39	**Kilmarnock** d.	...	...	...	0801	0900	...	...	1104	...	...	1303	...	...	1458	...	1700	...	1804	1904	1904	...	...	2104	...	2305
56	Troon **216** d.	...	...	...	0814	0912	...	...	1116	...	...	1315	...	...	1510	...	1712	...	1818	1916	1916	...	...	2116	...	2317
64	**Ayr** 🚌 **216** a.	...	...	...	0827	0923	...	...	1130	...	...	1328	...	...	1524	...	1723	...	1828	1927	1927	...	...	2127	...	2330
64	**Ayr** d.	0525	0621	0716	0828	0923	1026	1106	1131	1226	1227	1329	1424	1505	1525	1625	1724	1805	1829	1927	1927	1927	2032	2128	2230	2331
97	Girvan d.	0552	0648	0756	0855	0954	1055	1136	1201	1253	1253	1359	1453	1535	1555	1652	1754	1835	1856	1958	1958	1953	2059	2153	2257	0001
121	Barrhill d.	...	...	0816	...	1013	...	1155	1220	...	1318	1418	...	1554	1614	...	1813	1854	...	2017	2017	2017	...	...	...	0020
162	**Stranraer** a.	...	...	0852	...	1049	...	1231	1256	...	1354	1454	...	1630	1650	...	1849	1930	...	2053	2053	2053	...	...	...	0056

	✕	✕	✕	✕	✕	✕	✕	⑦	✕	⑦	✕		✕	⑦	✕	✕	✕	⑦	✕	✕	✕	⑦	⑥	Ⓐ	✕	✕
Stranraer d.	...	...	0702	...	0858	...	1106	1041	...	1241	1304	...	...	1440	1500	...	1659	1740	...	1903	...	1940	2103	2103	...	...
Barrhill d.	...	...	0736	...	0932	...	1140	1116	...	1316	1338	...	...	1514	1534	...	1733	1814	...	1937	...	2015	2137	2137	...	...
Girvan d.	0557	0653	0754	0900	0952	1100	1159	1134	1300	1334	1357	...	1500	1533	1553	1658	1751	1833	1901	1956	2104	2033	2157	2157	2230	2302
Ayr a.	0627	0721	0823	0928	1020	1128	1229	1202	1328	1402	1429	...	1528	1601	1626	1727	1820	1901	1929	2026	2132	2101	2225	2225	2309	2330
Ayr 🚌 **216** d.	...	0722	0824	...	1021	...	1229	...	...	...	1430	...	...	...	1627	1728	1821	...	...	2027	...	...	2226	2226	...	...
Troon **216** d.	...	0732	0833	...	1029	...	1238	...	...	...	1441	...	...	...	1638	1739	1829	...	...	2038	...	...	2239	2239	...	...
Kilmarnock a.	...	0749	0852	...	1044	...	1254	...	...	...	1456	...	...	...	1653	1756	1844	...	...	2055	...	...	2256	2303	...	...
Kilmarnock 214 d.	...	...	0857	...	...	...	...	...	...	...	...	...	...	...	...	...	1857	...	...	...	...	...	...	...	...	...
Glasgow Central **216** a.	...	...	0937	...	...	...	...	...	...	...	...	...	...	...	...	...	1937	...	...	...	...	...	...	...	...	...

A – Runs Ⓐ from Glasgow, ✕ from Kilmarnock.
B – Runs ⑥ from Glasgow, ✕ from Kilmarnock.

☛ 🚌 connections to/from Cairnryan are available from Ayr for pre-booked Rail & Sail ticket holders - www.stenaline.co.uk/rail

Typical off-peak journey time in hours and minutes
READ DOWN ↓ READ UP ↑

Journey times may be extended during peak hours on Ⓐ (0600 - 0900 and 1600 - 1900) and also at weekends.
The longest journey time by any train is noted in the table heading.

GLASGOW CENTRAL - AYR — Longest journey: 1 hour 04 minutes SR

km	△				△
0	0h00	↓	**Glasgow** Central ...... d.		0h49
43	0h25		Kilwinning .... d.	↑	0h22
48	0h29	↓	Irvine .... d.		0h18
56	0h37		Troon .... d.	↑	0h11
61	0h41	↓	Prestwick Airport ✈ .. d.		0h07
67	0h52		**Ayr** .... a.	↑	0h00

From Glasgow Central: On ⚒ at 0015②–⑥, 0600, 0630, 0700, 0730, 0746, 0800, 0830, 0838, 0900, 0930, 1000, 1030 and every 30 minutes until 1500, 1530, 1600, 1628, 1640, 1701, 1716Ⓐ, 1728Ⓐ, 1730⑥, 1747Ⓐ, 1800 and every 30 minutes until 2330.
On ⑦ at 0900 and every 30 minutes until 1900, 2000, 2100, 2200, 2300.

From Ayr: On ⚒ at 0513, 0540, 0602, 0620Ⓐ, 0633, 0650, 0705, 0717, 0732Ⓐ, 0740, 0805, 0829, 0851, 0924, 0948 and at the same minutes past each hour until 1525, 1548, 1623, 1654, 1706, 1724, 1753, 1805, 1825, 1850, 1915 and every 30 minutes until 2215, 2300.
On ⑦ at 0845 and every 30 minutes until 1945, 2045, 2145, 2300.

△ – Trains at 0015⚒ - 0838⚒ and 1900⚒ - 2330⚒ and all day on ⑦ call additionally at Paisley Gilmour Street.

GLASGOW CENTRAL - ARDROSSAN - LARGS — Longest journey: 1 hour 10 minutes SR

km					
0	0h00	↓	**Glasgow** Central ...... d.	↑	0h59
12	0h10		Paisley Gilmour St .... d.		0h46
43	0h29	↓	Kilwinning .... d.	↑	0h25
50	0h38		**Ardrossan** Sth Beach .. d.		0h17
64	0h49	↓	Fairlie .... d.	↑	0h05
69	0h56		**Largs** .... a.		0h00

From Glasgow Central: On ⚒ at 0615, 0715, 0848 and hourly until 1448, 1548, 1631, 1714⑥, 1723Ⓐ, 1749, 1850, 1945, 2045, 2145, 2245, 2315①②③④⑥, 2345⑤. On ⑦ at 0940 and hourly until 2140, 2242.

From Largs: On ⚒ at 0642, 0722Ⓐ, 0742, 0833Ⓐ, 0853⑥, 0953 and hourly until 1553, 1648, 1733, 1852, 1952, 2052, 2152, 2252.
On ⑦ at 0854 and hourly until 2154, 2300.

SR 2nd class — GLASGOW - OBAN, FORT WILLIAM and MALLAIG — 218

km		⚒	⚒	⚒ A	Ⓐ Ba	⚒ 🍷	⚒ 🍷	⑦ d	⑦ c	⑦ 🍷	⚒ 🍷	Ⓐ Bb	⑦ 🍷	⑦ 🍷 d	⚒ 🍷	⚒ 🍷		Ⓐ	⚒ 🍷	⑦ 🍷	⑦ 🍷	⚒ 🍷	①–④ 🍷	⑤ 🍷	⑥ 🍷
	Edinburgh **220** .... d.	...	...	0450	...	*0715*	*0715*	...	0808	*0830*	*0930*	...	*1100*	*1100*	*1114*	*1114*	...	...	*1530*	*1700*	*1700*	*1715*	*1715*	*1715*	*1715*
0	**Glasgow** Queen St ..... d.	...	0520	0548‡	...	0821	0821	...	│	0956	1037	...	1220	1220	1221	1221	...	...	1637	1820	1820	1821	1821	1821	1821
16	Dalmuir .... d.	...	0538	0604	...	0842	0842	...	0927**u**	1016	1056	...	1234	1234	1242	1242	...	...	1657	1834	1834	1841	1841	1841	1841
26	Dumbarton Central .... d.	...	0547	0615	...	0851	0851	...	│	1025	1105	...	1247	1247	1251	1251	...	...	1706	1847	1847	1850	1850	1850	1850
40	Helensburgh Upper ..... d.	...	0603	0632	...	0906	0906	...	0952	1040	1127	...	1306	1306	1306	1306	...	...	1722	1905	1905	1904	1904	1904	1904
51	Garelochhead .... d.	...	0614	0645	...	0917	0917	...	1003	1051	1140	...	1318	1318	1318	1318	...	...	1733	1916	1916	1917	1917	1917	1917
68	Arrochar & Tarbet .... d.	...	0634	0709	...	0937	0937	...	1023	1111	1201	...	1338	1338	1338	1338	...	...	1757	1936	1936	1937	1937	1937	1937
81	Ardlui .... d.	...	0652	0724**x**	...	0950	0950	...	1037	1127	1214	...	1356	1356	1356	1356	...	...	1810	1951	1951	1951	1951	1951	1951
95	**Crianlarich** .... a.	...	0708	0745	...	1006	1006	...	1053	1144	1230	...	1412	1412	1412	1412	...	...	1826	2007	2007	2007	2007	2007	2007
95	**Crianlarich** .... d.	...	0718	0747	...	1015	1021	...	1056	1146	1233	...	1418	1424	1418	1424	...	...	1829	2014	2020	2014	2020	2020	2020
	Dalmally .... d.	...	0751	│	...	1042	│	...	1122	1214	1259	...	1444	│	1444	│	...	1705	1855	2040	│	2040	│	│	│
	Taynuilt .... d.	...	0811	│	...	1103	│	...	1142	1240	1320	...	1504	│	1505	│	...	1724	1920	2100	│	2100	│	│	│
162	**Oban** .... a.	...	0835	│	...	1127	│	...	1206	1304	1343	...	1527	│	1528	│	...	1747	1943	2124	│	2124	│	│	│
115	Bridge of Orchy .... d.	...	...	0818	...	...	1048	...	...	...	...	...	...	1449	...	1449	...	...	...	...	2047	...	2045	2045	2045
140	Rannoch .... d.	...	...	0846	...	...	1109	...	...	...	...	...	...	1512	...	1512	...	...	...	...	2108	...	2108	2108	2108
177	Roy Bridge .... d.	...	...	0931**x**	...	...	1148	...	...	...	...	...	...	1550	...	1550	...	...	...	...	2146	...	2146	2146	2146
183	Spean Bridge .... d.	...	...	0939	...	...	1155	...	...	...	...	...	...	1556	...	1556	...	...	...	...	2153	...	2153	2156	2153
197	**Fort William** .... a.	...	...	0955	...	...	1208	...	...	...	...	...	...	1609	...	1609	...	...	...	...	2206	...	2206	2209	2206
197	**Fort William** .... d.	0830	...	...	1015	...	1212	1212	...	...	...	1430	...	1619	...	1619	...	...	...	...	2214	...	2214	2217	2214
223	Glenfinnan .... d.	0905	...	...	1122	...	1246	1246	...	...	...	1545	...	1655	...	1655	...	...	...	...	2247	...	2247	2250	2247
251	Arisaig .... d.	0938	...	...	│	...	1319	1319	...	...	...	│	...	1727	...	1727	...	...	...	...	2320	...	2320	2323	2320
259	Morar .... d.	0946	...	...	│	...	1327	1327	...	...	...	│	...	1736	...	1736	...	...	...	...	2328	...	2328	2331	2328
264	**Mallaig** .... a.	0953	...	...	1225	...	1334	1334	...	...	...	1629	...	1743	...	1743	...	...	...	...	2335	...	2335	2338	2335

	⚒ 🍷	⚒ 🍷	⚒	⚒	⚒	⑦	⑦ d	Ⓐ	Ⓐ Ba	⑦	⑥		Ⓐ	⑦ c	⚒	⚒	⑦	⑦	⑦ A	⑦ d	⚒	⚒	Ⓐ A	Ⓐ Bb
Mallaig .... d.	...	0603	...	...	1010	...	1010	...	1410	...	...	...	...	...	1605	...	1605	...	...	1815	1815	...	...	1838
Morar .... d.	...	0609	...	...	1017	...	1017	...	│	...	...	...	...	...	1612	...	1612	...	...	1822	1822	...	...	│
Arisaig .... d.	...	0619	...	...	1027	...	1026	...	│	...	...	...	...	...	1621	...	1621	...	...	1831	1831	...	...	│
Glenfinnan .... d.	...	0651	...	...	1059	...	1059	...	1518	...	...	...	...	...	1654	...	1654	...	...	1904	1904	...	...	1947
Fort William .... a.	...	0725	...	...	1132	...	1132	...	1600	...	...	...	...	...	1728	...	1728	...	...	1937	1937	...	...	2031
Fort William .... d.	...	0744	...	...	1140	...	1140	...	...	...	...	...	...	...	1737	...	1737	...	1900	...	...	...	1950	...
Spean Bridge .... d.	...	0757	...	...	1156	...	1156	...	...	...	...	...	...	...	1751	...	1751	...	1920	...	...	...	2010	...
Roy Bridge .... d.	...	0804	...	...	1202	...	1202	...	...	...	...	...	...	...	1757	...	1757	...	1927**x**	...	...	...	2017**x**	...
Rannoch .... d.	...	0847	...	...	1242	...	1242	...	...	...	...	...	...	...	1838	...	1838	...	2015	...	...	...	2107	...
Bridge of Orchy .... d.	...	0907	...	...	1303	...	1303	...	...	...	...	...	...	...	1858	...	1858	...	2048	...	...	...	2135	...
Oban .... d.	0521	│	0857	1211	│	1211	│	1441	...	1611	1611	...	1611	1711	│	1811	│	1811	│	...	...	2036	│	...
Taynuilt .... d.	0544	│	0920	1235	│	1238	│	1506	...	1638	1634	...	1634	1737	│	1833	│	1833	│	...	...	2101	│	...
Dalmally .... d.	0603	│	0940	1300	│	1259	│	1526	...	1658	1654	...	1654	1758	│	1856	│	1856	│	...	...	2120	│	...
Crianlarich .... a.	0631	0931	1008	1332	1327	1326	1332	1554	...	1726	1722	...	...	1825	1922	1927	1922	1927	2118	...	...	2147	2205	...
Crianlarich .... d.	0633	0933	1014	1337	1337	1337	1337	1556	...	1727	1724	...	...	1826	1932	1932	1932	1932	2119	...	...	2148	2206	...
Ardlui .... d.	0651	0951	1029	1355	1355	1355	1355	1611	...	1743	1742	...	...	1841	1952	1952	1952	1952	2140**x**	...	...	2204	2227**x**	...
Arrochar & Tarbet .... d.	0710	1005	1043	1409	1409	1409	1409	1627	...	1757	1756	...	...	1855	2006	2006	2006	2006	2158	...	...	2218	2245	...
Garelochhead .... d.	0730	1032	1104	1431	1431	1429	1429	1649	...	1819	1819	...	...	1917	2026	2026	2026	2026	2224	...	...	2238	2311	...
Helensburgh Upper .... d.	0742	1044	1116	1443	1443	1440	1440	1700	...	1831	1831	...	...	1929	2037	2037	2040	2040	2238	...	...	2249	2325	...
Dumbarton Central .... a.	0756	1059	1129	1459	1459	1457	1457	1713	...	1847	1844	...	...	│	2050	2050	2053	2053	2252	...	...	2302	2339	...
Dalmuir .... a.	│	1109	1138	1509	1509	1506	1506	1723	...	1856	1853	...	...	1955**s**	2104	2104	2104	2104	2304	...	...	2311	2351	...
Glasgow Queen St .... a.	0837	1130	1156	1529	1529	1526	1526	1748	...	1917	1919	...	...	│	2122	2122	2119	2119	2329¶	...	...	2333	0014¶	...
Edinburgh **220** .... a.	*0951*	*1239*	*1307*	*1639*	*1639*	*1655*	*1655*	*1851*	...	*2024*	*2021*	...	...	2109	*2256*	*2256*	*2221*	*2221*	0024	...	...	...	0110	...

A – Ⓡ. 🛏(12) (limited accommodation), 🛏 1, 2 cl. and ✕ London Euston - Fort William and v.v. (Table **161**).
B – THE JACOBITE – 🚂. Ⓡ. National Rail tickets **not** valid. To book ✆ 0844 850 4685 or visit www.westcoastrailways.co.uk.

a – Apr. 14 - Oct. 27 (also ⑥⑦ June 17 - Oct. 1).
b – May 15 - Sept. 15 (also ⑥⑦ July 1 - Sept. 3).
c – June 25 - Aug. 27.
d – May 21 - Oct. 29.
s – Calls to set down only.

u – Calls to pick up only.
x – Calls on request.
‡ – Low-level platforms. Calls to pick up only.
¶ – Low-level platforms. Calls to set down only.

⛴ SCOTTISH ISLAND FERRIES — 219

Caledonian MacBrayne Ltd operates numerous ferry services linking the Western Isles of Scotland to the mainland and to each other. Principal routes – some of which are seasonal – are listed below (see also the map on page **90**). Service frequencies, sailing-times and reservations: ✆ +44 (0)800 066 5000; fax +44 (0)1475 635 235; www.calmac.co.uk

Ardrossan – Brodick (Arran)
Ardrossan – Campbeltown (Kintyre)
Barra – Eriskay
Claonaig – Lochranza (Arran)
Colintraive – Rhubodach (Bute)
Fionnphort – Iona (Iona)
Kennacraig – Port Askaig (Islay)
Kennacraig – Port Ellen (Islay)
Kilchoan – Tobermory (Mull)
Largs – Cumbrae (Cumbrae)
Leverburgh (Harris) – Berneray (North Uist)
Lochaline – Fishnish (Mull)
Mallaig – Armadale (Skye)
Mallaig – Eigg, Muck, Rum and Canna
Mallaig/Oban – Lochboisdale (South Uist)
Oban – Castlebay (Barra)
Oban – Coll and Tiree
Oban – Colonsay, Port Askaig (Islay) and Kennacraig
Oban – Craignure (Mull)
Oban – Lismore
Portavadie (Cowal & Kintyre) – Tarbert Loch Fyne
Sconser (Skye) – Raasay
Tayinloan – Gigha
Tobermory (Mull) – Kilchoan
Uig (Skye) – Lochmaddy (North Uist)
Uig (Skye) – Tarbert (Harris)
Ullapool – Stornoway (Lewis)
Wemyss Bay – Rothesay (Bute)

220 EDINBURGH - GLASGOW

GR, SR, XC

EDINBURGH - FALKIRK - GLASGOW QUEEN STREET

km		⚒	⚒	⚒	Ⓐ	⚒	⚒	⚒	⚒	⚒	⚒	⚒	⚒	⚒		⚒	⚒	⚒	⚒	⚒	⚒	⚒	⚒
0	**Edinburgh** Waverley d.		0555	0630	0645	0700	0715	0730	0745	0800	0815	0830	0845	0900	and at	1800	1815	1830	1845	1900	1915	1930	2000
2	Haymarket d.		0600	0634	0649	0704	0719	0735	0749	0805	0820	0834	0849	0905	the same	1806	1820	1834	1849	1905	1920	1935	2005
28	Linlithgow d.		0615	0649	0705	|	0734	0750	0806	|	0835	|	0905	|	minutes	|	1836	|	1905	|	1935	1950	2020
41	Falkirk High d.		0626	0701	0714	0727	0743	0801	0815	0830	0847	0855	0917	0925	past each hour until	1826	1848	1855	1916	1925	1946	1959	2031
76	**Glasgow** Queen Street a.		0649	0725	0737	0751	0808	0825	0840	0855	0908	0919	0937	0952	☆	1850	1909	1922	1936	1951	2009	2024	2051

	⚒	⚒	⚒	⚒	⚒	⚒	⚒	⑦	⑦	⑦	⑦	⑦	⑦	⑦	⑦		⑦	⑦	⑦	⑦	⑦	⑦
Edinburgh Waverley d.	2030	2100	2130	2200	2230	2300	2330		0800	0830	0900	0930	1000	1030	1100	and at the same	2100	2130	2200	2230	2300	2330
Haymarket d.	2034	2105	2134	2204	2234	2304	2334		0804	0834	0904	0934	1004	1034	1104	minutes	2104	2134	2205	2234	2304	2334
Linlithgow d.	2049	2120	2150	2219	2250	2319	2349		0824	0854	0924	0954	1023	1049	1119	past each	2119	2149	2220	2249	2319	2350
Falkirk High d.	2058	2131	2159	2230	2259	2330	0001		0835	0903	0935	1003	1034	1058	1130	hour until	2130	2200	2231	2258	2330	0002
Glasgow Queen Street a.	2125	2151	2225	2251	2322	2359	0027		0859	0926	0955	1028	1055	1121	1151	⊡	2150	2228	2251	2322	2354	0025

	⚒	⚒	Ⓐ	⑥	Ⓐ	⚒	⚒	⚒	⚒	⚒	⚒	⚒	⚒		⚒	⚒	⚒	⚒	⚒	⚒	⚒	⚒
Glasgow Queen Street d.		0600	0630	0630	0645	0700	0715	0730	0745	0800	0815	0830	0845	and at the same	1800	1815	1830	1845	1900	1915	1930	2000
Falkirk High d.		0618	0651	0654	0707	0721	0734	0753	0804	0822	0834	0853	0904	minutes	1824	1834	1853	1905	1922	1933	1948	2022
Linlithgow d.		0629	0702	0705	0715	0732	0745	0800	0815	|	0843	|	0915	past each	|	1845	|	1916	|	1945	1959	2029
Haymarket ▽ a.		0645	0718	0720	0732	0750	0801	0818	0832	0846	0905	0915	0933	hour until	1844	1902	1918	1933	1946	2001	2018	2047
Edinburgh Waverley a.		0650	0723	0725	0737	0755	0806	0824	0837	0852	0911	0921	0939	☆**a**	1851	1907	1923	1939	1951	2007	2024	2052

	⚒		⚒	⚒	⑥	Ⓐ	⚒	⚒	⚒	⑦	⑦	⑦	⑦	⑦	⑦	⑦	⑦		⑦	⑦	⑦	⑦
Glasgow Queen Street d.	2030	...	2100	2130	2200	2200	2230	2300	2330		0748	0830	0900	0930	1000	1030	1100	and at the same	2200	2230	2300	2330
Falkirk High d.	2049	...	2122	2150	2222	2222	2249	2322	2352		0810	0848	0922	0949	1022	1048	1122	minutes	2222	2248	2322	2353
Linlithgow d.	2100	...	2129	2201	2229	2229	2300	2333	0003		0820	0859	0929	1000	1029	1059	1129	past each	2229	2259	2329	0004
Haymarket ▽ a.	2115	...	2145	2217	2245	2246	2315	2350	0021		0842	0920	0949	1020	1045	1115	1145	hour until	2245	2315	2345	0025
Edinburgh Waverley a.	2123	...	2150	2222	2250	2252	2322	2355	0026		0847	0925	0954	1025	1050	1120	1150	☆	2250	2321	2350	0030

EDINBURGH - MOTHERWELL - GLASGOW CENTRAL

km		⚒	⚒	⚒	Ⓐ2	⑥2	⑥A	ⒶA	⚒2	⚒A	⚒2	⚒A	⚒2	⚒A	Ⓐ2	⑥2	⚒A	⚒2	⚒2	⚒A	ⒶB	⑥A	ⒶA	⚒2
0	**Edinburgh** Waverley d.		0624	0727	0740	0754	0914	0918	1019	1111	1153	1312	1352	1512	1549	1548	1712	1740	1826	1911	2017	2113	2114	2313
2	Haymarket d.		|	0731	0746	0758	0920	0924	1024	1116	1158	1316	1357	1516	1554	1553	1717	1746	1831	1916	2022	2118	2119	2317
71	Motherwell a.		0704	0812	0833	0900	0954	1002	1133	1152	1309	1353	1504	1552	1635	1704	1752	1834	1933	1953	2103	2159	2207	0021
92	**Glasgow** Central a.		0722	0829	0855	0923	1015	1025	1154	1212	1325	1412	1525	1612	1657	1723	1811	1856	1954	2015	2125	2220	2224	...

	⑦	⑦	⑦A	⑦A	⑦A	⑦A	⑦A	⑦A	⑦B
Edinburgh Waverley d.		1023	1217	1313	1510	1711	1918	2112	2122
Haymarket d.		|	1221	1318	1514	1715	1923	2117	2126
Motherwell a.		1103	1258	1353	1554	1755	1959	2156	2203
Glasgow Central a.		1128	1318	1412	1611	1812	2019	2213	2226

	⚒	⚒A	⚒B	⑥2	Ⓐ2	⚒A	⚒A	Ⓐ2	⑥2
Glasgow Central d.		0601	0650	0703	0705	0750	0900	0933	0948
Motherwell d.		0616	0706	0721	0721	0805	0915	1000	1004
Haymarket d.		0657	0748	0822	0829	0851	0957	1050	1113
Edinburgh Waverley a.		0701	0752	0829	0834	0857	1002	1054	1121

	⚒A	⚒2	⚒A	⚒2	⚒A	⚒2	⚒A	⚒A	Ⓐ2	⑥2	⑥	Ⓐ		⑦	⑦A	⑦A	⑦A	⑦A		⑦A	⑦A	⑦	
Glasgow Central d.	1100	1146	1300	1405	1500	1546	1700	1900	1947	1948	2105	2105	...		1055	1200	1348	1455	...	1655	1900	2058	...
Motherwell d.	1116	1202	1316	1427	1516	1602	1716	1916	2006	2006	|	2122	...		1113	1217	1404	1512	...	1712	1915	2118	...
Haymarket d.	1154	1249	1354	1519	1556	1705	1754	1954	2054	2053	2154	|	...		1151	1256	1442	1552	...	1751	1959	2204	...
Edinburgh Waverley a.	1159	1256	1359	152	1600	1711	1800	1958	2100	2058	2159	2221	...		1156	1300	1447	1556	...	1755	2005	2208	...

OTHER SERVICES EDINBURGH - GLASGOW

EDINBURGH WAVERLEY – SHOTTS – GLASGOW CENTRAL

76 km Journey time: ±75 minutes (trains marked * ±90 minutes)

From Edinburgh Waverley:

⚒: 0552*, 0636 Ⓐ, 0641 ⑥, 0655*, 0757, 0825*, 0857, 0925*⑥, 0927*Ⓐ, 0956 and at the same minutes past each hour (⊡) until 1555, 1626*, 1656, 1720*, 1749, 1756*Ⓐ, 1758*⑥, 1856, 1926*, 2126* ⑤⑥ and 2256* ⑤⑥.

All trains call at **Haymarket** 4 minutes later and **Shotts** 38 minutes later (trains marked * 53 minutes later).

⑦: 1026, 1226, 1426, 1626, 1826 and 2026.

On ⑦ trains run **Edinburgh** to **West Calder** where a 🚌 connection is made serving **Shotts** and **Glasgow Central**. Journey time to **Haymarket** 4 mins; **Shotts** 78 mins; **Glasgow** 149 mins.

From Glasgow Central:

⚒: 0006*⑥, 0616*, 0700, 0713*, 0803, 0817*, 0903, 0917*, 1005, 1017*, 1103, 1117* and at the same minutes past each hour until 1703, 1717*, 1803, 1816 ⑥, 1818 Ⓐ*, 1903 Ⓐ, 1907 ⑥, 1917*, 2117 ⑤⑥* and 2303 ⑤⑥*

Trains call at **Shotts** 27 minutes later (trains marked * 36 minutes later) and **Haymarket** 59 minutes later (trains marked * 83 minutes later).

⑦: 0904, 1104, 1305, 1505, 1705 and 1905.

On ⑦ trains run **West Calder** to **Edinburgh**. A 🚌 connection runs from **Glasgow Central** calling at **Shotts** then **West Calder**. Journey time to **Shotts** 85 mins; **Haymarket** 160 mins and **Edinburgh** 164 mins.

EDINBURGH WAVERLEY – AIRDRIE – GLASGOW QUEEN STREET LOW LEVEL

71 km Journey time: ±74 minutes.

From Edinburgh Waverley:

⚒: 0607, 0621, 0638, 0651, 0707, 0720, 0737Ⓐ, 0739⑥, 0749 ⑥, 0751 Ⓐ, 0808, 0821, 0839Ⓐ, 0841⑥, 0849Ⓐ, 0852 ⑥, 0910, 0920⑥, 0922Ⓐ, 0937, 0949, 1008, 1022Ⓐ, 1024⑥, 1038, 1048, 1107, 1121, 1137, 1148, 1208, 1221, 1236, 1250 ⑥, 1255 Ⓐ, 1308, 1318 Ⓐ, 1322⑥, 1337, 1349, 1407Ⓐ, 1409⑥, 1422⑥, 1424Ⓐ, 1438, 1448⑥, 1450Ⓐ, 1507, 1522, 1539, 1552, 1608, 1621, 1638, 1648, 1707, 1718 Ⓐ, 1723 ⑥, 1737, 1753, 1807, 1823, 1839, 1848, 1919 ⑥, 1922 Ⓐ, 1951, 2022, 2051 ⑥, 2054 Ⓐ, 2120 ⑥, 2123 Ⓐ, 2150Ⓐ, 2153⑥, 2221Ⓐ, 2223⑥, 2250Ⓐ, 2252⑥ and 2307**c**.

⑦: 0838, 0906, 0938, 1006, 1040, 1110, 1140, 1210, 1240, 1308 and every 30 minutes until 1809, 1840, 1940, 2040, 2140 and 2240.

All trains call at **Haymarket** 4 minutes later, **Bathgate** 25 minutes later and **Airdrie** 44 – 49 minutes later.

From Glasgow Queen Street Low Level:

⚒: 0545Ⓐ, 0547⑥, 0601, 0616, 0637, 0647, 0707, 0717, 0738, 0747, 0808, 0816, 0838, 0848, 0909, 0918, 0938, 0946, 1007, 1016, 1038, 1047, 1108, 1117, 1138, 1147, 1208, 1217, 1238, 1247 and at the same minutes past each hour until 1808, 1817, 1838, 1847, 1908, 1938, 2009, 2039, 2109, 2138, 2208, 2237, 2308**b** and 2338**b**.

⑦: 0811, 0845, 0915, 0945, 1015, 1045 and every 30 minutes until 1815, 1845, 1945, 2045, 2145 and 2245**b**.

All trains call at **Airdrie** 23 minutes later, **Bathgate** 40 – 45 minutes later and **Haymarket** 63 – 67 minutes later.

A – To / from destinations on Tables **120** and **124**.
B – To / from London Kings Cross (Table **180**).
a – 1730 from Glasgow also calls at Linlithgow (d. 1803).
b – Terminates at Bathgate.
c – Terminates at Airdrie.
☆ – Timings may vary by ± 5 minutes.
▽ – Trains call to set down only.
⊡ – Timings may vary by ± 2 minutes.

221 EDINBURGH - TWEEDBANK

2nd class SR

km		⚒	Ⓐ	⑥	Ⓐ	⑥	⚒	⚒	Ⓐ	⑥	⚒	⚒	⚒		⚒	⚒	⚒	Ⓐ	⑥	⚒	⚒	Ⓐ	⑥	⚒	Ⓐ	⑥
0	**Edinburgh** Waverley. d.		0543	0555	0622	0625	0651	0723	0753	0756	0824	0855	0922	and at	1524	1552	1624	1652	1654	1722	1755	1823	1826	1854	1924	0925
13	Eskbank d.		0608	0614	0641	0644	0711	0743	0812	0815	0843	0914	0942	the same	1543	1613	1643	1713	1715	1743	1814	1842	1845	1914	1943	1945
15	Newtongrange d.		0612	0617	0644	0647	0714	0746	0815	0818	0846	0917	0945	minutes	1546	1616	1646	1716	1718	1746	1817	1845	1848	1917	1946	1948
43	Stow d.		|	|	0706	0709	0736	0808	0837	0840	0908	|	1008	past each	1608	|	1708	1738	1741	1808	1839	1907	1910	1939**a**	2008	2010
53	Galashiels d.		0644	0646	0715	0718	0745	0817	0846	0849	0917	0946	1017	hour until	1617	1646	1717	1747	1749	1817	1848	1916	1919	1948	2017	2019
57	**Tweedbank** a.		0648	0650	0719	0722	0750	0823	0850	0853	0922	0950	1021	♤	1623	1650	1722	1751	1754	1821	1853	1921	1923	1952	2021	2024

	⚒	Ⓐ	⑥	⚒	⚒	⚒	⑦	⑦	⑦		⑦	⑦
Edinburgh Waverley d.	1954	2053	2056	2153	2254	2354		0911	1011	and at	2212	2311
Eskbank d.	2014	2113	2115	2213	2314	0013		0930	1030	the same	2232	2330
Newtongrange d.	2017	2116	2118	2216	2317	0016		0933	1033	minutes	2235	2333
Stow d.	2039	2138	2140	2238	2339	0038		0955	1055	past each	2257	2355
Galashiels d.	2048	2147	2149	2247	2348	0047		1004	1104	hour until	2306	0004
Tweedbank a.	2053	2151	2153	2253	2354	0052		1008	1108	♡	2310	0009

	⚒	Ⓐ	⑥	⚒	Ⓐ	⑥	Ⓐ	⑥	⚒	⚒
Tweedbank d.		0520	0530	0558	0628	0629	0658	0700	0728	0758
Galashiels d.		0524	0534	0602	0632	0633	0702	0704	0732	0802
Stow d.		0533	0543	0611	0641	0642	0711	0713	0741	0811**a**
Newtongrange d.		0553	0603	0631	0701	0702	0731	0733	0801	0831
Eskbank d.		0556	0606	0634	0704	0705	0734	0736	0804	0834
Edinburgh Waverley a.		0615	0625	0656	0728	0724	0759	0755	0824	0854

	Ⓐ	⑥	⚒	⚒	⚒	⚒		⚒	⚒	Ⓐ	⑥	Ⓐ	⑥	⚒	Ⓐ	⑥	⚒	⚒	⚒d	⑦	⑦	⑦		⑦	⑦
Tweedbank d.	0828	0831	0859	0930	0959	1029	and at	1730	1759	1828	1832	1859	1903	1931	2029	2032	2129	2229	2328		0845	0945	and at	2145	2246
Galashiels d.	0832	0835	0903	0934	1003	1033	the same	1734	1803	1832	1836	1903	1907	1935	2033	2036	2133	2233	2332		0849	0949	the same	2149	2250
Stow d.	0841	0844	|	0943	|	1042	minutes	1743	|	1841	1845	|	|	1944	2042	2045	2142	2242	2341		0858	0958	minutes	2158	2259
Newtongrange d.	0901	0904	0931	1003	1031	1102	past each	1803	1831	1901	1905	1931	1935	2004	2102	2105	2202	2302	0001		0918	1018	past each	2218	2319
Eskbank d.	0904	0907	0934	1006	1034	1105	hour until	1806	1834	1904	1908	1934	1938	2007	2105	2108	2205	2305	0004		0921	1021	hour until	2221	2322
Edinburgh Waverley a.	0923	0926	0954	1028	1056**b**	1128**b**	♤**c**	1829	1856	1925	1931	1954	1959	2027	2125	2127	2228	2326	0023		0940	1040		2240	2341

a – Not ⑥.
b – Arrives 3 – 4 minutes earlier on Ⓐ.
c – The 1557 and 1658 departures also call at Stow on Ⓐ.
d – On ⑥ runs 3 minutes later.
♤ – Timings may vary by ± 4 minutes.
♡ – Timings may vary by ± 2 minutes.

Panel 1

km	Station	B	A	H				2	2	H		2	2	⑥	Ⓐ	⑦		H	⑥ E	Ⓐ E		Ⓐ	⑦	Ⓐ	⑥	⑦	⑥	Ⓐ
0	Edinburgh Waverley ..d.	...	...	...	...	0530	...	0629	0700	0728	...	0733	0800	0801	0804	0828	...	0832	0832	0900	0910	0928	0930	0915	...	...		
2	Haymarket ....d.	...	...	...	...	0534	...	0634	0704	0733	...	0738	0804	0807	0808	0833	...	0836	0836	0904	0915	0934	0934	0920	...	...		
42	Kirkcaldy ....d.	...	0520	...	0603	...	0706	0736	0802	...	0812	0836	0839	0840	...	0907	0910	0936	0950	...	1006	...						
54	Markinch ....d.	...	...	...	0612	...	0715	0745	...	0822	0845	0848	...	0916	0919	0945	...	1016	...									
82	Leuchars ....△ d.	...	0548	...	0633	...	0806	0825	...	0909	0911	0906	0925	...	1005	1014	...	1023	1037	...								
	Glasgow Queen Str d.	...	...	...	0556	...	0742	...	0841	...	0941	0941																
	Stirling ....d.	...	...	0625	...	0809u	...	0908	...	1008	1008																	
	Perth ....d.	...	0600	...	0700	0746	...	0842	0857	...	0942	0946	0949	...	1040	1040												
95	Dundee ....d.	0539a	0611	0625	0642	0652f	0723	0812	0822	0843	0904	...	0925	0927	0920	0940	1005	...	1022	1029	1034	1037	1052	1102	1102			
112	Carnoustie ....d.	0559a	0625	0640	...	0704	0735	...	0916	...	1117	1117																
123	Arbroath ....d.	0606a	0634	0648	0701	0712	0742	...	0859	0923	...	0936	0959	1021	...	1046	1051	1054	1109	1124	1124							
145	Montrose ....d.	0626	0650	0704	0716	0726	0757	...	0914	0938	...	0950	1040	...	1102	1105	1108	1124	1138	1144								
184	Stonehaven ....d.	0651	0715	0726	0737	0751	0821	...	0935	...	1010	1036	1102	...	1125	1126	1129	1146	1203	1212								
210	Aberdeen ....a.	0714	0739	0749	0757	0813	0847	...	0955	1017	...	1029	1055	1124	...	1147	1146	1149	1210	1223	1235							

Panel 2

Station	⑦	⑦ E	Ⓐ 2	⑥ 2		C		E	⑦	⑦ 2	⑥	Ⓐ	⑦ 2			⑦ 2	H		2	⑦	⑦	2	⑦ J
Edinburgh Waverley ..d.	...	0933	0935	0938	1000	1028	...	1036	...	1050	1100	1131	1134	1132	...	1136	...	1200	1230	...	1236	1241	...	1300	1327	1334
Haymarket ....d.	...	0937	0939	0943	1004	1033	...	1041u	...	1054	1104	1135	1138	1136	...	1141	...	1204	1234	...	1241	1245	...	1304	1331	1338
Kirkcaldy ....d.	...	1012	1013	1015	1036	1105	...	1113u	...	1123	1136	...	1208	...	1213	...	1236	...	1313	1314	...	1336	...	1410
Markinch ....d.	...	1022	1022	1024	1045	...	1122	...	1145	...	1217	...	1222	...	1245	...	1322	...	1345	...	1419
Leuchars ....△ d.	...	...	1105	1130	...	1147	1205	1224	1227	1239	...	1305	1323	...	1338	...	1405	1423	1441
Glasgow Queen Str. d.	0937	...	1041	1045	...	1141	1145	...	1241	...	1245												
Stirling ....d.	1010	...	1109	1111	...	1207	1211	...	1307	...	1311												
Perth ....d.	1047	1054	1054	1056	...	1139	1154	1142	...	1237	1256	1246	...	1339	1355	...	1342						
Dundee ....d.	1111	...	...	1122	1144	1202	...	1205	1210g	1221	1240	1241	1255	1300	...	1310	1321	1339	1402	...	1352	1407	1421	1437	1457
Carnoustie ....d.	1126	...	...	1312	...																		
Arbroath ....d.	1132	...	1202	1218	...	1227	...	1256	1258	...	1319	...	1326	...	1355	1418	...	1408	1423	...	1454
Montrose ....d.	1148	...	1218	1233	...	1241	...	1333	...	1341	...	1410	1433	...	1422	1439	...
Stonehaven ....d.	1213	...	1241	...	1303	...	1330	1331	...	1402	...	1431	1454	...	1446	1500	...	1527	...
Aberdeen ....a.	1237	...	1303	1313	...	1323	...	1350	1351	...	1415	...	1422	...	1450	1514	...	1506	1520	...	1549

Panel 3

Station	⑦ E	⑦ E		C	C	F		2	2	H	2			2 E	⑥	Ⓐ 2	⑦	H	2	⑦	CE 2
Edinburgh Waverley ..d.	...	1334	1356	1400	1428	1433	...	1435	1458	1528	1534	...	1535	1550	1600	1603	1605	1627	...	1632	1633
Haymarket ....d.	...	1340u	1400	1404	1433	1439	...	1441	1502	1534	1538	...	1540	1554	1604	1607	1609	1631u	...	1637	1638
Kirkcaldy ....d.	...	1411u	1432	1436	1506	1511	...	1513	1537	...	1610	...	1613	1626	1636	1639	1639	...	...	1713
Markinch ....d.	...	1420	...	1445	...	1522	1546	...	1621	...	1622	1635	1645	1648	1649	...	1722
Leuchars ....△ d.	...	1505	1531	1536	...	1606	1623	1642	...	1706	1708	1709	1725	...				
Glasgow Queen Str. d.	1341	1345	...	1441	1449	...	1541	1545	...	1611	1641	1645									
Stirling ....d.	1408	1413	...	1507	1518	...	1612	...	1639	1711e	1711	1722									
Perth ....d.	1438	1450	1450	1509	...	1540	1552	1555	...	1636	1647	1655	1707	...	1719	1741	1741	1756	1754
Dundee ....d.	1502	1513	...	1521	1548	1550	1602	1615	...	1622	1639	1658	1658	1710	...	1722	1724	1723	1740	1746	1804	1802	...
Carnoustie ....d.	1517	1525	...	1614	...	1710	...	1737	1803	1816	...
Arbroath ....d.	1524	1532	...	1605	1608	1621	1631	...	1655	...	1717	1726	...	1744	1756	1812	1813	1819	...
Montrose ....d.	1541	1548	...	1621	1624	1636	1645	...	1709	...	1732	1741	...	1759	1812	...	1837	...
Stonehaven ....d.	...	1610	...	1644	1647	...	1707	...	1733	...	1753	1805	...	1822	1837	...	1856	1858	...
Aberdeen ....a.	1626	1633	...	1707	1708	1715	1726	...	1753	...	1813	1825	...	1842	1901	...	1916	1918	...

Panel 4

Station	CE 2	⑦	Ⓐ 2	⑥ 2			⑦ E	⑦	Ⓐ 2	2	D	D	D	C	C		2	2	2	2	Ⓐ C	⑦ B	
Edinburgh Waverley ..d.	1632	1700	1705	1734	1736	...	1741	1750	1804	1806	1811	1810	1813	1833	1836	...	1837c	1855	1900	...	1915	1925	1929d
Haymarket ....d.	1637	1705	1709	1738	1741	...	1745u	1754	1808	1811	1815	1815	1816	1838	1841	...	1844	1859	1904	...	1919	1932	1933d
Kirkcaldy ....d.	...	1737	1739	1810	...	1816	1826	1840	...	1844	1847	1845	1913	1913	...	1919	...	1936	...	2002	...
Markinch ....d.	...	1746	...	1819	...	1826	1836	1850	...	1853	1857	1854	...	1929	1945	...	2011	...
Leuchars ....△ d.	...	1809	1804	1841	1834	...	1910	...	1914	1923	1915	1938	1937	...	2006	...	2032	...	2029	...
Glasgow Queen Str. d.	...	...	1704b	1741	1745	...	1841	...	1909	...	1941
Stirling ....d.	1723	...	1745	1816	1813	...	1907	...	1936	...	2015	...	2008
Perth ....d.	1758	...	1825	1855	1845	1858	1906	...	1943	2001	2035	...	2023	2038	2048	...	2043	2100
Dundee ....d.	2110	...	1825	1818	1857	1848	1856	1918	1909	...	1926	...	1930	1936	1931	1955	1952	2005	...	2023	2038	2048	...	2043	2100
Carnoustie ....d.	...	1919	1929	1921	...	2019	...
Arbroath ....d.	...	1835	...	1905	...	1936	1928	...	1949	1952	1947	2012	2009	2026	...	2059	2117
Montrose ....d.	...	1850	...	1922	...	1951	1944	...	2003	2006	2001	2028	2025	2041	...	2114	2131
Stonehaven ....d.	...	1912	...	1944	...	2015	2009	...	2024	2027	2023	2051	2048	...	2135	2155
Aberdeen ....a.	2225	...	1935	...	2007	...	2035	2029	...	2042	2048	2042	2113	2110	2122	...	2156	2215

Panel 5

Station	⑦ E	⑦ 2	Ⓐ D	⑥ D	Ⓐ C		2	⑦	⑦	G	⑦		2	⑥	Ⓐ		2	⑦	2	⑥	⑦	⑦ 2	2
Edinburgh Waverley ..d.	...	1941	2000	2015	2014	2032	...	2037	2100	2105	2143	...	2134	2150	2153	2208	2225	2236	2237	...	2309	2319
Haymarket ....d.	...	1945	2004	2018	2037	...	2041	2105	2109	2147	...	2139	2155	2157	2212	2229	2241	2241	...	2313	2323
Kirkcaldy ....d.	...	2017	2047	...	2052	2111	...	2115	2135	2151	2215	...	2255	2312	...	2324	...	2356	...
Markinch ....d.	...	2026	2056	2103	2102	...	2124	2144	2200	...	2256	2258	2306	2321	...	2333	...	0005	0024
Leuchars ....△ d.	...	2116	2127	2128	2139	...	2205	2222	2239	...	2328	2342	...	0025
Glasgow Queen Str. d.	1945	...	2041	...	2142	2124h	...	2248r	2248	2313t	2321k
Stirling ....d.	2012	...	2108	...	2208	2212	2225	...	2328	...	2333	2333	0005	0020
Perth ....d.	2047	2100	...	2143	2158	...	2241	2247	2304	2333	2333	...	0008	0013	0009	0044	0057	...	0057
Dundee ....d.	2110	...	2132	2142	2143	2153	2209	...	2221	2238	2253	2303	2310	...	2344	2358	...	0036	...	0041	...
Carnoustie ....d.	...	2220	...	2320	2322	...
Arbroath ....d.	2126	...	2211	2227	...	2240	...	2309	2327	2329	...
Montrose ....d.	2141	...	2227	2241	...	2255	...	2324	2341	2344	...
Stonehaven ....d.	2205	...	2250	2302	...	2316	...	2345	0005	0005	...
Aberdeen ....a.	2225	...	2310	2322	...	2339	...	0007	0027	0025	...

222 ABERDEEN - DUNDEE - EDINBURGH and GLASGOW

🍷 on most trains — GR, SR, XC

km		Ⓐ C	Ⓐ 2	⚒	⑥ 2	Ⓐ	⚒ 2	⚒	⚒ D	⚒ 2	⑥ 2	Ⓐ 2	⚒	⚒	⚒ 2	⚒ 2	⑦ 2	Ⓐ 2F	⑥ 2F	⚒	⚒	⚒ G	⚒ 2	⑦ 2	⚒ F	⑦ 2
0	**Aberdeen** d.	...	...	...	...	...	...	...	...	...	...	...	0526	0546	...	...	...	...	...	0633	...	0703	...	...	...	...
26	Stonehaven d.	...	...	...	...	...	...	...	...	...	...	...	0546	0603	...	...	...	...	...	0652	...	0720	...	...	...	...
65	Montrose d.	...	...	...	...	...	...	...	...	...	...	...	0611	0624	...	...	...	...	...	0715	...	0744	...	...	...	...
87	Arbroath d.	...	...	...	...	...	...	...	...	...	...	...	0626	0638	...	...	...	...	...	0728	...	0758	...	...	...	...
97	Carnoustie d.	...	...	...	...	...	...	...	*0603*	...	...	...	|	0645	...	...	...	...	...	0735	...	0805	...	...	...	...
115	**Dundee** d.	...	...	...	...	...	0553	0604	0632	...	...	...	0650	0658	0709	0738	0724	...	...	0753	0817	0820	0828	...	...	...
149	**Perth** d.	...	0513	0518	0536	0614	0619	|	|	0639	0656	0656	0715	|	|	|	|	0801	0802	0814	0841	|	|	...	0850	0850
202	Stirling d.	0526	|	0554	|	|	0655	|	|	0717	|	|	0753	|	|	|	|	|	|	0845	0915	|	|	0905	|	|
249	**Glasgow** Queen Str a.	|	|	0634	|	|	0734	|	|	|	|	|	0834	|	|	|	|	|	|	0915	0948	|	|	|	|	|
	Leuchars △ d.	|	|	...	|	|	...	0617	0646	|	|	|	...	0712	0723	0751	0737	|	|	...	...	|	0841	|	|	|
	Markinch d.	|	0546	...	0607	0646	...	0640	0710	|	0737	0737	...	|	0747	0812	0759	0830	0831	...	...	|	0903	|	|	0919
	Kirkcaldy d.	|	0555	...	0616	|	...	0649	0721	|	0746	0746	...	0741	0757	0821	0809	0840	0841	...	...	|	0912	|	0925	0929
	Haymarket a.	0611	0642	...	0703	0754	...	0735	0758	0814	0821	0825	...	0818	0839	0858	0858	0916	0920	...	...	0925	0956	0959	1003	1018
	Edinburgh Waverley a.	0617	0647	...	0708	0800	...	0740	0804	0819	0826	0830	...	0823	0846	0906	0903	0921	0926	...	...	0931	1001	1006	1008	1023

	⑦	⚒ J	⑦ 2	⚒ C	⚒ D	⑦ 2	⚒ 2	⑦ 2	⚒ CF	⚒ 2	⚒	⚒	⑦ 2	Ⓐ 2	⑥ 2	⚒ 2	⑦	⚒ H	⑦ C	⚒ C	⑦ 2	⚒	⑦ CF	⚒ F	⑦	⚒
Aberdeen d.	...	0739	...	0752	0820	...	...	...	...	...	0842	0907	...	...	...	...	0924	0935	0947	0952	...	...	...	...	1030	1038
Stonehaven d.	...	0756	...	0810	0838	...	...	...	...	...	|	|	...	...	...	...	0941	0954	1005	1010	...	...	...	...	1047	|
Montrose d.	...	0817	...	0833	0859	...	...	...	...	...	0918	0946	...	...	...	...	1005	1016	1028	1033	...	...	...	...	1108	1114
Arbroath d.	...	0831	...	0849	0915	...	...	...	...	...	0932	1000	...	...	...	...	1020	1030	1044	1049	...	...	...	...	1123	1128
Carnoustie d.	...	0838	...	|	|	...	...	...	...	...	0939	|	...	...	...	...	1027	1036	|	|	...	...	...	...	|	1135
Dundee d.	0845	0854	...	0907	0932	0924	0943	...	...	...	0954	1017	...	1032	1034	...	1046	1054	1103	1107	1120	1128	...	...	1144	1150
Perth d.	0906	0915	0916	|	|	|	|	0936	0957	1003	1016	|	1010	|	|	1102	1108	1116	|	|	|	|	1159	1202	1209	1212
Stirling d.	0939	0943	0951	|	|	|	|	|	1032	|	1044	|	1046	|	|	|	1143	1144	|	|	|	|	1235	|	1243	1243
Glasgow Queen Str a.	1014	1018	|	|	|	|	|	|	|	|	1115	|	|	|	|	|	1214	1216	|	|	|	|	|	|	1314	1315
Leuchars △ d.	...	...	|	0921	0946	0937	0956	|	|	|	...	1030	|	1045	1047	|	...	...	1117	1123	1133	1141	|	|	...	...
Markinch d.	...	...	|	|	1009	0959	1019	1005	|	1032	...	|	|	1106	1108	1132	...	...	|	|	1155	1202	|	1231	...	...
Kirkcaldy d.	...	...	|	0945	1017	1009	1028	|	|	1042	...	|	|	1116	1118	1141	...	...	1141	1147	1205	1212	|	1241	...	...
Haymarket a.	...	...	1040	1019	1049	1055	1109	1111	1112	1123	...	1126	1135	1151	1158	1217	...	...	1216	1220	1240	1247	1313	1319	...	...
Edinburgh Waverley a.	...	...	1046	1025	1055	1100	1115	1116	1118	1130	...	1132	1141	1156	1203	1222	...	...	1222	1226	1245	1252	1321	1324	...	...

	⚒	⚒ J	⑦ D	⑥ 2	Ⓐ 2	⑦ F	⚒ F	⑦ J	⚒	⑦ C	⚒ J	⑦ 2	⚒ 2	⚒ 2	⑦	⚒	⑦	⚒	⚒ 2	⚒ F	⑦	⚒	⑦ C	⚒ 2	Ⓐ	⑥
Aberdeen d.	...	1103	1110	...	...	...	...	1129	1142	1147	1205	...	...	...	1229	1240	1245	1308	...	...	1331	1337	1347	...	1404	1404
Stonehaven d.	...	1120	1127	...	...	...	...	1145	|	1205	1224	...	...	...	1246	1256	1305	1325	...	...	1348	1356	1405	...	1421	1421
Montrose d.	...	1144	1148	...	...	...	...	1208	1218	1228	|	...	...	...	1307	1320	1330	1346	...	...	1409	1418	1428	...	|	|
Arbroath d.	...	1158	1204	...	...	...	...	1222	1232	1244	1258	...	...	...	1322	1334	1344	1400	...	...	1424	1432	1444	...	1458	1458
Carnoustie d.	...	|	|	...	...	...	...	|	1239	|	|	...	...	...	|	|	1351	|	...	...	|	1439	|	...	|	|
Dundee d.	1213	1217	1224	1234	1236	...	...	1243	1254	1302	1317	1320	1332	...	1343	1354	1407	1417	1434	...	1445	1454	1502	1513	1517	1517
Perth d.	1238	|	|	|	|	1255	1302	1305	1316	|	|	|	|	1402	1406	1415	|	|	|	1504	1508	1516	|	1537	|	|
Stirling d.	1313	|	|	|	|	|	|	1338	1344	|	|	|	|	|	1438	1444	|	|	|	|	1542	1544	|	1614	|	|
Glasgow Queen Str a.	1348	|	|	|	|	|	|	1409	1416	|	|	|	|	|	1509	1518	|	|	|	|	1614	1618	|	1648	|	|
Leuchars △ d.	...	1230	1237	1247	1249	|	|	...	...	1317	1330	1333	1345	|	...	...	1420	1430	1447	|	...	...	1516	...	1530	1530
Markinch d.	...	|	1258	1308	1310	1323	1331	...	...	|	|	1355	1406	1431	...	...	|	|	1508	1531	...	...	|	...	|	|
Kirkcaldy d.	...	|	1307	1318	1320	1332	1341	...	...	1342	|	1405	1416	1441	...	...	1446	|	1518	1541	...	...	1541	...	|	|
Haymarket a.	...	1323	1337	1353	1357	1407	1417	...	...	1420	1423	1440	1453	1520	...	...	1518	1523	1553	1620	...	...	1618	...	1623	1626
Edinburgh Waverley a.	...	1333	1343	1358	1404	1412	1424	...	...	1426	1428	1445	1458	1525	...	...	1523	1531	1600	1625	...	...	1625	...	1628	1633

	⑦ 2	⑦ F	⚒	⚒ 2	⑦	⚒	⚒ C	⑦	⑦	⚒	⚒ 2	⚒ 2	⚒ J	⑦ F	⑦ 2	⚒ 2	⑦	⚒ F	Ⓐ	⑥	⚒ K	⑦	Ⓐ 2	⑥ 2	⚒ 2	⚒
Aberdeen d.	...	...	...	...	1431	1439	1452	1509	1528	1533	...	...	1602	...	...	...	1628	...	1627	1636	1709	1709	...	...	...	1736
Stonehaven d.	...	...	...	...	1448	|	1510	1529	1544	1549	...	...	1619	...	...	...	1645	...	1645u	1655	|	1725	...	...	...	1753
Montrose d.	...	...	...	...	1509	1515	1533	1550	1609	1610	...	...	|	...	...	...	1706	...	1710	1717	1751	1747	...	...	...	1817
Arbroath d.	...	...	...	...	1524	1529	1549	1604	1623	1624	...	...	1655	...	...	...	1721	...	1726	1731	1805	1800	1821	1821	...	1831
Carnoustie d.	...	...	...	...	|	1536	|	1610	|	|	...	...	1702	...	...	...	|	...	|	|	|	|	1827	1827	...	1838
Dundee d.	1515	...	1534	...	1545	1551	1607	1624	1643	1646	1649	...	1718	...	1721	1734	1742	...	1748	1750	1822	1818	1845	1845	...	1854
Perth d.	|	1532	|	1600	1608	1613	|	|	1705	1711	|	1703	|	1722	|	|	1805	1806	1814	1814	|	|	|	|	1911	1916
Stirling d.	|	|	|	|	1640	1641s	|	|	1738	1743	|	|	|	|	|	|	1837	|	1844	1844	|	|	|	|	|	1945
Glasgow Queen Str a.	|	|	|	|	1713	1718	|	|	1812	1817	|	|	|	|	|	|	1908	|	1915	1915	|	|	|	|	|	2017
Leuchars △ d.	1528	|	1547	|	...	...	1622	1637	...	...	1702	|	1731	|	1734	1747	...	|	...	...	1835	1831	1858	1858	|	...
Markinch d.	1550	1600	1608	1629	...	...	|	|	...	...	1723	1732	|	1750	1756	1810	...	1835	...	...	|	|	1919	1919	1940	...
Kirkcaldy d.	1600	1610	1618	1639	...	...	1646	1702	...	...	1733	1742	|	1800	1806	1820	...	1845	...	...	|	1856	1929	1929	1950	...
Haymarket a.	1635	1645	1653	1714	...	...	1720	1734	...	...	1817	1822	1827	1835	1841	1855	...	1920	...	...	1930	1928	2004	2008	2027	...
Edinburgh Waverley a.	1640	1650	1659	1722	...	...	1726	1740	...	...	1825	1828	1832	1842	1846	1901	...	1926	...	...	1936	1933	2010	2013	2032	...

	⑦ G	⑥	Ⓐ C	⑦ 2	⚒ 2	⚒	⚒ J	⑦	⚒ 2	⑥ F	Ⓑ F	⑦	⚒	⑦	⚒ J	⚒	⚒	⚒ F	⑦	⚒	⚒ 2	Ⓑ B	⑦	①–④	⑥	⑤
Aberdeen d.	1747	1818	1818	...	...	1828	1911	1907	...	...	...	1936	1946	2006	2009	2042	2104	...	2129	2131	...	2143	2226	2226	2226	2323
Stonehaven d.	1804	1836	1836	...	...	1849	1928	1924	...	...	...	1952	2005	2026	2025	2059	2121	...	2146	2149	...	2201u	2246	2246	2246	2343
Montrose d.	1828	1859	1859	...	...	1912	1952	1945	...	...	...	2014	2027	2050	2046	2120	2145	...	2207	2210	...	2226u	2310	2310	2310	0007
Arbroath d.	1843	1915	1915	...	...	1926	2006	1959	...	...	...	2028	2041	2104	2100	2134	2159	...	2223	2226	...	2244u	2324	2324	2324	0021
Carnoustie d.	|	|	|	...	...	1933	|	2006	...	...	...	|	|	|	2107	|	|	...	|	|	...	2253u	2331	2331	2331	0028
Dundee d.	1903	1932	1933	1916	...	1949	2023	2022	2042	...	...	2050	2101	2121	2119	2156	2216	...	2241	2245	...	2306u	2349	2349	2348	0046
Perth d.	1926	|	|	|	2002	2011	|	|	|	2106	2106	2111	2122	|	|	2217	|	2238	|	|	2243	|	0012	0012	...	0110
Stirling d.	1958	|	|	|	|	2042	|	|	|	|	|	2144	2150	|	|	2248	|	2310	|	|	|	|	...	...	...	...
Glasgow Queen Str a.	2029	|	|	|	|	2115	|	|	|	|	|	2234d	2235t	|	|	2336r	|	0004v	|	|	|	|	...	...	...	...
Leuchars △ d.	...	1946	1947	1929	|	...	2036	2035	2055	|	|	...	...	2134	2132	...	2229	...	2254	2258	|	2325u	...	...	...	...
Markinch d.	...	|	|	1951	2032	...	|	|	2116	2133	2133	...	...	2157	2154	...	2251	...	2316	2319	2312	|	...	...	...	...
Kirkcaldy d.	...	2011	2011	2001	2041	...	|	2101	2126	2143	2143	...	...	2206	2203	...	2300	...	2324	2328	|	2354u	...	...	...	...
Haymarket a.	...	2043	2044	2047	2117	...	2130	2133	2211	2216	2221	...	...	2238	2250	...	2346	...	2357	2358	0022	...	...	...	...	...
Edinburgh Waverley a.	...	2048	2050	2052	2124	...	2136	2138	2216	2221	2228	...	...	2243	2255	...	2351	...	0002	0007	0027	...	...	...	...	...

OTHER SERVICES EDINBURGH and GLASGOW - STIRLING

From Edinburgh Waverley to Stirling: *75 km* Journey time: 54 minutes

⚒: 0518, 0633 and every 30 minutes (⊡) until 1933, 2033, 2134⑥, 2135Ⓐ, 2233, 2304Ⓐ, 2305⑥, 2333.

⑦: 0934, 1035 and hourly until 2135, 2236 (also 1106 and hourly until 1806).

All trains call at **Haymarket** 4 minutes later, **Linlithgow** 22 minutes later and **Falkirk Grahamston** 35 minutes later.

From Stirling to Edinburgh Waverley:

⚒: 0530, 0637, 0717, 0749Ⓐ, 0807 and every 30 minutes (⊡) until 1837, 1937, 2007, 2037, 2107, 2207, 2317.

⑦: 0905, 0951, 1046, 1110 and hourly until 1810, 1919, 2010, 2110, 2210 (also 1046 and hourly until 1646).

Trains call at **Falkirk Grahamston** 17 minutes later, **Linlithgow** 30 minutes later and **Haymarket** 50 minutes later.

From Glasgow Queen Street to Stirling: *47 km* Journey time: 45 minutes

⚒: 0556, 0614, 0648, 0718, 0749, 0818, 0849, 0920, 0949 and every 30 minutes (⊡) until 1948, 2048**e**, 2118**e**, 2148**e**, 2218**e**, 2248**e**, 2319**e**, 2348**e**.

⑦: 0937, 1015 and hourly until 2015, 2115**g**, 2215**g**, 2345**g**.

From Stirling to Glasgow Queen Street:

⚒: 0554, 0623, 0655, 0723, 0739, 0753, 0811, 0823 and every 30 minutes (⊡) until 1723, 1751, 1819, 1853, 1923, 1953, 2021, 2053**e**, 2123**e**, 2153⑥, 2155Ⓐ**e**, 2223**e**, 2253**e**.

⑦: 0926, 1026, 1125 and hourly until 2025, 2125**g**, 2144**g**.

B – Ⓡ. 🛏 1, 2 class and 💺 Aberdeen - London Euston. Train stops to pick up only. See Table **161**.
C – To destinations on Table **180**.
D – To destinations on Table **124**.
F – From Inverness (Table **223**).
G – From Inverness (Table **225**).
H – From Dyce (Table **225**).
J – From Inverurie (Table **225**).
K – From Dyce on Ⓐ; from Inverurie on ⑥.

d – Arrives 2218 from Sept. 17.
e – ⑤⑥ only May 26 - Sept. 1; ⚒ from Sept. 8.
g – From Sept. 17.
r – Arrives 2318 on ⑤⑥ May 26 - Sept. 1 and ⚒ from Sept. 8.
s – Stops to set down only.
t – Arrives 2221 on ⑤⑥ May 26 - Sept. 1 and ⚒ from Sept. 8.
v – Arrives 2344 on ⑤⑥ May 26 - Sept. 1 and ⚒ from Sept. 8.

⊡ – Timings may vary by up to ± 5 minutes.
△ – Frequent 🚌 connections available to / from **St Andrews**. Journey 10 minutes. Operator: Stagecoach (routes 94, 96, 99).

Most Inverness trains convey 🍷.

km		⚒	⚒	⚒	⚒	⚒	⚒	⑦	⑦	⚒	⚒	⚒	⚒	⑦	⑦	⚒	⚒	⚒	⚒	⑦	⑦	⑦	⚒	⚒	⑦	⑦	⚒
			A	2						2				2		2						P	2				
0	**Edinburgh** Waverley d.	...	...	0629	...	...	0832	...	0933	0935	...	...	1036	1035	...	1136	...	...	1334	...	1356	...	1435	...	...	1550	...
2	Haymarket d.	...	...	0634	...	...	0836	...	0937	0939	...	...	1041u	1039	...	1141	...	...	1340u	...	1400	...	1441	...	...	1554	...
42	Kirkcaldy d.	...	...	0706	...	...	0907	...	1012	1013	...	...	1113u	|	...	1213	...	...	1411u	...	1432	...	1513	...	...	1626	...
54	Markinch d.	...	...	0715	...	...	0916	...	1022	1022	...	...	1122	|	...	1222	...	...	1420	...	|	...	1522	...	...	1635	...
	Glasgow Queen St. d.	...	...	|	0710	0841	|	0937	|	|	1010	1041	|	|	1111	|	1209	1341	|	1345	|	1438	|	1507	1545	|	1641
	Stirling d.	...	0455	|	0736	0908	|	1010	|	|	1037	1109	|	1126	1141	|	1237	1408	|	1413	|	1507	|	1537	1612	|	1711a
91	**Perth** d.	0508	0539	0745	0810	0941	0950	1046	1055	1056	1116	1138	1155	...	1217	1256	1313	1437	1451	1449	1513	1546	1555	1617	1646	1708	1740
116	Dunkeld & Birnam d.	0525	0600	...	0830	...	|	...	1111	...	1137	...	|	...	1235	...	1329	...	1508	...	1529	|	...	1634	...	1725	...
137	Pitlochry d.	0538	0616	...	0843	...	1022	...	1124	...	1150	...	1224	...	1248	...	1342	...	1521	...	1542	1613	...	1647	...	1738	...
148	Blair Atholl d.	0547	0628	...	0852	...	1031	...	1134	...	|	...	1233	...	|	...	1352	...	1530	...	1552	|	...	1656	...	|	...
186	Dalwhinnie d.	0613	0659	...	0917	...	1056	...	1158	...	|	...	1259	...	|	...	|	...	1555	...	1622	|	...	|	...	|	...
202	Newtonmore d.	|	0711	...	0927	...	|	...	1208	...	|	...	1309	...	|	...	|	...	|	...	1633	|	...	1728	...	|	...
207	Kingussie d.	0643	0719	...	0936	...	1109	...	1213	...	1235	...	1315	...	1334	...	1428	...	1608	...	1638	1657	...	1733	...	1822	...
226	Aviemore d.	0704	0743	...	0950	...	1123	...	1225	...	1247	...	1333	...	1346	...	1439	...	1619	...	1649	1710	...	1744	...	1833	...
237	Carrbridge d.	0719	0756	...	0959	...	|	...	1232	...	|	...	1341	...	1359	...	|	...	|	...	1659	|	...	1752	...	|	...
282	**Inverness** a.	0749	0838	...	1027	...	1158	...	1301	...	1329	...	1415	...	1427	...	1523	...	1654	...	1727	1745	...	1821	...	1908	...

	⚒	⑦	⑦	⚒	⚒	⑦	⑦	⚒	⚒	⑥	Ⓐ
	K		K					P			
Edinburgh Waverley d.	1632	...	1632	...	1741	1750	...	...	...	1941	1942
Haymarket d.	1637	...	1637	...	1745u	1754	...	...	...	1945	1946
Kirkcaldy d.	|	...	|	...	1816	1826	...	...	...	2017	2019
Markinch d.	|	...	|	...	1826	1836	...	...	...	2026	2028
Glasgow Queen St. d.	|	1645	|	1741	|	|	1811	1811	1941	|	|
Stirling d.	1723	1711	1722	1816	|	|	1841	1842	2008	|	|
Perth d.	1802	1738	1801	1852	1859	1906	1917	1921	2037	2101	2101
Dunkeld & Birnam d.	|	...	|	...	1918	...	1933	1938	...	2118	2118
Pitlochry d.	1831	...	1832	...	1931	...	1946	1951	...	2133	2133
Blair Atholl d.	|	...	|	...	|	...	1956	2001	...	2142	2142
Dalwhinnie d.	|	...	|	...	|	...	2019	2025	...	2207	2212
Newtonmore d.	|	...	|	...	|	...	2030	2035	...	2217	2223
Kingussie d.	1916	...	1917	...	2014	...	2035	2040	...	2222	2228
Aviemore d.	1929	...	1931	...	2026	...	2046	2052	...	2234	2239
Carrbridge d.	|	...	|	...	|	...	2054	|	...	2242	2247
Inverness a.	2006	...	2008	...	2101	...	2124	2126	...	2310	2316

	⚒	⚒	⚒	⚒	⚒	⚒	⚒	⚒	⑦	⑦	⚒	⚒
	2				L			2	L			
Inverness d.	0536	...	0650	...	0755	...	0845	...	0940	...	0941	...
Carrbridge d.	|	...	|	...	|	...	0916	...	1011	...	|	...
Aviemore d.	0612	...	0725	...	0830	...	0924	...	1019	...	1027	...
Kingussie d.	0627	...	0738	...	0843	...	0936	...	1032	...	1039	...
Newtonmore d.	|	...	|	...	|	...	0940	...	1037	...	|	...
Dalwhinnie d.	0640	...	|	...	|	...	|	...	|	...	1053	...
Blair Atholl d.	0712	...	|	...	|	...	|	...	1109	...	1114	...
Pitlochry d.	0726	...	0818	...	0924	...	1023	...	1123	...	1124	...
Dunkeld & Birnam d.	0739	...	0830	...	|	...	1034	...	1137	...	1137	...
Perth d.	0801	0813	0850	0915	0957	1016	1056	1102	1159	1209	1202c	1212
Stirling d.	|	0845	|	0943	1032	1044	1129	|	1235	1243	|	1243
Glasgow Q St a.	|	0915	|	1018	|	1115	1213	|	|	1314	|	1315
Markinch d.	0830	...	|	...	|	...	...	1132	|	...	1231	...
Kirkcaldy d.	0840	...	0925	...	|	...	...	1141	|	...	1241	...
Haymarket a.	0920	...	1003	...	1112	...	...	1217	1313	...	1319	...
Edinburgh W a.	0926	...	1008	...	1118	...	...	1222	1321	...	1324	...

	⚒	⚒	⑦	⑦	⑦	⚒	⚒	⑦	⑦	⚒	⚒	⑦	⑦	⚒	⚒	⑦	⑦	⚒	⚒	⚒	⚒	⑦	⑦	⚒	⚒	⑦	Ⓐ
											2						2		2							B	B
Inverness d.	1045	...	1050	...	1243	1253	...	1330	...	1447	...	1522	...	1551	...	1624	...	1730	...	1846	...	1850	...	2015	...	2026	2044
Carrbridge d.	|	...	|	...	1315	1325	...	|	...	|	...	|	...	1627	...	1658	...	1807	...	1916	...	1922	...	2059	...	|	|
Aviemore d.	1123	...	1125	...	1323	1333	...	1406	...	1522	...	1557	...	1635	...	1710	...	1814	...	1928	...	1931	...	2107	...	2115	2134
Kingussie d.	1136	...	1137	...	1335	1345	...	1418	...	1534	...	1609	...	1647	...	1722	...	1826	...	1940	...	1943	...	2119	...	2129	2151
Newtonmore d.	|	...	|	...	1340	1349	...	|	...	|	...	|	...	1651	...	|	...	|	...	1945	...	1947	...	2123	...	2135	2157
Dalwhinnie d.	|	...	1151	...	|	|	...	|	...	1548	...	|	...	|	...	|	...	|	...	1957	...	1959	...	2135	...	2150	2211
Blair Atholl d.	|	...	|	...	1411	1420	...	|	...	|	...	|	...	1723	...	1755	...	|	...	2019	...	2021	...	2156	...	2215	2238
Pitlochry d.	1224	...	1220	...	1421	1431	...	1459	...	1617	...	1650	...	1733	...	1805	...	1906	...	2029	...	2031	...	2206	...	2229	2250
Dunkeld & Birnam d.	1237	...	1235	...	1434	1443	...	|	...	1634	...	1702	...	1745	...	1818	...	1918	...	2042	...	2042	...	2219	...	2243	2304
Perth d.	1302c	1316	1255	1305	1454	1504	1516	1532	1608	1654	1703	1722	1805	1806	1814	1839	...	1938	2002	2106c	2122	2106	2111	2238	2243	2306	2330
Stirling d.	|	1344	|	1338	1524	|	1544	|	1640	1729	|	|	1837	|	1844	1909	1919	2015	|	|	2150	|	2144	2310	|	2353	0016
Glasgow Queen St. a.	|	1416	|	1409	1558	|	1618	|	1713	1810	|	|	1908	|	1915	1941	|	2045	|	|	2235f	|	2234t	0004r	|	...	...
Markinch d.	1331	...	1323	...	...	1531	...	1600	...	...	1732	1750	...	1835	...	...	|	...	2032	2133	...	2133	...	...	2312	...	...
Kirkcaldy d.	1341	...	1332	...	...	1541	...	1610	...	...	1742	1800	...	1845	...	...	|	...	2041	2143	...	2143	...	...	|	...	...
Haymarket a.	1417	...	1407	...	...	1620	...	1645	...	...	1822	1835	...	1920	...	...	2011	...	2117	2221b	...	2221	...	...	0022	...	...
Edinburgh Waverley a.	1424	...	1412	...	...	1625	...	1650	...	...	1828	1842	...	1926	...	...	2018	...	2124	2228b	...	2228	...	...	0027	...	...

A – 🅁. 🛏 1, 2 class and (2) London Euston - Inverness. Departs London previous day. Train stops to set down only. See Table **161**.
B – 🅁. 🛏 1, 2 class and (2) Inverness - London Euston. Train stops to pick up only. See Table **161**.
K – From London (Table **180**). Via Falkirk Grahamston (d. 1704).
L – To London (Table **180**). Via Falkirk Grahamston (d. 1046⚒/1249⑦).
P – To Elgin (Table **225**).

a – ⑥ only.
b – Arrives Haymarket 2216, Edinburgh 2221 on ⑥.
c – Arrives 5–6 minutes earlier.
f – Arrives 2221 on ⑤⑥ May 26 - Sept. 1 and ⚒ from Sept. 8.
r – Arrives 2344 on ⑤⑥ May 26 - Sept. 1 and ⚒ from Sept. 8.
t – Arrives 2218 from Sept. 17.
u – Calls to pick up only.

km			⚒	⚒	Ⓐ	⚒	⚒	⚒	⚒	⚒	⚒	Ⓐ	⑥	⚒	⚒	⚒	⚒	①–④	⑥		⑦	⑦	⑦	⑦	⑦	⑦	⑦
			A	🍷		C		2🍷	🍷	2🍷	2🍷	A		🍷	🍷	2		2	2		🍷	2🍷	C	2🍷	B	2🍷	B
0	**Inverness** d.	⚒	0453	0554	...	...	0709	0900	1057	1246	1427	...	...	1529	1714	1813	2004	2040	2133	⑦	0959	1233	1529	1713	1800	2103	2142
24	Nairn d.		0508	0609	...	...	0725	0916	1114	1301	1442	...	...	1546	1730	1828	2020	2055	2148		1014	1248	1544	1729	1815	2118	2157
40	Forres d.		0519	0620	...	...	0737	0927	1125	1312	1453	...	...	1557	1741	1839	2031	2106	2158		1025	1259	1555	1740	1826	2129	2208
59	**Elgin** d.		0533	0634	...	...	0752	0952	1141	1330	1509	...	...	1611	1759	1857	2047	2020	2213		1039	1313	1609	1754	1841	2143	2223
89	Keith d.		0554	0655	...	...	0813	1011	1202	1349	1530	...	...	1635	1820	1919	...	2141	2234		1100	1334	1631	1815	...	2205	...
109	Huntly d.		0609	0711	0746	...	0839	1026	1216	1403	1545	...	...	1650	1847	1942	...	2203	2251		1120	1352	1646	1830	...	2221	...
130	Insch d.		0624	0729	0802	...	0857	1048	1235	1419	1603	...	...	1706	1902	1958	...	2219	2306		1136	1408	1702	1851	...	2237	...
147	**Inverurie** d.		0637	0743	0816	...	0909	1100	1247	1431	1616	...	...	1719	1915	2010	...	2233	2319		1148	1420	1714	1903	...	2249	...
164	Dyce ✈ d.		0651	0759	0830	0907	0921	1113	1302	1443	1630	1639	1705	1735	1929	2024	...	2246	2332		1201	1435	1728	1917	...	2301	...
174	**Aberdeen** a.		0702	0811	0841	0917	0933	1125	1313	1455	1641	1650	1717	1746	1940	2035	...	2257	2343		1212	1446	1739	1928	...	2313	...

		⚒	⚒	⚒	⚒	⚒	⚒	⚒	⚒	⚒	⚒	Ⓐ	⑥	⑥	Ⓐ	⚒	⑤⑥	①–④	⑥	Ⓐ	①–④		⑦	⑦	⑦	⑦	⑦
			2		2D	2		2🍷	2🍷	🍷	2🍷			🍷	🍷C	2🍷	2🍷	2🍷	A	A	A		🍷	🍷	🍷	🍷	🍷
Aberdeen d.	⚒	...	...	0614	0715	0819	0849	1013	1200	1338	1527	1619	1644	1722	1726	1822	2014	2039	2156	2201	2205	⑦	1000	1300	1522	1801	2127
Dyce ✈ d.		...	...	0623	0727	0830	0857	1022	1209	1347	1537	1629	1652	1732	1735	1831	2024	2048	2205	2210	2214		1009	1309	1531	1810	2136
Inverurie d.		...	...	0639	0743	0843	...	1034	1221	1359	1549	...	...	1750	1751	1844	2037	2100	2217	2222	2232f		1021	1321	1543	1822	2148
Insch d.		...	...	0651	0755	0858	...	1047	1234	1412	1602	...	...	1803	1803	1857	2049	2113	2229	2234	2244		1034	1334	1556	1835	2201
Huntly d.		...	...	0713	0812	0914	...	1103	1250	1428	1618	...	...	1820	1820	1913	2107	2136	2250	2255	2300		1050	1351	1612	1858	2222
Keith d.		...	...	0727	0826	0928	...	1118	1305	1443	1640	...	...	1834	1834	1928	2121	2151	2304	2309	2315		1108	1406	1635	1913	2236
Elgin d.		0658	0723	0753	0847	0950	...	1140	1329	1508	1702	...	...	1857	1857	1950	2142	2212	2325	2330	2336		1129	1427	1656	1935	2257
Forres d.		0711	0743	0806	0902	1004	...	1153	1342	1522	1716	...	...	1913	1911	2003	2205	2226	2339	2344	2349		1142	1440	1710	1949	2311
Nairn d.		0727	0754	0817	0918	1015	...	1204	1353	1545	1731	...	...	1924	1922	2021	2216	2237	2350	2355	0002		1153	1451	1730	2000	2322
Inverness a.		0745	0812	0835	0936	1033	...	1222	1411	1603	1749	...	...	1942	1940	2039	2234	2255	0008	0013	0020		1211	1509	1748	2018	2340

Other trains **Inverurie - Dyce - Aberdeen**: On ⚒ at 0713**C**, 0817⑥, 0846Ⓐ, 1038**A**, 1134**A**, 1333, 1524**A**, 1638⑥**A**, 1647Ⓐ, 1751, 1845**A**, 1946**A**, 2124①–④, 2131⑤⑥;
On ⑦ at 1102**C**, 1255, 1458, 1620, 1730, 2122.
Other trains **Aberdeen - Dyce - Inverurie**: On ⚒ at 0750**E**, 0958**A**, 1103**A**, 1250, 1457**A**, 1552**F**, 1652Ⓐ, 1754**A**, 1918**A**, 2055⑤⑥, 2103①–④, 2250⑤⑥;
On ⑦ at 1035, 1225, 1426, 1550, 1648, 2035.

A – To/from Edinburgh (Table **222**).
B – From Glasgow (Table **223**).
C – To/from Glasgow (Table **222**).
D – From Dundee on Ⓐ; Montrose on ⑥ (Table **222**).
E – From Perth (Table **222**).
F – From Edinburgh on ⑥ (Table **222**).
f – Arrives 2226.

① – Monday ② – Tuesday ③ – Wednesday ④ – Thursday ⑤ – Friday ⑥ – Saturday ⑦ – Sunday Ⓐ – Monday to Fridays, not holidays 83

226 INVERNESS - THURSO, WICK and KYLE OF LOCHALSH

2nd class SR

km		⚒🍷	⚒a	⚒🍷	⚒a	⚒		⚒a	⚒🍷	⚒	⚒		⚒a	⚒🍷	⚒	⑤⑥	⑦	⑦	⑦	⑦	⑦🍷	⑦b	⑦
0	**Inverness** d.	0702	0855	1038	1100	1142	...	1335	1400	1450	1712	...	1754	1828	2106	2333	0940	1059	1253	1533	1754	1754	2108
16	Beauly d.	0717	0910	1053	1115	1157	...	1350	1415	1505	1727	...	1809	1843	2121	2348	0955	1115	1308	1548	1809	1809	2123
21	Muir of Ord d.	0725	0916	1059	1121	1206	...	1356	1423	1511	1733	...	1815	1849	2127	2354	1001	1121	1314	1556	1815	1815	2129
30	Dingwall d.	0740	0929	1112	1132	1218	...	1411	1437	1524	1747	...	1829	1905	2140	0007	1014	1134	1327	1609	1831	1833	2142
49	Garve d.	|	0952	|	1155	...	...	1433	|	|	|	...	1853	|	|	|	|	1158	|	|	|	1855	|
75	Achnasheen d.	|	1018	|	1221	...	...	1500	|	|	|	...	1920	|	|	|	|	1225	|	|	|	1922	|
104	Strathcarron d.	|	1048	|	1253	...	...	1530	|	|	|	...	1949	|	|	|	|	1255	|	|	|	1951	|
116	Stromeferry d.	|	1105	|	1310	...	...	1547	|	|	|	...	2006	|	|	|	|	1312	|	|	|	2008	|
124	Plockton d.	|	1117	|	1322	...	...	1559	|	|	|	...	2018	|	|	|	|	1324	|	|	|	2020	|
133	**Kyle of Lochalsh** a.	|	1130	|	1335	...	...	1612	|	|	|	...	2031	|	|	|	|	1337	|	|	|	2033	|
51	Invergordon d.	0758	...	1130	...	...	...	...	1454	1541	1804	...	...	1926	2157	0024	1032	...	1345	1626	1848	...	2200
71	Tain d.	0817	...	1149	...	...	...	...	1513	...	1824	...	...	1945	2216	0043	1050	...	1403	...	1901	...	2218
93	Ardgay d.	0833	...	1205	...	...	...	...	1529	...	1839	...	...	2001	...	...	...	...	...	...	1923	...	...
108	Lairg d.	0853	...	1221	...	...	...	...	1545	...	...	...	...	2017	...	...	...	...	...	...	1942	...	...
136	Golspie d.	0918	...	1246	...	...	...	...	1610	...	...	...	...	2042	...	...	...	...	...	...	2007	...	...
146	Brora d.	0929	...	1257	...	...	...	...	1621	...	...	...	...	2053	...	...	...	...	...	...	2018	...	...
163	Helmsdale d.	0947	...	1312	...	...	...	...	1636	...	...	...	...	2108	...	...	...	...	...	...	2033	...	...
201	Forsinard d.	1021	...	1346	...	...	...	...	1712	...	...	...	...	2142	...	...	...	...	...	...	2107	...	...
237	Georgemas Jcn a.	1045	...	1410	...	...	...	...	1736	...	...	...	...	2206	...	...	...	...	...	...	2131	...	...
248	**Thurso** a.	1059	...	1424	...	...	...	...	1750	...	...	...	...	2220	...	...	...	...	...	...	2145	...	...
248	**Thurso** d.	1102	...	1427	...	...	...	...	1753	...	...	...	...	2223	...	...	...	...	...	...	2148	...	...
237	Georgemas Jcn d.	1114	...	1439	...	...	...	...	1805	...	...	...	...	2235	...	...	...	...	...	...	2200	...	...
260	**Wick** a.	1131	...	1456	...	...	...	...	1822	...	...	...	...	2252	...	...	...	...	...	...	2217	...	...

	⚒	⚒	⚒a	⚒🍷		⚒🍷	⚒	⚒a		⚒a	⚒	⚒🍷	⚒a	⚒🍷	⚒	⚒	⑦	⑦b	⑦	⑦🍷	⑦	⑦	⑦
Wick d.	...	...	...	0618	...	0802	...	...	...	...	...	1234	...	1600	...	...	...	...	...	1158	...	...	...
Georgemas Jcn. d.	...	...	...	0636	...	0820	...	...	...	...	...	1252	...	1618	...	...	...	...	...	1216	...	...	...
Thurso a.	...	...	...	0646	...	0830	...	...	...	...	...	1302	...	1628	...	...	...	...	...	1226	...	...	...
Thurso d.	...	...	...	0650	...	0834	...	...	...	...	...	1306	...	1632	...	...	...	...	...	1230	...	...	...
Georgemas Jcn. d.	...	...	...	0703	...	0847	...	...	...	...	...	1319	...	1645	...	...	...	...	...	1243	...	...	...
Forsinard d.	...	...	...	0727	...	0913	...	...	...	...	...	1347	...	1711	...	...	...	...	...	1309	...	...	...
Helmsdale d.	...	...	...	0800	...	0946	...	...	...	...	...	1421	...	1744	...	...	...	...	...	1342	...	...	...
Brora d.	...	...	...	0816	...	1002	...	...	...	...	...	1436	...	1800	...	...	...	...	...	1358	...	...	...
Golspie d.	...	...	...	0825	...	1012	...	...	...	...	...	1447	...	1810	...	...	...	...	...	1408	...	...	...
Lairg d.	...	0628	...	0852	...	1038	...	...	...	...	...	1512	...	1836	...	...	...	...	...	1433	...	...	...
Ardgay d.	0616	0645	...	0907	...	1054	...	...	...	...	...	1530	...	1852	1928	...	...	...	...	1449	...	...	...
Tain d.	0632	0701	...	0923	...	1110	...	...	...	...	...	1546	...	1908	1946	2221	1055	...	1408	1505	...	...	2223
Invergorgon d.	0651	0720	...	0942	...	1131	...	...	...	...	1550	1606	...	1925	2005	2240	1114	...	1427	1524	1631	...	2242
Kyle of Lochalsh d.	|	|	0612	|	...	|	...	1208	...	1346	|	|	1713	|	|	|	|	1020	|	|	|	1512	|
Plockton d.	|	|	0628	|	...	|	...	1221	...	1359	|	|	1726	|	|	|	|	1033	|	|	|	1525	|
Stromferry d.	|	|	0640	|	...	|	...	1233	...	1411	|	|	1738	|	|	|	|	1045	|	|	|	1537	|
Strathcarron d.	|	|	0659	|	...	|	...	1252	...	1430	|	|	1757	|	|	|	|	1103	|	|	|	1556	|
Achnasheen d.	|	|	0727	|	...	|	...	1320	...	1501	|	|	1825	|	|	|	|	1131	|	|	|	1624	|
Garve d.	|	|	0754	|	...	|	...	1347	...	1527	|	|	1852	|	|	|	|	1157	|	|	|	1651	|
Dingwall d.	0710	0739	0817	1001	...	1153	1245	1410	...	1550	1610	1626	1919	1941	2024	2258	1135	1220	1445	1543	1649	1714	2300
Muir of Ord d.	0724	0752	0830	1014	...	1205	1258	1422	...	1603	1624	1638	1931	1952	2037	2311	1148	1232	1457	1555	1702	1726	2313
Beauly d.	0729	0758	0835	1019	...	1210	1303	1427	...	1608	1629	1644	1936	|	2042	2316	1153	1237	1502	1601	1707	1732	2318
Inverness a.	0744	0813	0850	1034	...	1225	1318	1442	...	1623	1646	1701	2000	2010	2057	2331	1208	1252	1517	1616	1722	1747	2333

a – Conveys 🍷 on ①–⑤.

b – May 21 - Sept. 24.

227 🚌 INVERNESS - ULLAPOOL - STORNOWAY

Valid from March 31, 2017

	①–⑥ 🚌	①–⑥ ⛴	⑦a 🚌	⑦a ⛴	①–⑤ 🚌	①–⑤ ⛴	⑦b 🚌	⑦a 🚌	⑦ ⛴	⑥ 🚌	⑥ ⛴
Inverness d.	0810	...	0910	...	1500	...	1540	1610	...	1640	...
Garve d.	0844	...	0944	...	1534	...	1614	1644	...	1714	...
Ullapool a.	0930	...	1030	...	1620	...	1700	1730	...	1800	...
Ullapool d.	...	1030	...	1130	...	1730	...	...	1830	...	1900
Stornoway a.	...	1300	...	1400	...	2000	...	...	2100	...	2130

	①–⑥ ⛴	①–⑥ 🚌	⑦a ⛴	⑦a 🚌	①–⑤ ⛴	①–⑤ 🚌	⑦b ⛴	⑦b 🚌	⑦a ⛴	⑦a 🚌	⑥ ⛴	⑥ 🚌
Stornoway d.	0700	...	0800	...	1400	...	1430	...	1500	...	1530	...
Ullapool a.	0930	...	1030	...	1630	...	1700	...	1730	...	1800	...
Ullapool d.	...	0950	...	1050	...	1650	...	1720	...	1750	...	1820
Garve d.	...	1032	...	1132	...	1732	...	1802	...	1832	...	1902
Inverness a.	...	1110	...	1210	...	1810	...	1840	...	1910	...	1940

a – June 25 - Sept. 3.

b – Not June 25 - Sept. 3.

☛ Latest passenger check-in for ⛴ is 30 minutes before departure.

Operators: 🚌 Scottish Citylink (service **961**). www.citylink.co.uk. ✆ (0) 871 266 3333.
⛴ Caledonian MacBrayne. www.calmac.co.uk. ✆ (0)800 066 5000.

228 🚌 INVERNESS - FORT WILLIAM - OBAN

Valid from May 22, 2017

Service number	**915**	**919**	**919**	**19**	**919**	**916**	**919**	**919**	**919**	**19**
		①–⑥	①–⑥	①–⑥				①–⑥	⑦	①–⑤
Inverness bus station d.	...	0905	1105	1300	1405	...	1735	1905	1915	2000
Fort Augustus bus stance d.	...	1008	1208	1403	1508	...	1838	2008	2018	2107
Invergarry Jct. bus bay A82 d.	0948j	1023	1223	1423	1523	1738j	1853	2023	2033	2113
Fort William bus station a.	1030	1105	1305	1500	1605	1820	1935	2105	2115	2150
Service number		**918**			**918**					
		①–⑥			①–⑥					
Fort William bus station d.	...	1115	...	...	1710	...	...	...	...	...
Ballachulish Tourist Office d.	...	1142	...	...	1737	...	...	...	...	...
Oban Station Road a.	...	1242	...	...	1837	...	...	...	...	...

Service number	**919**	**19**	**919**	**916**	**918**	**915**	**919**	**19**	**918**	**919**	**917**
	①–⑥	①–⑥	①–⑥		①–⑥		①–⑥	①–⑤	①–⑥	⑦	
Oban Station Road d.	...	...	...	...	0930	...	...	...	1500	...	...
Ballachulish Tourist Office d.	...	...	...	...	1029	...	...	...	1559	...	...
Fort William bus station a.	...	...	...	...	1058	...	...	...	1628	...	...
Service number					**919**				**919**		
					①–⑦				①–⑥		
Fort William bus station d.	0625	0730	0855	1015	1115	1400	1415	1520	1645	1700	1840
Invergarry Jct. bus bay A82 d.	0707	0807	0937	1054j	1157	1439j	1457	1615	1727	1742	1919j
Fort Augustus d.	0722	0819	0952	...	1212	...	1512	1630	1742	1757	...
Inverness bus station a.	0825	0920	1055	...	1315	...	1615	1731	1845	1900	...

j – On A87 at Invergarry Hotel.

Operator: Scottish Citylink. www.citylink.co.uk. ✆ (0) 871 266 3333.

229 ISLE OF MAN RAILWAYS

2017 service ✆ +44 (0)1624 662525

Please confirm all journeys locally as the exact service available may vary from that shown below

km	*Manx Electric Railway*	A	A	A	A	A	A	A		
0	**Douglas** Derby Castle ‡ d.	0940	1040	1140	1240	1410	1510	1610	...	...
4	Groudle d.	0952	1052	1152	1252	1422	1522	1622	...	...
11	Laxey d.	1010	1110	1210	1310	1440	1540	1640	...	...
29	**Ramsey** a.	1055	1155	1255	1355	1525	1625	...	...	...

	A	A	A	A	A	A	A		
Ramsey d.	...	1110	1210	1340	1440	1540	1640	...	...
Laxey d.	1055	1155	1255	1425	1525	1625	1725	...	...
Groudle d.	1113	1213	1313	1443	1543	1643	1743	...	...
Douglas Derby Castle ‡ a.	1125	1225	1325	1455	1555	1655	1755	...	...

km	*Snaefell Mountain Railway*	B	B	B	B	B	B	B		
0	**Laxey** d.	1015	1115	1215	1315	1400	1455	1545	...	...
8	**Summit** a.	1045	1145	1245	1345	1430	1525	1615	...	...

	B	B	B	B	B	B	B		
Summit d.	1110	1215	1315	1415	1500	1555	1645	...	...
Laxey a.	1140	1245	1345	1445	1530	1625	1715	...	...

km	*Isle of Man Steam Railway*	C	C	C	C			D✕		
0	**Douglas** Railway Station ‡ d.	0950	1150	1350	1550	...	...	1900	...	...
9	Santon d.	1011x	1211x	1411x	1611x	...	...	|	...	...
13	Ballasalla d.	1120	1220	1420	1620	...	...	1940	...	...
16	Castletown d.	1027	1227	1427	1627	...	...	1947	...	...
25	**Port Erin** a.	1050	1250	1450	1650	...	...	2015	...	...

	C	C	C	C		D✕		
Port Erin d.	1000	1200	1400	1600	...	2115	...	...
Castletown d.	1027	1227	1427	1627	...	2142	...	...
Ballasalla d.	1035	1235	1435	1635	...	2149	...	...
Santon d.	1047x	1247x	1447x	1647x	...	|	...	...
Douglas Railway Station ‡ a.	1105	1305	1505	1705	...	2230	...	...

A – Mar. 9 - Oct.1 (not Mar. 13, 17, 20, 24, 27, 31, Apr. 3) (also ⑥⑦ in Oct.). Minimum service shown. Additional services operate on most dates. A reduced service operates on ②③④ Oct. 10 - Nov. 2; also ⑥⑦ Oct. 28 - Nov. 5.

B – Apr. 7 - Nov. 5 (not Oct. 2, 6, 9, 13, 16, 20, 23, 27, 30, Nov. 3). Minimum service shown. Additional services operate on most dates June - September.

C – Mar. 18 - Nov. 5. **Does not run every day**. Enhanced services with different timetables operate on most ④⑥⑦ in July and ④⑤⑥⑦ in August and on certain other dates.

D – ④ June 15 - Nov. 2. Reservation essential.

x – Calls on request.

‡ – 🚌 services **1**, **1H**, **2A**, **12**, **12A**, connect Derby Castle and Lord Street Bus Station which is near the Steam Railway Station.

 For explanation of standard symbols see page 1

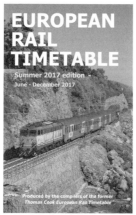
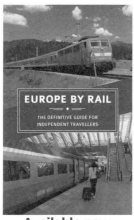

⊖ Frontier point

IRELAND

GREAT BRITAIN

NETHERLANDS

Cambridge   15a   Ipswich

15a 2235   Harwich   15a 2235

LONDON   9 10 15 17 20 21 3   Dover

32 40 42 44 45 47 56   10a

Calais

Boulogne

Brugge   12 9 15 18

Lille   BRUSSELS   BELGIUM

9 11 12 16 18 18a 20 21 56

10a

Antwerpen

Namur   Liège

Sterpenich

Luxembourg

AMSTERDAM   Bad Bentheim   22

Den Haag   15 15a   18

9 15 18   Amersfoort   22

Utrecht   28

Hoek van Holland   15 15a   Arnhem

15a   Rotterdam   28   Emmerich   Dortmund

470   Essen   20 56 66 68

13   Duisburg   20 56 66 70

Eindhoven   Düsseldorf

Venlo   802

12 20 21 56   Aachen   KÖLN

20 21 56   21 28 48 66

12   68 70 73

Mainz   24 30 48

54 56 73

9 10 10a 11 17 18 18a 20   Mannheim   54 56 73

21 31 32 40 42 44 45 47   Saarbrücken   32 68

PARIS   9 11 13 17 40   Metz   30   Heidelberg

11   24 30 32 40 56   Forbach   32

Rennes   9 13 17 31 40 42 44   Karlsruhe   32

11   24 30 32 40 56   Kehl

Nantes   Strasbourg

FRANCE   40 42   40 48   54 73

Besançon   Mulhouse

9 11 13 17 31 44   40 42 48   Basel   40 54 73 75

Dijon   40 73 82   ZÜRICH

48   42 48   Bern   Luzern

Vallorbe   Interlaken

13   Mâcon   Lausanne   Montreux   40 42 73

9 31 44   13 31   Brig   40 73 82

11 45 47   Genève   42 44 82   Iselle

9 St Gervais   Chiasso

Limoges   Lyon   9 44   73 82   40 44

44   Bourg St Maurice

Chambéry   9   MILANO

45 47   44   Modane   25 44 90

Bordeaux   44   Torino

44   Genova

Biarritz   13   25 90

Hendaye   Toulouse   San Remo

San Sebastián   Irún   11 13 48   Avignon   Ventimiglia

/ Donostia   11 13   11 13 48   Nice

45 47   11 13   Montpellier   11 90   25 90

Burgos   Narbonne   11 13 17 48

Aix en Provence

13   Marseille

Medina del   Cannes

Campo   Cerbère   Toulon

45 46 47   47   Portbou

45 46 47   13

LISBOA   SPAIN   Barcelona

Zaragoza   13

MADRID   13

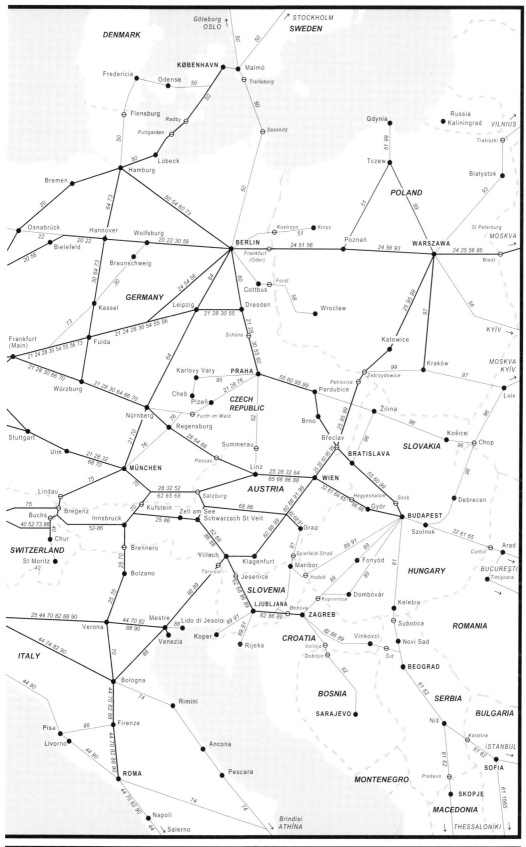

MP Middleton Press
EVOLVING THE ULTIMATE RAIL ENCYCLOPEDIA

Easebourne Midhurst GU29 9AZ. Tel:01730 813169
www.middletonpress.co.uk   email:info@middletonpress.co.uk
A-978 0 906520 B- 978 1 873793 C- 978 1 901706 D-978 1 904474
E - 978 1 906008 F- 978 1 908174 G - 978 1 910356

All titles listed below were in print at time of publication - please check current availability by looking at our website - *www.middletonpress.co.uk* or by requesting a Brochure which includes our *LATEST* RAILWAY TITLES also our TRAMWAY, TROLLEYBUS, MILITARY and COASTAL series

A
Abergavenny to Merthyr C 91 8
Abertillery & Ebbw Vale Lines D 84 5
Aberystwyth to Carmarthen E 90 1
Allhallows - Branch Line to A 62 8
Alton - Branch Lines to A 11 6
Andover to Southampton A 82 6
Ascot - Branch Lines around A 64 2
Ashburton - Branch Line to B 95 4
Ashford - Steam to Eurostar B 67 1
Ashford to Dover A 48 2
Austrian Narrow Gauge D 04 3
Avonmouth - BL around D 42 5
Aylesbury to Rugby D 91 3

B
Baker Street to Uxbridge D 90 6
Bala to Llandudno E 87 1
Banbury to Birmingham D 27 2
Banbury to Cheltenham E 63 5
Bangor to Holyhead F 01 7
Bangor to Portmadoc E 72 7
Barking to Southend C 80 2
Barmouth to Pwllheli E 53 6
Barry - Branch Lines around D 50 0
Bartlow - Branch Lines to F 27 7
Bath Green Park to Bristol C 36 9
Bath to Evercreech Junction A 60 4
Beamish 40 years on rails E94 9
Bedford to Wellingborough D 31 9
Berwick to Drem F 64 2
Berwick to St. Boswells F 75 8
B'ham to Tamworth & Nuneaton F 63 5
Birkenhead to West Kirby F 61 1
Birmingham to Wolverhampton E253
Blackburn to Hellifield F 95 6
Bletchley to Cambridge D 94 4
Bletchley to Rugby E 07 9
Bodmin - Branch Lines around B 83 1
Boston to Lincoln F 80 2
Bournemouth to Evercreech Jn A 46 8
Bournemouth to Weymouth A 57 4
Bradshaw's History F18 5
Bradshaw's Rail Times 1850 F 13 0
Bradshaw's Rail Times 1895 F 11 6
Branch Lines series - see town names
Brecon to Neath D 43 2
Brecon to Newport D 16 6
Brecon to Newtown E 06 2
Brighton to Eastbourne A 16 1
Brighton to Worthing A 03 1
Bristol to Taunton D 03 6
Bromley South to Rochester B 23 7
Bromsgrove to Birmingham D 87 8
Bromsgrove to Gloucester D 73 9
Brunel - A railtour D 74 6
Bude - Branch Line to B 29 9
Burnham to Evercreech Jn B 68 0

C
Cambridge to Ely D 55 5
Canterbury - BLs around B 58 9
Cardiff to Dowlais (Cae Harris) E 47 5
Cardiff to Pontypridd E 95 0
Cardiff to Swansea E 42 0
Carlisle to Hawick E 85 7
Carmarthen to Fishguard E 66 6
Caterham & Tattenham Corner B251
Central & Southern Spain NG E 91 8
Chard and Yeovil - BLs a C 30 7
Charing Cross to Dartford A 75 8
Charing Cross to Orpington A 96 3
Cheddar - Branch Line to B 90 9
Cheltenham to Andover C 43 7
Cheltenham to Redditch D 81 4
Chester to Birkenhead F 21 5
Chester to Manchester F 51 2
Chester to Rhyl E 93 2
Chester to Warrington F 40 6
Chichester to Portsmouth A 14 7
Clacton and Walton - BLs to F 04 8
Clapham to Beckenham Jn B 36 7
Cleobury Mortimer - BLs a E 18 5

Clevedon & Portishead - BLs to D180
Consett to South Shields E 57 4
Cornwall Narrow Gauge D 56 2
Corris and Vale of Rheidol E 65 9
Coventry to Leicester G 00 5
Craven Arms to Llandeilo E 35 2
Craven Arms to Wellington E 33 8
Crawley to Littlehampton A 34 5
Crewe to Manchester F 57 4
Cromer - Branch Lines around C 26 0
Croydon to East Grinstead B 48 0
Crystal Palace & Catford Loop B 87 1
Cyprus Narrow Gauge E 13 0

D
Darjeeling Revisited F 09 3
Darlington Leamside Newcastle E 28 4
Darlington to Newcastle D 98 2
Dartford to Sittingbourne B 34 3
Denbigh - Branch Lines around F 32 1
Derby to Stoke-on-Trent F 93 2
Derwent Valley - BL to the D 06 7
Devon Narrow Gauge E 09 3
Didcot to Banbury D 02 9
Didcot to Swindon C 84 0
Didcot to Winchester C 13 0
Dorset & Somerset NG D 76 0
Douglas - Laxey - Ramsey E 75 8
Douglas to Peel C 88 8
Douglas to Port Erin C 55 0
Douglas to Ramsey D 39 5
Dover to Ramsgate A 78 9
Drem to Edinburgh G 06 7
Dublin Northwards in 1950s E 31 4
Dunstable - Branch Lines to E 27 7

E
Ealing to Slough C 42 0
Eastbourne to Hastings A 27 7
East Cornwall Mineral Railways D 22 7
East Croydon to Three Bridges A 53 6
Eastern Spain Narrow Gauge E 56 7
East Grinstead - BLs to A 07 9
East Kent Light Railway A 61 1
East London - Branch Lines of C 44 4
East London Line B 80 0
East of Norwich - Branch Lines E 69 7
Effingham Junction - BLs a A 74 1
Ely to Norwich C 90 1
Enfield Town & Palace Gates D 32 6
Epsom to Horsham A 30 7
Eritrean Narrow Gauge E 38 3
Euston to Harrow & Wealdstone C 89 5
Exeter to Barnstaple B 15 2
Exeter to Newton Abbot C 49 9
Exeter to Tavistock B 69 5
Exmouth - Branch Lines to B 00 8

F
Fairford - Branch Line to A 52 9
Falmouth, Helston & St. Ives C 74 1
Fareham to Salisbury A 67 3
Faversham to Dover B 05 3
Felixstowe & Aldeburgh - BL to D 20 3
Fenchurch Street to Barking C 20 8
Festiniog - 50 yrs of enterprise C 83 3
Festiniog 1946-55 E 01 7
Festiniog in the Fifties B 68 8
Festiniog in the Sixties B 91 6
Ffestiniog in Colour 1955-82 F 25 3
Finsbury Park to Alexandra Pal C 02 8
French Metre Gauge Survivors F 88 3
Frome to Bristol B 77 0

G
Galashiels to Edinburgh F 52 9
Gloucester to Bristol D 35 7
Gloucester to Cardiff D 66 1
Gosport - Branch Lines around A 36 9
Greece Narrow Gauge D 72 2

H
Hampshire Narrow Gauge D 36 4
Harrow to Watford D 14 2
Harwich & Hadleigh - BLs to F 02 4
Harz Revisited F 62 8

Hastings to Ashford A 37 6
Hawick to Galashiels F 36 9
Hawkhurst - Branch Line to A 66 6
Hayling - Branch Line to A 12 3
Hay-on-Wye - BL around D 92 0
Haywards Heath to Seaford A 28 4
Hemel Hempstead - BLs to D 88 3
Henley, Windsor & Marlow - BLa C77 2
Hereford to Newport D 54 8
Hertford & Hatfield - BLs a E 58 1
Hertford Loop E 71 0
Hexham to Carlisle D 75 3
Hexham to Hawick F 08 6
Hitchin to Peterborough D 07 4
Holborn Viaduct to Lewisham A 81 9
Horsham - Branch Lines to A 02 4
Huntingdon - Branch Line to A 93 2

I
Ilford to Shenfield C 97 0
Ilfracombe - Branch Line to B 21 3
Industrial Rlys of the South East A 09 3
Ipswich to Diss F 81 9
Ipswich to Saxmundham C 41 3
Isle of Man Railway Journey G 02 9
Isle of Wight Lines - 50 yrs C 12 3
Italy Narrow Gauge F 17 8

K
Kent Narrow Gauge C 45 1
Kettering to Nottingham F 82-6
Kidderminster to Shrewsbury E 10 9
Kingsbridge - Branch Line to C 98 7
Kings Cross to Potters Bar E 62 8
King's Lynn to Hunstanton F 58 1
Kingston & Hounslow Loops A 83 3
Kingswear - Branch Line to C 17 8

L
Lambourn - Branch Line to C 70 3
Launceston & Princetown - BLs C 19 2
Leek - Branch Line From G 01 2
Leicester to Burton F 85 7
Lewisham to Dartford A 92 5
Lincoln to Cleethorpes F 56 7
Lincoln to Doncaster G 03 6
Lines around Stamford F 98 7
Lines around Wimbledon B 75 6
Liverpool Street to Chingford D 01 2
Liverpool Street to Ilford C 34 5
Llandeilo to Swansea E 46 8
London Bridge to Addiscombe B 20 6
London Bridge to East Croydon A 58 1
Longmoor - Branch Lines to A 41 3
Looe - Branch Line to C 22 2
Loughborough to Nottingham F 68 0
Lowestoft - BLs around E 40 6
Ludlow to Hereford E 14 7
Lydney - Branch Lines around E 26 0
Lyme Regis - Branch Line to A 45 1
Lynton - Branch Line to B 04 6

M
Machynlleth to Barmouth E 54 3
Maesteg and Tondu Lines E 61 8
Majorca & Corsica Narrow Gauge F 41 3
March - Branch Lines around B 09 1
Market Drayton - BLs around F 67 3
Market Harborough to Newark F 86 4
Marylebone to Rickmansworth D 49 4
Melton Constable to Yarmouth Bch E031
Midhurst - Branch Lines of E 78 9
Midhurst - Branch Lines to F 00 0
Minehead - Branch Line to A 80 2
Mitcham Junction Lines B 01 5
Monmouth - Branch Lines to E 20 8
Monmouthshire Eastern Valleys D 71 5
Moretonhampstead - BL to C 27 7
Moreton-in-Marsh to Worcester D 26 5
Morpeth to Bellingham F 87 1
Mountain Ash to Neath D 80 7

N
Newark to Doncaster F 78 9
Newbury to Westbury C 66 6
Newcastle to Hexham D 69 2

Newport (IOW) - Branch Lines to A 26 0
Newquay - Branch Lines to C 71 0
Newton Abbot to Plymouth C 60 4
Newtown to Aberystwyth E 41 3
Northampton to Peterborough F 92 5
North East German NG D 44 9
Northern Alpine Narrow Gauge F 37 6
Northern France Narrow Gauge C 75 8
Northern Spain Narrow Gauge E 83 3
North London Line B 94 7
North of Birmingham F 55 0
North Woolwich - BLs around C 65 9
Nottingham to Boston F 70 3
Nottingham to Lincoln F 43 7

O
Ongar - Branch Line to E 05 5
Orpington to Tonbridge B 03 9
Oswestry - Branch Lines around E 60 4
Oswestry to Whitchurch E 81 9
Oxford to Bletchley D 57 9
Oxford to Moreton-in-Marsh D 15 9

P
Paddington to Ealing C 37 6
Paddington to Princes Risborough C819
Padstow - Branch Line to B 54 1
Pembroke and Cardigan - BLs to F 29 1
Peterborough to Kings Lynn F 32 1
Peterborough to Lincoln F 89 5
Peterborough to Newark F 72 7
Plymouth - BLs around B 98 5
Plymouth to St. Austell C 63 5
Pontypool to Mountain Ash D 65 4
Pontypridd to Merthyr F 14 7
Pontypridd to Port Talbot E 86 4
Porthmadog 1954-46 - BLa B 31 2
Portmadoc 1923-46 - BLa B 13 8
Portsmouth to Southampton A 31 4
Portugal Narrow Gauge E 67 3
Potters Bar to Cambridge D 70 8
Princes Risborough - BL to D 05 0
Princes Risborough to Banbury C 85 7

R
Railways to Victory C 16 1
Reading to Basingstoke B 27 5
Reading to Didcot C 79 6
Reading to Guildford A 47 5
Redhill to Ashford A 73 4
Return to Blaenau 1970-82 C 64 2
Rhyl to Bangor F 15 4
Rhymney & New Tredegar Lines E 48 2
Rickmansworth to Aylesbury D 61 6
Romania & Bulgaria NG E 23 9
Romneyrail C 32 1
Ross-on-Wye - BLs around E 30 7
Ruabon to Barmouth E 84 0
Rugby to Birmingham E 37 6
Rugby to Loughborough F 12 3
Rugby to Stafford F 07 9
Rugeley to Stoke-on-Trent F 90 1
Ryde to Ventnor A 19 2

S
Salisbury to Westbury B 39 8
Sardinia and Sicily Narrow Gauge F 50 5
Saxmundham to Yarmouth C 69 7
Saxony & Baltic Germany Revisited F 71 0
Saxony Narrow Gauge D 47 0
Seaton & Sidmouth - BLs to A 95 6
Selsey - Branch Line to A 04 8
Sheerness - Branch Line to B 16 2
Shenfield to Ipswich E 96 3
Shrewsbury - Branch Line to A 86 4
Shrewsbury to Chester E 70 3
Shrewsbury to Crewe E 48 2
Shrewsbury to Ludlow E 21 5
Shrewsbury to Newtown E 29 1
Sierra Leone Narrow Gauge D 28 9
Sirhowy Valley Line E 12 3
Sittingbourne to Ramsgate A 90 1
Skegness & Mablethorpe - BL to F 84 0
Slough to Newbury C 56 7
South African Two-foot gauge E 51 2
Southampton to Bournemouth A 42 0
Southend & Southminster BLs E 76 5
Southern Alpine Narrow Gauge F 22 2
South London Line B 46 6
South Lynn to Norwich City F 03 1
Southwold - Branch Line to A 15 4
Spalding - Branch Lines around E 52 9
Spalding to Grimsby F 65 9 6
Stafford to Chester F 34 5

Stafford to Wellington F 59 8
St Albans to Bedford D 08 1
St. Austell to Penzance C 67 3
St. Boswell to Berwick F 44 4
Steaming Through Isle of Wight A 56
Steaming Through West Hants A 69 7
Stourbridge to Wolverhampton E 16 1
St. Pancras to Barking D 68 5
St. Pancras to Folkestone E 88 8
St. Pancras to St. Albans C 78 9
Stratford to Cheshunt F 53 6
Stratford-u-Avon to Birmingham D771
Stratford-u-Avon to Cheltenham C253
Sudbury - Branch Lines to F 19 2
Surrey Narrow Gauge C 87 1
Sussex Narrow Gauge C 68 0
Swaffham - Branch Lines around F 91
Swanage to 1999 - BL to A 33 8
Swanley to Ashford B 45 9
Swansea - Branch Lines around F 38
Swansea to Carmarthen E 59 8
Swindon to Bristol C 96 3
Swindon to Gloucester D 46 3
Swindon to Newport D 30 2
Swiss Narrow Gauge C 94 9

T
Talyllyn 60 E 98 7
Tamworth to Derby F 76 5
Taunton to Barnstaple B 60 2
Taunton to Exeter C 82 6
Taunton to Minehead F 39 0
Tavistock to Plymouth B 88 6
Tenterden - Branch Line to A 21 5
Three Bridges to Brighton A 35 2
Tilbury Loop C 86 4
Tiverton - BLs around C 62 8
Tivetshall to Beccles D 41 8
Tonbridge to Hastings A 44 4
Torrington - Branch Lines to B 37 4
Tourist Railways of France G 04 3
Towcester - BLs around E 39 0
Tunbridge Wells BLs A 32 1

U
Upwell - Branch Line to B 64 0
Uttoxeter to Macclesfield G 05 0

V
Victoria to Bromley South A 98 7
Victoria to East Croydon A 40 6
Vivarais Revisited E 08 6

W
Walsall Routes F 45 1
Wantage - Branch Line to D 25 8
Wareham to Swanage 50 yrs D098
Waterloo to Windsor A 54 3
Waterloo to Woking A 38 3
Watford to Leighton Buzzard D 45 6
Wellingborough to Leicester F 73 4
Welshpool to Llanfair E 49 9
Wenford Bridge to Fowey C 09 3
Westbury to Bath B 55 8
Westbury to Taunton C 76 5
West Cornwall Mineral Rlys D 48 7
West Croydon to Epsom B 08 4
West German Narrow Gauge D 93 7
West London - BLs of C 50 5
West London Line B 84 8
West Wiltshire - BLs of D 12 8
Weymouth - BLs A 65 9
Willesden Jn to Richmond B 71 8
Wimbledon to Beckenham C 58 1
Wimbledon to Epsom B 62 6
Wimborne - BLs around A 97 0
Wisbech - BLs around C 01 7
Witham & Kelvedon - BLs a E 82 6
Woking to Alton A 59 8
Woking to Portsmouth A 25 3
Woking to Southampton A 55 0
Wolverhampton to Shrewsbury E444
Wolverhampton to Stafford F 79 6
Worcester to Birmingham D 97 5
Worcester to Hereford D 38 8
Worthing to Chichester A 06 2
Wrexham to New Brighton F 47 5
Wroxham - BLs around F 31 4

Y
Yeovil - 50 yrs change C 38 3
Yeovil to Dorchester A 76 5
Yeovil to Exeter A 91 8
York to Scarborough F 23 9